THE MEN OF CAJAMARCA

LATIN AMERICAN MONOGRAPHS, NO. 27
Institute of Latin American Studies
THE UNIVERSITY OF TEXAS AT AUSTIN

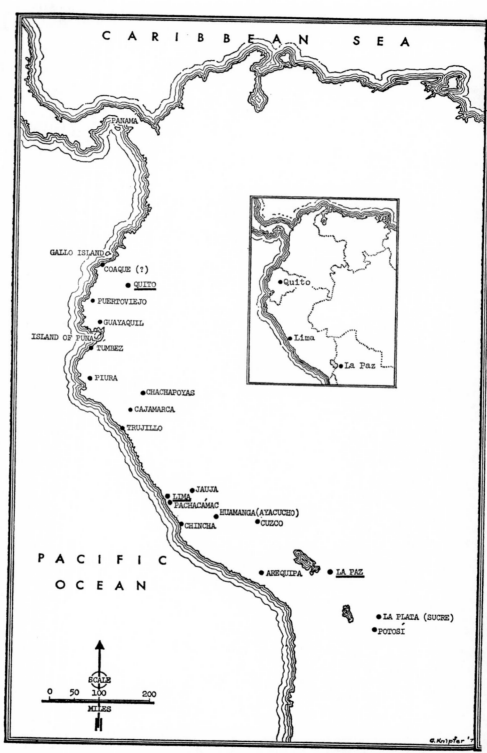

Peru and Tierra Firme in the conquest period.

The Men of Cajamarca

A SOCIAL AND BIOGRAPHICAL STUDY OF THE FIRST CONQUERORS OF PERU

by James Lockhart

PUBLISHED FOR THE INSTITUTE OF LATIN AMERICAN STUDIES
BY THE UNIVERSITY OF TEXAS PRESS, AUSTIN

Library of Congress Cataloging in Publication Data

Lockhart, James Marvin.
  The Men of Cajamarca.

  (Latin American monographs, no. 27)
  Bibliography: p.
  1. Peru—History—Conquest, 1522–1548—Biography.
I. Title. II. Series: Latin American monographs
(Austin, Tex.) no. 27.
F3442.L77   985'.02'0922[B]   72-185236

Composition by G&S Typesetters, Austin

ISNB 978-0-292-73563-7
First paperback printing, 2012

To Mary Ann

CONTENTS

TABLES

The 168 Spaniards who captured the Inca emperor at Cajamarca, Peru, in 1532 constitute the subject of the present book. An extension of the work begun in the author's *Spanish Peru, 1532–1560*, it covers a selected smaller portion of the same ground more intensively and embodies a slightly different, complementary technique within the same current of social history. (A fuller discussion of the relation between the methods and conclusions of the two books will be found in Part I, chapter 6.) The book was first conceived in 1964–1965, midway in the course of research for *Spanish Peru*, and thereafter the author scanned everything that came into his hands for the purposes of the second topic as well as the first.

Whether scholars intend it or not, their paths converge. A later survey of the relevant historical literature made it apparent that the project stood at the intersecting point of two separate traditions in writing about early Spanish immigrants to America, or conquerors. One of these has expressed itself in a small body of work dedicated to the study of groups and group characteristics, rather than of individuals. There is Tomás Thayer Ojeda's *Valdivia y sus compañeros*, which analyzes the first conquerors of Chile from several points of view. Rafael Loredo, too, at times emphasizes groups as groups in his documentary publications, *Los repartos* and *Alardes y derramas*. Far the most refined, concentrated study of the conquerors' social characteristics and the patterns in their activity is Mario Góngora's splendid *Grupos de conquistadores en Tierra Firme (1509–1530)*. It represents, in the aspect of group history, the present book's only serious predecessor. Since the conquest of Peru is immediately subsequent to Góngora's time period and the Peruvian conquerors came from Panama, this study can be seen in part as a direct continuation of Góngora's work, and as such might have been entitled "A Group of Conquerors in Peru (1530–1550)." This close and exclusive relationship means that at times *The Men of Cajamarca* becomes almost a conversation with Góngora—always a respectful one, usually in a framework of general agreement.

The second tradition is much more widely practiced: biographical writing about celebrities or men taking part in notable events. The capture of Emperor Atahuallpa in 1532 was a notable event if there ever was one, and there has been a more sustained interest in the men who did it than in any other similar body. The whole list of their names figured in a contemporary chronicle and continued to appear in publications of the seventeenth century. In the nineteenth century interest revived, as Peruvians began to write about their national history, and it continues today. There is a goodly scattering of older biographical notes and articles, but two names of this century stand out as contributing most to the literature on the men of Cajamarca. Raúl Porras Barrenechea wrote much on Francisco Pizarro, who is, after all, one of the men, and prepared masterly editions of two chronicles by first conquerors. In the course of his work he assembled comments or articles on about thirty figures, which appear as notes to the chronicles and documents he edited. Porras's work is superb, characterized by depth, finesse, and high accuracy, for the most part. One could wish that the mores of his time and place had permitted source references. Source references in abundance will be found in the extensive, conscientious writing of José Antonio del Busto, who has published articles in various journals and reviews on perhaps half of the men, including humble ones. Busto has some sense for the social and does not knowingly distort the truth, but he also loves a colorful narrative and sometimes uses the methods of the historical novelist. The reader will find in this volume numerous challenges of factual points in Busto's work. These are not malicious, but result from the broader documentary base and more precise social focus employed here; the author realizes that all research of this type, including his own, involves a certain irreducible minimum of error. To date, no unified publication on the captors of Atahuallpa has appeared, though one hears that Busto means to publish a multivolume biographical dictionary on the Peruvian conquerors in general.

In accordance with its double tradition, *The Men of Cajamarca* is in two parts. The first contains several analytical chapters on general pat-

terns, social, collective, or organizational. The second contains short
biographies of all the men, insofar as that is possible. Social scientists
will probably think that Part I is the body of the work, followed by an
appendix, while humanists may consider it a prologue, and the biographies the body. The author gives equal weight to both parts.

Part I speaks for itself. Part II stands as substantiation, with more
detail and subtlety. It can also serve as a reference work on a good portion (not all) of the early conquerors of Peru and as a tool for further
research of several kinds. Primarily it is meant as a panorama of common social types, which if read attentively could do much to change
that most pernicious and pertinacious of clichés, the common image of
the Spanish conqueror. While none but enthusiasts will read this part
from start to finish, it is roughly organized into chapters on the basis
of type or function, so that one may quickly get a general picture by
reading one or two biographies in each section. The sketches vary considerably. Where little is known, every detail is included, so that as
much of the man as possible can be inferred from the fragment, as with
a broken statue. Where there is more, emphasis is on the structure of
the career rather than on external events, though the most salient even
of these are reported. In those cases where a mass of information was
available, it was possible to go beyond career patterns to an extensive
discussion of the interrelation of social background, experience, and
mentality.

A book of this nature can never be complete. In the author's opinion the work had reached the point where the main patterns were well
enough established, with examples sufficiently full to illustrate them.
All the archival collections and subsections thought likely to contain
concentrated relevant material were examined, with one large exception: the local archives of the many places to which the conquerors returned in Spain. These could doubtless tell us much, yet to investigate
them thoroughly would be the work of years. Perhaps the desired data
can come out of research aimed primarily at Spanish regional history.
Without any doubt more information will come to light. It is hoped,
indeed, that this study will help scholars working on related materials
to see the potential value of scraps they might have discarded.

Acknowledgments go again to all those previously cited for bibliographical, archival, and financial help with my previous book. It
should not be left unmentioned that Professor Enrique Otte guided me

to the ships' registers in the Archive of the Indies' Indiferente General 1801, which were invaluable in identifying returning conquerors. Paul B. Ganster located and filmed some important documents for me in the Peruvian archives, and David Szewczyk surveyed the Lilly Library for my purposes. The University of California, Los Angeles, and the Institute of Latin American Studies of The University of Texas at Austin subsidized a part of my writing time. My wife, Mary Ann, contributed even more to research than before; most of the lists and compilations are her work.

JAMES LOCKHART

ABBREVIATIONS

AGI   Archivo General de Indias, Seville
AHA   Archivo Histórico de Arequipa
AHC   Archivo Histórico Nacional del Cuzco
ANP   Archivo Nacional del Perú, Lima
APS   Archivo de Protocolos, Seville
BNP   Biblioteca Nacional del Perú, Lima
CDIAO *Colección de documentos inéditos relativos al descubrimiento, conquista y colonización de las posesiones españolas en América y Oceanía*
CDIHC *Colección de documentos inéditos para la historia de Chile*, José Toribio Medina, ed.
CDIHE *Colección de documentos inéditos para la historia de España*
CDIHN *Colección Somoza. Documentos para la historia de Nicaragua*
DHA   *Documentos para la historia de Arequipa*, Víctor M. Barriga, ed.
HC   Harkness Collection, Library of Congress
PA   The "Protocolo Ambulante," a collection of notarial documents in Peru in 1533–1537; in ANP
RAHC   *Revista del Archivo Histórico del Cuzco*
RANP   *Revista del Archivo Nacional del Perú*
RA PC   Real Audiencia, Procedimientos Civiles; in ANP
RIPIG   *Revista del Instituto Peruano de Investigaciones Genealógicas*

In the notes, a proper name following AHA, AHC, or ANP denotes a document issued by a notary of that name, contained in that archive. A number following the name denotes the year or years of the register. Thus ANP, Gutiérrez 1545–1555, f.100, means folio 100 of a register of Diego Gutiérrez for the years 1545–1555, in the Archivo Nacional del Perú.

Part I: Social Phenomena

1. NARRATIVE PRELIMINARIES

Cajamarca and Other Episodes in the Conquest of Peru

IN THIS STUDY THE PRIMARY INTEREST is not the conquest but the pattern in the lives of the conquerors; therefore the familiar procedure of using social material as background to a narrative presentation will be reversed. In any case, history and anthropology have made such strides since Prescott or Kirkpatrick that an adequate narrative of the Peruvian conquest would require another volume the size of this one.[1]

Rather than narrative properly speaking, the brief calendar or summary below will be episodic. Episodes are the building blocks of the

[1] John Hemming's *Conquest of the Incas* comes close to adequacy, though not geared to the specific purposes and perspectives of this book. Much of the material in this chapter is common knowledge among experts. Standard chronicles and other sources agree on many salient facts, so in most cases there is no need for footnoting. In the main, only several passages from Pedro de Cieza's little-used *Te,cera parte* are cited, and some other new or controversial items.

conquerors' careers. Participation in some of them and not in others is an important part of any individual's life pattern and sets him off in some way from other men. This effect is strongest and most visible in the case of Spaniards who had any part in capturing the Inca emperor, but it operates in many other less notable happenings as well. Thus presence at certain events becomes a diagnostic trait, and, with that, those events become an integral part of the study's vocabulary. The main purpose of what follows is to give the reader a preliminary comprehension of some occurrences that will be used in this work again and again as reference points. Since the men of Cajamarca are our special concern, events of 1531–1533 will naturally receive the fullest treatment.

Balboa Sees the Pacific

The conquest of Peru might be said to have started when Vasco Núñez de Balboa and some sixty men first glimpsed the "South Sea" in the Panama region in 1513. A few of Peru's conquerors were already in the Isthmian area at that time, and one of them, Francisco Pizarro, was present as Balboa's chief lieutenant.

Balboa's discovery brought in its wake a shift to the west, mainly carried out under Governor Pedrarias de Avila. The latter arrived in the area in 1514; the great expedition he headed included some few of the future men of Cajamarca, among them Hernando de Soto. In 1519 Pedrarias shifted the capital of Tierra Firme to the new west coast city of Panama. From that base advances were made along the coast in both directions.

The Conquest of Nicaragua

In the first years after Panama's foundation the thrust north and west toward easily accessible Nicaragua was stronger than that toward the treacherous coast of South America. An expedition under Gil González de Avila, starting in 1521, explored Nicaragua, then returned. A few of that expedition's members, probably seamen, were later to come to Peru. Just afterward perhaps a dozen future conquerors of Peru took part in some stage of the effective conquest of Nicaragua in 1523–1524, under Pedrarias's captain, Francisco Hernández de Córdoba. Soto was a prominent leader in this movement, as was Sebastián de Benalcázar, at a little lower level.

The Discovery of Peru

In 1524, previous attempts having led to little, Pedrarias agreed to let Captain Francisco Pizarro with his associates explore and conquer toward the "Levant," or in the direction of present Colombia.[2] A first venture produced small profit and discovered little new, probing along a coast populated mainly with enough mosquitoes "to do battle with all the armies of the Grand Turk."[3] A second expedition of 1526, in which Pizarro's partner Almagro figured with increasing prominence as a near equal and a potential rival, advanced farther down the coast but suffered greatly from disease and hunger. For this and other reasons, very few veterans of the early expeditions took part in the actual conquest of 1531–1532—far fewer men than from Nicaragua. Late in 1526, pilot Bartolomé Ruiz reconnoitered far ahead of the main group, finding the first promising signs of the central Andean peoples and their great wealth. The whole expedition reached the settled town of Atacames (in northern Ecuador).

Gallo Island and the Thirteen of Fame

Nevertheless, the situation of the men continued to deteriorate; lacking the strength to take Atacames, they retired to desolate Gallo Island, off the far southern coast of Colombia. Complaints from there reached Governor Pedro de los Ríos (Pedrarias's successor) in 1527, whereupon he sent out a lieutenant with orders to bring back to Panama all the men who wished to come. If any substantial number wanted to continue the venture, they could do so. Pizarro spoke for continuing, in a way simpler, more matter of fact, and at the same time more moving than is usually reported. Nor did the men express their choice so theatrically as is often thought. It was decided that some thirteen men (more or less) would stay on the nearby island of Gorgona, which was better provisioned, and await reinforcements to carry on south.[4] Most of the Spaniards returned to Panama, many of them disillusioned or disaffected, but this was not the case with all. Some were wounded, or ill, and did not intend to abandon the venture permanent-

---

[2] See below, pp. 68–73, and 142–144.
[3] Cieza, *Tercera parte*, in *Mercurio Peruano* 32 (1951):150.
[4] Ibid., pp. 148–149.

ly, as they later showed by their actions. Others were on specific missions for Pizarro, including pilot Ruiz himself.

After a few months Ruiz returned to Gorgona with a ship and sailors, but no further reinforcements. In the first half of 1528, Pizarro, the Thirteen, and the sailors reconnoitered the Peruvian coast as far south as Santa (a third of the way down the coast of modern Peru), several times going on shore and seeing something of the magnificence of the Incan empire. South of Túmbez they picked up the Indian boys who would later interpret at Cajamarca.[5] Feeling that enough had been seen to attract men and support, Pizarro returned to Panama with some gold pieces, llamas, and Indians.

Back to Spain

From late 1528 until January, 1530, Pizarro was in Spain. His main business was to obtain a capitulation with the crown, granting him the governorship of Peru and the authorization to conquer it. He also recruited men for the conquering expedition, particularly in the area of his homeland, Extremaduran Trujillo. He returned to Panama with three of his brothers, many Extremaduran compatriots new to the Indies,[6] a long string of offices and honors for himself, and nothing for his partner Almagro.

The 1531 Expedition

In Pizarro's absence, Almagro, the manager and organizer of the two, along with Bartolomé Ruiz and others, had made considerable progress toward financing and manning the expected conquest. Ruiz had been to Nicaragua to collect men, and he and Almagro had begun negotiations with important leaders there, to persuade them to contribute ships and bring their followings to Peru. When Almagro discovered how he had been slighted, the partnership temporarily collapsed, but promises overcame his resentment. Around January, 1531, an expedition of three ships, perhaps 180 men, and some thirty horses left Panama, with Pizarro in command.[7]

---

[5] Ibid. 34 (1953):314.
[6] Cieza estimates that Pizarro arrived in Nombre de Dios with 125 men (ibid. 36 [1955]:463).
[7] Estimates vary, but no one was in a position to know the number better than Pizarro's secretary, Francisco de Jerez (*Verdadera relación*, II, 322). Cieza's esti-

Coaque

Within a short time the men were in the vicinity of the north Ecuadorian coast, but upon landing they found the first Indian towns deserted. They advanced to a large settlement called Coaque, which they attacked and occupied, taking a respectable profit in gold and silver pieces.[8] This treasure Pizarro sent to Panama and Nicaragua in the ships, which were to bring back reinforcements. To await them, the expedition settled down in Coaque for several months; many of the men fell victim to a strange disease which caused walnut-sized growths on their faces and bodies. At last a ship came from Panama under entrepreneur Pedro Gregorio (in connection with Almagro), bringing supplies, the three royal treasury officials, possibly twenty-odd men, and about thirteen horses.[9] Thereupon the main body advanced south by land.

---

mate is identical: 180 men, 36 horses (*Tercera parte*, in *Mercurio Peruano* 36 [1955]:465). Another of the men, Cristóbal de Mena, estimates 250 ("Conquista del Perú," p. 79); so does Diego de Trujillo (*Relación*, p. 45). Pedro Pizarro (*Relación*, V, 171) thinks there were about 200.

[8] Jerez (*Verdadera relación*, II, 322) states that the take was 15,000 pesos of gold and 1,500 marks of silver (worth 7,500 pesos if "good silver" is meant). Trujillo (*Relación*, p. 48) mentions 18,000 pesos of gold and some poor silver; Juan Ruiz (*Advertencias*, p. 79) also 18,000. Agustín de Zárate (*Historia*, II, 474) gives the figure of 30,000 pesos. Pedro Pizarro (*Relación*, V, 170) thinks the total was worth 200,000 pesos, doubtless a late fantasy. But he seems to be right in his statement that after Coaque no further appreciable amounts of money accrued until Cajamarca, a year and a half later.

[9] Accounts vary considerably on the subject of the main reinforcing parties. Particularly there is a tendency in Estete, Jerez, and Pizarro not to mention Benalcázar at all, or to consider that he arrived while the main group was at Coaque. Juan Ruiz, one of Benalcázar's men, says that they actually did land north of Coaque, then reached the town after Pizarro's men had left, staying there a week to recuperate. Pizarro sent a party of three men back to get them, and they then went the thirty leagues down the coast to where he was (*Advertencias*, pp. 78–80).

According to Cieza, Gregorio brought thirteen horses and an unspecified but not large number of men; Benalcázar brought twelve horses and about thirty men (*Tercera parte*, in *Mercurio Peruano* 36 [1955]:468–470). Pedro Pizarro also puts Benalcázar's contingent at about thirty (*Relación*, V, 172), as does Hernando Beltrán, one of the men (AGI, Patronato 90, no. 1, ramo 11). Jerez ignores Benalcázar, but does consider that two ships arrived at Coaque, with a total of twenty-six horsemen and thirty footmen, or fifty-six altogether (*Verdadera relación*, II, 322). One may justifiably conclude that Jerez totaled Gregorio's and Benalcázar's men to arrive at these figures; his twenty-six horses agrees closely with Cieza's thirteen plus twelve. By the same token, subtracting thirty from his fifty-six leaves an estimated twenty-six for the number of men coming with Gregorio. Miguel de Estete (*Rela-*

Benalcázar Arrives

They had gone only as far as Puertoviejo when two ships appeared on the coast with news that a party of about thirty men and twelve horses, under Sebastián de Benalcázar, had arrived from Nicaragua and was proceeding toward them by land from the north.[10] In a few days Benalcázar's men joined the main group and were well received, though there was some grumbling at their small number. Apparently this was not the large party expected from Nicaragua.

Puná and the Arrival of Soto

As the expedition worked its way painfully down the coast, still suffering from diseases, it came near to the large island of Puná, in the gulf of Guayaquil. Seeking a place of recuperation and refuge from seasonal rains, the Spaniards crossed to the island, but they chose poorly, for the Indians of Puná gave them some of the hardest fighting of the whole campaign.[11] The greatest event of the stay on Puná, however, was the expected arrival from Nicaragua and Panama of Hernando de Soto's party: two ships, perhaps a hundred men, and twenty-five horses.[12] With this reinforcement the expedition prepared in February, 1532, to return to the mainland and enter Inca territory.

---

ción, pp. 13, 15) considers that Soto's contingent were the men sent for in Nicaragua.

[10] Cieza (*Tercera parte*, in *Mercurio Peruano* 36 [1955]:470) and Juan Ruiz (*Advertencias*, pp. 78–80) are in basic agreement on the time and manner of arrival; but both speak of only one ship.

To this writer's knowledge, no chronicles or histories mention the exact date of Benalcázar's arrival in Peru, or the names of his ships and their masters. Treasury records of the expedition, preserved in AGI, Contaduría 1825, give certainty on this question. It there appears that two ships arrived at Puertoviejo from Nicaragua on November 15, 1531: the *Santiago*, master Juan Fernández, and the *San Pedro*, master Pedro de Veintemillia.

[11] The expedition was at Puná on December 1, 1531 (footnote 12, below), having been at Puertoviejo on November 15 (footnote 10, above). Cieza (*Tercera parte*, in *Mercurio Peruano* 36 [1955]:473) states that the men were on the island for over three months. Mena estimates four or five months ("Conquista del Perú," p. 79). They were still there, a part of them at least, on February 3, 1532 (AGI, Justicia 724, no. 6).

[12] Cieza (*Tercera parte*, in *Mercurio Peruano* 37 [1956]:82) tells of the arrival but gives no numbers. Pedro Pizarro (*Relación*, V, 171–172) and Trujillo (*Relación*, p. 52) agree that there were two ships; Trujillo says Soto brought "many men, horses and supplies," and Pedro Pizarro estimates that he had about a hundred men.

The Foundation of San Miguel

Túmbez had been the most impressive settlement that Pizarro and the Thirteen had seen in the 1528 reconnoitering; the intention now was to make it the capital of Peru, and several men on the expedition already had royal appointments to the council of the future city. But epidemics and a war with Puná had since ravaged the region, which seemed dry and without mineral wealth, in any case. For several months the expedition occupied the Túmbez region quite uneventfully,[13] then after a time of exploration headed south to look for a better place to found a city.

The Spaniards were now beginning to see Inca highways, herds of livestock, and warehouses. They met no more resistance than occasional skirmishing, flight, or rebellion after submission. The place they chose for a settlement was San Miguel (Piura) about a hundred miles south of Túmbez, thought to be well-watered, populous, and not far from a good port.[14] Some forty Spaniards—the older, weaker, and infirm—became citizens and received encomiendas in the area.[15] The rest, hearing of the Inca emperor's presence at Cajamarca in the highlands, set out to encounter him.

Juan Ruiz (*Advertencias*, p. 85) asserts there were twenty-five horsemen—as many as the other two reinforcements put together.

One important reference which seems not to have been noticed before apparently gives the exact date of Soto's arrival, with names of ships and masters. Treasury records in AGI, Contaduría 1825, state that on December 1, 1531, two ships arrived at the island of Puná from Panama. Both were named *La Concepción*; the masters were Juan de Avendaño and Cristóbal Quintero. The last port of call had been Panama, where Soto must have touched. It is true that Soto's name does not appear specifically, but it is not known that any other two ships arrived at this time, and the records mention no others.

[13] Definitely in Túmbez by April, 1532 (AGI, Patronato 28, ramo 55), the expedition left there on May 16 (Jerez, *Verdadera relación*, II, 323). Mena says they were at Túmbez two or three months ("Conquista del Perú," p. 79).

[14] San Miguel was in existence by August 1, 1532, at which time the ship *Santa Catalina*, master Juan Pichón, and the bark *Santo Domingo*, master Juan de San Juan, both from Panama, registered arrival there (AGI, Contaduría 1825). The expedition left San Miguel on September 24 (Jerez, *Verdadera relación*, II, 325).

[15] Cieza (*Tercera parte*, in *Mercurio Peruano* 37 [1956]:88) gives the attributes of the men. Juan Ruiz (*Advertencias*, p. 87) says forty men stayed in San Miguel. According to the precise figures of Jerez there were forty-six citizens and ten or twelve noncitizens, joined by another nine who returned after the general muster made a little farther on (*Verdadera relación*, II, 325). San Miguel was founded on a site called Tangarará, and only later moved to the nearby site of Piura, retaining its corporate identity.

The First Interview with Atahuallpa

During their ascent the Spaniards were often mystified or made suspicious, but never attacked. In the afternoon of November 15, 1532, they made an unmolested entry into the deserted central square of Cajamarca;[16] Emperor Atahuallpa and his thousands of followers were encamped some distance away at a spring. The governor sent out Hernando de Soto and some of the best horsemen, whose mission it was to invite the emperor to visit the Spaniards, with the intention of capturing him according to standard procedure. Soto was not long gone when Pizarro had misgivings about sending such a small group, and sent another of the same size under his brother Hernando. Exactly how many men went, and what was said, has been obscured by greatly varying reports, but to have ridden on the mission was a feather in a man's cap. After making the Spaniards wait, Atahuallpa agreed to come to the Spanish camp the following day.

Cajamarca

The morning of November 16 found the Spaniards prepared to assault Atahuallpa whenever he should appear before them. Most of the some sixty horsemen were distributed in three large buildings on as many sides of the square, under the captaincy of Soto, Benalcázar, and Hernando Pizarro. A few others supported Governor Pizarro and some twenty-five footmen in a building on the fourth side. Perhaps seventy footmen were posted in small detachments to guard the several entryways to the enclosed square. Pedro de Candía, with a few artillerymen and musketeers, was atop a fortress that lay either in or on the square. At the proper moment, Pizarro's ensign was to hoist his standard, upon which the trumpets would sound, the artillery would fire, and the onslaught would begin.

From earliest morning Atahuallpa had begun to move his thousands. Messengers went back and forth, saying first that Atahuallpa would come unarmed, then that he would bring weapons, while Pizarro replied that it made no difference—perhaps the truest word uttered that day on either side.[17] It was late afternoon before the Inca's forces, filling the fields, came to rest some hundreds of yards from the square.

---

[16] The date is given in Jerez, *Verdadera relación,* II, 330.
[17] Mena, "Conquista del Perú," p. 84.

Again Atahuallpa needed persuasion to come farther, and Spaniard Hernando de Aldana visited his camp.

At last the emperor advanced toward the square, his following now reduced to a few thousand. The Spaniards were impressed by the hundreds of nobles who accompanied him in checked livery, singing in unison while they swept away straws and pebbles in his path. The Indians were armed, but only with small maces and slings. Once the whole entourage was inside the square, the Dominican fray Vicente de Valverde came out with an interpreter to speak to Atahuallpa. The Spanish intention, standard in such cases, was to get the chieftain into their power peacefully if possible. Words passed between the two, but Atahuallpa soon became agitated, and Valverde returned, shouting.

At this the signal was given and the attack began, though not quite as planned, since not all the guns went off, and, when the Spaniards rushed out, many of the inexperienced footmen around the governor became frightened and fell to one side.[18] Nevertheless, Pizarro and those remaining pressed into the crowd of Indians toward the litter of Atahuallpa. Miguel Estete de Santo Domingo is said to have first laid hands on him, and Pizarro himself to have taken him prisoner. Meanwhile the horsemen were having the effect of an earthquake on the mass of Indians inside the plaza. Many were trampled, and others trampled each other, until by sheer force they knocked over one of the walls around the square and began to escape into the open fields. The Spaniards then went out into the fields to meet a great horde of fully armed warriors, whom they quickly routed and pursued until darkness fell, killing thousands and collecting gold and silver objects in unprecedented quantity. No Spaniard had lost his life.

The Treasure

Atahuallpa, now a prisoner, promised to fill a room with gold and silver in return for his life, and, as most say, for his liberty as well. The Spaniards agreed. As for Atahuallpa's liberty, it is hard to see how they can have been serious, unless, as Juan Ruiz states, they intended to send him to his homeland of Quito,[19] for the whole expedition was predicated on the assumption of permanent Spanish rule in Peru under Governor Pizarro. The conquerors now settled down at Cajamarca to await the assembly of the treasure and also the arrival of

[18] Ibid., pp. 86–87.
[19] Ruiz, *Advertencias*, p. 95.

further reinforcements. The country appeared calm, but many of the emperor's "captains" in other areas seemed disposed to assert their independence.

Hernando Pizarro Goes to Pachacámac

As the months stretched on, through the spring of 1533, the Spaniards grew impatient and insecure, and began to take a more active part in the treasure collection. In one of the most famous exploits of the whole campaign, Hernando Pizarro took a small body of horsemen and footmen far across the country to the great temple of Pachacámac, near the future site of Lima. Though the gold there proved far less than expected, the Spaniards cast down the idol, and on their way back intercepted a great fortune in the hands of an Inca captain at Jauja.[20]

Emissaries to Cuzco

In the same period, three Spaniards were sent under safe conduct to Cuzco, the Inca capital, partly to take possession for Spain, but mainly to hasten the removal of treasure.[21] More successful than Hernando Pizarro, they brought back hundreds of loads of gold, and their feat became legendary, though often attributed to the wrong men.[22]

Distribution of the Treasure

Over these months pressures continued to build up. The governor wished to get on with the conquest. The royal treasury officials arrived from San Miguel and were unhappy to see so much gold and silver accumulating, without their being able to dispatch the king's fifth to Spain. In April, 1533,[23] a body of some two hundred men arrived from Panama under Almagro, to learn that they would not receive a share of the growing hoard. They could not complain overmuch of this on principle, but became rapidly disaffected as it began to appear that the whole vast wealth of the country would go to the captors of Atahuallpa while they would not receive a penny. On top of all this, reports and rumors began to be heard about large-scale movements of Indian warriors through the countryside; whether true or not, they disturbed the conquerors considerably.

[20] Dates in Jerez, *Verdadera relación*, II, 337, 342.
[21] Dates in ibid., pp. 337, 343.
[22] They were Zárate, Moguer, and Bueno.
[23] Date in Jerez, *Verdadera relación*, II, 337.

Thus the interests of almost all the Spaniards were converging on the necessity of eliminating Atahuallpa and distributing the treasure quickly. Assaying and melting down of the metals began in mid-May, in anticipation of Atahuallpa's execution. This then took place in the latter part of July, at about the same time as the distribution of the treasure.[24]

The total gold and silver, spoils and ransom together, turned out to be worth over 1.5 million pesos,[25] beyond anything seen or dreamed of in the Indies to that date. All but the king's fifth went to the more than 160 men of Cajamarca, the subjects of the present study. Even lowly footmen now had fortunes exceeding what captains had been able to get in Mexico, Guatemala, or Nicaragua.

Some twenty lucky men were permitted to return home with their wealth. The impact of their arrival in Spain was without parallel, particularly on the crown, which soon sent chief emissary Hernando Pizarro back to Peru for more of the same.

Jauja

The rest of the Spaniards, both men of Cajamarca and new arrivals, continued the conquest, for so they considered it. Only later would the idea arise that the Inca empire had collapsed with one thunderbolt. The conquerors advanced in formation, expecting resistance and often meeting it, apparently most often from Quito compatriots of Atahuallpa, who were still in central Peru after the Incan civil wars. Leaving Cajamarca in August, 1533, the Spaniards reached Jauja in the central highlands in just two months.[26] There was discussion of making the town their capital, and a Spanish municipality and council were formed, though only provisionally.

Vilcaconga

In late October the expedition departed for Cuzco, leaving the royal treasurer, Riquelme, with a substantial party, to hold Jauja and guard the treasure left there. Soto started out several days in advance of the main body with a mounted vanguard. About a week into November,

---

[24] Dates in ibid., p. 343; Loredo, *Los repartos*, pp. 71, 72, 117.

[25] This despite probable gross underevaluation.

[26] Dates from the time of departure from Cajamarca to arrival in Cuzco are well covered in José A. del Busto Duthurburu, "La marcha de Francisco Pizarro de Cajamarca al Cuzco," *Revista Histórica* 26 (1962–1963):146–174.

well over halfway to the Inca capital, Soto and his men experienced the worst military disaster of the Peruvian conquest. Trying to get to Cuzco and its riches first, Soto's party had gone too far ahead of the rest and, even worse, had tired out both men and horses. As they were ascending a long slope at Vilcaconga, Indians attacked them with a hail of stones and weapons from above. They barely managed to reach the top, with more casualties than the expedition had suffered in all the rest of the action since Túmbez. A relief party under Almagro extricated them.

Cuzco

The Spaniards entered Cuzco on November 15, 1533, and after some skirmishes with the Indians from Quito were well enough received by the rest of the population. During the months that the conquerors quartered in the Inca palaces and other buildings in the center of the city, another great treasure was collected, this time with more silver than gold, and distribution to the men duly took place in early March, 1534. On March 23, 1534, the governor founded a Spanish municipality in Cuzco. Some eighty conquerors enrolled as citizens and received encomiendas in the district, but only forty stayed to guard the town, while all the others returned in the direction of Jauja.[27] The expedition as a band of men was dispersing, and the conquest proper was over.

The Exodus

Returning to Jauja with most of the conquerors in April, 1534, the governor reestablished the town, and in July and August proceeded to assign encomiendas to its citizens.[28] At the same time he issued a general license for Spaniards to leave Peru, and about sixty conquerors, most of them men from Cajamarca, departed immediately for Spain. Since Jauja was soon found to be too inaccessible, the governor with general agreement evacuated the town, incorporating it into the new capital, Lima, founded on the coast in January, 1535. A little later he established Trujillo, named for his home town, near the coast to the north.

[27] Raúl Porras, "Dos documentos esenciales," *Revista Histórica* 17 (1948):9–133; Raúl Rivera Serna, *Libro primero de cabildos del Cuzco*, p. 28.
[28] Porras, "Jauja," *Revista Histórica* 18 (1949–1950):118, 136.

Offshoots: Quito and Chile

After the distribution of treasure at Cajamarca in 1533, Sebastián de Benalcázar went back to preside over the town of San Miguel. There he began independently organizing an expedition to carry out the conquest of the Quito area, which he and his men accomplished in the course of 1534. But Pedro de Alvarado invaded Quito with a large band of Spaniards from Guatemala; at the same time Almagro arrived in the area after the conquest of Cuzco and achieved a settlement in favor of Governor Pizarro. A few men of Cajamarca were in Quito accompanying Benalcázar and Almagro, but none stayed except Benalcázar himself.

Almagro now had the title of Marshal, and he was shortly to become governor and *adelantado* of an undefined area to the south of Pizarro's, named New Toledo (the kingdom of Toledo being his home region). Returning to central Peru, he took Alvarado's men and other newcomers with him to Cuzco, and in 1535 left with a large expedition on his disastrous exploration of Chile. A small number of the men of Cajamarca went with him.

The Great Rebellion and Siege of Cuzco

If a people's first resistance to an invasion is unsuccessful, it is invariably soon followed by a second resistance or rebellion. This phenomenon occurred in Peru in 1536–1537. Under their traditional leadership, the Indians rose in all parts of the country. Lima was briefly besieged, while the less than two hundred Spaniards in Cuzco were cut off from the coast for over a year. These conflicts cost the lives of several of the first conquerors, who were now encomenderos of the large towns.

The Almagrist Wars

Almagro and his men returned to Cuzco in the spring of 1537, having found no evidence of significant amounts of precious metals in upper Peru or Chile. The great silver mines of Charcas were still unsuspected. Putting an end to the Indian siege, Almagro seized Cuzco as his own, and before long laid claim to the whole southern half of Peru. In reply, the Pizarros organized an army and marched into the highlands. At Salinas, near Cuzco, they defeated Almagro badly and had him executed shortly afterward. Men of Cajamarca participated in the fighting, mainly on the side of the Pizarros.

After this the Spaniards founded subsidiary towns, such as La Plata (Charcas), Arequipa, Huamanga, and Huánuco. A second, more mod-est and successful Chile expedition went out under Pedro de Valdivia, in company with Pedro Sancho de Hoz, a first conqueror, in 1539–1540.

In 1541 partisans of don Diego, Almagro's mestizo son, assassinated Francisco Pizarro and put don Diego in power. A new royal governor, Vaca de Castro, soon entered the country, and at the head of most of the encomenderos of Peru defeated the younger Almagro in 1542 at Chupas, once again near Cuzco. This time only three or four first con-querors were with the Almagrists.

The Gonzalo Pizarro Rebellion

Vaca de Castro cheated Pizarro's youngest brother, Gonzalo, of the governorship of Peru, which Francisco had bequeathed to him by a previous royal concession. Had Gonzalo not been leading an expedi-tion into the Amazon region at the time of his assassination, he might have challenged Vaca de Castro openly. As it was, he was left discon-tented, with powerful allies.

In 1544 Viceroy Blasco Núñez Vela arrived in Peru with royal di-rectives which would have cut deeply into the significance of the en-comienda, the basis of Spanish occupation. With wide support Gon-zalo raised an army in Cuzco, marched to Lima, and forced the *audien-cia* to receive him as governor. He then ruled Peru for four years in the face of all challenges, winning several battles. A majority of the surviving first conquerors supported him at least for a time; some were prominent leaders in his cause. A few suffered his wrath for disloyalty.

When royal emissary Licenciado Gasca entered the country in 1547 with pardons for all and repeal of the offending measures, most of the conquerors and other encomenderos went over to his side. The battle of Jaquijahuana (for the third time near Cuzco) was an easy royal victory. Gonzalo Pizarro's execution terminated the last major external event in the lives of the first conquerors.

2. BEFORE THE EVENT

Backgrounds, Characteristics, and Types

B EING PRECEDES ACTION. The background of the men of Cajamarca has a primordial interest unmatched by that attaching to
any other facet of their history. The policies and stratagems they may
have devised, the goals they set for themselves, their subsequent fates,
and their impact on the invaded country, all depend in the clearest way
upon the group's composition at the moment of impact, in terms of
social types and previous experience. A group like this can also serve
social history as a good random sampling of Spanish immigration at a
given moment. For both purposes it is crucial not to let posterior fame
distort the picture. This chapter will be devoted to the men as they
were in 1532, ignoring for the moment what became of them later.

The Military Aspect

Inevitably we must ask to what extent the men we are concerned
with can be considered "soldiers." This term has been the main category used to describe the Spanish conquerors for the last four hundred

years, and, though it has led to one misconception after another, it will probably continue to have currency.[1] At least, perhaps, our understanding of the word can be modified enough to allow for some needed rectification of the conquerors' image.

The men of Cajamarca were no more professional soldiers (and no less fighting men) than the general body of immigrants into Peru in the first thirty years after the conquest.[2] Just as conquest and settlement were one process, conqueror and settler were of the same type, when not actually the same individual. Early and late, almost all men were fighters, but not only that; being a soldier did not distinguish any one group from another. The whole soldier–civilian contrast so familiar to the twentieth century was invalid in sixteenth-century Spanish America. If there were few true military men, there were hardly any "civilians." Even the clergy, surgeons, and declared merchants often took part in Indian fighting.[3] The word "soldier" was part of the vocabulary, at least, whereas there was simply no equivalent for "civilian."

The subtleties of contemporary usage can, in fact, tell us a good deal. How did the conquerors of Peru use the word "soldier"? The first thing that stands out is how little they used it. Any good modern account of the conquests, from Prescott through Kirkpatrick to Parry and Gibson, will speak of soldiers repeatedly, using the term as the primary designation for the Spaniards. Yet "soldier" never occurs, not even once, in the first two important chronicles of the Peruvian conquest by eyewitnesses Cristóbal de Mena and Francisco de Jerez. (The same appears to be true for many other on-the-spot accounts.) Nor will one find "soldier" used in the voluminous testimony, much of it very colloquial, that the conquerors gave about each other's deeds. Pi-

---

[1] If there is any category worse and more misleading than "soldier," it is that of "troops." Nothing justifies the use of this word, and it will not be discussed here.

[2] As described by the author in *Spanish Peru*; see particularly pp. 137–141.

[3] A scholar as sophisticated as Charles Gibson, whom this author greatly admires, uses the soldier-civilian classification system when he declares (*Spain in America*, p. 49) that the encomenderos were former conquerors and "leading civilian colonists." Yet even the most sedentary encomendero had to go through the motions of maintaining horse and arms. With practically all of them it was more than a pretense. Certainly there were some noncombatants at times—declared merchants and others—but they were by that fact ineligible for encomiendas. If a priest refrained from fighting, as many did, he still was not a "civilian." The question of whether fray Vicente de Valverde fought at Cajamarca has never been raised, much less settled. One source says that he was armed, at least (Gonzalo F. de Oviedo, *Historia general*, V, 92).

zarro's companions, whether spoken of in the aggregate, as small detachments, or as individuals, appear in all these sources only as "people," "men," "Spaniards," "Christians," "footmen" and "horsemen." Even chronicler Agustín de Zárate, who came to Peru in 1544 and wrote still later, retains this usage.

Generally speaking, as one moves farther away from the events in time and space, the vocabulary used to describe the conquest becomes more military. Zárate speaks of the footmen as "infantry," a term not employed by any strict contemporary.[4] Oviedo, writing at the time of the conquest, but stationed in Santo Domingo, once refers to the conquerors as soldiers.[5] Gómara, who not only wrote later, but was never himself in the Indies, also uses the word, and with him it starts to take on pejorative connotations. Perhaps like many Spaniards at home, who were seeing the growth of a more professional mercenary soldiery dedicated to the European wars, Gómara was beginning to associate the word "soldier" with rootlessness, imprudence, and quick wealth followed by quick poverty.[6] This conception of the soldier has dominated conquest historiography down to the present day. A good statement of it may be found in a recent text by a perceptive scholar: "Many a feckless foot-soldier had no other ambition than to stagger back to Spain with a sackful of silver on his back, or else to move on to fresh adventures and further rapine."[7]

Actually the conquerors were no different from any other Spaniards in this respect. Practically all who reached the Indies had intentions of returning to Spain, essentially with an eye to founding a family on their home ground. What most often kept them from realizing that ambition was purely and simply the lack of liquid wealth, a handicap that, by and large, only the first conquerors, large merchants, and a few others could overcome. The common idea that the Spanish conquerors often moved from one place to another out of adventurousness is without base. Spaniards all over the Indies tended to stay in any reasonably tolerable established position. The successful man (an encomendero, usually) either remained where he was or returned to Spain. If the

4 Zárate, *Historia*, II, 476.
5 Oviedo, *Historia general*, V, 54. Ironically the word appears in the chronicle of Francisco de Jerez, which Oviedo included in toto in his own. But comparison with Jerez's original shows that the passage is written by Oviedo, and stylistic analysis confirms it.
6 Francisco López de Gomara, *Hispania victrix*, I, 231.
7 J. H. Parry, *The Spanish Seaborne Empire*, p. 99.

area was unusually poor he might be pulled to an unusually rich one;
otherwise the only thing that could impel him to go elsewhere in the
Indies was the chance to govern his own region. The seekers after El
Dorado (leaders excepted) were new arrivals or men without position.

The concept of the footloose mercenary or professional soldier, then,
was largely imposed on the Spanish American conquest period from
European analogies, with the aid of overripe literary imagination and
anachronistic thinking. All implications following from it are a priori
suspect—for example, François Chevalier's premature assumption that
the conquerors of Mexico, "for the most part professional soldiers,"
lacked the interest and the ability to develop the economies of their
encomiendas.[8]

The conquerors knew the word "soldier," of course, and semidelib-
erately chose not to apply it to themselves. Why? To them the term
had a connotation nearer to its etymological derivation, quite different
from the ruling concept among literati and cosmopolites. It implied a
person who was being paid a salary and therefore was another person's
dependent, with little claim to direct rewards. (*Soldada* was still the
name for any contract whereby one man entered the service and pay of
another.) In Central America by 1520 or earlier, full-fledged members
of an expedition were being paid little or nothing, though they might
receive credit or loans. Partners in a joint enterprise, they expected a
share of all profits, whether treasure, encomiendas or honors. *Com-
pañero* ("partner" or "companion") was one of their favorite self-
designations.

Contrary to common opinion, according to which the early "soldiers"
were soon supplanted by settlers, the use of the word "soldier" greatly
increased with time, at least in Peru. It never referred to the first conquerors; surviving conquerors became encomenderos and were usually
referred to as *vecinos* ("citizens") of the Peruvian towns. Only nonencomenderos without a well-defined calling or position were called
"soldiers." The word in this meaning occurs constantly in the chronicles of the Peruvian civil wars and in correspondence of the late 1540's
and 1550's.

A very sophisticated attempt to grapple with the "military" problem
can be found in Mario Góngora's *Grupos de conquistadores*. With un-

[8] François Chevalier, *Land and Society in Colonial Mexico. The Great Hacienda*,
pp. 24, 25, 27.

usually complete and authentic background information, showing large numbers of men who had worked as artisans, farmers, sailors, and the like, Góngora sees that the objects of his study, the founders of Panama, cannot be considered soldiers in any exclusive sense. However, he still attempts to distinguish "men of arms" from the rest. He puts into this category hidalgos and others without a specific occupation; then he adds the mariners, and thus arrives at a figure of 50 percent for men of "martial callings."[9] Though "men of arms" is a great improvement on "soldiers," systematic distinctions among the conquerors cannot be made even on this basis. In the Indies all bore arms equally and, to judge by the results, efficiently. Probably in Spain itself most knew how to handle weapons. There are cogent objections to classifying almost any of the main branches of Spanish life under martial callings. Conceivably one could so class the hidalgos, who certainly received instruction in arms as a standard part of their education, though lineage and wealth were equally important in defining their status. But why include retainers and henchmen, as Góngora does? More often than not these men were business managers. Sailors are even less acceptable as military men. Though they, too, in practice, could fight and often joined the others, there was a clear contemporary distinction between conquerors and sailors. The only noncombatants in the very early stages of the conquest of Peru were the sailors who conveyed men and supplies from Panama and Nicaragua, then returned. On the other hand, Góngora excludes from the men of arms the members of the urban professions; yet many notaries had hidalgo pretensions, with matching martial skills and ethos. Hernando Cortés was a notary. And by excluding artisans, Góngora omits from his category such men as the swordsmiths, gunsmiths, and horseshoers, who had professional skill in arts necessary to war.

Profession and status thus throw very little light on the question of "soldiers." The only remaining criterion for assessing the broadly military element among the conquerors of Peru is experience. How many had any direct European military experience? Only two, to our certain knowledge; perhaps three or four. One was the Greek, Pedro de Candía, who had served as an artilleryman in Italy and subsequently spent years in the Spanish royal guard. He is the only man of all 168 who can comfortably be described as a professional soldier. (His Aragonese

---

[9] Mario Góngora, *Los grupos de conquistadores en Tierra Firme*, pp. 81, 90.

friend, Martín de Florencia, crossbowman and artilleryman, might have been a comparable case, but we cannot be sure.)

The second was Hernando Pizarro, who had been appointed captain of infantry in Navarre while there as a youth in the company of his father, also a captain. Having held captaincies in royal service far from home for two generations, the Pizarros had a certain claim to professional soldiery. Yet Hernando was a well-rounded hidalgo, manager of affairs, and courtier. If he devoted himself to any military activity in the time between his father's death (1522) and the conquest of Peru, there is no record of it. Francisco Pizarro himself may have been briefly in Italy as a youth, though he waited until suspiciously late to claim so, and how such an episode fits into his career is not clear.

No other European veterans appear. Conceivably some are hidden among the lesser-known figures. There may have been other men from families with a tradition of military service or border fighting; Juan Ruiz claimed that his father had fought in Granada and Navarre, and his grandfather against the Portuguese.[10] But none of the important men who later presented memorials of their services had fought in Europe; they would have been sure to mention it if they had. Many others came to the Indies too young to have campaigned previously.

Only a very small minority of the first conquerors of Peru, then, had any professional European military experience. But this minority was crucially placed, including two important captains and possibly the governor himself.

New World Experience

The military question is like many others involving unspecialized early moderns; one cannot discuss it fully without going beyond it. The conquerors' previous experience in the Indies was of greater importance in this matter than any experience in the European wars. Anyone who had lived for many years in Panama, Nicaragua, or the Caribbean in the first decades of the sixteenth century, was ipso facto an experienced Indian fighter, whatever else he was. "Indian fighter," indeed, is what we should mainly mean when we call the conquerors soldiers, if we are to continue using the word at all. This is the sense that Oviedo gave it: "skilled men, veterans and experienced soldiers

---

[10] Juan Ruiz de Arce, *Advertencias*, p. 69.

with Indians."[11] He used these words in specific reference to the men of Cajamarca, and he was of the opinion that "most" were of that type. The evidence, as far as it goes, tends to bear him out. Of 101 men whose previous experience is known or surmised as of 1532, 64 had been in the Indies for some time, 52 of them for five years or more.[12]

Table 1. Experience in the Indies, 1532

Years in Indies	No. of Men	
Under 5 years	12	
c. 5	28	
c. 10	14	
c. 15	2	
c. 20	7	
c. 25	1	
	—	64
None or almost none		37
		101
Unknown		67
Total (men)		168

Even allowing for the unknowns and the vague dividing line between new men and old, it seems safe to assert that over half of the men at Cajamarca were veterans of the Indies by any standards. There were certainly enough of them to set the tone and preserve the developing subculture (institutions, techniques, procedures, and values) of the New World Spaniards. The captains were almost all old hands. The great leaders—Pizarro, Benalcázar, and Soto—had been in the Panama region some twenty years or more. Captains Mena and Salcedo were at least ten-year veterans. The only leaders with less experience

[11] Oviedo, *Historia general*, V, 54 (the same passage referred to in footnote 5 above).

[12] Except in the case of those men who presented a memorial of services, it is hard to get any exact idea of the number of years an individual had been in the New World. His first appearance in the records is in most cases probably not the date of his arrival. Direct statements on the subject tend to be vague. Table 1 is therefore offered only as a rough approximation. The apparent anomaly that there are more men in the twenty- than in the fifteen-year category reflects the great expedition of Pedrarias de Avila to Panama in 1513–1514.

were the European military men, Candía (six years) and Hernando Pizarro (no experience).

The predominance of veterans is all the more striking because the expedition was one of the few major ones originally organized in Spain itself. The numbers of new recruits the Pizarros brought from Spain in 1530 had dwindled drastically from disease, desertion, and battle; only about thirty of them can be identified among the conquerors still with Pizarro in November, 1532. The general Spanish pattern of conquest, in relay fashion, from one new settlement to the next, was thus able to reassert itself.

In what part of the Indies had the veterans operated? The extreme vagueness and inclusiveness of their own statements make geographical precision impossible. Nevertheless it can be said that the overwhelming majority had been denizens of the domain of Pedrarias de Avila—Panama and Nicaragua—the pacified areas closest to Peru. Nicaragua, point of departure of both Soto and Benalcázar, was especially important. Only one man is known certainly to have been in Mexico, though one other originally left Spain meaning to go to Yucatan. A few had been in Honduras, which they left for Nicaragua. All must at least have traversed the Caribbean, but hardly any are known to have spent more than a brief transitional period on the islands, except for Francisco Pizarro himself.

The effect of the specifically American experience is hard to pinpoint. In the main, new social types had not yet matured, and the behavior of most of the veterans is quite readily explained directly from their peninsular backgrounds. But there are two cases of "men of the Indies" among our conquerors: Francisco Pizarro and Sebastián de Benalcázar, who by 1532 had each spent over half of his life in the New World. The imprint on them was all the deeper because they had little to look to in Spain, one being a marginal and illegitimate member of an hidalgo family and the other of frankly humble origins.

Each had a strong sense of identification with the Indies, nearly the equivalent of the emotional tie of a Spaniard to his home region. They raised almost to the status of religion the trilogy of comprehensive values which protected all their customs and privileges—respect for seniority, disdain for greenhorns, and belief in the superiority of the ways of the Indies.

By no means all of the Spaniards in Panama and Nicaragua were rough backwoodsmen; the courtly type appeared as early as 1514 with the entourage of Pedrarias de Avila. But there was also a type specific to the Isthmus, which was already becoming somewhat anachronistic by the 1530's, and to which Benalcázar, Pizarro, and Pizarro's partner, Diego de Almagro (who chanced not to be at Cajamarca), all belonged. These were men who had energy and ability, but were illiterate and retained a striking simplicity of manner. Zárate might appear to be indulging in literary fantasy in his famous chapter describing the similarities in life style of Pizarro and Almagro.[13] Actually he is close to the mark; what he is really doing is describing the Isthmian type.

None of the three, all of whom became *adelantados*, ever married or considered marriage. It is impossible to imagine a match. Their power and ambition required duchesses, their manners the humblest of women; in any case, they lived all their lives with Indian servant-mistresses. In some ways they were quite violently deviant from the general Spanish social ideals which were to be manifest in the Peru of the 1530's and 1540's. They resisted resplendent dress; they sometimes shook off their retinues to drop in on friends unannounced. Pizarro went to bed early and rose before dawn. As don Alonso Enríquez said, even after all his success he never ceased to be "a very good companion, without vanities or pomp."[14]

A question related to the men's experience is how many of them belonged to families previously associated with the Indies. The mechanism of relative appealing to relative accounted in one way or another for a very large proportion of the immigration to Spanish America. (Surely the same has been true at all times and in all parts of the world, from Carthage to Australia.) Whatever the proportions, the process was qualitatively important in building up continuous traditions which transcended and compensated for the newcomer's inexperience. Information on this aspect of our men's background is not available in a quantity to allow for methodical study or tabulation. We need to know not only that someone of the same name as a given conqueror took part in the earlier Caribbean phase, but that this predecessor was actually connected with the man of Cajamarca. The limited repertory of Spanish names practically restricts tracing of family continuities to those with rare or foreign names, or to those few cases where documents make the connection explicit.

---

[13] Agustín de Zárate, *Historia*, II, 498–499.
[14] Alonso Enríquez de Guzmán, *Libro de la vida y costumbres*, p. 153.

The oddly named Iñigo Tabuyo turns out to have been preceded by several relatives in the Caribbean. Two men at Cajamarca, Cataño and Pinelo, bore the names of Andalusia-based Genoese families which had participated in New World finance and commerce since the time of Columbus. Francisco Pizarro himself followed his uncle to the Caribbean. Alonso Peto belonged to a family involved as shipmasters and merchants in the trade between Seville and the Indies. Several men had older relatives prominent in Panama or Nicaragua; one was Gonzalo del Castillo, son of a Panamanian notary. Examples like these imply that family continuity, if we knew all the facts, would loom very large indeed, and that the cumulative experience of the expedition members was even greater than might appear from their life histories alone.[15]

Ages

The men's ages in 1532 correspond to their experience; the captains were all over thirty; Benalcázar was over forty, and Pizarro over fifty. The veterans of Nicaragua were mainly in their late twenties and early thirties. Many of the newcomers were in their early twenties. The general distribution is shown in Table 2.

Table 2. Age at the Time of Cajamarca

Age (years)	No. of Men
c. 15–19	5
c. 20–24	29
c. 25–29	41
c. 30–34	19
c. 35–39	8
c. 40–44	3
c. 45–49	1
c. 50–55	1
	107
Unknown	61
Total	168

[15] Sebastián de Torres, Pedro de Salinas de la Hoz, Alonso de Toro, and probably Hernando de Sosa accompanied older relatives. Juan de Porras was preceded by a relative in the Caribbean. Molina, Mendoza, Melchor Palomino, the Estetes, and Sotelo had relatives in Panama and Nicaragua.

Of the men whose ages are known, it could be said that most of them (70) were in their twenties; 32 were over thirty, and 5 were under twenty. Of 107 men, 75 were under thirty. However, it is also important to bring out how many of the conquerors were at the time of life that could be called youthful maturity and that can be expressed statistically as twenty-five to thirty-five. Of the 107, no less than 60 were in this age group, with 11 over thirty-five and 34 under twenty-five.[16] These men were the backbone of the force, largely identical with the Nicaraguan veterans and the best horsemen.

Spanish Regional Origins

The men of Cajamarca were a fairly standard sample of Spanish immigration in the third decade of the sixteenth century, when each year more men from central and northern Castile were joining the Andalusians who had been overwhelmingly predominant in the Caribbean phase. The one major deviation is a plurality of Extremadurans, the residue of the recruiting carried on in Trujillo and surrounding regions in 1529.[17] Despite great losses among the new recruits, Extremadura remained the largest regional unit, advancing from its usual second position to displace Andalusia.

Castile, in a broad sense, predominated. Of 131 men, all but 6 were from areas directly under the crown of Castile; even excluding Biscay,

[16] The data available on the men of Cajamarca lead in most cases to only approximate figures for their ages. Most of the ages estimated in this book rest on legal testimony by the individual involved. To arrive at the precise age of a given man on November 16, 1532, one would have to know the date of testimony to the month and day, which is not always available, as well as the man's age at that time in terms of months, which is never given. Thus, even in the most precise cases, one must allow a year's leeway in either direction; and since the age always appears modified by the remark "a little more or less," it is prudent to allow two years. The frequent statements that an individual is "about twenty-five," or "about thirty," allow for a variation of three or four years either way. Also, some ages are known only as an upper or lower limit, and some are merely estimated crudely on the basis of circumstantial evidence. Thus there is some technical impropriety in tabulating the ages in five-year periods as presented in Table 2; the aim is not to achieve statistical precision, but to underline a general pattern.

[17] The author has considerable confidence in the accuracy of the attributions of regional origin in Table 3, including those arrived at by deduction or association. It proved possible to determine a higher proportion of birthplaces than ages, one more indication of the importance of regionalism to the Spaniards. The data are here tabulated according to Spanish regions in terms of twentieth-century provinces. For the rationale and limitations of this procedure see James Lockhart, *Spanish Peru*, pp. 237–238.

Table 3. Regional Origins

Region	No. of Men
Extremadura	36
Andalusia	34
Old Castile	17
New Castile	15
Leon	15
Biscay	8
Navarre	2
Aragon	2
Greece	2
	131
Unknown	37
Total (men)	168

117 were from regions that were Castilian-speaking and Castilian-ruled. The old heartland of Leon and the two Castiles contributed 47, in a sense the largest regional group. No less than 83 were from the central provinces, compared to 48 from provinces on the periphery of the peninsula, plus 2 non-Iberians. One may note that the south was still very strong, since Extremadura and Andalusia together form a majority of 70 over 61. Yet it would be well to keep in mind that Extremadura, though often counted "southern," lies mainly side by side with New Castile on the central plateau.

The great Spanish regions as conventionally defined cannot serve all purposes of analysis. The Spaniards' primary loyalties were to smaller units, some of which had significant idiosyncrasies. In the case of Extremadura, there are marked subregions and internal rivalries, particularly important here because of the expedition's Extremaduran leadership. Sixteenth-century Extremadura divides most naturally not into the present-day provinces, but into an eastern region, Trujillo-Cáceres, the most pastoral and backward part, and the home of the Pizarros; a western region, dominated by Badajoz, with closer connections to both Seville and Portugal; and a southern region, mainly identical with the Order of Santiago's Maestrazgo de León, affected by strong Sevillian commercial influence. The standard relationship of these three regional subgroups to each other was hostility and suspicion, particularly between Badajoz and the northeast. The Extremaduran contingent is ana-

Table 4. Origins of the Extremaduran Contingent

Region	No. of Men	
Trujillo-Cáceres		
Trujillo	14	
Deleitosa	1	
Casas del Puerto or		
Las Piñuelas	1	
La Zarza	1	
		17
Cáceres	2	
Plasencia	1	
San Martín de Trevejo	1	
		4
		21
Badajoz	2	
Valencia de Alcántara	1	
Alburquerque	2	
Jerez	2	
		7
Maestrazgo and La Serena		
Maestrazgo in general	1	
Guareña	1	
Miajadas	1	
Puebla del Prior	1	
Segura de León	1	
Villafranca de los Barros	1	
Zalamea de la Serena	1	
		7
Far North		
La Garganta	1	1
Total (men)		36

lyzed in Table 4. Almost all the men from Trujillo-Cáceres accompanied the Pizarros from Spain in 1530, whereas almost all the Badajoz men were veterans. The 1529 recruiting effort apparently extended into the Maestrazgo and La Serena, since several of the men from there were new arrivals, but the main effect of the recruiting was an unusual predominance of eastern over western and southern Extremadurans.

It is also of interest to subdivide the contingent from Andalusia, to emphasize how many were from the commercial-maritime western part, and how few from the east and Granada. In fact "Andalusia," in the everyday usage of the sixteenth century, mainly referred to the present provinces of Seville and Huelva. The home town of Sebastián de Benalcázar, though in the jurisdiction of Córdoba, lies to the northeast of

Table 5. Origins of the Andalusian Contingent

Region of Origin	No. of Men	
West		
Seville		
Seville in general	7	
City of Seville	5	
Cádiz	2	
Cazalla	1	
Chiclana	1	
Lebrija	1	
Guadalcanal*	1	
Paterna del Campo	1	
Sanlúcar	1	
Santa Olalla	1	
	—	21
Huelva		
Moguer	2	
Palos	2	
Lepe	1	
	—	5
East		
Córdoba	2	
Belalcázar	1	
	—	3
Jaén	1	
Baeza	1	
Quesada	1	
	—	3
Granada	2	
		34

* Guadalcanal was in the Maestrazgo de León in the sixteenth century, a domain which stretched over southern Extremadura.

the Extremaduran Maestrazgo, with close affinities to that area and La Serena. In view of this it could be said that all the group's captains (except the Greek Candía) were from central Spain.

Regionally the expedition was a striking example of the internal consistency so characteristic of the Spanish occupation. Regional diversity among immigrants might have led to exclusive concentration of certain groups in given areas. But it never did. In area after area of the Indies, in one kind of group after another, a broad regional spread is found. With the Peru expedition, the original Extremaduran near-monopoly at the time of departure from Spain dissolved, leaving tension between Trujillan leadership and a body of men from every region in Spain.

Social Origins

Spanish social terminology of the sixteenth century is such a muddled subject that one is tempted simply to ignore the question of who the nobles were and who the commoners among the conquerors. A welter of Spanish words designated some degree of gentility or nobility; none had any unequivocal meaning. At the opposite end of the scale, we have not the slightest notion of what really constitutes a peasant; the term tends merely to cover that portion of the populace which scholars know nothing about. Once categories are established, it is most difficult to fit individuals into them. Nevertheless, the attempt must be made. Whereas no distinction between military and nonmilitary members of the expedition really existed, and groups cannot be set up on that basis, there was some sort of distinction, however blurred, between noble and plebeian members.

Contemporary Spaniards were tending to use the word "hidalgo" indiscriminately to indicate all gentlemen and nobles. But, accepting this usage, one still cannot uncritically count as hidalgos all who may have claimed to be at some later time, or, even worse, all who have had the claim raised for them by descendants. On the other hand, many who clearly were hidalgos never had occasion to say so. No one criterion sufficient for attribution can be found. The hidalgo is to be recognized in a combination of factors—the ring of his name, the quality of his signature, the nature of his associates, the respect accorded him, and the rewards given him. In the absence of ironclad evidence of a type that is too rarely available, one must decide a given individual's social quality subjectively out of a detailed acquaintance with his career. The author's

personal evaluations of the social quality of the men of Cajamarca are
embodied in Table 6.

Perhaps one in four of the conquerors, then, had some trace of gentle birth, or the appearance of it, which comes to almost the same
thing. Most were very small gentry, of the type that this writer likes to
call "ordinary hidalgos." While any classification based on the word
"hidalgo" or its synonyms is bound to remain somewhat vague, there
are certain other less equivocal indicators which tend to place the hidalgos of Cajamarca low on the scale. The higher nobility, consisting
of dukes, counts, lesser feudal lords, and their close relatives, almost
invariably bore the title of "don" from birth. Not a single "don" was
at Cajamarca. Even more revealing, very few of the men's female relatives could boast the "doña." This title was used much more liberally
than "don," so that a very large proportion of the wives of local Spanish hidalgos (themselves without title) were doñas. Yet only two or
three doñas appear among the mothers of our men. In this they were
quite typical of the general stream of Spanish immigration, as a glance
through the Sevillian registers will show, but they had far fewer doñas
in their background than the prominent people who came to Peru in
subsequent years, after its wealth was fully demonstrated.

As to the regional origin of those considered hidalgos above, nearly
all were from central Spain; Andalusia contributed only four, and Biscay proper none. The Extremaduran leadership reflects itself very clearly. Two main types of hidalgos are discernible. There were the Extremadurans, who could be called true hidalgos at least in the sense that
they manifested no strong affinity for any particular civil pursuit
(though they were in most cases more than adequately literate). Most
of these were from prominent Trujillan families, brought to the Indies

Table 6. Presumed Social Rank

Rank	No. of Men
Hidalgos	38
Borderline cases	6
Plebeians	91
	135
Unknown	33
Total	168

Table 7. Regional Origins of Hidalgos

Region of Origin	No. of Men
Extremadura	12
Old Castile	7
New Castile	7
Leon	6
Andalusia	4
Navarre	1
Unknown	1
Total	38

by Pizarro. Several petty hidalgos from the two Castiles, on the other hand, were close to the urban professions. Some were notaries, others from families which included clerics, lawyers, and even merchants. The most illustrious hidalgos among the men of Cajamarca had connections with the kingdom of Leon. Juan Morgovejo and Juan de Valdevieso were both sons of doñas; members of their immediate families had been municipal council members or magistrates. Morgovejo was connected through the Quiñones with the royal court, and Valdevieso's father belonged to one of the military orders. From Leon came also two hidalgos bearing the famous name of Maldonado.[18]

In regard to the commoners, one would like to subdivide them into two classes, separating a quasi-yeoman type from the rock-bottom plebeians and marginal members of society. The categories existed, in the terms *hombre de bien* (goodman) for the former, and *hombre vil y bajo* (vile and low person) or *villano* (peasant) for the latter. However, "hombre de bien" had almost passed out of currency; mainly it will be found in fossilized form in the headings of royal orders. "Hombre vil" was more misused than used; most often it merely indicated an attempt to denigrate the opposing party in litigation. "Villano" was a true category, though also a term of insult. The main objection to it is that Spaniards in the Indies successfully hid their peasant origins behind a general plebeianism. In no source known to this writer is any man of Cajamarca ever referred to as a *villano*, or even a *labrador* (farmer), though some of them must have been such.

---

[18] One, Diego Maldonado, was born in Dueñas near Palencia, which, though it borders Leon, is generally considered to be in Old Castile; however, he had connections with the Maldonados of Salamanca.

A gulf stretched between the capabilities and possible rewards of such literate commoners as the notary Francisco de Jerez or the merchant Diego Gavilán and such illiterate, irredeemable plebeians as trumpeter Alconchel and tailor Chico. But the difference cannot be systematized. It did not rest on occupation alone; there was great variety in the single class of artisans, or even in a single trade, like tailoring. Again, a careful subjective assessment is perhaps better than none. It can be estimated that of the 91 called plebeians above, only some twenty were of the sort whose external behavior and appearance branded them as belonging to the humblest station. The others circulated freely among the hidalgos, and under the right conditions could pass effectively into their ranks.

While no one factor determined whether or not this would happen, a crucial element was education, which became of increased importance because the situation tended to submerge some other distinctions. All were men of arms, and lineage proper could be brought to bear only for the most illustrious, since most men were not aware of each other's exact social origins. Degree of education thus becomes a matter of great interest; yet the formal education of our men remains a mystery. Only fray Vicente de Valverde is known to have attended a university. Morgovejo, Valdevieso, Hernando Pizarro, and some of the notaries, like Miguel Estete and Jerónimo de Aliaga, might well have done so, to judge by their articulateness and polish. No less than six of the men composed accounts of the conquest substantial enough to be considered chronicles, and only two of these works show signs of having been dictated.

For the rest, our knowledge of the expedition members' educational background is limited to the index of their literacy, compiled in Table 8. The twentieth century draws a sharp, somewhat artificial line between literates and illiterates. The sixteenth knew three categories, adding the intermediate one of those who could sign their names. Laughable though this may seem, there was a real distinction. The person who might not be able to read and write well enough to handle the sixteenth century's complicated script and forms of written expression, yet could sign decently, had invariably been exposed to a year or two of education of the grammar-school type, with corresponding effects on his values, manners, and ambitions. The distinction leaps to the eye in the difference between the signatures of those effective illiterates who were

Table 8. Extent of Literacy

Extent		No. of Men
Definitely literate		51
Could sign		
Doubtless truly literate	25	
Literacy cannot be deduced	24	
Crude signature, probably		
illiterate	8	
		57
Definitely illiterate		33
		141
Unknown		27
Total		168

taught as children, and the misshapen, awkward scrawls or empty ru-brics of those who learned to "sign" as adults.

It may be noted that, to our definite knowledge, 108 of the men could sign their names, 33 could not. Of the whole group, 76 were al-most certainly functioning literates, 41 not, with 51 unknown.[19] The relatively high proportion of literates tends to reinforce the conclusion stated just above—that most of the expedition's commoners were not at the very lowest level of Spanish society. The core of the expedition, both the preponderance of its numbers and its main strength, was in its marginal hidalgos and upper plebeians, who for many purposes may be considered a single group.

What of Spain's subordinated ethnic minorities, Moorish, Jewish, and Negro? As is well known, imperial directives to exclude such peo-ple from the Indies were dead letters, though they did help induce at-tempts at self-disguise. Were any among the first conquerors of Peru? If there were any Moriscos or men of Moorish descent, they remain hidden, though a Cristóbal de Burgos who had taken part in the earlier stages of the discovery was reputedly of Morisco origin. Two men of

[19] Only occasionally does one meet with a direct statement on the literacy of one of the men. However, the inability to sign constitutes unequivocal negative evidence. On the other hand, such evidence as a holograph letter, the practice of a certain pro-fession, or membership in a certain type of family is equally clear positive proof. For a large intermediate group, the only evidence is the quality of the individual's signature, not a certain indicator, yet it is often fluent enough or crude enough to allow one to deduce the person's state of literacy reasonably well.

African or partly African descent can be identified among the conquerors (aside from the unknown—apparently not large—number of black slaves the Spaniards had with them). One was black Juan García, born in Old Castile, who served the expedition in the stereotyped role of crier and piper. He was counted a partner of the general company, but one of its lowest members. The other was mulatto Miguel Ruiz from Seville, probably the son of a Spaniard and his slave-woman. He too circulated among the plebeians, but at a much higher level, as a horseman with the expectation of a double share of any profits.

The question of Jews is much more difficult. All remaining Spanish Jews were by this time New Christians, at least nominally converted from Judaism. For more than a generation they had been industriously hiding their identity. To try to identify them at this remove in time involves one in endless innuendo and speculation, all the more so because the term "Jew" was an insult and curse word the Spaniards would resort to frequently and irresponsibly either in the heat of an argument or to discredit an enemy. José Antonio del Busto feels he has identified three New Christians among the conquerors.[20] Two of these attributions seem, at least to this writer, extremely speculative; for the third man, the half-Italian Aragonese, Martín de Florencia, there is a quite strong circumstantial case. Nor are these the only possibilities. Equally strong indications point to a *converso* origin for the company's only ecclesiastic, fray Vicente de Valverde. If one is to speculate, there is no stopping place. Prominent conqueror Juan de Barbarán was all his life little more than a pawnbroker, and his mother bore the surname San Pedro (many *conversos* took saints' names). Notary Jerónimo de Aliaga, for another example, was a stunningly successful negotiator who won permanent high office in Peru and married into a family of great nobles; yet he failed to gain entry into the Order of Santiago—the one honor usually denied New Christians.

Certainty about the *converso* descent of any of the men of Cajamarca will have to await genealogical studies extending back into the era when Jews did not hide themselves. We cannot, of course, assess the nature and the significance of their role until we have some firm examples with which to work. At most one can voice the suspicion that New Christians were indeed present, not restricted to any conventional role,

---

[20] José A. del Busto Duthurburu, "Tres conversos en la captura de Atahualpa," *Revista de Indias* 27 (1967):427–442.

but distributed in a variety of functions. It would be natural enough for some conversos to be found in a group dominated by petty hidalgos, subprofessionals, and substantial commoners.

Trades and Skills

For most of the characteristics of the first conquerors we have a numerical sampling of two-thirds or better. Not so with their occupational background. This writer views with considerable awe and envy the muster of the founders of Panama, where each man declares his peninsular trade in the plainest words.[21] Nothing comparable exists for the men of Cajamarca, and the research net which gathered in their regional origins or ages unfortunately let their trades mainly slip past. Therefore Table 9 does not have quite the same significance as those above.[22]

[21] Printed in full in Góngora, *Grupos de conquistadores*, pp. 70–75.

[22] In Table 9, the notary-secretaries are judged to be Jerez and Sancho; the notaries, Aliaga, Barrera, Narváez, and San Millán; the accountants, Azpeitia, Estete, Félix, Paredes, Pineda, and Zárate. (All appear in Part II, chapter 9.) These attributions are based on what the men happened to be doing at the moment. Some would qualify for two, or for all three subcategories, and all probably had the same basic notary's training, though Félix, Paredes, and Pineda may have been specialized accountants. The regional distribution of the men is: Old Castile, 5, Andalusia, 3, Biscay, 2, New Castile, 1, Navarre, 1. Four other men of Cajamarca had notaries in their immediate families, and very likely received the same training: Briceño, Castillo, Miguel Estete de Santo Domingo, and Melchor Palomino. To include them would change the distribution to: Old Castile, 6, Andalusia, 5, Biscay, 2, New Castile, Leon, and Navarre, 1 each. In neither computation is a single man from Extremadura.

As to the men of affairs, this group appears together in Part II, chapter 10. Their regional distribution is: Old Castile, 4, Andalusia, 3, Extremadura, 3, New Castile, 1, Navarre, 1, unknown, 1. Some others who might have been included are Diego Maldonado, Mesa, Alonso Pérez, Hernando Pizarro, Sotelo, Valdevieso, and Verdugo, but several of these are clearly hidalgos with diverse activities, and one other circulated more among the seamen. If they are included, the regional distribution of this category becomes: Old Castile, 6, Andalusia, 5, Extremadura, 4, New Castile, 2, Leon, 2, Navarre, 1, unknown, 1.

The artisans are: tailors, Chico, Francisco González, Juan Jiménez, Francisco Martínez, Robles, Páramo; horseshoers, Calderón, Juan de Salinas; artillerymen, Candía, Florencia; carpenters, Escalante, Anadel; cooper, Palomino; swordsmith, Alonso Jiménez; barber, Francisco López; trumpeters, Alconchel, Segovia; and crier and piper, Juan García pregonero. Their biographies are in Part II, chapter 12, except for Candía's, which is in chapter 7, and Anadel's, in chapter 13. Their regional distribution is: Extremadura, 4; New Castile, 4; Andalusia, 3; Old Castile, Leon, Biscay, Aragon, and Greece, 1 each; unknown, 3.

So elusive are sure attributions for the calling of mariner that only Bartolomé Sánchez, called a sailor on the roll of Cajamarca, and Hernando Beltrán were included definitely as mariners. Anadel, under "artisans," was also a seaman, and so

Table 9. Known and Presumed Occupations

Occupations	No. of Men	
Ecclesiastics		1
Clerks or notaries		
Notary-secretaries	2	
Notaries	4	
Accountants	6	
		12
Men of affairs (merchants,		
managers, entrepreneurs)		13
Artisans, etc.		
Tailors	6	
Horseshoers	2	
Artillerymen	2	
Carpenters	2	
Coopers	1	
Swordsmiths	1	
Stonemasons	1	
Barbers	1	
Trumpeters	2	
Criers and Pipers	1	
		19
Seamen		2
Total		47

Very possibly it is not truly representative of the group as a whole; certainly it does not include all those who were trained for some special calling. On the other hand, it probably does include a majority of those who were still practicing their trades at the time of the conquest, and may be indicative of the skills in demand by the conquerors. There is a subjective element in some of the attributions, particularly of the men of affairs, who were included mainly on the basis of visible activities rather than because of any titles they bore.

---

may have been the cooper, Palomino, and artilleryman Candía. Various hints indicate that several others, included in Part II, chapter 13, may once have been men of the sea. All together this would make 15, who would be regionally distributed as follows: Andalusia (all Seville-Huelva), 8, Biscay, 2, Greece, 2, Catalonia, 1, unknown, 2.

Almost all of these skills were being actively used to further the purpose of the expedition. Only the stonemason, one of the seamen, and perhaps one or two of the entrepreneurs had not recently exercised their trades. It is indeed lamentable that fuller information on the original trades of the remaining men has not been forthcoming. The hierarchy of occupations made up a far more complete, articulated, and realistic system of social organization than the noble-plebeian distinction. Complete knowledge of the occupational background of the men would be the best possible indicator of their social origins and general potential. In its absence the only recourse is informed speculation. There are hints that several additional men were trained as clerks, and the entrepreneurial types were even more numerous, though hard to pin down. Well over a dozen men had probably been mariners at some time. Most of the remaining commoners must have been brought up to some branch of artisanship or agriculture; if they were like their close predecessors, the founders of Panama, there were considerably more artisans among them than farmers.

Of the forty-seven men listed in Table 9, only a few had specifically martial skills: the two artillerymen and the swordsmith, certainly, and in this context one should probably count also the two horseshoers and the three musicians. Only one person had a specifically religious calling. By and large the specialists were involved in organization, record-keeping, supply, and maintenance. The number of notaries may appear amazing at first sight, but it is in keeping with the great general strength of this profession in the Indies. The magnitude of the expected tasks of treasure distribution, revenue collection, governing and city-founding fully justified their presence. Why there were so many active tailors is rather puzzling, even though tailors were regularly the most numerous craft group in the Indies. Whatever the conquerors' propensities, before Cajamarca they lacked the money to pay for any large amount of new clothing. One would expect tailoring to be dormant, and the tailor to conceal his trade beneath a conqueror's role, as many artisans did. Yet tailors still suffered themselves to be called tailors—one of them appears on the roll of Cajamarca as "Robles, tailor"—and they cemented their identity by close association with each other. It should be made clear that although many of the merchants and other entrepreneurially oriented conquerors were engaged in the active management of affairs on thir own behalf and for others, none appeared in the guise of a merchant at the time. The declared merchants,

with their shipments of merchandise from Panama, stayed at first mainly in the ships, and at most came as far as Piura.

In regional origin the trade groups are from the usual scattered regions, but there are some peculiarities, stemming partly from the
smallness of the sampling, partly from the expedition's Extremaduran
origin. Extremadura was Spain's least developed area technically and
commercially; on most listings of Spaniards with special skills, Extremadura is hardly present. In this case, the Pizarros apparently made a
conscious effort when recruiting in their home region in 1529 to
acquire men with the necessary expertise, and the results are evident
in Extremadura's respectable showing on Table 10. The situation was

Table 10. Regional Origins of Occupational Groups

Place of Origin	Professionals and Subprofessionals	All Occupational Groups
Old Castile	9	9
Andalusia	7	10
Extremadura	3	8
New Castile	3	7
Biscay	2	3
Navarre	2	2
Leon	0	1
Aragon	0	1
Greece	0	1
Unknown	1	1
	27	43

still grim enough for Trujillan leadership. Only three of the men of
affairs were Extremaduran, and not a single one of the twelve notaries.
The Pizarros would be forced to rely mainly on men from other
regions.

Perhaps the mere operation of chance in a small sample has determined the fact that Andalusia, home of trades and commerce, is unusually weak in the occupational listings, in second place under all
three of the main headings of Table 9, and ahead of Old Castile overall
only on the strength of its seamen. Old Castile is the leader in the
literate skills. If one makes a category "professionals and subprofessionals" of the ecclesiastic, the clerks, the men of affairs, and the barber-

surgeon, Old Castile precedes Andalusia. These comparative positions may relate to the period of Old Castilian domination of commerce (even in Andalusia) in the early decades of the sixteenth century, before the Andalusians came to the fore. For some reason, Leon is very poorly represented among the occupations, despite the numerical strength of its contingent at Cajamarca.

The active occupations of the first conquerors were somewhat weighted toward the skills necessary to maintain an expedition, then to conquer and govern a country. But those trades and professions were mainly identical with the ordinary range of Spanish activity. Making little or no deliberate effort to duplicate peninsular society or to provide for all that was needed to implant a civilization, our men nevertheless represented in themselves the whole hierarchy of Spanish occupations. With this came the principal elements of European learning and technology, as well as the essence of Spanish social organization.

The Background in Sum

Spanish society in the Indies seems to have been like certain organisms which can regenerate themselves from any detached segment, however small. One never finds a group, whether an expedition, a town population, or an army, that is all of a piece. Always there is diversity —of region, of social rank, of occupation, of experience. Everything combined to produce this result: the pattern of Spanish expansion, which was unplanned or at most locally planned; the piecemeal character of immigration and its varied sources; the limited opportunities for a given calling in any one Spanish settlement, so that occupational groups naturally dispersed. Any expedition had to have men with a variety of skills merely in order to survive. Tropical diseases alone assured that not all the Spaniards in any one place would be newcomers.

So it was that the men of Cajamarca came from every region of Spain, represented every social position from the son of a slave to the relative of a courtier, and between them practiced all the major Spanish callings and crafts. As a group, their reputation for illiteracy is totally undeserved.[23] One in ten was a notary; twenty or thirty would not have

---

[23] See J. H. Cohen's introduction to his translation of the chronicle of Agustín de Zárate, entitled *The Discovery and Conquest of Peru*, where Cohen makes the incredible statement (p. 8) that "none of Francisco Pizarro's companions on the march to Cajamarca was more than barely literate." As so often, the conquerors must suffer the condescension of those who have not taken the trouble to understand them. Cohen is so unfamiliar with sixteenth-century Spanish that he (p. 207)

been out of place at the royal court, where some few did indeed later flourish. It is true that the group had an overall plebeian flavor. Its main strength, numerically and qualitatively, was in capable, literate commoners, lower-ranked professionals, and marginal hidalgos—three types with much in common. To establish a Spanish society in Peru would require more men, but not men of a different kind.

The expedition members also had their share of New World experience, indeed more than their share, for not only did they boast experienced leadership, but over half the men were themselves veterans. The vast distance from the base of recruitment in Spain and the deadly Panamanian climate had worked to reduce drastically the number of newcomers. On the other hand, since Peru's wealth and greatness had been confirmed, men in mineral-poor Nicaragua and Panama who had previously viewed the Peruvian venture cautiously hastened to join it. The traditions and techniques of the Spanish Indies would therefore go immediately and effortlessly into operation in Peru.

---

translates *por maravilla* ("very seldom") as "surprisingly," thinks *yanacona*, a word meaning Indian servant, is the name of an ethnic group, and (p. 208) translates *puñal* ("dagger") as "hilt."

3. AFTER THE EVENT

Life Patterns of Repatriates and Settlers

MANY NEW STRANDS APPEAR in the lives of the conquerors after the happenings of Cajamarca divided their careers sharply into two parts. Though the processes and tendencies to be found in the present chapter are common to all the Indies, in their proportions and magnitude they are as unique as Peru itself, so that the material here does not have quite the immediate, general applicability of the chapter on backgrounds. The treasure of Peru altered the rate of return, sending far more conquerors back to Spain than from poorer areas the Spaniards occupied, and the decisiveness of the victory meant that the men of Cajamarca were in a category by themselves. By common definition they and they alone were entitled to be called "first conquerors," though actual usage was somewhat looser.[1]

[1] Pedro de Cieza, *Tercera parte*, in *Mercurio Peruano* 39 (1958):570; Garcilaso de la Vega, *Obras*, II, 259.

Staying and Returning

The choice between remaining in Peru or returning to Spain presented itself to the captors of Atahuallpa in an acute form. They had stronger incentives in both directions than the vast majority of Spaniards in the Indies. If they stayed, they could expect large encomiendas and positions of honor in the wealthiest area in the New World. Yet the first harvest of that wealth was already in their hands. The treasure of Cajamarca alone made them immensely wealthy in a time before the silver of Potosí brought inflation; a year later many added an almost equal amount from the conquest of Cuzco. Their wealth, in liquid form, could easily be taken to Spain; they had little experience or expectation of the crown's confiscation policy, which in any case gave them highly desirable annuities.

To have so much bullion early in the game was highly unusual. The first rewards of conquerors of other areas were not remotely comparable. Most Spaniards, including encomenderos, had to spend years to amass such sums, in the process enmeshing themselves ever more deeply in local affairs. Aside from the momentum of their activities and their growing attachments, they could never transfer their total wealth and position back to Spain. (The one group which could—the import merchants—had the greatest tendency to return.)

In the days immediately after the distribution of treasure at Cajamarca in 1533, there was no doubt which way the scales were turning. Everything the men had was portable. All they would leave behind was potentiality; encomiendas had not yet been distributed, and there was danger as well as promise in the future. As individuals, the conquerors were overwhelmingly in favor of returning.[2] Only the governor and some other men of long experience and great ambition, like Benalcázar and Soto, were immune to the fever. But since much of the force was needed merely to secure what had been won, and letting any substantial number go would have posed an almost insoluble problem of choosing the lucky ones, Governor Pizarro was able to enforce a general policy of denying the conquerors license to leave the country.

Certain exceptions were made, however. Messengers and money had to be sent to Spain. The conquerors had an excellent understanding of the demonstration effect, and knew that nothing could better hasten reinforcements to Peru than the sight of men returning from there

[2] Despite William H. Prescott, *History of the Conquest of Peru*, p. 964.

with great fortunes.[3] Altogether, some twenty chosen men departed in July and August 1533.[4] A first small contingent accompanied Hernando Pizarro, with an advance on the king's fifth. As more Spaniards kept arriving in Peru, the governor felt confident enough to let another small group follow close on the heels of the first.[5] Indeed, most reports treat the two groups as one.

Who received the much-desired license? The chroniclers say that it went to old veterans, along with the sick and wounded.[6] Thirteen of the first returnees can be identified, and they tend to confirm the chroniclers' assertions.[7] Seven were older men, all but one of them veterans of the Indies. Two had been wounded, to our knowledge. But this did not preclude other considerations. Captains Mena and Salcedo were not so much receiving the reward for their long service as going reluctantly into exile. The Pizarros also saw to it that their personal interests were reflected in the group. Besides Hernando Pizarro, at least two Pizarro stewards went to Spain at this time—Juan Cortés and Martín Alonso.

The first set of returnees was thus selected for compelling reasons having to do, if not always with the interests of the conquering expedition as a whole, then at least with those of the Pizarro faction. Not until a year later did the conquerors get the opportunity to make a clear-cut choice between Spain and Peru.

By July, 1534, Governor Pizarro was back in the central Jauja region, after the Spanish foundation of Cuzco. The conquest of Peru appeared complete; citizenship had been assigned, and distribution of encomiendas had begun. With a flood of newcomers, Pizarro no longer needed manpower, and the first conquerors, with their valid claims,

[3] Pedro Sancho says this in so many words (Sancho, *Relación*, p. 15).

[4] Cristóbal de Mena, one of the men departing, gives the round number of twenty-five ("Conquista del Perú," p. 98). An account published in France in 1534, based on letters of officials at Panama, estimates the returnees more precisely at twenty-two or twenty-three (Raúl Porras, *Relaciones primitivas*, p. 77).

[5] So says Francisco de Jerez (*Verdadera relación*, II, 345). On pp. 345–346 he gives the arrival time of the ships bringing the men to Seville, with the names of some of the ships and masters.

[6] Jerez, *Verdadera relación*, II, 345; Sancho, *Relación*, p. 15. A letter from witness Nicolás de Heredia agrees (Raúl Porras, *Cartas*, p. 119), as does one from Gaspar de Marquina (below, p. 459).

[7] Aguirre, Alonso, Anadel, Baena, Carranza, Cortés, Cristóbal Gallego, Jerez, Mena, Molina, Hernando Pizarro, Salcedo, Juan de Salinas de la Hoz. Porras, speculating, presents a list including several men who actually returned later (*Relaciones primitivas*, p. 98).

were as much a burden to him as a support, since he began to be pressed for enough encomiendas to distribute to important people. These considerations and the clamor of the conquerors moved him to issue a general license for Spaniards to leave the country.[8]

In response, most of the conquerors quickly made their final decisions. Throughout late 1534 and early 1535, perhaps some sixty of the men of Cajamarca left for Spain.[9] This great exodus was the last important group movement among the first conquerors, and fixed once and for all their profile in the matter of staying in the Indies or going home (Table 11). Only eight or ten stragglers later left Peru for Spain, in exchange for about the same number of men who reappeared in Peru. As seen in Table 12, the division between the two hemispheres was approximately equal, although the proportion of repatriates may actually be slightly greater than indicated.[10]

Table 11. Rate of Return to Spain

Year	No. of Returnees
1533	13
1534	39 ⎫
1535	13 ⎭ 52
1536	3
1539	1
1540	1
1550	1
Year unknown (probably early)	3
Total	74

[8] Of the seventy-four listed in Table 11, 8 came back to Peru permanently. At least 3 of them never meant to stay in Spain. One, Hernando Pizarro, came back to Peru, then went to Spain once again. Late visits to Spain by Verdugo and Benalcázar were not taken into account here.

[9] Juan Ruiz, one of them, puts the number at sixty (*Advertencias*, p. 111). Diego de Ojuelos also refers to the general license of 1534 (*CDIHN*, III, 480). The best single source for identifying some of the men and the amounts they took home is AGI, Indiferente General 1801, containing records of the ships *Santa Catalina* and *San Miguel* for 1535.

[10] It is not in all cases documented that the repatriates died in Spain (Table 12), but since they reached there and did not come back to Peru, the presumption is justified. It does not seem possible to come any closer to an estimate of total returnees with present evidence. One might add the twenty-two or twenty-three of 1533 to the

Table 12. Final Destination of the Men of Cajamarca

Died in the Indies	
Peru	63
Other	3
	66
Died in Spain	66
	132
Unknown	36
	168

What lay behind the men's choices? Not pure chance or caprice, and hardly individual mentality, unless as an intermediary link in a process which began in more general factors. Anyone who studies the conquerors closely will soon get a sense of how strongly and uniformly such general forces operated, but they are of such complexity that they resist schematic interpretation.

No categories yet discovered seem to coincide exactly with the group pair of those staying versus those returning. The closest approach to such a thing is the distinction based on possession of a horse—not a comical circumstance, if we consider the values associated with the horse in Spanish society, added to its crucial role in war and profit-getting in the Indies. The tendency was for horsemen to go home and for footmen to stay in the Indies (Table 13).[11]

Naturally the horse in and of itself was not the principal determining factor. Of most immediate importance was the fact that a horseman got a standard share of the Cajamarca treasure which was double the share of even the best footman. In a word, the men with the biggest shares tended to return to Spain, the reason being too apparent to need

estimated sixty of 1534–1535, plus known stragglers, minus retrogressors, but this would give a false conclusion, because an unknown number of the returnees of 1534 were conquerors of Cuzco, who had not been at Cajamarca. It might be suspected, as the author's research centered on Peru and the Archive of the Indies, and Peru had so many fewer Spaniards than Spain, that more than half of the unknowns were returnees. Yet this cannot be measured, and it seems best to stay with an estimate of approximate parity between the groups, realizing that the "unknown" category may have a bias toward returnees.

11 Fray Vicente de Valverde is included among the footmen. Of course the reference is to horsemen and footmen at the time of Cajamarca itself; after that almost everyone had a horse.

Table 13. Final Destination of Horsemen and Footmen

Destination	Horsemen	Footmen	Totals
Spain	40	26	66
Indies	19	47	66
Unknown	3	33	36
	62	106	168

explanation. Only leading captains, for whom governorships of whole areas in the Indies were now a real possibility, were relatively unaffected by the temptation to terminate their New World careers with an unprecedented fortune. Owning or not owning a horse also tended to correlate, in a somewhat less direct way, with two other factors which, independently, had their effect on the choice between Europe and America.

Though it did not operate in any simple fashion, one of the most potent of these factors was experience in the Indies (often approximately parallel to age). While the statistical contrasts which this characteristic produces, as seen in Table 14, are clear enough, they are still less striking than its true effects. Even a rough compilation like this shows that almost two-thirds of the experienced men returned while a slight majority of the new men stayed. A very interesting phenomenon is the number of men of unknown experience among the settlers. In all probability the "unknown" category has a bias toward men with little or no experience in the Indies, so that if we knew the whole truth, there would be as large a majority of new men staying as there is of experienced men returning.[12]

To complicate matters, the accumulation of experience did not lead to the constant reinforcement of a single tendency. Rather, with the addition of years, a man often reached a point of diminishing desire to return that finally culminated in a positive desire to stay in the Indies. This was manifest in the careers of Pizarro and Benalcázar, and only less so for some other old hands.

This internal variation, in which the same statistical variable points

[12] The numbers are not large enough, nor the subcategories clear enough, to go beyond a simple distinction between "experienced" and "new" in Table 14. Those who had any Indies background at all are therefore included in the former group.

Table 14. Indies Experience Related to Final Destination

Indies Experience	Returned to Spain	Stayed in the Indies
Experienced	38	22
New	15	19
Unknown	13	25
Total	66	66

in two directions, demands that we attempt to go beyond correlation to a more direct understanding. The effect of experience on the oldest veterans is the more immediately comprehensible of the two reactions. These men gradually became so adapted to the ways of the New World that they felt more at home there than anywhere else. Indeed, this process of adaptation, enmeshment, and identification seems to have been the primary effect of experience in the Indies in general, and the strong opposite tendency had to do with the displacement involved in the conquest of Peru in particular.

The local identification that most of the experienced conquerors had built up was with Central America—above all, Nicaragua. Leaving that area for another as distant and distinct as Peru was quite a wrench, equivalent in a way to tearing up all roots and going home to Spain, so that the Nicaraguan veterans must have been in an unsettled mood, ready for yet another large move. Then, too, almost all had been dissatisfied in Central America. Many had been on one expedition after another without attaining either treasure or an encomienda; others had held marginal encomiendas hardly productive enough to sustain them. Even the most established had reason to be discontented with Nicaragua's lack of negotiable assets. After Cajamarca, such men must have had a sense of completion. They had searched and they had found, and there was nothing more to expect. Also, almost all of these veterans and "older men" were still young enough to look forward to decades of a new life if they returned to Spain (conversely, the really older men like Pizarro lacked any such incentive to return).

The new men, on the other hand, were in a different frame of mind. They had prepared themselves for a New World career, and a year and a half spent on an expedition could hardly represent the culmination of it. A fresh momentum carried them forward; perhaps they looked for more in the future because they could not compare Peru to austere Nicaragua as the veterans could. They were so young, most of them, that they could expect to accumulate wealth and honors for ten years and still go home at a good age if they cared to. In actual fact, few went home who did not go early, since Spanish and Indian wars took their toll, and the "new men" soon built up their own experience and local attachments, while the full extent of Peru's unparalleled wealth became ever more apparent. The neophytes were mainly footmen; both of these attributes contributed to relatively small shares of the treasure, creating in them a desire to stay and attain amounts equal to those of their superiors.

Experience alone, however elaborated upon, cannot serve as a sole explanation of the men's further destiny, any more than possession of a horse, or the size of their shares. Men of all degrees of experience ended on each side of the Atlantic. Another important determinant, more valid than the first for Spanish settlement in America generally, was the social standing of the individual. The better a person's social position in peninsular Spain, the more likely he was to return there (and conversely, the worse it was, the more likely he was to stay in the New World). The workings of this principle can be seen in the Pizarro family itself, where the legitimate member returned and the three illegitimate members died in Peru. It asserts itself at all levels, and is visible even when measured with the crude and subjective categories of "hidalgo" and "plebeian" (Table 15).[13] Nowhere is it clearer than in the cases of those few who tried to make a life for themselves at home in Spain, then gave up and returned to Peru—whether Diego de Trujillo, Hernando del Tiemblo, or Juan García de Santa Olalla, these are uniformly men of low degree.

The rationale of the tendency is not far to seek. The aim of any

Table 15. Presumed Social Rank Related to Final Destination

Rank	Spain	Indies
Hidalgos	26	20
Plebeians	30	36
Unknown	10	10
	66	66

[13] These categories are explained above, in chapter 2.

returning conqueror was to live in splendor in familiar surroundings. The wealth and, secondarily, the fame of the first conquerors of Peru would give them a powerful boost in local society, but there were limits to such action. What is more, the conquerors knew there were limits. Therefore those who could expect a good reception were the most prone to go home.

But, as with the factor of experience, the principle must admit not only of casual exceptions, but of cases where it seems to operate positively in the opposite direction. For there were instances of men leaving Peru precisely because of their humbleness. This, too, can be reduced to a more general formulation—the conquerors tended to choose a place of residence where they would meet with a social reception as comfortable as possible. Generally it was easier for a man to find a niche in the Indies, where exact lineage was often unknown or ignored and seniority of arrival was a strong redeeming factor. But as Peru began to settle down a little, and the remaining first conquerors turned to founding cities and exploiting their encomiendas, a certain shift took place. A horde of new arrivals, nonencomenderos, made up the majority of the Spanish populace; the encomiendas of the conquerors were vast and extremely lucrative. The encomenderos became the functioning heads of society and were expected to live in a seigneurial manner. Most of the men of Cajamarca, even most of the plebeians, were capable of acting the part of the patriarch without appearing ridiculous. But a few—Alconchel the trumpeter, Chico the tailor, Juan García the black crier, Escalante the carpenter, and others from the lowest reaches of Spanish society—could not. These were individuals whom the most casual glance would reveal as peasantlike in look and manner. Out of place as Peruvian encomenderos, they might either live unobtrusively on the margin—the choice of Alconchel—or they might escape from an uncomfortable position by returning to Spain. This was the alternative chosen by Juan García. His move was probably not altogether voluntary, since people had begun to murmur about him; and Escalante claimed on arrival in Spain that he had been ejected from Peru.

With this we begin to enter the realm of politics, which will be further discussed in the next chapter. Suffice it to say at present that politics and its concomitant of Spanish regional origin groupings must be taken into consideration. The governor's friends and compatriots tended to remain, his enemies and his regional rivals tended to return to Spain.

Having dealt with the main determinants of the conquerors' ultimate residence, we may ask what effect the selection process had upon Spanish Peruvian society, of which the remaining men of Cajamarca were important leaders and style-setters. If the most experienced and best-born men, with the largest shares, returned to Spain, was Peru left with plebeian mores and out of contact with the accumulating traditions of the Indies? The answer is no. First, not literally all the men in the groups so inclined actually went home; though two-thirds of the horsemen left, one-third stayed, and those remaining included the most experienced and best-educated of them all, starting with Francisco Pizarro and fray Vicente de Valverde. Moreover, by the time of the mass departure of 1534–1535, the new men had lived in close companionship with the veterans for some four years and had fully absorbed their ways. Finally, the men of Cajamarca were closely followed by other immigrants, some of whom had both Indies experience and good Spanish background, and among these men the incidence of return was far lower.

The Accumulation of Honors

In most respects we must deal with our men under two different headings, according to their destination in Spain or in the Indies. But in truth the lives of both groups are closely parallel, and nowhere is this clearer than in the matter of honors. The honors awarded the men of Cajamarca are a sensitive measure of their further progress. True enough, the conquerors actively sought many of these distinctions, and often paid for them. Yet they represent achievement of status and, by their nature, may lay bare a desire to attain something lasting.

Each of the men hoped for a coat of arms to adorn his person and family; as a maximum goal he aspired to membership in the Order of Santiago. Each man hoped for a municipal council seat or magistracy, the repatriate in the capital of his home region, the settler in the Peruvian town of his residence. Other honors—captaincies,[14] governorships, titles of "don" and "adelantado," Valverde's bishopric—did mainly go to men staying in the Indies, as can be seen in Table 16. Coats of arms went more often to those who returned and could be

[14] Of twenty-two men holding captaincies, two received permanent title as His Majesty's captain. Seven of the men were already captains at the time of Cajamarca.

Table 16. Honors Related to Final Destination

Honors	Indies	Spain	Totals
Common distinctions			
Coats of arms	10	17	27
Municipal office in Indies	34	7	41
Municipal office in Spain	1	11	12
Captaincies	17	5	22
High distinctions			
Governorships	5	0	5
Title of Marquis	1	0	1
Title of Adelantado	3	0	3
Habit of Santiago	3	1	4
Bishopric	1	0	1
Title of Don	5	1	6
Notary Major of Peru	0	1	1
Chief Constable of Audiencia of Granada	0	1	1

present at court.[15] The habit of Santiago was also awarded to men then in Spain, though all but one spent the rest of their lives in the Indies.[16] Altogether sixty-eight men, to our knowledge, obtained some distinction or other, many of them several. Probably more returnees held municipal office in Spain than appear, since research could not be done in all the scattered Spanish towns where they settled.

Not honors that had to be awarded, but recognition nonetheless, were the endowed chaplaincies the conquerors set up to perpetuate their memory, usually in the place where they settled permanently. Only fragmentary documentation of this aspect is available, but some idea emerges from the example of Huamanga: the families of four of the five first conquerors settling there had local chaplaincies still functioning in 1585.[17]

[15] Don Martín, the Indian interpreter, has not been integrated into any of the statistics in chapters 2 and 3, being clearly in a totally different category. Yet it is interesting to note that he too was granted arms, and, like most of those who were, he eventually "returned" to Spain, though involuntarily.

[16] Francisco Pizarro achieved this honor and many others before Cajamarca; only an elaborate escutcheon and the title of marquis came afterward.

[17] Jiménez de la Espada, *Relaciones geográficas*, I, 196–199.

In a sense, Table 16 tells the whole story of the fate of the men of Cajamarca. But to spell out its implications in more detail, a closer look at the conquerors' careers is needed.[18]

The Repatriates

Having established who returned to Spain, let us look into what came of the men returning. Even though the subject seems to lead away from the history of the New World proper, it is part of the rhythm of conquest. The conquerors, seen back in their homeland, not only throw light on the whole series of men and events; their return generated further developments directly affecting the Indies, notably the emigration of their relatives and compatriots. Research in the local Spanish archives on the men returned from the Indies would reap rich rewards, either for the general history of Spain and America, or for the conquerors of Peru alone. Even in advance of such research, however, there is much that can be said.

The process of return varied little from one man to the next. Like Pedro de Anadel and Gregorio de Sotelo, the returning conquerors bore letters and memoranda from companions, and they were loaded down with as many small lots of treasure as they could be persuaded to take, to be delivered to relatives in Spain. Often they were to negotiate favors at court for those remaining in Peru.

Each man's one real concern in the voyage was to convey his own fortune safely to Spain, that being the cornerstone of the life he hoped to live, the family he would found, the property he would buy, the honors he would attain. Everyone who returned at all went rich; otherwise there was no point. The exact degree of wealth is hard to establish. Only for a limited number of men do we have the amounts listed in the registers of ships arriving in Seville; in some cases close to 40,000 pesos, in others as little as 5,000.[19] But while this provides a rough guide, we know that much treasure was brought unregistered, and that some of the returnees handed over parts of theirs to companions, in order to distribute the risk.

Perhaps we had just as well accept the testimony of repatriate Juan Ruiz (1534–1535), who will be used here on various occasions as an

[18] The figures in Table 16 merely represent the present state of knowledge, and it may later appear that yet other conquerors won such distinctions. However, the only category likely ever to increase much is that of municipal office in Spain.

[19] AGI, Indiferente General 1801.

example, since he is the most articulate and best-documented of our men on the subjects of the return to Spain and life there afterward. Ruiz says that of the sixty conquerors, there were some who carried 40,000 pesos, others 30,000, and others 25,000; none had less than 20,000.[20] Ruiz himself registered 17,500 gold pesos and 1,700 silver marks, or a total of about 26,000 pesos.[21]

The journey to Spain took several months, with a long wait for re-shipping at the Isthmus, and shorter stops at ports in the Caribbean. Ruiz and his contingent took just a year. Along the way and on arrival in Seville they amazed onlookers with their golden jars and figures, and even more with the sheer amount of gold and silver, often measured in *arrobas* rather than the usual modest pesos. In the words of Gómara, "they filled the Contratación of Seville with money, and all the world with fame and desire."[22]

Arrival at the Casa de Contratación marked the end of this phase. There the treasure was received and almost invariably seized by royal officials to meet extraordinary expenses, usually one of Emperor Charles's wars. Seizure did not of course really strip the conquerors of their fortunes. Though the action was involuntary, sometimes it was clothed in the form of a loan. The donors were left with ready spend-ing money. And as principal compensation they received *juros*, annui-ties based on such established royal revenues as the tax on Granada silk. This was not only an acceptable solution, it was one that many of the conquerors actually desired. Those sending money home often gave specific instructions that it be used to buy *juros* in Spain. The *juros* represented security, social prestige, and a steady money income with-out management responsibility; they were thought to be the best basis of a lasting family fortune. The negotiations attendant on the confisca-tions and annuities were probably what held many of the conquerors for months in Seville, rather than the attractions of the Andalusian metropolis.

After Seville, the destination was home, with many men first mak-ing a visit to the royal court at one of the central Castilian cities. Juan Ruiz says that of his sixty companions twelve were with him at court in Madrid. The main purpose there was to acquire a coat of arms; in

---

[20] Ruiz, *Advertencias*, p. 111.

[21] AGI, Indiferente General 1801, records of ship *San Miguel*, 1535.

[22] Francisco López de Gomara, *Hispania victrix*, I, 231. This he writes despite the aspersions he elsewhere casts on Peru's wealth.

order to appear deserving, many brought along testimonials of their splendid services and good birth, which they had had prepared while still in Peru. Some, having lacked foresight, had to put together hasty memorials in Seville, before the conqueror-witnesses should disperse to the winds.

As far as we know, the conquerors' petitions for escutcheons were all successful, lubricated as they no doubt were by the hefty bribes and honoraria the men of Cajamarca could afford to pay. Apparently the lowest of the low, such as Escalante and Juan García, knew better than to apply, but arms were granted to men as far down the scale as Juan de Salinas, the horseshoer. The court made much of the two main contingents of Peruvian conquerors, particularly the first, but the very attentions lavished on them involved great expense for clothes, tournaments, festivities, and largesse. Juan Ruiz complains of the costs, and says some of the conquerors departed from court without money (though hardly without their *juros*).[23]

They then went "each to his country," in Juan Ruiz's words. With or without an interlude at court, most were soon living permanently in their home municipalities (Table 17). The inclusiveness of the Spanish city prevents us from obtaining any exact idea of the actual residence place, or even whether most of the men had been born in the cities proper or in the countryside. The majority seem to have chosen residences inside the city on their return, though we do know of a few who went to outlying hamlets, doubtless their birthplaces, while retaining citizenship in an organized municipality. Several more went to large towns near their home region. The mountains

Table 17. Residence Pattern of Repatriates

Residence	*No. of Men*
Home municipality	32
Nearby large city	7
Hamlet of birth	6
Farther from home	5
Unknown	16
Total	66

[23] Ruiz, *Advertencias*, p. 112.

of northern Castile in particular lacked cities where repatriates could unfold a life of any splendor, so some men from there went to Burgos or to a court town. The same conditions held in the Basque country, but the Basques tended to stick close to home nevertheless. Very few men indeed came to rest outside their general region, and they only for very compelling reasons. One New Castilian was attracted to the commerce and magnificence of Seville, where a relative had prepared his way; a Segovian went to live in the palace of the great nobleman whose daughter he married; a Basque seaman took the Andalusian port of Málaga for his base, while still visiting home frequently.[24]

Once home, the order of the day was to outfit oneself for the seigneurial existence that was the general Spanish ambition. Permanent revenues, a large town establishment, the noblest wife possible, and an ostentatious manner of living were its hallmarks. No better description of it has come down to us than that of the household of Juan Ruiz when back in his native Alburquerque. Though the testimony originated thirty years after his death, it is that of an eyewitness, and while doubtless exaggerated, it at least conveys the impression Juan Ruiz made on the town public.[25] "He had twelve squires who served him at table, and many more servants, pages, lackeys, Negroes and horses, armor, and much table ware, silver and gold, and many mules at his service; the pitchers he sent to the fountain were all of silver of much value. When he went out to hunt or other places he took along many horsemen, the cream of the town, and his squires as servants. He kept hunting dogs, falcons and hawks, horses, parrots and other animals. At his death they gave mourning clothes to twenty-four people besides all his servants and squires." An establishment of this type built up the individual's public reputation and served to perpetuate the status thus gained for his lineage, if not indeed, for many of our men, to start a new lineage. Even the second generation of their offspring often looked back to them for the family's principal claim of eminence, as in the case of Juan Ruiz himself, Alonso Romero, Pedro and Juan de Salinas de la Hoz, and others.

The culminating symbol of attained position was a municipal council seat. We know that twelve returning conquerors reached this goal, three of them on the nationally famous councils of Seville, Granada,

24 Vergara, Aliaga, Aguirre.
25 Antonio del Solar and José de Rújula, in their edition of Juan Ruiz's *Servicios en Indias*; also quoted by Rafael Loredo (*Los repartos*, p. 24).

and Toledo.[26] It is probable that many more held such posts at one time or another—perhaps half the repatriates, if one may guess. Others definitely did not. Though the offices were essentially bought in one form or another with money from Peru, a man ordinarily had to be literate and a reasonable approximation of an hidalgo to sit on a Spanish council. The man with well-known humble family connections had no chance of office in his home locality, no matter how rich he had become.

Returning conquerors had the strongest kind of impact on the council of Trujillo, the Pizarros' home town. Most of the surviving well-born Trujillans recruited in 1529 returned home at the first opportunity, and no less than four of them came to hold council seats, in addition to another man of Cajamarca born elsewhere. Finally the Pizarros themselves acquired the prestigious municipal office of *alférez mayor*. But the plebeians among the Trujillan repatriates had no luck; not Pizarro retainer Martín Alonso; nor illiterate Juan García, the black crier at Cajamarca, though he began to call himself Juan García Pizarro; nor Calderón the horseshoer, though he became "Pedro Calderón del Perú"; nor Diego de Trujillo, who grew so disgusted that he made his way back once again to Peru and ended on the council of Cuzco.

Holding municipal office did not make bureaucrats of the conquerors, of course. The posts, requiring little time or effort, were merely an integral part of that gentleman's life to which almost all adhered. Such a life could include the management of financial and commercial affairs, as in the example of Hernando Pizarro. But it does not appear that many repatriates carried on active careers in any branch of endeavor other than responsibility for their own estates. One man, Luis Maza, obtained the post of chief constable of the powerful High Court of Granada. While this position too was honorific, it was probably more than a sinecure, particularly in view of the fact that Maza had long been involved in law enforcement. Another man continuing professional activity was notary-attorney Pedro de Barrera, who became a solicitor in the Council of the Indies; he could follow the court in its progress through central Castile without getting far from his native Madrid. Several of the men settling in Seville were at one time or an-

[26] Vergara, Carranza, Sancho, respectively. Counted among the twelve are three who held subsidiary posts in the municipal governments of Seville and Granada, these positions being more than equal to a council seat in most Spanish towns.

other involved in commercial ventures, mainly in the direction of the Indies. They did this a little indirectly, however, never stepping out the role of gentleman entrepreneur into that of merchant.

As in the cases just mentioned, some connection with the New World often remained alive after return. Some men maintained correspondence with companions left in Peru, and many of the repatriates sent younger relatives off to follow their example. Whether they wished it or not, they were drawn into litigation about the treasure of Cajamarca, as Spanish relatives tried with little success to recover the estates of those who died in Peru. For the older veterans among them, a lifetime of intense experience was not easily forgotten. Old Indies hand Alonso Pérez de Vivero sat in Seville and watched for New World news with every fleet, interrogating every returning Spaniard he encountered.

The repatriates were prudent men, men with roots. They managed to preserve the bulk of the treasure they had won at Cajamarca and Cuzco, to convey it thousands of miles across the ocean, and to use it to attain a lasting position in the areas of their birth. The great majority returned to within a few miles of their birthplace. Their aim was conventional, to better themselves within existing society, and almost all did so, establishing their families in the upper or middle strata, with variations according to their original social rank. Some apparently made most impressive marriages. Those who failed to achieve the permanent place they hoped for were most often lowly men whose acceptance was hindered by Spanish peninsular conservatism and the limitations of their own education, not by any rebelliousness or rootlessness.

Fates of Men Remaining

The conquerors—about half of the total—who remained in the Indies met more diverse fates than did the repatriates. They too had a standard pattern of advancement, but many fell victim to the dangers of a newly occupied land. The rate of attrition from all causes can be seen in Table 18.

Three men staying in the New World were lost to Peru because they went on to take prominent part in the occupation of other areas, two of them adjoining. The greatest hazards to the conquerors left in Peru were Indian conflicts and the Spanish civil wars, which took an almost equal toll. More men seem to have died in subsequent indige-

Table 18. Rate of Attrition of the Men of Cajamarca

Year	Men Alive in the Indies
1536	58
1540	41
1545	27
1550	18
1560	11

nous rebellions than in the conquest itself. In the civil wars, five died in battle, nine were executed, and one, Francisco Pizarro himself, was assassinated. More died fighting against the Pizarros than for them. Only a small minority remained to play the role of legendary patriarchs when peace finally came in the 1550's.

Even those who lived no longer than the late 1530's, however, had a significant impact on the country, often establishing positions that were later successfully defended by their relatives or heirs. Word that a man had been killed in the conquest could attract relatives who would try to collect the inheritance and then stay on.

Genealogical continuity extending into the future from the men of Cajamarca is hard to trace. We know of twenty-three men whose relatives, often several, followed them to Peru, but the list is far indeed from being complete. Data on marriage are also fragmentary. Of the some forty men who were still alive in Peru by c.1540, twenty are known to have married, all but one to Spanish women. At least eleven of these left sons who successfully inherited their encomiendas, and at least five founded dynasties which retained fame and wealth in Peru for a century or more.[27] The clearest case of such continuity was, ironically, the Aliaga family, located still in the twentieth century on the site of Jerónimo de Aliaga's original lot in Lima, though the founder himself left for Spain after a substantial career in Peru.

The Great Men of Peru

The schematic representation of ultimate fates in Table 19 does not reveal that in the essentials the conquerors staying behind were all set upon the same path. Any man of Cajamarca in Peru almost automatically became a large encomendero of one of the more important Peru-

[27] Agüero, Aliaga, Barbarán (through the Lezcanos), Cornejo, Navarro.

Table 19. Causes of Death of Those Staying in Peru

Natural causes		21
Indian fighting		
Conquest	4	
Great Rebellion (1536–1537)	7	
Later outbreaks	5	
		16
Civil wars		
"War of Salinas" (1537–1538)	2	
"War of Chupas" (1541–1542)	6	
Gonzalo Pizarro rebellion (1544–1548)	6	
Francisco Hernández rebellion (1552–1554)	1	
		15
Miscellaneous*		1
Unknown		10
Total		63

* Juan de Barbarán, killed by runaway black slaves.

vian cities. Other things being equal, he received preference for office and honors over any later arrivals. Nothing could dislodge a man from that position but death, voluntary renunciation, or armed rebellion against the Pizarros.

In 1534–1535, when the main Peruvian municipalities were formed, the men were largely free to choose citizenship where they pleased. Cuzco was the first conquerors' preferred location, reflecting the initial importance of the "great city" as the Inca capital, which many incorrectly imagined would be the Spanish headquarters as well. Their second choice was the city which actually became the Spanish capital, Lima (with its predecessor, Juaja, incorporated into it in 1535). Cuzco and Lima together accounted for nearly all (Table 20), since those with citizenship in Arequipa and Huamanga in most cases retained encomiendas originally in the first two cities, which were merely reclassified when new districts were carved out of the old.[28]

Thus our men sought and received positions near the true center of

[28] Those who were citizens in more than one town in succession are counted each time in Table 20.

Table 20. Peruvian Citizenship of the Men of Cajamarca

Citizenship	No. of Men
Cuzco	44
Lima	26
(Jauja)	(19)
Arequipa	5
Huamanga	5
La Plata (Charcas)	3
Trujillo	2
Huánuco	1
Quito	1

wealth and power in Peru of the early 1530's. The inflexibility of the encomienda system and the strong competition for encomiendas meant that the first conquerors could hardly shift their location. To that extent their fortunes could deteriorate in absolute terms as the Indian population of coastal encomiendas plummeted, or in relative terms as the silver of the Charcas region became the real base of the Spanish Peruvian economy (after the mid-1540's).

Municipal office went to the first conquerors with great frequency (Table 21). At first only well-born or important men were chosen,

Table 21. Peruvian Municipal Offices Held by the Men of Cajamarca

Municipality	Council Seats	Positions of Alcalde	Lieutenant-governorships
Cuzco	13	5	5
Lima	9	5	2
Jauja	6	2	0
Huamanga	5	4	1
Arequipa	2	3	1
Trujillo	2	?	0
Túmbez	2	0	0
Huánuco	0	1	0
La Plata	1	0	1
Quito	0	0	1
Piura	0	0	1
Total	40	20	12

but as time went by the others joined them, until finally almost all the survivors held some office or other.[29] Only some special disability could prevent it. Of the men who survived the conquest proper and stayed in Peru, there were sixteen who collected no such honors. Seven of these were killed before 1538; four more were Almagrists who died by 1542, in fighting against the Pizarros or the king. Two were men who first returned to Spain and then came back. Only three lived into the 1550's, never having left Peru, without garnering some recognition beyond their encomiendas. One of them, Pedro de Alconchel, was an utter plebeian; the second, Juan Delgado, stayed active too long as a Pizarro retainer and then was overinvolved in the Gonzalo Pizarro rebellion; the third, Pedro de Mendoza, was an open and inveterate merchant.

Before long the first conquerors and their junior partners, the conquerors of Cuzco, lost collective dominance of the Lima council, hardest hit by new currents. They dominated longer in highland Cuzco, and longer still in remote Huamanga, where they were often a majority even into the later 1550's. Shifts in socioeconomic domination followed the same pattern.

But if group dominance inevitably faded, individually the men enjoyed eminent prosperity and public honor from the late 1530's as long as they lived. They were not easily or quickly pushed aside, as some have imagined. They lived as great encomenderos in a seigneurial-capitalistic fashion which, in brief, was much like that of repatriate Juan Ruiz back in Spain, with encomienda labor and tribute replacing royal annuities as the principal revenue. Their relative status was even better than that of the repatriates, for they had no superiors and few peers. In the 1540's and 1550's there were no more powerful men in Peru, economically and politically, than Diego Maldonado, Melchor Verdugo, or Lucas Martínez. As time went on they came to be surrounded by a mythic aura, in which even such secondary figures as Diego de Trujillo fully participated.

Some Parallels

What separated the two groups, repatriates and settlers? Less than appears. Both owed their wealth and position to the same circumstance —participation in the climactic events of the Peruvian conquest. Both

[29] Some individuals held different positions at different times. The offices enumerated in Table 21 were held by a total of forty-one men, of whom seven eventually returned to Spain.

acted with determination and considerable success to preserve that wealth and build something permanent. Both shared the double goal of a seigneurial life for themselves and lasting honor and wealth for their families. They pursued the same distinctions and held the same kinds of offices.

While many met reverses, few indeed can be found who hurled their prospects away. If there were any substantial number of such men, they must be hidden among the score or so of the most obscure figures. Of the rest, only the very few who left Peru for Chile could be called adventurers or wastrels, and even in these cases weighty objective factors influenced their action. As for those who went to Spain and then returned, they met such unforeseen catastrophes as piracy on the sea voyage, failure of business ventures, and lack of acceptance in proud peninsular society. Neither vagabonds nor squanderers, the conquerors acted as tough and capable men, just as we would expect from the earlier study of their background.

The principal factor impelling one group to stay, the other to go, was the individual's judgment of where he could best attain the common goal. Behind this lay considerations of size of share, age, social status, and the like. No distinction of psychology or ideology is visible. There was not a true rebel or dissenter in either group. Neither fear of danger nor love of adventure played any appreciable role, nor did, on the other hand, the desire to construct something new, unless perhaps in the minds of old Indies veterans Francisco Pizarro and Benalcázar. It might be said of these two, along with Soto, that a burning desire for power, fame, and great achievement kept them in the Indies and separated them from the mass. The truth is, however, that others shared the ambition and lacked only the means of carrying it out. Rather than looking to psychological factors, we understand best by pointing out that these men were the three most powerful and experienced captains of the expedition, with the best chance of carving out their own jurisdictions. The governorships they sought were merely a maximum embodiment of the general seigneurial ambition, which these three were in the best position to fulfill.

4. ORGANIZATION, POLITICS, AND FACTION

WHILE THE CONQUERORS' BACKGROUNDS and life patterns have broad, lasting significance, their internal organization represents a more finite subject, for the special set of practices surrounding expeditions and spoils was abandoned once the conquest was over. Yet even such ephemeral phenomena have their context, their parallels, and their consequences. What began as an expedition grew into the administration of a country. Impulses arising in internal rivalries of the Peruvian conquerors affected, indeed almost dictated, the timing and manner of the conquest of other areas. The factionalism so evident at every step was a Hispanic and Mediterranean trait that had prevailed from time immemorial and would project indefinitely into the future.

The Expedition

The Iberians had a special tradition of campaigns and raids which resulted in the same characteristic expedition type—under such names as *entrada, cabalgada, conquista*—wherever they went in Spanish America and Brazil. Within this unity, there were variations; practices were adapted to the individual region and the purpose of the moment. In particular, an evolution took place as Spanish expansion made the transition from its Caribbean phase to the conquest of the great mainland populations. Essentially this development consisted in the shift from an operation patterned on a commercial company, with a few employer-investors and a mass of mere employees, toward a company of men, a body of conquerors, each one outfitting himself and later receiving a share of the gain, rather than wages. In other words, there was an evolution away from the Italian commercial model instituted in the Caribbean by Columbus and other Genoese, toward a revived warlike company of men in the tradition of the Spanish Reconquest.

No one has shown better than Mario Góngora how the two elements —commercial company and band of men—existed side by side, intertwining and alternating. By the time of the Panamanian-Nicaraguan phase, in the second and third decades of the sixteenth century, the Iberian tradition of shares for the body of men had won out formally, though in fact the leaders, large investors, and high officials still took the lion's share of the profits and exercised overwhelming organizational dominance. Góngora intentionally stops short of the conquest of Peru, as a major break and different subject matter. However, development followed along the same lines, in a many-faceted continuity. In Peru the trend continued for the men to get ever better shares, proportionately and absolutely, and to assert themselves more; yet the leaders were still domineering and grasping, so much so that this aspect is the first to impress the uninitiated.

Maximum democratization and decommercialization occurred almost automatically where no capital was available. As Góngora suggests,[1] the high point of group rule may have been the occupation of Darién and the Caribbean coast of Panama around 1509–1513, the time of Enciso, Balboa, and, significantly, Francisco Pizarro. With little treasure, no expeditions covering long distances, and not even a legitimate governor in residence, the men shared everything, and created or expelled leaders at their pleasure. It would be interesting to know whether this reconstitution of the Castilian band was deliberate, or the result of favorable conditions alone. Since much age-old Spanish terminology was used, presumably the Spaniards were at least somewhat conscious of reviving traditional practices.

[1] Mario Góngora, *Grupos*, p. 58.

On the Pacific coast of the Isthmus, after 1517 or 1519, there was a renewed need for ships and long expeditions. At the same time more capital became available, as bullion supplies increased, while credit could be had through Governor Pedrarias de Avila, Licenciado Espinosa, and some other high officials, entrepreneurs, and encomenderos. Therefore investor dominance began to reassert itself, though not in the pure form of a commercial company.

Share winning rather than wage earning remained the framework, if only, at times, as little more than a fiction. Often a considerable number of the men were retainers, even slaves, of certain important backers or captains, and the shares they earned went all or in part to the employer, though nominally awarded to the lowly band member. Most of the men were free agents, not in the direct hire of anyone else, but even they often fell into the hands of the organizers. They borrowed money to outfit themselves, or they bought their equipment from the outfitters on credit, so that their shares were not really their own unless the expedition made an unusual profit. Some of the horses they rode belonged to investors, who received the horse's share. The captain or captains actually leading the expeditions took along supplies, sometimes including horses and slaves, which they hoarded and later sold to their men in time of need, for prices that were anything but low.[2]

The expeditions organized by Pizarro and Almagro to explore south and east from Panama, starting in 1524, not only were in this general tradition, but were an outstanding example of all the tendencies. To take just one of the contemporary descriptions and complaints, Licenciado Castañeda wrote in Nicaragua in 1529 that two hundred men had died of hunger, disease, and bad treatment in Pizarro and Almagro's expeditions.[3] In apparent reference to Peru, he said that those who equip expeditions do so ungenerously, and subjugate the men mercilessly once they are in the new country. At the time of setting out they lend the members money with their shares as security, then hold this over their heads till they dare not speak. All the profit goes to the outfitters.

It is in this context that we can interpret the happenings on Gallo Island in 1527, when complaints grew so general that Governor Ríos of Panama sent permission for any and all expedition members to return. Those coming back to Panama must have been mainly undersup-

2 This is largely a synthesis of Góngora's description in *Grupos*, pp. 53–59.
3 *CDIHN*, I, 494–495. Others in Raúl Porras, *Cartas*, first part.

plied debtors, while the heroic Thirteen staying were probably investors and creditors for the most part. It is for a related reason that many of the Thirteen did not take part in the later conquest. In their experience, investors came off best; now that a rich area had been discovered, they hoped to profit primarily by staying in Panama and supplying the conquerors. But the wealth of Peru quickly revolutionized the business of expeditions, making it far more profitable to be on the spot, contrary to the expectations of the old hands.

Conditions in the wet tropical Isthmus area often led to such mortality from disease that it was hard to keep an expedition in existence long enough to accomplish its mission. To cope with this problem a special technique evolved, as Rolando Mellafe has pointed out.[4] The expedition's ships would deposit the main body of men on the coast, then run constantly back and forth between Panama and the point the men might have reached in a slow coastal advance, bringing supplies, but more importantly, men. Or a part of the leadership would stay behind in Panama to continue recruiting, then follow later. The contingent already on the ground would often be immobilized for months waiting for reinforcements.

Pizarro and Almagro had adopted this practice as their own and may even have had some share in its evolution. At any rate, it was their principal tactic in the early voyages of discovery and continued in full force for the conquering expedition of 1531–1532.

At that time Almagro stayed behind to recruit and equip a second large contingent, which, as it happened, did not arrive in Peru until after Cajamarca. Upon the main group's landfall near Coaque, they waited for several months until a ship came from Panama carrying some merchandise and a few men, whereupon they continued south along the coast. They also expected reinforcements from Nicaragua. Negotiations had long been going forward there with Soto (and probably with Benalcázar also). Some of the first treasure sent back from Coaque went to facilitate Soto's departure. After a slow march south, the expedition waited again on the island of Puná, just off central Peru, until Soto arrived, prior to crossing over to Túmbez. Even after the victory of Cajamarca, Pizarro waited for Almagro and his men before he would push on into the Inca heartland.

A peculiar burden of the expeditions in Panama had been the neces-

---

[4] Rolando Mellafe and Sergio Villalobos, *Diego de Almagro*, pp. 46–47.

sity for the captain or captains who actually directed the enterprise to share profits and authority with the absent governor. The Peru venture initially had to suffer from this as much as any. First Governor Pedrarias had attempted to extract gain without much investment, then later Governor Ríos intervened directly with almost disastrous effect. By the time of the final expedition, however, this hurdle had been passed. Pizarro himself was governor, and the expedition combined governor and commander in one man, present on the spot.

The exact details of the outfitting of the final Peru expedition are not known, nor can we even say with any certainty what arrangements were made for the ordinary expedition members. Pedro Pizarro, an eyewitness (though writing years later), says that the men received no payments or advances and had to pay their own expenses, including even passage money.[5] Conqueror Jerónimo de Aliaga, who arrived with the first reinforcement ship at Coaque, also claimed he paid for everything himself. Witnesses to his testimonial agreed, but they were of two opinions on whether or not he had to pay for his passage from Panama.[6]

Notarial records preserved from Coaque give the impression that the Pizarros were not at that time deeply engaged in the supply business (almost the only evidence of such a thing are the several pigs Hernando Pizarro brought along).[7] Rather, the ordinary men are observed freely trading back and forth among themselves; they did accept some credit from crew members of the ship arriving there, which then returned to Panama. Only Captain Cristóbal de Mena is to be seen engaging in some speculative selling.[8] Records of four ships which joined the expedition at various times show diversified ownership of goods carried on them, with the masters the largest investors.[9] From these glimpses, from the absence of documented debt repayment after Cajamarca, and from the fact that so many men were later able to return to Spain with substantially their full shares of Peruvian treasures, we may conclude that indebtedness to the captains by the rank and file was at this time not a large factor, or was at least a far smaller one than it had been in the conquest of Nicaragua. It is true that the unprecedented

---

[5] Pedro Pizarro, *Relación*, V, 171.

[6] *RANP* 1 (1920):431, 541.

[7] Diego de Trujillo, *Relación*, p. 50.

[8] HC 1–31.

[9] AGI, Contaduría 1825. These are the ships arriving at Puná and San Miguel. See above, chapter 1, footnotes 11 and 14.

shares of Cajamarca would easily have wiped out almost any amount of debt from the austere pre-Cajamarca phase. Whatever the exact shape of financial investment, the end result was a distribution of power in the form of widespread personal possession of equipment and discretion over its use. Equipment was even more important to success than men. Nothing could be more instructive than Pizarro's reaction when several disillusioned conquerors wanted to abandon the enterprise at Túmbez. Pizarro told them they were free to take ship for Panama—if they would leave their horses and arms behind.[10]

Ever since the Caribbean period, investors in expeditions had contracted their own private partnerships or companies outside the framework of general sharing among the band of men. Any such private arrangement, whether short or long term, specific or universal, commercial or not, was called a *compañía* ("company"). The word and the institution were extremely popular and becoming ever more so. Confusingly enough, the technical term for a band of men earning shares was the almost identical word *compaña* (which would also translate as "company").[11] Though not much heard in everyday speech, this expression was employed consistently in documents of the Panama area, and continued to be used by the Peru expedition at least until the distribution of treasure in Cuzco in the spring of 1534.[12]

The company (*compañía*) most essential to the Peru expedition was the long-standing universal partnership of Pizarro and Almagro. At the time of Cajamarca, Almagro was far away, but if Pizarro lived up to the spirit of their agreement, Almagro in some fashion received half of Pizarro's share. Whatever the arrangement between the two, much of the governor's share must have gone to pay off the debts accumulated over several years of outfitting expeditions and building or hiring ships.

Sometime partner Hernando de Luque, who died several months after the expedition set out, was no longer an equal member of the association, if indeed he had ever been; the famous contract promis-

---

[10] Pedro de Cieza, *Tercera parte*, in *Mercurio Peruano* 37 (1956):85; *RANP* 1 (1920):526–527.

[11] See Mario Góngora, *Grupos*, p. 39.

[12] Rafael Loredo, *Los repartos*, pp. 96, 97, 101. Since the word was dying out, it was very susceptible to being confused with "compañía." Modern transcribers have also made this error. Some examples appear in Loredo's own book (*Los repartos*, pp. 72, 118). A passage in Cristóbal de Mena's chronicle has "compañía" where the sense demands "compaña" ("Conquista del Perú," p. 98). The same error appears in the version of the roll of Cajamarca that has come down to us.

ing him a one-third share of the gain is a forgery. The fraud was discovered independently by Raúl Porras[13] and Rolando Mellafe.[14] In this writer's view, they are correct beyond all dispute, and future treatments of the Peruvian conquest had best leave the contract unmentioned. However, some of the reasoning offered by Porras and Mellafe needs discussion and updating, particularly in view of Guillermo Lohmann Villena's recent attempt to rehabilitate the document. Lohmann admits the unauthenticity of certain of its aspects, and even draws attention to new discordant elements, but inconsistently enough applies his critique only to the dating and other details of the instrument, assuming that the contract must indeed have been made at some time or other.[15]

1. Mellafe believed the contract impossible because Pizarro was absent from Panama and in Chochama at the time it was allegedly signed (March 10, 1526), but this cannot be proved conclusively. Though Pizarro was indeed avoiding Panama during these months, and is specifically reported in Chochama no more than two weeks before the contract date,[16] the voyage from Chochama to Panama could have been made quickly in a canoe. This can only be a contributing argument.

2. Porras and Mellafe objected that the contract, in speaking of the "reino del Perú," (kingdom or realm of Peru) goes beyond the usage of 1526 and betrays an origin at the earliest at a time subsequent to 1530. They are right, but the argument is not as strong as they imagined. Without going into the details of the evolution of the word "Peru," dealt with by Porras, it can now be asserted that "Peru" was being used in specific connection with the discoveries of Pizarro and Almagro earlier than Porras and Mellafe thought it had been. Góngora has published a document of 1525 referring to "Captain Francisco Pizarro and the men with him on the coast of Peru and its provinces."[17] Only the use of the world "realm" is left as clearly anachronistic in a document of 1526.

3. The lack of contemporary reference to any such agreement remains the most serious objection to its validity. Luque's heirs did not bring the contract to bear in settling his claims with Pizarro and Alma-

---

[13] Raúl Porras, "El Nombre del Perú," *Mar del Sur* 6, no. 18 (1951):26.

[14] Mellafe and Villalobos, *Diego de Almagro*, pp. 57–58.

[15] Guillermo Lohmann Villena, *Les Espinosa*, pp. 206–220. Lohmann gives several additional false or suspicious aspects of the document not alluded to here. He includes the full text of the contract on pp. 253–256.

[16] Góngora, *Grupos*, p. 126.

[17] Ibid., p. 124; and Lohmann, *Les Espinosa*, p. 209.

gro in the 1530's, nor does word of it appear in any document or book of the time. It is first mentioned in 1567, almost forty years later, by the heirs of Licenciado Gaspar de Espinosa, who were guilty of various misrepresentations in their own favor. They refer to the contract in connection with another equally suspicious document granting Luque's share to Licenciado Espinosa. The earliest known actual copies of the document are of the early seventeenth century, and it was not until then that the idea of the 1526 tripartite contract and Luque's great monetary contribution became current among officials, chroniclers, and historians.[18] Everything points to deliberate forgery, not committed, as Mellafe thought probable, by Licenciado Espinosa himself, but by his heirs at a time when no survivors were left to challenge them.

4. Another suspicious circumstance in the contract, not emphasized by Porras, Mellafe, or Lohmann, is the size of the loan. Twenty thousand pesos in gold bars, physically present in one sum, would have been an almost incredible amount to be lent by a single individual in the time before Cajamarca.

5. Another of the contract's unauthentic traits has escaped notice until now; in the mind of this writer, it is the most conclusive of them all. The document depicts Francisco Pizarro declining to sign, on the ground that he could not. Now it is true that Pizarro in his whole life never learned to sign his name, but by the early 1520's he began to make a rubric, and all known documents issued by him from them until his death contain that rubric, along with the statement that Pizarro signed. The earliest known example is from 1522.[19] Pizarro also signed the authentic capitulation with Governor Pedrarias, made in May, 1524.[20]

That very document is one of the weightiest pieces of evidence known tending to demonstrate that Luque was ever involved with Pizarro and Almagro as an equal partner, more than the various other people who collaborated in the venture at some time or other.[21] The agreement provides that Pedrarias was to pay one-fourth of the cost

[18] See Lohmann, *Les Espinosa*, pp. 207–208, 216–217, based on AGI, Lima, 145 and 149.

[19] José T. Medina, *Descubrimiento*, II, 475–477.

[20] Góngora, *Grupos*, pp. 132–133.

[21] Substantial loans or investments were made in 1524 by pilot Bartolomé Ruiz, and by Juan Vallejo, a citizen of Panama. Mellafe and Villalobos, *Diego de Almagro*, p. 40. Vallejo was originally a blacksmith, as seen in the list of founders of Panama, in Góngora, *Grupos*, p. 73.

of the ships, the other three parties paying the remaining three-fourths, with freighting profits to be divided in the same proportion. The internal division among the three is not made explicit. While there would be a symmetry in imagining three equal parts, the document treats Pizarro as the principal partner, mentions his investments alone, and provides that he could not be removed from the captaincy.[22]

In the long run it is not crucial to historical interpretation whether Luque was a major financial contributor or not; apparently he was. The more essential point is that he was not the *principal* source of financing for two impoverished conquerors, since the Pizarro-Almagro interests were by themselves among the strongest in Panama.

Each of the two subexpeditions of the Peru venture, those of Soto and Benalcázar, also had a private company at the top. Soto's arrangement with Hernán Ponce de León was remarkably similar to that between Pizarro and Almagro. It was a long-standing universal partnership in which Soto was the more active captain and Hernán Ponce the business manager; Soto came to Peru while Ponce stayed in Nicaragua to see to their affairs, then followed much later. Benalcázar had an agreement with the shipmaster Juan Fernández, apparently of a more temporary and limited nature. All three companies served the purpose of capitalizing and organizing a venture adequately, but each arrangement ended in serious dispute among the partners at a later time.

As far as we know, there were no other company arrangements binding members of the expedition to anyone outside it. Within the expedition itself, companies were rife. No less than eighteen partnerships are fairly well authenticated among the men of Cajamarca, and there is good reason to think that in fact there were many more.[23] These

[22] In Almagro's 1526 *probanza*, principal emphasis is on Pizarro and himself, but both he and the witnesses make statements implying that Luque's resources were spent together with theirs, and that Luque was a member of their consortium in building and outfitting the expedition's ships (*CDIHC*, IV, 6–47).

[23] The best-documented partnership among the ordinary men is that of Lucas Martínez and Alonso Ruiz, discussed in their biographies. The other pairs are not all specifically called partners (*compañeros*) in the records, but the relationship can be deduced from their repeated appearance together. Some of the sets were: Aliaga and Sebastián de Torres; Aguirre and Anadel; Baena and Barrera; Beltrán and Alonso Pérez; Carranza and Maza; Cataño and Vélez; Hernández Briceño and Medina; Fuentes and Castillo; Marquina and Azpeitia; Rojas and Olivares; Moguer and Bueno; Miguel Ruiz and Chico; Quincoces and Beranga; Romero and Nuño González; Candía and Florencia; Valencia and Sánchez de Talavera; Valdevieso and Gonzalo Maldonado; Morales and Alonso Jiménez; and probably Francisco López and Lozano.

were all general partnerships, basically the same as those of the great captains, but since they were subjected to less strain, they held up better. Such relationships were not a phenomenon exclusively related to expeditions. Some of the companies among the men of Cajamarca had existed for as much as ten years, while others continued long into the future. Several sets of partners went home to Spain together, and one or two received joint encomiendas in Peru.

Nevertheless, this buddy system, if we may call it that, where the partners held their property in common and were constantly together at all hours of day and night, was peculiar to the time of conquests and expeditions, and faded quickly as a more settled manner of life developed. While most of the partnerships among our men antedated 1531, some were formed as a direct consequence of the expedition, particularly among the neophytes.

The origin of this custom remains to be established. Perhaps it grew out of the commercial companies so prevalent in Seville and the Indies; some of the partners were making common investments for gain, and, in a few cases, like that of Beranga and Quincoces, business became the dominant note. Yet most of these arrangements did not rest on a written contract, as the commercial company so often did, and full partner equality was more typical than the investor-factor relationship. Perhaps the partnership was of maritime origin; an undue proportion of the seafarers among the men of Cajamarca were partners, and the custom remained prevalent among mariners along the Peruvian coast long after it had died out among other Spaniards. But perhaps, too, the pairing of men is a trait with a background in the Spanish Reconquest; or perhaps it spontaneously asserts itself on new and dangerous frontiers, as it did in the American West.

At any rate, it was a way of trying to attain greater security in a fluid situation. Therefore partners had to be sure of each other, and we find almost all the companies based on strong common bonds of some description—regional origin, profession, social status, long experience together, and often all of these combined.

Capitalization was a factor of third importance, after security and actual companionship. We find no more than three or four pairs investing in merchandise together or making joint loans; one other shared the profits from their artisanry. For their extensive commercial and entrepreneurial activity, the men did not hesitate to step outside the general partnership to make more limited agreements. One such arrangement common at the time of the conquest proper was sharing the profits from a horse. Two men bought a horse together; two-thirds of the horse's share went to the rider, one-third to the other man. Or the owner of two horses might let another man ride one, sharing the profits from it equally.[24] In the time before Cajamarca most of these agreements are hidden from us, but there is reason to suspect that the horse ridden by Miguel Ruiz at Atahuallpa's capture was owned by expedition member Juan Alonso, who was left behind at Piura. Ownership of more than one horse seems to have been rare or nonexistent until Inca treasure made it possible; but after Cajamarca, on the way to Cuzco, there were some men with two horses, and Juan Pizarro had three.[25]

If investment was well distributed and association patterns were free, in what consisted the great dominance of the leaders, and specifically, of the Pizarros? It began in personal and regional considerations: the formidable eligibility of Francisco and Hernando Pizarro for leadership and their inclination to make use of power, both of which can be seen in their biographies; the presence of no less than four Pizarro brothers; a loyal group of Trujillan relatives and compatriots who constituted the largest, most coherent subregional group.

But to proceed to the organizational side, Pizarro dominance expressed itself in the overlapping of three nominally separate structures: the government of Peru, the expedition, and the Pizarro estate or body of direct retainers. Whereas, on some expeditions, rival captains scrambled for the upper hand, each expecting favor from a distant governor, in this case Governor Pizarro was present, with clear authority to name captains and depose them. For his chief lieutenant he naturally settled on his brother Hernando. Young Juan also received commands, and even the stripling Gonzalo was pushed into some prominence. As governor, Pizarro also had the undisputed authority to assign citizenship and encomiendas. His power to punish and reward was thus great, and no one dared challenge him directly. One part of his government, the royal treasury officials, did hamper him somewhat, since they were appointed independently by the crown. Pizarro therefore managed to leave them behind time and again; none of the three was present at Cajamarca. In their absence the governor would appoint trusted associates as temporary deputies. The expedition as a royal arm also

24 ANP, PA, passim.
25 Loredo, *Los repartos*, p. 400.

helped pay certain expenses, including a salary for carpenter Escalante.

As in Central America in previous decades, the *compaña*, or band of conquerors, had a juridical existence separate from the royal government. Though the treasury officials were responsible for the king's fifth and the marking of all gold and silver, the treasure belonged in the first instance to the *compaña*, which had its own treasurer and accountant and carried out the distribution of spoils. The whole body of men elected representatives whose duty it was to assign shares to each individual.[26] However, in Peru, the *compaña* was to a large extent a legal fiction, as indeed it apparently had already become in Nicaragua. Its clerks were Pizarro's personal secretaries; its treasurer was Gonzalo de Pineda, Pizarro's own hired man, as were probably its other officials. The representatives whom the men "elected" were simply the Pizarros, another important captain or two, and the *compaña* officials once again.[27] At San Miguel, Pizarro melted down what gold had been taken and, after paying the fifth, appropriated the rest in the form of a forced loan from the *compaña*, in order to pay off pressing debts to shipmasters on the coast.[28]

Already in the *compaña* we can see emerging an organization which was at the expedition's heart, the corps of retainers who had been directly hired by the Pizarros, owing them unconditional loyalty and obedience. Since they functioned also as free members of the band, the governor could put them in all sorts of responsible positions and act autocratically while preserving appearances.

It is possible to identify at least thirteen of our men who were in the Pizarros' pay around the time of Cajamarca, plus the secretaries Jerez and Sancho. They range from a figure as high-ranking as Juan Cortés, who took part in the highest councils, to obscure men of artisan background, like Rodrigo de Herrera or Juan Delgado. Their functions were many. Juan de Valdevieso was the governor's chamberlain, Gaspar de Marquina one of his pages. Hernando de Toro was Hernando Pizarro's squire; Pedro Navarro was once in charge of conveying the governor's gear from the island of Puná to Túmbez on a raft. Whatever their position, almost all acted as stewards and managers, so they were mainly literate, capable men. In the records they appear as Pizarro's *criados* ("servants") or "majordomos." Most worked specifically

[26] Mena, "Conquista del Perú," p. 97.
[27] Raúl Porras, *Relaciones primitivas*, p. 98; roll of Cajamarca.
[28] Francisco de Jerez, *Verdadera relación*, II, 325.

for Francisco, while others were Hernando's men, but the distinction was not great, since the Pizarro interest was so unified.

No actual contracts have come down to us; very possibly the agreements were never formalized. We do not know whether the retainers at this time received actual pay in money, or merely protection, sustenance, and promises of favors. A little later, some Pizarro stewards were receiving fixed salaries.[29] We do have some powers of attorney granted to Navarro, Valdevieso, and Crisóstomo de Hontiveros, allowing them broad leeway in buying, selling, receiving, hiring, and firing.[30] The Pizarros favored Trujillo compatriots as retainers, but there were few who understood business affairs, so they grasped men from all regions of Spain. Of the fifteen men mentioned above, only four were from Trujillo or any other part of Extremadura. In the long run, this disproportion proved a great weakness of the Pizarro faction. The Trujillans were hired in Spain in 1529, and most of the others apparently in Panama in 1530. More were added in the course of the expedition, pulled out of the followings of Benalcázar and Soto almost immediately after arrival. Such men as Juan de Barbarán and Navarro, however, had probably known Pizarro for years in Central America.

A final element of great importance in the expedition's organization was the plurality and miscellaneity of its origin. The two contingents arriving from Nicaragua were expeditions in themselves, organized much like the larger one, and they did not immediately lose all internal coherence. Soto had his own retainers; Pedro de Torres was still functioning openly as such after Cajamarca. Each new group almost inevitably became a unit to be sent on missions, under the captaincy of Benalcázar or Soto. These two leaders could not be constrained from acting with a certain independence, and serious conflicts arose, which will be discussed a little further on.

Thus there were two countervailing, well-matched forces in evidence in the expedition. Through organization and leadership, the Pizarros moved toward a total dominance. On the other hand, the ordinary expedition members carried much weight, because their persons, experience, and equipment were the sine qua non of the conquest, and two subgroupings were present which did not owe their origin to the Pizarros directly.

[29] HC 79, 92; ANP, PA 689–690.
[30] HC 49, 220.

The Distribution of Treasure

The first major precipitation of the power relationships sketched above were the shares the individuals received of the treasure of Cajamarca. There is no better measure of the actual leverage of any one man on the expedition, nor of the general balance of power.

What was distributed has often been referred to as Atahuallpa's ransom, and that was the bulk of it perhaps, but the clerks described it in more inclusive terms, as everything "that had been taken on the way from the city of San Miguel to the town of Cajamarca, and what was taken in the capture of Atahuallpa, and what Chief Atahuallpa himself gave to the Spaniards who seized him, and everything else that was had until the governor left the said town with the Spaniards."[31] The greatest political coup and power play involved in the whole process of distribution appears only indirectly in the documents themselves. The names of the citizens of San Miguel and of the men who arrived with Almagro are absent. That is, the whole profit of the Peru expedition from September, 1532, through July, 1533—the first important amount accruing since early 1531—was awarded only to the men who happened to be present the day Atahuallpa was captured. Abstract justice spoke in favor of a share for the men left in San Miguel, who had taken part in the general combats and hardships for over a year and a half; but they were few, mainly older or infirm, and could safely be ignored. Almagro's men, on the other hand, were on the spot, numerous and well-equipped, but they had arrived only in April, 1533, having done no fighting, and it was not impossible to convince them that they had no right to what others had won, particularly in view of the further treasure to be expected in the immediate future. This was one issue, of course, on which the whole body of the men of Cajamarca stood united. The deprived groups received token payments as a small gesture of conciliation. That this was a matter of expediency and politics rather than pure custom can be seen in the fact that, a little later, those staying in Jauja and returning to Piura received shares from the conquest of Cuzco—they would not otherwise agree to stay behind.[32]

After fending off interlopers, subtracting the king's fifth, and paying expenses, those responsible for the distribution divided the treasure

---

[31] Loredo, *Los repartos*, p. 72.
[32] Loredo, *Los repartos*, p. 99; ANP, PA 746.

into shares of 4,440 gold pesos and 181 silver marks, worth altogether 5,345 gold pesos at the standard conversion rate.[33] Reports vary on how many of these shares there were, but arithmetic tells us that about 217 of them went to our men. Almost all sources agree that the criteria used in assigning shares were the performance and social quality of the individual. Pedro Pizarro adds that the performance of the horse was also important.[34] In effect, the value of a man's performance usually coincided with his degree of experience in the Indies. The norm was one share for a footman, two shares for a horseman (one for the rider, one for the horse), and something beyond that for captains. The partitioners showed approval and respect, or the opposite, by departing from the norm. In general they really seem to have followed objective factors for the bulk of the men; among the captains politics came more into play.

There was great variety among the footmen. Without going into subtleties, we can say that only a minority, experienced or well born, received a full share. A larger number, mainly the new men, got a three-quarters share. Lower plebeians or inferior performers got perhaps a half share; this was also the "tailor's share." While some similar variation is found among the horsemen, most got very close to the standard double share, showing not only the crucial role of the horse, but also the fact that the horsemen by no accident were mainly experienced and influential men.

Among the captains there was again wide variation. Francisco Pizarro as governor took 13 shares and the customary "governor's jewel," in the form of Atahuallpa's gilded seat, worth about 2 shares.[35] Her-

[33] Five pesos per mark. A peso of "good gold" was worth 450 maravedises; a mark of "good silver," 2,200.

[34] The roll of Cajamarca and the related documents published by Loredo in *Los repartos* are the only reliable guides in these matters. Chroniclers' descriptions of the mechanics of distribution are in Pedro de Cieza, *Tercera parte*, in *Mercurio Peruano* 39 (1958):569, 573–574; Mena, "Conquista del Perú," pp. 97–98; Miguel de Estete, *Relación*, p. 41; Jerez, *Verdadera relación*, II, 343; Juan Ruiz de Arce, *Advertencias*, p. 96; Pedro Pizarro, *Relación*, V, 184–185; Francisco López de Gómara, *Hispania victrix*, I, 231; Agustín de Zárate, *Historia*, II, 479. Pedro Pizarro reports that Almagro argued in favor of giving half the treasure to Pizarro and himself, restricting the others to a thousand pesos—or two thousand at most. We must suspect that this is nothing more than a malicious Pizarrist rumor, but that someone made the suggestion is not unlikely. It would have been in the Central American tradition.

[35] Loredo, *Los repartos*, p. 74. This did not enter into the general partition, and is not taken into account in the figures below. It contained 18,000 pesos of gold judged to be of 15 carats; that is, metal with only two-thirds the gold content of "good

nando Pizarro received 7, and the younger brothers got portions of $2\frac{1}{2}$ and $2\frac{1}{4}$ respectively. These were large amounts, though by no means excessive in the terms of the Panamanian-Nicaraguan precedent. The striking thing was that the Pizarros were able to hold the other captains down to such minimal rewards. Soto, without whose arrival the conquest could hardly have gone forward in 1532, received only 4 shares, 3 less than Hernando Pizarro. Even more amazing, Benalcázar received only $2\frac{1}{4}$ shares. Captain Salcedo got still less, and Captain Mena actually got less than an ordinary horseman. The Pizarros now had enough men for the conquest, and their own candidates for captaincies, so they were in a position to brush off their chief rivals, making them choose between insignificance and departure from Peru.

All in all, the ordinary members did very well for themselves, whether measured relatively or absolutely. The horsemen fared particularly well, revealing themselves once more as the expedition's real core. Of a total of 217-odd shares, 135 and a fraction went to 62 horsemen (including captains), 81 and a fraction to 105 footmen. Only 24 of the 217 went to the Pizarros, and only 39 to all the captains together. In absolute amounts, converted and rounded off, 1.16 million pesos were distributed to our men, 724,000 to horsemen and 436,000 to footmen; the Pizarros got 131,000; all captains together 209,000.[36] This may be compared with a partition planned in Nicaragua a decade earlier, in which the governor and the important men appropriated to themselves 28,000 pesos of a total 33,000.[37]

The above analysis and calculation (see also Table 22) rest on the basis of the ostensible amounts distributed. Though taking records at face value has caused many a false turn in the interpretation of Spanish American history, we may assume that there was a certain validity in an operation watched so closely by so many hostile and interested parties. Some direct testimony seems to indicate that the nominal share was indeed the bulk of what the men received,[38] and Cristóbal de Mena cer-

---

gold" of $22\frac{1}{2}$ carats. It would thus have had a value of 12,000 of the good gold pesos used as the unit of reckoning in the distribution.

[36] The two younger Pizarros are included with the captains, as is Hernández Briceño, though it is not clear that he held any command until after Cajamarca. This makes ten men altogether, who, even as mere horsemen, would have been entitled to 107,000 pesos. To obtain the totals, the share of Juan de Sosa, the small amount donated to the Church, and the pay for the secretaries were subtracted.

[37] Góngora, *Grupos*, p. 55.

[38] See p. 93.

Table 22. Distribution of Shares of Treasure to the Men of Cajamarca

Detail		Résumé	
Number of Shares Each	No. of Men	Number of Shares Each	No. of Men
13	1		
7	1		
4	1	4 and over	3
2–2½	10		
2	30	2–2½	40
1½–2	13		
1–1½	4		
1	30	1–2	47
¾–1	12		
¾	38		
½–¾	13		
½	7		
Under 12	7	Under 1	77
Total	167	Total	167

tainly complained bitterly enough about his substandard portion.[39] Yet it would be naive to believe that the men obeyed literally the governor's injunction to bring every piece of gold and silver to the common heap;[40] indeed legends formed to the effect that they did not.[41]

In this writer's opinion, the nominal shares reflect accurately enough the relative profits of the men, except that it hardly seems possible for even Pizarro power and partisanship to have depressed the shares of Soto and Benalcázar to their ostensible levels. Possibly some adjustment was made by allowing them to retain what they had taken themselves. One piece of evidence indicates that Benalcázar, at least, came off with more than the listed twelve thousand pesos; his friend Alonso Pérez de Vivero, an important and knowledgeable man, once testified

[39] Cristóbal de Mena, "Conquista del Perú," p. 98.
[40] Pedro Pizarro (Relación, V, 171), claims they did fulfill the order, being afraid not to.
[41] Garcilaso de la Vega, Obras, I, 250.

that Benalcázar's share at Cajamarca amounted to more than thirty thousand pesos.[42]

Factionalism and Its Aftermath

It has already been seen that rivalry, faction, and cutthroat competition crop out wherever one examines the expedition's operation. In truth, the Spaniards appeared more actively concerned with internal rivalries than with the Indians, and naturally so, since their fellows were a greater threat to their well-being, particularly to their prosperity. This strong tendency of the Spanish conquerors has drawn much attention, but it is not a strange thing. The Indians too gave great importance to internal conflicts while neglecting external enemies, and at much greater hazard to themselves. History is full of such examples. The mere fact of constant mistrust and competition shows little about the conquerors, unless that they were human. It is more important to recognize the rationale, pattern, and consequences of the rivalries.

Many of the divisions went back for years. Pizarro, Soto, and Benalcázar had known each other well in Central America. Pizarro's eminence antedated the arrival of Pedrarias in 1514, while the other two were Pedrarias's creatures. Pizarro probably considered the others, experienced though they were by the time of the Peruvian conquest, as upstarts and inferiors; indeed he had once had Soto under his direct command.

Nor were Benalcázar and Soto capable of uniting against Pizarro; they failed even to agree on a joint voyage from Nicaragua to Peru. By 1530 both were leaders of enough renown that they might aim at independent governorships, as so many captains had done before them. To accomplish this in some fashion or other was their maximum objective in coming to Peru, and by itself it was enough to make rivals of the two. Nicaraguan politics had pulled them farther apart. Benalcázar remained a strong partisan of Pedrarias until the latter's death in 1531, whereas Soto allied himself with Licenciado Castañeda in seeking an independent position. The two men came into direct conflict over the election of the town council of Nicaragua's capital, León, for 1530.

Serious political conflicts first burst onto the surface in the 1531 expedition in the form of competition for captaincies. A captain's title

[42] Quito, *Colección de documentos . . . Benalcázar*, p. 391.

was no light matter in the Spanish conquest period. It had unparalleled prestige; even more to the point, it meant an increased share of the profits, and some years as a subsidiary captain were usually prerequisite to becoming a leader of expeditions of one's own. As Oviedo said, "One of the principal assets or instruments of gain is this name of captain."[43]

Pizarro was faced with the problem of reconciling the claims of three groups: his brothers; the senior men and the expedition as it left Panama; and the later additions, Soto and Benalcázar. One might think it a sheer impossibility to create several captaincies in a body of men that never counted much above two hundred. But ever since the Central American phase, if not earlier, the Spaniards had been accustomed to having several "captains" in small groups. A captain's title was not a rank in a hierarchy and did not imply a squadron of any given size; rather the word simply meant "leader," someone who could act independently and take responsibility. Even the smallest expeditions often needed to split up into detachments, perhaps for days or weeks at a time.

Thus, at first, enough room was found. In the early stages, the younger Pizarros and the lesser figures from Trujillo were so green that their claims were not urgent; only Hernando Pizarro, who had been a captain in Spain, had a clear right to a place, which his brother Francisco gladly gave him. Otherwise, captains seasoned in the Indies were dominant in the months after the expedition touched land in the north at Coaque; two of the most important of these, and the only two to reach Cajamarca, were Cristóbal de Mena and Juan de Salcedo. Mena in those days sometimes acted as second in command after the governor, but before long Hernando Pizarro was permanently ensconced in that position. With this began a process in which the old captains were gradually pushed to the margin. The pressing nature of other claims may have made this inevitable, since Mena and Salcedo had no leverage in the form of ships or an independent following.

Their position was worsened by their common regional origin—another element of capital importance in Spanish factionalism. Factions were often neither more nor less than regional groupings around a leader from a given area. In this case, both Mena and Salcedo happened to be from New Castile, the region of Pizarro's partner and now

---

[43] Oviedo, *Historia general*, III, 208.

arch-rival, Almagro, who was at that moment suspected of planning to conquer part of Peru on his own or even to usurp Pizarro's position. All through the civil wars to come, an important thread was to be the alignment of Trujillo and Cáceres for the Pizarros, Toledo and Ciudad Real for the other side. Mena especially was from the immediate area of Ciudad Real; the Pizarros apparently looked upon him as little more than a spy, with much justice, since in Spain, later, Mena did act as Almagro's agent against Pizarro interests.

The arrival of Benalcázar, and shortly thereafter of Soto, completed the eclipse of the two New Castilians. The new captains now got the important missions, and their word carried weight in the high council. Mena and Salcedo are hardly heard of thereafter, except in the chronicle that Mena himself wrote. At the partition of treasure they received small shares. Taking the hint, they departed for Spain immediately afterward, since Peru offered them no future.

The newcomers brought new tensions, and a tug-of-war began, with the Pizarros trying to get the upper hand, while Soto and Benalcázar looked for possibilities of shaking loose, or failing that, of achieving some autonomy under the Pizarro regime. Soto had previously bargained with Pizarro for a permanent lieutenant governorship of the capital city.

The Pizarros tried in every way possible to weaken their rivals, without openly affronting them. The main technique was to woo men away from their following while at the same time infiltrating trusted Trujillans among them. This succeeded quite well with Benalcázar, who brought fewer men than Soto and had less prestige and dash. By the time of Cajamarca he had sunk to a poor third behind Hernando Pizarro and Hernando de Soto, with hardly half a dozen loyal followers. Soto proved irrepressible; he had the best horses and horsemen and not only retained the loyalties of many, but picked up the allegiance of other expedition members from his native region of Badajoz. Soon the Pizarros decided to give him his head, letting him ride out in command of the vanguard, where he might exceed his orders and plot mutinies, but was at least out of the way.

With the arrival of Almagro, the time of greatest dependence on the Nicaraguan captains was past. At the distribution of treasure, as we have seen, their shares told them clearly that they must look elsewhere. Benalcázar, treated by far the worst, reacted immediately. Hardly had he received the lieutenant-governorship of Piura (a form of banishment from central Peru), than he took advantage of it to organize and carry out the conquest of Quito on his own. When the Pizarros later pursued him there, he took his independent career as governor and conqueror yet farther north into Popayán and New Granada. Soto was longer in responding, partly because he could look forward by previous agreement to the lieutenant governorship of rich and famous Cuzco, at least for a while, and partly because he hoped to find some opportunity for an independent governorship to the south. But after the Chile venture fell to Almagro, and dickering for a captaincy-general in that conquest had failed, Soto left Peru in 1535 to seek a governorship elsewhere—in North America, as it turned out. He was not literally forced out of Peru, but he could not fulfill his ambitions, and such a powerful subordinate was intolerable in the long run to the Pizarros; they had already cut into his position in Cuzco. Many of Soto's faithful supporters left at about the same time, and so did all the men of Badajoz, who probably experienced in lesser degree the strains felt by Soto.

Thus, within a short period, the Pizarros managed to eject all other leaders among the men of Cajamarca who threatened independence, belonged to other factions, or merely stood in the way of the advancement of themselves and their Trujillo compatriots. As the campaign proceeded, new men came into captaincies; they were either of the Trujillo faction, like Juan Pizarro and Diego de Agüero, or were prepared to operate within a framework of Pizarro dominance, like Juan Morgovejo. The ejections were not forceful, nor even very abrupt, but a subtle push-and-pull action, exercised mainly through the distribution of shares of treasure. Those shares were small enough to arouse a sense of injustice among the men affected, implying that they would find little favor in the future. At the same time the amounts were large enough to enable those leaving to achieve their aims outside Peru: for Mena and Salcedo, to go to Spain; for Soto and Benalcázar, to conquer new areas. Thus it was the rivalries of the conquerors, in conjunction with the treasure, that brought about the quick occupation of other regions.

It is much more difficult to trace the workings of faction and regional group among the ordinary members of the expedition. Tabulating the regional origin of repatriates and settlers gives us some notion of them. In Table 23 it can be seen that both men staying and men returning, taken as groups, reflect the general regional composition of the expedition quite well, with one considerable exception. More Extremadurans stayed, and fewer returned, clearly the result of favored treatment by their compatriot the governor. Actually Extremadura is too broad a category. As mentioned above, Soto's Badajoz compatriots went home, so that an overwhelming majority of the Extremadurans staying were from Trujillo, Cáceres, and the surrounding region. This area accounted for thirteen of the nineteen remaining in the Indies, one of the other six being Soto himself, who ended in North America, and another Rodrigo Núñez, who went to Chile.

Mainly from humble or unimpressive backgrounds, the Trujillans remaining in Peru were at first completely dependent on the Pizarro tie; all were strong Pizarro partisans, many actual retainers. These people received encomiendas of the very best, and were often preferred to council seats before their individual eminence would have merited it. The Pizarros made a concerted effort to pack the Peruvian town councils with compatriots and retainers. Possibly the height of this kind of dominance was reached with the council of Cuzco of 1537, analyzed in Table 24.[44] Usually, however, they bowed to the local situation, and permitted several representatives of other interests to sit on the council. The men appointed as Pizarro spokesmen did their job as instructed, but at the same time sought to cement their position and to begin building an independent base. The non-Trujillans were generally most

Table 23. Regional Origin Related to Final Destination

Origin	Indies	Spain
Extremadura	19	15
Andalusia	12	19
Old Castile	8	8
New Castile	7	8
Leon	6	6
Biscay	1	6
Navarre	2	0
Aragon	2	0
Greece	1	1
Unknown	8	3
Total	66	66

[44] The table rests on a mass of data from the sources for the individual men, but the composition of the council may be seen in *CDIHC*, IV, 398.

successful or determined in this effort; Juan de Valdevieso, for example, in 1541 attained the post of chief majordomo to the then governor, Vaca de Castro, who was from Leon like himself. Few of the retainers became captains or faction leaders on their own; during the Gonzalo Pizarro rebellion of the later 1540's, however, several attained prominence as Pizarrist captains or local lieutenant governors: Almendras, Hontiveros, Lucas Martínez, Alonso de Toro.

The whole series of civil wars engulfing Peru until 1550 grew out of tensions already evident at the time of Cajamarca. The ramifications of this vast subject cannot all be considered here, though there is hardly an aspect of it that does not relate significantly to the conquest proper and the backgrounds of the conquerors. There was the Pizarro-Almagro struggle, with its attendant Extremadura–New Castile rivalry; there was the subtler struggle between Pizarro rule and the officials of the royal government; and, at the root, there was the contest already seen in the distribution of Cajamarca treasure—the issue of whether the

Table 24. The Council of Cuzco, 1537

Members	Men of Cajamarca	Pizarro Retainers	From Trujillo-Cáceres	Pizarro Partisans
Lieutenant governor				
Hernando Pizarro	*	——	*	*
Alcaldes				
Gabriel de Rojas	——	——	——	——
Francisco de Villacastín	——	——	——	*
Councilmen				
Diego Maldonado	*	——	——	——
Hernando de Aldana	*	——	*	*
Juan de Valdevieso	*	*	——	*
Gonzalo de los Nidos	——	——	*	*
Lucas Martínez	*	(?)	*	*
Francisco de Almendras	*	(?)	*	*
Rodrigo de Herrera	*	*	——	*
Clerk				
Diego de Narváez	*	——	——	——

NOTE: An asterisk (*) denotes possession of attributes indicated; a dash (——), absence of attributes indicated; a question mark (?), doubtful status.

narrow Pizarro party was to be overwhelmingly predominant, or whether a diversity of interests was to prevail. Within a few years the Almagrists had lost utterly, but the other factors all remained strong. In 1554 Gonzalo Pizarro made a last attempt to assert total Pizarro dominance, but after some years of apparent success, based on the temporary coincidence of interests of the Pizarros and the majority of encomenderos, the combined elements of royal authority and the general Spanish population won a decisive victory. In 1548 the Pizarro party was destroyed, and the factionalism stemming from the conquering expedition came to an end, though many old Pizarrists remained among the encomenderos.

In the civil wars no more than a small number of the men of Cajamarca ever opposed the Pizarros directly, if only because they owed to them the encomiendas which were the base of their wealth and influence. Those doing so were almost all either New Castilians or marginal figures of one kind or another who were unhappy with the treatment accorded them. A few were resentful of poor shares of Cajamarca treasure. Altogether, five men are thought to have gone on Almagro's Chile expedition; two of these and three others died fighting on the Almagro side in the civil wars.

The importance of the New Castilian factor does not emerge in the raw figures telling who stayed and who returned. For one thing, the region proves as usual too broad a category. New Castile includes Madrid, too far away from Almagro's Ciudad Real to have much affinity with it; the effects are visible only in the men of Toledo and of Ciudad Real itself.[45] Mena, a Ciudad Real native, was an Almagro agent, as we have seen; Francisco de Peces, from Sonseca, a little to the north, took Almagro's side in the "War of Salinas" despite an encomienda and a council seat in Cuzco; tailor Juan Jiménez, from nearby Consuegra, probably accompanied Almagro to Chile; Alonso de Mesa, from Toledo, repeatedly came under suspicion of Almagro partisanship, and suffered for it.[46]

One of the more noted figures to join Almagro was Rodrigo Núñez.

[45] Madrid man Barrera was no enemy of the Pizarros; Baena was their ally, and Barbarán actually their retainer.

[46] Alonso de Morales, from Moral de Calatrava near Ciudad Real, came from Spain with the Pizarros and was their retainer for a time; nevertheless, he went home early and later complained of his treatment. He is last seen in Peru in the following of Almagro in 1534 (Antonio de Herrera, Décadas, XI, 43). Pedro de León of Ciudad Real also went early to Spain, though we know nothing more specific.

Though Pizarro named him *maestro de campo* when he arrived in Peru with Benalcázar, he received no authority with the post, and he got a simple horseman's share of the treasure. In resentment he took a similar assignment with Almagro's Chile expedition. Several Pizarro enemies were clearly marginal men. They include Pedro de San Millán, the expedition's only authenticated wastrel; Pedro de Ulloa, who, though a Cáceres man, got the Peru expedition's smallest share; the Greek, Pedro de Candía, his Aragonese-Italian friend Florencia, and Diego de Narváez from Navarre.

Conclusion

The slave raiding on the Caribbean, the spoils seeking in Central America, and the great conquests are all on the same line of development. In the evolution of Spanish-American expeditionary enterprises from the investor-dominated commercial company toward a band of men winning shares, the Peru venture had gone far toward the latter, not only formally, but in the diversification of investment and the plurality of independent interests. On the other hand, the Pizarros were strong in organization and in the number of their faction. Gradually they expelled or destroyed all prominent individuals who could challenge them, but an indestructible counterweight to their power existed in the numbers, equipment, and skill of the ordinary Spaniards. The whole organizational-political aspect of the expedition and its aftermath was characterized by this struggle between Pizarro-Trujillo dominance and the self-assertion of the body of men, with the result long inconclusive.

Through all the maneuverings and battles, most of the men acted on a realistic assessment of their own self-interest. Their factions rested on ties of common region and common experience. We need never have recourse to the concepts of treachery or adventurousness to explain the conquerors' conflicts and movements. Treachery perhaps is in evidence, though never as a gratuitous factor; adventurousness is simply not applicable, since those few who went on to farther frontiers had essentially been expelled. After twenty years the conflicts died down; meanwhile they had had major repercussions on the settlement of other parts of South America, and even of Florida. Indeed, the workings of faction go far to explain the speed of the Spanish occupation of the Indies.

5. THE ROLL OF CAJAMARCA

THE EXISTENCE OF A LIST of the participants in Atahuallpa's capture, on the whole amazingly accurate and complete, is what makes the present book possible. Besides giving a framework and a starting place, the list provides much essential information about the individuals—their roles, social standing, associations, and occasionally even their occupations. Yet we do not know the original of the list, nor any contemporary copy, nor any direct copy made in later times. All the known versions extant are at least third-hand.

A document with such a masked origin deserves to have its history traced. What has come down to us is a record of the distribution of the treasure, rather than a roll of the participants as such. It omits Fray Vicente de Valverde, who participated but received no share; any other Spanish participants who might have been deprived of shares would also fail to appear, though it is unlikely that there were any. On the other hand, the list includes Juan de Sosa, who received a share but was not present. Whether or not a full roster of participants ever existed is unknown. Expeditions do seem sometimes to have maintained a general roster. Such a document for the Peru expedition would presumably have listed all the Spaniards who had entered the country, including those who stayed behind in Piura.

The earliest version that is definitely known to have existed actually consisted of *two* documents prepared by the secretaries Francisco de Jerez and Pedro Sancho. One list recorded the distribution of silver, the other of gold; some individuals were omitted entirely from one or the other listing. These documents eventually came into the hands of the chief notary of the realm, Jerónimo de Aliaga, and were in his possession in Lima around 1550.

At this time the chronicler Pedro de Cieza de León consulted the lists and prepared a version which he inserted in the third part of his Peruvian histories. Cieza was interested above all in perpetuating the first conquerors' names; for that reason, and because he thought the division of the treasure unjust, he omitted the shares. By his own statements Cieza would appear to have used only the silver list. One of the omissions on his list can be traced back to this procedure.[1] If an authentic reproduction of Cieza's list had come down to us, it would probably be the best we have. But most of Cieza's writings had to wait centuries for publication, and by the twentieth century the third part of his chronicle of Peru, dealing with the conquest, was considered lost. At last Peruvian Rafael Loredo located a copy, of which he has published sections in *Mercurio Peruano*, including the Cajamarca list.[2] But Loredo's copy, apparently made in the eighteenth century or later, is garbled in many places, and Loredo's own editorial practices are veiled and arbitrary. Cieza's list thus reaches us twice removed from the original. Even so, it has much value. Despite many misspellings and impossible forms, it gives correct renditions of several names which are in-

---

[1] Cieza does not specifically say that he used only the silver list, but at the end of his list he gives only the quantity of silver distributed. In the shares as given by Caravantes, two men, Gaspar de Marquina and Diego Escudero, received no silver. Checking this against Cieza, we find that Cieza has omitted Marquina as would be expected; but Diego Escudero does appear on his list, though in a far different location than on the Caravantes-Salinas list. The present writer thinks that Cieza did in fact use the silver list, then glanced through the gold list and caught Escudero, but not Marquina. Cieza has probably given Escudero the location he occupied on the gold list. Cieza's other apparent omissions must be merely defects in the available copy, since Herrera's list, derived from Cieza's, omits only Marquina.

[2] Pedro de Cieza, *Tercera parte*, in *Mercurio Peruano* 39 (1958):570–574. Loredo has consistently refused to reveal the provenance of his copy. However, there can be no reasonable doubt that it is essentially authentic.

correct in the better-known versions. Cieza also at times presents a more logical order of names, probably reflecting the original lists. (When he puts two tailors together, neither of whose occupations he could have known, there is no doubt that he follows the original. However, when he puts two men with the same surname together, he may be checking or rationalizing rather than copying directly.) Cieza alone preserves the original *gente de a pie* ("footmen") as the heading for the second section, rather than the militarizing *infantería* ("infantry") of the later writers.

At some later time, probably around the 1580's, in the era of Viceroy Toledo, when efforts were being made to preserve the history of the conquest, someone made another copy.[3] Not long thereafter the originals disappeared. The copier reproduced the wording of the official act of distributing the silver, a short summary of the act of distributing the gold, and a combined list of all persons receiving shares, with the exact amounts of silver and gold going to each person. The combined list was not prepared in 1532 by Pedro Sancho, as Loredo thought.[4] The statement made there that the lists are combined in order to avoid writing the list twice is only a parenthetical remark by the later copier. It is highly improbable that a member of the Peru expedition would have had to guess whether a comrade's name was Rodrigo or Francisco, or would not know whether a prominent captain was named Mena or Medina.[5] Also, we know that Cieza in 1550 had no amalgamated list to work from.

In the early seventeenth century Francisco López de Caravantes, a treasury official in Lima, copied this list in its entirety and inserted it in his manuscript "Noticia general de las provincias del Perú, Tierra Firme y Chile," of which various parts were completed between 1614 and 1632.[6] The fact that Caravantes was a treasury accountant may

[3] The time was certainly no later than the early seventeenth century, when Caravantes and Salinas y Córdoba used the list, and long enough after the conquest that the calligraphy of 1530 was becoming difficult to read.

[4] Rafael Loredo, *Los repartos*, p. 92. Loredo's discussion of the history of the document, with several acute remarks, covers pages 91–95.

[5] These alternatives appear in both Caravantes and Salinas y Córdoba, so they must have been in this copy, along with the many other mistakes those two versions have in common. Because the two have so many common errors, but each has correct readings not in the other, one may deduce that an independent list existed, rather than that one of these two was based on the other.

[6] The unpublished manuscript of Caravantes's work is in the Biblioteca de Palacio in Madrid; a description is to be found in Jesús Domínguez Bordoña, *Manuscritos*

well indicate that the copy was preserved in the Lima offices of the royal exchequer. Caravantes's version of this late-sixteenth century copy is the standard one today and the only source available which gives the men's individual shares of gold and silver. There is no way to check closely the accuracy of the amounts, but internal evidence, comparison with other fragmentary information,[7] and the congruence of Caravantes's totals with those given elsewhere,[8] all point to a high degree of reliability. As to the names, Caravantes, like the copy before him, is extremely reliable in reproducing all the elements, and usually their order. The spelling, however, is highly corrupt. Many names are completely erroneous, though plausible, while others are improbable, and several are so garbled as to be impossible in Spanish or any other language. A majority of the mistakes are Caravantes's own, but a good number were already in the copy he used.

Around the same time as Caravantes, or a little later, the Franciscan friar Buenaventura de Salinas y Córdoba again used the copy which served Caravantes, including a version of it in his *Memorial de las historias del nuevo mundo Pirú*,[9] published in 1630. Salinas y Córdoba changed the orientation of the listing by omitting the shares and attempting to account for all the participants. At the end of the list of horsemen he added the name of Fray Vicente de Valverde. One might naturally suspect that Salinas y Córdoba merely used Caravantes, but though the two tally in most details, the Franciscan has many correct readings which are mistaken in Caravantes, besides a few new mistakes of his own. In general, Salinas y Córdoba gives a better rendering of the names, and, in one case, of the order of their common source, though he does make two omissions. Having served as the basis of the two versions, the late-sixteenth-century copy in Lima must have disappeared. Neither its original nor any other direct copies are known today.

Cieza, Caravantes, and Salinas y Córdoba are the three principal

---

de América, pp. 179–181 and 182. The Cajamarca document therein contained has been published many times, perhaps most completely and clearly in Enrique Torres Saldamando, *Libro primero de cabildos de Lima*, III, 121–126.

[7] See, for example, Oviedo's assertion that Hernando Pizarro got seven shares, or Gaspar de Marquina's mention in a letter that he possessed "tres mil ducados largos."

[8] See Loredo, *Los repartos*, pp. 67–86, for an extensive treatment of the amount and quality of the treasure of Cajamarca.

[9] Buenaventura de Salinas y Córdoba, *Memorial*, edited by Luis E. Valcárcel and Warren L. Cook. The list is on pp. 78–90.

sources for the Cajamarca list. Each has independent value; each contains correct readings not in any other version, as well as confirmation
or refutation of the others. A fourth copy, included by Antonio de Herrera in his *Décadas*,[10] is far less valuable. Roughly contemporary with
Caravantes and Salinas y Córdoba, Herrera's listing is almost exclusively based on Cieza's. Scholars have long known that Herrera relied heavily on Cieza, and that he used the subsequently lost third part of Cieza's
work. Again and again Herrera's list agrees with Cieza's, in order as
well as in spelling of names. Most indicative of all is the fact that Herrera follows Cieza in mistakes, such as Hernando Martínez for Hernán Muñoz, Juan Martínez for Juan Muñoz, and Nicolás de Aspa for
Nicolás de Azpeitia. Herrera shows no sign of having known the other
two versions, or any other form of the list. His considerable deviation
from Cieza comes from an ill-informed attempt to correct apparent
mistakes, and to supplement the listing from individual bits of outside
testimony. Not knowing that there really were two Miguel Estetes, he
banished one from the list, putting in his place one Pedro Alonso Carrasco, who was not at Cajamaca. Herrera also eliminated one of the
two Juan de Salinases to make room for Captain Pedro de Vergara, an
artillery captain who arrived in Peru only late in the 1530's. Herrera's
listing would have no independent value at all if the original of Cieza's
were available. That original is lost, however, and since Herrera used
either the original or a good copy of it, many of his renderings are
more faithful to Cieza than the bad copy of the *Tercera parte* published by Loredo. Particularly, Herrera's copy proves that Cieza did not
originally omit five names from Pedro de Anadel to Diego Ojuelos, as
he seems to, in Loredo's edition.

To the analysis and comparison of these four versions, much other
evidence can be added. Accounts in chronicles, and testimony in trials
and *probanzas*, give direct evidence that many of these men were indeed participants at Cajamarca. Much powerful circumstantial evidence
is available in notarial documents and treasury records from Cajamarca
in early 1533 and from Coaque in 1531. The web of reciprocal confirmation is thick and strong. Such corroboration cannot be made explicit
here, but the underpinnings may be found in the references to each
biography in Part II. While a few of the men, particularly those without first names on the list, are not certainly identified, the writer has

[10] Antonio de Herrera, *Décadas*, XI, 177–178.

little doubt that all the names on the version presented below are correct, with the exception of Juan de Niza.

Going beyond its history to analysis of the document itself, the significance of the names and amounts will be immediately apparent. Far less apparent is the meaning hidden in the order of listing. Generally speaking, the list is arranged in order of precedence, from high to low. The largest shares come first; the horsemen precede the footmen, the hidalgos the commoners, the captains the men. But this principle is not carried out consistently. There are many slips and anomalies. It seems almost that each of the two sections consists of a small number of clearly prominent men arranged in strict order of precedence at the top, followed by a large middle group without much attention to ranking, and then a smaller group of obviously inferior members at the end. (Though the first section appears to include only horsemen, some of the captains at the beginning of the list fought on foot. It is true that they owned horses, which was the important thing when it came to distributing the treasure.)

Another principle is the listing together of associates, partners, and men of the same trade. Partners Alonso Ruiz and Lucas Martínez appear together, as do at least four other pairs. Trumpeters Alconchel and Segovia are paired, and there are two sets of tailors: Chico and Robles, and González and Martínez. Such associations make one wonder if the list did not originate in a queue. Perhaps the compilers would have made these connections mentally in any case.

Whole units may be concealed in the list. It is not sure that the expedition had any permanently organized subunits of horse or foot; we hear rather of a certain leader being assigned so many men for a given mission. The closest thing to units were the bodies of horsemen loyal to Soto and Benalcázar respectively, the "artillery" under Candía, and a body of twenty crossbowmen that Jerez says was formed about a month before Cajamarca. In the list of horsemen, the seven men from "Alonso Pérez" to "Juan Ruiz" were veterans of Nicaragua who probably arrived with Benalcázar. It is not quite certain that the next two, Fuentes and Castillo, arrived with him, but they did accompany him back to Piura after Cajamarca. This grouping could be the nucleus of Benalcázar's squadron; nevertheless, others who came with him are located elsewhere. Men loyal to Soto are even more widely spread. The artillery—mainly musketeers—might be concentrated in the vicinity of Rodrigo de Herrera, musketeer, Martín de Florencia, crossbowman and subsequently artilleryman, and Jorge Griego, Greek friend of Captain Candía. But musketeer Juan García is at some distance. There surely must be many other elements hidden in the structure of the listing. Any new item of information about the men, added to what is already known and applied to the list, can confirm hunches or produce further insights.

A version of the Cajamarca list, based on a comparison of the four versions described above and combined with the best information that could be derived from other sources, follows. No list exactly like this one ever existed. It does not attempt to reconstruct the original separate lists for gold and silver; it is not an exact reconstruction of the late-sixteenth-century combined list, which had various errors. Rather, it gives the latter list as it would have been if all the readings had been correct.

The notes give some of the principal variants in the four versions, in both names and order, except that Herrera's partly derivative, partly arbitrary order is ignored. No account is taken of purely orthographic differences, or of the presence or absence of connectives and articles. The spelling of the names has been modernized and standardized.

All figures for shares are taken from Caravantes, the only known source at present. The occasional omission of a man from one or the other of the lists is not a mere oversight, since the original consolidator of the gold and silver lists made a written note in each case that he had searched and could not find a given name on a given list. The omissions must go all the way back to Cajamarca, and it is highly unlikely that oversights would be permitted in a matter of such pressing importance to individuals. There is a strong presumption that those missing from a given list actually received nothing.

GENTE DE A CABALLO

	(Silver marks)	*(Gold pesos)*
La Iglesia[11]	90	2,220
El señor gobernador por su persona y las lenguas y caballo	2,350	57,220
Hernando Pizarro	1,267	31,080

[11] The consolidated list, and presumably the originals, prefaced all entries with an *a* ("to"), which is omitted here. "La Iglesia" is omitted in all versions except Caravantes's.

	(*Silver marks*)	(*Gold pesos*)
Hernando de Soto	724	17,740
El padre Juan de Sosa		
vicario del ejército[12]	310 6/8	7,770
Juan Pizarro	407 2/8	11,100
Pedro de Candía	407 2/8	9,909
Gonzalo Pizarro	384 5/8	9,909
Juan Cortés	362	9,430
Sebastián de Benalcázar	407 2/8	9,909
Cristóbal de Mena[13]	366	8,380
Ruy Hernández Briceño	384 5/8	9,435
Juan de Salcedo[14]	362	9,435
Miguel Estete[15]	362	8,980
Francisco de Jerez	362	8,880
Más el dicho Jerez y Pedro Sancho		
por la escritura de compañía[16]	94	2,220
Gonzalo de Pineda	384	9,909
Alonso Briceño[17]	362	8,380
Alonso de Medina	362	8,480
Juan Pizarro de Orellana	362	8,980
Luis Maza	362	8,880
Jerónimo de Aliaga	339 4/8	8,880
Gonzalo Pérez	362	8,880
Pedro Barrantes[18]	362	8,880
Rodrigo Núñez	362	8,880
Pedro de Anadel[19]	362	8,880
Francisco Maraver	362	7,770
Diego Maldonado	362	7,770
Rodrigo de Chaves[20]	362	8,880
Diego Ojuelos	362	8,880

[12] Correctly omitted by Cieza and Herrera as not at Cajamarca.

[13] Caravantes and Salinas y Córdoba give Cristóbal de Mena or Medina.

[14] Caravantes and Salinas y Córdoba give Juan de Salazar.

[15] Herrera substitutes Pedro Alonso Carrasco, thinking the two Miguel Estetes are a mistake.

[16] Cieza and Herrera omit this; Salinas y Córdoba puts in only the name Pedro Sancho, then includes him again later. The original may well have said "compaña," which was still the standard word for the body of men constituting an expedition. See above, p. 70.

[17] Cieza reverses the order here, putting Medina before Briceño.

[18] Caravantes and Salinas y Córdoba have Pedro de Barrientos.

[19] This and the four names following are omitted in Cieza.

[20] Caravantes has Ramiro or Francisco de Chastes; Salinas y Córdoba has Rodrigo or Francisco de Chaves.

	(Silver marks)	(Gold pesos)
Ginés de Carranza[21]	362	8,880
Juan de Quincoces	362	8,880
Alonso de Morales	362	8,880
Lope Vélez	362	8,880
Juan de Barbarán	362	8,880
Pedro de Aguirre	362	8,880
Pedro de León	362	8,880
Diego Mejía	362	8,880
Martín Alonso	362	8,880
Juan de Rojas	362	8,880
Pedro Cataño	362	8,880
Pedro Ortiz	362	8,880
Juan Morgovejo	362	8,880
Hernando de Toro	316	8,880
Diego de Agüero	362	8,880
Alonso Pérez	362	8,880
Hernando Beltrán	362	8,880
Pedro de Barrera	362	8,880
Francisco Baena	362	8,880
Francisco López	371 4/8	6,660
Sebastián de Torres	362	8,880
Juan Ruiz	339 3/8	8,880
Francisco de Fuentes	362	8,880
Gonzalo del Castillo	362	8,880
Nicolás de Azpeitia[22]	339 3/8	8,880
Diego de Molina	316 6/8	7,770
Alonso Peto	316 6/8	7,770
Miguel Ruiz	362	8,880
Juan de Salinas herrador	362	8,880
Juan de Salinas de la Hoz[23]	248 7/8	6,110
Cristóbal Gallego	316 6/8	—
Rodrigo de Cantillana	294 1/8	—
Gabriel Félix	371 4/8	—
Hernán Sánchez	262	8,880

[21] Cieza has Pedro de Carranza, Herrera has Gómez de Carranza.

[22] Cieza gives the surname as Aspa and Herrera gives it as Azpa. Cieza may have meant what he wrote as an abbreviation, but Herrera definitely did not understand it as such.

[23] Salinas y Córdoba gives Juan del Hoz, Caravantes gives Juan Olz, or Loz. It would appear that the copy used by both of them had only "Hoz," omitting "Salinas." Herrera puts Pedro de la Hoz Salinas, then below, under the footmen, he puts Pedro de Salinas de la Hoz, a different form of the same man's name.

	(Silver marks)	*(Gold pesos)*
Pedro de Páramo[24]	271 4/8	6,115

GENTE DE A PIE[25]

	(Silver marks)	*(Gold pesos)*
Juan de Porras	181	4,540
Gregorio de Sotelo	181	4,540
Pedro Sancho	181	4,440
García de Paredes	181	4,440
Juan de Valdevieso	181	4,440
Gonzalo Maldonado	181	4,440
Pedro Navarro[26]	181	4,440
Juan Ronquillo	181	4,440
Antonio de Vergara	181	4,440
Alonso de la Carrera	181	4,440
Alonso Romero	181	4,440
Melchor Verdugo	135 6/8	3,330
Martín Bueno	135 6/8	4,440
Juan Pérez de Tudela	181	4,440
Iñigo Tabuyo[27]	181	4,440
Nuño González	181	—
Juan de Herrera	158	3,385
Francisco de Avalos	181	4,440
Hernando de Aldana	181	4,440
Martín de Marquina	135 6/8	3,330
Antonio de Herrera	135 6/8	3,330
Sandoval	135 6/8	3,330
Miguel Estete de Santo Domingo	135 6/8	3,330
Juan Borrallo	181	4,440
Pedro de Moguer	181	4,440
Francisco Peces[28]	158 3/8	3,880
Melchor Palomino	135 6/8	3,330
Pedro de Alconchel	181	4,440
Juan de Segovia	136 6/8	3,330
Crisóstomo de Hontiveros	135 6/8	3,330
Hernán Muñoz	135 6/8	3,330
Alonso de Mesa	135 6/8	3,330

24 Salinas y Córdoba adds the name of fray Vicente de Valverde after Páramo.
25 Herrera has "Infantes"; Caravantes and Salinas y Córdoba have "Infantería."
26 Salinas y Córdoba omits Pedro Navarro.
27 Caravantes and Salinas y Córdoba have Iñigo Taburco, Cieza has Iñigo Zalvio, and Herrera has Iñigo Talbio, the latter doubtless being what Cieza's original said.
28 All four versions have Francisco Pérez.

	(Silver marks)	(Gold pesos)
Juan Pérez de Oma[29]	135 6/8	3,885
Diego de Trujillo[30]	158 3/8	3,330
Palomino tonelero[31]	181	4,440
Alonso Jiménez	181	4,440
Pedro de Torres	135 6/8	3,330
Alonso de Toro	135 6/8	3,330
Diego López	135 6/8	3,330
Francisco Gallego	135 6/8	3,330
Bonilla	181	4,440
Francisco de Almendras	181	4,440
Escalante	181	3,330
Andrés Jiménez	181	4,440
Juan Jiménez[32]	181	3,330
García Martín	181	4,440
Alonso Ruiz	135 6/8	3,330
Lucas Martínez	135 6/8	3,330
Gómez González	135 6/8	3,330
Alonso de Alburquerque[33]	94	2,220
Francisco de Vargas	181	4,440
Diego Gavilán	181	3,884
Contreras difunto	133	2,770
Rodrigo de Herrera escopetero[34]	135 3/8	3,330
Martín de Florencia	135 6/8	3,330
Antonio de Oviedo	135 6/8	3,330
Jorge Griego	181	4,440
Pedro de San Millán	135 6/8	3,330
Pedro Catalán	93	3,330
Pedro Román	93	2,220
Francisco de la Torre	131 1/8	2,775
Francisco Gorducho	135 6/8	3,330
Juan Pérez de Zamora[35]	181	4,440
Diego de Narváez	131 1/8	2,775
Gabriel de Olivares	181	4,440
Juan García de Santa Olalla	135 6/8	3,330

[29] Herrera and Salinas y Córdoba have Juan Pérez de Osma.
[30] Cieza and Herrera give Alonso de Trujillo.
[31] Salinas y Córdoba has Pedro Palomino.
[32] Caravantes reverses the order of Juan Jiménez and García Martín; Salinas y Córdoba omits Juan Jiménez.
[33] Cieza and Herrera say simply Alburquerque.
[34] Salinas y Córdoba has Diego de Herrera.
[35] Caravantes gives Juan Pérez de Gómara.

	(Silver marks)	(Gold pesos)
Juan García escopetero[36]	135 6/8	3,330
Pedro de Mendoza	135 6/8	3,330
Juan Pérez	135 6/8	3,330
Francisco Martín	135 6/8	3,330
Bartolomé Sánchez marinero	135 6/8	3,330
Martín Pizarro	135 6/8	2,330
Hernando de Montalbo	181	3,330
Pedro Pinelo	135 6/8	3,330
Lázaro Sánchez	94	2,330
Miguel Cornejo	135 6/8	3,336
Francisco González	94	2,220
Francisco Martínez[37]	135 5/8	2,220
Zárate	182	4,440
Hernando de Sosa	135 6/8	3,330
Juan de Niza (?)[38]	195 6/8	3,330
Francisco de Solares	94	3,330
Hernando del Tiemblo[39]	67 7/8	2,220
Juan Sánchez	94	1,665
Sancho de Villegas	135 6/8	3,330
Pedro de Ulloa	94	—
Juan Chico[40]	135 6/8	3,330
Robles sastre[41]	94	2,220
Pedro Salinas de la Hoz	125 5/8	3,330
Antón García[42]	186	2,000
Juan Delgado[43]	139	3,330
Pedro de Valencia	94	2,220
Alonso Sánchez de Talavera	94	2,220
Miguel Sánchez	135 6/8	3,330

[36] Caravantes and Salinas y Córdoba put Pedro de Mendoza between the two Juan Garcías.

[37] Caravantes says Francisco Martínez and adds that he appears in the gold list as Francisco Cazalla; Cieza has Francisco Núñez; Herrera has Francisco Martínez. Doubtless Cieza's original had Martínez as well.

[38] Cieza has Juan Deuscar, Herrera has Juan de Orfán. In another document from Cajamarca the name appears to be Juan de Nizar.

[39] Salinas y Córdoba has Hernando Temblo; Caravantes has Hernando de Jemendo.

[40] Caravantes places Chico before Ulloa.

[41] Caravantes has Rodas sastre; Herrera and Salinas y Córdoba have simply Robles, without "sastre."

[42] Caravantes has Antón Esteban García; Salinas y Córdoba has Antonio Esteban García.

[43] Caravantes gives Juan Delgado Menzón; Salinas y Córdoba gives Juan Delgado Monzón.

	(Silver marks)	(Gold pesos)
Juan García pregonero	103	2,775
Lozano	94	2,220
García López	135 6/8	3,330
Juan Muñoz[44]	135 6/8	3,330
Juan de Beranga[45]	180	4,440
Esteban García	94	4,440
Juan de Salvatierra	135 6/8	3,330
Pedro Calderón	135	—
Gaspar de Marquina[46]	—	3,330
Diego Escudero[47]	—	4,440
Cristóbal de Sosa[48]	135 6/8	3,330

[44] Cieza and Herrera have Juan Martínez.

[45] Caravantes and Salinas y Córdoba have Juan de Berlanga; Cieza has Juan de Verarga; Herrera has Juan de Vergara. Cieza and Herrera place Esteban García ahead of this man.

[46] Omitted by Cieza and Herrera.

[47] Placed by Cieza (and Herrera after him) far above, just after Alonso de Toro.

[48] Caravantes has Cristóbal de Soto; Cieza places Cristóbal de Sosa higher on the list, just after Hernando de Sosa.

6. SOME GENERAL REFLECTIONS

MANY OF THE ANALYSES CARRIED OUT in earlier pages escape the question of representativeness or typicality by operating at a depth where that question does not arise. Implications for the image of the Spanish conqueror have emerged—views of the social types, ideals, patterns of behavior, and functions—that need no further discussion. Still, some delimitation and comparison may be helpful.

Perspective in Peru

Within Peru itself, it has not been the intention to assert here that our 168 men bore the whole burden of early Peruvian history, or that the events of Cajamarca had an utterly unparalleled effect on them. They *are* an "important" body of men in the usual sense, but the author was moved to write about them primarily because they are a varied group whose total membership is known and for whose lives minimally adequate data exist. It is unfortunate that the citizens of San Miguel are not well enough identified and documented to be studied jointly, in the same way, since they had been an integral part of the expedition for over a year and a half. As far as one can gather, they were of the same types, except that they were older; they would tip the scales even farther in the direction of maturity and experience in the Indies. In their subsequent careers the men of San Miguel do stand in some contrast to the others. Though local notables, they did not receive significant shares of Inca treasure at any point, and their own region was exceedingly poor in precious metals. Correspondingly few, it appears, went back to Spain. This tends to reinforce what was said above, that wealth and good social standing were the basic factors impelling return, while the strong correlation with experience was due to somewhat unusual circumstances.

If the conquerors left behind in San Miguel shared the pre-Cajamarca phase, the men arriving with Almagro shared the experiences of the captors of Atahuallpa for the rest of their lives. The study of this contingent also presents difficulties, though when the document of partition of treasure at Cuzco becomes available, the problem may not be insurmountable.[1] At any rate, for the present book they would have more than doubled the number of men, rendering the subject nearly unmanageable. In the absence of a methodical study of this group, some impressionistic assessments may have their value.

Almagro's men (so we often call them, though not nearly all were his partisans) shipped from Panama, rather than from Nicaragua, after the town had been drained twice previously. It stands to reason that a relatively high proportion of them were new arrivals to the Indies. On the other hand, a further small shipload of men from Nicaragua joined them on the way. Once again they seem types essentially similar to the men of Cajamarca. But because they received less than half as much treasure as the first conquerors, even with participation in the distribution of Cuzco, far fewer of them returned to Spain, or so it appears.[2]

---

[1] In possession of Rafael Loredo, at this writing.

[2] Pedro de Cieza describes the circumstances surrounding Almagro's expedition in *Tercera parte*, in *Mercurio Peruano* 38 (1957):260–262. As Loredo and others have pointed out (*Los repartos*, p. 113), the treasure of Cuzco was worth slightly more than that of Cajamarca. But, since it was divided among many more men, individual shares were smaller. The scraps published concerning the partition at Cuzco mention few shares strictly comparable to those at Cajamarca. Governor Pizarro got gold and silver worth 51,000 pesos, compared to his 68,000 at Cajamarca; Soto got 12,000, compared to 21,000. But in these cases, particularly Soto's, political exigencies were important. The only ordinary member whose share at Cuzco is known is Juan Pérez de Tudela; his case is complicated by the fact that, having been a footman at Caja-

A larger proportion of them accompanied Almagro to the conquest of Chile, as well they might, having closer connections with him and having received fewer favors from the Pizarros. Even so, most stayed behind as encomenderos of Peru, and these had careers closely paralleling those of the men of Cajamarca who still remained in the country. They sat on the same councils, fought in the same wars, received the same honors, and held encomiendas in the same city districts, though it is true that coming second, some were pushed off into peripheral areas.

Before long the two groups felt a strong solidarity of interest and were often viewed by later arrivals as a single entity. There was a difference, but one of degree only. It was no doubt true, as Garcilaso says, that the conquerors of Cuzco greatly honored the men of Cajamarca,[3] and overall it seems to be true that the latter were somewhat more prominent. By 1548, however, we find the distinctions of "first conqueror" and "conqueror of Cuzco" fading, with both groups considered "conquerors" pure and simple. That category remained important in the award and retention of encomiendas and was used around 1550 with considerable accuracy for these two sets of men and no others.[4]

As time went by, a further shift occurred. The dramatic events of Cajamarca came to symbolize the whole conquest, whether it was a matter of praising the conquerors or paying restitution to the Indians, when this gesture became fashionable.[5] It is in the late period, after 1560, that we first hear the term *los de Cajamarca*, translated here as "the men of Cajamarca."[6] Neither of the two men so called were in fact at Cajamarca—they had been left in San Miguel. The later generations no longer knew who actually took part in the capture of Ata-

marca, he had become a horseman by the time of the conquest of Cuzco. Many of the men of Cajamarca now had horses, in fact, and this increased the discrepancy between their shares and those of the new men, who could not yet afford mounts. At any rate, Juan Pérez de Tudela's share as a horseman at Cuzco was worth 7,668 pesos; since this was presumably a double portion, a single share at Cuzco would have been worth 3,834 pesos, compared to 5,345 at Cajamarca (see Loredo, *Los repartos*, pp. 99, 12, 400–403).

[3] Garcilaso de la Vega, *Obras*, II, 259.

[4] See for example the 1548 list of the encomenderos of Huamanga, in Loredo, *Los repartos*, pp. 211–213.

[5] Nicolás de Ribera el viejo, one of the Thirteen of Gallo, who arrived with Almagro in 1533 and had a long and active career in Peru, ordered in his will of 1563 that 6,000 pesos be paid as restitution to Indians, "despite the fact that I was not at Cajamarca" (*RAHC* 4 [1953]:105–108).

[6] In a Mercedarian memorial of services of 1570. Víctor M. Barriga, *Mercedarios*, I, 4.

huallpa, and, despite the growing emphasis on Cajamarca, imagined that the conquerors of Cuzco and other early arrivals must also have been there. Although Garcilaso gives a strict, standard definition of "first conqueror," in fact he applies it equally to all these groups. He, himself, with all his special knowledge, apparently had no exact idea of who participated and who did not.

To combine the whole corps of conquerors of Peru—the citizens of San Miguel, the men of Cajamarca, and the conquerors of Cuzco—would result in a group with a level of experience and social origins very similar to those of the men studied here; the forces, patterns, and variables operating on and in them were the same. One major quantitative difference would appear, in the form of a far larger proportion of settlers to repatriates. Also one would doubtless find the strength of the contingent from the Trujillo region less striking, with Andalusia probably regaining its usual numerical predominance among the regions.

Comparison with Other Areas

That the men of Cajamarca were closely akin to the conquerors of other parts of Spanish America is past all doubting. They operated within a whole network of well-formed Indies traditions, with which the long experience of many rendered them perfectly familiar; not a few had themselves been conquerors of Nicaragua and even of Panama. In their ideals they were strongly Spanish; in their social and regional origin they were closely parallel to the general stream of Spanish immigration in the early and middle sixteenth century.

Once a deep and subtle understanding of a subject has been achieved through close study, the business of comparative investigation is, first, to make a quick, superficial check as to the range of applicability, and, second, more importantly, to discern the pattern in regional variation. In the present case such comparison is severely limited by the lack of similar work for many other important areas. The peers of the men of Cajamarca are the conquerors of Mexico, on whose lives unfortunately no adequate research has been performed. Some partial studies exist, which enable us to see that the patterns of the conquerors' advancement and perpetuation within the county were much the same.[7] But in

---

[7] Francisco A. Icaza, *Conquistadores y pobladores de Nueva España*; Edmundo O'Gorman, *Catálogo de pobladores de Nueva España*.

most categories of our interest the information is inadequate or even suspect. Above all, completeness has not been attained and is perhaps hardly to be hoped for, with the large and miscellaneous body of Mexico's conquerors, so that we can have no certainty about proportions.

While it would be possible here to offer some observations on political similarities, or to speculate on the probable effect of the small amounts of Mexican treasure in holding down the rate of return to Spain, there is one remark that can be made in advance of closer study. Similar though they appear to be, the two great conquests and sets of conquerors were remarkably separate. The exchange of personnel was nearly nil. It was seen above that only one, or perhaps two, of the Peruvian conquerors had ever been in Mexico. No Mexican rivalries, friendships, or practices reflect themselves in Peru, as do those of Panama and Nicaragua.

There are two watersheds of conquest—one toward Central America, then Peru, the other toward Cuba, then Mexico, each with its own continuities, inside a broad framework of contemporaneity and similar dynamics. It is hard to say in which the characteristic forms of mainland expansion and occupation first evolved—probably Panama-Peru. Fortunately, studies do exist which allow a comparative view of at least some aspects of the groups of Spaniards involved at three important steps along this southern path of conquest: the founders of Panama, the men of Cajamarca, and the conquerors of Chile.

Góngora in his *Grupos de conquistadores* takes that truly remarkable document, the census of the first encomenderos of Panama in 1519–1522, and analyzes it for social history in categories approaching those used here, though not always identical.[8] The document and con-

---

[8] The document appears in entirety in Mario Góngora, *Los grupos de conquistadores*, pp. 70–75, and Góngora's discussion of it on pp. 75–84. There are two possible objections to using the founders of Panama for purposes of comparison: (1) the foundation of Panama was merely a strategic shift of Spaniards already in the country, rather than an expedition of conquerors; and (2) the document used lists only encomenderos, not literally every Spaniard present, as in the other two cases. To the first one may answer that the broader Panamanian area at this time was still in the conquest phase, and Panama was established as a base for expeditions. To the second one can reply that the small, often meaningless Panama encomiendas went to a broad sampling of the men present, including some very humble ones. It was not until the settlement of Peru and Mexico that the encomienda acquired its full seigneurial significance. Also, Góngora studies other elements of the local population, without discovering any additional types beyond auxiliary blacks and mulattoes.

There is a group that would have been still better for our purposes: the discoverers of the Pacific with Balboa in 1513. A unitary list exists (See Oviedo, *His-*

sequently Góngora's treatment of it are purely in terms of origins and background, with little information on current activity and nothing on later fate.

Tomás Thayer Ojeda in *Valdivia y sus compañeros* has examined the group characteristics of the conquerors of Chile, as to both background and subsequent careers. Lacking a unitary base document, he nevertheless assembled, through years of work, a list of Chile's first conquerors that can be considered literally complete. Though the methods of an earlier generation of scholars, together with a certain generous patriotism and Hispanism, have combined to render much of Thayer's background information suspect or unacceptable, his treatment of subsequent fates is reliable and admirably full.

In these circumstances, comparison must inevitably be uneven. The one aspect in which a thorough comparison can be carried out is that of regional origin. This in itself is significant. Whenever one undertakes a serious study of a group of Spaniards of any kind in the Indies, he will discover where most of them were born, if he finds nothing else. The Spaniards themselves considered regional origin of such importance, as a primary element of their social and political life, that they insisted on declaration of origin at every turn. For Panama, we have the origins of over 95 percent, for the men of Cajamarca, 77 percent, for the conquerors of Chile, 72 percent. The confrontation of percentages in Table 25 makes little contribution to the history of Spanish immigration generally, as it is emerging in the work of Peter Boyd-Bowman, this author's *Spanish Peru*, etc. But it does serve to emphasize several points. The conquering groups were always of diverse origin, in roughly the same proportions as the broad Spanish population in the Indies at the time. The general tendency for Andalusians to diminish in number, while remaining generally the largest regional division, is reflected very well in the three successive groups. The entry of a minority of mestizos among the conquerors of Chile (1540) paral-

---

toria general, III, 213, 214, 217), and a beginning was made on the men's biographies by José Toribio Medina in chapter 15 of his life of Balboa (*Descubrimiento*, I, 297–327). However, not only does this information need synthesis, much of it is patently in error; rechecking of the original archival sources and further research would be required to build up a reliable picture of group characteristics. For the present one can only point to some readily recognizable traits: diverse regional origin, including the usual scattering of foreigners and blacks or mulattoes; the presence of some artisans and seamen; the fact that several of the men six years later entered the lists of Panama's first encomenderos, the very group studied by Góngora.

lels a general phenomenon. Once again we see that conqueror and settler, conquest and settlement are the same.

At the same time, in these relatively small groups, the origin of the
leadership or other variable factors could throw the balance off, with
strong political implications, as already seen in chapter 4, above. In
fact, yet another repercussion of the Extremaduran dominance in Peru,
with the consequent poor position of Almagro's New Castilians, is visible in the composition of the conquerors of Chile. Even though Almagro's Chile venture failed, the New Castilian tradition remained, as
well as the Pizarro hostility in Peru. So even though Pizarro named his
Extremaduran compatriot Valdivia to head the second expedition, New
Castilians were still the second-largest regional group—far larger than
usual—with Extremadurans only third. Valdivia had to face the hostile
New Castilians, the men of Leon or western Old Castile under his
rival Pedro Sancho (man of Cajamarca), and the indifferent Andalusians, with an insufficient regional following of his own; the situation expressed itself in repeated mutinies.

In the matter of experience, the founders of Panama, like the men
of Cajamarca, fell into two groups: men of little experience who ar-

Table 25. Regional Origins Compared

Regions of Origin (first six in expected order)	Founders of Panama, 1519 (percent)	Men of Caja-marca, 1532 (percent)	Conquerors of Chile, 1540 (percent)
Andalusia	34.7	25.9	22.5
Extremadura	21.4	27.5	15.4
Old Castile	10.6	13.0	7.2
New Castile	9.5	11.4	16.2
Leon	5.9	11.4	12.6
Biscay	8.3	6.1	10.8
Asturias	2.0	0.0	0.0
Galicia	0.0	0.0	1.8
Navarre	0.0	1.5	0.0
Aragon	1.1	1.5	0.9
Murcia	0.0	0.0	0.9
Canaries	0.0	0.0	0.9
Foreign countries	5.9	1.5	5.5
Indies	0.0	0.0	5.5

rived in a body with the governor, and old veterans, there long before.[9] Since, in the case of Panama, the main expedition had arrived some time ago, almost the whole group were veterans of a few years, and over half had been in the area for more than five years.[10] Thus even the great armada of Pedrarias de Avila had been unable to impose a monolithic uniformity on the local Spanish population, or to halt the evolution of that population's local traditions.

Thayer Ojeda's analysis of this subject is vitiated by his too liberal use of the *Pasajeros a Indias*.[11] Nevertheless, the general picture seems valid. The great majority of the conquerors of Chile had arrived in the Indies only two to four years before. Only a few had longer experience, mainly the veterans of Almagro's first Chile expedition, though it is true that the several young mestizos had lived all their lives in the Indies. This probably indicates a trend. The time was coming to an

[9] In Table 25, the figures for the founders of Panama are taken unchanged from the table Góngora inserted in *Grupos*, p. 77, except that Old Castile and the Montaña are combined to achieve comparability.

With the conquerors of Chile the situation is far more complex. Although himself a man of the broadest knowledge, Tomás Thayer Ojeda was forced by blindness late in life to use untutored help in compiling *Valdivia y sus compañeros*. Many errors crept in, including some very obvious ones, putting Spanish towns in the wrong regions. This writer has adopted the procedure of correcting the known errors, making one addition from other sources, and recalculating. The changes are as follows: (1) Alonso de Chinchilla, said to be from Medina del Campo, is changed from Murcia to Old Castile; in fact, the man was probably from Medina de Ríoseco, Old Castile, in any case (see below, pp. 280–281); (2) Francisco and Pedro de León, from Moral de Calatrava, are changed from Andalusia to New Castile; (3) Diego García de Cáceres is changed from Leon to Extremadura because he was from Cáceres, not Palencia, as is apparent from the entry in *Valdivia*, p. 43, alone; (4) Diego Gutiérrez de los Ríos is changed fom Asturias to Andalusia because he was not from Naveda but from Córdoba; see don Alonso Enríquez de Guzmán, *Vida y costumbres*, p. 162; (5) Francisco Rodríguez de Hontiveros, from Hontiveros, is changed from Extremadura to Old Castile—Hontiveros is the modern Fontiveros; (6) Antonio Zapata, from Palencia, is changed from Leon to Old Castile. By some criteria Palencia can be considered Leon, but more usually Old Castile, and it is so considered in both the other listings; (7) Juan Romero is added to Leon as being from Zamora. The author disagrees with Thayer on the exact origin of Pedro Sancho, but both place him in Old Castile (see below, pp. 280–281).

[10] Góngora (*Grupos*, p. 78) declines to be specific about the times of arrival, alleging with good reason the men's vague manner of speaking. Also, they refer only to their arrival in "estas partes," which here proves mainly equivalent to the immediate Panama region, so that they could have been on the islands earlier. Nevertheless, some idea is better than none. The author finds that eighty-two men stated how long ago they had arrived: two under two years; thirty-seven between two and five years; thirty-one between five and ten years; and twelve between ten and fifteen years.

[11] Tomás Thayer Ojeda, *Valdivia*, pp. 84–86.

end when conquest was the mainstream of Spanish American evolution, when any experienced and wealthy members of the Spanish population were willing to devote themselves primarily to the opening up of new regions. The great heartlands were occupied; now began the business of sending unhappy young newcomers out of the country. The conquest of Chile was one of the first, and the most successful, of the numberless *entradas* leaving Peru in all directions in the 1540's, 1550's, and 1560's.

As to social origins, Panama's founders seem hardly distinguishable from the men of Cajamarca: the same upper-ranking group of modest hidalgos, with one or two fairly near the courtly nobility, followed by notaries, artisans, seamen, and lower plebeians, all in much the same proportion, as far as we can tell. Such differences as there are seem to be of terminology (Panama's *escuderos* were Peru's hidalgos),[12] or of the different state of knowledge, since the background information in the Panama census far exceeds what has been pieced together about the men of Cajamarca, particularly as to the humbler trades. A predominance of artisans over "peasants" or small agriculturalists in Panama seems very significant both in itself and for the implication that, in this aspect too, the Peruvian conquerors were probably similar, though we have no firm evidence. The Panama list identifies no declared merchants, nor could Góngora locate a trace of any in the Panama of the time.[13] Nevertheless, they were there,[14] as they were later in Peru. It is true that the full-time declared merchants stood aside from the conquest proper; when any joined the ranks of the conquerors, they dropped their label and open activity. Perhaps there were no trained merchants among the encomenderos of Panama at that early time (the city was soon to be crowded with merchants), but it would be possible to identify several individuals who were primarily entrepreneurs and men of affairs, much like those among the men of Cajamarca.

Thayer Ojeda's data are again less satisfactory. Góngora himself chided Thayer for an overly facile acceptance of spurious hidalgos;[15] nor was the identification of trades a particular interest of his. Nevertheless, something emerges. For one thing, the conquerors of Chile

[12] See James Lockhart, *Spanish Peru*, p. 35.
[13] Góngora, *Grupos*, pp. 88–89.
[14] Enrique Otte, "Mercaderes vascos in Tierra Firme," *Mercurio Peruano* 45, nos. 443–444 (Libro Jubiliar de Víctor Andrés Belaúnde), March–April, 1964, pp. 81–89.
[15] Góngora, *Grupos*, p. 69.

were the first of our three groups to have among their number anyone titled "don"; there were, in fact, two of them.[16] Word of the wealth of Peru had had its effect in Spanish courtly circles, and some marginal members of the high nobility were now willing to try a hand at conquest. There was not, however, any wholesale transformation of the conquering group. Discounting Thayer's known tendencies, reading between the lines of his data, and using one's informed imagination, one can see the same familiar concatenation of types and skills. This would remain, of course, to be proved in detail. At least the elements were there; among 154 men Thayer found five notaries, ten artisans, and three merchants.[17] Thayer's index of his men's literacy is too vague and generous to make comparisons.[18] Some 20 percent of the men were definitely functioning literates; according to Thayer, practically all the rest for whom there is any evidence at all could sign their names, with only 9 percent of the men surely illiterate. This would considerably improve on the performance of the men of Cajamarca, if true. The author's own experience does confirm that in Peru at least the quality of the signatures of the Spanish population as a whole was improving over the 1540's and into the 1550's; perhaps the conquerors of Chile were part of this general movement.[19]

Proceeding from backgrounds to further careers, the Panamanian data here almost forsake us. An impression of impermanence arises from a general knowledge of the area's history and is confirmed by Góngora's treatment. The reasons for this are apparent: the rampant diseases of the Isthmus; the lack of local wealth; the fact that the town was founded as a staging area to conquer north and south; the commercial revolution and the constant stream of passers-through after the Peruvian conquest, when the whole function of the city changed. We know of several men who left Panama for Nicaragua and then left again for Peru. But what proportion did this? Perhaps not as great as

[16] Thayer Ojeda, *Valdivia*, pp. 75–83.
[17] Ibid., pp. 108–109.
[18] Ibid., pp. 92–96.
[19] Thayer Ojeda also gives information on the men's ages (*Valdivia*, pp. 65–68, and passim), but he arbitrarily assumed that anyone whose age he did not know was twenty years old in 1540. On the other end of the scale, misuse of the *Pasajeros a Indias* led him to identify some conquerors of Chile with men of the same name who had come to the Indies many years before. Thus some longevity appears that is most unusual for the time: one man is said to have lived over one hundred years, six between eighty and ninety, nineteen between seventy and eighty.

one might think, if wholesale displacement is imagined. With a knowledge of the Spaniards in early Peru certainly not complete, but extensive, this writer can identify no more than sixteen of the ninety-three
founders of Panama who ever came to Peru—a significant movement
in any case. Only three of the men of Cajamarca ended anywhere else
in the Indies than Peru, and those went to be governors. The rate of
return to Spain among the Panamanians is not known.

The ultimate fates of the conquerors of Chile, on the other hand,
are known with accuracy and completeness. Chile was the opposite of
Panama, and indeed was far the most stable situation of the three
examined, despite the Indian wars. The conquerors of Chile were there
to stay. Of 154, only 7 returned permanently to Spain. Another 9 did
go back to Peru.[20] A trend of increasing permanence appears to obtain
for this whole southern current of Spanish conquest. But it depends
more on the location of Peru and Peru's wealth than on any general
stabilizing tendency. Peru pulled people on from Central America
and back from Chile. Its treasure was the springboard by which many
of its conquerors returned to Spain; the conquerors of Chile, and probably those of Panama, could hardly afford passage home, much less an
ostentatious life there. In the broad picture of the Spanish Indies, the
situation of the conquerors of Chile was common; that of the men of
Cajamarca exceptional. It was poverty that kept the Chileans in Chile,
not a mission to colonize constructively, which some have imagined
distinguished them from putatively more rapacious conquerors of
other areas. Whatever the reason, it is true that there was a constant
trend toward de-emphasis of treasure seeking, together with more emphasis on encomiendas and permanent settlement within the framework of conquest proper. The process had already gone far in Peru
itself, with encomiendas in San Miguel preceding Cajamarca; the
leaders were intent on permanent rule, not treasure, and even the partition of the treasure, important as it was, was geared to that end.

In the shape of their further lives the conquerors of Chile confirm
fully that the place accorded the men of Cajamarca in Peru was but
an instance of the general treatment first conquerors received in other
areas of the Indies. The effect was even stronger and lasted longer in
Chile, the flow of later immigration to the area being so much weaker.

[20] These figures are calculated from the catalog of the conquerors, in Thayer Ojeda,
Valdivia, pp. 31–61, rather than from the list of those leaving Chile (ibid., p. 117),
which omits two names.

Almost all who lived there any time became encomenderos, clustered in the two main cities of Santiago and Concepción.[21] Offices and honors were heaped on them: three became adelantados; four, members of the Order of Santiago; seven, governors (they long rotated in the governorship of Chile); nine, lieutenant governors or corregidors; and a whole horde, council members of the Chilean cities; apparently only three men survived long without holding some honorific post or other. The expedition's chief ecclesiastic became Chile's bishop, as Valverde had in Peru.[22] As in Peru, Indians and Spanish internal conflicts accounted for many of the conquerors' deaths; but, given Chile's less sedentary, more fragmented Indian population, the former outweighed the latter fifty to nine, whereas in Peru the two factors appear to have been almost equal.[23] With so much less wealth than Peru, Chile did not originate major expeditions into other areas on the order of Soto's and Benalcázar's, but the impulse was there, and one of the first conquerors was later governor of Tucumán across the Andes.[24]

Up and down this path of conquest, from Panama to Peru to Chile, the men were much the same: groups with great internal diversity of social and regional origin, occupation, and faction. They were principally commoners, perhaps with an urban and maritime bias, led by a substantial minority of modest hidalgos. Over the years there was a slight tendency for the general social level to rise. These men operated in the same traditions of action and organization, with the same general and individual goals. In this respect, however, change and evolution are much more visible, as the whole body of the men assumes ever more independence of the leaders and outfitters, and emphasis changes from distribution of treasure to permanent occupation.

It is in the pattern of the lives of the men after the conquest that we see the most variation. The processes were the same, but the proportions varied enormously, particularly in the matter of stability of settlement in the new country. That the backgrounds were so much more similar than the subsequent careers shows the force of the environment in the individual areas: the mineral wealth of Peru was the all-important factor in that environment, with the nature and numbers of the local Indian population at first only a very strong undercurrent.

21 Ibid., pp. 110–114.
22 Ibid., pp. 75, 105–107.
23 Ibid., pp. 115–116.
24 Ibid., p. 32.

Aspects of Method and Theory

The reader would doubtless not submit to a long discourse on the method of social history.[25] Nevertheless, the study of method and sources is the epistemology of the discipline, without which we could as well accept chroniclers' accounts as the pure, complete truth, and have done. Some discussion of these matters is necessary to an under-standing of one large part of the significance of the present work.

One way to study the society of a country or large region is to read widely in all available sources which show the daily functioning of its members at various levels, assembling a multitude of pertinent exam-ples of contractual agreements and careers, then sorting out the main social types and processes as therein embodied. Such a study was *Span-ish Peru*. Work of this type rests on the most direct sources and discov-ers basic patterns of an inherent intelligibility. Yet there is no doubt that the approach is somewhat selective. While the observations of pat-terns, functions, and structures can hardly be less than valid, the pro-portions are estimates. Wide-ranging investigation can bypass regulari-ties whose locus falls somewhere between the individual and the whole society.

Such surveys can be usefully supplemented by intensive, exhaustive studies of strategically placed small groups within the larger society, thus reducing the element of selectivity to a minimum. This is the ra-tionale of *The Men of Cajamarca*. And indeed this sampling shows the same functioning cross-section of Castilians, the same society in em-bryo, as did the broader overview. Such a result not only confirms the conclusions of the earlier work, it extends them, since *Spanish Peru* concentrated especially on the constructive period of about 1538 to 1555, resorting to somewhat impressionistic reporting for the time of the conquest proper. The inseparability of conquest and settlement now stand as fully established. The extreme earliness of decisive quasi-national development emerges even more strongly than before.

The method used in *The Men of Cajamarca* could find many appli-cations, but it may prove hard to find another group so manageable in size, so relatively well documented, and so exactly in the center of a

25 A discourse of this type is James Lockhart, "The Social History of Colonial Latin America: Evolution and Potential," *Latin American Research Review* 7 (1972), which restates the methodological part of what is said here, elaborates upon it, and puts it in the general context of social history research strategy.

vast historical process. It is important to have some kind of reliable unitary contemporary listing as a basis. Otherwise one might spend years in the mere identification of the group, or end by doing no more than a narrow selective study instead of a broad one.

The present work has several implications for the general theory of Spanish immigration to the New World and the establishment of a new society there. One way to broach this subject is to compare our findings with the ideas of anthropologist George M. Foster, whose explanation of the process is particularly attractive because of the small role it posits for conscious innovation.[26] Foster accounts for the possibility of a special variant or subculture of Hispanic civilization in America, in the face of constant new immigration from the metropolis, by the special advantage that experience with the New World gave to those already there. The earliest stages were especially important, because then the settlers were literally forced to make certain adaptations to the new environment. Once made, these adaptations quickly hardened into local traditions, and new arrivals adapted to them in turn.

We find this fully confirmed in the Peruvian conquest and accompanying movements. Seniority pervades everything. The leaders are those with the longest Indies experience; the largest shares go to the most experienced. Those who arrive first get the most rewards, honors, and positions, while succeeding immigrants look up to them and presumably imitate them. In the powerful old veterans Pizarro and Benalcázar we see a pride in the customs of the Indies and an insistence on forcing compliance with their ways.

The other main aspect of Foster's ideas is the contention that a simplification of Spanish culture had to take place in America in order to transmit its rudiments across the barriers of different language and concepts. Now, insofar as it refers to rural Indians, much can be said for this explanation. Even in the Spanish centers, something like simplification occurred, but at this point we must begin to question the nature of the phenomenon. A frequently quoted example is the evolution of plow forms; the many Spanish regional types of plow gave way to a single type in America. But here as in other cases, deeper consideration will tell us that rather than true simplification, this is mere loss of diversity—standardization or unification. No one region in Spain itself

---

[26] George M. Foster, *Culture and Conquest: America's Spanish Heritage*, especially chapters 2 and 17.

had many plow types. The technique and function are fully preserved in the New World.

Even in so small a sample as the Peru expedition, we can see that no truly essential elements of Spanish culture are being lost, not even the subtleties, present in such members as Valverde, Morgovejo, and Aliaga. There is some loss of variety, consequent on the simple reduction of numbers, and a process of standardization goes on as various Spanish regional groups clash, without any one group able to predominate absolutely. This same process has occurred regularly in settler colonies, including North America, and has nothing at all to do with Indians. In Foster's thinking the preoccupation of the whole discipline of anthropology with the concept of acculturation (from which it is now apparently beginning to recover) has led to the belief that when two societies come into contact, acculturation must explain almost everything.[27] The set of processes that has been called acculturation has its undeniable importance, even, in the long run, for the Spanish nuclei in America. But we should recognize the ability of a dominant group to maintain its traditions, even when a minority of the total population. Scholars have usually underestimated the structural importance of Indians—the way that they determined the nature of Spanish settlement as a primary environmental factor—while overestimating their direct impact on the Spaniards and Spanish culture.

The final parts of chapters 2 and 3 above have already sufficiently emphasized that the operation of such structural or general factors as the varying wealth of the new regions and the nature of long-standing Spanish social ideals far outweigh ideology and individual psychology in explaining what went on in the Indies, either countrywide, or in the career of a single Spaniard. This is not said in that sense in which scholars so often believe their own subject matter more important than another. Rather the assertion is being made that ideology and individual psychology did not bear on the process *at all*, as determinants. Utopianism can be dismissed out of hand. Not a trace of it appears in the

27 Foster shows several times in chapter 2, *Culture and Conquest*, that he realizes the importance of various factors having to do purely with the establishment of a new offshoot of a parent culture, regardless of the original inhabitants of the new area. Yet he also on occasion expresses open puzzlement about certain parts of the normal process of standardization (p. 16), and his primary focus is on the modification of what he considers a donor culture in relation to a recipient culture. He speaks in terms of "conquest" or "contact" culture, where in this writer's opinion one could more properly speak of "expansion," "colonial," or perhaps "frontier" culture.

Peruvian conquerors' words or actions, except perhaps for the death-
bed contrition into which zealous friars forced certain men who survived to the 1560's. Far from having any motive of dissent, the conquerors opposed innovation in any form, either in Spanish culture or
in the customs of the Indies. It appears that practically all Spaniards favored the expansion of Spain and Christianity. But this would apply to
one Spaniard as much as to another, and to all non-Spanish, non-Chris-
tian peoples equally. It could never explain why some Spaniards left
Spain and others did not, or why more went to some areas than others,
or why they did different things in different areas.

It should be apparent that group temperament or frame of mind
does not explain the immigrants' actions. Only the most naive would
think the conquerors of Panama a group of insecure, shifting individuals, those of Peru a contentious lot, and those of Chile constructive
colonists. The situation in each case gave the men good reason to act as
they did. Nor was there really a "conqueror mentality" causing conquest and a "settler mentality" causing peaceful occupation; the same
men often manifested both, as conditions changed.

It is true that attitudes of this kind can become so fixed that they are
an independent factor. But they still derive from the environment,
from experience, or from social condition. Some of the oldest veterans
had a positive emotional attachment to the Indies—not because of any
predisposition or act of will, but because they were humble and poor
fellows who had had to live at the edge of nowhere so long that it
grew on them, as would happen to anyone subjected to the experience.
The temperament of the conquerors—energetic, capable, laconic—was
adapted to the challenges and the pressures that faced their generation.
The creole idlers and talkers who often succeeded them represented the
almost universal response of sons for whom everything has been done
by their fathers. Such mentalities and temperaments whirl in front of
us in never-ending variety. But finally they are as nothing compared to
the Spanish desire to keep a large establishment and enhance the family name, a motivation actively shaping the lives of loquacious and taciturn, stable and unstable, low and high, settlers and repatriates.

Part II: The Men

7. LEADERS

HERE ARE BROUGHT TOGETHER life histories of the principal leaders of the Peruvian expedition as it approached Cajamarca. This may tempt some readers to concentrate on prominent individuals at the expense of the body of men who were the expedition's strength and to view the leaders apart from the general context. Yet the leading figures conform perfectly to the trends of their time and place. Indeed, since the careers of several of them are known in greater detail than those of the other conquerors, one can demonstrate by their cases more clearly than usual the shaping effect of general forces present in the environment and the background. It is often only with the leaders that we have the kind of information allowing us to perceive patterns of a psychological order, though these of course existed among all men. What appear at first to be idiosyncratic habits of mind often later reveal an intimate relation to social origin and experience.

If the men here were to be included in other sections, most would be listed with the hidalgos. Candía, with his special manual skill, would most nearly fit among the artisans, and Benalcázar would take his place among the plebeians, in all probability the lower plebeians. There is also, however, the specific type of the leader, usually a man respected for his lineage and experience. Juan and Gonzalo Pizarro are hardly of this type, since in 1532 their position was still purely dependent on their brother the governor. The youngest of the Pizarros, Gonzalo, was at this time perhaps not yet a leader at all. Nevertheless, he belongs with his kinsmen; his share of the treasure and his position on the roll of Cajamarca intimate that he was soon to be a captain like the rest.

Sebastián de Benalcázar

Age at Cajamarca: Over 40
Role: Captain of horse
Share: 2¼ shares of gold and silver

Place of origin: Belalcázar, in the
    province of Córdoba
Extent of literacy: Illiterate

Few indeed of the men of Cajamarca achieved greater fame than Sebastián de Benalcázar, yet his origins and even the early stages of his career in the Indies are no better known than those of many lesser figures. Much of the information current about Benalcázar's life comes from a single late and dubious source, Juan de Castellanos. This versifying chronicler of New Granada, who wrote his *Elegías* in the late sixteenth century, offers us one picturesque detail after another. In Castellanos's sketch, Benalcázar was one of twins born to a peasant family; since his parents died in his infancy, he was raised by an older brother. Once he took a mule to fetch wood, Castellanos says, and killed the animal by accident while trying to get it out of the mud. Rather than face the consequences, he fled from home. After some wandering Castellanos then has him arrive in Seville, where recruiting chanced to be in progress for the famous expedition of Pedrarias de Avila to the Isthmus of Panama (1513). Sebastián joined, taking the name of his home village, Benalcázar, for lack of another surname. In the Panama region his daring and liberality soon made him a popular leader. He was a close friend of Pizarro and Almagro, and he and Pizarro served as godfathers of Almagro's son. Later he went with Pedrarias to conquer Nicaragua, where he was alcalde of the capital, León, in the year of its foundation. All of this, to repeat, rests solely on Castellanos's account.

How much of it is true? The incident of the mule is nearly identical to a tale told by Gómara of how Francisco Pizarro as a boy lost a herd of pigs. Both are without doubt fabrications. Pedrarias did not conquer

Nicaragua in person, as is well known. If Castellanos was wrong on such a basic point, he cannot be accepted on the related matter of Benalcázar's position as first alcalde of León (though it is not impossible that he was). And the godfather relationship to Almagro's son fits too well with Castellanos's romanticizing tendency for us to put much faith in it, though once again it is not utterly implausible. Oviedo, a contemporary and personal acquaintance, said Benalcázar had been the friend of Almagro and Pizarro for a long time before the conquest of Peru.

Castellanos was himself conscientious, and his sources were not all corrupt. Benalcázar was indeed from the village of that name in the jurisdiction of Córdoba, well into the hill country to the north. He may even have been born a twin; Garcilaso de la Vega makes him one of triplets. Garcilaso, an equally late source, might be thought to be as suspect as Castellanos, but in this instance he was informed by a priest acquainted with the family. According to Garcilaso, Sebastián did not lack a surname; his name was originally Moyano, but, once out in the world, he took the name of his home town because it was better known. This is confirmed by Benalcázar's mention in his will of a nephew named Pedro Moyano.

Whether the Moyanos were literally "peasants" or not, they were certainly very humble people. Sebastián was illiterate and never learned to sign his name beyond an awkward rubric. Though he once said he knew no trade, he never laid any claim to good birth. Unlike his peers, Francisco Pizarro and Soto, he did not receive a cross of Santiago, and even after he became an *adelantado* as they did, there was a noticeable reluctance to call him "don." In his will there is not, as with Soto and Pizarro, any mention of his parents' names. As late as 1546 the viceroy of Peru dared throw in Benalcázar's face the statement that since the king had made him a cavalier, he would do well to fight like one. The judicious Cieza de León called him a man "of little knowledge and low intellect." All in all, one must conclude that Benalcázar was plebeian to the core.

The time and place of Benalcázar's arrival in the New World are also matters of uncertainty, because of his own conflicting testimony. In Panama in 1522, he said he had arrived nine and a half years before (this would anticipate the arrival of Pedrarias by a year or two). A later memorial of his services also affirms that his first destination in the Indies was the area of the Isthmus (Darién and Tierra Firme). Yet

in a letter to the Crown he once stated in so many words that he came
to Santo Domingo in 1507, and then later went on to Darién and the
rest. However this may be, Benalcázar was one of the senior figures
among the conquerors of Peru, bowing only to Francisco Pizarro. In
1532 he had already been in the Indies for some twenty years at least—
most of his adult life. Like Pizarro he was a creature of the Indies,
feeling a native's attachment to the new country. Indeed, with no sense
of incongruity he once suggested to the crown that every realm should
have native governors: "Here, men of the Indies, as in Spain Spaniards."

And like Pizarro, Benalcázar had long been a man of eminence.
That he was an actual "captain" from soon after Pedrarias's arrival, as
both he and Castellanos later claimed, remains uncertain. Oviedo's extremely thorough list of the captains of Pedrarias does not mention
Benalcázar. Nevertheless, he held responsible positions from an early
time. He was an encomendero of Panama in 1522. Then he went with
Francisco Hernández de Córdoba to the conquest of Nicaragua, and
was the first messenger back to Pedrarias; as such he received mention
in a letter to the crown in 1525. If not a first alcalde of León, Nicaragua, he was at least at times on the municipal council, as he had previously been elsewhere.

Both before and after Pedrarias arrived in Nicaragua to take over
the governorship, Benalcázar was his close follower, possibly his henchman. He was prominent in the party going under Diego Albítez to
Honduras in 1527, to assert Pedrarias's rights there (in Honduras he
was seized and sent to Santo Domingo, but soon returned to Nicaragua). In 1530 we find him taking the side of Pedrarias in a dispute
with alcalde mayor Licenciado Castañeda and his following, which included Hernando de Soto. Benalcázar agreed with Pedrarias's refusal to
appoint Soto alcalde in León, testifying that Soto had performed poorly in that post in the past. As Soto's friend, Benalcázar said he had
pleaded unsuccessfully with him to carry the staff of office more often,
and that in any case Soto knew little of judicature and had too quick a
temper for a judge. Thus a long-standing rivalry, both factional and
personal in nature, existed between Benalcázar and Soto.

At that time, in January of 1530, Benalcázar had already been discussing with Soto the possibility of coming to Peru. By November of
the next year he was already there, on the coast of present Ecuador, at
the head of a party of some thirty men, twelve or fourteen of them

mounted, in two ships. Whether or not he had a previous agreement with Pizarro and Almagro, as Castellanos asserts, and as his rival Soto certainly had, is not known; doubtless he had been approached. Incorporating himself into Soto's contingent would have been repugnant to him, so he had set about organizing his own expedition, probably immediately after the death of Governor Pedrarias, in March, 1531, when the realm of Nicaragua seemed close to anarchy. Benalcázar's partner in organizing the expedition was the shipmaster and pilot Juan Fernández. Their company may have been limited to the maritime aspects of the venture, and Juan Fernández must have been part owner of the ships, one of which he piloted to Peru, though Benalcázar referred to the ships as his own. After Cajamarca, Fernández came to claim his share of the profits, and went back unsatisfied to Nicaragua, there, according to Cieza, to incite Pedro de Alvarado to attempt the conquest of the Quito region. Benalcázar's men were mostly old hands in the Indies, several of them veterans of Gil González de Avila's expedition from Santo Domingo to Honduras in 1524.

By beating Soto to Perú, Benalcázar put himself in a good bargaining position; when he arrived, the Peru expedition was at a low point. Several of Benalcázar's men immediately received positions of honor, and he himself was made captain of horse, his squadron consisting of the riders he brought with him. He thus achieved a position nominally equal to that of Soto, who arrived with a larger contingent very shortly afterward. Yet he had much reason to be dissatisfied; of the three cavalry captains he was clearly the least regarded. The attitude not only of the Pizarros, but of all concerned, is expressed in the chronicle of Cristóbal de Mena, who calls both Soto and Hernando Pizarro "señor capitán," but leaves Benalcázar's name unadorned. Hernando Pizarro was also "general," or second in command, and Soto got most of the missions of prestige. In the most basic matter of all, the division of the treasure of Cajamarca, Benalcázar also suffered. Not to speak of the astronomical share of Hernando Pizarro, Soto got almost twice as much as Benalcázar, and even young Juan Pizarro got more. Benalcázar's share was indeed not much above that of the standard horseman. Through subterfuge and special bargaining Benalcázar may actually have received more than appears on the list (one companion speaks of 25,000 pesos, another of 30,000), but the message was clear. With the advent of more men and more leaders, the Pizarros no longer considered Benalcázar indispensable. He probably realized already that he had no future in Peru commensurate with his eminence and ambition.

When Pizarro went on to Jauja with the main body in 1533, he sent Benalcázar back with some ten men to guard the city of Piura and rule it in his name. The assignment meant considerable independent power and responsibility; it also removed Benalcázar from the main current of the conquest of Peru. With this, a pattern was set for the rest of Benalcázar's life. Henceforth he was to maintain his independence on the northern marches of Peru, a senior and formidable figure, yet also a bit disreputable, and far from the centers of wealth and power. There were probably individual encomenderos in Cuzco and Charcas whose revenues were greater than anything Benalcázar ever attained, though he led the conquest of Quito and Popayán.

For the purposes of the present book, there would be little point in relating the rest of Benalcázar's life in any detail. A man whose career includes such a significant chain of events will certainly someday find his biographer.

For years a seesaw struggle went on, Benalcázar trying to break loose and establish an independent jurisdiction, Pizarro trying to stop him, with the issue in doubt. Benalcázar on his own initiative organized the conquest of the Quito area in 1533–1534; but, faced with the double challenge of Almagro coming to reassert Pizarro's authority, and Pedro de Alvarado invading from the outside, he ceded and accepted subordination to Pizarro. The crown subsequently refused to allow Quito to be taken from Pizarro's province, though it did not discourage Benalcázar's initiative. Continuing to act like a governor, Benalcázar organized further conquests to the north, at first through lieutenants. Then he abandoned Quito, taking with him many residents, both Spanish and Indian, and by 1538 he had carved out for himself a large region to the north, not very well defined or cohesive, which came to be named officially after the city of Popayán, but was more often called simply Benalcázar's (*lo de Benalcázar*). Pizarro finally determined to rid himself of such an independent subordinate, and in 1538 sent a lieutenant to take over Quito and Popayán and arrest Benalcázar. Pizarro's man succeeded in the former mission, but the latter was beyond his capacity. The path of conquest had led Benalcázar to Bogotá, where he met two other sets of conquerors under Quesada and Federmann. The rivals settled their dispute by embarking for Spain and the royal court; direct access to the crown, free of Pizarro's restraint, may have actually been Benalcázar's primary goal at the time.

At court in 1540, Benalcázar apparently asked for and was denied the governorship of Quito, but he received a lifetime appointment as governor of Popayán, with the title of *adelantado*. At this time he legitimated three natural children, presumably mestizo, and arranged the marriage of the oldest, don Francisco de Benalcázar, already grown and with him in Spain, to a doña María de Herrera, of Burgos. When they returned to Popayán by 1541, Benalcázar soon disposed of the claims of Pascual de Andagoya to a shadowy area of San Juan, overlapping Popayán. The old man of the Indies had only caustic comments for the polished, ineffectual Andagoya, who, according to Benalcázar, did nothing but lie in soft beds and think of new names for the cities other men had founded.

The continued civil strife in Peru caused Benalcázar far more trouble. In 1541 Peru's governor, Vaca de Castro, who stopped in Popayán before going on to Peru to fight the rebellious younger Almagro, insisted that Benalcázar accompany him until, south of Quito, disagreements between the two caused Vaca de Castro to order him back. In 1545 rebel Gonzalo Pizarro chased Viceroy Blasco Núñez Vela into the Popayán region, and the viceroy forced a reluctant Benalcázar to return with him to Quito. In January, 1546, Benalcázar, though nearing sixty years of age and vociferously opposed to both the campaign and the battle, fought on the viceroy's side against Pizarro's overwhelming force and was badly wounded. Pizarro finally let him return to Popayán, probably afraid to act arbitrarily against a man of such seniority and influence. Then, in 1548, Benalcázar was once again drawn into Gasca's campaign against Gonzalo Pizarro, this time going all the way to Cuzco in the capacity of cavalry captain.

However, peace in Peru was even worse for Benalcázar than war. In the unsettled conditions of the middle and late 1540's, he had succeeded in staving off a threatened royal visitation. In 1546 he executed a former subordinate who was invading the northern part of his territory, and went unpunished for the time being. But with the end of troubled times, a royal visitor was able to enter Popayán, arrest Benalcázar, and sentence him to death for the execution. Benalcázar was allowed to appeal the sentence (perhaps not intended literally), and departed for Spain. He died of illness on the way, in Cartagena, in April, 1551, and was given a poor burial, all that his small estate could afford. He left instructions that the accounts of his faithful majordomo were not to be audited, an example of the evenhanded treatment of underlings for which he was well known, however harsh he might have been in defending his rights.

In his will he mentioned numerous heirs: "don Francisco, don Sebastián, don Lázaro, doña Magdalena and other sons and daughters." The prolific old bachelor's eldest, don Francisco, was an important figure even in his father's lifetime. He must have been born in Panama or Nicaragua; his father assigned him a guardian or tutor, and already in 1542 he was serving as lieutenant governor in the city of Popayán. He remained a citizen of Popayán for many years after his father's death; at times he was alcalde, and he held one of the few encomiendas in the Popayán region with an income comparable to some of those in Peru. His descendants were among the illustrious of the area all the way down to the time of Colombian independence.

NOTES. Benalcázar's name also appears as Belalcázar, which is without doubt more correct and was probably preferred by Benalcázar himself, but was nevertheless little used. In León, in 1530, Benalcázar said he was about forty (*CDIHN*, II, 514–518, which also includes his remarks about Soto). In Panama, in 1522, he declared himself to be a native of Belalcázar (Góngora, *Grupos*, pp. 74–75).

Two documentary publications of the municipality of Quito are essential sources for Benalcázar's life. One is *Testamento del señor capitán don Sebastián de Benalcázar*, a copy of his testament of 1551. The second is the monumental *Colección de documentos inéditos relativos al adelantado capitán don Sebastián de Benalcázar*. This contains two *probanzas de servicios*, most of the known cédulas relating to Benalcázar, and much of his correspondence (the above quote from him is on p. 175), as well as documents concerning his son don Francisco. Juan de Castellanos's writings on Benalcázar are in *Elegías de varones ilustres de Indias*, pp. 441–506; the anecdotal section about his early career is on pp. 445–446. A biography, *Sebastián de Benalcázar*, by J. Jijón y Caamaño, is not without merit; it traces portions of Benalcázar's life on an almost day-to-day basis, but the work was never completed, and adds nothing to knowledge of Benalcázar's background or pre-Peruvian career.

Some valuable, because scarce, information on the pre-Peruvian stage of Benalcázar's life will be found in *CDIHN*, I, 128, 191; Garcilaso, *Obras*, III, 36; Góngora, *Grupos*, pp. 48, 74–75; Medina, *Descubrimiento*, II, 448; Oviedo, *Historia*, V, 23–24.

Other references are in AGI, Contaduría 1825, records from Puerto Viejo, Nov. 15, 1531; Justicia 432, no. 2, ramo 3; Patronato 90, no. 1, ramo 11; ANP, PA 7, 33, 40, 55, 58, 90, 94, 103, 107, 171, 172; HC 70,

71, 430; *CDIHC*, IV, 197, 198, 202, 203; Busto, "Una relación y un estudio," *Revista Histórica* 27 (1964):280–319; Calvete, *Rebelión de Pizarro*,
IV, 281, 363–364, 408; V, 18; Cieza, *Chupas*, pp. 3, 61, 63–85, 97, 142,
145, 162–163, 166, 186, 188, 192–195; Cieza, *Quito* (Serrano y Sanz,
ed.), p. 168; Cieza, *Tercera parte*, in *Mercurio Peruano* 36 (1955):470;
37 (1956):82; 39 (1958):581; Cieza, *Salinas*, pp. 296–300; Diego Fernández, *Historia*, I, 80, 83–84, 86, 221, 227; Gómara, *Hispania victrix*, I,
228, 234; Gutiérrez de Santa Clara, *Quinquenarios*, III, 22, 31, 36–37; IV,
108, 172; *Libros de cabildos de Quito*, I, sect. 1, passim; Loredo, *Los repartos*, pp. 99–100; Mena, "Conquista del Perú," p. 85; Oviedo, *Historia*,
I, 188–189; III, 93, 343–351; IV, 195; V, 18–20, 23–25, 269–270, 272–
274, 277–278; Pedro Pizarro, *Relación*, V, 172, 199; Porras, *Cartas*, pp.
76–77, 106, 128, 329; Porras, *Cedulario*, II, 70, 399; Porras, in Trujillo,
Relación, pp. 81, 82; Pérez de Tudela, ed., *Relación de las cosas del Perú*,
V, 290–291; Trujillo, *Relación*, p. 50; Zárate, *Historia*, II, 474, 532, 533,
537, 539, 540.

Pedro de Candía

Age at Cajamarca: About 38   Place of origin: Crete
Role: Captain of Artillery   Trade: Artilleryman and founder
Share: 2¼ shares of gold and silver   Extent of literacy: Very crude signa-
                                  ture, but possibly semiliterate

The most exotic figure of all the men of Cajamarca was the Greek
Pedro de Candía, yet he was no monstrous exception in the world of
the Spanish Indies in the sixteenth century. Landlocked Castile, suddenly embarked upon the greatest maritime enterprise in history, had
to draw sailors from every available source. Many came from the Mediterranean, which in navigation was but a single unit from Catalonia to
Greece, with men and techniques in constant movement back and forth
over the whole expanse. The Greeks were experts in artillery, often
called on by the Spaniards in their Mediterranean naval battles and
their Italian wars. Thus it was that a good number of the sailors in the
New World, and literally a majority of the artillerymen, were Greeks.
Pedro de Candía was one of them.

He had served, so he claimed, under the Spanish flag since about
1510—against the Turks, in Italy, and then in Spain with the king's
guards. He had married a Spanish woman of Villalpando (Zamora),
and maintained a home there. In 1526 he came to the Indies with Governor Pedro de los Ríos of Panama. When Ríos arrived, Pizarro and
Almagro, who were then painfully working their way south along the

Pacific coast, asked the new governor for help, and he let Candía join them as an artillery expert and a man experienced in the things of war. With these auspices Candía was a figure of importance from the beginning, in particular favor with Francisco Pizarro. A letter written when the expedition was on Gallo Island in 1527 reports that everyone there was on the verge of starvation except Pedro de Candía, who was permitted to eat at Captain Pizarro's table. It is just as well that he was the one to get extra rations, for he is said to have been the largest man seen in Peru in his time.

Late in 1527 the expedition was threatened by the arrival of envoys from the governor, bearing permission for all to return to Panama who wished to do so. Having become closely identified with the enterprise, Pedro de Candía was one of the Thirteen (or whatever number) who agreed to stay with Pizarro and wait for a ship to come back from Panama and carry the discovery forward. The ship eventually arrived and in a short time Pizarro and his Thirteen were coasting off the land of the Incas. Pedro de Candía was one of the first to go on shore in Túmbez, coming back with tales of great stone palaces and fortresses, filled with wealth and magnificence of all kinds. He also, it is said, miraculously tamed a lion and a tiger that the Indians loosed on him. Candía's trip to shore became legendary almost immediately. The sober truth of the matter was that Túmbez was impressive, but built of adobe rather than stone. As to the lion and tiger, reading Cieza one can infer that the Indians let loose the animals (a jaguar and a puma) in Candía's vicinity to see what would happen. Candía discharged his musket, and the beasts ran. Candía with his tales of oriental opulence and his miracles is cast in the mold of his fellow Mediterranean, Christopher Columbus. Their flowery stories are in the strongest contrast to the terse reports of the Spaniards, telling usually of a good place to settle, a temperate climate to grow wheat, good mining prospects, and the like. Only for such truly miraculous victories as Cajamarca and the siege of Cuzco did the Spaniards call on the supernatural for explanation. Back in Panama, Pizarro decided to take Candía with him to Spain to help convince the royal court of Peru's riches. Candía took along a painting or map he had made, and a written account of what he had seen. But he was more hindrance than help, for his extravagant words aroused skepticism, and Pizarro finally had to silence him.

In the agreements reached in Toledo in 1529, Candía was appointed royal captain of artillery, with a small salary which he later wished had not been assigned him; in the conquest the other captains said his share should be reduced because he was paid for his work. On the expedition of 1531–1532 he was in charge of some small pieces of artillery and a few musketeers, no more than seven or eight at most. With these he produced the thunder of Cajamarca, though there were malicious Spaniards who claimed that he had only two guns, that only one of these could be made to work, and that he shot too late.

After the events of Cajamarca, Candía was one of the magnates of Peru. His share of the treasure equaled that of Captain Sebastián de Benalcázar and was exceeded only by Soto and the Pizarro brothers. He was alcalde of Cuzco at its founding, in 1534, and got one of the richest encomiendas. The Pizarros treated him very carefully, with a good deal of suspicion, as they did all those who had an independent base of power. Candía had some independence, since he held a royal title, was known at court, and was already a legendary figure in Peru, aside from possessing skills in high demand. He quickly built up a great fortune, and before long began to collect a band of fellow Greeks around him. Among the Spaniards he always remained a foreigner, not only because of his accent and his predilection for association with his compatriots, but also because his eccentric mind and his active involvement in matters like manufacturing gunpowder and founding cannon set him off from the other captains and great encomenderos. The Spaniards did not understand him. Cieza de León says on one occasion that he was ingenious, then again that he had little understanding. Both statements were true. Candía applied lively intelligence to a variety of technical skills, but was erratic and effusive, and had little understanding of what was required in a leader of Spaniards: good lineage or the pretense of it, a dignified presence, and a grasp of the Spanish politics of regional and family ties.

The Pizarros soon fell out with Candía. He was not, as would have been expected, the Pizarrist captain of artillery in the battle against Almagro at Salinas in 1538. Shortly after the Pizarro victory, Candía financed and led an expedition of discovery into the jungle-covered valleys east of Cuzco. This was a high honor, but also a form of exile. Such expeditions as this were always hampered by the impossible terrain and the lack of prospects, but Candía's venture failed unusually soon and resoundingly. The primary reason, we are told, was the Spaniards' lack of respect for their foreign leader. The group was returning to Cuzco with uncertain plans when Hernando Pizarro rode out to meet them, brusquely removed Candía from command, hanged one of his lieutenants for planning sedition, and gave charge of the men to a Spanish captain.

The insult left Candía in a state of burning resentment against the Pizarro family. He was one of only two or three senior and powerful men who joined the rebellion of the younger Almagro in 1541. By this time, according to the report of Governor Vaca de Castro, he had a following of fifteen or twenty Greeks. With their help, Candía succeeded —after several tries—in founding more than a dozen bronze cannon, some of them twelve feet long. This battery far exceeded what the other side could muster, and it was the Almagrists' main hope for victory at the battle of Chupas in September, 1542. Their hopes came to nothing. According to some accounts Candía repented of his allegiance with the rebels; even his supposed difficulties in founding the cannon had been intentional, and at the battle he misdirected his guns so as to do no damage. Other accounts say that the guns were moved to a disadvantageous spot over his protests. At any rate, young don Diego de Almagro became convinced of Candía's treason, attacked him furiously, and killed him. Despite his eminence, Candía's foreignness had pushed him into an ever more marginal position. He left a mestizo son who grew up in Cuzco as a friend of the chronicler Garcilaso de la Vega.

NOTES. In 1534 Candía twice stated that he was forty (AGI, Lima 204, *probanza* of Hernán González, and Patronato 93, no. 4, ramo 1). He never made any formal statement about his place of origin, but the chroniclers call him Greek and say he was a native of Crete (cf. Zárate, *Historia*, II, 464; Garcilaso, *Obras*, III, 29). A *probanza de servicios* made by Candía in Panama in 1528 is in AGI, Patronato 150, no. 3, ramo 2. Much narrative detail and many source references will be found in Busto's long article, "Pedro de Candía, artillero mayor del Perú," *Revista Histórica* 25 (1960–1961):379–405. "Candía" is the older Spanish name for Crete, and therefore presumably not Candía's original surname.

Other references are in AGI, Contaduría 1824, records from Cuzco, 1536; Patronato 93, no. 6, ramo 4; 109, ramo 4; ANP, PA 38, 131, 133, 147; CDIHC, VI, 409; CDIHE, XXVI, 230; RAHC 8 (1957):53; Cieza, *Chupas*, p. 213; Cieza, *Salinas*, pp. 104, 339; Cieza, *Tercera parte*, in *Mercurio Peruano* 32 (1951):158 ff.; 38 (1957):254; 39 (1958):584; Estete, *Relación*, pp. 19–20; Garcilaso, *Obras*, III, 31, 196; Lockhart, *Spanish Peru*, pp. 125–126; Loredo, *Alardes y derramas*, pp. 116, 128; Loredo, *Los repartos*, pp. 128–132; Mena, "Conquista del Perú," pp. 85–86; Pedro

Pizarro, *Relación*, V, 177–178, 220–221; Porras, *Cartas*, pp. 12, 472, 475, 493, 498–501, 503; Porras, *Cedulario*, I, 14, 16, 113, 135; II, 101, 102, 117; Romero, *Los héroes de la Isla del Gallo*, p. 42.

Cristóbal de Mena

Age at Cajamarca: Probably 30 or more

Role: Captain

Share: 1⅞ shares of gold; 2 shares of silver

Place of origin: Ciudad Real (New Castile)

Extent of literacy: Literate

The chronicler Oviedo, who knew Mena personally, called him an hidalgo, and though Oviedo often used the word somewhat loosely, there is no reason to doubt his judgment in this case. Mena had the kind of prominence in the Indies that most often went with good birth, he was fully literate, and later he proved able to function very well at the royal court of Spain.

Mena is first seen in the Indies in 1526 or 1527, but his experience must stretch back considerably farther, since he was already at that time a captain, encomendero, and council member in the town of Granada, Nicaragua. In July, 1529, he was sent to Nicaragua's port of Realejo to prevent the illegal departure of two ships for Panama with men and slaves to be used in the conquest of Peru.

He failed, and then very shortly went to Panama himself to join the expedition as one of the principal captains, perhaps the chief figure after Francisco and Hernando Pizarro. He seems to have invested a certain amount in horses and slaves to be sold to expedition members, a common practice for the leaders and organizers. When the main party left Panama in early 1531, Mena stayed behind with one of the boats to bring any last-minute recruits and those who could not yet leave because of unpaid debts. He had to bear the brunt of official disapproval of Pizarro's failure to comply with the regulations for expeditions, yet he successfully got his boat out of the harbor when the time came, and soon joined Pizarro.

On land on the northern coast, Mena continued to be assigned missions of honor and responsibility, and at times acted as second in command in place of Hernando Pizarro. But his importance faded with every passing day. Benalcázar, and then Soto, arrived at the head of men loyal to themselves, and they could not be denied positions of command; on the other hand, Francisco Pizarro was not willing, perhaps not able, to reduce the claims of his own brothers. Mena's position was made worse by his origin in Ciudad Real, the home region of the Pizarros' great rival, Diego de Almagro; Almagro and Mena were good friends, and Mena was correspondingly suspect among the Pizarros. By the time of Cajamarca, Mena's situation was untenable. All important missions went to Soto, Benalcázar, or the Pizarro brothers, and still other men were beginning to rise, while Mena sat idle. It is doubtful that he had any position of command during the events of Cajamarca, and his share was not only the smallest of all the captains', but actually less than that of an ordinary horseman. This amounted to an invitation to leave, which Mena accepted, asking for and receiving license to return to Spain with the first contingent in 1533.

In Mena's baggage as he returned was a chronicle of the conquest of Peru, which he published anonymously in Seville in 1534. To all appearances it was actually written by Mena himself, rather than merely dictated. It shows a man with a good grasp of strategy and tactics in general, expressing himself with more freshness and individuality than the official chroniclers Jerez and Sancho. It is more fair and objective toward the other leaders than one might reasonably expect, though the bitterness shines through at times.

Mena also carried money and powers of attorney from Diego de Almagro, who with good reason did not trust Hernando Pizarro's promise to negotiate honors and offices for him at the royal court. In fact, once there, Hernando tried to denigrate Almagro by bringing criminal action against him. Mena too was present at court. According to Oviedo, he managed to stop the suit against Almagro, and publicized Almagro's requests and his merits to such an extent that Hernando Pizarro saw he could not prevent Almagro from being granted the government of a region to the south of the Pizarros. The original provisions were given to Hernando, who delayed things as far as he could by holding on to them, but Mena thwarted even this to a certain extent by sending copies back to Almagro. Mena also tried to sue Hernando Pizarro directly, but that was hopeless, in view of the gold Pizarro was showering about the court. Almagro's agent, Juan de Espinosa, came to Spain in 1536 and paid Mena and others for their trouble, though they complained of Espinosa's stinginess, and Almagro himself later said they should have received more. After this Mena disappeared, probably to reside in Ciudad Real.

NOTES. Mena's age is calculated on the presumption that a man who had acquired prominence and municipal office by 1526 or 1527 must have been born at least twenty-five years earlier. As to his regional origin, the chronicler Oviedo says that he knew "an hidalgo called Mena," from Ciudad Real, in Granada, Nicaragua, in 1528 (*Historia*, IV, 382). If there is any doubt that this was the Mena of Cajamarca it is resolved when we see him enjoying the special confidence of the Ciudad Real native Diego de Almagro.

Basic for Mena's life and writing is Porras's treatment in his *Relaciones primitivas*, pp. 45–46. Included in that volume is an edition of Mena's "La conquista del Perú." This writer accepts Porras's attribution of authorship to Mena; all the additional data seen in the preparation of the present book only serve to confirm his thesis. Porras also arrived at complete understanding of the process by which Mena was pushed aside, and here too this writer agrees with and follows him, having reached the same conclusion independently. In one respect Porras's findings cannot be accepted. Knowing full well what Mena's name was, he nevertheless picked up the appearance of Mena on the seventeenth-century version of the roll of Cajamarca as "Cristóbal de Mena or Medina," searched out the Cristóbal de Medinas in the *Pasajeros a Indias*, and came to a totally unjustified conclusion as to Mena's regional origin.

Other references are in AGI, Contaduría 1825, Penas de Cámara, 1532; Contratación 2715, no. 1, ramo 1; ANP, PA 92, 652, 653, 654, 656, 658; HC 2, 27; *CDIHN*, I, 253, 502; II, 63–65; Cieza, *Tercera parte*, in *Mercurio Peruano* 36 (1955):465, 469; 37 (1956):83, 84; 39 (1958):575; Enríquez de Guzmán, *Vida y costumbres*, p. 156; Jerez, *Verdadera relación*, II, 345; Cristóbal de Mena, "La conquista del Perú," particularly pp. 97–98 for personal details about Mena; Oviedo, *Historia*, V, 109–110; Porras, *Cartas*, pp. 63, 66, 67.

El Señor Gobernador (Francisco Pizarro)

Age at Cajamarca: About 54
Role: Commander in chief and
    captain of foot
Share: 13 shares of gold and silver

Place of origin: Trujillo, Extremadura
Parents: Captain Gonzalo Pizarro
    and Francisca González
Extent of literacy: Illiterate

The discoverer, conqueror, and first governor of Peru presents no little challenge to the interpreters of his life. More than most famous men, Pizarro is hidden by his taciturnity and illiteracy; his pattern of behavior is complex, not shaped totally by any one ideal or force. An ill-conceived legend, starting among such hostile sixteenth-century contemporaries as Oviedo and Gómara, and reaching its fullest expression in the nineteenth century with Prescott, converted Pizarro into a swineherd in his childhood and a humble, ignorant old man by the time of the discovery of Peru. At last Porras Barrenechea and others justly reacted against this myth, but produced instead the image of a farseeing founder, noble and benign, which is equally lacking in verisimilitude. For readers of English, it is probably the "porcine legend," as Porras called it, that still is the primary obstacle to comprehension. Without exaggerating—for no amount of verbiage can make him literate or legitimate—we must learn to see that in a great many ways, including lineage, Francisco Pizarro had the attributes of a leader of expeditions and was the indicated man to lead the conquest of Peru.

First, one must ask who the Pizarros were. Of course a name is not a family; there were noble and wealthy Pizarros, and others who were cobblers or less. But the name was known in eastern Extremadura, and the term "the good Pizarros of Extremadura," as used by chronicler Pedro Pizarro, conveyed a meaning. The genealogist and Extremaduran patriot Muñoz de San Pedro has traced the Pizarros of Trujillo back for some generations before the time of Francisco and Hernando. Though Muñoz de San Pedro makes all the people he writes about seem equally noble, one can deduce from his work that the Pizarros long prominent in Trujillo's bitter family feuding were more local hidalgos or minor gentry than nobility or lords. Perhaps the most important conclusion to be drawn from the work of Muñoz de San Pedro is that the line leading to the conqueror of Peru was in effect a new branch. Francisco's great-grandfather was an Hinojosa; contrary to usage, all the male descendants took the maternal surname of Pizarro, and that alone, without a second surname. In effect, they were somewhat separate from both the Hinojosas and the other Pizarros.

Porras, with little empirical evidence but unerring intuition, has said that the Pizarros were among the recent hidalgos residing around the plaza of Trujillo, just rising out of the professional, commercial, or other classes. (Next door to Pizarro's father lived a notary.) This is probably as close to the truth as we can approach without a complete social history of Trujillo in the fifteenth and sixteenth centuries. The effective founder of the Pizarro family in the narrower sense was Hernando Alonso Pizarro, grandfather of Francisco and Hernando. Many of the witnesses at the investigation made into Francisco's lineage in 1529 remembered Hernando Alonso, and most pointed to his membership on the town council of Trujillo, "where the councilmen are gentle-men" (*caballeros*). Hernando Alonso's son Gonzalo went yet farther toward success than his father, achieving an eminence beyond Trujillo itself as a royal captain of infantry. He served in the wars of Granada and later in Navarre; Porras thinks that he rose from a position of semidependence on the Chaves family. It was Captain Gonzalo who through marriage first acquired a family patrimony, the village of La Zarza in the hills southeast of Trujillo. As well as one can tell from Gonzalo's will, his claim to La Zarza rested on property rights rather than feudal domain. By the second decade of the sixteenth century, Captain Gonzalo had reached a position which put his branch of the family on a new level. One sign of this is the royal appointment of his son Hernando to a captaincy while still a raw youth. Another indication can be found in the names and titles of the Pizarro women. None, in-cluding Gonzalo's wife and even his legitimate daughters, who were born around the turn of the century, had the coveted title of "doña." Only his youngest—illegitimate, but born after he had become promi-nent—was called "doña Graciana." This same upward movement of the family under Gonzalo can be seen in the way Francisco Pizarro later described his origin; instead of referring to the Pizarros of Trujillo, he again and again called himself most specifically "son of Captain Gon-zalo Pizarro."

This Pizarro branch, then, could definitely claim hidalgo status; it was more notable for its rising tendency and for the military leadership of Captain Gonzalo than for resplendent nobility, wealth, or great do-mains. In the Indies, to have come from such a family was a great asset. Just this combination of *hidalguía* and military reputation was what the Spaniards expected or desired in the background of a captain, and what, contrary to common opinion, they too rarely found.

Having established provisionally the characteristics of the Pizarro family, we must inquire into Francisco's exact position within it. This is a far cloudier matter, in which much uncertainty will remain, but some basic aspects emerge clearly enough. First of all, there is little room for doubt that Francisco was indeed Captain Gonzalo Pizarro's son. Such doubt might reasonably arise from the fact that Francisco alone of Gonzalo's many children is not mentioned in his will of 1522, and that a gap of at least twenty years separates Francisco from the oth-ers. More than one humble, ambitious Spaniard appropriated a noble name in order to ease the way to success; in Peru of the conquest period there were at least two famous examples, Rodrigo de Orgoños and Francisco de Carvajal. Yet Francisco's brothers and other relatives immediately accepted him and followed his lead when he returned to Spain in 1529. He was tall like all the other sons of Gonzalo Pizarro "the Long," and he bore the Pizarro name from the time he can first be located in the Indies. Above all, witnesses to the 1529 inquiry unanimously considered Francisco to be Captain Gonzalo's son, and one had seen him as a child in the house of his grandfather Hernando Alonso Pizarro.

Pizarro's mother was Francisca González, daughter of humble farmers who without much qualification may be considered peasants. Witnesses for Francicso in 1529 claimed they were honest folk and Old Christians, and Francisca herself worked at least for a time as a servant of the nuns of a Trujillan convent. On the other hand, an old friend of the family was named Inés Alonso "la barragana," a name with disreputable connotations (though it is quite possibly merely a feminine version of the surname Barragán). Francisco Pizarro was born in the house of a Juan Casco, who was probably, as Porras deduces, the second husband of Francisca's mother.

Given that Francisco was the authentic son of Gonzalo Pizarro and Francisca González, how was he treated and brought up? To what extent was he recognized? Perhaps it is unnecessary to say that we cannot accept the story of Gómara—that Francisco was left at the church door, suckled for a time by a sow, then later (reluctantly) recognized by his father, and put to herding swine. One day he was supposed to have lost his charges to some infection, and then to have run away from home rather than return to report the bad news. The mythical nature and the malice of this account are manifest (see the similar tale told of Benalcázar). No other source than Gómara exists for a single element of it. Gómara was long in the hire of Pizarro's great rival, Cortés, and he goes to great lengths to reduce and malign all of Pizarro's accomplishments, down to the amount of treasure produced by Peru as compared to Mexico. The chronicler Garcilaso asks cogently where Gómara, writing more than half a century after the events, found out such details about a child so obscure. There is not the slightest reason to believe any part of Gómara's story.

Garcilaso goes on to ridicule the idea that a man as prominent as Captain Gonzalo Pizarro would allow his recognized son to herd pigs. This plausible argument has one weak link. There is no indication that

Gonzalo Pizarro ever recognized Francisco in the full legal sense. He certainly never had him legitimated; no public document of donation or recognition is known to exist, and on the most natural occasion, his final testament, Gonzalo conspicuously failed to act. Spaniards of the medieval and early modern periods had a whole set of social practices concerning the innumerable illegitimate children their system produced. The fully recognized child would grow up in his father's home and receive almost the same education as the legitimate heirs. But if the mother was of bad repute or very low social status, or if the father was not absolutely sure of the child's paternity, the child might grow up neither recognized nor rejected. He would take the father's name, and the father would tacitly assume some responsibility for him, while taking care not to recognize him legally, in order not to jeopardize the inheritance of preferred children or legitimate kin. Such a child might live in his father's house in a subordinate, almost servile, position, or he might stay with his mother's family all or part of the time. Cases of this kind are known among the progeny of Garcilaso and of Hernando de Soto, to mention only an illustrious example or two. Francisco Pizarro seems to fit somewhere in this category. In his case, the factor preventing formal recognition and more active parental tutelage may have been more his father's youth than his mother's reputation. If Captain Gonzalo was still siring children far into the sixteenth century, he must have been very young indeed when Francisco was born, sometime around 1478. Not for many years would Gonzalo have an independent position, or even his own household.

Whatever the reason, Francisco received far less attention than all his younger brothers. Some of this we may attribute to the greater poverty of the Pizarros in the earlier time, but differences remain. The names Hernando, Gonzalo, and Juan, given respectively to his brothers, were all common among the Pizarro lineage, but not a single Francisco appears. The conqueror's name must have been chosen by his mother, if indeed he was not named after her. Of the brothers, Hernando was highly literate; Juan and Gonzalo could sign their names well; Francisco never got beyond a simple rubric, and even that was so helpless that he must have learned how to make it when already grown. Francisco also differed from his brothers, including the illegitimate ones, in his numerous strongly plebeian tastes and characteristics, which we will discuss further on.

All of these things serve to raise again the question of exactly where

Francisco grew up. While we know that as a child he frequented his grandfather Pizarro's house, we do not know for sure that he lived there, or, if he did, that he lived there for his whole childhood. One must suspect that Francisco spent much time during his formative years with his humble maternal relatives, and that this accounts in large part for his lifelong plebeian culture. Though there is no reason whatever to go back to the swineherd story, it is quite possible that Pizarro at this time did agricultural work or practiced a manual trade. If as a child Pizarro lived with his mother, a further question arises. At some time Francisca González left Trujillo, for her son Francisco Martín de Alcántara, Francisco Pizarro's half brother, was born in Castilleja del Campo, near Seville. Indeed, Pizarro would seem to have told don Alonso Enríquez de Guzmán that his mother was actually *from* Sanlúcar de Alpechín in that area. This does not seem likely, since there is much testimony to the effect that Francisca and her parents before her were natives of Trujillo. At any rate, she lived part of her life in the area of Sanlúcar, and it might well be, as Porras has suspected, that Francisco Pizarro also lived there for a time. However, according to direct testimony in 1529, Pizarro lived in Trujillo at least until he was about fourteen or fifteen. We do know that he kept in touch with his maternal relatives. Unlike Juan Pizarro, who could not bring to mind the names of his maternal half brothers and sisters, Francisco sought out his half brother Francisco Martín in Spain and brought him to Peru, where he became Pizarro's right-hand man, his constant companion, and the guardian of his children.

While we will never know all the details, Francisco Pizarro reached young manhood as a true son of Trujillo, home of grim, quiet men. He bore a good name and was imbued with the ambitions that accompanied it, yet his upbringing was more plebeian than noble.

In the end his parental heritage decided the shape of his career. Like his father he sought his fortune on the outer borders of Spanish endeavor. He seems to have been in Italy for a while as a very young man, though probably for only a short time, and in some minimal role such as page or attendant. In his first detailed memorandum of services to the crown, he failed to say anything about Italy, then in a later version put in a perfunctory mention. Even a slight experience of professional military activity on the continent would have given him an edge over most Spaniards in the Indies.

It is not known—assuming that he did go to Italy—whether Francisco went under parental auspices, or merely to emulate his father. When he came to the Indies in 1502, however, there is some reason to imagine that his Pizarro relatives might have had a hand. By his own statement Francisco arrived in the fleet of Governor Ovando of Hispaniola; Ovando was from Cáceres, near Trujillo, and brought with him large numbers of his Extremaduran compatriots. Francisco was not the only Pizarro of his branch who was in the Indies around this time. Captain Gonzalo, Francisco's father, mentions in his will of 1522 that his brother Juan Pizarro had died in the Indies, leaving much money and property; before that, Juan had sent money home to Gonzalo and other members of the family. Captain Gonzalo, then, was in direct contact with relatives in the Indies. It would seem very likely that young Francisco accompanied his uncle Juan to Santo Domingo, or possibly that Captain Gonzalo sent Francisco to join Juan, knowing that Juan was already there. Such a connection would have made it easier for Francisco to capitalize on Pizarro family prestige and advance to positions of command, as he did before too many years passed.

The process of Pizarro's rise while on Hispaniola is hidden from us, but not the fact of it. By the time he joined Alonso de Ojeda's expedition to the Gulf of Urabá in 1509, he was a leader. After a short time in Urabá, Ojeda returned to Santo Domingo, ostensibly for reinforcements, and made Pizarro his lieutenant general to take charge of all those remaining. In this role Pizarro first appears in the chronicles of the Spanish conquest. Peter Martyr calls him a *nobilis vir*, it not being clear from the Latin whether the nobility was thought to inhere in personal qualities or in lineage. The situation was uncannily like what Pizarro would later face in the discovery of Peru. Then he would again work his way along a heavily overgrown tropical coast with no clear goal, enduring in the face of hunger, disease, storms, and the arrows of indomitable forest Indians.

Pizarro was soon superseded by Bachiller Enciso, with superior authority from Ojeda, and after that by Balboa, who had previous experience of the area, as well as much dash and incisiveness. As for Pizarro, he was never flashy, and was usually slow to reach decisions. He receded for a time to the role of a senior man and respected captain, not at the very top but always close to it. On the list of the first sixty-seven Spaniards to see the Pacific, in 1513, Pizarro's name comes right after Balboa's.

After the arrival of Governor Pedrarias de Avila in the Isthmus area in 1514, Pizarro played his now accustomed role of second in command in several expeditions important enough to be mentioned in the chronicles. He stood out in one of the early forays made on the west coast by Pedrarias's cousin Gaspar de Morales. In support of a large seaborne venture by Licenciado Gaspar de Espinosa into Veragua, Pizarro led a column of a hundred men along the coast to a rendezvous with the main body. (At that time Hernando de Soto was with Pizarro, going ahead as a scout.) The well-educated, well-connected luminaries that Governor Pedrarias brought with him as captains were often young and always without experience. Thus when Luis Carrillo, young brother-in-law of royal secretary Conchillos, headed an expedition to the province of Abraime, Pedrarias sought out Pizarro to go as his top aide and probably de facto commander. From time to time Pizarro led expeditions himself, though they were neither large nor lucrative.

One of Pizarro's most meaningful missions was to arrest Balboa in the name of Pedrarias. There was a half-conscious symbolism in this. Often the man who seized a rebel or criminal was rewarded with his encomienda, property, or command. In a way, the enterprise of the discovery and conquest of Peru devolved from Balboa onto Pizarro.

When Panama was founded on the west coast in 1519, as principal city for the Isthmus area, Pizarro as a matter of course was a prominent citizen, council member, and one of the largest encomenderos. What his position was by then can be seen from records of the detailed inquiries Pedrarias made into the background and experience of Panama's encomenderos in 1519 and 1522. Each man had to give his status in Spain, whether farmer or hidalgo, notary or cobbler. Only a few captains and prominent men were allowed to stand on the position they had won in the Indies, including Gonzalo de Badajoz, who was Pedrarias's lieutenant governor; Francisco Hernández de Córdoba, who was to conquer Nicaragua; and Francisco Pizarro. In the 1522 listings he is described as "Captain Francisco Pizarro, who came with Governor Alonso de Ojeda, and was his lieutenant governor and captain, and has been council member and alcalde in this city, and is also inspector [of encomiendas]."

By 1523–1524, when the organization of the Peru expedition entered its initial stages, Pizarro was senior in the Indies to almost anyone else then in Panama and had commanded men on the mainland longer than any other Spaniard in the New World. His relatively large encomienda, added to the smaller one of his junior partner and business manager Diego de Almagro, gave him a source of supplies and financial credit for the organization of expeditions. Thus Pizarro more than any other man was indicated to undertake one of the larger ventures on the Pacific coast. Rather than wonder how he came to command the conquest of Peru, we must explain how it was that others than he conquered Nicaragua and undertook the first explorations to the south and east of Panama. The root reason was the mutual rivalry between Governor Pedrarias and the men who had been in the area before he came in 1514. Balboa's execution is the clearest example of the conflict. But in general the old veterans resented newcomer Pedrarias, and Pedrarias in turn mistrusted them, fearing they would become too independent. Thus he gave almost all major assignments to men who came with him and whom he imagined he could control. Pedrarias, along with Licenciado Espinosa, who arrived with Pedrarias and was from a banking family, also tried to assume control of the avenues of credit, vital for any larger expedition.

Pizarro was left with secondary commands and small ventures, while Francisco Hernández, followed by Pedrarias himself, went to the easily accessible and exploitable area of Nicaragua. Licenciado Espinosa and Pedrarias's retainer Pascual de Andagoya made the first expeditions toward the south. But though it was known that large populations and probably mineral wealth lay somewhere in that direction, the forbidding coast and unfavorable winds put quick success out of their reach. After a few attempts, the main concern of the Pedrarias interests was diverted toward the immediate benefits to be found in Nicaragua and elsewhere. At this point pre-Pedrarias continuities could assert themselves. Pizarro requested the command and received it.

The title of captain, with military command and direction of the whole enterprise, went to Francisco Pizarro and to him alone—not to a three-man junta composed of Pizarro, Almagro, and Luque. Financial support was to be given by these three and supposedly by Governor Pedrarias as well; all parties were to share in the profits. But the enterprise at this stage was principally Pizarro's. The relationship between the three partners (for Pedrarias was only nominally involved) will bear some examination. It was not an equal partnership; as seen in Part I, chapter 4, the famous tripartite company pact of 1526 has been proved unauthentic. The priest and entrepreneur Luque stood apart from the other two. Pizarro and Almagro were partners before and after their connection with Luque, and their association was closer and more constant during the whole Panama period. As Rolando Mellafe has shown, Pizarro and Almagro bore the brunt of the Peru enterprise, and Hernando de Luque was not the only person giving them significant support. In their final, not very generous, settlement with the Luque interests, Pizarro and Almagro said that Luque had at times retired from the company.

But the Pizarro-Almagro alliance was itself not equal. Pizarro had lineage and seniority, and for a decade and a half had borne a captain's title. Almagro had no known family; he arrived in the area with Pedrarias, when Pizarro had been in the Indies twelve years, and he was never a captain until he became one in the course of the Peru enterprise itself. In the beginning Almagro was little more than Pizarro's man— his majordomo or steward. As such, Almagro managed the adjoining encomiendas the two held in the Panama district; Pizarro's had almost twice as many Indians as Almagro's. This is not to say that Almagro was superfluous. Pizarro had not the slightest capacity in business matters, whereas managing affairs was Almagro's specialty. He became a splendid organizer of expeditions and acquirer of credit. Pizarro was forbidding and closemouthed; for recruiting he relied on Almagro, who had spontaneity, liberality, and warmth. In the whole pre-Cajamarca phase of the conquest, Pizarro would have been lost without Diego de Almagro. Pizarro knew this very well, and by all accounts he valued Almagro's person and contribution. Yet he could never learn to look upon him as anything but a subordinate. He was resentful when he found out that Pedrarias had made Almagro a captain; he never lifted a finger to help Almagro get any title or honor, and he did what he could to prevent it. His conception, incredibly narrow but sincere, was that the Peru enterprise and later Peru itself were his alone, and that all honors and titles should go to him, after which he would share wealth and even power with his trusted subordinate, making him his alter ego. Almagro of course could not reconcile himself to such a role, particularly after the organizational aspects of the expedition became more important, with its long extension over time, and the differences between the two in title and seniority evened out. The later interposition of Pizarro's brothers between them ended any possibility of harmony.

There is little point in tracing here Pizarro's further career, almost identical with the early history of Peru: the arduous "discovery"; the trip to the Spanish court in 1529 and Pizarro's appointment as governor; the conquest itself; the founding of Spanish cities and the reorganization of the country; the Indian rebellion; the first civil strife; and Pizarro's assassination in Lima in 1541, after nine years of governing. But it will be well to discuss a few of the threads in Pizarro's activity in Peru, as affected by the background already described. Three things we can see working strongly on Pizarro: his experience on the Isthmus; the plebeian side of his education; and that complex of family, religion, and region that can be subsumed under the heading of "Trujillo." The first two often reinforced each other, for the whole Isthmian phase of the Spanish occupation, like the Caribbean phase before it, had a decided maritime-plebeian cast.

"Bred in the Indies," fray Vicente de Valverde called Pizarro. In large measure it was true. Among the men of Cajamarca only Benalcázar could compare with Pizarro in the extent to which he was steeped in the customs of the Spanish Indies, where he spent over two-thirds of his life and all his adulthood. He had contempt for greenhorns, and he defended the special ways of the Indies against the canons of conventional Spanish legalism. *Antigüedad*, seniority in the Indies in general and in any given country in particular, seems almost to have been his highest value. It was, at any rate, the value he felt most personally and vehemently, and it often roused him to spontaneous, forceful expressions of opinion which reach us even through the secretaries who wrote them down.

When the members of the council of Lima voted for alcaldes for the year of 1537 and presented Governor Pizarro with four names from which to pick two, he did not choose in strict accordance with the majority's vote. Councilman Rodrigo de Mazuelas, a notary and legal expert, objected. Pizarro thought it over for a day, then came back with a strong and for him unusually long reply. The election was valid, he said; governors in the Indies have chosen whichever they please of the four names presented by the council.

The main thing that is usually considered in these parts and even in Spain is that when a man is a councilman one year they make him alcalde the next, if he is a person with the qualities required; and as is notorious Francisco de Avalos is such a person, besides being one of the first conquerors and settlers of this land, which means much more than the one vote that Montenegro says he defeated him by, because he is not as senior in this country as Avalos; and he might have bought the vote, as is often done to win and have such offices, all of which is avoided if the election is given to the governor as is done in all these parts; and this is his reply to Rodrigo de Mazuelas, so that he can see how little good it does him to try to make an alcalde, because it is to be done as they do it in all these parts of the Indies.

The events of Cajamarca meant much less to Pizarro than to most of the others. To him many of the men there were upstarts, and their quick victory less deserving of reward than the long years of struggle along the jungle coasts from Panama south. By the laws of reality Peru had to be given to the men who conquered it. But Pizarro preferred his old companions from the Isthmus and the time of the discovery. Whenever he could, he gave them important temporary posts, such as alcalde or lieutenant governor, and eventually he found encomiendas for most of them, though not the largest. He named two veterans of Panama, newly arrived in Peru, to pick out the site of Lima. Pizarro gave few recommendations, but most of the ones he did issue, and the most heartfelt, were for veterans, like illiterate old peasant Alonso Martín de Don Benito, fellow discoverer of the Pacific, or equally illiterate Cristóbal de Burgos, widely reputed to be a Morisco, who accompanied Pizarro in the years of the discovery of Peru.

In Pizarro's eyes, the merit of such services was so great that kings and governors had a binding obligation to reward them. It seems to be true that, as the chronicles claim, Pizarro had a generally respectful attitude toward the Spanish crown, but, when he felt there was any threat to his governing all of Peru, he (like other Spaniards of his time) came very near to disrespect. He told the king that since he had won Peru he deserved to keep it; "as first discoverer and settler and sustainer Your Majesty as grateful lord has the obligation to give me the reward that is owed me." The Indies morality of first-there-gets-everything was so strong in Pizarro that he could not believe the king meant to award southern Peru to someone else, "since he is born and bred in our pious faith, and will not permit his conscience to be burdened with me." Even if he lived for only four more days, and were disloyal, Pizarro wrote to his solicitor, the king would have to let him govern what he had won.

As a veteran, Pizarro bitterly resented any and all royal or ecclesiastical supervision. Bishop Berlanga of Panama came to Peru in 1535 on a royal commission to investigate the conduct of the treasury officials and other affairs. On Berlanga's arrival Pizarro said openly that when he went with a knapsack on his back conquering the country he never received any aid, and now that he had it conquered they sent him a step-father. Whether the matter was the royal treasury or conversion of Indians, Pizarro wanted to retain the practices worked out over three or four decades in the Caribbean and on the Isthmus. While there was much parochialism and self-interest in his attitude, at bottom local practices *were* better adjusted to reality. Francisco Pizarro was a living illustration of how and why the American variant of Hispanic culture could harden and attain some independence, rather than be completely overwhelmed by currents from Spain.

Close examination can find many other ways in which his Isthmian experience affected Pizarro. Most striking is how twenty years of traversing jungle coasts alienated him from that embodiment of Hispanic prestige, the horse. Of course he owned horses and rode them for travel and display, but in Panama, as in Peru, when it came to fighting Indians he was a footman. In the conquest he was always with the footmen of the main body, while others rode in the vanguard. On the day of Cajamarca, according to eyewitness Miguel Estete, he said he wanted to fight on foot, "which he knew how to do better than on horseback." In tactics generally Pizarro bore the mark of the Isthmus. Seizing the cacique (in this case Atahuallpa) had been standard practice there, and long before; one need not presume that Hernando Cortés was a direct precedent. Other Isthmian techniques were not well adapted to Peru, but Pizarro was set in his ways. He was particularly enamored of the Isthmian manner of sending successive small detachments of men to reinforce the main body. This was proper in Panama, where the main enemies were disease and hunger. In Peru it would have been far more appropriate to keep at least a hundred men together; but during the siege of Cuzco Pizarro sent out one thirty-man column after another, each of which was massacred in mountain passes.

To fight afoot rather than on horseback is a plebeian trait, as well as Isthmian. So it is with many of Pizarro's characteristics. The plebeian side of his upbringing was reinforced by the atmosphere prevailing in the Isthmus area in the first quarter of the sixteenth century. This aspect of Pizarro is also somewhat hard to distinguish from the backwardness of Extremadura and the simple austerity of the pre-Hapsburg period when Pizarro grew up.

Pizarro and Almagro were sometimes accused of, and sometimes praised for, an addiction to plebeian activities and to low company—sailors, millers, muleteers, and the like. This trait in Pizarro, in conjunction with his constant gambling and sporting, is extremely well authenticated. Thus his enemies the Almagrists complained that he was forever going off to a limekiln outside Lima, to watch the work, in order to avoid the duties of office; and sometimes they found him at midday in the sun and open air, reaping wheat with the Indians, "doing what he enjoyed and was his trade." Friendly Agustín de Zárate puts the same behavior in a different light, as part of Pizarro's strong interest in building up Peru's cities and European agriculture. According to him, Pizarro built two milldams in Lima's river, "in whose construction he spent all his leisure time, urging on the workmen who were building them." Neutral Cieza mentions in passing that when the big bell for Lima's cathedral was forged, Pizarro personally worked the bellows. In a contemporary lawsuit we can read that shoemaker Juan Pizarro was a good friend of Marqués Pizarro because they were both from Trujillo. His gambling is documented in equal depth, bowling by day and cards by night, with all players treated as equals. There may be truth to the Almagrists' charge that he collected what he won and left unpaid what he lost. Gambling cannot be called plebeian in itself, for the Spanish royal court was a center of it; but in this case there was a connection, going beyond the lowly partners the governor often chose. Pizarro had not the slightest training or competence in business affairs or law; he had never been taught the delights of noble pastimes like the chase. When not discovering, conquering, or founding cities, Francisco Pizarro did not know what to do with himself.

This same illiteracy and incompetence in the subtleties of law—as opposed to questions of substance, which he understood very well—go far to explain other parts of his behavior, such as his excessive leaning on literate Hernando Pizarro; his irresolution, as he wavered between one well-educated advisor and another; his ambivalent attitude toward his secretaries, now distrusting them, now granting them carte blanche.

Pizarro's commonness is socially significant and humanly attractive, and the attraction is not merely projected onto the materials from the perspective of later equalitarianism, but was felt and repeatedly expressed at the time. This side of Pizarro was important in disarming the sort of pure hate aroused by his brother Hernando's unmitigated haughtiness. But it was not what made Pizarro a conqueror and governor. For the core of his being we must look to Trujillo and Extremadura. If there is anything that stands out in the typology of Spanish regions, it is the difference between the loquacious, externalized Anda-

lusian and the tight-lipped, hard-bitten Extremaduran. No one could
have been more typical of Extremadura in this respect than Pizarro. A
man "of short conversation," his acquaintance Oviedo calls him, and
everything confirms the description. No governor ever sent home fewer
or less informative reports; whenever he testified before a notary, his
testimony was sure to be the shortest of all the witnesses. Pizarro retained his sangfroid under all conditions; never did he let himself get
carried away, or say anything flowery or high flown. The people who
made up the speeches and gestures of Gallo Island had no conception
of the man. He never had generous words except for a relative or a
companion of twenty years. As his page Pedro Pizarro said, "he had
the custom that whenever they asked him for something, he always said
no." Whether, as some Pizarro partisans maintained, he performed secret charities underneath this brusque exterior, cannot be known and
may be doubted. His tendency was to give without measure to those
few with whom he had identified himself, including his paternal
brothers, his maternal brother Francisco Martín, Francisco de Chaves
of the proud family of Trujillo, and a few more. For all others, Spanish or Indian, he had bone-chilling indifference. This dichotomy is also
a marked Extremaduran trait.

Even when Pizarro testified in favor of someone, his tendency was to
belittle. Jerónimo de Aliaga, the notary and great schemer who was
with him at Cajamarca, managed to persuade the governor to testify in
one of his memorials of services. But Pizarro gave no praise. In response to a question expecting a strong affirmative answer to the propo-
sition that Aliaga was a resplendent hidalgo, ideal for the high posts he
had held, Pizarro made no mention of the word hidalgo, merely saying
that Aliaga was a "good person," capable of filling the posts he gave
him. In 1539 one Diego Rodríguez claimed to have accumulated merits in a hundred martial endeavors all over the Indies, culminating in
the heroic siege of Cuzco. Pizarro in his testimony volunteered the information that Diego Rodríguez did not fight in the siege of Cuzco,
because he was sick the whole time, though he did give his horse and
arms for someone else to use. Understatements of this sort sometimes
have almost a tinge of laconic wit, as close as Pizarro ever approached
to that quality. When the Indians of the island of Puná were outdoing
themselves in festivities, to divert the Spaniards from their plan to sink
them all as they crossed over to the island, Pizarro is supposed to have
said to Benalcázar, "No me parece bien tantas fiestas," the pithiness of

which this writer does not know how to retain in English: approximately, "I don't like so much celebrating."

This hard-bitten way of seeing and expressing things was closely related to or identical with a trait that was vital to Pizarro's success, the ability to rip right through all verbiage, pretense, and sentiment, to the heart of the matter in terms of naked power. The overriding concern with essentials, plus the instinct for recognizing and manipulating them, was also Extremaduran, and indeed it was seen in the Indies above all among men from Pizarro's eastern central subregion. Pizarro, Cortés, and Valdivia each singlemindedly overcame all obstacles and rivals to conquer a land and found a permanent Hispanic society. The dashing cavaliers of western Badajoz—Balboa, Soto, and Alvarado—were more explorers than conquerors or governors, and are associated with exploits rather than with countries.

From an early time Pizarro identified himself deeply and permanently with the Peruvian venture, not just or mainly for treasure, but as governor of Peru. When Pizarro and the Thirteen were reconnoitering the central Peruvian coast in 1528, seeing riches on every hand, Cieza reports that he could not contain himself for impatience to return with more Spaniards and govern the country. From the moment the 1531 expedition left Panama, if not before, Pizarro was called "the Governor," to the practical exclusion of his other titles of *adelantado* and captain general. When Pedro de Alvarado in a letter once refers to him as Adelantado Pizarro, there is an unfamiliar ring to the words. Almagro on the other hand, when he finally received the same titles as Pizarro, was called *adelantado*, not governor, and the difference is expressive. Only in his final years did Pizarro's title of *marqués* supersede that of governor. The new title also conveyed identity with the region: since no precise definition of Pizarro's domain was carried out, his marquisate in effect was Peru.

Thus the personal became the national. We have seen Pizarro's strong personal interest in improving the country, as he understood improvement. His personal concern for ruling everything and perpetuating his position for his descendants was a strong force in maintaining the integrity of what was to be the Peruvian viceroyalty. Pizarro sought for and achieved permanence in all his city foundations and jurisdictional arrangements. If he did it with an eye to his patrimony rather than out of high-flown imperial-strategical considerations, he did it nonetheless.

Pizarro was convinced, beyond the power of logic to dissuade him, that he alone had conquered Peru. He knew as well as anyone that he had had first to await Soto's men and later Almagro's, before he dared proceed to complete the conquest. Surely he must have realized that it was the ensemble of European skills and weapons, brought together in a whole group of Spaniards, that was the decisive force. The difference between 1528 and 1532 was in numbers of Spaniards, not in Pizarro. Moreover, beyond the one transcendental act of personally seizing Atahuallpa, whom he was to replace, Pizarro did little in the campaign of 1532–1533. Soto and others took all the dangerous missions; on the way south, from Cajamarca to Cuzco, both Soto and Almagro rode ahead and did most of the fighting.

Yet when Pizarro and Almagro met at Mala in 1537, after Almagro had returned from Chile to seize Cuzco as his own, Pizarro faced Almagro with great anger and asked him (says Cieza), "What is the reason why you took the city of Cuzco, that I won and discovered with so much toil?" He was impervious to Almagro's telling reply, "Look out what you're saying, that I took Cuzco from you and it was won by your person; you know very well who won it. And the land is the king's to give me, not pasture of Trujillo." To maintain what was his own against all comers, Pizarro, like Pedrarias before him and Valdivia after him, would resort readily to tricks and bribes and violation of his given word, with no sense of injustice. Just before the Mala meeting an emissary came to Pizarro and accused him of planning to seize Almagro unawares, which was true. Pizarro here too showed anger; he accused the Almagrists in turn of the vile scheme, in his eyes, of building a boat to send dispatches to the king. "What could they write him, except tell him that they want to take and usurp what I won with such travail?" So he had the boat intercepted. Francisco, Hernando, and Gonzalo Pizarro were all alike in this unmeasured persecution of their enemies, pushing them off the very face of the earth. They were infinitely suspicious and utterly implacable, with no consideration or conception of the counterfeelings they would arouse in men who were not their strict partisans. For this reason Hernando Pizarro never won an independent base of power in Peru; Gonzalo was deserted by his followers at the critical moment; and in 1541 all Lima watched unmoved as a dozen Almagrists murdered Francisco.

The cultural content of the hegemony Pizarro established in Peru was prehumanistic and conventional—Spanish, Extremaduran, Truji-

llan—but deeply felt. It had nothing to do with the conversion of
Indians or with legal philosophy. Its pillars were family, region, and
religion. The religious part was social and ceremonial, rather than
moral-philosophical; it led right back to the other two, of which it was
an expression. Pizarro had the Extremaduran devotion to Our Lady of
the Immaculate Conception. Both the Cathedral of Lima and the
church he wanted to endow in Trujillo were to be dedicated to her. On
Gallo Island he and the Thirteen sang the Salve Regina in the eve-
nings, and he wanted it sung on Saturdays in his Trujillo church too.
That church was to be located as near as possible to the house of his
father, Captain Gonzalo Pizarro, and was to display his father's and his
own coat of arms in prominent places. Pizarros were to be patrons of
both ecclesiastical foundations in perpetuity. Region, family, and religion are here linked in a chain of reciprocal enhancement.

In 1529 Pizarro brought a good contingent of Trujillans and other
eastern Extremadurans with him from Spain, and he favored them in
every way he could. After word of Peru's wealth reached Spain, more
Trujillans arrived, and they too received preferred treatment. The most
conspicuous example was Francisco de Chaves, from an important Trujillan family that had been close to the Pizarros, perhaps their benefac-
tors. Though Chaves arrived long after the conquest was over, Pizarro
gave him a huge encomienda and posts of command and honor; when
both were killed in 1541, Chaves was thought by some to be the most
important man in the country after the governor.

It is evident that Pizarro's ties to Trujillo were in the most direct
kind of conflict with his close attachment to the Indies. Awards to Trujillan newcomers flew in the face of his devotion to old comrades and
his cherished principle of seniority. It was inconsistent to endow a lavish church in Trujillo to perpetuate his name and then request burial in
Lima. Peru was to be his patrimony, yet if and when the governor of
Peru should not be a Pizarro, his children were to be sent to Trujillo.
The conflict was most apparent of all in his treatment of his brothers.
No sooner were the three greenhorns on land in Panama than Pizarro
admitted them to the nucleus of the enterprise. All others were now
outsiders. At Túmbez, in 1532, he said he was determined to go ahead
"even if no one went but his brothers and himself." In order to have
commands and appanages for them, he first pushed out veteran captains Mena and Salcedo; then his sometime subordinate Soto; and
above all his old partner Almagro.

This great shift in Pizarro's allegiances, after he renewed the Trujillo tie in 1529, could not fail to result in tensions. Juan and Gonzalo caused little trouble at first. They were too young to assert themselves, and they were ready to follow Francisco's lead. But Hernando, legitimate and educated, was more than willing to assert himself, and his word carried weight. From the first he feuded bitterly with Almagro, in the purest imaginable duel between position in Spain and experience in the Indies. He won out again and again, and he usually had his way with Francisco too, but one can detect resentments in the older brother. If Francisco sent Hernando to Spain with the king's gold and silver in 1533, he did it partly to get rid of him; he sent him back again in 1539, to face punishment for the death of Almagro. In late 1537, too, after Almagro had released Hernando from custody, the two brothers argued so bitterly that Hernando was preparing to go to Spain until friends reconciled them. This report comes from their enemy Oviedo, but Francisco's words as given by Oviedo have the ring of authenticity —that he had conquered much territory without Hernando, then Hernando had stirred up a revolt and lost it; now he would conquer it again without him. So many brothers gave the Pizarro interests depth, ubiquity, and resilience, but they made Francisco's government of Peru the more difficult.

In the life of this hollow-cheeked, thin-bearded Trujillan and man of the Indies, continuities and patterns abound. There is not a single element in his motivation, culture, or behavior that is at all out of the ordinary. Seniority and lineage explain much of his success, and lack of education many of his failures; Trujillan elementality and insensitivity had much to do with both. But as his heritage was unusually complex, and there was only one Peru, with one first governor, his case is unique.

NOTES. There is no need to document the birthplace of Francisco Pizarro. As to his age, Cieza makes the unusually precise statement that he was sixty-three years and two months old when he died (*Chupas*, p. 114), which would result in a birthdate of April, 1478. In 1522 Pizarro said he was about forty (Medina, *Descubrimiento*, II, 475); in 1539 that he was about sixty (AGI, Lima 204, *probanza* of Diego Rodríguez). Zárate says that Pizarro and Almagro were each at least sixty-five at death (*Historia*, II, 498).

Pizarro had in succession two Indian mistresses, by whom he sired a total of four mestizo children. The first was doña Inés Yupanqui Huaylas; her name is given in various orders and versions, and the Spaniards mainly called her just doña Inés. She was a daughter of Huayna Capac by an Indian noblewoman from the Huaylas region, Contarhuacho. Pizarro must have lived with her from around the time of the conquest of Cuzco; in 1534 their daughter, doña Francisca Pizarro, was baptized in Jauja. Doña Inés went to live with Pizarro in Lima, where another child was born, don Gonzalo Pizarro, probably before 1536. By 1537 Pizarro had had both children legitimated.

During the siege of Lima by Indian rebels in 1536–1537, doña Inés came under some sort of suspicion. Pedro Pizarro claims that out of envy she told Pizarro that a sister of hers, then in Lima, had ordered the siege, upon which Pizarro had the sister killed without waiting to find out if the story was true. It proved false. Perhaps this finished Pizarro and doña Inés, or perhaps she was herself suspected of sympathy with the rebellion. As the mother of the governor's legitimated children, she could not be treated brusquely, so Pizarro had her married at this time to his retainer Francisco de Ampuero. Ampuero became a councilman of Lima, and her children by him eventually reached the same prominence. Doña Francisca and don Gonzalo were given into the care of Pizarro's half brother Francisco Martín de Alcántara and his wife, doña Inés Muñoz.

Pizarro's second mistress was Cuzco noblewoman doña Angelina or Añas Yupanqui, also a daughter of royalty, though some say of Atahuallpa and others of Huayna Capac. Pizarro may have consorted with her before he abandoned doña Inés, since at Mala in 1537 he accused Almagro of taking his "india," which would imply she had been in Cuzco when Almagro entered in April, 1537, and had consequently been there through the siege. If so, Pizarro may have known her in Cuzco when he was there in 1535. His two childen by her were born in 1539 or after, named don Francisco and don Juan. They were not legitimated. After Pizarro's death, Gonzalo Pizarro had doña Angelina marry Spaniard Juan de Betanzos, renowned as an interpreter. The pair held an encomienda and lived in Cuzco.

All four of Pizarro's children were in Lima when he was killed. Juan de Barbarán, Pizarro custodian and man of Cajamarca, was their guardian for a year or two. In April of 1543 they were all still alive, now under the guardianship of their uncle Gonzalo Pizarro. Don Juan seems to have died very young. Legitimated don Gonzalo died around 1546, perhaps ten years old. Don Francisco grew up in Cuzco with his mother, doña Angelina, and was a companion of El Inca Garcilaso. In 1551 he was sent to Spain; he married doña Inés Pizarro, mestizo daughter of his uncle Gonzalo, and died in 1557. The most famous and long-lived of the children was legitimated doña Francisca Pizarro, who grew up in Lima in the care of don Antonio de Ribera and doña Inés Muñoz, and held a large encomienda as her father's successor. Sent to Spain at the same time as don Francisco, she married her uncle Hernando, to unite the Pizarro wealth and entails, and bore him several children; she survived him and, before 1584, married the son of the Count of Puñoenrrostro, a relative of former Governor Pedrarias de Avila of Panama.

The chronicles and documents of Peru are full of Francisco Pizarro, in every chapter and on every page. Here only a small selection of significant sources will be mentioned. In studying Pizarro one is made very conscious of the work of Raúl Porras. The monumental biography he planned never came into being, but he published and commented on some documents of transcendental importance. One of these is the 1529 investigation into Pizarro's lineage, in "Dos documentos esenciales," *Revista Histórica* 17 (1948): 9–73. Another is *Testamento de Pizarro*, a transcription of Pizarro's 1537 testament and the ceremony of its opening, with a masterly introduction and copious biographical notes which are articles in themselves. Porras's *Cartas del Perú* contains Pizarro's known correspondence, with particularly revealing letters on pp. 5–6, 147–149, 228, 250–253, 303–304, 400–403. Less enlightening but equally necessary is Porras's two-volume *Cedulario*, particularly the Toledo capitulation at the beginning and the grants of coats of arms with résumés of Pizarro's career based on his own statements, in I, 76–78, and II, 393–395. Porras's overall view of Pizarro is perhaps best expressed in "Las conferencias del Dr. Raúl Porras Barrenechea sobre el conquistador del Perú," *Documenta*, I (1948):159–174. See also his "Francisco Pizarro," *Revista de Indias* 3 (1942):5–40.

Cúneo-Vidal's *Francisco Pizarro* has merit, but Porras was correct, or even too mild, in chastising him for "incredible levity." References are totally lacking, of course; names and dates vary wildly. Yet Cúneo somehow located, utilized, and partly reproduced documents that neither Porras nor this writer has managed to find again. Muñoz de San Pedro, for all the valuable work he has done, is almost as lighthearted as Cúneo. After working for a decade on the subtleties of Pizarro genealogy, he recently, on one page, gave wrong names for the mothers of both Francisco and Gonzalo Pizarro. Nevertheless, two articles of his are essential for the Pizarro background: "Doña Isabel de Vargas, esposa del padre del conquistador del Perú," *Revista de Indias* 11 (1951):9–28; and "Francisco Pizarro debió apellidarse Díaz o Hinojosa," *Revista de Estudios Extremeños* 6 (1950): 503–542. Busto's recent *Francisco Pizarro* is a popularizing work, first outline of a more serious biography. The will of Captain Gonzalo Pizarro, which fails to mention Francisco, is in Luisa Cuesta, "Una documentación interesante sobre la familia del conquistador del Perú," *Revista de Indias* 8 (1947):866–871.

Zárate's chapter describing and comparing the characters of Pizarro and Almagro (*Historia*, II, 498–499) is a masterpiece, and, though slightly laudatory, amazingly authentic. Equally informative in its way is the description by Pizarro's page Pedro Pizarro, *Relación*, V, 210–211 and 224–225. General descriptions by various chroniclers are in Cieza, *Chupas*, pp. 106–107; don Alonso Enríquez, *Vida y costumbres*, pp. 139, 153; Garcilaso, *Obras*, III, 186–187; Gómara, *Hispania victrix*, I, 245; Herrera, *Historia general*, XI, 165–166; Oviedo, *Historia*, III, 344; V, 30, 32–33. The main lines of Prescott's conception of Pizarro emerge in *Conquest of Peru*, pp. 834–836 and 1090–1097. An outstanding portrait by a present-day historian is that by Pérez de Tudela in *Crónicas del Perú*, I, xvii–xxvi. The image that Pizarro wished to project of himself may be seen in Jerez, *Verdadera relación*, II, 320. His view of his relationship with Almagro can be seen most clearly in *CDIHC*, V, 454–455.

Some more miscellaneous and direct evidence for Pizarro's character will be found in BNP, A208 (for relationship with Juan Pizarro, shoemaker); *CDIHC*, VI, 414, 423; Cieza, *Quito* (Jiménez, ed.), p. 147; Cieza, *Salinas*, pp. 194, 198; Estete, *Relación*, p. 29; Porras, *Cartas*, pp. 177, 190, 193, 319; Torres Saldamando, *Libro primero de cabildos*, I, 114–116. Legal testimony by Francisco Pizarro is in AGI, Lima 204, *probanza* of Diego Rodriguez; *RANP*, I (1920):430–431; Medina, *Descubrimiento*, II, 475–477. In the latter it is seen that Pizarro was already making a rubric in his accustomed fashion as early as 1522.

Essential for the Isthmian period are the descriptions of Pizarro's position included in Medina, *Descubrimiento*, II, 454, and Góngora, *Grupos*, p. 71. The latter has an appendix with Isthmian treasury records that tell much about the expeditions of the period and Pizarro's standing, as well as copies of the agreements of 1524 and 1526 between Pizarro, Almagro, Luque, and Pedrarias. Pizarro's activity in expeditions in the Isthmus area is discussed in *CDIAO*, X, 5–119; Las Casas, *Historia*, II, 401, 407, 596; III, 48–49, 53, 85, 88, 392–394; Gómara, *Hispania victrix*, I, 188–189; Pietro Martire d'Anghiera, *De Orbe Novo*, I, 220; Oviedo, *Historia*, III, 141–142, 213–217, 243.

For the discovery period, see Mellafe, *Descubrimiento del Perú*, and the various *probanzas* in *CDIHC*, vol. IV. Of the chronicles, the one with the most unduplicated and authentic information on this period is Cieza's *Tercera parte*.

On doña Inés Yupanqui see AGI, Lima, 204, *probanzas* of Francisco de Ampuero of 1537 and 1538; ANP, Castañeda, reg. 1, f.15; Salinas 1542–1543, ff.32–38 (second series); Pedro Pizarro, *Relación*, V, 224. For doña Angelina see BNP, A29, ff.2–3; A607, f.1; Garcilaso, *Obras*, IV, 140; Ella Dunbar Temple, "Don Carlos Inca," *Revista Histórica* 17 (1948):145; Pérez de Tudela, *Gasca*, II, 272.

For Pizarro's children see the above and ANP, Salinas 1542–1543, f.143;

HC 499; *CDIHC*, VIII, 147, 235–236; Cúneo-Vidal, *Francisco Pizarro*, pp. 569, 574–575, 582, 585–586, Loredo, *Los repartos*, pp. 219, 227, 231; Porras, *Cedulario*, II, 142; Porras, *Testamento de Pizarro*, pp. 56–57, 63–64, 77, and passim.

For Francisco Martín de Alcántara and doña Inés Muñoz, see AGI, Patronato 93, no. 9, ramo 2; 192, no. 1, ramo 32; Cobo, *Obras*, II, 430; Lockhart, *Spanish Peru*, pp. 44, 154; Porras, *Cartas*, p. 545; Vargas Ugarte, "El monasterio de la Concepción de la ciudad de Los Reyes," *Revista de Indias* 6 (1945):419. Captain Francisco de Chaves is called "el principal de la tierra, después del Marqués" in Zárate, *Historia*, II, 497. Both Chaves and Francisco Martín figure prominently in the chroniclers' accounts of Pizarro's final days.

Hernando Pizarro

Age at Cajamarca: About 30
Role: Captain of horse
Share: 7 shares of gold and silver

Place of origin: Trujillo, Extremadura
Parents: Captain Gonzalo Pizarro and Isabel de Vargas
Extent of literacy: Fully literate

Something of the nature of the Pizarro family's dominance in the conquering expedition can be seen in the fact that Francisco was by far the most senior figure in the Indies, while Hernando had incomparably the best position in Spain. As discussed just above, the Pizarro branch to which Hernando and Francisco belonged had a clear claim to hidalgo status. Though there were men at Cajamarca who came from nobler families—Juan de Valdevieso, Juan Morgovejo, and perhaps others—none could match Hernando in actually attained preeminence, as opposed to potentiality. The others were second sons, or at least had not come into their inheritance. Hernando was not only an eldest (and only) legitimate son, he had already inherited his father's estate and was the functioning head of his family. Though the Pizarros did not yet have a legally instituted entail, Hernando had received as inalienable property the core of the rather meager Pizarro holdings, consisting of their family residence on the square of Trujillo and their rights to the village of La Zarza, and so in effect he was in the envied situation of a *mayorazgo*.

Hernando was also one of the very few men at Cajamarca who had had any experience in large-scale European military action; he was the only one to have held positions of command. When still very young he had accompanied his father, Captain Gonzalo Pizarro, to the wars in Navarre. There, in 1521, hardly twenty years old, he received (through his father's influence) a royal appointment as captain of infantry. Whether he continued in such positions after his father's death is not known, though a friend once asserted he had "done good things in wars." But the mere fact of having held a captaincy in the metropolis put Hernando in a different category from everyone around him. This manifest superiority of birth, education, and above all, attained position in peninsular society, relative not only to the other Spaniards, but to his own brothers, is a key trait in explaining the nature of Hernando's behavior and the direction of his career. Of course there were other factors; he was as Extremaduran as Francisco—elemental, efficient, and inconsiderate—and he had a transparent self-centeredness, coldness, and lack of charm that were all his own. That he was the governor's brother rather than the governor was also important. Yet almost everything Hernando did related in one way or another to his peculiar advantages of background.

Hernando's position as head of the Pizarro house gave him an immediate ascendancy over his brothers. He had literally been the guardian of Juan and Gonzalo; he stood infinitely closer to the family center than Francisco, and the latter found in him at last an educated advisor who could be trusted implicitly. Thus from the beginning of the Peruvian expedition until his last days in Peru, Hernando played the role of a near-governor, plenipotentiary, and power behind the throne. This is not to say that, as legend and some historians would have it, Hernando manipulated Francisco at will. As seen above, Francisco essentially stood his ground, and it may have been he who was in the end the true manipulator. But he seems also to have held Hernando somewhat in awe, and certainly he allowed him extraordinary leeway and initiative.

Complaints that Hernando was running everything began to come out of Peru long before the expedition reached Cajamarca. Aside from holding a cavalry captaincy, Hernando exercised general tactical command as Francisco's lieutenant general, and at times he was called captain general, a title usually retained by the governor himself. Hernando then and later carried out functions commonly exercised personally by governors in the Indies. A good many of the original titles to Peru's encomiendas were issued by Hernando rather than Francisco. Hernando was in complete charge of the conduct of the "War of Salinas" in

1538, and of course it was he who ordered the execution of Almagro.

In the matter of rewards and prerogatives, too, Hernando showed a tendency to keep almost even with his brother the governor. His huge share of the treasure of Cajamarca was above what any individual captain, however important, might reasonably expect. Like Francisco, Hernando had encomiendas in several jurisdictions and houses in more than one town. The first time he returned to Spain, in 1534, he was admitted to the Order of Santiago as Francisco had been before him. The process of screening him for admission was hurried, hardly more than perfunctory. Since his was a clear case, the investigation into his lineage was not carried out in Trujillo, as it had been with Francisco; instead, enough witnesses were found at court in Toledo. On Hernando's return to Peru, there was an incipient tendency to call him "don" like his brother the governor and *adelantado*, but the title did not take hold, and in the end Hernando's name remained unadorned for the rest of his long life. At times people also called him "Vuestra Señoria," another form of address generally restricted to governors and bishops.

Hernando owed all his riches and power to his peninsular position and his relationship with Francisco, rather than to the seniority in the Indies that was so important for most of the men, including Francisco himself. To belittle American experience and uphold Spanish distinctions was therefore in his interest; it was also his inclination as a metropolis-made man among provincials. There was nothing to hold back his vituperation, for his position was unassailable while his brother lived. One often sees in history how the king or governor can manifest a certain diplomacy and goodness, while a younger brother, as hatchet man, acts with cruelty and arrogance. Hernando loosed insults on all who crossed him. The choicest were reserved for Almagro, his rival for Francisco Pizarro's favor, and his exact antithesis, since Almagro was a creature of the Indies, with no visible social origins in Spain. On more than one occasion Hernando referred to Almagro as a circumcised Moor, and it was apropos of him that he said, shortly after his arrival in Panama, "dámele vaquiano y dártelo he bellaco," which might be rendered "give me an old hand and I'll give you a son of a bitch." Hernando insulted Captain Alonso de Alvarado by openly reminding him of a humiliating rout he had suffered at Abancay. He called the council of Cuzco a bunch of peasants, and asked for a stick to make them obey his orders. His insults stopped nowhere. According to Diego de Trujillo, Hernando got the Inca emperor to emerge from his seclusion for a first interview by saying to the interpreter, "Tell the dog to come out here this minute."

Indeed, Hernando's demeanor may have struck a responsive chord in Atahuallpa. The emperor is supposed to have said that he had seen no Spaniard who acted like a lord, unless it was Hernando Pizarro. This may seem a strange remark, since the Spanish conception of the leader as an awe-inspiring figure, grave and dignified, is close to the Indian ideal. Yet the Spanish captain or governor ordinarily took care not to trample the dignity of his subordinates, particularly the more important ones, whereas one of the principal manifestations of the Indian concept of majesty was the king's ostensible contempt for his lieutenants. Of all the Spaniards, only Hernando Pizarro had a similarly boundless arrogance and lack of consideration.

It is commonly observable, both among the men of Cajamarca and among other Spaniards in the Indies in the sixteenth century, that those who were highest in Spanish peninsular society were the quickest to return to Spain and the last to identify themselves permanently with the new country. (See Part I, chapter 3, above.) Hernando fits this pattern perfectly. First in peninsular rank, he was first to depart from Peru, even before the distribution of the treasure was complete. His own inclinations were not the only determinant, since many of the conquerors undeniably desired to be rid of him, and his rank and experience made him the best emissary to the Spanish court. But his goals corresponded very well to the role assigned him. Unlike Francisco, whose consuming ambition was to hold and govern Peru, Hernando wanted above all to extract wealth to improve his position at home in Trujillo. His first act on arriving in Spain was to acquire the elements of a princely estate in the form of lands and steady income from annuities. Though Hernando had a more adequate notion of the duties, limitations, and opportunities stemming from the conquest of Peru than did Francisco, the new country failed to engage his emotions deeply. He seemed to have no sense whatever of permanence, and he once said openly that he was not concerned with the welfare of the Spanish citizens of Peru.

While he did return to Peru in 1535, it was only with the mission of garnering more treasure for the king and himself, and he would have been in Spain within one year rather than five, if the Indian rebellion and the war with Almagro had not detained him. More than any of the other conquerors, Hernando could be accused of an all-absorbing interest in "gold," though even he wanted precious metals only for what they could do for him in Spain. In that first trip home he saw that treasure could do much for him indeed, as he received the adulation of everyone up to the Council of the Indies and the emperor. With his hyperintense thrust toward essentials, Hernando directed his effort single-mindedly to the job of amassing treasure in one way or another. His more heroic exploits were mainly by-products of that effort. Just after Cajamarca, he took some twenty men on a hazardous four-month trip through still unpacified country to throw down the great idol of Pachacámac—and collect the immense treasure thought to be there. With about 180 men he withstood the prolonged siege of Cuzco by thousands and thousands of Indians; yet he had come there only to force the citizens of Cuzco to "serve" the king with large amounts of gold and silver. Despite the Spaniards' desperate situation, he would not receive individual Indians as allies unless they would pay a certain quota of gold.

By more testimony than his own, it appears that Hernando had a better idea of the necessity of being politic with the Indian authorities than did his brothers or many other Spaniards; he saved Chalcuchimi from burning, and released Manco Inca from captivity. But his only purpose was to secure more treasure, like the two golden statues Manco gave him. When pressed for time, Hernando (not alone) quickly resorted to the torture and burning of chieftains to extort money. He was also obsessed with hunting for hidden treasure, and when he left Peru in 1539, at a time when many Spaniards were turning their thoughts to a methodical exploitation of their encomiendas' economies, Hernando was still spinning elaborate plots to get at the gold-rich burial sites he was sure existed.

Related to his gold hunting was Hernando's extensive business activity, at least insofar as it was a means of getting liquid assets out of Peru. Though he used many stewards and agents, ultimately he managed his affairs himself. His education had provided him with a good understanding of subtle financial maneuverings which were a closed book to all his brothers and to most central Extremadurans of any background. Hernando poured capital into his silver mine at Porco, probably the richest in the country outside of Potosí, and sent to work in it one of the largest parties of Negro slaves to be imported into Peru during the whole conquest period. In the time around 1537–1538 Hernando was probably Peru's greatest single importer of European merchandise, which he sold to the Peruvian Spaniards both through his own stewards and through merchants hired for the purpose. Once back in Spain, Hernando successfully applied his ingenuity to the difficult art of getting funds from Peru into Spain, past the officials of the Contratación of Seville. For the rest of his life in Spain, Hernando manipulated bonds, mortgages, and annuities of dizzying complexity, and, despite the great misfortunes suffered by the Pizarro family and himself, died in possession of a vast estate and income.

Of all the differences between Hernando and his brothers, stemming ultimately from their different upbringing, none is more striking than Hernando's articulateness. If he lacked the light, spontaneous ease of communication of a Sevillian like don Alonso Enríquez de Guzmán, he was capable, when the need arose, of a stream of words, either in speech or writing, as massive and overwhelming as his own person. At such times he could make the most outrageous distortions and lies seem plausible, as in his replies to the Almagrists' accusations in Spain in 1540, or in his various letters to Charles V. His long letter to the Audiencia of Santo Domingo, reporting on the main events of the conquest (with emphasis of course on his own role), alone puts him in the first rank of the chroniclers of Peru.

Closely related was Hernando's wit, almost totally lacking in his brothers, and the only humanly attractive (rather than merely formidable or astounding) trait this writer has managed to discover in him. The flavor of Hernando's witty remarks was unvarying, and, amazingly enough, slightly self-deprecatory, in the sense that they tended to admit openly that Hernando would violate chivalric standards to obtain advantage under certain conditions. When he was accused of going against a truce by destroying a bridge in Cuzco in order to prevent Almagro's entry, he replied that "for every traitor like that there have to be two perfidious wretches like don Alonso Enríquez and me." After Almagro had seized Cuzco and Francisco Pizarro was thinking of making an interim agreement whereby the city would be handed over to three neutrals, Hernando praised the idea and proposed that the three neutral persons should be the legitimate son of Gonzalo Pizarro; Hernando Pizarro; and himself.

So plausible, so imbued with intelligence are many of Hernando's statements and writings, that it would be easy to believe him universally and unjustly maligned despite the other evidence. Yet, reading closely, we find him convicted out of his own mouth. While he explained any one situation to perfection, he did not trouble himself to be consistent from one time to the next. We have already seen his frank admission that he cared nothing for the well-being of the Peruvian Spaniards, a statement made in the context of his attempt to show that his only desire was to increase the king's revenue. If he proved successfully that in many ways he was judicious and mild with Indian chiefs, when it came to asserting his supposed great concern for the lives of Spanish citizens (elsewhere denied), he said he had told the Indians he would burn any of them who touched a Spaniard. The responsible witness we see seems far from the man accused of ordering poisonings and assassinations of his enemies, yet Hernando offered, in justification of his execution of Almagro, the remark that he could easily have had him secretly murdered instead.

If almost all the above aspects of Hernando's character and action seem to relate to advantages of position and education, as compared to his brothers and the other conquerors, eventually one must come to grips with qualities that seem more individual, or at least less obviously related to a general pattern. Where Francisco Pizarro was tall, lean, and sinewy, Hernando was massive—not only tall, but heavy. Physically as well as psychologically he was more apt to inspire awe and fear than affection. But for all his formidability, he was not a fine rider and dashing warrior like his younger brothers Juan and Gonzalo. At Cajamarca he fell off his horse and had to be carried to shelter. At the battle of Salinas his enemy Pedro de Lerma nearly unhorsed him, and he was saved only by friends and servants. Even his partisan and relative Pedro Pizarro admits that Hernando was a heavy man on a horse.

An outstanding characteristic of Hernando, beyond what his position will explain, was the stark quality of his selfishness or aloneness. The typical Spaniard, and perhaps even more the Extremaduran, tended to identify himself with a small group of relatives, subordinates, and neighbors, and to treat all others as outsiders. In Hernando this trait reached its culmination; the favored group shrank until it included only himself. Even his brothers were outside it. He ignored his younger brothers, except when they could give him something, as when Gonzalo, as rebel governor of Peru, controlled the flow of silver. He generally said good things about Francisco because his whole career depended on him, yet repeatedly in correspondence he implied that his older brother could not have conquered Peru and held it without his own superior judgment. Many a Spaniard stood alone in the world except for his household of trusted servants; Hernando lacked even that, for though there were people willing to be loyal to a now famous name and great fortune, he mistrusted almost everyone, and he was sure that all his employees were robbing him. His final will contains none of the usual statements that certain well-deserving stewards should not have their accounts audited, and no relatives or important citizens were witnesses to the document, as was usually the case.

A perfect example of Hernando's self-centeredness, which can be found in all his expressions, is his best-known writing, the letter he sent to the Audiencia of Santo Domingo in 1533 and which has often been printed among the chronicles of the conquest. It is in the form of a general account, and indeed Hernando says more, and more penetrating, things about the Incas and the Peruvian landscape than most of the other chroniclers—far more, in proportion to the length of the statement. Yet he totally omits the names of all other Spaniards, and he never mentions anything good that anyone else did. Governor Francisco himself is only mentioned when really necessary, or when Hernando gave him good advice. Hernando skips quickly past the fighting at Cajamarca, where he did poorly, and dwells on the two episodes where he shone: the interview with Atahuallpa and the trip to Pachacámac. Of course these same tendencies may be seen in the letters of Hernando Cortés and in the writings of other individualistic men of the Renaissance, but the purity of Hernando's individualism is chilling.

The only things outside himself to which Hernando gave evidence of a deep attachment were the Pizarro name and his home region of Trujillo. Through all the family's reverses—Francisco's assassination, Gonzalo's rebellion, and his own imprisonment of more than two decades in Spain—Hernando did his best not merely to keep himself afloat, but to preserve and consolidate the patrimony of the Pizarro heirs. The biggest step in this direction was his marriage, not long after her arrival in Spain in 1550, to his niece, doña Francisca Pizarro, Francisco's daughter by an Indian princess. Of course Hernando himself gained much through this match, but its main purpose was to combine all the Pizarro claims and entails in one coherent body. Hernando's purely personal inclination would probably have been to marry the daughter of a duke or count, like Hernando Cortés. After Hernando's death in 1578 doña Francisca herself married the son of the Count of Puñoenrrostro.

In all the long years he was away from Trujillo, Hernando never gave any thought to establishing himself in some larger center, but remained determined to graft the wealth and honors gained in Peru directly onto the Pizarros' Trujillan roots. He built a palatial residence on the site of his father's house facing the Trujillo square, and another one in the nearby village of La Zarza, the heart of the family patrimony. The permanent identification with Trujillo was cemented by Hernando's acquisition for his heirs of the honorific post of Trujillo's *alférez mayor*. The whole current of Hernando's career from 1532 until his death was away from Peru and toward Trujillo, using Peru only as a stepping-stone. It was fitting, then, that the crown ultimately exiled Hernando and his descendants from the Indies. On the other hand, it is somewhat paradoxical that doña Francisca and Hernando retained important economic interests in Peru, in the form of encomiendas and mines, as long as they lived.

At his death, in his late seventies, Hernando was blind, or nearly so, but unchanged in temperament and still in command of his affairs. His unusual energy, endurance, and initiative, plus a penetrating intellect, had enabled him to achieve some spectacular things, and he was equal in a way to any situation. His natural gifts, together with his advantages of position and education, led to an infinite arrogance, selfishness, and overconfidence that made him the most unpopular man of his time. Though greatly feared, he always had to remain dependent on Francisco for the ultimate sources of power, wealth, and honor. Hernando had the putative qualities of the Extremadurans and the Pizarros in excess; in him their concern with essentials reached the extreme of placing complete confidence in naked power and money, neglecting all else. Even four centuries after he lived, it is hard to attain a proper serenity of attitude toward Hernando Pizarro.

N O T E S . Hernando's regional origin is variously documented, among other places in his father's will, published in Luisa Cuesta, "Una documentación interesante sobre la familia del conquistador del Perú," *Revista de Indias* 8 (1947):866–871. Hernando's own will is in the same place, pp. 879–891. Related is the "Información sobre el linaje de Hernando Pizarro," published by Miguel Muñoz de San Pedro in *Revista de Estudios Extremeños* 22 (1966):209–227. For the Pizarro family in general see the article above on Francisco Pizarro.

The question of Hernando's birthdate has been discussed authoritatively by Porras in *Testamento de Pizarro*, though without giving the references. Hernando states his age in AGI, Patronato 93, no. 4, ramo 3; no. 185, ramo 20; Justicia 1124, no. 5, ramo 2; *CDIHC*, VI, 158.

Hernando and doña Francisca had three children: don Francisco, don Juan, and doña Inés. Don Francisco inherited the principal entail, and his son don Juan Fernando Pizarro became the first "Marqués de La Conquista," the village of La Zarza at that time being formally put under Pizarro overlordship and renamed La Conquista. Eventually the legitimate branch died out, and the title went to descendants of doña Francisca Pizarro, Hernando's daughter by doña Isabel Mercado, who had been his mistress in the early years of his imprisonment. This doña Francisca married Hernando de Orellana, son of the Juan Pizarro de Orellana of Cajamarca. See Muñoz de San Pedro, "La total extinguida descendencia de Francisco Pizarro," *Revista de Estudios Extremeños* 20 (1964):467–472. Other information on Hernando's children and his wife, doña Francisca, is in his will and in Lohmann Villena, "Documentos interesantes a la historia del Perú en el Archivo Histórico de Protocolos de Madrid," *Revista Histórica* 25 (1960–1961):450–477, which includes doña Francisca's will. More references and information relative to doña Francisca will be found in the notes on Francisco Pizarro, above.

A basic document for Hernando Pizarro's life is the lengthy statement he made in Madrid on May 15, 1540, in reply to a series of accusations by the Almagrists. Published in *CDIHC*, vol. V, it ranges in great detail over Hernando's whole Peruvian career and also constitutes a magnificent psychological self-portrait. Equally important, if less consolidated, are Hernando's many letters, most of which can be found in Porras, *Cartas*; Pérez de Tudela, *Gasca*, and AGI, Justicia 833. It is worthy of note that the significant letter in Porras's *Cartas*, pp. 448–450, dated May 6, 1542, must actually be from 1540. Hernando's letter-chronicle of 1533 is in Porras, *Cartas*; Conde de Canilleros (Muñoz de San Pedro), *Tres testigos de la conquista del Perú*; and Oviedo, *Historia*, V, 84–90. Porras's *Cedulario* is also essential, particularly the series of royal orders of 1534 which show how Hernando at that time enjoyed the almost unlimited confidence of the crown and the Council of the Indies because of the incredible treasure he had brought from Peru.

Their contemporaries did not write nearly as many general descriptions of Hernando Pizarro as of Francisco, or even of Gonzalo. Those that exist are very short. See don Alonso Enríquez, *Vida y costumbres*, pp. 154–155; Oviedo, *Historia*, V, 33; Pedro Pizarro, *Relación*, V, 211. That of the hostile Oviedo may be quoted in full for what it is worth: "Of all of them (the four brothers), only Hernando was legitimate, and more legitimated in arrogance: a heavy man, tall of stature, with thick lips and tongue, and the tip of his nose fleshy and red; this was the disturber of the peace of all, and especially of the two old partners Francisco Pizarro and Diego de Almagro." Cieza, *Salinas*, p. 450, has kinder words, on the basis of Hernando's comprehension of the necessities of the king's service and his treatment of the Indian lords. Among modern assessments, Pérez de Tudela shows a deep understanding of Hernando in the prologue to his *Crónicas del Perú*, I, xxiv–xxvi; so does Porras, in his note on Hernando in *Testamento de Pizarro*, pp. 61–63, which is also the best short chronological survey of Hernando's life. The biographical introduction to Conde de Canilleros (Muñoz de San Pedro), *Tres testigos de la conquista del Perú*, is written in a spirit of praise for Extremadura. Cúneo-Vidal, *Francisco Pizarro*, is full of errors, but reproduces valuable documents concerning Hernando, including his appointment to a captaincy.

Information on Hernando's encomiendas and mines will be found in Loredo, *Alardes y derramas*, pp. 115, 127; Loredo, *Los repartos*, p. 166; Cúneo-Vidal, *Francisco Pizarro*, pp. 527–531; CDIHC, VII, 175; RAHC 4 (1953):33; and scattered through his letters and the indexed Pérez de Tudela, *Gasca*. Evidence of the extent of his Peruvian mercantile activity is in ANP, PA 393, 408, 409, 535, 596, 598, 627, and HC 79, 226, 231–238, 311. See also Lockhart, *Spanish Peru*, pp. 86, 92–93. His later business dealings in Spain can be seen particularly in his letters in AGI, Justicia 833, his will, and Lohmann, "Documentos interesantes a la historia del Perú."

A summary of the records of Hernando's long trial is in Ernst Schaefer, "El proceso de Hernando Pizarro por la muerte del Adelantado Almagro," *Investigación y Progreso*, 5 (1931):43–46. On Hernando's part in the first interview with Atahuallpa and the events of Cajamarca, see AGI, Patronato 90, no. 1, ramo 11, testimony of Pedro Cataño; Gómara, *Hispania victrix*, I, 228; Mena, "Conquista del Perú," pp. 83, 85; Oviedo, *Historia*, V, 85–86; Pedro Pizarro, *Relación*, V, 177; Trujillo, *Relación*, pp. 56–57. For Hernando's trip to Pachacámac, see AGI, Patronato 93, no. 4, ramo 4; 150, no. 6, ramo 2; Jerez, *Verdadera relación*, II, 338–342; Oviedo, *Historia*, V, 87–90; Porras, in Trujillo, *Relación*, p. 110; Trujillo, *Relación*, p. 59.

The sayings of Hernando's that are quoted in the text above come from Cieza, *Salinas*, pp. 30, 313; Oviedo, *Historia*, V, 119, 189; Porras, *Cartas*, p. 384; CDIHC, V, 429, 435; VI, 17. In Lima on October 24, 1537, a notary wrote Hernando's name as "comendador don Hernando Pizarro," then crossed out the "don" (ANP, Castañeda, register 4, f. 30).

Other valuable miscellaneous information about Hernando will be found in ANP, PA 675, 689; HC 15, 28, 220, CDIAO, XX, 391; XLII, 98–100; CDIHC, V, 55, 102–103; VI, 311, 316–317; VI, 139–140; RANP 1:486; Cieza, *Salinas*, pp. 28, 86, 270–274, 316, 323–325, 329, 352–353, 420, 442, 449–450; Cieza, *Tercera parte*, in *Mercurio Peruano* 37 (1956):78; 39 (1958):567, 575; don Alonso Enríquez, *Vida y costumbres*, pp. 156

and passim; Gómara, *Hispania victrix*, I, 228; Oviedo, *Historia*, V, 109–110, 123, 190, 195; Pedro Pizarro, *Relación*, V, 201, 206; Porras, *Cartas*, p. 34; Trujillo, *Relación*, pp. 50, 52. Needless to say, there are hundreds or thousands of other informative documentary references to Hernando Pizarro.

Juan Pizarro

Age at Cajamarca: Probably about
   22 or 23
Role: Not definitely established
Share: 2½ shares of gold;
   2¼ shares of silver

Place of origin: Trujillo, Extremadura
Parents: Captain Gonzalo Pizarro
   and María Alonso
Extent of literacy: Could sign
   his name

Though early death kept Juan Pizarro from equaling the fame of his three brothers, he was a significant figure during the first years of the conquest, clearly senior to Gonzalo, and at times almost rivaling Hernando. Illegitimacy did not prevent his recognition; in his testament Juan's father made adequate provision for him. Indeed, the context leads one to suspect that Juan was living with Captain Gonzalo in Navarre at the time of the latter's death in 1522.

Most of what we know about Juan's background comes from the will he dictated in 1536. There he says that Estefanía de Vargas, matriarch of the Pizarro household in Trujillo, brought him up. Apparently he meant this in a general sense, since he later mentions being raised by a succession of four nurses. Juan was unable to remember the names, the sex, or even the number of children his mother had by Bartolomé de Soto. It is safe to assume that at an early age he was taken out of his mother's care, to grow up in the Pizarro home under the tutelage of his aunt Estefanía and his legitimate older brother Hernando. No original example of Juan's handwriting seems to survive, but copies of his will prove that he could make a signature. Perhaps this was the limit of his accomplishments, as apparently it was with his full brother Gonzalo. But since Juan received preferred treatment in some ways, he may have been closer to Hernando's complete mastery of the arts of literacy. At any rate, his father clearly meant him to live in the style of an hidalgo, with a mount and a portion of the family patrimony. There was much basis for the mistake Agustín de Zárate made in reporting that Juan, as well as Hernando, was legitimate.

Several of the best-informed chroniclers assert that Juan, unlike the other Pizarros, was magnanimous, affable, and popular. On the strength of such statements, William Prescott turned Juan into a "true and valiant knight," whose daring was tempered by mildness and courtesy and who stood out strongly from his brothers. Later, Porras, in his capacity as chief defender of Francisco Pizarro, objected to such an interpretation, pointing to the revolting ill-treatment Juan meted out to Manco Inca. Yet the truth is that Juan was guilty only of an almost universal failing of Spaniards of his time, and of other human beings before and since, who are fair to their peers and recognize few claims of those beyond the pale. A given Spaniard's treatment of Indians had little to do with the nature of his social and moral behavior among his fellows. Judging Juan Pizarro in the Spanish context alone, one would first have to voice the suspicion that his reputation for magnanimity came mainly from a lack of opportunity, in his short life, to manifest the famous Pizarro vindictiveness and parsimony. Pedro Pizarro relates an episode in which Juan accused Hernando de Soto of favoring Almagro, then chased him at the point of a lance through the streets of Cuzco. Juan apparently had the same narrow, unquestioning partisanry as the other Pizarros; he also shared with his full brother Gonzalo an impetuosity which was less evident in Francisco and Hernando.

For more objective testimony to Juan's human qualities, one can only have recourse to his will, which strongly tends to confirm what the chroniclers say. This document, drafted hastily when Juan was dying of a head wound during the siege of Cuzco, manages to mention (and benefit) more Pizarro relatives, legitimate and illegitimate, than any other Pizarro will, including the elaborate and leisurely testament of Francisco. Juan also left legacies to religious and charitable establishments all over western Spain and the Indies, and made a donation to all the inhabitants of La Zarza, the Pizarro family domain near Trujillo. If we add to this the directions he left not to trouble his debtors overmuch and not to quibble over debts he owed under fifty pesos, we must admit that Juan was indeed unusually magnanimous and considerate for a Pizarro.

In the conquest of Peru, Francisco Pizarro placed Juan in positions of responsibility almost from the beginning. If Juan did not at first receive the title of captain or a permanent command, this was more because of the surplus of captains than because of his greenness. He led groups of horsemen on various missions, on the island of Puná and during the march south on the mainland. Often he was in Hernando de Soto's vanguard, to try to rein in the excessive independence that the Pizarros deplored in Soto. Juan was a natural choice for the role; his own dash, impetuosity, and popularity made him more like Soto than any of his brothers.

Juan's role in the events of Cajamarca is in doubt. According to one version, he had a very important place. Pedro Pizarro claims that Francisco Pizarro divided the main body of foot into two equal groups, with Juan in charge of one of them. When the Spaniards were about to attack, Francisco was unable to tell which of two chiefs being carried in litters was Atahuallpa, so he sent Juan and his men toward one of them, while he himself went toward the other. However, no other chronicler reports this. Pedro Pizarro was not at Cajamarca himself, and his version of what went on there diverges from all others in some aspects. It is not at all likely that the Spaniards still could not tell who Atahuallpa was after his interview with fray Vicente de Valverde. Most reports fail to mention Juan at Cajamarca; Agustín de Zárate says that he shared responsibility for the cavalry with his brothers Hernando and Gonzalo. Whatever his exact role, Juan's place on the roll of Cajamarca is very high. He stands fourth in order and in the size of his share, after only his two older brothers and Hernando de Soto; all the other captains, even Benalcázar and Candía, are well behind and below him. This is more a testimony to Pizarro hegemony than to Juan's personal qualities, of course, but it does serve to measure his position.

By the time the expedition reached Cuzco, in 1533, Juan was being called Captain Juan Pizarro. He sat on the council of Cuzco in the year of its Spanish founding, and he was for some time top representative of the Pizarro interests in the Cuzco area, since Francisco traveled about so much, inspecting the country and founding cities, and Hernando returned to Spain after Cajamarca. In 1535 Juan was the protagonist of the first great Pizarro-Almagro clash. Hernando de Soto was in charge in Cuzco, in the position called alternately corregidor or lieutenant governor, when Francisco Pizarro sent Almagro there to take over and reallot the city's encomiendas. Just at this time Almagro got word that the crown had made him governor of the area to the south, and, instead of governing Cuzco in Pizarro's name, he made an attempt to claim it for his own. Soto's attitude was equivocal. Juan Pizarro gathered the whole Pizarro faction into the Inca palace he shared with his brother Gonzalo and from there resisted Almagro. Francisco Pizarro soon sent orders revoking Almagro's powers, confirming Soto as corregidor and

Juan as "captain general." The two camps remained at loggerheads until Francisco arrived in person and worked out a reconciliation with
Almagro.

After this crisis, Francisco made Juan corregidor of Cuzco, Soto having gone to Spain and Almagro to Chile. Hernando Pizarro then returned to Peru from the king's court, and promptly directed himself to
Cuzco. But by now Juan was too important a figure to be pushed aside
without ceremony. Though Francisco made Hernando corregidor, and
Hernando immediately took effective command on reaching Cuzco,
Juan kept his title of captain general. Only after Juan's death did Hernando take that post for himself. By 1535 Juan had his own following
and retainers, and his own large fortune. Fellow Trujillans Alonso de
Toro and Juan de Herrera (q.v.) were very close to him; Herrera took
25,000 pesos to Spain in Juan Pizarro's name. Don Alonso Enríquez
estimated that Juan was worth 200,000 ducats. The Pizarro brothers
came into conflict with each other more than once. Just before the siege
of Cuzco, in 1536, Juan and Hernando argued over the imprisonment
of Manco Inca. In this case Hernando had his way, but when the great
Indian siege began and Hernando planned to evacuate the city, Juan,
Gonzalo, and others protested successfully.

Juan died in the most heroic episode of the whole Peruvian conquest,
full though it was of improbable successes at arms. At the beginning of
the siege, in 1536, the Indians took over the great fortress of Sacsahuamán, which stood above the town with a sheer drop-off on one side and
a series of three dentated walls of house-sized stones on the other. Sixty
Spaniards, with Juan Pizarro at their head, took the fortress in a single
nighttime assault. One source says simply that Hernando Pizarro ordered Juan to command the attack; another would have it that Juan
insisted he must be the one to take the fortress, because it was lost
through his fault (since it was he who had decided that a fortress guard
was superfluous). Juan was already suffering from a jaw wound and
could not put his helmet on over the bandages. Thus he went to battle
bareheaded, meaning to stay with the reserves while his brother Gonzalo led the actual attack on the walls. But after the first barrier was
passed the Spanish effort flagged, and Juan rushed in with the remaining men. With this reinforcement the Spaniards penetrated into the
heart of the fortress, but the stones rained down on them, and one dealt
Juan a crushing blow on the head. Even after that he stayed in the
fight, but before long had to be carried back down to the town, where

he died within two weeks, leaving his full brother Gonzalo as his principal heir. Had he lived, he, rather than Gonzalo, would have explored the Amazon and led the great rebellion of the late 1540's. Perhaps he would have conducted himself in a milder fashion, and not have brought upon the Pizarros their utter removal from the Peruvian scene. When the Inca Garcilaso de la Vega last saw Cuzco, in 1559, Juan was buried in the cathedral under a great unmarked slab of blue stone.

NOTES. The voluminous legal testimonies of the conquest period, main source of our knowledge of the Spaniards' birthdates, apparently contain no exact statements of their ages by Juan and Gonzalo; one must rely on indirect methods and relation of one brother to another, with results that remain very imprecise. There are two lines of evidence.

  1. Gonzalo has always been considered the youngest of the Pizarro brothers, with Juan next older. This is confirmed generally by the order of preeminence in which they were treated by Francisco and others, and more specifically by the will granted by their father, Captain Gonzalo Pizarro, in 1522 (*Revista de Indias* 8 [1947]:866–871). Therein the father urges Hernando, already a captain himself, to watch over and direct Juan and Gonzalo. Juan was presumably at least in his early teens, since his father gave him a mount. Gonzalo was to receive a small legacy and be put in some gentleman's service "siendo de edad de doce años" (being twelve years old). This would seem to leave hardly any doubt that Gonzalo was under twelve in 1522, or at least that his father thought he was, and conversely that Juan was over twelve, but not grown. Don Alonso Enríquez, an eyewitness, put some upper limit on Juan's age by his statement that he was a young man of twenty-five when he died in 1536 (*Vida y costumbres*, p. 150). Though Porras takes this information as exact (*Testamento de Pizarro*, p. 69), it can only be regarded as a general estimate, in the roundest of numbers. Combining and evening out the two sources, one might conclude that Juan was about twenty-two or twenty-three at Cajamarca, and Gonzalo younger, but old enough to bear arms—somewhere between eighteen and twenty-one. Two recorded statements that Gonzalo had occasion to make about his age are both compatible with this conclusion; in both 1540 and 1543 he said he was "over twenty-five" (AGI, Lima 204, *probanza* of Pedro del Barco; *RANP* 1:457). Ordinarily a Spaniard would do this type of rounding off by fives; if a man was over thirty, he was not yet thirty-five. But twenty-five was the vaguest of all, since, in asking a witness how old he was, the purpose was merely to ascertain whether he was legally of age (twenty-five). If we take Gonzalo to mean in each case only a little over twenty-five, he might have been born as late as 1517—an

impossibility. We can conclude from his statements only that he was born sometime before 1515. One last, if uncertain, testimony to Gonzalo's relative youth is the statement of Pedro Hernández Paniagua in 1547 that he was young and robust and might expect to live forty years more (Pérez de Tudela, *Gasca*, II, 315). In this connection one may remember that Hernando Pizarro lived to be about eighty.

2. If all the above evidence seems to indicate that Juan and Gonzalo were in their early twenties or less at Cajamarca, there is also evidence for a different conclusion. Chronicler Agustín de Zárate, in Peru in the 1540's and very knowledgeable, judged Gonzalo to be about forty in 1544 (*Historia*, II, 522). Calvete de Estrella, basing himself apparently mainly on Zárate, but conceivably also on information in the Gasca papers that is now lost, states that Gonzalo was forty-two years old in 1548 (*Rebelión de Pizarro*, V, 21). Pedro Gutiérrez de Santa Clara agrees, declaring Gonzalo to have been about forty-five at the time (*Quinquenarios*, IV, 171). Gutiérrez de Santa Clara is often derivative, and in this case his statement is definitely based partly on Zárate and on Calvete; on the other hand, he is most original and trustworthy when talking about just this period of the later 1540's when he was in Peru himself, and he had many occasions to see Gonzalo Pizarro in the flesh. If Zárate and Calvete were right, Gonzalo would have been about twenty-six or twenty-eight at Cajamarca, Juan a year or two older.

Weighing all this, and considering also that Gonzalo did not begin to come into prominence on his own until 1536 or 1537, this writer has decided that, until further evidence appears, the probabilities are stronger for the later birthdates. Gonzalo was most likely born around 1512, Juan around 1509 or 1510.

Juan's will says that his mother's name was María Alonso. His half brother, Blas de Soto, gave his parents as Bartolomé de Soto and María de Aguilar (ANP, Salinas 1542–1543, f.627). Such alternate names were not uncommon at the time, particularly for women. The name Aguilar is interesting because it was also used by the Pizarros themselves. Hernando Pizarro's grandmother and his full sister used the surname Rodríguez de Aguilar (Muñoz de San Pedro, "Doña Isabel de Vargas," *Revista de Indias* 11 [1951]:9–28). Juan's unnamed and unknown half brothers and sisters included the just-mentioned Blas de Soto and Isabel de Soto, to whom Blas donated 1,000 ducats Juan bequeathed him. The money was doubtless for Isabel's dowry, since it was she whom Diego de Carvajal, a former retainer of Juan's in Peru, married after he returned to Trujillo sometime before 1541 (AGI, Justicia 1053, no. 5). Juan's sister María de Aguilar, who died before he did and is mentioned by no one else, was probably also a maternal relative. The only direct piece of evidence relating to the social quality of the Soto-Alonso family is Blas de Soto's total illiteracy. Blas came to Peru by the early 1540's, to be well received by his surviving half brother Gonzalo. He married a daughter of an *audiencia* judge, received an encomienda, and was beginning to appear in positions of command when he died of dysentery in Cuzco around 1545 (Gutiérrez de Santa Clara, *Quinquenarios*, III, 10–11). Juan's legacy to the people of La Zarza may indicate that his mother's family lived there, like the Martín Alonso (q.v.) who accompanied the Peru expedition.

Juan Pizarro never married, though at home in Trujillo he had had some clandestine romance that caused him to leave a veiled legacy in his will. In Peru he left behind at least one mestizo child. Here his magnanimity deserted him; in his testament he referred only to an unnamed girl, born to an Inca noblewoman who had served him, and said he did not consider the child his daughter. Nevertheless, he left her 2,000 ducats for a dowry and requested Hernando Pizarro to see to her marriage. Presumably this girl was the same doña Isabel who was accepted by the Pizarros as a daughter of Juan (AHA, Antonio Cerón, document of December 22, 1548, signed by Diego Velázquez). In 1547 she was living in Cuzco in company with the mestizo daughter of Gonzalo Pizarro, doña Inés (Pérez de Tudela, *Gasca*, I, 444–445). During much of the Gonzalo Pizarro rebellion the two girls enjoyed the usufruct of an encomienda in Arequipa. After the war Gasca planned to send them to Spain (Calvete, *Rebelión de Pizarro*, V, 36).

Porras thought that the child Juan referred to in his will was a "Francisca" (doubtless originally doña Francisca), daughter of Juan Pizarro and a (doña) Francisca Inquill Coya (*Testamento de Pizarro*, p. 69). No doubt this person existed and claimed to be Juan's daughter, but she did not receive the recognition given doña Isabel.

Juan Pizarro's will has been published by Luisa Cuesta in *Revista de Indias* 8 (1947):872–878, along with wills of his father and Hernando, taken from Madrid's Archivo Histórico Nacional, Consejos, Ejecutoria 3822. While mainly reliable, the printed version contains certain errors of transcription and omits mention of Juan's sister Francisca Rodríguez. These faults are remedied in Cúneo-Vidal's partial transcription (*Vida del . . . Pizarro*, pp. 539–543), from an unknown source, yet still other errors make their appearance. A contemporary copy of the will is in AGI, Justicia 1053, no. 5.

Various writers' portraits of Juan Pizarro are in *CDIHC*, VII, 473; Garcilaso, *Obras*, III, 130–131; Herrera, *Historia general*, XI, 66; Pedro Pizarro, *Relación*, pp. 200–201, 211; Porras, *Testamento de Pizarro*, pp. 68–69; Prescott, *Conquest of Peru*, pp. 1026–1027; Zárate, *Historia*, II, 486.

There are references to Juan Pizarro in AGI, Contaduría 1824, records from Cuzco, March, 1536; Justicia 1082, no. 1, ramo 4; Patronato 109, ramo 4; ANP, PA 149, 669, 798; *CDIHC*, IV, 199, 207; V, 409–412; VI, 313–316; VII, 470–473; *RAHC* 8:53; Cieza, *Tercera parte*, in *Mercurio Peruano* 37 (1956):82; 38 (1957):268; 39 (1958):584–585; Cieza, *Salinas*, p. 198; Luisa Cuesta, "Una documentación interesante sobre la familia del conquistador del Perú," *Revista de Indias* 8 (1947):890; Enríquez de Guzmán, *Vida y costumbres*, pp. 150, 154; Gómara, *Hispania victrix*, I, 225, 237; Loredo, *Los repartos*, p. 400; Oviedo, *Historia*, V, 92; Pedro Pizarro, *Relación*, V, 175, 177, 178, 196, 200–204, 211; Porras, "Jauja," *Revista Histórica* 18 (1949–1950):135; Porras, "Dos documentos esenciales," *Revista Histórica* 17 (1948):91–92; Porras, *Testamento de Pizarro*, pp. 68–69, and passim; Zárate, *Historia*, II, 464, 474–475.

Gonzalo Pizarro

Age at Cajamarca: About 20
Role: Horseman
Share: 2¼ shares of gold;
  2⅛ shares of silver

Place of origin: Trujillo, Extremadura
Parents: Captain Gonzalo Pizarro
  and María Alonso
Extent of literacy: Could sign
  his name

Because of the great Peruvian rebellion which he headed in the later 1540's, an aura of power and swaggering arrogance surrounds the name of Gonzalo Pizarro, making it easy to forget that he was the youngest and long the least prominent of the four Pizarro brothers. It is largely by analogy with his full brother, Juan Pizarro, that we must deduce the nature of Gonzalo's upbringing. Like Juan he was recognized by his father, and presumably he too was taken out of his mother's hands at an early age and put in the care of the nurses who looked after Juan in the Pizarro family home.

However, there may not have been strict parity between the two. Juan had precedence as the elder, and may have been more in the company of their father, Captain Gonzalo Pizarro. Captain Gonzalo left a mount to Juan, and none to young Gonzalo, though probably this merely reflects the boys' respective ages. Gonzalo was to be put in some gentleman's service at the proper age, a provision omitted for Juan. Yet once again this could have been merely because the older Juan no longer needed to have his education furthered by a period as a page; the service that their father mentioned must be construed as that standard gentleman's apprenticeship, not as the performance of menial tasks.

Actual direct evidence as to the education Gonzalo received is meager indeed: a random remark or two in the chronicles, and Gonzalo's signature. Diego Fernández el Palentino, in explaining Gonzalo's small aptitude for affairs of state, emphasizes the point by maintaining that he could not even read. Gutiérrez de Santa Clara, who must have known Gonzalo at least slightly, agrees, though perhaps he is only repeating Diego Fernández, as in other portions of his work. No other writers touch on the matter.

But if Gonzalo would appear to be left in the same class as utterly illiterate Francisco, such is not the case. He arrived in Peru in 1531 able to sign his name legibly and with complete fluency. He would have won no awards for penmanship, and he did not sign with the effortlessness of a notary, merchant, or lawyer, but his signature could stand unnoticed among those of many hidalgos and commoners who were functionally literate, though not professional men. There is no doubt that Gonzalo underwent some sort of organized instruction during childhood, as his brother Francisco did not.

Some Peruvian nationalists have been led to assert that Gonzalo not only could sign, but really knew how to read and write. This appears dubious. While no trustworthy evidence has appeared that would demonstrate beyond doubt that Gonzalo was ignorant of the alphabet, we can be sure that he made almost no use of his skills, if he had them. We know that he had associates read letters and books aloud to him, though it is true that this service was commonly performed even for truly literate masters by their secretaries and servants. More importantly, a great deal of Gonzalo's correspondence is preserved from the time when he was rebel governor of Peru, and nowhere do we find anything in Gonzalo's hand beyond his signature itself. This may be compared with the letters of Hernando Pizarro, of which most of the more personal and important ones are written in his own clear, vigorous script. Hernando was unusual in this respect; most gentlemen-correspondents roughed out a first draft and then had a secretary write a final clean version. In the combined Gasca-Gonzalo Pizarro papers there are many such handwritten first drafts by Licenciado Gasca, but all of Gonzalo's notes are in a secretary's hand. Often the gentleman writer would append to the final draft of his letter a few sentences of purely personal remarks in his own hand, and almost invariably he would himself write out the concluding polite formulas. This Gonzalo never did, and one is led to presume that he was unable to.

Gonzalo's signature is not the only indication that he received some rudiments of a gentleman's education. He lacked his brother Francisco's fondness for plebeian companions and pastimes. All his life he showed great concern for living up to chivalric and other codes. Gonzalo's great passion was for the arts of hunting, riding, and war, which he cultivated as sports, in the fashion of the gentry. He prided himself on keeping only the finest, most spirited, horses, and he was universally praised for his horsemanship. An excellent shot with a musket or crossbow, he may not have been the "best lance in the New World," as Garcilaso called him, but at least the legend existed. Above all, he loved the hunt, both shooting and hawking. After defeating viceroy Blasco Núñez Vela near Quito in 1545, he spent most of four months hunting on a rural property outside the town. Once Gonzalo said (of course with only partial truth) that if fate had not forced him into the governorship, he would have preferred to spend his time relaxing and hunting.

On first coming to Peru, Gonzalo, because of his youth and the prior claims of his brothers, existed as much on the sidelines as could be permitted a Pizarro. During the whole campaign of conquest from 1531 to 1534, he appears in the records only very infrequently, and never in a position of command. He is reported to have ridden out under Soto to the interview with Atahuallpa, and to have gone with Hernando Pizarro to Pachacámac. Cieza does say that Gonzalo, or rather Juan and Gonzalo, did much in the conquest. But rather than beginning to develop a following as Juan soon did, Gonzalo consorted almost as an equal with a group of the younger men from the Trujillo-Cáceres region. Still, his relationship to the governor gave him a reflected eminence. He appears seventh on the Cajamarca roll, along with the captains, and his share of the treasure was correspondingly large. At the Spanish founding of Cuzco he was still not called captain, like his brother Juan, but he did receive a seat beside him on the council.

By the time of the siege of Cuzco, in 1536–1537, Gonzalo begins to emerge as a prominent actor, with his own well-defined personality. Partly this was because he was coming of age, partly because the death of Juan Pizarro early in 1536 left a position open for him. Hernando Pizarro made him captain of horse, and chronicler Pedro Pizarro lists him prominently among the dozen vigorous young horsemen who were Cuzco's main defense.

Almost every reference to Gonzalo at this time gives him the character of an impetuous, imprudent firebrand, a quality exaggerated no doubt by his youth, but hardly to be tempered as he grew older. Once during the siege Gonzalo took twenty horsemen far into Indian territory, "with more spirit than prudence," and had to be retrieved by a second party at great risk to all. A little later, as the siege ended and Almagro's men approached Cuzco, Gonzalo urged attacking them before they could organize mischief for the Pizarros. After termination of the first civil war with Almagro's execution, when Hernando Pizarro was returning to Spain, Gonzalo told him it would be better to stay in Peru and await what might come, lance in hand. A decade later, Gonzalo would continue to take the same attitude.

It was this perennial adolescence of sporting, posturing, and bravado that caused Gonzalo's reputation for lack of sense, rather than any truly subnormal intelligence. The notion that Gonzalo was something less than wise had wide currency. All the standard chroniclers, following Zárate, who had direct experience of him, cast aspersions on his intellect in one way or another. Don Alonso Enríquez, who was with him at Cuzco, said he was *necio*—foolish or dim-witted. Of them all, sympathetic Pedro Pizarro was perhaps most nearly right in asserting that Gonzalo "knew little."

The chroniclers go on to say that despite his small understanding Gonzalo declared his ideas well in a crude way. We find considerable direct evidence of this, generally in statements of a blustering nature. Cieza seems to have caught his tone very well in reporting what he said when he learned in 1539 that the Indians of Charcas were massing forces against his small party of Spaniards. (The passage characteristically includes an oath by the Virgin, to whom Gonzalo had a special devotion, even stronger, or more openly expressed, than Francisco's.)

By Our Lady, as soon as I'm mounted on a horse, I don't care whether there are a thousand Indians or a hundred thousand; I don't know what makes these simpletons want to try their luck against the Spaniards, since through experience they ought to have learned how little they are worth against us, since two hundred thousand of them joined together to kill a hundred and eighty of us in Cuzco, and all they got from that feat that they thought to accomplish was over eighty thousand of them left dead; so let them come now, and not think that things will be any different.

In the time when he had seized power in Peru, Gonzalo asked a messenger from the loyalist forces in Panama how long he thought he could expect to live. The messenger replied forty years, and Gonzalo said he would rather live ten and be governor. Lest we get an inflated idea of his eloquence, a probably far more typical remark of Gonzalo's has come down to us, redolent of adolescent arrogance. Gonzalo was told that Emperor Charles had asked who that Gonzalo Pizarro was that was causing so much trouble, and Gonzalo replied that he would show him who that Gonzalo Pizarro was. After that he repeated this jewel every day.

In physique, Gonzalo was the most lordly of the Pizarros. He was tall as they all were, but where Francisco was hollow-cheeked, leathery, and sparse-bearded, and Hernando was a massive hulk, Gonzalo was well proportioned and graceful, with a handsome dark face and a beard that grew black and full as he matured. So often does one see Gonzalo thus described that historian Rafael Loredo, after years of studying the civil wars, felt sure of only one fact, that Gonzalo Pizarro's physical appearance was uncommonly striking.

Gonzalo also had a capacity for camaraderie unusual among the Pizarro brothers; he was far less insensitive than Francisco or Hernando. He developed close friends and strongly felt his duty toward them, as well as their reciprocal duty toward him; a sense of outrage and necessity for revenge overcame him when they failed him. As governor he tended to view the whole Spanish Peruvian population as his faithful friends or personal enemies, with ultimately bad results for his cause. Yet except for his full brother who died early, he was the only Pizarro who had much potentiality for true popularity.

Gonzalo's overdone knightliness, his overconcern with a gentleman's duties, and his excessive assertion of chivalric values, seem to originate in his social position within the Pizarro family. Whereas Francisco stood almost outside that family in many respects, an independent-minded plebeian and man of the Indies, and Hernando was so firmly ensconced within its center that he gave no thought to a knightly exterior, Gonzalo was in the middle, in an insecure position. He had no plebeian side to call upon, yet he was illegitimate, youngest born, and placed behind both Hernando and Juan. His early reaction must have been to overcompensate, insisting on what he was not sure of. Having to follow after the unusual achievement of Francisco and Hernando did nothing to alleviate the condition, so that it became a permanent marked characteristic.

As the older brothers fell aside, any bearer of the Pizarro name was bound to come to the fore, and Gonzalo, as we have seen, had considerable merit and attraction to add to the name. By the time of Juan's death it was becoming apparent that Hernando was going to be in Spain more than in Peru. If there was any remaining doubt, it was settled by his departure in 1539 and his imprisonment in 1540. After the end of the "War of Salinas" in 1538, Governor Francisco Pizarro began grooming Gonzalo to take Hernando's place as his second man. Gonzalo received command of the party sent to occupy Charcas, the mining region of far Upper Peru, and was the effective founder of La Plata (Chuquisaca or Sucre). He took an encomienda there, without giving up his previous one in Cuzco. By the mid 1540's he held top rank encomiendas in Charcas, Cuzco, and Arequipa, and he also had a silver mine, though not as productive as Hernando's.

In his will, Francisco Pizarro named Gonzalo, in Hernando's absence, as the person to hold the governorship of Peru until his own son should come of age. In 1540, though he had no real right to do so, Francisco sent Gonzalo to the Quito region, not merely as his lieutenant, but as actual "Governor of Quito." Francisco had seen that the whole vast area of the Inca empire was ungovernable from one center, and, foreseeing effective division, thought thus to prevent the northern segment from going out of the family's hands, probably to Benalcázar. At the same time, Francisco wrote to the Council of the Indies requesting formal sanction for his move. It was never given, and though Gonzalo was received in Quito as governor, he actually exercised power as a subordinate of Francisco.

The great event of the Quito period of Gonzalo's life was his large-scale expedition into the Amazon area. Though the ultimate hopelessness and adventuresomeness of the enterprise make it appear in retrospect well suited to Gonzalo's imprudent character, it had its origins in very serious considerations which might have moved the most realistic Spaniard to action. Persistent Indian reports told of the Amazonian region's wealth in gold and spices, and there was no more apparent reason for disbelief than there had been in the case of Peru itself. Perhaps even more important was the prospect that if Gonzalo really found a settled area, his claim to govern the whole Quito region would be cemented. Finders keepers was not only the Pizarros' maxim, but the rule of life everywhere in the Indies, repeatedly recognized by the crown itself. Therefore all the political and economic power of the Pizarro interests went into organizing an expedition of over two hundred men, far better equipped and provisioned than the conquerors of Peru had been in 1531–1532.

Of course Gonzalo failed to discover what did not exist, and the Pizarro doggedness with which he long pushed on the search only increased the losses from starvation and disease. Nevertheless, the "Cinnamon" expedition was far from a personal failure for Gonzalo. His capacity for enduring hardship proved equal to Francisco's, and he kept the respect, even in many cases the affection, of the few survivors. When he finally reappeared near Quito in 1542, he had become not only a power, but a legend; he had experienced command, and gained the elements of a personal following. With his sense for dramatic gestures, Gonzalo refused the horses sent him from Quito, and he and his men entered the city on foot and in their rags.

He found the situation in Peru transformed, with most of the elements of his rebellion already given. Francisco Pizarro had been assassinated, and governing in his place was the man originally sent to adjudicate the Pizarro-Almagro disputes, Licenciado Cristóbal Vaca de Castro. The resentments of a Pizarro, by now a veteran of the Indies, on seeing the governorship taken away from his family to be awarded to an utter greenhorn, are readily imaginable. Against this general background there were more specific claims which Gonzalo could and did put forth. The crown had granted Francisco the right to name a successor, and in his will Francisco had named Gonzalo, in the clearest of language. There was also the legally more questionable appointment of Gonzalo to the governorship of Quito. It was of great subjective importance that Gonzalo had for two years been accustomed to acting the part of a governor.

Gonzalo made no attempt to hide his feelings, but said openly that he should have been made governor of Peru. The Peruvian Spaniards had been pusillanimous to accept Vaca de Castro, and the king had been ungrateful to name him. Finally, out of necessity, Gonzalo brought himself to a surly acceptance of Vaca de Castro's rule. In his absence Vaca had already won the allegiance of the majority of Peru's encomenderos, and on the other hand he had not completed the task of putting down the Almagrist rebels, who were still formidable militarily. Gonzalo's offer of help in the campaign was respectfully declined, and he moved slowly toward central Peru in great state, his entourage full of seditious murmuring. When he reached Cuzco, after Vaca de Castro's victory, tension and incidents ensued, and at last Vaca had to banish Gonzalo to Charcas under a polite pretext.

Thus the situation simmered until Peru's first viceroy, Blasco Núñez Vela, arrived in the country in 1544 with royal ordinances, the New Laws, which, if taken literally, would have come near to destroying the encomienda system, the social and economic base of the Spanish presence. Blasco Núñez gave every sign of taking the ordinances literally, and Peru's alarmed encomenderos flocked to the indicated person, Gonzalo Pizarro, for help. Their aim was to block the legislation and get rid of Blasco Núñez, while Gonzalo's aim was to be governor; the two purposes very largely coincided, at least in the early stages. Thus began the most explosive of Peru's long series of civil wars and rebellions. It was different from the rest, not in being more revolutionary, but in being more serious, for this time the "rebels" were senior and powerful men—the council members, captains, and great encomenderos. Almost the only dissenters from the movement, at first, were latecomers, compatriots of the viceroy, and Almagrists, or others who had reason to be hostile to the Pizarros.

Without too much urging from Gonzalo, the Peruvian cities named him their procurator and captain general. He quickly organized an army of enthusiastic Spaniards and marched from Cuzco to Lima, where he found the viceroy already ejected by the *audiencia*. In the face of his guns, but in any case not very reluctantly, the *audiencia* named Gonzalo governor of Peru, and he entered Lima in triumph in October, 1544.

To do narrative justice to the following segment of Gonzalo's life, and Peru's history, would require a volume. In brief, viceroy Blasco Núñez reorganized his forces in the north of the country; Gonzalo, at the head of an army of Peru's finest, pursued him, eventually defeating and killing him near Quito at the end of 1545. At this point the interests of Gonzalo and the Peruvian Spaniards began to diverge, as he himself saw: "It is best that those in this country should have encomiendas granted by me, because these men will work to support me in the time of necessity, and for the others, once the ordinances are revoked, it will make very little difference whether one man governs or another." Nevertheless, despite some uprisings in the south of Peru, Gonzalo maintained himself handily until the advent of royal emissary Licenciado Pedro de la Gasca, bearing effective repeal of the offending laws, and the offer of a pardon for all. With these inducements he won over the men Gonzalo had sent to control Panama, then came to Peru late in 1547 to find adhesion almost as general as that previously given to Gonzalo in 1544. Gonzalo defeated his enemies once more in the far south, but when he met Gasca and the main forces of Spanish Peru near Cuzco in April, 1548, a battle hardly took place. After some skirmishing almost all of Gonzalo's army went over to the king's side; he himself surrendered, to suffer execution the next day.

Though he does not appear on the official lists of viceroys and governors, Gonzalo had ruled Peru for three and a half years, as far as anyone could be said to have ruled it in the first decades of its existence as a Spanish possession. The most real power of the governor—granting and removing encomiendas—he exercised abundantly.

Gonzalo might appear to have been merely a dynastic figurehead. In some ways he was. Peru's encomenderos used him, and, in a later phase, there were rebellious, marginal figures urging him on. Among them was the evil, incomparable Francisco de Carvajal, who took nearly complete control of Pizarrist military strategy and fought several important battles all by himself. Throughout, Gonzalo's more important policy statements were written by lawyers and notaries who filled their pages with "just war" and "natural law" and other terms and arguments that would never have entered Gonzalo's head.

Yet all that held the two successive phases of the rebellion together was Gonzalo Pizarro and his desire to govern. He was as determined to be governor as had been Francisco, from whom he had without doubt caught the urge, and he also had Francisco's tenacity and his rationale that the conqueror deserved to rule the conquered country. At the end of each fancy letter the lawyers wrote he would express this sentiment —in almost exactly the words Francisco had used—that no one could take from him what he had gained with such sweat and toil. He repeated the same thing when he was brought face to face with Gasca the day before his execution.

If Gonzalo was no born political manipulator, yet he had a sense for the political realities, as expressed in the quote from him above. The support initially given him he accepted in order to achieve his own ends; if the encomenderos were exploiting him, the opposite was also true. Knowing that the structure of his alliance with them would weaken after the viceroy's final defeat, he did what he could to strengthen the connection or find a surrogate. He took so many magnates with him on his 1545 campaign not so much because he needed them militarily, but in order to involve them in an extreme, irretrievable gesture of support for him. Gonzalo divided, reassigned, and shuffled encomiendas, trying to fill the encomendero ranks with men whose rights would depend on him alone.

Increasingly he resorted to exemplary punishment, usually execution of the unfaithful. This policy started as early as 1544, and one can distinguish several of its ingredients. In part it was the consistent Pizarro implacability toward enemies, from Almagro downward; in part it was the result of Gonzalo's neurotic outrage at any betrayal by "friends." The reign of terror was exaggerated by the pathological tendencies of Francisco de Carvajal, who accounted for most of the executions, including those of several men of Cajamarca. But we discover in Gonzalo's correspondence that Carvajal was not acting completely on his own. Gonzalo did not hesitate to give Carvajal orders, both general and specific. He often urged him to be strict in the punishment of wrongdoers. Occasionally he recommended the execution of certain individuals, and even complained of Carvajal's overlenience. He enjoyed frightening people with Carvajal's name, and wanted to project an image of himself as a remote and fearsome figure. As the Pizarrist situation grew worse in 1547 and 1548, the terror grew, and the various motives for it melted into habit and desperation.

In other ways too, Gonzalo put his stamp on the movement. The Spanish Peruvians in general were in a mood of arrogance and overconfidence in the middle 1540's, but it was Gonzalo's own brand of blustering big talk that was the fashion during the whole time he governed, from one end of Peru to the other. His great concern to fulfill a Christian gentleman's duties also emerges clearly in his governorship. He put more personal effort than had governors before him into the recruiting of priests to instruct the Indians, and he even tried to investigate their actual conduct. His letters are full of instructions to his lieutenants to respect the Indians' livestock and provisions. Under Gonzalo a serious attempt was made to observe all the formalities of Spanish legalism, particularly in respect to the royal treasury. Of course all such efforts were superficial, just as the sentiments that caused them were not at the center of Gonzalo's psyche. He used more clerics to manage his estates and support his cause than he ever recruited to teach Indians; his own campaigns were the greatest destroyer of Indian life and property, and he even went to the extreme of granting tiny "encomiendas" of ten or fifteen Indians, an abusive measure not resorted to by any other governor. Not a penny of the royal revenue left Peru during the time of his rule. In his final days he gave up all pretense of legality, as when he filled the council of Cuzco with men who were not even citizens.

His name and his association with the Pizarro interests had brought Gonzalo to power, aided by his good presence, his reputation as a warrior, and his ambition. Once there, his great popularity and the extensive congruence of his interests with those of the Spanish Peruvians, if managed flexibly and moderately, might have made him unassailable and attained the acquiescence of the crown in his governorship. At any time before 1548 he could have been pardoned, retaining his economic base and possibly receiving a noble title. But he was inflexible, because of his small education and rash temperament, plus Pizarro tenacity and the determination to govern that he imbibed from his brother Francisco. The Pizarro-Extremaduran characteristics did not serve Gonzalo well in a position that was no longer the overwhelming dominance of the early period, when Francisco could ride roughshod over others. Through narrow partisanry and ruthless punishment of enemies, Gonzalo destroyed the popularity and cohesion so necessary to him; though he needed to spread benefits to all, and even thought he was doing so, he was the most parsimonious of all the Pizarros beneath his fair and gentlemanly exterior, and in the end he gave little to anyone. These tactics, which brought bad enough results in the 1530's, were utterly inadequate to the complex play of interests in the quickly growing, ever more wealthy Peru of the following decade. Gonzalo's support disintegrated and he was left, like the leaders of the other Peruvian rebellions, at the head of an easily defeated fringe group.

The personal and family assets Gonzalo possessed, following normal processes of continuity, enhancement, and accretion, might have assured him and his descendants an informal dominance in Peru surpassing that of the Cortés family in Mexico. Instead, through his inability to adjust to a changed situation, Gonzalo lost his life and his estate and brought about the total expulsion of the Pizarro dynasty from Peru. Only the name remained. Chronicles and official writings long pointed to Gonzalo as the most horrible example of a "tyrant" (traitor). Popular legend, on the other hand, picked up the thread of his former popularity, and, centering on the scene of his execution, made of him a gallant warrior and conqueror, unjustly brought low through the ingratitude of officialdom and the inconstancy of his peers.

NOTES. For Gonzalo's origin and age, see under Juan Pizarro above. Perhaps in view of statements by Cúneo-Vidal and more recently by Muñoz de San Pedro ("Información sobre el linaje de Hernando Pizarro," *Revista de Estudios Extremeños* 22 [1966]:209) that Gonzalo's mother was María de Biedma, it is necessary to prove in detail that his mother was the same as Juan's, María Alonso or María de Aguilar. Chronicler Gómara says that Juan and Gonzalo were full brothers (*Hispania victrix*, I, 225). Blas de Soto, whom the chroniclers repeatedly assert to have been Gonzalo's half brother, was by his own statement Juan's brother as well (ANP, Salinas 1542–1543, f. 627). To use only statements by parties directly involved, Isabel de Soto was sister of both Juan (ANP, Salinas 1542–1543, f. 627) and Gonzalo (AGI, Justicia 1053, no. 5, testimony of Diego de Carvajal).

Gonzalo had a mestizo son, don Francisco, who was legitimated through the influence of Hernando Pizarro around 1544, and a mestizo daughter, doña Inés, who grew up in the company of Juan Pizarro's mestizo daughter, doña Isabel. Both of Gonzalo's children were sent to Spain in 1550, and doña Inés, in pursuance of Hernando Pizarro's policy of family consolidation, married her cousin don Francisco Pizarro, unlegitimated mestizo son of Francisco. Garcilaso mentions another son of Gonzalo, don Hernando, supposed to have been in Cuzco in 1548, but there appears to be no other notice of him. In 1546 a Spanish woman, María de Ulloa, who had been Gonzalo's mistress while he was in Quito, bore him a child who died the day of its birth. See *CDIHC*, VIII, 236; Garcilaso, *Obras*, III, 308; Pérez de Tudela, *Gasca*, I, 168, 279–280; Porras, *Testamento de Pizarro*, p. 75; Zárate, *Historia*, II, 534, 540; and the references to Juan Pizarro's children in the note above.

Because of the great masses of contemporary chronicles and reports on the subject of the Gonzalo Pizarro rebellion, there are probably more sources available for Gonzalo's life, at least during that time, than for the lives of any of his brothers. Most, however, are in a very diluted form, invariably mixed with the general history of the period and seriously distorted by the backward reflection of Gonzalo's ultimate fate. Hardly a chronicle of Peru, or a general one of the Indies, fails to throw some light on this phase of Gonzalo's career. Perhaps the most consistently informative and generally trustworthy chronicler is Zárate, who combines direct personal experience with good education and judgment. Gutiérrez de Santa Clara supplies much authentic unduplicated information, along with much embroidery, plagiarism, and error. By the time of the rebellion, Oviedo had developed into a hardened enemy of the Pizarros, and his accounts need correspondingly close scrutiny. For the prerebellion period, much more sparsely documented, the most generous and accurate chronicler is, as usual, Cieza, in his *Tercera parte*, *Salinas*, and *Chupas*. Particularly see his account of the Amazon expedition, in *Chupas*, passim.

The chronicles appear to contain quite a large number of general descriptions of Gonzalo, usually on the occasion of his execution. But the appearances are deceptive. Many of the later versions are only variations on two root passages, to which later authors added bits of often untrustworthy information. One of the originals is Gasca's report of Gonzalo's capture and execution, really a bare account of events, with little description beyond a reproduction of Gonzalo's remark that he had won Peru. The second, and more important, is that of Zárate (*Historia*, II, 522), which may well be given here not only because other chroniclers copied it, but because it is such a concise and just portrait, every element of which (except for Gonzalo's age) this writer has found confirmed in other kinds of sources:

Gonzalo Pizarro when he began to get into this tyanny was a man of about forty, tall of body and with well-proportioned members. His face was dark and his beard black and very long. He was inclined to the things of war and a great sufferer of its hardships; he was a good horseman in both saddles and a great musketeer; and while a man of little understanding, he declared his concepts well, though in very rough words; he could not keep secrets, from which much trouble resulted in his wars. He had too much to do with women, both Indian and Castilian.

Zárate's account of Gonzalo's death rests largely on Gasca's letter, with a few additions; he does not there repeat his general description. Gómara (*Hispania victrix*, I, 272) follows this part of Zárate, also without a description. Calvete (*Rebelión de Pizarro*, V, 19–21), takes the capture and execution straight from Gasca, then appends Zárate's description almost word for word. This gives us an opportunity to assess the value of Calvete's remark that Gonzalo was forty-two at his death, the most exact statement of his age that we have; one might well imagine that it came out of the Gasca papers, Calvete's main source, and ultimately from Gonzalo's confession. Yet since almost every word in this passage comes either from Gasca's letter (which does not give Gonzalo's age) or Zárate's description, we can give little credence to Calvete's estimate.

Diego Fernández reverts to Gasca's letter alone (*Historia*, I, 228), though he elsewhere includes a slight reminiscence of Zárate (*Historia*, I, 117), with the added remark that Gonzalo could not read. Gutiérrez de Santa Clara (*Quinquenarios*, IV, 171) repeats Zárate, mainly literally, with an interpolation or two. Garcilaso gives a romanticized version of both Gonzalo's character and his death (*Obras*, III, 309, 386, 402). He reflects the bias of his father's political sympathies and the shape oral legend had taken by the time he wrote; nevertheless, his main description is structured on Zárate's. Perhaps even the short and homely description by Pedro Pizarro (*Relación*, V, 211), who knew Gonzalo well, contains some echo of Zárate (above), or perhaps the justice of both portraits caused them to coincide. The reader may judge for himself: "Gonzalo Pizarro was valiant, knew little, had a good face and beard; a tight man and not generous, and a very good horseman." Don Alonso Enríquez's description of Gonzalo as *necio* is in *Vida y costumbres*, p. 272. Two valuable modern treatments of Gonzalo are in Pérez de Tudela's prologue to *Crónicas del Perú*, and Porras, *Testamento de Pizarro*, pp. 73–75.

Among more direct documentation, some important pieces are lost or never existed. Since his estate was confiscated, Gonzalo made no will, though he is mentioned in the wills of the other brothers and his father (q.v.). A document of great potential would be the record of the lengthy confession taken from Gonzalo after his surrender, but it has apparently disappeared.

Far and away the most important publication concerning Gonzalo Pizarro is Pérez de Tudela, *Gasca*, a transcription of documents whose originals are in the Huntington Library. Aside from most of Gasca's reports to Spain, it contains dozens of letters Gonzalo sent to his lieutenants and others during his period of rule, as well as great numbers of hardly less informative letters sent to him. The most spectacular document in the two volumes is a letter of Pedro Hernández Paniagua (II, 300–326) telling of his interviews with Gonzalo and giving a magnificent portrayal of Gonzalo's behavior at the height of his power; however, the letter must be used with some caution, since Paniagua, to impress Gasca, to whom the letter was directed, overdramatized his account and was probably guilty of making Gonzalo somewhat more fearsome than the actuality, to emphasize the danger he was in. Legal testimony by Gonzalo, showing him almost as taciturn as Francisco, is in AGI, Lima 204, *probanza* of Pedro del Barco, and *RANP* I (1920):457–459.

Gonzalo's encomiendas are described in Loredo, *Alardes y derramas*, pp. 118, 127, and Loredo, *Los repartos*, pp. 150, 194, 195. Characteristic remarks by Gonzalo, including those quoted in the text above, will be found in Cieza, *Chupas*, p. 290; Cieza, *Salinas*, pp. 27, 433, 450; Pérez de Tudela, *Gasca*, I, 79, 96; II, 150–151, 152–153, 165, 170, 178, 181, 188, 195, 203, 315, 319, 413.

Some valuable miscellaneous references to Gonzalo in the time before the great rebellion are in AGI, Justicia 1071, no. 1, ramo 8; 1082, no. 1, ramo 4; ANP, PA 54, 634; HC 12, 13, 274–308 passim; *CDIHC*, VII, 68;

Cieza, *Tercera parte*, in *Mercurio Peruano* 38 (1957):268; Oviedo, *Historia*, V, 92; Pedro Pizarro, *Relación*, V, 20; Porras, "Dos documentos esenciales," *Revista Histórica* 17 (1948):91–92; Zárate, *Historia*, II, 486.

Juan de Salcedo

Age at Cajamarca: About 38 to 40	Place of origin: Cazalegas, near Talavera de la Reina in New Castile
Role: Captain	
Share: 2⅛ shares of gold; 2 shares of silver	Extent of literacy: Could sign his name

One of the principal figures of the Peruvian expedition, Salcedo was an experienced veteran and proven leader. He had taken part in the earliest phases of Pizarro's explorations, from 1524 to 1527; apparently he is the Salcedo who was *alférez*, or ensign, on the first voyage of discovery in 1524. Around 1528 he was in Nicaragua serving as a captain under Governor Pedrarias de Avila. An old Nicaragua comrade, Captain Cristóbal de Mena, said that Salcedo was a prudent man and skilled in the ruses of war (meaning war with Indians). As to his social background, someone called him a "gentleman of Talavera" and he was at least not overtly plebeian. It seems that he had been part of the 1531 expedition from the time of its organization in Panama.

Salcedo acted principally as a captain of foot. He was in charge of the rear guard at the crucial time when the expedition was climbing from the Peruvian coast up steep slopes to the highland plateau. Whether he actually held command responsibility on the day of Cajamarca is not clear; from most accounts it appears that Governor Pizarro commanded the bulk of the footmen himself, though Salcedo may have been in charge of some of the guards posted around the entries to the plaza.

After Cajamarca, Salcedo received license to go home to Spain, leaving about the end of July, 1533. The reasons were various. Many of the Spaniards were clamoring for permission to return with their unheard-of wealth, and it was given only to the wounded, the sick, and a few older men like Salcedo. But Salcedo also, like his colleague Captain Mena, was doubtless resentful over the share allotted him—less than Soto, Benalcázar, Candía, and all four of the Pizarro brothers. The expedition had too many captains, and in the future was likely to favor men of the Cáceres-Trujillo contingent rather than New Castilians like Salcedo and Mena. The early departure of these two leaders contained an element of rejection and exile. Back in Spain, Salcedo quickly went to the Talavera region. He was living in the village of Cazalegas near Talavera in 1554, still styling himself Captain Juan de Salcedo. At that time he testified in favor of secretary Francisco de Jerez, whom he had known ever since the two of them joined Pizarro and Almagro's first ventures.

NOTES. A comrade calls Juan de Salcedo a native of Talavera de la Reina in ANP, PA 139: In 1554 Salcedo was a citizen of Talavera, resident in Cazalegas, and said he was over sixty (AGI, Patronato 98, no. 4, ramo 3, a *probanza* by Francisco de Jerez).

Other references are in ANP, PA 11, 99, 138, 139; *CDIHN*, I, 342; II, 321; Cieza, *Tercera parte*, in *Mercurio Peruano* 27 (1946):415; 39 (1958):39, 575, 576, 579; Mena, "La conquista del Perú," p. 82; Porras, *Cartas*, pp. 131–132; Zárate, *Historia*, II, 475.

Hernando de Soto

Age at Cajamarca: About 35
Role: Captain of horse
Share: 4 shares of gold and silver

Place of origin: Jerez de Badajoz, in western Extremadura
Parents: Francisco Méndez (de Soto) and Leonor Arias (Tinoco)
Degree of literacy: Literate

Except for Francisco Pizarro, Soto is better known to world history than any of the other men of Cajamarca. In the United States, where his name has taken on the odd, rather laughable form "De Soto," his fame exceeds even Pizarro's. There is a mass of contemporary narrative concerning his action in the Indies, and several (unsatisfactory) biographies of him have been written in the nineteenth and twentieth centuries. This is not the place to trace his varied career in any detail, though the task would be challenging and materials for it abound. But our format provides plenty of room to discuss the little that is known about Soto's background.

The most copious reporter of Soto's doings, Garcilaso de la Vega, knew so little about his subject's antecedents that he gave him the wrong birthplace. Yet Soto did not rise from the dust like Benalcázar, nor was his status tainted by illegitimacy, like Francisco Pizarro's. He was the legitimate (apparently second) son of parents who were plausible hidalgos. Though not illustrious, they bore names well known in

Badajoz and its satellite, Jerez, and Garcilaso was probably not wrong in considering Soto an hidalgo "on all four sides." The circle of their acquaintance included a member of the council of Badajoz. A relative of Soto's, who later went to Florida with him, was a Dominican friar, and a more distant connection was a bachelor at law from the University of Salamanca. The women of the family were not doñas; by 1539 the youngest sister had become one, but probably only by virtue of her relationship to the then governor of Florida. In Spain, Soto was a true if somewhat marginal hidalgo. In the Indies he always passed for an hidalgo of good standing, much the same as Alonso de Medina of Badajoz (their families were acquainted). Soto was literate, but if he had a formal grounding in Spanish legalism or any other professional training, he did not show the effects of it. By temperament he was neither a lawyer nor a manager.

In the English-speaking world Soto has had a reputation as a shining knight, an embodiment of various imaginary virtues, as opposed to the unmitigated vices of other conquerors. Porras Barrenechea has convincingly destroyed this legend for all who will listen. Soto shared the values of his fellows. He never seriously questioned the validity of the conquest of the New World, or his own right to govern a large part of it, and toward this end he killed as many Indians as the next man, resorting to torture and exemplary mutilation when he thought necessary. If he opposed Atahuallpa's execution, Atahuallpa alive augured better for him than for the Pizarros. Porras was right in saying that the Anglo-Saxons engaged in their image-building of Soto mainly for the puerile reason that Soto could be considered an explorer of the United States. Still, if he was no saint or image of benevolence, Soto does stand out as a knight of sorts, hasty, dashing and gallant. Like the Pizarros in his inordinate ambition to govern, he lacked their coldness, calculation, and vindictiveness. Whereas Hernando Pizarro was no horseman, Soto performed one feat of spectacular horsemanship after another. We have conflicting evidence as to whether Soto was a small man or above medium size, but there is no reason to contest Garcilaso's assessment that he was one of the best lances in the Indies. As Oviedo and others commented, he was particularly good at the mobile tactics of Indian fighting. His whole tendency was to rush ahead, to be first to do battle.

Nor do Anglo-Saxon distortions of Soto's role mean that his importance in Peru is merely a backward projection of his later fame. He was the most powerful single independent figure of the expedition after Francisco Pizarro, since the other Pizarro brothers were ultimately Francisco's creatures, and Benalcázar was clearly not Soto's equal. As with Pizarro, Soto's eminence was a direct carry-over from a long career in Central America.

He seems to have arrived in the Indies with the great expedition of Pedrarias de Avila to the Isthmus in 1513–1514. Then a boy in his later teens, he was naturally not much heard of for some time. But before many years had passed he was being called Captain. Around 1517 he entered into a long-lasting universal partnership or "company" with two other prominent men, also captains and reputedly hidalgos. Apparently the senior member was Francisco Campañón, of much the same type as Soto. Campañón died in Nicaragua around 1527, but Soto remembered him long afterward, and ordered masses for him in his will of 1539. The third member was Hernán Ponce de León from Talavera de la Reina, who, though a captain, was less a leader of ex-peditions than a manager and man of affairs. Soto and Ponce's tendencies conflicted yet complemented each other, and their association lasted until after the conquest of Peru.

Soto first appears in the chronicles of the Panama area around 1520, already with a reputation for swiftness. The episode, given by Las Casas, shows Soto's tendencies and abilities fully formed. That is perhaps not surprising, but it is rather flabbergasting to see that the rela-tionship between Soto and Francisco Pizarro was prefigured over a decade before the conquest of Peru. As part of a large expedition, partly seaborne, under the general command of Licenciado Gaspar de Espinosa, Pizarro led a hundred men along the coast toward Veragua; Soto went ahead of Pizarro with thirty followers to scout out the countryside. Far in advance of Pizarro, Soto and his men chanced on Espinosa's main body, which had landed and was now sorely beset by Indians. Soto attacked them by surprise and saved the day. This was the conquest of Peru in miniature: commander Pizarro with a column of foot, subordinate Soto in the vanguard and performing dashing feats.

The three partners went with Francisco Hernández de Córdoba to the conquest of Nicaragua in 1524. They were then, and afterward remained, among the principal leaders after the governor; Oviedo names only three captains accompanying Francisco Hernández, and Campañón and Soto are two of them. Soto and his partners held some of the best encomiendas in Nicaragua, with corresponding wealth. By 1530, the two survivors, Soto and Ponce, were such luminaries that they were often referred to merely as "the captains." Soto himself was alcalde of Nicaragua's chief town, León, in its very early days. He did not repeat in the office, because (according to Sebastián de Benalcázar, at any rate) he showed little interest in exercising his duties and proved too hasty and passionate when he did. During the interlude of the governorship of Diego López de Salcedo in 1527, Soto was captain of the new governor's guard, then leader of a mutiny against Salcedo and in favor of his old master Pedrarias. After Pedrarias came to Nicaragua to assume the governorship himself, he and Soto fell out; Soto and Ponce allied themselves with Pedrarias's rival, alcalde mayor Licenciado Castañeda, against the supporters of Pedrarias, who included future men of Cajamarca as important as Benalcázar and Sebastián de Torres. In 1530, Licenciado Castañeda engineered a majority vote for Soto as alcalde of León, but Pedrarias refused to allow him to take office.

By 1530, then, Soto, though only in his mid-thirties, was a senior man of unusual prestige, with wealth and a following. His excessive independent power was at the root of his rivalries with Pedrarias. Now he was growing increasingly anxious to acquire a governorship of his own. When Pizarro came back from the south with tales of riches, Peru seemed to offer the hoped-for opportunity. Soto and his partner Ponce explored all the possibilities. With a Peruvian expedition in mind, they began building two ships in company with Licenciado Castañeda. They conferred with Benalcázar. They negotiated seriously with Pedrarias, but, according to Cieza, they failed to come to an agreement; Soto and Ponce were ambitious to rule for themselves, while Pedrarias wanted to send his representative along with them and keep the new land under his own jurisdiction. Given Pedrarias's earned reputation for cutting down subordinates, these were not attractive terms.

Around 1529–1530, the Pizarro interests sent to Nicaragua to try to interest Soto and Ponce in joining them. According to Cieza again, Hernán Ponce agreed to be in Panama when Pizarro returned from Spain. He was, and the two parties hammered out some sort of informal agreement. The informality allowed each side to retain its own interpretation. That of the Pizarros is recorded for us in some detail by Pedro Pizarro. In the Pizarros' eyes, Soto and Ponce were only contributing ships. In return, the Pizarros would pay freight and passage.

They would reward the owners with good encomiendas and, for Soto, a captaincy and a "lieutenant governorship of the main city." From Coaque, Pizarro sent some money to Soto in Nicaragua; he allowed him to serve as captain of horse in the conquest, and then made him lieutenant governor briefly in Túmbez, Cajamarca, and Cuzco (each at the time considered the principal city). With this the Pizarros considered the bargain complete. Soto apparently had another view of the matter. He knew that the men and horses he was bringing were essential to the conquest and that he was their leader and organizer, not merely a shipper for the Pizarros. He thought the agreement was that he was to be Pizarro's effective and permanent second in command or "general." On arrival in Peru he was much offended to find Hernando Pizarro firmly established in that post. The Pizarros were determined not to share real power. Unable to attain a position of truly independent command and unwilling to accept subordination, Soto went through the conquest in an ambiguous position. It was clear that he would have to carve out his own province or leave Peru; and Soto's fate would to a large extent parallel that of his following, particularly the Badajoz contingent.

Almost nothing is known about the actual organization of Soto's expedition. Doubtless Hernán Ponce took care of most of the details. Definitive preparations had to wait until March, 1531, and the death of Pedrarias, who had effectively opposed the removal of any large number of men from Nicaragua. Personal and factional rivalries kept Soto and Benalcázar from combining their similar ventures, and, as it happened, Benalcázar's improvised expedition arrived before Soto's. This may be explained partly by Soto's stopover in Panama. In chronicles and other sources, Soto usually appears to have come directly from Nicaragua. Pedro Pizarro, for example, speaks of Soto raising about a hundred men, then arriving with them "from Nicaragua" at the isle of Puná. The impression that the bulk of Soto's men came with him from Nicaragua is not false, but some of them may have joined him in Panama. The two ships arriving at Puná on December 1, 1531, registered Panama as their point of origin.

The mission which naturally devolved on Soto in the conquest of Peru was to lead a mounted vanguard. All the anecdotes and crises concerning him in Peru are variations on this theme. So many factors indicated such a role for him that it does not seem that either Soto or the Pizarros necessarily invented it for selfish advantage, though it offered that to both parties. Soto had performed in this capacity for Pizarro before. He was a renowned rider, scout, and Indian fighter; he brought fresh horses and a group of men personally loyal to him, some from the Badajoz region, who constituted a natural unit. For Soto, the arrangement satisfied his restless forward urge and his penchant for being first; it also gave him an independence in which he could hatch plans to further his own ambitions, and a chance to look over new areas which might one day be governed by Hernando de Soto. First chance at booty was also not to be sneered at. For the Pizarros, Soto's vanguard role got him away from the center of power and out of the councils; they were willing to grant Soto the glory of going first, in the transparent hope that he would get killed.

Type-cast as the dashing, untrustworthy, but valuable forward rider, Soto performed consistently. He led the advance all the way from Túmbez to Cuzco. A little south of Túmbez, he was involved in a near mutiny, or so says Pedro Pizarro; possibly he hoped to attempt the conquest of Quito on his own. After that the Pizarros leavened his men with some trusted friends. Soto was first to see something of the wonders of the highland, with the Inca highway and the great llama herds.

At the head of a dozen horsemen, he went as the Spanish emissary into the Inca camp and was the first to meet Emperor Atahuallpa. Characteristically he tried to impress the emperor by rearing and wheeling his horse almost in the Inca's face. Around this time Pizarro made Soto temporarily his chief lieutenant, and he was a member of the board that determined the allocation of the treasure of Cajamarca; but soon he was back in his accustomed place. (His position among the allocators was not enough to get him the second largest share, which he would seem to have deserved by almost any standards. He received a poor third, after Hernando Pizarro, as seen in Part I, chapter 4.)

Most of the chroniclers and other witnesses, including his enemies, have asserted that Soto was especially opposed to Atahuallpa's execution. Garcilaso says that the attachment between the two was mutual, the emperor taking a fancy to him as the first Spaniard he had seen. This last is more dubious; the same claim of Atahuallpa's special favor was also raised for Hernando Pizarro. Soto's actions at the time of Atahuallpa's execution are once again related to his perennial outrider function. When the Spaniards heard reports that Atahuallpa was raising forces at Cajas to attack them, Soto went to establish the truth. Perhaps the Pizarros and others sent him on this mission in order to have him out of the way while they proceeded against the Inca, for Soto's insistence on literal fulfillment of agreements was one of his best-known and most authentic traits. At Cajas Soto discovered no sign of hostile Indians; for that reason alone he would have opposed the execution, which he found already completed when he returned. Soto's attitude toward Atahuallpa had elements of fairmindedness, generosity, and chivalry, but there was also another dimension, even if it should not be true that, as Garcilaso avers, the emperor showered gifts and favors on Soto. Atahuallpa alive and free would represent a threat to the rulers of Peru, the Pizarros, but for Soto, already in the process of being pushed out, such a fluid and insecure situation might bring with it great opportunities. Soto lacked Francisco Pizarro's long-range view of Peru or of the problem of government in general.

As the Spanish advance southward continued, Soto was the first to view the great valley of Jauja. On the final march to Cuzco, Soto and his men became too impatient to reach the rich Inca capital. For both worthy and unworthy reasons, and against Pizarro's orders, they rode far ahead of the main party. A near defeat, and the greatest loss of men in the whole campaign, came when the Indians ambushed Soto's column during its weary ascent of a slope at Vilcaconga. As usual, Soto was the first man to reach the top. It is not strange that to so many authentic exploits a persistent legend added an apocryphal one—that Soto and a Pedro del Barco were the first emissaries sent to Cuzco, while Atahuallpa was still alive, to claim the city for Spain and collect its gold (the three men of the party actually were Bueno, Moguer, and Zárate).

After the campaign reached its goal, Cuzco, late in 1533, Soto still continued in his usual role. Made lieutenant governer and great encomendero of Cuzco at its Spanish founding in 1534, he nevertheless left almost immediately to pursue the hostile Inca general Quizquiz northward into unknown territory. Pizarro once again assigned Soto to the lieutenant governorship of Cuzco for a time in late 1534 and 1535, but he could not last in the position. The major problem then facing the Spaniards in Peru was the question of who was to conquer and rule the areas to the south. Soto was intensely interested, and in many ways he was the man indicated to lead the southern expedition, if not to govern the area. As things developed, he had to make way for Almagro, who came on the scene with both royal sanction and Pizarro toleration for his Chile venture. There was much conflict, however, between Pizarrists and Almagrists over the possession of Cuzco itself, and Soto as local man in charge gave Almagro partial treatment, hoping to gain a position of command or partnership in the Chilean expedition. For this the Pizarros retracted the conditional support they had given him.

Soto was exceedingly anxious to get some control of the Chile expedition. He is said to have offered Almagro 200,000 pesos if he would name him general; apparently Soto understood or hoped that Almagro would stay in Cuzco and leave the entire undertaking to him. Almagro seems to have sensed that Soto was too eager for, and capable of, independence. In the end he chose another man as his chief lieutenant and accompanied the expedition himself.

No possibilities remained for Soto in Peru unless he was willing to accept subordination—by now his reputation was such that the Pizarros probably would not have accepted him as a subordinate in any case. Accordingly, he decided to take his burning ambition to the Spanish court. By August, 1535, he was in Lima on his way home, and he reached Spain in the spring of 1536. In charge of his remaining Peruvian affairs was his partner Hernán Ponce de León. Ponce had followed Soto to Peru after the end of the conquest; he held a large encomienda for a time and was caught for a year in the Indian siege of Cuzco, but he never took root. In Cuzco, in 1535, Soto and Ponce renewed and reaffirmed their long-standing partnership, probably at the initiative of Soto, since the interests of the two now began to diverge. Soto's principal aim was to win the leadership of some great enterprise in the Indies; that of Ponce to enjoy in Spain the fruits of their past efforts.

Garcilaso asserts that Soto originally meant to return to Peru, but this is extremely unlikely. Hardly had Soto left when Ponce in his name relinquished Soto's Cuzco encomienda to Almagro. We can judge Soto's intention better from a memorandum he wrote to a lawyer at court in 1536. He expressed the desire to get the governorship of Quito, which would be taken away from Pizarro, in order to undertake an expedition inland (the Amazon venture later attempted by Gonzalo Pizarro). Failing that, he wanted to govern Guatemala, with license to explore along the Pacific (the arrangement previously made by the crown with Pedro de Alvarado). In any case, he wanted the title of *adelantado* and membership in the Order of Santiago. He was not interested then in any specific area, but in a governorship, high honors, and the opportunity to carry out a major expedition of conquest and exploration in the Indies.

Neither of the commands he desired was available, but Soto had brought to Spain so much Peruvian treasure (100,000 pesos, according to Oviedo) and such a reputation as a captain in Nicaragua and Peru, that he was certain to conclude some major agreement with the crown. In April, 1537, he acquired the right to conquer "Florida," stretching indefinitely into the North American heartland, and also the governorship of Cuba as a base of operations. Into the bargain Soto received his title of *Adelantado* and his cross of Santiago; a provision for a future marquisate made him the nominal equal of Pizarro and Cortés. He had reached the pinnacle of ambition for Spaniards of the Indies. That Florida turned out to lack the liquid resources of Peru and Mexico was, in a way, a chance circumstance.

Soto's further career, the best-known part of his life, need not concern us here, except as it relates to his Peruvian interlude. Without Peruvian wealth Soto could never have negotiated his titles or financed the Florida expedition, but otherwise Peru hardly touched the vital center of his life. The Central American experience which took up all his young manhood shaped Soto definitively. It is symptomatic that rather than marrying someone from Badajoz, or some relative of the Pizarros, Soto sought an alliance with the daughter of Pedrarias de Avila, who dominated Panama and Nicaragua in the fifteen formative years Soto spent there. The characteristics of Soto's behavior in North America—erratic forward advance, mobility, military glory, and little permanent residue of his action—all tally with his role in Peru. Ultimately it would seem that Soto in Peru was a free agent, responding to the dynamics of his own being, rather than a pawn of the Pizarros.

Peru, and Cajamarca, were crucial nonetheless. Like the conquests of Ecuador, Colombia, and Chile, the first exploration of the southeastern United States was an offshoot of the Peruvian expedition and received much of its impetus from the events of November 16, 1532, at Cajamarca.

NOTES.   The estimate of Soto's age is a compromise between his statements in 1535 that he was about thirty-five (Medina, *Descubrimiento*, II, 356), and in 1536 that he was about forty (AGI, Justicia 719, no. 9). Soto's regional origin has been a matter of fiery controversy, based on the local patriotism of several towns in western Extremadura. There is no doubt, as Porras has shown, that Soto considered himself to be a native of Jerez de Badajoz (Solar and Rújula, *Soto*, p. 210; AGI, Justicia 719, no. 9; Patronato 93, no. 6, ramo 1). But other claims are not without foundation. The royal officials investigating Soto's lineage for membership in the Order of Santiago were under the impression that he was from Badajoz, and actually carried out their investigation there. In a way their procedure was not in error. Not only was Soto's mother of a Badajoz family; Soto felt allegiance to a region of which Badajoz was the center. In Peru he was the rallying point for the Badajoz faction, and his Florida expedition drew from all over the Badajoz hinterland, stretching into Portugal. The claims of Barcarrota are harder to substantiate; essentially only Garcilaso pronounces in its favor (Garcilaso, *Obras*, I, 251). Soto repeatedly expressed a primary allegiance to Jerez de Badajoz and even to a specific parish within that town. Yet all that we can assert categorically, given the usage of the times, is that Soto felt himself to be from Jerez or its environs, which might include Barcarrota for all we know, however injurious that conclusion might be to Barcarrota civic pride. The municipal claims are not mutually exclusive. If Soto was from Jerez, that does *not* prove that he was not from Barcarrota.

No children resulted from Soto's marriage, in Valladolid, in 1536, to doña Isabel de Bobadilla, daughter of Governor Pedrarias de Avila. In Nicaragua he left an illegitimate daughter, doña María de Soto, presumably mestizo, who married a Spaniard named Hernán Nieto. She receives mention in Soto's 1539 testament.

In Peru, Soto consorted with a daughter of Huayna Capac called Tocto Chimbu, and later doña Leonor; she had been one of Atahuallpa's wives, and after his death the new Inca gave her to Soto. By her he had a daughter, doña Leonor de Soto. On leaving Peru Soto placed his daughter in the care of Hernán Ponce de León, who soon departed in turn, but not without finding a new guardian. Soto did not lose sight of doña Leonor; as late as 1540 the crown issued orders at Soto's petition that she was to be returned to the guardian he had assigned. Yet he failed to mention her in his will. In the 1550's doña Leonor was married in Cuzco to Spaniard García Garrillo, whose only asset seems to have been the prospect of trading on the memory of Soto's deeds. Though doña Leonor inherited her mother's estate in 1546, the couple lived partly through the charity of don Carlos Inca, only encomendero among the Indian nobility. Perhaps doña Leonor and her husband exaggerated their poverty. They did manage to maintain themselves, and they were alive in Cuzco in 1573, at which time they were still being served by some fifteen *yanaconas* (permanently attached Indians) who had come down to them from doña Leonor's mother and Soto.

The most basic source for Soto's background is Solar and Rújula, *El Adelantado Hernando de Soto*, a mainly documentary publication. The central piece in the book is a full transcription of the investigation into Soto's lineage carried out in Badajoz in 1538. Also included are Soto's will of 1539, his dowry agreement with doña Isabel de Bobadilla, the confirmation of his company with Hernán Ponce, signed in Cuzco, 1535 (original in HC 83), and much else. The memorandum that Soto wrote of his ambitions for governorships is in Porras, *Cartas*, p. 273.

Garcilaso's flowing reports of Soto's actions in Florida carry conviction, but for all that they are often less reliable than earlier accounts; his treatment of Soto's personal characteristics seems nearer the mark. All of *La Florida*, in a way, is about Soto, but for personal details see particularly *Obras*, I, 251–252, 269–271, 309, 404, 441, 462, the latter being a general description. Shorter descriptions of Soto are in Pedro Pizarro, *Relación*, V, 211, and Oviedo, *Historia*, III, 351. Contemporary accounts of the Florida period are in Edward G. Bourne, ed., *Narratives of the Career of Hernando de Soto*. Of the biographies of Soto, two of the least bad are Theodore Maynard's *De Soto and the Conquistadores* and Francisco Blanco Castilla's *Hernando de Soto, el centauro de las Indias*, but even these are ill-informed and novelistic, particularly the latter. Porras's scathing remarks about "Soto the Good" are in Trujillo, *Relación*, pp. 91–93, 119–120.

Further references to the less documented pre-Peruvian phase of Soto's life are in *CDIHN*, I, 130; II, 131–138, 500, 506, 515–516, 532; IV, 536, 538, 541, and passim; Las Casas, *Historia*, III, 392–394 (the episode with Pizarro and Espinosa); Cieza, *Tercera parte*, in *Mercurio Peruano* 36 (1955):458–459, 464; Góngora, *Grupos*, pp. 47–48; Medina, *Descubrimiento*, I, 225; II, 292, 316, 356, 360; Oviedo, *Historia*, III, 208, 302, 351; Pedro Pizarro, *Relación*, V, 170–171.

Mention of Soto in the records multiplies for the later period of his life. Some important references to Soto in the Peruvian period and later are in AGI, Contaduría 1825, records from Puná, December 1, 1531; records from Cajamarca, May, 1533; Contratación 576, f.164; Justicia 1124, no. 3, ramo 2; no. 5, ramo 3, testimony of Miguel de Estete; Patronato 109, ramo 4; 185, ramo 11; HC 2, 67, 86, 97; *CDIAO*, X, 256, 257, 269–272; *CDIHC*, IV, 199; *CDIHN*, III, 467; *RAHC* 8 (1957):68–69; *RANP* 1 (1920):441; Cieza, *Tercera parte*, in Loredo, *Los repartos*, p. 387; in *Mercurio Peruano* 37 (1956):82–84, 87; 38 (1957):249, 250; 39 (1958): 566, 584–585; Gómara, *Hispania victrix*, I, 228, 229, 235, 237; Herrera, *Historia General*, X, 171, 351; Mena, "Conquista del Perú," pp. 80, 83, 85; Oviedo, *Historia*, III, 351; V, 92, 196; Pedro Pizarro, *Relación*, 5:170–172, 174–177, 188, 189, 198–201; Porras, *Cartas*, pp. 165, 167; Porras, "Dos documentos esenciales," *Revista Histórica* 17 (1948):91–93; Trujillo, *Relación*, pp. 52–54, 57, 60–62; Zárate, *Historia*, II, 477.

For doña Leonor de Soto and her mother, see AGI, Lima 565, vol. III, May 23, 1540; Patronato 109, ramo 4; ANP, Salinas 1546–1548, ff.1144–1146; *RAHC* 4 (1953):125; Solar and Rújula, *Soto*, pp. 46, 49–51, 185–196.

Fray Vicente de Valverde

Age at Cajamarca: Over 30   Place of origin: Oropesa (western New Castile)
Role: Chaplain   Parents: Francisco de Valverde and
Share: Nothing   Ana de Vallejeda
    Extent of literacy: Highly literate

Of all the men of Cajamarca, there is no more familiar figure than fray Vicente de Valverde, who held the famous parley with Atahuallpa just before the Spanish onslaught. Yet his is the only name missing on the Cajamarca roll, for among the participants he alone received no share of the treasure. It is quite indicative of the difference between regular and secular clergy that another ecclesiastic, the priest Juan de Sosa, did receive a share, though he was not actually present.

Valverde's legendary fame produced over the centuries a good deal of distorted information about his background, particularly in those rich mines of error, the seventeenth-century ecclesiastical chronicles. It was sometimes claimed, starting in almost contemporary times, that Valverde was from Trujillo, and, more extravagantly, that he was an actual relative of the Pizarros. Nevertheless, there is no doubt that he was from Oropesa; perhaps his father had been born in Trujillo or Cáceres, or had relatives there, though this is by no means certain. Any kinship between the Pizarros and the Valverdes remains unestablished and is highly unlikely, since the Pizarros gave great publicity to their family ties. The report of a late chronicler that fray Vicente's mother was a cousin of the Count of Oropesa is a sheer fabrication. Fray Vicente's father, Francisco de Valverde, was a servant of the Count. Porras Barrenechea, usually well informed, says that Francisco was the Count's chamberlain, and that the family of fray Vicente's mother was reputed to be *converso* (of Jewish descent). The servants of a high nobleman were in an ambiguous position. Francisco de Valverde doubtless partook of the attributes of both steward and hidalgo. Fray

Vicente's mother, it appears, was without the "doña." His sister came
to Peru in 1538 as doña Maria de Valverde, but she may have assumed
the title only on the strength of fray Vicente's new position as bishop.

Fray Vicente was by all odds the best educated of the men of Cajamarca, the only one known to have gone beyond the informal school-
ing given notaries and hidalgos to actual university training. He
studied for some years at Salamanca; at least this conclusion can be
drawn with some certainty from the fact that no sooner had he pro-
fessed in the Dominican order in Salamanca, in 1524, than he went to
the Colegio Mayor de San Gregorio in Valladolid and became a
colegial or full-fledged member. San Gregorio was a Dominican institution dedicated to advanced study and the preparation of university
instructors. For five years fray Vicente studied theology and philosophy
there and also perhaps helped with teaching. All the late Dominican
chroniclers say that he received the degree of master of theology, but
his modern biographer, Alberto María Torres, though also Dominican,
remains dubious on this point; indeed, no known contemporary source
confirms the chroniclers. Master or not, fray Vicente de Valverde was
formidably educated and fully cognizant of all aspects of the Spanish
tradition, both secular and ecclesiastic. He understood the total implications of the Spanish presence in Peru better than any other member
of the expedition, with the possible exception of Hernando Pizarro.
His letters show us a man with a well-rounded intelligence and emotional maturity, though not graced by exceptional elegance, vitality,
or originality.

The capitulations between Pizarro and the crown in 1529 provided
that six Dominicans should accompany the Peru expedition under fray
Reginaldo de Pedraza, receiving a modest royal subsidy. Just how fray
Vicente came to be picked, or offered himself, is not known. Of the six
friars who left Spain with Pizarro, only fray Vicente reached central
Peru; two died, and the rest gave up for reasons that are not clear. The
leader, fray Reginaldo, gave a poor account of himself. From Coaque
he returned to Panama, where he soon died and was found to have a
fortune in emeralds sewn into his clothes. Before long, fray Vicente
was the chief ecclesiastic of the expedition, cast in a pseudo-episcopal
role, and clearly predominant over the three or more secular priests
who took part in the conquest at various stages. Though it is doubtful
that he exercised great influence on decision making, fray Vicente was
regularly a part of Pizarro's high council, along with the royal treasury

officials, whether the matter at hand was the founding of a city or the execution of the Inca emperor.

It was natural, then, that fray Vicente rather than the secular priest Juan de Sosa should accompany the expedition in its climactic phase, the march to Cajamarca and the encounter with Atahuallpa. That encounter itself is so overlaid with myth and polemic that unequivocal statements on the subject become nearly impossible to make. It appears to the present writer that the purposes of Valverde's interview with the Inca were two: to fulfill the conditions of just war as provided through the Requirement, and, more immediately, to entice Atahuallpa into Pizarro's power if possible. Not only have the words of Valverde and Atahuallpa been reported in a hundred different versions, they were in all probability not understood by the distant onlookers at the time. It is certain that fray Vicente gave Atahuallpa a breviary; Atahuallpa hurled it down and rose in his litter, whereupon fray Vicente returned to the Spaniards, agitated and shouting. The shouts, whatever their actual content, were interpreted by the Spaniards as an exhortation to begin the attack as already planned.

Fray Vicente's real reward for his part in the events at Cajamarca was the bishopric of Cuzco (including all Peru). He was in any case eminently qualified, and, given his presence at Cajamarca, there was no doubt whom the Peruvian conquerors would pick as their candidate. Valverde departed for Spain in July or August of 1534, at the same time as the largest contingent of returnees, but his intention was different from theirs. With him went letters from the council of Jauja, and probably from Pizarro and others as well, requesting that Valverde be named bishop of Peru. A compatriot of fray Vicente's wrote to the Count of Oropesa asking him to intercede at court in favor of the son of faithful servants. Which of these various influences worked strongest on the king and the Council of the Indies is not known, but there was no reason for the crown to resist the petition, since it had already accepted far less promising candidates in similar cases. By August, 1535, the crown had presented fray Vicente for the new bishopric. After extensive deliberations with the Council of the Indies, he received instructions to investigate and report on all aspects of Peruvian life and government, including such delicate subjects as the distribution of encomiendas, the extent of tributes, and the management of the royal treasury. The Council commissioned him to carry out an actual audit of the Peruvian treasury accounts. In general it is clear that the

Council, following a classic design, hoped to create in Valverde an independent arm and check on Pizarro's government, as well as a source of information beyond what the tight-lipped Pizarro was prepared to divulge.

Not until January, 1537, did Pope Paul III finally issue the bulls creating the new diocese and making Valverde bishop. The crown, impatient, had already authorized fray Vicente to embark, but the bulls reached Spain before his departure in the spring of 1537. He arrived in Lima in April, 1538, at the head of a contingent of Dominicans, to find the first of the great civil wars already in progress.

Valverde's action as bishop was moderate and conscientious; his very moderation tended to favor the Pizarros, but he was not blatantly partisan. He pleaded (though without effect) for the life of the elder Almagro, and he requested (though again unsuccessfully) that Pizarro give the governorship of Almagro's area to his designated successor, Diego de Alvarado; he even married his sister to an Almagrist. The Almagrists, nevertheless, were left with the impression that he was their enemy. In his overall policies Valverde showed no signs whatever of having been influenced by his fellow Dominicans Las Casas and Victoria. His ideas fell within a more general pattern. He defended the church's jurisdiction, revenue, and privileges against secular encroachment; he opposed Indian slavery and permanent personal service (*yanaconaje*) for broad religious and human reasons; he worked for peace and against bloodshed. But he accepted as given the encomienda system and a permanent Spanish presence in Peru. The reports he sent back on the state of the land are extensive and full of a realistic wisdom. His suggestions for the subdivision of the area into governmental districts anticipated the modern boundaries of Bolivia, Peru, and Ecuador.

Several contemporaries praised Valverde's blameless life; Licenciado Gaspar de Espinosa said he was "without covetousness for temporal things." The judgment is essentially correct, but this does not mean that fray Vicente refrained from practices condoned by all Spaniards. Though he received no formal share at Cajamarca, he must have been given something for sustenance and his trip to Spain. Pizarro granted him an encomienda in Cuzco and another smaller one near Lima, for his personal service. As an individual he owned farm land outside Lima as well as a valuable lot next to the site of the future cathedral. (These things lend substance to an unverified report that Valverde planned to change the seat of his diocese from Cuzco to Lima.) As was standard practice, he hired a steward and an accountant for his estate. He is not known to have undertaken any special entrepreneurial activity, although in one letter to the Council he waxed enthusiastic about a search for emeralds in the Guayaquil area, the same interest that was the downfall of his colleague fray Reginaldo de Pedraza. His estate did not make him rich. At his death all he left behind, aside from the aforementioned land and lot, were numerous debts and some personal belongings. Among them were his books— theology, Terence, Nebrija.

Like many prominent churchmen, fray Vicente used his position to advance the welfare of his relatives. When he returned to Peru in 1538, he brought with him his brother Francisco, his sister doña María, some nephews, and other associates. By 1540 Francisco was an encomendero in Guayaquil. While in Spain, fray Vicente had arranged a marriage between doña María and Pedro Orgoños, brother of Rodrigo Orgoños from Oropesa, who was the elder Almagro's second in command and received the exalted title of Marshal. Pedro Orgoños soon received an encomienda in Lima; when he died, fray Vicente arranged for doña María to marry his own associate Dr. Juan Blázquez, whom he had also brought to Peru. At the time of Francisco Pizarro's assassination in 1541, Dr. Blázquez was serving as Lima's lieutenant governor.

The assassination and the ensuing rebellion of the younger Almagro indirectly brought fray Vicente's career to a close. The news reached him in the highlands, and he hurried to Lima, where he found his brother-in-law Dr. Blázquez being held prisoner; he himself was called on by the Almagrists to negotiate for the surrender of Cuzco, then in the hands of Pizarrists. Fray Vicente refused, publicly opposing the Almagrists' plans to take Cuzco. On All Saints' Day, 1541, he escaped from Lima by ship, accompanied by Blázquez and a party of friends and relatives, with the intention of meeting Vaca de Castro, the new royal governor, who was then in the Quito area. In Túmbez, fray Vicente disembarked and wrote a letter to the Audiencia in Panama (dated November 11), before continuing with his following toward the Guayaquil estuary in some Indian boats or rafts. On the way the intractable Indians of the island of Puná, who caused the Spaniards much grief at one time or another, attacked the party and killed them all. Gory details about fray Vicente's death, found in late sources, are probably nothing more than embroidery.

The Valverde family continued to be prominent in Peru. Though his brother Francisco died before many years, fray Vicente's nephew Francisco de Valverde Montalbo became an encomendero of Quito and eventually a knight of Santiago. Doña María de Valverde, after the death of Dr. Blázquez, married Licenciado Rodrigo Niño from Toledo, who became one of the great men of Lima. It also seems reasonable to suppose that a Pedro de Valverde from the archdiocese of Toledo, who came to occupy a canonry in the cathedral of Lima in 1553, owed his position to some kinship with Spanish Peru's most famous ecclesiastic.

N O T E S . Most of the sources for Valverde's life are brought together in *El Padre Valverde, ensayo biográfico y crítico*, by Alberto María Torres, O.P. Torres was able to consult documents from Dominican archives which the present writer has not seen. Porras in his "Diego de Silva," *Mar del Sur* 5, no. 15 (1950–1951), p. 32, mentions documents proving that fray Vicente's father, Francisco de Valverde, served as chamberlain of the Court of Oropesa, but was criticized for his marriage to Ana de Vallejeda, considered to be from a family of *conversos*. Porras gives no source, but he is to be trusted as always when he makes a categorical statement about the contents of a document. Porras does not specifically say that fray Vicente's mother was without the "doña," but he gives her name without it, while including the "doña" with other women who indeed had the title. Torres gives her name as "doña Ana Alvarez de Vallegeda y Toledo," basing himself on Marchese's *Sacro diario domenicano*, published in Naples in 1681 (*El padre Valverde*, p. 33). Using the same source, Torres states that fray Vicente was born "toward the end of the fifteenth century." More convincingly, he reasons that fray Vicente must have been born in 1501 or before in order to have completed so much study by 1524 that he could enter the Colegio Mayor de San Gregorio as a *colegial*.

The evidence reported by Porras makes fray Vicente the most nearly authenticated New Christian among the men of Cajamarca. Certainty in such a cloudy matter is hardly to be attained. But it is noteworthy that Rodrigo Orgoños, who was so close to Valverde that they arranged an alliance through marriage, was also widely considered to be of Jewish descent, and in his case there is copious court testimony (*CDIHC*, VI, 126–130).

An important source for Valverde is Porras, *Cartas*, full of references which are there indexed. Particularly essential are Valverde's own letters, pp. 309–311, 311–335, 428–432 and references to him on pp. 73 and 132. Also instructive are royal directives and appointments in Porras, *Cedulario*, II, 104, 112, 131, 133, 142, 155–157, 165, 167, 170, 173, 177–182 (general instructions to Valverde), 184, 187, 189, 192, 242, 287–288, 315, 323–324. Porras's short general discussion of Valverde is in Trujillo, *Relación*, pp. 69–70.

For Valverde's role in the events of Cajamarca, see *RANP* 1:567; Jerez, *Verdadera relación*, II, 332; Mena, "Conquista del Perú," pp. 85–86; Oviedo, *Historia*, V, 92; Pedro Pizarro, *Relación*, V, 178; Porras, *Cartas*, p. 80; Porras, in Trujillo, *Relación*, pp. 107–109; Trujillo, *Relación*, pp. 58–59. For his worldly affairs, see ANP, Salinas 1542–1543, ff.3, 10, 11, 536; HC 438, 451, 623, 630–645. Dr. Juan Blázquez is mentioned in *CDIHE*, XXVI, 195, and Cobo, *Obras*, II, 304–305; for doña María de Valverde see ANP, Salinas 1542–1543, ff.3, 49, 16 (2nd series), 115–116.

Further references are in AGI, Lima 565, vol. III, November 8, 1539; HC 38, 321, 450; *CDIHC*, VI, 411; *CDIHE*, XXVI, 195; *RANP* 1 (1920) :568; Cieza, *Chupas*, p. 129; Cobo, *Obras*, II, 304–305, 361, 386, 387; Egaña, *Historia*, p. 43; Gutiérrez de Santa Clara, *Quinquenarios*, III, 222, 224–226, 228; Pedro Pizarro, *Relación*, V, 185, 227, 229; Porras, "Dos documentos esenciales," *Revista Histórica* 17 (1948) :90; Porras, "Jauja," *Revista Histórica* 18 (1949–1950) :135; Vargas Ugarte, *Historia de la iglesia*, I, 134.

8. HIDALGOS

PERHAPS NOT ALL THE MEN included in this chapter were born to clear hidalgo status—there is reason for doubt in the cases of Agüero, Torres, Mesa, and two or three others. But most were of demonstrably gentle birth. Even more important, all passed for rather grand hidalgos in Peru. However hard it is to define the word "hidalgo" or to specify its exact range of application, by studying the lives of such men as these one can acquire a good subjective understanding of its meaning. These men and others like them define the word as it was being used in Peru in the 1530's.

Not all of the expedition's hidalgos will be found here. Most of the leaders (chapter 7) were also hidalgos of good standing, as were some of the clerks (chapter 9), and the men of affairs (chapter 10). Very petty or dubious hidalgos appear in chapter 11, and some famous names appear among the little-known figures of chapter 15.

Diego de Agüero

Age at Cajamarca: About 22 or 23	Place of origin: Deleitosa (north-
Role: Horseman and standard-	eastern Extremadura)
bearer	Parents: García de Agüero and
Share: 2 shares of gold and silver	María de Sandoval
	Literacy: Illiterate

Something of the fame of Diego de Agüero came down to the Lima of the nineteenth and twentieth centuries as an authentic, almost un-interrupted tradition, borne by generation after generation of his illustrious descendants. The stamp of nobility resulting from such a process is at the same time indelible and highly suspect. In his lifetime, Agüero was indeed a noble, imposing figure and one of the most important men in Peru, but his eminence stemmed more from personal qualities than from lineage or breeding.

Diego de Agüero was one of the men Pizarro recruited in Extremadura in 1529. Word of the enterprise of Peru must have been brought as far as the little town of Deleitosa, some twenty miles north of Trujillo—as provincial and isolated a village as there was in Spain. But no Spanish town was without some leavening of old and famous names. Agüeros from various places had been notable in feats of arms and in the royal court since the mid-thirteenth century. This the genealogists have shown beyond a doubt, but they have not shown any definite link between these noble Agüeros and the Agüeros of Deleitosa, other than the name itself. It is true that the name of Diego's father, García de Agüero, occurred also in the noble branch. This allows us to presume some connection, without telling us anything of its nature. The bearer of such a name could have been anything from the head of an extended noble house to his Moorish houseboy. The Deleitosa Agüeros may have been somewhere in the middle; the mere fact that Diego mentioned his parents in his will means that he was not unduly ashamed of them. As with all but a few of the men of Cajamarca, Diego's mother was not a "doña," though her name, Sandoval, had a good ring.

The model education which one enthusiast has praised in Diego de Agüero did not include the skills of reading and writing. He arrived in Peru unable to sign his name, and did not prove an apt pupil when he had to learn. This can be compared with the formidable literacy of the legitimate son of the Pizarro family, Hernando. In the first memorandum of his services prepared to be sent to the Spanish court in 1536,

Agüero did not claim to be an hidalgo, something never omitted by oversight, but rather based his whole petition for a coat of arms on his own actions. And when that honor was forthcoming, there was no mention of any previous family coat of arms to be incorporated into the new one, as the Pizarros and some others had. On balance, while Diego de Agüero may have had some hidalgo connections, there were many of his fellows who could surpass him in degree at birth.

The main quality of Agüero was that he was an authentic hero, not only with the typical Spanish heroism of austerity, undergoing hunger and disease and facing great odds, but with the dashing individual heroism of the Romans. At the civil war battle of Chupas he snatched away the enemy's banner; in the conquest of Quito he dismounted and attacked a band of Indians who were fortified on a stone bridge, an incident depicted on his coat of arms. Agüero was one of the first three Spaniards to see the valley of Jauja. After the conquest of Cuzco he and a companion were the first to explore upper Peru as far as Lake Titicaca. He was one of the very few men present at the conquest of both Cuzco and Quito. If some of the claims in his memorials appear exaggerated, they receive corroboration from other sources. The most powerful confirmation of their general truth was the way Diego de Agüero began to become legendary; his name might be supplied for any heroic act whose real performer had been forgotten. Thus the chronicler Gutiérrez de Santa Clara would have him among the first advance party of Spaniards to set eyes on the marvels of Cuzco.

Another aspect of Agüero was his generally upstanding character, combined with a certain disinclination to the partisanry that so permeated the Peruvian civil wars. Essentially allied with the Pizarros, he became the chief messenger between the two camps in the early days of the conquest. He brought the first news of the capture of the Inca to Almagro, and later the news of Almagro's agreement with Pedro de Alvarado to Pizarro. Each time the mission must have gone beyond message-bearing to diplomacy; Agüero was to get the consent of the other party to basic policy decisions taken without its knowledge. When royal provisions arrived, outlining the area to be governed by Almagro, Agüero in a now accustomed role rushed ahead with the news. But this time he went without being sent by the grudging Pizarros. It is told, without certain foundation, though it would fit the character of both Agüero and Pizarro, that Agüero not only hailed the new governor personally, but without authorization offered Almagro congratulations on behalf of the Pizarros. In 1537 Agüero spoke out against the Pizarrist plan to seize Almagro at a conference. Agüero was one of the few Spanish Peruvians admired and sought after by both sides in the civil wars. When the Almagrists held Lima briefly, in 1541, they took him into custody, but they allowed him to continue on the town council of Lima, as they did not some of their more bitter enemies, and when they retired to the highlands they took him along, still hoping to attract him to their side, until he managed to flee. But the Pizarrists were willing to put the interpretation on this that the Almagrists had seized Agüero as one of Pizarro's greatest friends. Agüero's goodness also spawned legends; one still current in the seventeenth century told of his maiming a prize horse to prove to his Indians that he valued human souls above animals.

Agüero's qualities earned him recognition from an early date. In the progress south in 1531 he was already leading small groups of men on dangerous missions, though because of his youth and the surfeit of leaders on the conquering expedition, he was not yet a captain. At Cajamarca he was one of the standard-bearers or ensigns; by 1536 he was being called captain; and in 1538 he reached the top of the ladder as captain of cavalry at the battle of Salinas. His encomienda of Lunahuaná was one of the best in the jurisdiction of Lima. He was a regidor on the council of Lima from the day of its foundation to his death, one of the three perpetual regidors named by Pizarro and then confirmed by the crown. He was one of only two of the conquerors to hold a permanent title as His Majesty's Captain.

Agüero's personal affairs flourished. In 1538 he married doña Luisa de Garay, daughter of Adelantado Francisco de Garay, ill-fated governor of Pánuco in Mexico. His son and namesake, born in 1542, had Governor Vaca de Castro for a godfather. He managed his estate well, and though he was no accountant himself, he entered into partnership with another man who was, and amassed holdings of houses, lands, and livestock equal to any in Lima.

His whole heritage, both property and aura of grandeur, passed on to his son when he died of an illness in October, 1544. Diego de Agüero the younger held the position of alcalde in Lima more often than any other man in Lima's history. In the mid-seventeenth century the Agüero entail was still held by a namesake, great-grandson of the original, and was considered by the chronicler Cobo to be the richest in Peru, if not in the Indies. By the eighteenth century most of the aristocrats of Lima had Diego de Agüero somewhere among their ancestors.

NOTES. Agüero said in 1537 that he was about twenty-eight (AGI, Lima 118, *probanza* of Sebastián de Torres); in 1541 that he was about thirty (AGI, Lima 204, *probanza* of Juan de León). He declares himself a native of Deleitosa in his will, published in *RANP* 6 (1926):157–170. A codicil is in BNP, A33, ff. 260–261. Two *probanzas de servicios* of Agüero are in AGI, Patronato 93, no. 6, ramo 3; and 92, no. 3.

Other references are in AGI, Lima 565, vol. III, Sept. 6, 1538; Patronato 93, no. 10, ramo 1; 132, no. 2, ramo 1; ANP, PA 17, 72, 108, 162, 168, 248, 689, 690, 738, 795; Salinas 1538–1540, ff.79, 481; Salinas 1542–1543, f.595; HC 14, 33, 290, 328, 432–434; *CDIHC*, IV, 198, 412–413, 417; *RANP* 11:226; Borregán, *Crónica*, p. 43; Busto, "El capitán Melchor Verdugo," *Revista Histórica* 24 (1959):323; Cieza, *Salinas*, p. 186; Cieza, *Tercera parte*, in *Mercurio Peruano* 36 (1955):472; 38 (1957):262; 39 (1958):584; Cobo, *Obras*, I, 380, 381; II, 298, 304; Diego Fernández, *Historia*, I, 15, 33, 35; II, 128; Garcilaso, *Obras*, III, 193; Gutiérrez de Santa Clara, *Quinquenarios*, II, 160, 171, 172, 247, 249–251, 253, 258, 259, 262, 265, 276; III, 226, 403; *Libros de Cabildos de Lima*, I, 15; Lohmann Villena, "Restitución por conquistadores," *Anuario de Estudios Americanos* 23 (1966):21–89; Loredo, *Los repartos*, pp. 82, 227; Pedro Pizarro, *Relación*, V, 198, 200, 228; Porras, *Cartas*, pp. 412, 436, 452, 477; Porras, *Cedulario*, II, 357, 386; Torres Saldamando, *Libro primero de cabildos*, I, 388, 389; II, 49–50; Urteaga, "Don Diego de Agüero y Sandoval," *RANP* 6 (1928):149–155.

Information about Agüero's descendants will be found in his will, above, and in ANP, Gutiérrez 1545–1555, f.783; Salinas 1546–1548, ff. 1163–1164; HC 747, 790; *RANP* 11 (1938):226; *Libros de Cabildos de Lima*, VI, 1, 332; Torres Saldamando, *Libro primero de cabildos*, II, 33–48.

Hernando de Aldana

Age at Cajamarca: About 32
Role: Footman
Share: 1 full share of silver and gold

Place of origin: Valencia de Alcántara (western Extremadura)
Parents: Mother, Mari Prieto; father not known, but doubtless an Aldana
Literacy: Could sign well, probably literate

Recruited in Spain in 1529, Hernando de Aldana was related to a prominent family of Cáceres who sent their share of men to Peru, including Lorenzo de Aldana, renowned for his high lineage, arrogance, and ability to govern. Though kept at a little distance by his Cáceres relatives, Hernando considered himself an hidalgo, and no one disputed the claim. Not only was he one of the very few able to get a personal royal recommendation at the time of the Toledo agreements, before the success of the Peruvian enterprise opened all doors, but the document contained the key formula "relative of servants of ours," which always meant good connections, if not gentle birth.

Aldana had a conspicuous part in the events at Cajamarca. Through varying reports it can be discerned that he had learned to speak a little Quechua by that time—he was perhaps the first Spaniard to do so. When Atahuallpa halted his procession near the waiting Spaniards and began to pitch tents, Pizarro sent Aldana alone to persuade him to come before sunset. During the interview Atahuallpa asked for, or by some accounts even tried to seize, Aldana's sword, and Aldana left in a hurry, having secured a promise that the Inca would come soon.

At the founding of Cuzco in 1534 Aldana settled there and received a good encomienda. Within a few years he seemed on his way to becoming one of the *principales* or leading men of Peru. He performed well during the year-long siege of Cuzco by the Indians, and in 1537 was on the city council, closely associated with the Pizarro party, as was normal in view of his Cáceres-Trujillo connections. Yet in the following years he was little heard of, and he failed to cooperate with the rebellion of Gonzalo Pizarro in 1544. So alienated did he become that in 1546 a lieutenant of Gonzalo's hanged him for suspicion of plotting against the Pizarro cause. His death, accompanied by prolonged laments, was a pitiful spectacle that turned many against the rebellion once and for all.

NOTES. Hernando's relation to the Aldanas of Cáceres is based mainly on the following evidence: That Francisco de Godoy of Cáceres, whose mother was an Aldana, gave Hernando a power of attorney in Jauja in October, 1533 (HC 33), and that Hernando appeared in the company of Lorenzo de Aldana in Lima in October, 1537 (HC 278, 287). The Cáceres Aldanas did not make much of their connection with Hernando, as can be seen from the way the three most illustrious representatives of the clan, Francisco de Godoy, Lorenzo de Aldana, and Perálvarez Holguín published their relationship as cousins and were much in each other's company, but left Hernando out of consideration. Lorenzo de Aldana, an informant of Cieza de León, told about his reunion with Perálvarez when he returned from Chile, but never mentioned that he knew Hernando de Aldana, though he was thrown together with him in even more striking circumstances (Cieza, *Salinas*, pp. 21–30).

In 1540 Hernando said that he was about forty (AGI, Lima 204, *probanza* of Pedro del Barco). He seems not to have made a direct statement about his birthplace, though his associations leave little doubt that he must have been from Extremadura. The money he sent home with Gonzalo de Pineda in 1535 was listed as belonging to "Hernando de Aldana, native of Valencia" (AGI, Justicia 723, no. 1). Spain has many Valencias, but the one in closest connection with Cáceres was Valencia de Alcántara. Aldana gives his mother's name in ANP, PA 119. Other references are in AGI, Indiferente General 1801, records of ship *San Miguel*, 1535; ANP, PA 138; HC 260; *CDIHE*, XXVI, 221–232; *DHA*, I, 40; Cieza, *Quito* (Serrano y Sanz, ed.), p. 203; Cieza, *Tercera parte*, in *Mercurio Peruano* 38 (1957):253–254; Gutiérrez de Santa Clara, *Quinquenarios*, II, 186; III, 84–85; Oviedo, *Historia*, V, 86, 175, 280; Pedro Pizarro, *Relación*, V, 178, 208, 211; Porras, *Cedulario*, I, 9; II, 127; Porras, in Trujillo, *Relación*, p. 106; Roa y Ursúa, *El reyno de Chile*, pp. 11–12; Trujillo, *Relación*, p. 57.

Pedro Barrantes

Age at Cajamarca: About 25
Role: Horseman
Share: Double share of gold and silver

Place of origin: Trujillo (Extremadura)
Degree of literacy: Good signature, probably literate

The Barrantes family was a well-known house of Trujillo, connected with the Pizarros and the Orellanas. When an inquiry was held in Trujillo in 1529 into Francisco Pizarro's lineage for admission to the Order of Santiago a Juan Barrantes was among the witnesses, one of the very few granted the epithet "señor." Pedro Barrantes must have been this man's relative, perhaps his son, and he was also related to Juan Pizarro de Orellana, thought by Porras Barrenechea to be the noblest representative of the Pizarros in Peru. He had blood ties with the immediate family of Hernando Pizarro as well. There is little doubt, then, that Barrantes was an hidalgo, by local standards, and that he joined the expedition when Pizarro was in Trujillo in 1529.

Most of the well-born among the 1529 recruits returned home to Trujillo quickly. Barrantes took part in the conquest through the

HIDALGOS 215

Spanish foundation of Cuzco; he left in 1534 when Pizarro issued a blanket license for all to return who wished to do so. Back in Trujillo, his wealth brought him a position on the municipal council, where he still sat in 1550.

NOTES. In Seville, in 1535, Barrantes said he was about twenty-five and also declared himself a native of Trujillo (AGI, Patronato 93, no. 5, ramo 2). In 1550, a citizen and regidor of Trujillo, he said he was about forty-three (AGI, Justicia 1082, no. 1, ramo 4). See also ANP, PA 125; CDIHC, VII, 153; Busto, *Francisco Pizarro*, p. 47; and Porras, "Dos documentos esenciales," *Revista Histórica* 17 (1948):29–32, 52.

Alonso Briceño

Age at Cajamarca: About 26 or 27
Role: Horseman
Share: 2 shares of silver;
  1 8/9 shares of gold

Place of origin: Benavente, near
  Zamora (León)
Degree of literacy: Literate

By now the reader doubtless recognizes the Thirteen, the alleged heroes of Gallo Island, who stayed with the Peruvian enterprise when it reached a low ebb in 1527 and who accompanied Pizarro and Bartolomé Ruiz on the first survey of the coast of Peru proper. Though their names have become synonymous with perseverance, only two arrived with Pizarro at Cajamarca—the Greek Pedro de Candía and Alonso Briceño. Briceño had come to the area of Panama and Nicaragua around 1525; as to his Spanish background we have the testimony of his beautiful and fluent signature and his connection with an Antonio Briceño of Benavente, a notary. Also, one of his fellows considered him an expert judge of the quality of silver—but that could be said of many of the conquerors.

It does not appear that Briceño, as a very young man not long in the Indies in 1527, had at that time developed an independent position or fortune like some of the others of the Thirteen, who were able to stand somewhat aside from the rigors of the conquest and profit from it commercially. That is perhaps the explanation for Briceño's presence in the expedition of 1531–1532. As one of the Thirteen, he was treated with respect; his name stands high on the roll of Cajamarca, just after the captains. Both his background in Spain and his seniority in the conquest made it natural that he should be appointed to the council of Jauja in 1534. This could have been the beginning of a princely career in Peru, but instead Briceño left the country before serving out even his one-year term as regidor. By September, 1534, he had arrived in Panama, en route to Spain, with a fortune in gold and silver, leaving of the Thirteen only Pedro de Candía, Nicolás de Ribera, and Juan de la Torre to stay in Peru permanently. What he did in Spain is not known. No doubt he went to his home town, Benavente. Later, in 1545, probably through his influence, another Briceño from Benavente was appointed a secretary to the Royal Audiencia of Peru.

N O T E S . Briceño's portion of gold fell five hundred pesos short of two full shares and may have been arrived at by arbitrarily taking away that amount, rather than by using fractions. The reason for the deduction was probably an accidental or objective factor, such as a lame horse, and not any displeasure with Briceño.

In 1534 Briceño gave his age three times; twice as thirty (AGI, Patronato 93, no. 4, ramo 1, and Lima 204, *probanza* of Hernán González), and once as twenty-eight or twenty-nine (AGI, Patronato 150, no. 6, ramo 2). Gregorio de Sotelo, also from the Zamora area, once testified that Briceño was a native of Benavente (AGI, Patronato 185, ramo 11, or printed in *CDIAO*, X, 243). Zárate, *Historia*, II, 464, also gives Briceño, one of the Thirteen, as from Benavente.

Other references are in AGI, Indiferente General 1801, records of ship *San Miguel*, 1535; Lima 566, vol. V, June 27, 1545; Patronato 150, no. 3, ramo 2; ANP, PA 18, 25, 84, 124, 133, 138; HC 37, 38; Busto, "Alonso Briceño," *Mercurio Peruano* 42 (1961):479–485; Carlos A. Romero, *Los héroes de la isla del Gallo*, p. 41; Montoto, *Nobiliario*, pp. 324–325.

Ginés de Carranza

Age at Cajamarca: About 22
Role: Horseman
Share: Double share of gold and silver

Place of origin: Probably the Granada area
Extent of literacy: Good signature, doubtless literate

For a time Carranza had been in the entourage of Governor Pedrarias de Avila of Nicaragua, along with his good friend Luis Maza, and he came directly from there to Peru, probably in Hernando de Soto's contingent. His career in Peru was brief indeed, but he had one of the best horses, and he accompanied Soto on the hazardous first interview with Atahuallpa, thereby winning mention in one of the chronicles of the conquest. He returned to Spain among the first to receive license in 1533, possibly sick or wounded, since he certainly was not old. In Spain he proceeded to Granada, where he became a *veinticuatro*, or city councilman, a high enough honor anywhere, and all the more so in a center of the importance of the old capital of the Moors. As *veinticuatro*, Carranza called himself "don," a title eluding all others except the three *adelantados*. No doubt his new wealth acquired him the post, but a certain degree of education and the appearance of good breeding were prerequisite to eligibility, making it certain that Carranza's origins were, at the least, not blatantly plebeian. His comrade Luis Maza joined him in Granada around 1535 or 1536, and both were there together in 1539. Carranza remained in Granada into the 1540's, when he gave testimony on behalf of Hernando Pizarro.

N O T E S . Carranza declared in 1539 that he was twenty-nine (AGI, Justicia 1124, no. 5, ramo 1). His residence and position in Granada at that time is the basis for assigning his regional origin. Ordinarily such evidence would be sufficient for practical certainty, but since Granada was a new area as well as an important one attracting people from various places, one must leave room for possible doubt. Use of the title "don" may have been more liberal in Granada than in other places. Luis Maza, as high constable of the Audiencia of Granada, also appears with the title, but it is then dropped, whereas with Carranza it is repeated. Other references are in ANP, PA 34, 119; *CDIHC*, VII, 156; Oviedo, *Historia*, V. 92.

Rodrigo de Chaves

Age at Cajamarca: About 25
Role: Horseman
Share: Double share of gold
and silver

Place of origin: Ciudad Rodrigo
(kingdom of Leon)
Extent of literacy: Excellent signature, doubtless literate

While many of the men of Cajamarca had experience in Nicaragua and Panama, Chaves was one of only four or five who had taken part in the earlier stages of the discovery of Peru. He was not among the Thirteen of Gallo Island, yet he seems to have been in the good graces of the leaders of the expedition of 1531–1532, for he received a royal appointment to the council of Túmbez in April, 1530, long before the Spaniards had reached the Peru of the Incas. In the end, Túmbez did not become a Spanish city and Chaves could not occupy his seat.

This probably disturbed him very little; no sooner had the main body of the conquerors returned to Jauja, in 1534, after taking Cuzco, than Chaves began making preparations to return, and he reached Seville by 1535. He may have been influenced in his decision by a bad leg wound suffered in a skirmish with Indians on the outskirts of Cuzco. In Spain he returned immediately to his home, Ciudad Rodrigo, and was on the municipal council there by 1541. That he was able to do so sheds a certain amount of light on his social origins, making it appear that he had at least some connection with the proud Chaves clans of the western border country of Spain.

N O T E S . It has often been assumed, as this writer originally assumed, that Rodrigo de Chaves was from Trujillo, because the Chaveses were an important family there, close to the Pizarros, and many of them went to Peru, including at least one Rodrigo de Chaves. But the name Chaves, originally Portuguese-Galician, was common from north to south, and there was a branch in Ciudad Rodrigo. The Chaves of Cajamarca is declared a native of Ciudad Rodrigo in AGI, Justicia 1126, no. 2, ramo 1, in a memorandum of Gregorio de Sotelo. In the same *legajo* Chaves twice declares himself a citizen of Ciudad Rodrigo. Here and in some other sources he gives his age in round numbers which would result in a birthdate between 1506 and 1509; his most exact statement is that he was twenty-six or twenty-seven in 1534 (Patronato 150, no. 6, ramo 2).

There are other references to Chaves in AGI, Contaduría 1825, records from Cajamarca, May, 1533; Lima 204, *probanza* of Hernán González; Patronato 93, no. 4, ramo 1; 150, no. 3, ramo 2; ANP, PA 18, 52; HC 32, 37, 38, 40; Porras, *Cedulario*, I, 88; Trujillo, *Relación*, p. 63.

Ruy Hernández Briceño

Age at Cajamarca: About 29
Role: Horseman
Share: 2 1/8 shares of gold and silver

Place of origin: Badajoz (western Extremadura)
Extent of literacy: Very good signature, doubtless literate

Hernández Briceño had both of the standard ingredients of success in the Indies—good lineage (or fairly good) and long experience. As to his lineage, in 1534 he raised the modest enough claim that he was an "honored person and hidalgo," this being not nearly as strong as the reverse word order, but at the time few of his companions were prepared to claim even that much. In the matter of experience, he had been in Panama and Nicaragua since the early 1520's, and had had an encomienda in Nicaragua. When he left Panama with the 1531 expedition, in the company of his best friend, Alonso de Medina, also a Badajoz man, he brought with him a good horse, equipment, and slaves.

These qualities, added, we may assume, to a good presence, achieved quick recognition. Hernández Briceño's name appears near the top of the roll of Cajamarca, among the captains, and he received a larger share than Captains Mena and Salcedo. It is possible that he had some position of command on the day Atahuallpa was taken. We do know that immediately afterward he acted as captain of Governor Pizarro's guard. He was named to the first council of Jauja, the forerunner of the country's capital. But all this was not enough to hold him. Hernández Briceño left Peru in 1534, still accompanied by Alonso de Medina. On the ship to Seville he registered gold and silver worth some 24,000 pesos; also among his effects was a personal recommendation to the king from Francisco Pizarro. He was back in his native Badajoz before the end of 1535. There he founded a family that in 1589 still looked back to him and tried to exist on his reputation and services.

NOTES. In 1534 Hernández Briceño gave his age as about thirty-one (AGI, Patronato 150, no. 6, ramo 2). An acquaintance testified that he was a Badajoz native (AGI, Patronato 185, ramo 11), and his associations confirm this again and again. His *probanza de servicios*, made in Jauja in 1534, is to be found in AGI, Patronato 93, no. 4, ramo 1.

Other references are in AGI, Contaduría 1825, records from Isle of Puná, December 1, 1531; Indiferente General 1801, records of ship *San Miguel*, 1535; Justicia 723, no. 1; 1126, no. 2, ramo 1; ANP, PA, 113, 139, 140, 146, 148, 169; HC 30; Busto, "Ruy Hernández Briceño, el guardián de Atahualpa," *Cuadernos del Seminario de Historia del Instituto Riva-Agüero*, no. 7, pp. 5–7; Porras, *Cartas*, p. 121. Busto considers that Ruy Hernández as captain of Pizarro's guard was responsible also for guarding Atahuallpa, which is probably true.

Juan de Herrera

Age at Cajamarca: About 19	Place of origin: Trujillo
Role: Footman	(Extremadura)
Share: ¾ share of gold;	Extent of literacy: Good signature,
⅞ share of silver	doubtless literate

Herrera was so young and new in the Indies, having left Spain with the Pizarros in 1530, that he stayed very largely within the bounds of his Trujillo regional group. Though cast largely in the role of a dependent, he was treated with a certain respect, apparently because of family connections in Trujillo.

After Cajamarca, Herrera went on to Cuzco and enrolled as a citizen there, but by 1535 he was on his way to Spain, carrying the then vast sum of 25,000 pesos to Trujillo for Juan Pizarro. En route, in Lima, he took some of the amount entrusted to him to buy a horse that Juan Pizarro wanted. But back in Trujillo, Pizarro representative Juan Cortés sued Herrera for the missing money and collected, despite crystal-clear proof that the transaction had taken place and that Juan Pizarro had approved of it. All this left Herrera understandably bitter, and he was henceforth more enemy than friend of the Pizarro family, particularly of Hernando Pizarro. However, even after the conquest of Peru, Trujillo was more than a Pizarro bailiwick. By 1544 Juan de Herrera was on the Trujillo city council, and he was still holding a seat in the year of 1577, having won a lifetime of honor and importance by spending some four years of his youth in the Indies.

N O T E S . Herrera's share of the silver was 158 marks, only a fraction from 7/8; his exact share of the gold was 3,385 pesos, 55 pesos more than 3/4. Possibly the amount is a mistake for 3,885, which would have been 7/8, like his silver share, or possibly the distributors started to give Herrera 7/8, then decided it was too much for a mere boy and arbitrarily reduced it by 500 pesos.

The estimate of Herrera's birthdate as c.1513 is based on his statement in 1545 that he was thirty-two (AGI, Justicia 1174, no. 1, ramo 3), ignoring his statement in 1577 (AGI, Patronato 93, no. 4, ramo 3) that he was sixty-one, not only on the general grounds that many Spaniards did not keep reliable count of their age over fifty, but because this would have made him about fourteen on leaving Spain and sixteen at Cajamarca; yet Pedro Pizarro, who was left in San Miguel as too young to fight, was already about seventeen. In Seville, in 1535, Herrera is called a native of Trujillo (AGI, Justicia 723, no. 1).

Proceedings initiated by Herrera to recover the money paid for Juan Pizarro's horse, with extensive testimony, are in AGI, Justicia 1053, no. 5. Other references are in AGI, Indiferente General 1801, records of ship *San Miguel*, 1535; Justicia 1052, no. 3, ramo 3; Patronato 109, ramo 4;

APS, 1536, oficio XV, libro II, October 4; ANP, PA 64, 118, 121, 125; *CDIHE*, XXVI, 221–232; Porras, "Dos documentos esenciales," *Revista Histórica* 17 (1948):31.

Diego Maldonado

Age at Cajamarca: About 26 or 28
Role: Horseman
Share: 1¾ shares of gold;
  2 shares of silver

Place of origin: Dueñas, in the
  district of Palencia in Old Castile
Parents: Francisco Maldonado and
  Catalina Nieto
Extent of literacy: Fully literate

Neither of the two Maldonados at Cajamarca was from Salamanca, where the noble family of that name had its roots. But though Diego Maldonado was born in the small Old Castilian town of Dueñas, he had a connection through his father with the Maldonados of Salamanca, and indeed was often thought to be a Salamanca native. Diego had a good education, and that, added to his identification with an illustrious lineage, sufficed for him to pass as a very resplendent hidalgo in Peru.

An isolated reference seems to imply that Maldonado had been in the Indies since about 1525, but no more is known. He joined the expedition in Panama, more respected for himself than for the poor horse he rode, which brought his share of the treasure of Cajamarca down below the normal for a horseman. A better measure of his position was his appointment to the first council of Jauja in 1534. For some reason he thereafter changed his citizenship to Cuzco, where he was soon a permanent member of the council by royal appointment, as well as repeatedly alcalde. He was not particularly skilled or interested in war, and he never or hardly ever led a company in Peru's civil conflicts, but he did lead some men into an Indian skirmish in the early period and was ever after styled Captain Diego Maldonado.

Above all he was "Maldonado the Rich." He received the encomienda of Andahuaylas, on the northern edge of Cuzco's jurisdiction, variously rated from first to sixth in the whole Cuzco district, and by all odds one of the best in the country. With this base he carried on a massive and systematic drive to increase his wealth; by 1541 he had a large crew of stewards and tribute collectors working on the encomienda, while most of his fellows were still contenting themselves with from one to three or four. He came to own thousands of llamas, as well as increasing numbers of Spanish stock, and far-flung lands, farms, and real estate. Maldonado was one of the largest dealers in the supply trade to the mines of Potosí, which was Cuzco's lifeline after the middle 1540's.

In the civil wars Maldonado's action was mainly nondescript. He did become important in the Gonzalo Pizarro rebellion, more as a political than a military figure. At the beginning he was reluctant to support the movement. When Pizarro left him in charge of Cuzco in 1544, he precipitated an abortive counterrevolt and was only grudgingly pardoned. Later the Pizarrists tortured him to find out if he had been spreading defamatory letters against them as rumored. Maldonado's defection to the side of the king in 1547 was a major blow to the rebel cause. In 1554, during the revolt of Francisco Hernández Girón, Maldonado received a leg wound from which he never fully recovered.

Maldonado married a doña Francisca de Guzmán, but never had any legitimate heirs, so he legitimated his two children by an Indian noblewoman. He arranged the marriage of the daughter, doña Beatriz, to don Martín de Guzmán of Salamanca, with a huge dowry which don Martín soon dissipated. Doña Beatriz died in Salamanca. The son, Juan Alvarez Maldonado, became involved in the mestizo revolts of the 1560's, but eventually settled down, inherited the bulk of his father's estate, and became an important figure in Cuzco. Later in the decade he led an expedition to explore the eastern lowlands; it was a disaster of which he was almost the sole survivor. Diego Maldonado himself died of an illness in Ica in 1570, on his way from frequently visited Lima to Cuzco.

NOTES. Maldonado gave his age vaguely several times; his most definite statement on the subject was that he was about thirty in 1534 (AGI, Patronato 93, no. 4, ramo 1). His birthplace is given as Dueñas, in his will, in AHC, Antonio Sánchez, 4, ff. 538–549, extracted in *RAHC* 4 (1953):117. Garcilaso, in *Obras*, II, 265, says that he was a native of Salamanca. His *probanza de servicios* is in AGI, Patronato 93, no. 11, ramo 2. Extremely valuable is Busto's article "Maldonado el Rico, señor de los Andahuaylas," *Revista Histórica* 26 (1962–1963):113–145, which follows Maldonado's career closely through the conquest and the civil wars, using several sources not consulted by this writer. However, the psychological interpretation of Maldonado there given borders on flippancy.

Two important points of fact made by Busto require some discussion.

First, he is wrong in assuming (p. 114) that Diego Maldonado was the "Maldonado, servant of the Marqués," who was in Cuzco around 1534 or 1535. As Pedro Pizarro, source of the quote, makes clear later, this man was the Francisco Maldonado from Ledesma (near Salamanca), who later served Gonzalo Pizarro as envoy and captain, and was executed in 1548 (Pedro Pizarro, *Relación*, V, 196, 205; *CDIAO*, XX, 527). Second, it is not positive, indeed it is improbable, that our Maldonado was the one who distinguished himself, the chroniclers say, on the loyalist side in the battle of Chupas in 1542. Busto (p. 121) follows Garcilaso's comment that the man was "Diego Maldonado, who later acquired the surname of the Rich" (*Obras*, III, 206). This might stand unchallenged, except that Garcilaso took his list of those prominent at Chupas from Agustín de Zárate (*Historia*, II, 506), making slight changes where he saw fit. Zárate's original fails to call this Maldonado either "the Rich" or a citizen of Cuzco, but rather includes him among those who had previously belonged to the party of Almagro the elder. This does not seem to apply to our Diego Maldonado.

There were innumerable Diego Maldonados in Peru in the conquest period. The principal ones: (1) a veteran of the Isthmus who accompanied the 1531 expedition and at first overshadowed Maldonado the Rich, but who was not at Cajamarca; (2) a man who was prominent in Almagro's Chile expedition of 1535–1537 (this was probably the person mentioned for his action at Chupas); and (3) Diego Maldonado de Alamos, who came to Peru very early and, like Maldonado the Rich, was a citizen and encomendero of Cuzco. The two sat on Cuzco's council together for many years. Busto gives further information on these Maldonados and others (pp. 135–137), but it should be noted that Maldonado de Alamos was from Fontiveros in Old Castile, not from Salamanca as Busto says (ANP, Alzate, f. 692).

For Maldonado's children, see ANP, Salinas 1546–1548, f.280, and AGI, Patronato 93, no. 11, ramo 2. Doña Beatriz and her husband appear in AGI, Patronato 102, ramo 5, and ANP, Alzate, f.332. For Juan Alvarez Maldonado, who was also called Juan Arias Maldonado, see *RAHC*, pp. 115–116, 122, 141; Busto, "Maldonado el Rico," pp. 131–132; Garcilaso, *Obras*, II, 269–270.

Other references to Maldonado the Rich are in AGI, Contaduría 1824, records from Cuzco, March, 1536; Lima 110, Relación de la ciudad del Cuzco; 204, *probanza* of Diego Rodríguez; Patronato 97, no. 1, ramo 1; 109, ramo 4; 114, ramo 2; 185, ramo 11; 192, no. 1, ramo 4; AHC, Libros de cabildos de Cuzco, I, ff. 75–77, 153; *RANP* 1 (1920):513–518; Cieza, *Quito* (Jiménez, ed.), pp. 90–92, 95, 98; Cieza, *Tercera parte*, in *Mercurio Peruano* 36 (1955):465; Loredo, *Alardes y derramas*, p. 116; Pérez de Tudela, *Gasca*, II, 256, 356; Porras, *Cedulario*, II, 138.

Gonzalo Maldonado

Age at Cajamarca: In early 20's
Role: Footman
Share: 1 full share of gold
    and silver

Place of origin: Astorga, in the
    kingdom of Leon
Extent of literacy: Excellent signature,
    doubtless literate

Though Gonzalo Maldonado chanced to be on foot the day of the events of Cajamarca, he was as well considered as his mounted namesake, Diego Maldonado. There is no evidence that the two shared anything more than their noble-sounding name, even though they both joined the expedition in Panama and had family connections in the kingdom of Leon. Their homes were many miles apart, and there were many branches of Maldonados. Gonzalo appears on the roll of Cajamarca near the head of the infantry and next to Juan de Valdevieso, who was the clearest hidalgo of all the conquerors and Gonzalo's close friend. At the founding of Cuzco, Maldonado received the sought-after post of *alguacil mayor*, or chief constable. Taken all together, his name, his signature, his associations, and the treatment accorded him make it clear that Gonzalo Maldonado was or was thought to be of very good birth.

After resisting the impulse to return with the wave of 1534, Maldonado left the country in early 1536, arriving in Seville the same year, with his mind still not made up completely about his future. In Spain he went to court, as so many did, but rather than negotiate for a coat of arms, he obtained a royal recommendation to the governor of Peru and a license ex post facto to retain his encomienda while in Spain for a visit. Such licenses, however, were not worth the ink expended on them unless the licensee had made clear his intentions at the time he left Peru. Maldonado, either realizing this or seduced by his homeland, in the end never went back to the Indies. He settled in Ponferrada, near Astorga, and was still a citizen there in 1541.

NOTES. Maldonado said in 1541 that he was "thirty or over" (AGI, Justicia 1126, no. 2, ramo 1), which seems to justify placing his birthdate c.1508–1511, making him twenty-one or over at Cajamarca, but not by very much. Maldonado once said he was a native of Astorga (AGI, Patronato 93, no. 6, ramo 1), and another report concurs (*CDIAO*, X, 280); his setting in Ponferrada, a somewhat larger center nearby, conforms to a general pattern.

Maldonado and Juan de Valdevieso were extremely close friends, perhaps partners. They were from the same region, they appear together on the roll of Cajamarca and at the founding of Cuzco; Maldonado gave Valdevieso general powers to act on his behalf, and, when Maldonado left Peru, Valdevieso sent back a fortune in silver with him.

Other references are in AGI, Contaduría 1824, records from Cuzco, May–July, 1535; Justicia 1124, no. 2; Justicia 1125, suit over estate of Francisco Martín de Alburquerque; Patronato 109, ramo 4; 185, ramo 10; ANP, PA 776; HC 50; Porras, *Cedulario*, II, 206; Porras, "Dos documentos esenciales," *Revista Histórica* 17 (1948):91–93.

Luis Maza

Age at Cajamarca: About 28
Role: Horseman
Share: Double share of gold and silver

Place of origin: Probably the Granada area
Extent of literacy: Literate

Luis Maza had been in the Indies some eight or nine years, since about 1523 or 1524. For most of that time he had been in Nicaragua as a retainer of Governor Pedrarias de Avila. Since he was ubiquitous as a witness to notifications and statements, one presumes that he acted as a constable. Perhaps he was connected with the Bernaldino de Maza who was constable in the town of Trujillo, Honduras, in 1529.

After the death of Pedrarias in 1531, Maza and other dependents of Pedrarias were left without a patron, at the mercy of Pedrarias's old enemy Licenciado Castañeda, who as *alcalde mayor* succeeded to the governorship. Maza joined the contingent of Hernando de Soto, arriving in Peru at the island of Puná in late 1531, and from there all the way to Cuzco he was one of the horsemen at Soto's side in the missions of greatest peril and most honor. Like many others he left the country in 1534, never having shown any inclination to become involved in the affairs of Peru, though he would have been a good candidate for a seat on the council of one of the main towns. Back in Spain he went to Granada to join his old friend Ginés de Carranza, who had been with him in Nicaragua and Peru, but had gone to Spain right after Cajamarca, in 1533, and was now sitting in honor on the municipal council of Granada. Maza exceeded even this degree of success by becoming chief constable of the Audiencia of Granada. While he doubtless bought the post, no one but a literate, minimally able man could have held it. Apparently Maza was by profession a bureaucrat or law-enforcer, one of the very few of our men who could be so described. It is extremely likely that he was from the Granada area originally, in the broader sense of southeastern Spain. Not only did he return there, but the name Maza was very rare among Castilians and common in the region of Valencia. Of two Mazas in Peru later, one was from the kingdom of Aragon and the other from Baena, north of Granada. Sometime in the 1520's or 1530's a don Pedro Maza was governor of Alicante.

NOTES. In Granada, in 1539, Maza said he was "over twenty-five" (AGI, Justicia 1124, no. 5, ramo 1); in 1540 he made the more exact statement that he was thirty-six (AGI, Justicia 1052, no. 6). His *probanza de servicios*, made in Panama in 1534, is in AGI, Patronato 150, no. 6, ramo 2. Other references are in AGI, Indiferente General 1204, no. 44; ANP, PA 85, 93; *CDIHN*, II, 77, 81, 182, 194, 195, 504, 505; Oviedo, *Historia*, V, 92. See also Ginés de Carranza.

For the other Mazas, see ANP, Alzate, f.938; *CDIHN*, I, 369; Enríquez de Guzmán, *Vida y costumbres*, p. 19; Thayer Ojeda, *Formación*, II, 226.

Alonso de Medina

Age at Cajamarca: About 29	Place of origin: Badajoz
Role: Horseman	(western Extremadura)
Share: 1⁹⁄₁₀ shares of gold;	Father: Alonso de Medina
2 shares of silver	Extent of literacy: Could sign,
	probably literate

In Peru Alonso de Medina twice identified himself as the son of Alonso de Medina, citizen of Badajoz, as though his father were a well-known figure. Perhaps he was; in 1538 Alonso de Medina the elder was one of the witnesses called to prove Hernando de Soto's nobility of lineage so that he could be admitted to the Order of Santiago. The elder Medina had known Soto's parents and grandparents, so it is quite probable that young Alonso and Soto had been acquainted since childhood. Both seem to have belonged to the same sphere of responsible burghers and very minor gentry.

By the time of Cajamarca, Alonso de Medina was an experienced and respected man, much like his friend and Badajoz compatriot, Ruy Hernández Briceño. He had been in the region of Panama and Nicaragua since about 1524; in 1527 he was on the municipal council of the ephemeral city of Bruselas in the Costa Rican area. After that he was in León, Nicaragua, where he must have come into contact again with Hernando de Soto. Yet he did not accompany Soto to Peru, but in 1529 went with Bartolomé Ruiz to Panama and was with the 1531 expedition from the beginning. He is seen constantly in the company of other Badajoz men, particularly Ruy Hernández, from whom he was inseparable. Medina as far as we know held no posts of honor or command in Peru, but something of his position can be seen from his inclusion, along with Pizarro's brothers and other dignitaries, as a witness to the Spanish foundation of Cuzco.

Medina and Ruy Hernández Briceño left Peru together in 1534, Medina carrying 7,300 pesos for Francisco Pizarro, as well as a vast amount of his own gold, measured by *arrobas* rather than pesos. He arrived in 1535, and remained in Seville in 1536, but since he then called himself a citizen of Badajoz, he apparently still meant to return to his home.

N O T E S .   In Jauja, in 1534, Medina said he was thirty-one years old (AGI, Patronato 93, no. 4, ramo 1). His origin and his father's name appear in ANP, PA 140 and 146, as well as in other places.

Further references are in AGI, Contaduría 1825, records from Cuzco, March, 1534; Indiferente General 1801, records of ship *San Miguel*, 1535; Justicia 723, no. 1; 1126, no. 2, ramo 1; ANP, PA 113; *CDIHN*, II, 35–37; Busto, "Los fugitivos," *Mercurio Peruano* 43 (1962): 268–270; Porras, "Dos documentos esenciales," *Revista Histórica* 17 (1948):90; Solar y Rújula, *Hernando de Soto*, pp. 152–154.

Alonso de Mesa

Age at Cajamarca: About 18
Role: Footman
Share: ¾ share of gold and silver

Place of origin: Toledo (New Castile)
Parents: Alonso Alvarez de Toledo
    and Lucía Hernández (de Mesa)
Extent of literacy: Literate

To have arrived so young, Alonso de Mesa must no doubt have been recruited for the Peruvian venture in his native Toledo while Pizarro was there negotiating at court. He was apparently from a family of modest urban professionals, the kind of people who became merchants, notaries, or lower clergy; one of his brothers was a priest in the cathedral of Toledo, and the family planned that another, younger brother should enter the clergy as well. Though well brought up and literate, Mesa did not insist on his high lineage, and the chronicler Pedro Pizarro, who compiled a short series of descriptions of his comrades, fails to call him an hidalgo. The family was proudest of its connection, through Alonso's mother, with the Mesas, naming all three sons Mesa, yet it may have been a somewhat distant relationship, since the mother was usually called merely Lucía Hernández.

Despite his youth and inexperience, Mesa began early to attain a certain prominence. We are told that he was the second man to lay hands on Atahuallpa at Cajamarca, though he still received only the usual three-fourths share allotted new arrivals. He is said to have performed marvels in a fight with the retreating Indians of Quito in 1534 after Cuzco was conquered. Herrera says that he was a robust youth, with a good horse and good arms by that time. He became a citizen and encomendero in Cuzco, and his name began to be mentioned often by the time of the Indian rebellion of 1536. With his background he would probably soon have been on the council of Cuzco along with his intimate friend, the hidalgo of Toro, Juan de Valdevieso. But he showed himself favorable to Almagro in the first of the civil wars, and was thereafter suspect in the eyes of the Pizarros. They seem to have reduced his encomienda, which was rated only thirtieth of eighty-three in Cuzco in the 1540's. While the details of his action are not known, he probably did not actually fight on Almagro's side at the battle of Salinas. In that case he would have lost his encomienda altogether. The reason for his sympathy for Almagro is not far to seek—the affinity of the New Castilians with a governor who was their compatriot. In the second Almagrist war Mesa stayed on the loyal (and Pizarrist) side, attaining distinction at the battle of Chupas, but his old tendencies reasserted themselves in 1544 at the beginning of the Gonzalo Pizarro revolt. Mesa stayed in Cuzco as Pizarro advanced on Lima, and hardly was Pizarro gone when Mesa, together with Diego Maldonado the Rich, led an unsuccessful anti-Pizarrist uprising. Captured and sent to Lima, Mesa was in great danger of execution; Gonzalo Pizarro finally decided to pardon him and restrict punishment to the removal of his encomienda.

After Gonzalo Pizarro's defeat in 1548 and the fading of the Pizarros as a dominant active power in Peru, Mesa began to come into his own. In 1552 he was one of Cuzco's alcaldes. He had always shown

great ability and interest in managing his estate; already in the 1540's
he had large holdings of Cuzco real estate, lands, and black slaves. In
the 1550's, and afterward, he was one of Peru's wealthiest men.
Around 1554 rebels found a fortune in silver bars buried in his garden.
In the 1560's he is supposed to have offered to pay the crown over
35,000 pesos to achieve the perpetuity of encomiendas, and by this
time his own encomienda was rated fifth or sixth in Cuzco rather than
thirtieth.

Mesa's personal life was a little out of the ordinary. Most Spaniards
had a succession of Indian mistresses and servants; an encomendero
would under normal circumstances eventually marry a Spanish woman
and sire legitimate heirs who could inherit the encomienda. Mesa had
more mistresses and resisted marriage longer than most. In 1544 he
had in his house in Cuzco six mestizo children and their six Indian
mothers. By 1552 he was still unmarried, and when he did finally
marry late in life his wife was an Indian noblewoman, doña Catalina
Huaco Ocllo. Probably she had long been his mistress and had already
borne him sons, though the details are not known. Mesa was apparently the only man of Cajamarca to marry an Indian. His life was also
unusually long under the circumstances. He died in 1587, dictating a
long will containing the philanthropic gestures toward Indians that
were typical of latter sixteenth-century Peru.

N O T E S .   In 1539 Mesa said he was twenty-five years old (AGI, Lima
204, *probanza* of Diego de Narváez). Three testaments of Mesa's are
known. One, of 1542, in which he declares himself a native of Toledo, is
in *RANP* 5 (1927):5–12. A second, of 1544, long but incomplete, is in
BNP, A397, ff. 410–417. Mesa's children at that time were Luis de Mesa,
by Ciza; Miguel de Mesa, by Quipi; Antonio de Mesa, by Yugao; Juana de
Mesa, by Paycocha; Lucía de Mesa, by Inés or Tostocollo; and Antonía de
Mesa, by Angay. Another Indian woman, Lucía or Paycocollo, was preg-
nant, and Mesa apparently suspected that another boy, Francisquito, by his
black slave woman, Francisca, was his son, though he was not prepared to
recognize him. Mesa's final will, of 1587, is in the Archivo Nacional de
Chile, Jesuitas, Perú, 372 (ex: 206) ; though not actually seen by this
writer, it has been partially described by Lohmann Villena ("Restitución
por conquistadores," *Anuario de Estudios Americanos* 23 [1966]:85).
Some of Mesa's other children were a legitimate son, don Florencio
Hernández de Mesa; a natural son, Baltasar Hernández de Mesa, by María
Segura; Alonso Hernández de Mesa, by Luisa de Balboa; and a Bernardo

de Mesa. All of these died or made testaments by 1590 (*RAHC* 4 [1953]: 151, 154, 155). A mestizo son, called don Alonso de Mesa (whether legitimate or not is not known), was living at court in Valladolid in 1603 (Garcilaso, *Obras*, II, 384).

Other references are in AGI, Indiferente General 1801, records of ship *San Miguel*, 1535; Lima 110, Relación de la ciudad del Cuzco; 118, proceedings concerning the encomienda of Alonso de Mesa and petition of Rodrigo de Esquivel (1552–1553); 566, 5, June 18, 1546; Patronato 109, ramo 4; ANP, Salinas 1546–1548, f. 423; AHC, Libros de cabildos, I, f. 169; Gregorio de Vitorero, March 11, 1560, February 9, 1560; HC 15; Busto, "Maldonado el Rico," *Revista Histórica* 26 (1962–1963):122; Calvete, *Rebelión de Pizarro*, IV, 405; Cieza, *Tercera parte*, in *Mercurio Peruano* 38 (1957):256; Diego Fernández, *Historia*, I, 220; II, 19; Garcilaso, *Obras*, IV, 105; Herrera, *Décadas*, XI, 42; Loredo, *Alardes y derramas*, pp. 120, 130; Juan de Matienzo, *Gobierno del Perú*, p. 13; Pedro Pizarro, *Relación*, V, 173, 205, 208, 211; Porras, in Trujillo, *Relación*, p. 118; Trujillo, *Relación*, p. 52; Zárate, *Historia*, II, 506.

Juan Morgovejo

Age at Cajamarca: About 29
Role: Horseman
Share: Double share of gold
    and silver

Place of origin: Mayorga
    (western Old Castile)
Parents: Gonzalo Morgovejo and
    doña Brianda de Prado
Extent of literacy: Fully literate

Juan Morgovejo de Quiñones was well descended, as close as any of the men of Cajamarca to the higher nobility of Spain. He was one of only two or three whose mothers were "doñas," and his grandfather had been a council member of Mayorga. The names of his lineage, Quiñones and Morgovejo, were to be important in Peru; the wife of Licenciado Vaca de Castro, governor of Peru in 1542–1543, was a relative of his, and so was Vaca de Castro's chamberlain Antonio de Quiñones, a nephew of the chief almoner of Prince Philip. In the second half of the sixteenth century, Toribio de Mogrovejo, archbishop of Lima and saint of the church, was of the same family, a son of Juan Morgovejo's cousin; Francisco de Quiñones, corregidor of Lima and governor of Chile, was also a relative.

Morgovejo had been in Nicaragua since 1528 or earlier, at times in positions of leadership. When he came to Peru, with Benalcázar, he had formidable advantages of experience, reputation, and equipment, along with good education and high lineage. These qualities quickly made themselves felt. It does not appear that Morgovejo held a position of command in the pre-Cajamarca campaign, since Pizarro was already plagued with too many captains. But in October, 1533, when the main body of the conquerors advanced toward Cuzco from Jauja, Morgovejo stayed behind as captain of horse in the garrison left to protect the king's treasure. Jauja was founded provisionally as a Spanish city at this time, and Morgovejo was one of the first pair of alcaldes. In 1534 a second founding took place, with Morgovejo confirmed as alcalde of the city that was meant to be Peru's capital. Then, in 1536, he was named alcalde in Jauja's successor city, Lima.

Educated for high posts, with the lineage to make his authority respected, he seemed destined to be one of Peru's great; his position was buttressed by seniority and the favor of the Pizarros. But his career was cut short by the Indian rebellion of 1536. Governor Pizarro took him from his judicial post and made him captain of thirty of the best horsemen available, to ride through the highlands to the relief of Cuzco. To send so few men on such a mission may smack of insanity, yet the Spaniards believed from long experience that a body of as many as thirty horse was practically invulnerable. Indeed it was, on flat or rolling ground; but the Incas were learning that they could deal with fairly large groups of Spaniards if they could catch them in steep places or narrow passes. This was the fate of Morgovejo's expedition. The Spaniards succeeded in driving far along the way toward their goal before their horses finally tired and they turned aside to try to reach the coast. In a pass on the way they met an avalanche of stones from which only a few escaped. Morgovejo was last seen lying wounded on the ground with a faithful slave trying to defend him.

NOTES. The form "Mogrovejo" has become so standard that any other spelling tends to look ridiculous to Peruvians. Nevertheless, the man of Cajamarca always spelled his name "Morgovejo"; that this was no caprice can be seen from the present spelling of the place name related to the surname—also Morgovejo, a town in the homeland of the man of Cajamarca.

Our man at times called himself Juan de Quiñones de Morgovejo, but he was not the attorney Juan de Quiñones in Nicaragua or the regidor Juan de Quiñones in Lima. Though Juan de Quiñones, regidor, was in Lima in 1535 and 1536 at the same time as Morgovejo, their signatures are very different (Torres Saldamando, *Libro primero de cabildos*, I, Pls. opp. p. 2 and opp. p. 50), and in 1536 they appear together as distinct individuals in the same documents (ibid., p. 69). The other Juan de Quiñones was in Nicaragua at the same time as Morgovejo, in 1529, but he was still there in 1535, when Morgovejo had been in Peru for years (*CDIHN*, II, 109–111; III, 362).

In 1535 Morgovejo said he was thirty-two years old (AGI, Lima 204, *probanza* of Juan de Salinas). His regional origin and the names of his parents are in AGI, Justicia 1164, no. 2, ramo 1. Busto's article "Una relación y un estudio," *Revista Histórica* 27 (1964), contains, on pp. 314–318, a well-documented section on Morgovejo, particularly rich in background information, on which this writer has partly relied. For Morgovejo's relatives in Peru in later times see Busto's article; HC 466; James Lockhart, *Spanish Peru*, p. 47; Lohmann Villena, *Americanos en las órdenes nobiliarias*, II, 216.

Other references are in AGI, Justicia 1126, no. 2, ramo 1; Lima 204, *probanza* of Jerónimo de Aliaga; 565, III, September 5, 1539; Patronato 192, no. 1, ramo 4; ANP, PA 19, 55, 149, 169, 649; HC 56, 80; Cieza, *Chupas*, p. 256; Cieza, *Tercera parte*, in *Mercurio Peruano* 36 (1955):470; *Libros de cabildos de Lima*, I, 75–76; Oviedo, *Historia*, V, 92; Porras, *Cedulario*, II, 142, 206; Porras, in Trujillo, *Relación*, p. 82.

Gabriel de Olivares

Age at Cajamarca: About 22
Role: Footman
Share: 1 full share of gold
and silver

Place of origin: Avila or Segovia
(Old Castile)
Extent of literacy: Good signature,
doubtless literate

His companions were not quite sure whether Olivares was from Avila or Segovia, in either case a fine old town in the heart of Old Castile. Apparently he was born in Segovia, but had connections in Avila, where his uncle was a canon in the cathedral. One of his friends wrote that he was a "good hidalgo and person who has been held in esteem here." That he was indeed held in esteem can be seen from his portion of the treasure of Cajamarca, since very few of the young and inexperienced men received a full share, as he did. He would seem to have been from one of the many central Castilian urban families who sent their sons into broadly professional activities—whether as lawyers, notaries, churchmen, or merchants—and were marginal hidalgos as well. Olivares moved in a circle of young Castilians of this type, especially close to Juan de Rojas, who was frequently with him from the time they both joined the Peruvian expedition in Panama.

At first Olivares apparently considered staying permanently in Peru. He resisted the great exodus of July–August, 1534, when general permission to leave was first granted, though his friend Juan de Rojas left at that time, carrying four thousand pesos for him. He was still a citizen of Jauja when the city was transferred to Lima at the end of 1534. But almost immediately thereafter he was on his way to Spain, making such good speed that he arrived in Seville by September, 1535. He went to court and petitioned for a coat of arms, which was granted him in January, 1536. Then he presumably went home, probably to Avila rather than to Segovia, since he described himself as a citizen of Avila at the time of his arrival in Spain.

N O T E S . In Seville, in 1535, Olivares said he was twenty-five years old and a citizen of Avila (AGI, Patronato 93, no. 5, ramo 2). One fellow conqueror said he was from Avila (Porras, *Cartas*, pp. 145–146) and another that he was a native of Segovia (*CDIAO*, XX, 257). His relation to the canon in Avila is mentioned in Porras, *Cartas*, p. 232.

Other references are in AGI, Contaduría 1825, records from Jauja, Nov., 1534; Indiferente General 1801, records of ship *San Miguel*, 1535; ANP, PA 8, 62, 122; HC 5, 36, 52; *Libros de cabildos de Lima*, I, 8–10; Porras, *Cedulario*, II, 128.

Pedro Ortiz

Role at Cajamarca: Horseman
Share: Double share of gold
and silver

Place of origin: Probably Ampuero
(northern Old Castile)

Pedro Ortiz was one of the men with fast horses who often rode out under Hernando de Soto on reconnaissance missions, or in the vanguard ahead of the main body. Soto and Ortiz were the first men to reach the top of the slope in the battle, and near defeat, at Vilcaconga. Ortiz took part in the whole conquest and is last seen in Jauja in June, 1534. At that time a large contingent was preparing to leave the country for Spain, but there is no definite evidence that he joined them.

He would seem to be the same man as the Pedro Ortiz de Cariaga who appeared in Jauja in early 1534. In that case he almost certainly shared the background of a Diego Ortiz de Cariaga, from Ampuero, who was named to the council of Túmbez in 1529, and who must have been a person of consequence in courtly circles, to judge from the unusually strong royal recommendation he received at that time.

N O T E S . Pedro Ortiz is a name often heard in the Trujillo region of Peru, but the person concerned seems to be Bachiller Pedro Ortiz, a physician who came to Peru in 1534, then eventually abandoned his profession and stopped using his title, hoping to achieve an encomienda. (See Oviedo, *Historia*, V, 237–288 ff.; Pérez de Tudela, *Gasca*, II, 323, 566, 572; Porras, *Cedulario*, I, 198). This is mere conjecture; in any case there was no Pedro Ortiz among the first encomenderos of Trujillo (Vargas Ugarte, "La fecha de la fundación de Trujillo," *Revista Histórica* 10 [1936]:234–235), and there was still none in 1548 (Loredo, *Los repartos*, pp. 250–258), which alone excludes the possibility that the Pedro Ortiz of Cajamarca settled there.

Zárate mentions a Pedro Ortiz who conducted himself well, on the loyalist side, at the battle of Chupas in 1542, having previously been of the party of the Almagrists (*Historia*, II, 506). It is within the realm of possibility that this was the man of Cajamarca.

For references to the Pedro Ortiz of Cajamarca, see ANP, PA 117, 141; Herrera, *Historia general*, X, 351; Oviedo, *Historia*, V, 122. For Diego Ortiz de Cariaga see Porras, *Cedulario*, I, 9, 74; and AGI, Lima 565, vol. III, February 8, 1539. The last reference is to a royal cedula relating to Francisco, an Indian brought back from Peru by Diego Ortiz de Cariaga, *vecino* of Ampuero, the latter having died in Spain by that time.

Francisco Peces

Role at Cajamara: Footman   Place of origin: Sonseca, near Toledo
Share: ⅞ share of gold   in New Castile
  and silver   Extent of literacy: Literate

Peces joined the Peruvian venture in Toledo in 1529, while Francisco Pizarro was at court negotiating for the governorship. One of the first documents in the cedulary of Peru, issued even before the agreement with Pizarro, is a royal recommendation for Peces, with the formula "relative of servants of ours," which usually meant good birth, and always good connections. A neophyte in the ways of the Indies,

Peces received less than a full share of the treasure of Cajamarca, though more than the three-fourths share that went to most of the new men. With his court connections, Peces rose quickly to prominence; in 1534 he was sitting on the council of Cuzco by virtue of a royal appointment, secured probably over the heads of the Pizarros.

The future of Francisco Peces would have been assured had it not been for the accident of his regional origin. His home town of Sonseca was south of Toledo, near the domain of the Order of Calatrava, the homeland of Diego de Almagro. This regional affinity caused him to take Almagro's side in the Pizarro-Almagro quarrels in Cuzco in 1535, a first step toward his downfall. The differences were resolved amicably for the time being, and Peces decided to stay in Cuzco and keep his encomienda rather than accompany Almagro to Chile. When Almagro returned in 1537 and seized Cuzco, he found several of the Spaniards there thoroughly exasperated with the heavy-handed rule of Hernando Pizarro, and prominent among the malcontents was Francisco Peces. Almagro named Peces one of Cuzco's alcaldes, and from this moment he and the Pizarros were open enemies. He fought for Almagro at the battle of Salinas in 1538; afterward Hernando Pizarro took away his encomienda and ejected him from Cuzco's council.

Peces obtained royal orders, issued in September, 1541, reinstating him and granting him a coat of arms, but the provisions probably never reached him. By June, 1541, he had joined the rebellion headed by the younger Almagro, serving for a time as Almagro's alcalde in Lima. He stayed with the Almagrists until the end, as one of the leaders, if not actually a captain, and was executed by royal officials shortly after the battle of Chupas in 1542.

NOTES. Though all existing versions of the roll of Cajamarca give his name as Francisco Pérez, there is hardly any doubt that Francisco Peces was the man originally intended. The present writer decided this independently, then discovered that Porras had already reached the same conclusion in 1936. (See the valuable biographical note in Porras, *Testamento de Pizarro*, p. 55.) No Francisco Pérez appears in any of the original records of the men of Cajamarca or of the conquerors of Cuzco. We know definitely that Peces was with the expedition when it left Spain (Porras, *Cedulario*, I, 12), then at Puná in early 1532. (This can be deduced from the cedula of March, 1533, granting him a council seat in the principal city of Peru. The royal letters of that time were issued at the petition of Rodrigo de Mazuelas, who left Peru early in 1532, from the island of Puná.

See Porras, *Cedulario*, I, 136.) Peces appeared then at the founding of
Cuzco in early 1534, as citizen and encomendero (Porras, "Dos documentos esenciales," *Revista Histórica* 17 [1948]:92). Any man who was
at Puná and then an encomendero in Cuzco was almost ipso facto at Cajamarca, since practically all of those with the expedition who were not at
Cajamarca stayed at San Miguel and became citizens there permanently,
with no chance to go on to Cuzco. In addition to all this, there are many
known instances in all kinds of sources where Francisco Peces has been
rendered Pérez. The name occasionally appears as Francisco de Peces, but is
far more common without the "de."

A fellow Toledan, Antonio Téllez de Guzmán, said that Peces was a
"native of Sonseca, three leagues from Toledo" (AGI, Patronato 185,
ramo 11). The same statement will be found in *CDIAO*, X, 260, where
Sonseca is mistakenly given as "Fonseca."

Other references are in AGI, Contaduría 1824, records of levy on citi-
zens of Cuzco by Hernando Pizarro; records from Cuzco, 1536; Justicia
1054, no. 3, ramo 2; Lima 565, vol. III, December 29, 1539; 566, vol. IV,
September 22, 1541, November 24, 1541; Patronato 109, ramo 4; ANP,
PA 412, 489; HC 91, 246; *CDIAO*, X, 249; *CDIHC*, VI, 302; *RANP*
1:599; Cieza, *Chupas*, p. 284; Gómara, *Hispania victrix*, I, 248; Oviedo,
Historia, V, 163; Porras, *Cartas*, p. 412; Porras, *Cedulario*, I, 12, 136;
Porras, *Testamento de Pizarro*, p. 55.

Juan Pizarro de Orellano

Age at Cajamarca: About 21 or 22
Role: Horseman
Share: Double share of gold and
   silver, plus a token 100 pesos

Place of origin: Trujillo
   (Extremadura)
Parents: Hernando de Orellana
   and Juana García Pizarro
Extent of literacy: Fully literate

The name Orellana was one of the most illustrious in Trujillo, and
the magnificent signature of Juan Pizarro de Orellano indicates a man
educated with care. He was a distant relative of Pedro Barrantes, another of the very well born of the Trujillo contingent. Without doubt
he was a full-fledged hidalgo, and possibly higher on the Trujillan
scale than the immediate family of the Pizarro brothers, to which he
also bore some relationship. He was not a really close relative of Hernando and Francisco, or his share would have been even larger than it
was; the genealogists tell us that his great-grandfather was Hernando's

great-great-grandfather. Even this was enough to assure that Juan would be the only man to receive more than the usual horseman's double share without holding a post of command or special responsibility.

Coming from Spain with the other Pizarros in 1530, surely without previous experience in the Indies, Pizarro de Orellana was with the 1531 expedition from the beginning. Either a good horseman or the owner of a good horse, he was involved in most of the daring exploits of the campaign. He went with Soto to interview Atahuallpa, then with Hernando Pizarro to the great temple of Pachacámac. On the way south to Cuzco he rode among Soto's vanguard, and he distinguished himself in the battle of Vilcas. After the conquest he may have entertained briefly the thought of staying in Peru; he was named to the council of Jauja in 1534, but he left before the end of the year, carrying his own fortune and an even larger amount belonging to Juan Pizarro.

With his unique combination of connections, lineage, education, and dash he could have had anything he wanted in Peru. But, like the other Trujillan hidalgos, he preferred honors at home to honors in Peru. He reached Spain in 1535 and before long was sitting on the town council of his native Trujillo. Though he continued to be close to the Pizarro brothers, by 1550, when last heard of, he had come into conflict with that tightfisted clan over money. This did not keep his son Hernando de Orellana from marrying Hernando Pizarro's illegitimate daughter, whose descendants were eventually to inherit the Pizarro name and titles.

NOTES. Porras, through a slight misinterpretation of a statement by Garcilaso, concluded that Juan Pizarro de Orellana lived past 1560, as he may well have, but the passage does not say so (Porras, in Trujillo, *Relación*, p. 118; Garcilaso, *Obras*, III, 57).

Gregorio de Sotelo called Juan Pizarro de Orellana a native of Trujillo (*CDIAO*, X, 243, or AGI, Patronato 185, ramo 11). In 1534 Pizarro de Orellana said he was twenty-five (AGI, Patronato 150, no. 6, ramo 2); in 1545 that he was thirty-four (AGI, Justicia 1174, no. 1, ramo 3).

The names of Pizarro de Orellana's parents, with his genealogy for some generations back, appear in Muñoz de San Pedro, "Francisco Pizarro debió apellidarse Díaz o Hinojosa," *Revista de Estudios Extremeños* 6 (1950):531. While Muñoz de San Pedro is generally reliable as to names and lines of descent, his use of "don" and doña" is extraordinarily capricious. Juana García Pizarro appears in his text without "doña," and the present writer intuits that this is correct, because "doña Juana García" would sound faintly ridiculous in a sixteenth-century context, but there is no way of being sure.

Other references are in AGI, Justicia 833, letter of Hernando Pizarro, June 8, 1549; 1082, no. 1, ramo 4; ANP, PA 125; *CDIHC*, VII, 153; Porras, "Dos documentos esenciales," *Revista Histórica* 17 (1948):31; Trujillo, *Relación*, p. 61.

Juan de Porras

Age at Cajamarca: About 31 or 32   Place of origin: Seville
Role: Footman   Extent of literacy: Literate
Share: 1 full share of gold and
  silver, plus a token 100 pesos

The Sevillian family or group of families named Porras was closely connected with municipal government and maintenance of the peace. A Diego de Porras was *jurado*, or district alderman; his son Bachiller Juan de Porras registered to come to the Indies in 1517 and 1527. Another Juan de Porras, who was in Peru in the 1540's, had been the retainer of an alcalde of Seville. An Antonio de Porras, chief constable of Cuzco at one time, was also probably of this clan. They were literate, substantial people, no flashing nobles, but still claiming to be hidalgos.

The Juan de Porras of Cajamarca was solidly in this tradition. Having been in the conquest of Honduras around 1524, he, like others, soon left there for Nicaragua; he came to Peru with the Nicaraguan contingent of Benalcázar. Before long he was holding the position of *alcalde mayor* of the expedition, his main duty being to try minor cases of fighting, gambling, swearing, and the like. This post made him one of the expedition's leaders even though he happened not to possess the main appurtenance of prestige, a horse. As a gesture of respect, he was put at the very top of the list of footmen on the roll of Cajamarca, and he was one of only two of them to receive anything above the ordinary one share. After Cajamarca, Porras was soon on horseback. He continued to be the judicial authority of the expedition, as opposed to the authorities of the new municipalities which began to be set up. In late 1534 or early 1535 he left Peru, not tempted by the encomienda he was given in the silver-poor northern region. He arrived in Seville by late 1535 and lived there in some state for the rest of his life, "in the guise of a cavalier," displaying the coat of arms granted him by the king and sustaining himself from handsome royal annuities. For some reason Porras does not appear to have acquired any post in Sevillian municipal government like other returnees, even though his background gave him a special propensity and unusual qualifications. He was still living in Seville as late as 1562.

NOTES. Juan de Porras gave his age as thirty-five in 1535 (*CDIHN*, III, 470, 481–483) and in 1536 (AGI, Justicia 719, no. 9). In both of these references, as in many others, he is called a citizen of Seville. Of course many citizens of Seville were born and grew up elsewhere, but since Juan de Porras fits so perfectly, in name and characteristics, into a known family of Seville, he may be considered a born Sevillian. After the Gonzalo Pizarro revolt was defeated, orders went back to Spain to confiscate the property of a Juan de Porras, native of Seville, who had been involved. Authorities thought the man of Cajamarca was that Porras, and they took action against him. He made no attempt to prove that he was not a native of Seville, but he did prove his constant residence in Seville since 1535 in order to establish an alibi. (See Justicia 1073, no. 1.) Busto, in a section on Juan de Porras in his "Una relación y un estudio," *Revista Histórica* 27 (1964):304–309, also believes that Porras was from Seville. Jurado Diego de Porras and his son are mentioned in Bermúdez Plata, *Pasajeros*, I, 182, 243.

Other references are in AGI, Contaduría 1825, records from Cajamarca, May, 1533; Penas de Cámara, 1535; Patronato 93, no. 6, ramo 1; 98, no. 4, ramo 3; ANP, PA 31, 135; *CDIHN*, III, 415; Cieza, *Tercera parte*, in *Mercurio Peruano* 36 (1955):470; 39 (1958):566; Loredo, *Los repartos*, p. 131; Porras, *Cedulario*, II, 110.

Juan de Rojas

Age at Cajamarca: About 23
Role: Horseman
Share: Double share of gold and silver

Place of origin: Tordesillas or Segovia, in Old Castile
Extent of literacy: Literate

It would seem that Juan de Rojas was quite new to the Indies, since neither the veterans of Nicaragua nor the men of Panama had known him before about 1530. As to his background, he claimed even in Spain itself to be an hidalgo, and a comrade called him a cavalier; he sometimes used the noble-sounding surname of Solís. All these things are of somewhat dubious informative value, but taken together with his literacy they leave the impression of origins in very modest gentry and good townsmen, much the same as such Old Castilian "hidalgos" as Jerónimo de Aliaga and Melchor Verdugo, with whom he had connections.

Rojas joined the 1531 expedition before it left Panama, probably at the same time as his best friend, Gabriel de Olivares from Segovia, another of these modest professional people with pretensions to nobility. In the campaign Rojas figured as one of the first-line horsemen; he got the good horseman's full double share, and he was among the men chosen to accompany Hernando Pizarro on the hazardous trip to the coastal temple of Pachacámac. After seeing the conquest to its initial conclusion, Rojas availed himself of the general license issued in 1534, leaving Peru in July of that year and arriving in Seville in 1535. He carried thousands of pesos for his Old Castilian comrades, Olivares, Aliaga, and Verdugo, as well as his own fortune. Very shortly after his arrival he went to live in Tordesillas, and he was still there in 1554.

N O T E S .   In a letter to his family in Avila, Melchor Verdugo says that Rojas was from Segovia (Porras, *Cartas del Peru*, p. 232). However, it appears from the context of the letter that Verdugo knew Gabriel de Olivares, from Segovia, far better than he did Rojas, and indeed Verdugo and Olivares may have been related. Rojas's return to Tordesillas and his long residence there are strong evidence of origin. Verdugo was under the impression that Rojas was going to live in Segovia, which he did not. That Rojas did have a special tie with Olivares, however, is clear. Perhaps Rojas had relatives in Tordesillas as well as Segovia, both, in any case, in the heart of Old Castile.

Rojas said in 1534 that he was twenty-five years old (AGI, Patronato 150, no. 6, ramo 2). His belated *probanza de servicios*, where he appears as a citizen of Tordesillas in 1540 and 1554, is in AGI, Patronato 98, no. 4, ramo 6. The connections between Rojas and Olivares appear particularly in HC 5 and 52, and Porras, *Cartas*, p. 232.

Other references are in AGI, Indiferente General 1801, records of ship *San Miguel*, 1535; Justicia 723, no. 1; 1052, no. 2; ANP, PA 17, 105, 119, 133; HC 39, 67.

Gregorio de Sotelo

Age at Cajamarca: About 24
Role: Footman
Share: 1 full share of gold and
   silver, plus a token 100 pesos

Place of origin: Zamora, in the
   kingdom of Leon
Extent of literacy: Literate

Gregorio de Sotelo had good antecedents both in Spain and the Indies. An Alonso de Sotelo from Zamora, *comendador* of one of the military orders, governed the house of the Duke of Medina Sidonia in Seville. Gregorio may not have been a very close relative, for his wife, Antonía de Mella, was not a "doña." But he was trained in accounting and the management of affairs, as functionaries of the great noble houses usually were. Gregorio came to the Indies by about 1526, in the footsteps of his older brother Antonio de Sotelo, an important man in the area of Panama. By 1531, when he joined Benalcázar in Nicaragua and came to Peru, Gregorio was a man of experience, but he was still without his own independent position.

His background, connections, and skills brought him to quick prominence in Peru. Though he was without a horse, Sotelo, along with Alcalde Mayor Juan de Porras, was lifted almost out of the category of footman at Cajamarca, being placed at the top of the list and given an extraordinary share. He was named to the council of Jauja at its founding in 1534; he moved to Jauja's successor, Lima, in 1535, and became the first to hold the honorific position of majordomo of the church there.

The conquerors had extraordinary confidence in Sotelo's capability and trustworthiness with money and affairs. It was to him that comrades from his home region and elsewhere often turned, asking him to collect debts or handle their business when they were absent. In 1535, Bishop Berlanga of Panama, carrying out an investigation of the royal treasury, called on Sotelo to testify, as one most knowledgeable in such things, and was so impressed with him that he shortly afterward recommended him to the Council of the Indies as the best possible appointee for treasurer general of Peru. When Sotelo left Lima for Spain in January, 1536, he carried more of his fellows' money with him than any other returnee recorded. Besides really large consignments of thousands of pesos for two friends, he took the whole remaining estate of another man, and small amounts from some twenty or twenty-five other people, most of them from Zamora or Leon. Sotelo acquitted himself honorably, but the money did not reach its destination. As his ship was coming within sight of Spain, French pirates seized it and took every penny on board.

Another man of Cajamarca, Juan García de Santa Olalla, was on the same vessel and decided that the only recourse was to go back to Peru to mend his fortune. This Sotelo did not do, perhaps because it would have been hard to face so many disppointed people. What his intentions had been originally is not clear by any means. He had stayed in Peru while two separate waves of conquerors had left. At the time he went home, he received a royal license to retain his encomienda while he visited Spain briefly to get married; Bishop Berlanga in 1536 seemed to be under the impression that he meant to stay in Peru. Possibly, as so often happened, Sotelo had intended to go back to Peru, but once in Spain he was overcome by the attractions of home. In any case, he was not reduced to pauperdom, since he had sent money home with a friend earlier. He went to his native Zamora to settle and marry, and he was living there in 1538.

Though Sotelo left, several of his relatives followed him to Peru, two of whom became important figures. A brother, Cristóbal, arrived while Gregorio was still there, though already too late to get an encomienda. He went to Chile as one of Almagro's captains and fought for Almagro at the battle of Salinas. In 1541 he joined Almagro's son after the assassination of Pizarro and was so influential in the rebel camp that he was almost the de facto leader, until he was himself assassinated. Like his brother, he was admired for his prudence and capability, though fate had thrown him into a hopeless venture. Also presumably a relative, since he was from Zamora, was Gaspar de Sotelo, who was a prominent encomendero of Cuzco in the 1550's and 1560's.

NOTES. In 1538 Gregorio de Sotelo said he was thirty years old (AGI, Justicia 1124, no. 6, ramo 3). There, and in AGI, Justicia 758, no. 1, he is called a citizen of Zamora. The most comprehensive source for Sotelo is AGI, Justicia 1126, no. 2, ramo 1, which contains much testimony relating to Sotelo by other men of Cajamarca. Particularly, there is a copy of Sotelo's memorandum of all the money he was bringing home, from whom it came, and for whom it was destined. Most was to go to the kingdom of Leon, with some destinations as far afield as Segovia and the Basque country. Sotelo mentions his brothers, Antonio and Cristóbal, as well as a cousin, Cristóbal de Cisneros. Sotelo's revealing testimony about the conduct of the treasury officials of Peru is in *CDIAO*, XX, 240–244 and 285, and in AGI, Patronato 185, ramo 11.

Other references are in AGI, Lima 204, *probanza* of Juan de Salinas; Patronato 192, no. 1, ramo 4; ANP, Juzgado, December 30, 1535; PA 73, 136, 148, 149, 678; HC 37, 38, 260; a document of Dec. 10, 1535, among the Peruvian manuscripts of the Lilly Library; *CDIHN*, II, 35–37; *RANP* I (1920): 431–432; Cobo, *Obras*, II, 283, 286, 295; Loredo, *Los repartos*, pp. 425–431; Porras, *Cedulario*, II, 171; Porras, *Cartas*, p. 196 (mention by Bishop Berlanga).

For Sotelo's relatives and presumed relatives, see AGI, Justicia 1126, no. 2, ramo 1, described above, and for his wife and brother Antonio, AGI, Justicia 758, no. 1; for Comendador Alonso de Sotelo, Oviedo, *Historia*, I, 98; for his brother Cristóbal de Sotelo, *CDIHC*, VI, 272, 290, 300, 304; Cieza, *Salinas*, pp. 29 ff.; Porras, *Cartas*, pp. 412, 493, 528; for Gaspar de Sotelo, Garcilaso, *Obras*, II, 269–270, 359; IV, 73; for his cousin Cristóbal de Cisneros, ANP, PA 678.

Sebastián de Torres

Age at Cajamarca: About 30	Place of origin: Chiclana de la
Role: Horseman	Frontera, on the Andalusian coast
Share: Double share of gold	Parents: Hernando de Torres and
and silver	Beatriz Moral (or Muriel)
	Extent of literacy: Literate

While the knowledge we have about the origins of Sebastián de Torres does not define his background precisely, it does place him within certain bounds. His brother Hernando was an apothecary, that trade being either at the bottom of the professional world or high in the ranks of artisanship, depending on the circumstances. But there is no indication that Sebastián ever learned the family trade, if it was that, and he certainly did not practice it in the Indies. The only specialized activity he is known to have engaged in is shipbuilding, which was natural enough, as Chiclana is at the edge of the sea. A companion once testified that Sebastián "built the first ships to be made on the South Sea." This leaves us unenlightened as to whether Sebastián acted as entrepreneur, supervisor, or ship's carpenter. Besides, the claim to have built the first ships on the Pacific was made for so many individuals that it must be discounted to some extent. Torres's knowledge of ships may well have been merely that general maritime expertise one would expect of a coast dweller. After achieving prominence in Peru, Torres began to claim hidalgo status for himself and initiated proceedings in his home town to make his claim good. The mere obligation of proof usually (not always) indicated a very marginal kind of nobility; on the other hand, the audacity to bring up the matter at all in one's place of origin points to a claim with a certain verisimilitude.

To his respectable social origin Sebastián added the advantage of seniority. Still a boy, he registered in 1512 to come to the Indies in the company of his older brother Hernando; later that year two other brothers did the same. By about 1515 he was in the Panama region. From there he went to Nicaragua like so many others, and became, if he was not already, a man of consequence. He was at various times alcalde and municipal council member in León, Nicaragua's capital. In politics he tended to favor Governor Pedrarias de Avila and Benalcázar over the faction of Licenciado Castañeda and Hernando de Soto, but this did not prevent him from coming to Peru with Soto.

By experience and origin, then, Torres was prepared for the quick advancement which he received in Peru. He was alcalde in Jauja, first Spanish capital of Peru, at its effective founding in 1534, and then repeated as alcalde in the successor city of Lima in 1537.

Torres was among the first of the conquerors to marry in Peru, a fact he made much of in representations to the Council of the Indies. He claimed indeed that his wife was the first Spanish woman to arrive in the new country, or perhaps the first "honored lady" in his ambiguous language. Witnesses, however, merely confirmed that she was *one* of the first honored married women in Peru. The marriage took place in Jauja, presumably in 1534, and the lady, a widow with the rather plebeian name of Francisca Jiménez, was a native of the Caribbean capital of Santo Domingo. Torres claimed gentle birth for her, too, and got a royal cedula "confirming" her right to the title "doña," though it was a decade and more before conservative local usage could be brought to comply. Their children, though born by 1537, were of the third Spanish generation in the Indies.

Most close friendships among Spaniards in America rested ultimately on regional or professional ties, or on a history of shared experiences. None of these things explain why Torres and Jerónimo de Aliaga, the Old Castilian notary, should have become inseparable companions within a few months after Torres arrived in Peru. In 1534 they received, as partners, a joint encomienda in the area of Huaraz. They continued to be constant associates in Lima, and Aliaga's legal knowledge and connections were useful to Torres in negotiating for honors at the royal court.

Torres was one of the *principales* or important men of Peru by the time he was killed in 1539. He had gone out to inspect his encomienda and fell victim to a final outbreak of Indian rebellion that claimed at least four encomenderos of Lima, including two other veterans of Cajamarca. Torres's widow was immediately remarried, as was the custom, to the Sevillian Ruy Barba Cabeza de Vaca. Initially, the encomienda continued to be held in the name of Torres's infant son, Hernando, but by the late 1540's a process of diplacement or transferral had begun. Of the nominal fourteen hundred tributaries, Ruy Barba at that time held three hundred in his own name, and a nephew of Sebastián's, Cristóbal de Torres, held seven hundred. Sebastián's daughter, doña Juana de Torres, married a council member of Huánuco in 1557.

NOTES. In 1530 Torres gave his age once as thirty (*CDIHN*, II, 504–510), and once as thirty-five (*CDIHN*, II, 400), then, in 1535, as thirty-two or thirty-three (AGI, Lima 204, *probanza* of Juan de Salinas). Although the published calendar of the Harkness Collection gives his birthplace as Havana (p. 30), the original clearly says Chiclana (HC 117). His mother's name is given there as Moral, whereas in the *Pasajeros* it twice appears as Muriel. The departure of Sebastián and some of his relatives for the Indies is recorded in Bermúdez Plata, *Pasajeros*, I, 3, 34, 47. Torres's *probanza de servicios*, made in Lima in 1537, is in AGI, Lima 118. In 1537 Torres empowered his wife and nephews to make his will, also naming his children at that time (ANP, Castañeda, reg. 6, ff. 18–20).

Torres had two mestizo children, Hernando and Isabel de Torres. For many years after his death Isabel lived with his widow, Francisca Jiménez, apparently in a servile position (BNP, A34, ff.99–106). Two nephews of Sebastián followed him to Peru, Hernando and Cristóbal de Torres. Hernando was in the country at least by 1535 (ANP, PA 760), Cristóbal by 1537 (ANP, Castañeda, reg. 6, f.18v; HC 305).

The parents of Francisca Jiménez were Martín de Algaba and Marina González; her father owned a house in Santo Domingo when he died around 1537. A sister of Francisca's, Juana Ruiz, also lived in Lima in 1538; she was the wife of a Vicente de Béjar. Francisca's first husband was a Cristóbal García, and it is likely she came with him to Peru. She lived into the 1550's, gradually becoming "doña Francisca de Pineda." (See Lock-

THE MEN

hart, *Spanish Peru*, p. 154). Children from all three marriages survived.

Other references are in AGI, Lima 565, vol. III, September 6, 1538; Patronato 92, no. 3; 192, no. 1, ramo 4; ANP, PA 7, 18, 43, 116, 313, 508, 744, 749, 751, 760, 765; HC 64, 105, 117, 179, 217, 252, 330, 346, 382; *CDIHN*, II, 313, 326; *RANP* 1 (1920):439 (referred to unaccountably as Sebastián de Castro); IV (1926), 6; Cieza, *Chupas*, p. 57; Cobo, *Obras*, II, 283, 304; Loredo, *Los repartos*, p. 220; Montoto, *Nobiliario*, p. 383; Porras, *Cedulario*, II, 196, 391; Torres Saldamando, *Libro primero de cabildos*, I, 329. The Lilly Library at Indiana University has among its Peruvian manuscripts a document in which Torres grants power to Hernando de Soto to represent him at the royal court.

For Francisca Jiménez, and more on Torres's heirs, see AGI, Contaduría 1679, records from Lima, Sept. 1539, 1554; Lima 565, vol. III, August 9, 1538; Patronato 110, ramo 6; ANP, Castañeda, reg. 6, ff.18–20; reg. 7, ff.21–22; Salinas 1538–1540, ff.200, 461–462; 484, 555; Salinas 1542–1543, 10 (2nd series); 271, 272; BNP, A34, ff.99–106 (Francisca's testament), 138; A419, ff.112–113; HC 564, 616; Loredo, *Los repartos*, pp. 219, 220, 231.

Juan de Valdevieso

Age at Cajamarca: About 23 or 24
Role: Footman
Share: 1 full share of gold and silver

Place of origin: Barcial, near Toro, in the kingdom of Leon
Parents: Comendador Juan de Valdevieso and doña Isabel de Benavides
Extent of literacy: Fully literate

Among all the men of Cajamarca, Valdevieso is the clearest example of a true and well-established hidalgo of illustrious lineage in all branches of his family. His mother was a "doña," his father was a *comendador* of one of the military orders; one of his brothers was on the municipal council of Toro, and another was a Franciscan friar. This background won him quick recognition in Peru. Though he was young and apparently inexperienced in the Indies, he appears with his compatriot Gonzalo Maldonado near the top of the list of footmen, with a full share of the treasure rather than the three-quarters share that went to most of the greenhorns.

Apparently from the time he joined the expedition in Panama, Valdevieso was a retainer or servant of Governor Pizarro. "Servant" was one of the most ambiguous words in sixteenth-century Spanish usage.

To be the servant of another was a fate that all Spaniards did their utmost to avoid, yet in their patriarchal society most men were in some sense dependents of others. All aspired to be called servants of the king, and it was an honor to be chamberlain, treasurer, or usher of a high nobleman. Actual houseservants were despised, and yet pages who in practice functioned as such were only undergoing part of the standard training of a nobleman. Most commonly of all, "servant" meant steward or manager of affairs. Valdevieso was a little of all these things. In 1533 Pizarro empowered him and Pedro Navarro to collect money and receive shipments in his name. But even more than a steward, Valdevieso, with his lineage, was the courtier, the chief figure in the retinue that Pizarro began to build up. As the governor's chamberlain, Valdevieso carried Pizarro's daughter doña Francisca to the baptismal font at Jauja in 1534.

A man of such parts, who in addition was a respectable figure of a warrior, could not be kept long in purely subordinate positions. Pizarro named Valdevieso to the powerful council of Cuzco in the year of its founding; the intention was to pack the council with Pizarrists, yet a councilman could not help being an independent figure at the same time. In 1539 Valdevieso was one of Cuzco's alcaldes. As a capable man of affairs, he built up wealth through his encomienda, property-owning, and entrepreneurial activity (he had a large company with Licenciado Gaspar de Espinosa in Panama). Still, since he was from an established family in Spain, he kept one eye on his home city of Toro. In 1535 he sent home large amounts of money to be invested by his family in lands and annuities. There is some reason to think he meant to leave the country permanently when he came to Lima around 1540. He had already sold his houses and slaves in Cuzco to his close friend, Alonso de Mesa, leaving his mestizo children in Mesa's care, though it is true that Valdevieso made Mesa promise to let him buy his property back if he returned within two years.

Whatever his plans, they were changed when the Almagrists assassinated Pizarro. Valdevieso, a Pizarro man, went to join the new governor, Vaca de Castro, who had already arrived in the north. Since Valdevieso was from the kingdom of Leon like the governor, and also of good birth and with experience, Vaca de Castro made him his majordomo, or chief executive assistant. From Quito, Valdevieso went to the coast on a mission to recover royal funds then in San Miguel, in order to finance the oncoming campaign against the rebels. On the way, probably late in 1541, he was attacked and killed by the hardy Indians of the island of Puná, who had recently dealt in the same fashion with Bishop Valverde. Valdevieso left a mestizo son by a Cañari Indian woman. Also named Juan de Valdevieso, he was legitimized and lived on in Cuzco until 1588, maintaining a modest position.

NOTES. In 1539 Valdevieso gave his age twice, once as thirty (AGI, Lima 204, *probanza* of Diego Rodríguez), and once as over thirty (AGI, Lima 118, *probanza* of García Martín). His place of origin and the names of his parents and brothers are in AGI, Justicia 1124, no. 2; ANP, PA 776; Castañeda, reg. 4, f.21. Valdevieso once used the name of Juan Hurtado de Valdevieso (AGI, Contaduría 1825, records from Coaque, May, 1531), Hurtado being the name of some of the noblest families of Spain (and others, of course). For Valdevieso's son, see *RAHC* 4 (1953):148. Francisco Pizarro's power to Valdevieso as his servant is in HC 49.

There is some conflicting evidence about Valdevieso's final days. Pedro Pizarro, writing many years later and not as an eyewitness, thought Valdevieso fled Lima with Bishop Valverde and was killed with him (*Relación*, V, 229). Cieza, much closer but still not an eyewitness, says Valdevieso was on his way from Panama to Peru, presumably coming from Spain (*Chupas*, p. 162). It seems impossible, or at least unlikely, that he had already been to Spain, since he was definitely still in Peru in October, 1539 (HC 448); conceivably he could have reached Panama and then returned. For the most basic points, however, we have eyewitness reports. In AGI, Justicia 1055, a witness reports that Vaca de Castro made Valdevieso his majordomo, then sent him off on a special mission. The lieutenant governor of Guayaquil at the time describes that mission as recovering gold at San Miguel, and he tells of Valdevieso's death separate from Valverde's (Porras, *Cartas*, p. 544).

Other references to Juan de Valdevieso are found in AGI, Lima 566, vol. IV, June 18, 1540; Patronato 93, no. 11, ramo 2; 109, ramo 4; ANP, PA 778, 779, 787; Salinas 1542–1543, f.595; a document of 1537 among the Peruvian manuscripts of the Lilly Library; BNP, A397, ff.410–417; HC 50, 83, 300; CDIHC, IV, 199; RAHC 8 (1957):53; RANP 5 (1927):9; Pedro Pizarro, *Relación*, V, 208, 211; Porras, *Cedulario*, II, 206; Porras, "Dos documentos esenciales," *Revista Histórica* 17 (1948):92–93; Porras, "Jauja," *Revista Histórica* 18 (1949–1950):137–138.

A Juan de Valdevieso left Spain for Peru with Hernando Pizarro in late 1534 bearing a royal recommendation. This cannot have been the man of Cajamarca, who was then in Jauja, though it may well have been a relative. See Bermúdez Plata, *Pasajeros*, I, 363; Porras, *Cedulario*, II, 67.

Francisco de Vargas

Age at Cajamarca: About 26
Role: Footman
Share: 1 full share of gold
and silver

Place of origin: La Guardia del
Arzobispo, in New Castile
Father: Sancho Hernández
Extent of literacy: Doubtless fully
literate

The family of Francisco de Vargas maintained a certain position in the small New Castilian town of La Guardia, since his brother was a titled professional man, Bachiller Juan de Vargas; doubtless they considered themselves hidalgos, as did most Spaniards of any prominence. The extent of Vargas's experience in the Indies is not known; veteran or not, he was from the beginning treated with respect. After the conquest, he became a citizen and encomendero of Lima. He was a capable man of affairs, once entrusted provisionally with the custody of a large shipment of Hernando Pizarro's merchandise, but he does not seem to have been a full-scale Pizarro agent, nor was he as active in commerce and entrepreneurial ventures as some. He appeared to be headed toward the true eminence enjoyed by those who were both senior in the conquest and wellborn; the chronicler Cieza considered him a *vecino principal* or important citizen. In 1539 he held the honorific post of majordomo of the city of Lima. Soon he would have been sitting on the council itself, if Indians had not killed him in a late and final outbreak of rebelliousness that cost the lives of four encomenderos of Lima. Vargas left two daughters, one by an Indian servant woman and another by the Spanish—or possibly Morisco—woman, Lucía Hernández. The mestizo girl survived well into the 1540's, at least, under the guardianship of Vargas's comrade from Cajamarca, Jerónimo de Aliaga.

NOTES. Cieza, usually extremely reliable on origins, states that Vargas was from Campos, but this must be disregarded against multiple firsthand evidence. Vargas's origin and the names of his relatives and daughters are given in AGI, Lima 565, vol. III, May 23, 1540; vol. IV, August 13, 1540; Lima 566, vol. VI, December 8, 1550; BNP, A31, ff.149–151. In the last, unlike the many Spaniards who sent or tried to send their mestizo children to Spain, he says "my daughter María de la Cruz is the daughter of an Indian woman, and since she is mestizo she should not go to a place where she would dishonor my relatives." In 1535 Vargas gave his age as twenty-nine (AGI, Lima 204, *probanza* of Juan de Salinas).

Other references are in AGI, Indiferente General 1801, records of ship *San Miguel*, 1535; ANP, Juzgado, December 30, 1535; PA 246, 596; HC 201, 363, 443; Cieza, *Chupas*, p. 57; Torres Saldamando, *Libro primero de cabildos*, I, 297, 329, 335.

Melchor Verdugo

Age at Cajamarca: About 19	Place of origin: Avila (Old Castile)
Role: Footman	Parents: Francisco Verdugo
Share: ¾ share of gold	and Marina de Olivares
and silver	Extent of literacy: Fully literate

Melchor Verdugo was one of several Old Castilians among the men of Cajamarca who had affinities with the urban professions combined with certain hidalgo connections. Another such man was Verdugo's acquaintance Gabriel de Olivares, who may have been a distant relative on his mother's side. Verdugo's father and his mother bore the names of lineages well known in Old Castile, but, as usual in these cases, no details of their relationship to more illustrious family members are known. Conceivably Melchor was in some way related to fray Pedro Verdugo, *comendador mayor* of the Order of Alcántara, and in all probability he had family ties with Hernando Verdugo de Henao, a court functionary and employee of don Francisco de los Cobos, Charles V's secretary. Both of these Verdugos, at any rate, were from Avila. In his own family correspondence, Melchor mentions predominantly such people as a lawyer, a merchant, and a priest. Melchor enjoyed a reasonable education. He wrote letters in his own clearly legible hand, revealing an adequate (though hardly a professional man's) grasp of grammar and orthography, and he had a good understanding of affairs, both of business and of law. Personally he was quite single-mindedly devoted to his own advancement, a trait he shared with many Spaniards and human beings.

His father having died, Melchor left home early. He came to the Indies and Panama around 1529 or 1530, in the service of Licenciado Gaspar de Espinosa. Since Espinosa was closely connected with the Luque interests, it was natural that Melchor should be drawn into the Peruvian venture. He was not with the main group leaving Panama, however, but came with the first contingent of reinforcements that arrived in Coaque on the northern coast. In Panama, Melchor had apparently been Espinosa's page, or little better, and on the expedition he still did not cut much of a figure. Later, a royal prosecutor asserted that as a mere boy he did little at Cajamarca, a humiliating charge not leveled at any of the other conquerors. The prosecutor found several veterans who estimated Melchor's age at the time of the conquest as anywhere from eighteen to twenty-two and cast aspersions on his equipment, capacities, and reputation. It is apparent that he was an impoverished, poorly equipped, and untried youth, not then ready to stand on his own. Yet he received the standard three-fourths share of the younger and less experienced members, rather than the half share of the truly incapable or humble.

At the hands of the Pizarros, Melchor received ambiguous treatment. At first he seems to have been put off with promises; he received a lot in Cuzco, but no encomienda. Almost all the men of Cajamarca who stayed in Peru originally held encomiendas in the great central districts of Cuzco and Lima; Verdugo was one of the few pushed off to northern Trujillo. Only in March of 1535, at the time of Trujillo's foundation, did Melchor receive formal title to his encomienda. His grant was large, well-populated, well-endowed, and bore a famous name, since it included the town and province of Cajamarca itself. This might be taken as an indication of Verdugo's great importance, but there would be little ground for such an interpretation. As transcendental as were the events of November 16, 1532, Cajamarca as a site soon sank back into obscurity. It did not become a Spanish town, and it was not located on a major trade route. Verdugo's encomienda was among the largest and best in Trujillo, ranked first in income by some; yet his occasional complaints about having been slighted were not without some validity, as it became increasingly obvious that the best silver deposits were located far to the south in Upper Peru.

Though Melchor was apparently not on Trujillo's council at the time of its foundation, Francisco Pizarro soon made him a perpetual member, and the crown confirmed the appointment. For a time he was also chief constable of Trujillo.

Once his position was established on this basis, Melchor's activities went in the conventional directions. He sent money home to his mother, and he requested honors at the royal court. A coat of arms (with no mention of previous family arms) was granted him, but a

royal captaincy and membership in the Order of Santiago were not. He
built one of the finest houses in Trujillo on his lot at the corner of the
town square. He had a mestizo daughter legitimated. He developed his
encomienda intensively, including both silver mining in the Spanish
style under European supervision, and extortion of valuables from the
Indian chieftain (a standard technique of Panama that faded slowly in
Peru as its long-run incompatibility with steady revenue production
became apparent). He also exported provisions to Panama. On the
other hand, he had a church built in Cajamarca. The least standard
aspect of his behavior, and even that was nothing very unusual, was
his affair with the married daughter of Francisco de Fuentes, also a
man of Cajamarca.

By sixteenth-century Spanish standards it was not to be expected
that a stripling should distinguish himself in war, either by feats of
arms or in positions of command. Verdugo was hardly mentioned in
the civil wars until the "War of Chupas" in 1542. By some accounts
he shirked his duty, as did indeed many encomenderos of the north,
feeling the Lima-Cuzco rivalries were irrelevant to their vital interests.
Yet by other accounts Melchor stood out at the climactic battle of
Chupas, near Cuzco.

Verdugo's fame, or notoriety, came only with the Gonzalo Pizarro
rebellion of 1544–1548, and was brought on mainly by considerations
of Spanish regional origin. The first viceroy of Peru, Blasco Núñez
Vela, was also from Avila and therefore favored Verdugo in every
way from the moment he arrived in the country. Though Blasco
Núñez's general mission was to cut into the power of the encomienda
in Peru, and he usually acted the part of the martinet, he left Verdugo's
tributes untouched. When the revolt against Blasco Núñez began to
assume serious proportions, he made Verdugo one of the loyalist captains (his first such appointment). Verdugo was and remained one of
the viceroy's few allies among the encomenderos of Peru. When
Gonzalo Pizarro seized Lima and the governorship of Peru, Verdugo
only pretended to acquiesce. He excused himself from Pizarro's Quito
campaign against the viceroy by alleging leg trouble.

Thus he was left at home in Trujillo, in a position to carry out one
of the most bizarre, spectacular, and ambiguous exploits in the annals
of the Peruvian civil wars. While Pizarro's army was far to the north
in 1545, he conceived the notion of organizing a party in Trujillo to
go to the aid of his compatriot the viceroy. One day in late October

of that year he beguiled several prominent Trujillans into his house, seized them, and put them in irons. Then Verdugo, his immediate household of retainers and followers, and a few other loyalists took possession of the town. In the name of viceroy and king, Verdugo commandeered a passing ship, organized a company of men, and sailed from Trujillo. While his intentions seemed beyond reproach, Melchor used the opportunity to settle private accounts with fellow citizens in his own favor. To reward his men, he confiscated a large shipment of merchandise, including a good stock of fine stuffs and clothing.

As his expedition proceeded, its purpose became ever more unclear. Instead of going directly to the viceroy, Verdugo sailed to Nicaragua, where his men did more to disturb the peace than to save the country. Under pressure to leave quickly, they decided to go to the Caribbean and try to rejoin the viceroy from the north. Their hazardous trip to the sea in a fleet of small boats appears to have been the first navigation of the Desaguadero. Once on the Caribbean, Melchor and his men captured a ship and sailed south along the coast. But, hearing of the viceroy's death, they decided to attack the port town of Nombre de Dios, then in Pizarrist hands, rather than return toward Peru. In June, 1546, Verdugo took Nombre de Dios and the ships in its harbor; once again his action became the pretext for a large-scale confiscation of goods and money from merchants, and some of his men engaged in looting. Pizarrists from Panama soon arrived to expel Verdugo, and he left for Cartagena on the coast of New Granada (the present Colombia). There his men, in a now familiar pattern, again caused much trouble.

Shortly afterwards a new royal governor, Licenciado Gasca, arrived at Nombre de Dios to begin the task of putting down Gonzalo Pizarro's revolt. Verdugo returned to join him, but Gasca, who was to pacify Peru more by entreaty than by force, had to consider the interests of the merchants and other groups. He thanked Verdugo for his efforts, then ordered him to disband his men and make restitution to the merchants. This rebuff sent Verdugo off to Spain to protest at court. His main business did not go very well there; he barely managed to fend off official accusations that his campaigns were superfluous and that he had plundered innocent people.

In other ways, however, he had resounding success during his sojourn in Spain in 1548–1550. Above all, he succeeded in getting the great honor, earlier denied him, of membership in the Order of Santiago. Probably his personal presence at court was the crucial added factor, rather than his dubious "services." In any case it was quite an honor. Only three other men of Cajamarca became knights of Santiago—Francisco and Hernando Pizarro, and Hernando de Soto. Membership eluded as eminent a man as Sebastián de Benalcázar and as formidable a negotiator as Jerónimo de Aliaga (who also was in Spain for years). Around this time Verdugo married doña Jordana Mejía, from Espinar, within a few miles of Avila; she was the daughter of a captain of Viceroy Blasco Nuñez.

After this Verdugo lived as a great lord in Trujillo, if possible more ambitious and pretentious than ever. In 1554 he aspired to the position of *maestre de campo*, or second in command, of the army organized against rebel Francisco Hernández Girón; the offer of a cavalry captaincy merely angered him, and after rejecting it he soon went home "sick." In the latter 1550's Verdugo wooed Viceroy Cañete, and was sent back to Spain once more to represent the viceroy's interests against the *audiencia*. This time he had less luck than before. Soon he was weighed down with lawsuits, both civil and criminal, new and old. Finally, in 1562, he received a royal pardon, and he was back in Peru by 1564. He died in Trujillo in 1567, and since he left no legitimate children, his wife succeeded in the encomienda. A nephew became a council member of Lima, with a long line of descendants.

NOTES. A somewhat corrupt version of the title of Verdugo's encomienda is to be found in *RANP* 15 (1942):13–14. Around 1542 Governor Vaca de Castro gave a fourth of the encomienda to Hernando de Alvarado. This did not necessarily imply disapproval, since there was a general tendency to reduce some of the larger early grants at this time. Something of Verdugo's manner of operating his estate can be deduced from various known details. Verdugo claimed to be the first Spaniard to work silver mines in Peru. In 1542 he already had a large house and was maintaining five or six Spaniards, a priest, and several horses (AGI, Patronato 97, no. 1, ramo 1). In 1546 he kept a blacksmith in his house, and he was able to induce a shipmaster to come to see him because he intended to send some flour, maize, and Indian clothing to Panama (Gutiérrez de Santa Clara, *Quinquenarios*, III, 40–41). Around 1549 a commission reported that Verdugo's encomienda yielded some six thousand pesos from silver mines, with the encomendero supplying a Spanish miner and tools, and beyond this, the Indians delivered woolen goods, meat, maize, and wheat and supplied their master's house abundantly (Loredo, *Los repartos*, pp. 250, 255).

Melchor Verdugo's relationship to fray Pedro Verdugo is pure speculation, tempting because fray Pedro is known to have been friendly with
Viceroy Blasco Nuñez Vela, and because such a relationship would offer a
ready explanation for Melchor's cross of Santiago. (See don Francesillo de
Zúñiga, *Crónica*.) The circumstantial evidence for family ties with Hernando Verdugo de Henao, notary and majordomo for Secretary don Francisco de los Cobos, is stronger. The latter was in Peru in 1538–1539 on
business for Cobos. (See AGI, Justicia 1067, no. 2, ramo 1; HC 330, 357,
659; Keniston, *Cobos*, pp. 294, 312, 315.) No definite contact between
Melchor and Hernando at that time is established, but at the same time
there appeared in Lima a priest, Alonso de Henao, who in the early 1540's
joined Melchor in Trujillo as an aide or accountant and then accompanied
him on his journey to Nicaragua and Panama. A Sancho de Henao also
went along (Busto, "Verdugo," p. 380, n.105).

See Busto's long article "El Capitán Melchor Verdugo, encomendero
de Cajamarca," *Revista Histórica* 24 (1959):318–387, for a more detailed
account of Verdugo's activities in war and at court. Though at times using
the coy speculation of the historical novelist, and arriving thereby at a
literarily sinister picture of Verdugo, Busto has reconstructed Verdugo's
activity with great accuracy. The present writer has relied on Busto for
materials contained in AGI, Justicia 439, 776, 1081, and 1125.

Verdugo's *probanza de servicios* of 1542, with much other litigation and
testimony, is in AGI, Patronato 97, no. 1, ramo 1. There some of his fellows estimate his age as reported above in the text; he himself said in 1536
that he was twenty-three (AGI, Patronato 93, no. 6, ramo 3). Among the
many places where he is called a native of Avila are Calvete, *Rebelión de
Pizarro*, IV, 277, and Zárate, *Historia*, II, 535. A most enlightening personal letter from Verdugo to his mother is published in Porras, *Cartas*, pp.
231–233. Others are in AGI, Justicia 1125.

Other references may be found in AGI, Indiferente General 1801, records of ship *San Miguel*, 1535; Justicia 425, no. 4; 1052, no. 2; Lima 118,
probanza of Sebastián de Torres; 566, vol. IV, May 4, 1542; Patronato 109,
ramo 4; ANP, PA 78, 134, 375, 380; Alzate, ff.272, 274; HC 655;
RANP 4 (1926):18; Busto, "Maldonado el Rico," *Revista Histórica* 26
(1962–1963):115; Calvete, *Rebelión de Pizarro*, IV, 256; Castellanos,
Elegías, p. 502; Cieza, *Tercera parte*, in *Mercurio Peruano* 36 (1955):468;
Diego Fernández, *Historia*, I, 78–79; Gómara, *Hispania victrix*, I, 237;
Gutiérrez de Santa Clara, *Quinquenarios*, II, 281; III, 282; Moreyra Paz
Soldán, "Dos oidores del primer tercio del siglo XVII," *Mercurio Peruano*
27 (1946):549–550; Pedro Pizarro, *Relación*, V, 233–234; Porras, *Cedu-
lario*, II, 349, 385; Vargas Ugarte, "La fecha de la fundación de Trujillo,"
Revista Histórica 10 (1936):234; Zárate, *Historia*, II, 506.

Antonio de Vergara

Age at Cajamarca: About 23   Place of origin: Oropesa
Role: Footman   (western New Castile)
Share: 1 full share of gold   Father: Rodrigo de Vergara
   and silver   Extent of literacy: Literate

Vergara came from one of the local hidalgo families who made up the court, servants, and following of the Count of Oropesa. He was somehow related to Hernando de Soto's partner, Hernán Ponce de León, and also to the Orgoños family. He considered himself a cousin of Rodrigo Orgoños, the famous captain of Almagro; Rodrigo was illegitimate and may not have been a true member of the family at all, but his supposed father, Juan Orgoños, was an acknowledged hidalgo of Oropesa. Fray Vicente de Valverde was from yet another such family, connected with Orgoños through marriage. It is indeed quite possible that Vergara accompanied fray Vicente from Spain in 1530, since he is not known to have had previous experience in the Indies.

At any rate, Vergara was very well thought of by his companions on the Peru expedition; he was listed near the top of the footmen at Cajamarca, with the full share that went to less than a third of them. The only trace he has left of his activity in the subsequent course of the conquest is his cousin Rodrigo Orgoños's statement that he gave a good account of himself. He circulated mainly among compatriots from the Talavera-Oropesa region, and was enough of a man of affairs to be frequently entrusted with the business of his companions. He left Peru in 1534 with the main group of returnees, including fray Vicente; for Orgoños he carried 20,000 pesos of gold and 2,000 marks of silver, which was rather more than his own fortune. Vergara fell ill in Panama, but arrived safely in Seville in 1535. Once in Spain he had regrets, feeling he should have earned even more money and honor, and thought of going back, but in the end he did not. Perhaps he heeded Orgoños's advice, that he was plenty rich for his age, and that it was as well to be back in Spain young and rich as older and richer. Vergara appears to have gone first to his home in Oropesa, but before long he settled in Seville, where he attained a position almost any of his fellows in arms might have envied. By 1552 he was a *veinticuatro* on the council of Seville, the most prestigious municipal corporation in Spain. His compatriot or relative Ponce de León also came to Seville and obtained a seat on the council. Aside from a life of splendor, Vergara was active in the thriving commerce of Seville, and he may have grown richer as he grew older after all. He was still living in Seville in 1577, one of the last survivors of the men of Cajamarca in either hemisphere.

NOTES. Vergara gave his age in 1543 as thirty-four (AGI, Patronato 90, no. 1, ramo 1), and in 1577 as sixty-seven or sixty-eight (AGI, Patronato 93, no. 4, ramo 3). Lest there should be any doubt that the Vergara in Seville was the man of Cajamarca, at both of these times Vergara was a citizen of Seville and specifically testified to his participation in the capture of Atahuallpa. The Vergara who was *veinticuatro* was definitely the same man, as can be seen in his testimony on behalf of Cajamarca man Juan de Porras (AGI, Justicia 1073, no. 1). Vergara is called a native of Oropesa in ANP, PA 791. An essential source for Vergara's connections are the letters of Rodrigo Orgoños, in Porras, *Cartas*, pp. 131–133, 146, 164–168.

Other references are in AGI, Indiferente General 1801, records of ship *Santa Catalina*, 1535; ANP, PA 11, 39, 117, 124, 138, 139; HC 80; *DHA*, I, 141–142; Porras, "Medina y su contribución a la historia peruana," *Mercurio Peruano* 33 (1952):510, 513.

9. CLERKS

THE NOTARIES AND ACCOUNTANTS in this chapter require no further introduction than a brief mention of their affinities to the men in other categories. Many, if not most, were also men of affairs, like those in chapter 10; some few were clearly hidalgos (chapter 8), while others could find a place among the marginal hidalgos and upper plebeians (chapter 11). On the other hand, some further probable notaries can be found in the other sections (See Part I, chapter 2, n.22).

Jerónimo de Aliaga

Age at Cajamarca: About 24
Role: Horseman
Share: 2 shares of gold;
  1⅞ shares of silver

Place of origin: Segovia (Old Castile)
Parents: Juan de Aliaga and
  Francisca Ramírez
Degree of literacy: Highly literate
Profession: Notary

A great calculator and negotiator, very much in his element in the labyrinthine processes of Spanish law, Jerónimo de Aliaga was living proof that the first conquerors were not all ignorant fellows, quickly to be displaced from positions of power. He easily adjusted to changing conditions and ultimately achieved the double success of permanent high office in Peru and entry into courtly society in Spain.

Aliaga was a conqueror by the book. When he first arrived in Panama around 1529, he went to the veteran Blas de Atienza to ask what was needed to go on an expedition. Atienza obligingly wrote down a memorandum of the necessary things, which Aliaga proceeded to buy. Thus equipped, he gained experience in some small ventures in the Panama area before heading for Peru with the first boat of reinforcements arriving at Coaque in 1531. Thereafter he was in all the main events of the conquest and civil wars. But while he faced the hardships of exploration and the dangers of battle, the essential lines of his career can be seen in his advance as a notary. He came from Spain with a permanent title as His Majesty's notary, already one step ahead of the multitude of young secretaries in the Indies who had the training but lacked the money or connections to obtain a title from the royal court. Aliaga was the main practicing notary with the expedition from the time of the events of Cajamarca until after the conquest of Cuzco. The documents he has left—powers of attorney, loans, sales of horses—are the source of much of our knowledge of this period. In 1534 he acted as provisional royal inspector at the division of the treasure of Cuzco, and shortly thereafter he was the first clerk of the municipal council of Jauja, predecessor of Lima as the intended capital of Peru. Within a few months he delegated this post to a deputy and for several months in 1535 held the post of acting accountant general of all Peru. In 1538 Aliaga sent off seven thousand pesos to Juan de Sámano, secretary of Charles V, and in return was named chief government clerk of the kingdom of Peru. To this was added the chief secretaryship of the Royal Audiencia of Peru when that court was established in Lima in 1544.

Aliaga's success was soundly based on training and performance in his profession, plus tough negotiation at court. But the society in which he was immersed insisted on prowess at arms and gentle birth as prerequisites for advancement, so he turned his skill to enlarging upon his endowment in those respects. As to prowess in war and conquest, there is no reason to believe Aliaga met the incredible dangers and hardships of the time less than adequately. But the exploits abounding in the life of a heroic type like Diego de Agüero are lacking, and most of those alleged by Aliaga himself are suspect. After eighteen years in Peru, in his third memorial of services performed, Aliaga suddenly recalled that he had personally captured an Indian chieftain in Panama twenty years earlier. No one else could remember the incident, though one witness thought he might have heard something about it. The truth is, no doubt, that Aliaga was present—among others—at the chieftain's capture. According to Aliaga, he and Martín de Robles led a dangerous escape from the camp of rebel Gonzalo Pizarro in 1547, but looking in the chronicles one finds mention only of Robles. In his later years Aliaga always styled himself Captain, but he never held that position in combat until the battle of Jaquijahuana in 1548, famous for never having taken place. His main activity in this campaign was raising men and organizing supply and finance. The one truly responsible post of command Aliaga held was as deputy governor of the Lima district in 1542 just after its evacuation by rebel forces, a delicate but not a military mission. Of all his boasted exploits, the most truly genuine seems to have been that he was in the forefront of the cavalry at the battle of Chupas, fiercest fought among the Spaniards of Peru, for we find his name in the chroniclers' lists of those who distinguished themselves there.

As to that other lubricant of preferment, good birth, Aliaga was in a somewhat better position, and he pressed his advantage. That he was no very resounding nobleman can be deduced from the size of his patrimony, a yearly income of three thousand maravedises, or just eight ducats. His mother bore the plebeian name of plain Francisca Ramírez, and Aliaga shied away from her relative Ana Ramírez, who came to Lima and married off a daughter to old commoner Pedro de Alconchel. Aliaga waited until 1543, when he already had wealth and a coat of arms, to institute proceedings in Spain to prove that he was an hidalgo, and the necessity of doing so at that late date is itself mute testimony. Nevertheless, he certainly must have been related to some hidalgo family; he was connected with Rodrigo de Contreras, governor of Nicaragua, and with the Mercados, one of whom was later a judge on the Audiencia of Lima (possibly through Jerónimo's influence). The mere fact of having had a patrimony at all speaks for certain family pretensions. At any rate, Jerónimo in his 1535 memorial was one of the first of the men of Cajamarca to claim that he was an "hidalgo and person of honor." It is true that the witnesses turned the matter around, replying that he was a "person of honor and hidalgo," and some left out the hidalgo part entirely, but the claim was established.

In praise of his deeds and birth Aliaga obtained more pages of testimony than any two or three of the other conquerors, hoping to impress by bulk, for much of what the witnesses said is actually damaging, if read carefully. Above all, Aliaga secured the testimony of important people, including Hernando de Soto and Francisco Pizarro himself. Aliaga was a past master of the art of finagling. A good many of the conquerors got a royal license to come to Spain for a year or two; Aliaga alone got a license for three years. As secretary of the *audiencia*, he managed to play a prominent part in the seizure of Viceroy Blasco Núñez Vela in 1544 without seriously incriminating himself. It was this ability that won Aliaga the mission of *procurador*, or envoy, of the encomenderos of Peru to the royal court in 1549, after the Gonzalo Pizarro rebellion.

The same streak of calculation and management was dominant in Aliaga's personal life, but not so much so as to obscure certain very human qualities. In an elaborate memorandum to Gregorio de Sotelo, who took money home for him, it can be seen that he wanted half of his income in Spain to be spent on charity. He appears to have married his first wife in Lima in the 1530's for love rather than high lineage, though he soon transformed the girl from Beatriz Vázquez into doña Beatriz de Medrano. It is needless to say that he was one of the great encomenderos of Lima, and very rich in houses and lands. He instituted an entail for his heirs by doña Beatriz, but his favorite was his mestizo son don Jerónimo (all his sons were called don), to whom he bequeathed the lucrative secretaryship of the *audiencia*. In the elaborateness of his provisions he overstepped the bounds of clarity, and even made mistakes, omitting the name of his son don Juan at one crucial place. The result was a century of litigation among his heirs.

When Aliaga left for Spain in 1550, ostensibly to return soon, he had made a lasting mark on Peru. He may have known already that he would never come back; he took his favorite, don Jerónimo, with him, and left his legitimate sons in Lima to inherit the encomienda. Once in Spain, he had to go as far abroad as Flanders and Innsbruck to see the Emperor. Doña Beatriz had died in Peru while the Aliaga family was fleeing from Gonzalo Pizarro, and Aliaga soon married doña Juana de Manrique, daughter of the Count of Paredes. They retired to live at the count's residence of Villapalacios, though Aliaga was still in close touch with the royal court and the Council of the Indies. For a long time he maintained at least the pretense that his stay in Spain was temporary. This he dropped in 1565, when he received royal permission to exercise his offices through deputies. He died in Villapalacios in 1569, but in many essentials he should be counted among the settlers rather than the returnees. His heirs maintained the position in Lima that he had won for them. The only family of the men of Cajamarca to reach the twentieth century still intact and bearing the same name, they still possess their ancestral home, on the lot across from the governor's palace that was granted to Jerónimo de Aliaga in 1535.

N O T E S . Aliaga said he was about twenty-eight in 1536 (AGI, Patronato 93, no. 6, ramo 3), and in 1548 gave his age both as thirty-eight (AGI, Lima 204, *probanza* of don Juan de Sandoval) and as forty (AGI, Patronato 92, no. 3). Several sources make him a native of Segovia; for example, the royal grant of arms (Porras, *Cedulario*, II, 200). Aliaga's testament of 1547 is in *RANP* 14 (1941): 165–172; that of 1569 is in Loredo, "Documentos sobre el conquistador Aliaga," *Revista Histórica* 12 (1939):183–203. The foundation of Aliaga's entail is in *RANP* 2 (1921):137–154. His three *probanzas de servicios* are in *RANP* 1 (1920): 423–604. A remarkable memorandum Aliaga wrote to Gregorio de Sotelo reveals much about his connections, plans, and ambitions (Loredo, *Los repartos*, pp. 411–431). Aliaga's obligation to Secretary Sámano is in HC 330; his power to institute proceedings to establish *hidalguía* is in AGI, Justicia 1052, no. 1.

There are other references in AGI, Indiferente General 1801, records of the ship *San Miguel*, 1535; Justicia 1126, no. 2, ramo 1; Lima 177, *probanza* of Lorenzo de Aliaga; Lima 565, vol. III, November 8, 1539; Patronato 185, ramo 11; 192, no. 1, ramo 4; ANP, PA 20, 138, 248, 419, 650, 667, 678, 725, 735, 744, 745, 749, 759, 764; Salinas 1542–1543, f.28; BNP, A556, ff.27–28; HC 67, 150, 330, 382, 383; *CDIHC*, VI, 424; *CDIHE*, XXVI, 202–203; *DHA*, I, 141–142; *RANP*, 4 (1926):6, 201; 6 (1928):164; 7 (1929):201; 10 (1937):220; 11 (1938):227; 14 (1941):89; Angulo, "El capitán Gerónimo de Aliaga," *RANP* 2 (1921): 131–136; Bermúdez Plata, *Pasajeros*, I, 373; Calvete, *Rebelión de Pizarro*, IV, 390, 407; V, 13, 98, 113; Cieza, *Salinas*, p. 101; Cieza, *Tercera parte*, in *Mercurio Peruano* 36 (1955):468; Cobo, *Obras*, II, 303; Diego Fernández, *Historia*, I, 33, 42; Garcilaso, *Obras*, III, 506, 572; Gutiérrez de Santa Clara, *Quinquenarios*, II, 173, 235, 247, 252–254, 258, 262, 269, 275, 287,

288; IV, 108, 145, 151; Loredo, *Los repartos*, pp. 125, 219, 227, 231; Montoto, *Nobiliario*, p. 20; Pérez de Tudela, *Gasca*, II, 352, 353, 425, 430; Porras, *Cartas*, pp. 131, 196; Porras, *Cedulario*, II, 176; Porras, in Trujillo, *Relación*, p. 94; Torres Saldamando, *Libro primero de cabildos*, I, 205; Zárate, *Historia*, II, 506, 572.

Nicolás de Azpeitia

Age at Cajamarca: About 25 or 26   Place of origin: Azpeitia (Biscay)
Role: Horseman   Degree of literacy: Fully literate
Share: 2 shares of gold and   Profession: Accountant or secretary
  1⅞ shares of silver

His full name, as he used it in Spain, was Nicolás Sáenz de Evola, but like many Basques he took the name of his home town as a surname in the Indies. He probably joined the expedition in Coaque in 1531 with the first reinforcements sent by Almagro, since he worked for the royal treasurer, Riquelme, writing account books, and Riquelme arrived at that time. In Jauja in 1533 he was named provisional royal accountant in the place of Antonio Navarro, who was going on to Cuzco. His personal life was defined by Basque connections, starting with his Basque partner, Gaspar de Marquina. When his fellow Basques Anadel and Aguirre went home, in 1533, he was left in charge of winding up their affairs. For a time he lived with Francisco de Calahorra, factor of the Basque merchant Domingo de Soraluce, and it is more than possible that he was involved in their ventures himself, as commerce and accounting used one and the same technique. Azpeitia left Peru in the latter part of 1534, arriving in Spain in 1535, and returning soon to his birthplace, Azpeitia, in the Basque country, where he was still living in 1541.

N O T E S .   The name Sáenz also appears as Sánchez, and Evola as Hevola; our man also called himself just Nicolás de Evola. Azpeitia gave his age in 1534 as twenty-five (AGI, Lima 204, *probanza* of Hernán González), in 1538 as thirty-two (AGI, Justicia 1124, no. 5, ramo 1), and in 1541 as thirty-six (AGI, Justicia 1126, no. 2, ramo 1). In the latter two statements he appears as a citizen of Azpeitia. Information on his work for Riquelme is in AGI, Patronato 28, ramo 55. Further references are in ANP, PA 10, 19, 41, 117; HC 33, 43, 59, 66.

Pedro de Barrera

Age at Cajamarca: About 26   Place of origin: Madrid
Role: Horseman   Degree of literacy: Highly literate
Share: Double share of gold   Profession: Notary and attorney
  and silver

As early as 1522, if the memory of the chronicler Oviedo is correct, Pedro de Barrera was officiating as a notary in Panama; he also
dabbled in merchandise. Around 1524 or 1525, he moved to the
newly settled area of Nicaragua. There he seems to have acquired an
encomienda, at the same time continuing to work as a notary and advo-
cate. There is no evidence, however, that Barrera practiced his trade in
Peru.

Though he outstayed his Madrid compatriot Francisco de Baena,
who left in 1533, Barrera was even then thinking of home. When
Baena left he apparently took with him his friend's petition to be allowed to come to Spain for a year and a half without losing his encomienda; the petition was granted by the crown in Toledo in March,
1534. Whether Barrera actually had an encomienda, or had any serious intention of returning to Peru, is not known. At any rate he left
the country in July or August of 1534, long before the royal license
had time to reach him. Back in Spain, he went to court and obtained an
elaborate coat of arms. While he never made any attempt to return to
Peru, he did not lose touch completely; in 1552 he was a solicitor in
the Royal Council of the Indies.

N O T E S .   As indicated in the section of Francisco de Baena, Barrera
and Baena may well have been partners. Barrera's name also appears as
Pedro de la Barrera and Pedro de Barreda.
    In 1535 Barrera said he was twenty-eight or twenty-nine (*CDIHN*, III,
414), and in 1554 that he was forty-eight (AGI, Patronato 98, no. 4,
ramo 6). Both times he described himself as a citizen of Madrid, and the
chronicler Oviedo makes the flat statement that he *was* from Madrid
(*Historia*, V, 92). Barrera's position as solicitor emerges in AGI, Justicia
1073. A very brief statement of his career in the Indies is in AGI, Lima
565, vol. III, November 20, 1539.
    Other references are in AGI, Indiferente General 1204, *probanza* of
Pedro Cataño; Justicia 719, no. 9; 1126, no. 2, ramo 1; ANP, PA 1, 5, 39,

124, 138; *CDIHN*, II, 2, 5, 9, 128, 218, 225, 246, 521; III, 50; *RANP* 4 (1926):194; Oviedo, *Historia*, III, 276, 278; Porras, *Cedulario*, I, 146; II, 414.

Miguel Estete

Age at Cajamarca: About 24 or 25	Place of origin: Santo Domingo
Role: Horseman	de la Calzada (mountains
Share: Double share of gold	of Old Castile)
and silver, plus a token amount	Extent of literacy: Highly literate
of 100 pesos	Profession: Accountant, secretary,
	or notary

Both of the Estetes at Cajamarca came to the Indies in the train of Martín Estete, a notary and secretary who had long served Governor Pedrarias de Avila, first in Panama and then in the later 1520's in Nicaragua, where Pedrarias made him captain of some minor expeditions. After Cajamarca, when the riches of Peru became known, Martín Estete came there himself and settled in Trujillo.

Miguel Estete was doubtless trained as a notary like his relative Martín. His profession shines through not only in his beautiful and elaborate signature, but also in his activity as a treasury official and his authorship of a chronicle—almost all the chronicles of Peru were written by notaries, from Francisco de Jerez and Pedro Sancho to Diego Fernández el Palentino. When he got back to Spain and was rich, Estete claimed he was of very noble birth, an *hidalgo notorio de solar conocido*. It is hard to get at the truth of such a sweeping assertion; his better-known relative, Martín, certainly did not have the kind of reputation that would corroborate the claim, yet Estete did have connections, and he had an education that enabled him to circulate in the Spanish royal court with ease.

Miguel had been in Nicaragua with Martín Estete since about 1526 or 1527, and came to Peru under Hernando de Soto. He went on most of the hazardous missions of the campaign, with Soto and with others. Just after Cajamarca, Hernando Pizarro and a few men went to the coastal temple of Pachacámac to gather treasure, and Estete went along as treasurer and recorder, with the title of *veedor*. The journal he wrote of the trip was incorporated into two chronicles, those of Oviedo and Jerez. Estete also helped to arrange the general division of the treasure, having been chosen probably more for his expertise in accounting than to give substantive advice.

After seeing the conquest of Cuzco, he left Peru in 1534 with many others. Since he was by now an influential man, as well as knowledgeable in accounting and the ways of government, many of the other returnees asked him to register money for them, so that he arrived in Seville responsible for over 28,000 pesos of gold, aside from much silver. His knowledge and influence, however, failed to keep officials from seizing the whole amount. Estete soon settled in Valladolid, a court town within traveling distance of his birthplace of Santo Domingo de la Calzada. At some time not long after his return he wrote a vivid chronicle of the conquest of Peru, unusual among contemporary accounts in its incipient understanding (not always approval) of Inca culture and Peruvian geography. He lived on in Valladolid until 1550, at least.

N O T E S .   The name Estete often occurs in the variant Astete. Miguel Estete seems to have been enamored of the age twenty-seven. He was twenty-seven in 1534 (AGI, Patronato 150, no. 6, ramo 2), twenty-seven in 1535 (*CDIHN*, III, 413–414 and AGI, Justicia 719, no. 9), and still twenty-seven in 1537 (AGI, Justicia 1124, no. 6, ramo 3). At that rate he would have been twenty-seven in 1532 also, but the writer decided to disregard his last testimony and estimate his birthdate according to the other two as c.1507–1508. Porras Barrenechea opines that he was born in 1507.

On the testimony of Diego de Molina, one of the men of Cajamarca, the chronicler Oviedo says that Miguel Estete was a native of Santo Domingo de la Calzada (*Historia*, V, 92). We may be sure that the man referred to is not the other Estete, because on the day before Cajamarca he was on horseback, riding with Soto to meet Atahuallpa.

Estete's principal chronicle is published under the title *Relación de la Conquista del Perú* in the *Colección de libros y documentos referentes a la historia del Perú*, vol. VIII (2nd series), edited by Horacio H. Urteaga. Estete's account of Hernando Pizarro's trip to Pachacámac is included in Jerez, *Verdadera relación*, II, 338–343. Another version is in Oviedo, *Historia*, V, 68–78. Porras discusses Estete's life and writings in *Cronistas*, pp. 106–108.

Other references are in AGI, Indiferente General 1204, no. 44; 1801, records of ship *San Miguel*, 1535; Justicia 1124, no. 5, ramo 3; ANP, PA 34; Salinas 1538–1540, f.107; *CDIHC*, VII, 153; *CDIHE*, X, 312; *CDIHN*, I, 57; Altolaguirre y Duvale, *Vasco Núñez de Balboa*, p. 189; Medina, *Descubrimiento*, II, 390; Porras, *Cedulario*, II, 71; Porras, *Rela-*

ciones primitivas, p. 98; Porras, in Trujillo, *Relación*, p. 83; Lee, "Algunos documentos sobre los primeros conquistadores," *Revista Histórica* 8 (1925):196.
See also Miguel Estete de Santo Domingo in chapter 11.

Gabriel Félix

Age at Cajamarca: 26 or more   Extent of literacy: Fully literate
Role: Horseman   Trade: Accountant
Share: 2½₀ shares of silver; no gold

Gabriel Félix was accountant of the "company" (the expedition taken as a private venture, distinct from the royal treasury officials who also accompanied the conquest). Holding this job was tantamount to working for the Pizarros, and Félix may have been an acknowledged Pizarro retainer, like his counterpart, Gonzalo de Pineda, "company" treasurer. Given this connection and the responsibility of his position, it is quite surprising to see that his share was worth no more than the lowliest footman's. With some of the other men who apparently received no share of the gold, one might suspect that their names were omitted by mistake (in the copying process) but in this case we have Félix's later testimony that he got "a share of the silver" at Cajamarca. Perhaps his horse was to blame, for he soon bought a better one. With a tiny share, relegated to the end of the list of cavalry, he seems to have been in disgrace of some kind. His position was in no serious jeopardy, however, since he again acted as accountant in the division of the equally large treasure of Cuzco. After that he quickly returned to Jauja, and he arrived back in Spain in 1535. In 1541 he was still in Seville, a resident and citizen, making it probable, though by no means certain, that he had originally come out of the world of Andalusian commerce.

NOTES. The name Félix was extremely rare. Possibly Gabriel Félix was in some way connected with Alonso Félix de Morales, an early encomendero of Trujillo, who was from Córdoba.

In 1541 Gabriel Félix was a citizen of Seville in the district of San Vicente and declared his age as over thirty-five (AGI, Justicia 1112, no. 2, ramo 1). Other references are in AGI, Contaduría 1825, records from Jauja, Nov. 1534; ANP, PA 16, 37; Loredo, *Los repartos*, p. 96; Porras, *Relaciones primitivas*, p. 98.

For Alonso Félix de Morales see AGI, Patronato 116, no. 2, ramo 3, and Cabero, "El corregimiento de Saña," *Revista Histórica* 1 (1906):486–489, 510.

Francisco de Jerez

Age at Cajamarca: About 34 or 35	Place of origin: Seville
Role: Horseman	Father: Pedro de Jerez
Share: Double share of gold and silver	Extent of literacy: Fully literate
plus ¼ share for secretarial work	Trade: Notary

Jerez was one of the most experienced of all the men of Cajamarca and certainly the one longest associated with Francisco Pizarro in the Peruvian enterprise. He came to the Indies in 1514 with the armada of Governor Pedrarias de Avila, when he was still in his teens. Apparently he already had practical training as a notary, but not an official notary's title, probably being too poor to negotiate for a title at court. For almost twenty years he held notarial positions of all kinds, including that of notary public and council clerk in Acla on the Isthmus and that of registrar of mines in Panama, until finally, in 1533, when he was already on his way home to Spain, he received a royal appointment as notary. Jerez never presumed of high lineage, and was probably from a modest if not humble family, since in litigation he was once called "low, vile and of little account," terms usually reserved for plebeians.

In 1524 he went on the first voyage Pizarro made toward the "Levant," in the combined positions of the captain's secretary and notary-registrar for the whole expedition. Not deterred by the poor results of the first trip, he continued in the same post on the second voyage, by now a trusted confidant of the captain, or so we may judge by Jerez's credible statement that Pizarro "told me his secrets and everything he meant to do." He did not stay behind with Pizarro and the Thirteen on the Isle of Gorgona in 1527, but returned to Panama "destitute and ill." It is by no means certain that all those returning to Panama were actually deserting the venture. Jerez did not sign the well-known general letter of complaint to Panama that expedition members wrote from Gallo Island in August, 1527; a little later he showed solidarity with the Thirteen by testifying to the magnitude of their accomplishment.

When the conquering expedition of 1531 sailed from Panama, Jerez was not aboard, but it seems that he must have planned to help with arrangements for outfitting the first relief ship, and then to go with it to join the main body. This he subsequently did, arriving before the Spaniards had moved beyond their first halting place at Coaque. Jerez was closely identified with Pizarro even during the time when he was still in Panama. In April of 1531 Diego de Almagro, who was understandably resentful and suspicious of Pizarro after having been left out of any position of honor in the government of Peru, prepared a memorial to the crown to prove how important he had been in the discovery. One of the witnesses called was Francisco de Jerez, who made friendly statements about Almagro and said he deserved any honor that could be given him, but was noncommittal about Pizarro's neglect of his partner, and, in response to a query about whether Almagro persuaded Pizarro to continue when the latter was discouraged, denied that such a thing had happened, saying that "Captain Pizarro never could be convinced to return, nor ever had any such thought, but said he would die in the attempt rather than turn back."

From Coaque on to Cajamarca Jerez acted as Pizarro's secretary once again; perhaps it had been understood from the beginning that he would occupy his familiar position on arrival, though there was also a Juan Alonso who was "notary of the armada." At Cajamarca, Jerez had the misfortune to break his leg and was left lame for life. For this reason he returned to Spain without accompanying the conquest to its conclusion. He left Peru at the end of July, 1533, charged with carrying back to Spain the first full-scale official report of the expedition from Panama to Cajamarca, written by himself. (It is possible that Pizarro, who in Peru showed a tendency to change advisors and secretaries frequently, dismissed Jerez from his post. But Jerez had been with him for nine years, was loyal, and did not represent any threat of independent power, so it remains most probable that his physical condition really was the primary reason for his quick return.)

A month after Jerez arrived in Seville in 1534, his report was published as a chronicle, and such was the public's interest in Peru that it was republished in 1547, included in other chronicles, and also translated into Italian. Oviedo says that it "does not proceed with good style." It is certainly not in Oviedo's own vein of chatty journalism with humanistic overtones, but in its terseness and austerity it is far more expressive of the character of the conquerors of Peru than Oviedo's work, even if in some ways admittedly less informative.

With his wealth and notoriety, Jerez had considerable success in rising in Sevillian society. In the late 1540's he held the honorific municipal office of fiel ejecutor for two years, and, after the death of his first wife (of whom nothing is known), he made a good marriage to doña Francisca de Pineda. The Pinedas were prominent in the upper reaches of the notarial profession in Seville and considered themselves very noble; Jerez's children bore the impressive names of Pineda and Ponce de León. Jerez was active for a time in commerce with Panama and Peru, maintaining a factor on the Isthmus. But in the long run he lost more than he gained, and in 1554, alleging poverty, he announced his intention to return to the Indies, and petitioned for royal recommendations and grants of offices. The crown issued only a very mild recommendation to the viceroy of Peru to favor him, so it is not likely that he ever went back; at any rate there is no certain notice of it.

NOTES. Some years after returning to Seville, Jerez started calling himself Francisco López de Jerez, and finally by 1554 merely Francisco López, without using the Jerez at all. Pedro Pizarro, in his *Relación*, V, 198, says that Jerez was a native of Seville, and the assertion is repeated in Jerez's *Verdadera relación*, II, 346. An anonymous poem appended to the chronicle (p. 348) says that his father was Pedro de Jerez, an "honored citizen." In 1536 Jerez said that he was thirty-nine (AGI, Justicia 719, no. 9), and in 1554 that he was fifty-five (AGI, Patronato 98, no. 4, ramo 6). The quotes from Jerez given above, with much other interesting testimony about the discovery period, are in AGI, Patronato 150, no. 3, ramo 2, and *CDIHC*, 4:70, 128–131. Jerez's extensive *probanza de servicios* of 1554 is in AGI, Patronato 98, no. 4, ramo 3.

The report or chronicle written by Jerez, entitled *Verdadera relación de la conquista del Perú y provincia del Cuzco, llamada la Nueva Castilla*, is in Vedia, *Historiadores primitivos*, II, 319–349. Another version of it is inserted in Oviedo, *Historia*, V, 30–83. Oviedo makes certain omissions, adds many remarks of his own, and takes great liberties with Jerez's style. The "Relación Sámano-Jerez," Jerez's short account of Pizarro's early voyages, is in Porras, *Relaciones primitivas*. An indispensable discussion of the writings and also of the life of Jerez is in Porras, *Cronistas*, pp. 87–92.

Other references are in AGI, Justicia 724, no. 6; *CDIHC*, VII, 156; Góngora, *Grupos*, pp. 124, 127; Otte y Maticorena, "La isla de la Magdalena," *Mercurio Peruano* 41 (1960):260; Oviedo, *Historia*, V, 83, 84; Porras, *Cartas*, pp. 9–10; Porras, *Cedulario*, I, 133.

Diego de Narváez

Age at Cajamarca: About 21 to 23   Place of origin: Probably Navarre
Role: Footman   Extent of literacy: Fully literate
Share: ⅜ share of gold; ¾ share of silver   Trade: Notary

Diego de Narváez claimed to be an hidalgo, and the claim may have
had much substance, since his brother-in-law Felipe de Atienza held
the courtly sinecure of usher or lodger (*aposentador*) of the Infantas
of Spain. Despite his youth, he had already been in the New World
for several years. It was common for a young notary to arrive in the
Indies in his middle or late teens as part page, part amanuensis, in the
following of some important man. Narváez accompanied Pedro de los
Ríos in that capacity when he came from Spain in 1526 to be governor
of Tierra Firme, or Panama and surrounding area.

In Peru, Narváez never played the role for which his good birth and
experience had prepared him. At Cajamarca he got even less than the
three-fourths share given to most of the very young or uninitiated. He
never became a political or military leader, he does not seem to have
sat on a municipal council, and he was not even very rich; his encomienda in Cuzco ranked halfway down the long list of more than
eighty. He was the first clerk of the Cuzco council, but he retired from
the post around 1537 or 1538, since it was not the practice in Peru for
encomenderos to serve actively as notaries. Narváez also acted for years
as deputy accountant of the royal treasury in Cuzco, a post with a certain marginal prestige, but more avoided than sought after because of
the technical nature of its duties. To the notary Narváez there was no
difficulty in such a task, and indeed accounting may have been his
specialty. He acted as provisional treasurer at the distribution of gold
and silver in Cuzco in 1534, and he took care of the accounts of his
more prominent friend and citizen of Cuzco, Alonso de Mesa.

Narváez had more success at the royal court than in Peru. There he
garnered two separate grants of coats of arms and a royal recommendation; when he died the news hardly had time to reach Spain before the
court was ordering the recovery of his estate for relatives. The explanation for Narváez's comparative obscurity no doubt is to be found at
least partly in purely personal qualities, but his lack of close association
with any faction, party, or regional group strengthens the probability
that he was from Navarre or one of the other marginal and semi-
foreign Basque provinces.

In 1545 Narváez collaborated in an incipient uprising in Cuzco against rebel governor Gonzalo Pizarro, following the lead of his associate Alonso de Mesa. The next year the threat to the Pizarro revolt grew more serious, and Pizarrist captain Francisco de Carvajal came to Cuzco to deal with the trouble. His first act was the summary execution of Narváez and three or four other encomenderos on suspicion of further conspiracy. Killed with Narváez was another man of Cajamarca, Hernando de Aldana, both victims of the war that saw more executions of first conquerors than any other. Rodrigo de Narváez, Diego's mestizo son by an Indian noblewoman named doña Magdalena, lived in Cuzco until 1571.

NOTES. The name Narváez originated in and remains associated with Navarre. Of course with demographic movements there came to be people bearing that name in other parts of Spain, but in the sixteenth century there was still a very strong presumption that a Narváez actually was from Navarre. Two other Narváezes were in Peru in this period, one definitely from Navarre and the other almost certainly so, since he was among the heavily Basque group under Juan de Herrada that assassinated Francisco Pizarro (Cieza, *Chupas*, p. 108). That our Diego de Narváez also was from Navarre becomes a near certainty when we find him testifying in Cuzco in 1542 on behalf of an Andrés de Narváez who had served in Navarre in the royal guards (AGI, Patronato 93, no. 12, ramo 2). Of the ten witnesses, two were there because they had known Andrés de Narváez in New Spain, and two because they were in the siege of Cuzco; of the six remaining, no less than four were from Navarre or the Basque country, leaving Diego de Narváez and one other.

Diego de Narváez's share of silver, 131⅛ marks, is a little under a true ¾ share, which would be 135⅝. His share of the gold was exactly ⅝, and since a ⅝ share of silver would have been 113⅛ marks, it appears likely that a straight ⅝ share was originally intended and then revised upward slightly by arbitrarily altering 113 to 131. One other man, Francisco de la Torre, also got exactly this augmented ⅝ share.

Narváez declared his age several times; the upper and lower limits are represented by statements that he was twenty-eight in 1540 (AGI, Patronato 93, no. 9, ramo 7), and that he was twenty-nine or thirty in 1539 (AGI, Lima 118, *probanza* of García Martín). A *probanza de servicios* made by Narváez is in AGI, Lima 204. Mention of his courtly relative is in AGI, Lima 566, vol. V, April 23, 1548. His son appears in *RAHC* 4 (1953):120.

Other references are in AGI, Contaduría 1824, records from Cuzco,

March, 1536; Lima 204, *probanzas* of Diego Rodríguez and Pedro del Barco; Lima 566, vol. IV, August 20, 1540; vol. V, March 27, 1545, April 22, 1545; BNP, A397, 410–417; *CDIHC*, IV, 399; *DHA*, II, 49–50; *RAHC* 8 (1957):55; *RANP* 5 (1927):7; Calvete, *Rebelión de Pizarro*, IV, 277; Gutiérrez de Santa Clara, *Quinquenarios*, III, 84–85; Loredo, *Alardes y derramas*, pp. 122, 132; Loredo, *Los repartos*, p. 401; Oviedo, *Historia*, V, 280; Pérez de Tudela, *Gasca*, II, 527; Porras, "Dos documentos esenciales," *Revista Histórica* 17 (1948):93.

García de Paredes

Age at Cajamarca: About 32 to 36
Role: Footman
Share: 1 full share of gold
and silver

Place of origin: Medina del Campo
(Old Castile)
Extent of literacy: Literate
Trade: Probably accountant
or merchant

García de Paredes's home region of Medina del Campo had the reputation of a strongly commercial orientation, and this, taken together with his ability in accounting, might well indicate a mercantile background.

Paredes was a veteran, with six or seven years of experience in Panama and Nicaragua, where he may have held an encomienda, and at Cajamarca he got a veteran's full share of the treasure. He must have joined the expedition with one of the contingents arriving directly from Nicaragua, probably with the earlier one under Benalcázar, since he owed Benalcázar money for freightage. For a time Paredes functioned as provisional royal treasurer of the expedition, when Treasurer Riquelme was absent, having argued with the Pizarros. The respect in which he was held is reflected on the roll of Cajamarca, where he appears near the top of the infantry, next to Pedro Sancho, Pizarro's new secretary, and Juan de Porras, *alcalde mayor*. What part Paredes played in the rest of the conquest is not clear, but he did stay in Peru until after the founding of Cuzco. In 1535 he and a goodly fortune crossed the Atlantic from the Isthmus to Seville. Soon after his arrival in Spain he went to Medina del Campo and he still was a citizen there in November, 1538.

NOTES. The evidence for Paredes's place of origin is his citizenship in Medina del Campo and his statement that he came there directly from

Seville after arrival in Spain, indicating that he had already known his destination. He may, of course, have come originally from the surrounding
hinterland. Together the two items make a very strong case, which there
would be little need to discuss so explicitly if it were not that Busto, in
"Los presuntos peruleros," *Mercurio Peruano* 50 (1965):322–326, assumes that Paredes was from Cáceres. The name García de Paredes was
famous in Cáceres, particularly because of Diego García de Paredes, the
"Samson of Extremadura." Finding someone of this name in an expedition
with a strong Cáceres-Trujillo bias, one naturally makes the connection.
Yet there is no basis for doing so. With the man of Cajamarca, García was
a first name and a very common one, here added to the also common surname of Paredes, which was found all over Spain. García de Paredes
did not come from Spain with the Pizarros, but from Nicaragua, and very
few, if any, of the men of Nicaragua were from the Cáceres-Trujillo region. Then too, García de Paredes did not associate with the numerous
Cáceres people in Peru, but with veterans of Nicaragua and men from
Leon and Old Castile, as one would expect. Finally, the Cáceres-Trujillo
region was the last place in the world to spawn accountants, whereas accounting skills were very much in keeping with origin in Medina del
Campo.

A Diego García de Paredes, from Cáceres, was in Peru in the later
1540's. This was neither the hero of Cáceres nor the man of Cajamarca.
Numerous references to him will be found in Pérez de Tudela, *Crónicas
del Perú*. Busto's speculation in "Los presuntos peruleros" that the man of
Cajamarca might have been on Hernando de Soto's Florida expedition need
not be taken seriously, since Busto hardly does so himself. In any case,
García de Paredes was in Medina del Campo in November, 1538, when
Soto's fleet had already left Spain.

García de Paredes gave his age as thirty in 1530 (*CDIHN*, II, 530–534)
and as forty-two in 1538, when he was a citizen of Medina del Campo
(AGI, Justicia 1124, no. 6, ramo 3). Other references are in AGI, Indiferente general 1801, records of ship *Santa Catalina*, 1535; Justicia 1124, no.
6, ramo 3; ANP, PA 66, 67, 107; *CDIHN*, II, 184, 504.

Gonzalo de Pineda

Role at Cajamarca: Horseman
Share: 2¼ shares of gold;
  2⅛ shares of silver

Place of origin: Córdoba
Extent of literacy: Fully literate
Trade: Apparently accountant or notary

One of Pineda's companions called him a cavalier, a high-sounding
word of very loose meaning; in any case he was an educated man,

treated with respect by his fellows. Perhaps he was connected in some way with the Pineda family of Seville, who were high in municipal government as notaries and councilmen, and sent some of their number to Peru. Gonzalo had accounting skills, often a part of notarial training. Nothing is known of his experience in the Indies; on the 1531 expedition he acted as treasurer of the "company," or band of men, and was in charge of assembling the treasure of Cajamarca prior to distribution. He was also involved in the distribution itself, though probably mainly as a technical expert. At the same time, Pineda was a personal retainer of Francisco Pizarro.

All of this added up to a great deal of influence and responsibility, reflected in Pineda's position on the roll of Cajamarca, where he stands just below the captains, and in his share, which was actually larger than that of three of the captains. Pineda presumably continued in the same functions in the conquest of Cuzco and the distribution of treasure there. Then he left Peru with the exodus of July–August, 1534, arriving in Seville in 1535. As a man knowledgeable and trustworthy in financial matters, he carried large sums for several prominent people, the largest being ten thousand pesos for his employer Francisco Pizarro. Pineda soon settled in his native Córdoba and acquired the office of *jurado*, or district councilman, a seat on the general municipal council of Córdoba being so prestigious and expensive that it was possibly beyond his reach.

N O T E S .   Though Pineda never appears as anything more definite than a citizen of Córdoba, his origin is clear from the fact that he called himself that while still in Peru, and he and others knew that he was going straight to Córdoba and nowhere else (AGI, Justicia 1124, no. 6, ramo 1, where Pineda is called *jurado*; ANP, PA 120; Salinas 1538–1540, ff.118–120).

Other references are in AGI, Indiferente general 1801, records of ship *San Miguel*, 1535; Justicia 723, no. 1; ANP, PA 119, 122; Lee, "Algunos documentos sobre los primeros conquistadores del Perú," *Revista Histórica* 8 (1925):196; Loredo, *Los repartos*, p. 72; Porras, *Cartas*, p. 120; Porras, *Relaciones primitivas*, p. 98.

For some of the Pinedas of Seville see AGI, Justicia 1053, no. 5 (Bachiller Francisco de Pineda); Enríquez de Guzmán, *Vida y costumbres*, pp. 150, 273.

Pedro Sancho

Role at Cajamarca: Footman
Share: 1 full share of gold and
   silver, plus ¼ share for
   secretarial work

Place of origin: Probably near
   Medina de Ríoseco (Old Castile)
Extent of literacy: Highly literate
Profession: Notary

As author of one of the standard chronicles of the Peruvian conquest, and later, in many accounts, chief villain of the conquest of
Chile, Pedro Sancho de Hoz is a well-known historical figure. Yet
most aspects of his life are surprisingly obscure. His birthdate appears
nowhere. Even so basic a piece of information as his regional origin in
Spain has to be deduced in a roundabout fashion. Again and again he
was connected with people from the kingdom of Leon and western
Old Castile, centering on the town of Medina de Ríoseco; Medina or
its environs can be assumed with much probability to have been his
birthplace. As to his social origins, little is known beyond the perim-
eters set by his notarial profession. A late chronicler calls him an important hidalgo, and his relative success at the Spanish court would
indicate that he had the bearing of an hidalgo, if not actual good birth.
During the conquest of Peru he was known as plain Pedro Sancho;
only after returning rich to Spain did he assume the additional surname
of Hoz, which he used consistently thereafter.

If Sancho had any previous experience in the Indies, nothing is
known of it. He joined the Peru expedition in Panama, and by the
time of Cajamarca he had become an important member. Though still
on foot, he was almost at the top of the list of footmen on the roll of
Cajamarca. Indeed he probably had a hand in compiling the list, since,
along with Francisco de Jerez, he was paid for paperwork connected
with dividing the treasure.

When the injured Jerez left Peru with the first contingent of returnees in 1533, Sancho succeeded him as Pizarro's secretary and chief
government clerk for the whole province. In this capacity he served as
clerk at the execution of Atahuallpa, recorded the auction of the king's
share of the treasure of Cajamarca, and was officiating notary at the
founding of Cuzco as a Spanish city. He wrote an official chronicle,
signed by Pizarro, reporting on events up to July, 1534; together with
the chronicle of Jerez, to which it is the sequel, it forms the backbone
of the narrative history of the conquest of Peru. In its style, the work
is midway between the utterly laconic Jerez and the more discursive

Miguel Estete. Sancho also drafted that first series of encomienda titles which were in a real sense Peru's constitution.

Despite this crucial role, it is not clear that Sancho had much influence in substantive matters, as his successor Antonio Picado did. While Francisco Pizarro's illiteracy made him very dependent on his secretaries and retainers, it also made him very suspicious of them. An example of what was perhaps standard operating procedure is preserved in Sancho's own account of how Pizarro's reply to a complaint by the council of Jauja was drafted. Pizarro and Treasurer Alonso Riquelme first conferred on the substance of the reply, then went to Sancho's dwelling and told him in detail what to write; Sancho read the finished draft aloud to Pizarro and Riquelme, and they gave their approval. There is some reason to think that Pizarro had a low opinion of Sancho. Sancho's relinquishment of his post in early 1535, after two years, was doubtless not wholly voluntary. Nor was the parting amicable. During an inquiry into management of the royal exchequer in Peru, carried out by Bishop Berlanga of Panama, in Lima in 1535, Sancho gave the extremely damaging testimony that Pizarro had not paid the king's fifth on silver used to buy Pedro de Alvarado's fleet of ships.

However, Sancho may have been thinking for some time of returning to Spain. Though he resisted the exodus of 1534, he sent at that time for a royal license to visit Spain for a year and a half, retaining his encomienda in Cuzco. This license was granted in April, 1535, but it could not have reached him before he left Peru around November of that year. For that reason, and because Sancho did not leave the surety required in such cases, Pizarro soon felt free to give the encomienda to someone else.

While in Peru Sancho showed considerable interest in financial and entrepreneurial activity. He bought up the share of the treasure of Cajamarca that the priest Juan de Sosa (though not present) received, plus some debts owed to Sosa, and made a good profit on the transaction. He also undertook to collect the tithes of the district of Lima, apparently even after he left Peru, but this venture brought him nothing and the treasury officials confiscated the deposit he had left.

At any rate, he was apparently a very wealthy man when he reached Seville in 1536. His stay in Spain has been reported only from a great distance, and possibly not reliably. He seems to have made quite a display at the royal court, before settling down in the court town of

Toledo, marrying there the allegedly very noble doña Guiomar de Aragón, and acquiring a seat on the Toledo municipal council. His long-range intentions were never clear. While he gave every indication of staying in Spain permanently, he continued to secure extensions of the royal license to retain his Peruvian encomienda.

Before 1539, possibly reduced to penury by his social high flying, Sancho had decided to return to the Indies. His intention was still ambiguous. Though he had never held a captaincy and was low on funds, he negotiated an agreement with the crown whereby he would outfit two ships or more to explore south along the Pacific coast of South America, in return for the interim governorship of any lands he should occupy south of the Strait of Magellan. At the same time, perhaps realizing he lacked the resources for this venture, Sancho buttressed his position in Peru itself. Once more he had his encomienda confirmed by the crown and acquired the office of chief notary of mines for Peru.

Arriving in Peru late in 1539, Sancho got a very mixed reception. His Cuzco encomienda was still occupied by someone else, and Pizarro had no mind to return it to him. On his own authority, Pizarro had already entrusted to Pedro de Valdivia the conquest of Chile, an enterprise in almost direct competition with Sancho's. In December, 1539, in Cuzco, Pizarro arranged for the two ventures to be combined, Sancho and Valdivia becoming partners. Pizarro's reasons were probably those surmised by Bernardo de Mella, a witness; by sending Sancho on, he could avoid giving the encomienda back and he could give his friend and compatriot Valdivia the advantage of arms and supplies that Sancho, always inclined to big talk, claimed he could procure. Pizarro certainly did not do this in a spirit of friendliness to Sancho. One witness, whose partiality to Valdivia renders him somewhat suspect, reports remarks by Pizarro which nevertheless ring true. Pizarro was supposed to have said that "Pero Sancho had come back from Spain as stupid as he went," and, on hearing that Sancho was plotting against Valdivia, he expressed in pithy terms his confidence that Valdivia would easily be able to handle so unmanly and inept a person.

At any rate, in 1540, Valdivia started out toward Chile with a party of men, while Sancho, styling himself "Captain Sancho de Hoz," returned to Lima with an ambitious plan to acquire two ships, supplies, fifty horses, and two hundred breastplates, and then to catch up with Valdivia along the coast. The plan was strikingly similar to the operations of Pizarro and Almagro in the original conquest of Peru. But Sancho's talent for getting credit was not equal to Almagro's; before long he was in jail in Lima for debts. He managed to obtain his freedom on condition of leaving immediately for Chile, which meant that he was unable to fulfill his part of the bargain with Valdivia. When he finally arrived at Valdivia's camp be brought nothing more than a few horses and a very small band of followers, mainly compatriots and his wife's relatives.

From this point on, much more information about Sancho is available, but it all comes from his enemies. In the works of the historians of the conquest of Chile, and in the testimony by Valdivia's allies which is their source, Sancho figures as an incarnation of the evil spirit of rebellion, constantly plotting to overthrow Valdivia and assume the governorship. However, Sancho's role was determined not so much by his personal character as by his possession of a royal patent. This rendered him the inevitable head of any revolt, yet made Valdivia reluctant to execute him, lest Sancho's death prove as damaging to him as Almagro's was to the Pizarros.

On arrival at Valdivia's camp Sancho was promptly accused of plotting to kill Valdivia, though all that follows with certainty from testimony is that he desired to share in the command. Valdivia exiled Sancho's associates to Peru, but allowed Sancho himself to stay, yielding to his pleas not to be sent back to a debtor's prison. To assure his position, Valdivia forced Sancho to annul their partnership and agree to accompany the expedition as an ordinary member under Valdivia's leadership. Sancho was kept in irons until, after the founding of Santiago, he proved useful in Indian fighting.

Around 1542 a new plot to overthrow Valdivia came to light, leading to the execution of some six Spaniards, of whom at least two were close associates of Sancho. From much conflicting testimony it appears that, though the plotters meant to give the governorship to Sancho, it was not proved that Sancho had originated the plan, and indeed, by one statement, he may have been in custody already when it was conceived. In any case, Sancho was pardoned, or found innocent, and Valdivia gave him an encomienda in the Santiago district at the time of the general distribution.

Before 1546, however, Sancho had lost his encomienda. Once again he was suspected of a plot on Valdivia's life, and only the special entreaty of a friend dissuaded Valdivia from having him executed. By the time Valdivia went to visit Peru in early December, 1547, Sancho was living in enforced rustication some fifteen miles from Santiago, apparently engaged in building a mill. On hearing of Valdivia's departure he hastened to town and began planning to take command; he was indeed in a way the indicated person to do so. His plans became known through an incriminating letter he wrote, and Valdivia's lieutenant, Villagra, seized him, finding in his dwelling a staff of justice he had made to be used in the uprising. Since the discontent with Valdivia was great and the situation was explosive, Villagra had Sancho executed—decapitated by a slave—within an hour of his arrest. His head and body were briefly displayed in Santiago's plaza, and then he was buried near the church. A certain number of Sancho's allies came soon afterward to Peru to bring complaint, with little result. Plotter or not, Sancho was no match for Valdivia as a man of action and leader of men.

N O T E S .   The evidence for Pedro Sancho's regional origin is purely circumstantial. First of all, one must deal with the prima facie evidence of Sancho's possible origin in the Toledo region. Since returning Spaniards almost always went to the area of their birth, Sancho's citizenship in Toledo would seem to point to that area, but in fact the court towns of Valladolid and Toledo, along with the southern metropolis of Seville, on occasion drew returnees from areas far outside their respective local hinterlands.

It is a fact that can be confirmed repeatedly that Spaniards in the Indies, whether in matters of business, conquest, or rebellion, chose partners by preference from their own area, first from their actual home town or village, then from the broader region. Though certain individual associates of Sancho's were from Extremadura or Andalusia, many tended to be from western Old Castile or the kingdom of Leon. The examples follow.

In 1540 Sancho, on his way to Chile, stopped at Acarí, the encomienda of Pedro de Mendoza (q.v.), who was from Sahagún, in the province of Leon (*DHA*, I, 68). He and Mendoza made joint plans to outfit the Chile expedition; in pursuance of this they gave their power to Gaspar de Villarroel, from Sahagún (AGI, Lima 566, vol. VI, cedula of September 28, 1549) ; and Alonso de Chinchilla, from Medina de Ríoseco, thirty miles from Sahagún (see below, following paragraph). Also present was Diego García de Villalón, from Villalón de Campos, halfway between Sahagún and Medina de Ríoseco (AGI, Patronato 123, ramo 9; *CDIHC*, VIII, 364).

The grand plot of c.1542 in favor of Sancho included men of various origins, but the leaders were Chinchilla (above) and his father-in-law, Antonio de Pastrana, from Medina de Ríoseco. (For Pastrana, see *CDIHC*, VIII, 312; Thayer, *Valdivia*, p. 50; Bermúdez Plata, *Pasajeros*, II, 60. Chinchilla is said by the late and relatively corrupt chronicler Mariño de Lobera [*Crónica*, p. 262], to have been from Medina del Campo. Given Mariño's relative unreliability, the close connection between Chinchilla and Pastrana, and the fact that the two Medinas were often confused in this way, the present writer is sure that Chinchilla was actually from Medina de Ríoseco. A source more nearly contemporary than Mariño [*CDIHC*, VIII, 312], says merely that Chinchilla was from Old Castile.) When Sancho was in danger of execution a little later, he was saved by the intercession of Juan Bohón, from Medina de Ríoseco. (Thayer, *Valdivia*, p. 36; Bermúdez Plata, *Pasajeros*, I, 34; *CDIHC*, XXII, 627).

In the last years before his death Sancho had a servant and accomplice, Juan Romero, who was executed with him and who was said by many to have been from Sancho's region (*tierra*). (See *CDIHC*, XXII, 470, 537.) This man almost certainly must have been the Juan Romero from Zamora who came from Spain with Hernando Pizarro in 1534–1535 and was in Lima in 1536 (AGI, Justicia 1126, no. 2, ramo 1, memorandum of Gregorio de Sotelo; Bermúdez Plata, *Pasajeros*, I, 371). While Zamora and Medina de Ríoseco were rather far apart—some forty miles—to be comprehended within the same *tierra* by sixteenth-century Spanish notions, their respective jurisdictions reached much closer, perhaps touched. (It is impossible that, as Thayer Ojeda asserts, the Juan Romero in Chile should have been the man in *Pasajeros*, II, 281, who was from Cazorla [Jaén], because that Romero was going to Florida with Hernando de Soto and could not have accompanied the Chile expedition of 1540 as our Romero did. See Thayer, *Valdivia*, p. 53.) Hernán Rodríguez de Monroy, main coconspirator in Sancho's last plot, was from Salamanca, in the kingdom of Leon but considerably off to the south (AGI, Justicia 1082, no. 1, ramo 1).

Thayer Ojeda opines that Sancho was probably from Calahorra (Logroño), the son of Juan de Hoz and Juana Sánchez (Thayer, *Valdivia*, p. 54). He gives no source for his conjecture, but the present writer believes Thayer's guess was based on an entry in *Pasajeros*, I, 331. Thayer first saw the *Pasajeros* in his old age, and he used it like a new toy. The entry states that a Martín de la Hoz, son of Juan de la Hoz and Juana Sánchez, *vecinos* of Calahorra, registered on September 14, 1534, to go to the Strait of Magellan with Simón de Alcazaba. One sees why Thayer was tempted, but there is no reason whatever to make any connection between this man and Pedro Sancho.

According to Thayer, Sancho left a legitimate daughter and a mestizo son. Thayer estimates Sancho's age as thirty-three in 1547. There is no source for this estimate, which would make him about eighteen at Cajamarca. Yet Sancho's youth aroused no known comment, and such extreme youth is hardly compatible with the position of high responsibility that Sancho held at the time. Until presented with firmer evidence, the present writer is not prepared to place much confidence in Thayer's estimate.

Some testimony in the trials of Villagra and Valdivia seems to assert that Sancho kept his encomienda to the end and that in 1547 he was living in the Indian village of his own encomienda. But a list of the encomenderos of Santiago in July, 1546, does not include Sancho (*CDIHC*, VIII, 125–126). In 1547 Sancho was called *estante* rather than *vecino* (*CDIHC*, VIII, 155). The place where he was staying was the "madera de Flores," apparently a lumberyard or lumberpile of the German carpenter Bartolomé de Flores (*CDIHC*, VIII, 169).

Statements found in many histories that Sancho married doña Guiomar de Aragón in Toledo apparently originate in passages in Góngora Marmolejo (p. 88) and Mariño de Lobera (p. 286), both of whom were sadly confused about essentials of Sancho's life. They thought, for example, that Sancho was recently arrived in Chile in 1547. Porras (*Cronistas*, p. 100) goes slightly beyond the two chroniclers to assert that Sancho was a *regidor* of Toledo. As usual, he gives no source, but Porras's high general reliability adds to the authenticity of the Toledo episode in Sancho's life.

For the Chilean phase of Sancho's career, the main source is *CDIHC*. Volume VIII contains cedulas relating to Sancho's expedition (pp. 13–36), testimonials and inquiries about Valdivia that bear importantly on Sancho (pp. 154–172, 258–310), and scattered references (particularly pp. 95, 125–126, 324, 363–364). Volumes XXI and XXII, with litigation concerning Francisco de Villagra who executed Pedro Sancho, contain hundreds of references. Of particular interest is the testimony of secretary Juan de Cardenas, who reports Pizarro's opinions of Sancho, in vol. XXI, pp. 467–468.

Testimony by Sancho in Lima in 1535, revealing his attitudes toward Pizarro and the royal officials, as well as his modus operandi, is in *CDIAO*, X, 262–268, 281–282, 302–303 (from AGI, Patronato 185, ramo 11). Litigation with the priest Juan de Sosa in Seville is in AGI, Justicia 719, no. 9. Sancho's chronicle has been published, retranslated from the Italian by Joaquín García Icazbalceta, as *Relación de la conquista del Perú*. Porras's comments are in *Cronistas*, pp. 99–101.

Other references can be found in AGI, Lima 565, vol. III, May 31, 1538, May 23, 1540; Patronato 93, no. 6, ramo 1; 109, ramo 5; ANP, PA 714, 716; HC 26, 30, 33; Bermúdez Plata, Pasajeros, III, 14; Calvete, *Rebelión de Pizarro*, V, 44–47; Cieza, *Tercera parte*, in *Mercurio Peruano*

38 (1957):262; 39 (1958):569, 579; Góngora Marmolejo, *Historia*, p. 88 passim; Loredo, *Los repartos*, p. 127; Mariño de Lobera, *Crónica*, p. 286 and passim; Pedro Pizarro, *Relación*, V, 198; Porras, *Cedulario*, II, 87, 262; Porras, "Dos documentos esenciales," *Revista Histórica* 17 (1948):90–93; Porras, "Jauja," *Revista Histórica* 18 (1949–1950):134–135.

Pedro de San Millán

Age at Cajamarca: About 23
Role: Footman
Share: ¾ share of gold and silver

Place of origin: Segovia, in Old Castile
Extent of literacy: Fully literate
Trade: Notary, perhaps merchant

Two different chroniclers of Peru report that Pedro de San Millán belonged to the family of the Bocudos, important merchants of Segovia. Yet Pedro himself was apparently brought up to be a notary, since he practiced that trade briefly in Jauja in 1534. He had been in Nicaragua for five or six months, and presumably came from there to Peru with Soto or Benalcázar.

With his background, San Millán could have been expected either to return to Spain with a fortune second to none, or to rise quickly in Peru. He did neither, because, perhaps in overreaction against his commercial heritage, he was an inveterate spendthrift, *en extremo gastador*, in the phrase of Cieza de León. During the conquest he is seen constantly in debt, for horses, slaves, loans, or clothing, though he also had the ability to recoup his losses; perhaps something of the merchant can be glimpsed in his sale of a horse for three thousand pesos, one of the highest prices recorded. He took citizenship in neither Cuzco nor Jauja. In late 1534 he came to coastal Pachacámac as if he meant to leave for Spain, but no Spaniard would have left voluntarily without a fortune, and San Millán had reduced himself to near pennilessness again.

Restless and impoverished, San Millán returned to Cuzco, and he was one of the very few men of Cajamarca to go with Almagro's disastrous expedition to Chile in 1535–1537. Almost all of Almagro's men, whatever their previous experience or background, found themselves on his side in the ensuing civil wars, whether through circumstance or conviction, and San Millán was no exception. A relative, Luis de San Millán, also joined the Almagro faction.

Pedro fought for Almagro in the battle of Salinas in 1538, and afterward the victorious Pizarrists robbed him of his last possessions in Cuzco. Those few veterans of Cajamarca who had chosen Chile, Almagro, and poverty instead of a rich encomienda in Peru must have felt a very special bitterness. Three are definitely identified; all were implacable enemies of the Pizarros, and Pedro de San Millán most of all, since he became involved in Francisco Pizarro's assassination. After Salinas, San Millán managed to make a living somehow, even to thrive, perhaps through commerce; by 1541 he was in Lima. There seems no room for doubt that he did indeed participate in the assassination, since he was accused of it not only in several chronicles, but in the official interrogatory of the royal prosecution. According to Pedro Pizarro, San Millán had a crucial role. In his version, the plotters had almost decided to give up their project, when San Millán, though ordinarily weak of resolution and not valiant, was seized by the devil (more likely by bitterness and hate) and rushed shouting into the street, forcing the assassins to action because they were now discovered in any case.

After this, San Millán was prominent, though not a captain, in the forces of the younger Almagro. He was somehow rich again; according to Cieza, he spent and gave away over 80,000 pesos, an incredible amount, and in Cuzco he paid for a lavish general banquet. He was on Almagro's side at Chupas, in 1542, and survived that hardest fought of all the civil war battles; but afterward Governor Vaca de Castro summarily executed the remaining assassins of Pizarro, San Millán among them, and his body was quartered and displayed on stakes in the field.

N O T E S .   So few of the men of Cajamarca went to Chile that the chain of evidence for San Millán needs to be brought into the open. The Pedro de San Millán with the expedition in 1533–1534 contracted a debt of nine hundred pesos to Pedro de León (ANP, PA 145). León then left Peru and asked Gregorio de Sotelo to collect the money for him. In a memorandum, Sotelo said (AGI, Justicia 1126, no. 2, ramo 1) that he had collected part of the nine hundred pesos; his brother would collect the rest in Almagro's jurisdiction of New Toledo, because Pedro de San Millán was there.

San Millán said in 1539 that he was thirty (*DHA*, II, 58). Cieza (*Chupas*, pp. 229, 283) and Pedro Pizarro (*Relación*, V, 228) both say that he was from Segovia, and his relative Luis de San Millán is called a native of Segovia in AGI, Justicia 1126, no. 2, ramo 1, memorandum of Sotelo. That San Millán acted as a notary rests on notary Jerónimo de Aliaga's mention

(*CDIAO*, X, 247, or AGI, Patronato 185, ramo 11) of "San Millán, que a la sazón era escribano de Jauja." This must be Pedro; no other San Millán appears in any record, except Luis, who was in Spain as late as September, 1534, and therefore could not have been in Jauja, which ceased to exist in December of that year (Porras, *Cedulario*, II, 44).

Busto, in his article "Tres conversos," *Revista de Indias* 27 (1967):438–442, asserts that San Millán was of Jewish descent. His evidence is circumstantial—that Segovia was full of New Christians, that the San Millán or Bocudo family were merchants and lived in a district particularly renowned for its new converts, and that the name itself was taken from a Christian saint, like many of the names the Jews assumed on conversion. While these are cogent reasons, they are far from sufficient to make a definite attribution. The name San Millán was not necessarily new; there are several villages with that name in Old Castile and the Basque country.

Further references are in ANP, PA 16, 98, 132, 223, 705; *CDIHC*, V, 235; VI, 284, 399; *DHA*, II, 58–59; Cieza, *Chupas*, pp. 108–109, 229–230, 283–284; Gómara, *Hispania victrix*, I, 244; Gutiérrez de Santa Clara, *Quinquenarios*, III, 230; Pedro Pizarro, *Relación*, V, 228; Porras, *Cedulario*, II, 39–40.

Zárate

Role at Cajamarca: Footman
Share: 1 full share of gold
and silver

Place of origin: Orduña (Basque country)
Extent of literacy: Fully literate
Trade: Notary and accountant

Zárate (and that is in fact what the Spaniards called him, hardly ever using his first name, Juan) shared the common fate of the Basques, to perform essential tasks and yet be ignored. He was the key man, though not the leader, of the party of three sent from Cajamarca in 1533 to carry out a preliminary survey of Cuzco and gather treasure. The later chronicles give credit for this episode to well-known heroes like Hernando de Soto. Even Pedro Pizarro, almost an eyewitness, leaves out Zárate's name. The official chronicler Jerez comes closer by saying that the party consisted of two footmen and a notary, though with characteristic terseness he omits the names. Only Cieza de León (with Herrera following him) gives the names of all three: Moguer, Bueno, and Zárate. Since the Andalusians Moguer and Bueno were illiterate, the notary can only have been Zárate. This is confirmed by a document in which Zárate is associated with the royal treasurer and the accountant of the expedition, indicating in all probability that, like his Basque colleague, Nicolás de Azpeitia, he had been keeping accounts for the treasury officials.

From Inca Cuzco, Zárate brought back a record of how he had taken possession of the city in the name of the Spanish king, and another report on the towns along the road between Cuzco and Cajamarca. Both must rank high among the lost documents and chronicles of the conquest period. Zárate then took part in the rest of the conquest. He started to settle in Cuzco in 1534 but changed his mind and returned to Spain, probably by 1535. In 1538 he was back in his native Basque country.

N O T E S .   In March, 1533, the crown ordered that the estate of "Juan de Zárate violero," who had died in Peru, be recovered for the benefit of his widow, Mari Alvarez, and their children (Porras, *Cedulario*, I, 129). The presumed widow obtained the order on information given by Rodrigo de Mazuelas, who had left Peru in early 1532, before Cajamarca. It is hard to believe that there were two Juan de Zárates on the expedition. Perhaps Zárate had been dsperately ill or missing when Mazuelas left. This writer thinks it most probable that there was but one Juan de Zárate, who therefore would have been a mature man, with wife and children in Spain. There is also the intriguing word "violero," meaning "maker of stringed instruments," but this is not unequivocal, since rare or skilled crafts such as embroiderer (*bordador*) and coiner (*monedero*) were beginning to appear at this time as surnames.

Busto thinks that the Zárate of Cajamarca was a Pedro de Zárate who was a tailor in Panama ("Los innominados," pp. 95–96). Nevertheless, no man of this name appears in the expedition records. The only Zárate there is Juan, who is seen in Coaque in 1531 (HC 24) and at Cajamarca in May, 1533 (AGI, Contaduría 1825). Then, in 1538, Juan de Zárate, from Orduña, testifies, along with several other men of Cajamarca, whom he knows, about the estate of Juan de Beranga, for whom he brought money home (AGI, Justicia 1124, no. 5, ramo 3).

Further references are in AGI, Patronato 109, ramo 4; Cieza, *Tercera parte*, in *Mercurio Peruano* 38 (1957):263, 266; Herrera, *Historia*, X, 168; Jerez, *Verdadera relación*, II, 343.

10. MEN OF AFFAIRS

IN THIS VAGUE CATEGORY have been placed several men whose probable merchant origins are betrayed by their continuing activities or
family connections, as well as some of the principal business managers
for the Pizarros. Nearly all Spaniards in the Indies were men of affairs
and entrepreneurs to some extent. Most of the clerks (chapter 9)
would fit here very well; some of the most active managers are to be
found among the clear hidalgos (see Part I, chapter 2, n. 22). Also
many of the lesser figures in chapter 11 would probably appear mark-
edly entrepreneurial if we knew their activities in more detail. Only the
illiterates and lower plebeians were badly handicapped in this respect.
Thus the following thirteen men far from exhaust the expedition's
commercial-managerial capabilities. On the other hand, though they
embody the managerial impulse more clearly than most, they too are
versatile; at least three of them could reasonably claim hidalgo standing.

Martín Alonso

Role at Cajamarca: Horseman
Share: Double share of gold
   and silver

Place of origin: La Zarza, near Trujillo
   (Extremadura), now called La Conquista
Extent of literacy: Could sign,
   probably literate

La Zarza, Martín Alonso's birthplace, was the patrimony and part-time residence of the Pizarro family. When we add to this the fact that the mother of Juan and Gonzalo Pizarro was named María Alonso and apparently lived in La Zarza, we may surmise that when Martín Alonso came to the Indies with the four Pizarro brothers in 1530 he was on the fringe of the family entourage as a henchman or poor relative. The Alonsos were humble people, and Martín will have been no exception.

Like the higher-level Pizarro representative Juan Cortés, Martín returned to Spain right after Cajamarca in 1533 and became a citizen of Trujillo (not incompatible with residence in La Zarza), retaining his close Pizarro connections. In 1545 he participated in a ruse to try to get some of Hernando Pizarro's money past the officials in Seville during the rebellion of Gonzalo Pizarro. Sometime in the 1540's Martín testified in court in favor of Hernando; the opposing party objected to his testimony on the grounds that he was a person of low extraction and Hernando's servant, solicitor, and rent collector.

While most men of Cajamarca sooner or later aimed for independence, Martín Alonso stayed under the wings of the Pizarros. Probably having been born their dependent, he found it undesirable or impossible to pull away. This continuing relationship led to another unusual development, for around 1551, when Francisco Pizarro's daughter doña Francisca was sent to Spain, Martín Alonso went back to Peru to manage the encomienda that doña Francisca still held in the Lima area. The position entailed great influence, since it made Martín Alonso a major representative of the remaining Pizarro interests in Peru, and he acted in effect as an encomendero of Lima, yet for a veteran of Cajamarca to appear publicly as a majordomo at so late a date is unparalleled. By 1560 Martín had moved to Potosí in the same capacity, with authority over the Pizarro representative in Cuzco. He held this post until around 1564, when the Pizarros replaced him, along with other stewards in Peru. Whether he stayed in Peru after that or returned to Spain is unknown.

N O T E S . Porras, usually correct, asserts (in Trujillo, *Relación*, p. 121) that the Martín Alonso of Cajamarca was from La Zarza, but gives no source. In confirmation of Porras's finding, there is mention of a debt owed to Martín Alonso, citizen of Trujillo, born in La Zarza, in the will of Diego de Agüero, who is known to have had dealings with the Martín Alonso of Cajamarca (*RANP* 6 [1928]:161; ANP, PA 108).

The evidence definitely identifying the Martín Alonso of Cajamarca with the majordomo of the 1550's and 1560's is as follows: when doña Francisca's Peruvian majordomo, Martín Alonso, citizen of Trujillo, rendered accounts, he transferred to her, in compensation for debts he had incurred, 100,000 maravedies of annuities from taxes in Seville, the privilege of which had been granted him on November 20, 1534, just the time when most of the early returnees' fortunes were seized in return for Sevillian annuities. (Lohmann Villena, "Documentos interesantes a la historia del Perú," *Revista Histórica* 25 (1960–1961):457; see also pp. 452–453.)

Further references are in AGI, Justicia 833, letter of Hernando Pizarro, June 8, 1549; *CDIHC*, VII, 155; *RAHC* 4 (1953):33; and *Libros de cabildos de Lima*, V, 122–123.

Juan de Barbarán

Age at Cajamarca: About 31 or 32
Role: Horseman
Share: Double share of gold and silver

Place of origin: Illescas (between Madrid and Toledo)
Parents: Pedro de Barbarán and María de San Pedro
Extent of literacy: Fully literate

Juan de Barbarán became one of the great men of Peru. Though he never made such insistent claims to gentle birth as certain companions of his, like Jerónimo de Aliaga, he had respectable antecedents in Spain. He inherited property there, as Aliaga did, and he had his recognized family coat of arms incorporated into his personal arms, as Aliaga did not. He was the first of all the conquerors of Peru to receive this honor, negotiated for him by his Madrid compatriot Gonzalo Fernández de Oviedo, the chronicler. Barbarán's affinity for business and accounts points to the possibility of a mercantile background, not lessened by the fact that one of his wife's relatives was a merchant.

Barbarán appeared in Panama in the early 1520's, then soon moved on to Nicaragua. During this time he married María de Lezcano, from the Madrid area like himself, and a relative of the archpriest of the

church of Panama. In 1531 Barbarán came to Peru from Nicaragua
under Sebastián de Benalcázar, but he did not remain Benalcázar's man.
Francisco Pizarro appointed him to the council of Jauja at its first provisional founding in 1533, and he became alcalde of Jauja's successor,
Lima, in 1538. The chronicler Zárate says that Barbarán was Pizarro's
"servant" or retainer, and the statement rings true.

Barbarán managed his business affairs well and with enthusiasm. He
was as rich as any of the men of Cajamarca, but with more emphasis on
liquid assets than on houses and lands. His activity in lending money
was so extensive as almost to make him a banker or pawnbroker. When
he made a will in 1539, more than thirty people owed him debts large
and small. In that same year, after having been municipal custodian of
the property of the deceased the year previous, he is seen prepared to
make settlements with some of the heirs. Reading between the lines,
one may suspect that Barbarán had been lending out the "property" of
the deceased—most or all of it money. His main function with the Pizarros, too, seems to have been as a keeper of valuables.

It was left to Barbarán, very much in line with the rest of his efforts,
to bury Francisco Pizarro, at a time of great danger when no one else
came forward. Accounts of the burial vary in every particular except
that Barbarán was the protagonist. A throng of supposed well-wishers
later claimed credit, but their claim, reduced to its essence, was that
they aided Barbarán. Beyond dispute is the fact that Barbarán was the
first guardian of Pizarro's children, once again the faithful custodian.

By this time Barbarán's position was strong enough to survive the
death of his patron. He was soon alcalde in Lima again, and fought at
the ensuing battle of Chupas in a spirit of vengeance, distinguishing
himself; he won the grant of the encomienda of Lambayeque in the
Trujillo district, where his wife had many relatives, without having to
give up his citizenship in the capital, Lima. This was a privilege for
which many clamored, but which no others achieved.

Barbarán, while brave and formidable, had never been the man for
positions of command in battle. In 1545 he stayed behind in Lima
while the great captains of Peru went north under Gonzalo Pizarro to
fight the viceroy. So it happened that Barbarán was named head of a
party sent to root out a community of runaway Negro slaves, established in a canebrake on the coast not far away. He accomplished his
object, but not without such hard fighting that several Spaniards lost
their lives, and Barbarán himself got a leg wound of which he shortly

died. He left several heirs, and his wife, María Lezcano, though she never became a "doña," did become a matriarch and a legendary figure. The Lezcanos continued to be a power in Trujillo and Lima for a century at least.

N O T E S . In 1541 Barbarán gave his age as over forty (AGI, Justicia 432, no. 2, ramo 3). A will of 1539 and codicil of 1542 are in *RANP* 4 (1926):191–205. There Barbarán declares himself a native of Illescas. A posthumous *probanza de servicios* exists in AGI, Patronato 113, ramo 8; it is partly published in *DHA*, II, 316–324. There is an extensive biographical note on Barbarán in Porras, *Testamento de Pizarro*, pp. 76–77.

Other references are in AGI, Lima 565, vol. III, March 7, 1539, October 24, 1539; Patronato 93, no. 10, ramo 1; no. 113, ramo 8; ANP, Castañeda, reg. 7, ff.41–42; PA 486; Salinas 1542–1543, ff.48–50 (2nd series) ; 143, 160, 662, 673; HC 52, 53, 174, 330, 443, 444, 447, 455, 496, 514; a document of Nov. 22, 1535, among the Peruvian manuscripts of the Lilly Library; *RANP* 1 (1920):449, 450, 452, 453; Cabero, "El corregimiento de Saña," *Revista Histórica* 1 (1906):486–489; Cobo, *Obras*, II, 304; *Libros de Cabildos de Lima*, III, 31; Loredo, *Los repartos*, pp. 115, 250, 257; Porras, *Cartas*, pp. 436, 542; Porras, *Cedulario*, II, 102; Torres Saldamando, *Libro primero de cabildos*, II, 318; Zárate, *Historia*, II, 497, 506.

For the Lezcanos, see AGI, Contaduría 1680, 1681, 1683; Patronato 97, no. 1, ramo 4; ANP, Salinas 1542–1543, f.216; *CDIHN*, I, 204; Lockhart, *Spanish Peru*, pp. 158–159, 262, n. 10.

Juan de Beranga

Age at Cajamarca: Probably 30 or more	Place of origin: Village of Ballesteros in the valley of Trasmiera (Old Castile)
Role: Footman	Parents: Juan Gutiérrez de los Corrales and Juana Sáenz
Share: 1 full share of gold and silver	Extent of literacy: Could sign, doubtless literate

Beranga was from the mountains of Old Castile, as were Pedro de Torres and Miguel Estete, who took money home for him, and Juan de Quincoces, his business partner and fellow encomendero of Lima. His activity in business affairs suggests that he was at least fully literate, if not actually a merchant. That he was a man of some consequence can be deduced from his good encomienda in the Lima district and from the fact that he received a vote for *regidor* on the council of Lima in 1535.

He intended to go to Spain and bring back his wife, Mari Sáenz de la
Pila, but he died in 1536, apparently a casualty of the Indian rebellion
of that year, before the royal license could reach him.

N O T E S . Beranga's birthdate is estimated as 1502, or before, on the
assumption of approximate parity of age with his wife, who was thirty-six
years old in 1538, as appears in AGI, Justicia 1124, no. 5, ramo 3. This
document also lists Beranga's parents and calls him "vecino del lugar de
Ballesteros, que es en la merindad de Trasmiera." His connection with
Quincoces can be seen in the list of property of the deceased in AGI, Justicia 1074, no. 9.

Other references are in AGI, Contaduría 1825, records from Lima,
1535; Justicia 1125, proceedings concerning Francisco Martín de Alburquerque; ANP, PA 30, 41, 143, 676, 679, 680; HC 58, 61; *RANP* 4
(1925):198; Loredo, *Los repartos*, p. 212; Porras, *Cedulario*, II, 220,
379, 413; Torres Saldamando, *Libro primero de cabildos*, I, 55.

Rodrigo de Cantillana

Age at Cajamarca: Late 20's   Place of origin: Sanlúcar de Barrameda
Role: Horseman   (coast of Andalusia)
Share: 1⅝ shares of silver;   Parents: Diego de Jerez de las Islas
   no gold   and Leonor de Cantillana
                                   Extent of literacy: Literate

Cantillana came to the Indies as an employed agent of Diego de la
Tovilla, royal treasurer of the province of Nicaragua. In 1527, still in
Spain, treasurer Tovilla sent Cantillana to Ciudad Real on the responsible mission of arranging a 2,000-ducat bond. Judging from this, Cantillana would appear originally to have been a merchant, accountant, or
entrepreneur. Tovilla and his party left Spain late in 1527, and Cantillana presumably spent the time between then and 1531 in Nicaragua.

In Peru Cantillana left hardly a trace; he may have been one of the
first to leave the country in 1533. He appears again in 1543 as a citizen
of Seville, holding the honorific office of *jurado*, or district alderman,
and to all appearances connected with that city's thriving commerce.
He was still in Seville, and still a *jurado*, in 1554.

N O T E S . Absolutely unequivocal evidence is not at hand to prove that
Tovilla's employee, from Sanlúcar and with the parents listed above (Bermúdez Plata, *Pasajeros*, I, 241; *CDIHN*, I, 268–276) was the Cantillana at

Cajamarca. Yet the presence of someone with this reasonably rare name in Nicaragua, place of departure of so many of the men of Cajamarca, at just the right time, is an extremely strong indication. Furthermore, the Cantillana of Cajamarca went to Seville just as the Nicaraguan Cantillana would have been expected to. That the *jurado* of Seville was the man of Cajamarca rests on his direct testimony.

Cantillana said in 1543 that he was forty (AGI, Justicia 1067, no. 1, ramo 4), then in 1554 that he was forty-five (AGI, Patronato 98, no. 4, ramo 3). The two being rather too far apart to reconcile by compromise, the solution has been an indefinite statement, though, since Cantillana was already carrying on important business by 1527, the earlier birthdate seems much more probable.

Pedro Cataño

Age at Cajamarca: Probably about 28   Place of origin: Cádiz or Seville
Role: Horseman   Extent of literacy: Apparently literate
Share: Double share of gold and silver

The name Cataño, sometimes rendered Castaño by the Spaniards, was originally Italian. In the form Cataneo it was borne by a Genoese family long important in the commerce of Seville and Cádiz. In Genoa, where there was no contradiction between commerce and nobility, the Cataneos were a recognized house in both respects. In Spain they had at first been mainly commercial, but by the time of the conquest of Peru there were Cataños of every description: new and old, nobles and merchants, landsmen and sailors, all with some sense of family identity. Pedro Cataño seems to have belonged to a branch quite thoroughly acclimated in Spain; at any rate he was born in Spain and possessed formidable fluency and expressiveness in Spanish. As José Antonio del Busto has already observed, Cataño's sworn testimony on the events at Cajamarca is so voluminous and vivid that it practically constitutes a chronicle. At the same time, one wonders if there is not something of the Italian in such exceptional effusiveness.

The Cataños were commercially involved in the Indies both before and after Pedro's time. One of them lent money to Columbus, and they were still very active in the African slave trade at mid-sixteenth century. Pedro may well have been a factor for some firm of the Cataños when he first arrived in Santo Domingo around 1523 or 1524. But there was little of interest to international commerce in the petty conquests, raids, and sallies he took part in during the rest of the decade in the areas of Honduras and Nicaragua. In Peru, Cataño was not as active commercially as some of the other conquerors, though he does appear once as witness to a large transaction in which a merchant of Seville bought up a conqueror's silver in return for credit in Spain. His only known activity for material gain was to beat the royal treasurer, Riquelme, at cards.

Arriving in Peru from Nicaragua with Hernando de Soto, Cataño and his horse—one of the better ones—accompanied Soto on all his exploits. Cataño's partner, Lope Vélez, from Palos, was also usually with them. The two had been together ever since they met in Santo Domingo almost ten years before. Cataño may have worked for Soto in Nicaragua; he was at any rate a great partisan of Soto's. Perhaps for that reason he was left behind in Jauja when the main body went south to conquer Cuzco in 1533. The Pizarros did all they could to clip Soto's wings. In late 1534 Cataño left Peru; he reached Seville in the spring of 1535. He remained very loyal to Soto and proud of the connection with him. At first Cataño considered himself a citizen of Cádiz, but he ended by settling in the metropolis, where he lived until 1562 at least. He soon obtained the grant of an elaborate coat of arms, incorporating the arms of the Cataños, a simple arrangement of alternating blue and white stripes. A few years later Pedro further identified himself with the Cataño tradition by investing in the expedition of don Pedro de Mendoza to the Plata region, though it brought him nothing but loss and litigation, and he is not known to have burned his fingers again.

NOTES.   Cataño gave his age as thirty-two in 1536 (AGI, Justicia 719, no. 9), over thirty-five in 1543 (AGI, Patronato 90, no. 1, ramo 11), forty in 1552 (AGI, Justicia 1073, proceedings concerning Juan de Porras), and over forty in 1554 (AGI, Patronato 98, no. 4, ramo 3). His estimates vary widely; the writer has chosen the earlier indicated birthdate because Cataño on two different occasions claimed that he had served in the Indies as early as 1523. In the above references Cataño states that he is a citizen of Seville; in the cedula granting him arms (Porras, *Cedulario*, II, 134, and Montoto, *Nobiliario*, p. 79), he is called a citizen of Cádiz; Diego de Molina, a fellow man of Cajamarca, considered him a native of Seville (Oviedo, *Historia*, V, 92). There were Genoese colonies in both Cádiz and Seville, and Cataño might have been born in either place. This writer is inclined to think he was originally from Cádiz, since the move of a successful person to a metropolis was a normal procedure.

Cataño's extensive testimony about Cajamarca is contained in AGI, Patronato 90, no. 1, ramo 11, and is summarized in Busto's treatment of Cataño in "Una relación y un estudio sobre la conquista," *Revista Histórica* 27 (1964) :280–288. There Busto refers to some sources that this writer has not seen. A probanza concerning Cataño is in AGI, Indiferente General 1204, no. 44.

There are other references in AGI, Patronato 93, no. 6, ramo 1; 185, ramo 11, testimony of Alonso Jiménez (published in *CDIAO*, XX, 278); ANP, PA 127; *CDIHN*, IV, 519–521; Ruth Pike, *The Genoese in Seville*, pp. 2–4, 64, 99.

Juan Cortés

Age at Cajamarca: About 40	Place of origin: Trujillo
Role: Horseman	Extent of literacy: Literate
Share: 2 shares of silver;	
2⅛ shares of gold	

The Pizarros took Juan Cortés with them from Trujillo in 1529 as a close adviser. One account calls Cortés Hernando Pizarro's *escudero* ("squire"), but in fact he was an agent of all the Pizarros, in approximately the capacity of a chief steward. He was almost alone among the whole Trujillo contingent in having a head for finance and affairs, the only others being Hernando Pizarro himself, Martín Alonso, and Lucas Martínez Vegaso, who in 1530 was still an insignificant youth. Cortés must have been a fairly substantial citizen of Trujillo, something of an hidalgo and perhaps also an entrepreneur. In the conquest he was never among the light horsemen who so often rode ahead with Soto or one of the Pizarro brothers; but on the roll of Cajamarca he appears near the top of the list, among the captains, with more than a horseman's ordinary double share of the treasure.

In 1533, before the conquest proceeded beyond Cajamarca, Cortés was sent home to Trujillo to become the Pizarros' chief representative there. Gonzalo Pizarro and Juan Pizarro sent him large sums. He managed Hernando Pizarro's financial affairs in Trujillo at least into the 1540's. His importance was reflected by his seat on the council of Trujillo and his marriage to a doña María de Ribera. He was still active in Trujillo in 1550.

NOTES. The writer long imagined that the Juan Cortés of Cajamarca was identical with a man prominent in Lima in the 1540's and 1550's. But the other Juan Cortés was born around 1515, came to Peru about 1540, and was not well treated by the Pizarros. He became *regidor* in Lima in 1549, and later Viceroy Cañete named him *corregidor* of Chachapoyas.

Juan Cortés of Cajamarca was referred to many times as a citizen of Trujillo; see for example AGI, Justicia 1053, no. 5, or the published version in Cúneo-Vidal, *Vida de Pizarro*, p. 543. In 1550 Cortés said he was sixty years old (AGI, Justicia 1082, no. 1, ramo 4). Other references are in AGI, Contaduría 1825, records from Coaque, April, 1531; Justicia 833, letter of Hernando Pizarro, June 8, 1549; 1178, no. 2, ramo 8; *CDIHC*, VII, 154–155; Busto, *Francisco Pizarro*, p. 47; Pérez de Tudela, *Gasca*, II, 339; Pedro Pizarro, *Relación*, V, 170.

For the other Juan Cortés, see AGI, Justicia 432, no. 2, ramo 2; Lima 92, account of *corregidores* of Peru under Cañete; *Libros de cabildos de Lima*, IV, 43, 194; Oviedo, *Historia*, V, 279.

Diego Gavilán

Age at Cajamarca: Probably in his twenties
Role: Footman
Share: ⅞ share of gold; 1 full share of silver

Place of origin: Guadalcanal, on the edge of Extremadura and Andalusia
Parents: Diego González Gavilán and Leonor González
Extent of literacy: Literate
Trade: Merchant

It is at times hard to identify the merchants among the Spanish population in the Indies in the sixteenth century, not because there were few, but because commercialism pervaded all activity. Generally it is best to accept the criterion of the time and call merchants only those men who accepted the label. Yet after having been at Cajamarca, no man with an ordinary sense of propriety would openly use that label, so that some of the merchants among the conquerors must escape unnoticed. In a few cases there is evidence of such strong and sustained activity of a specifically mercantile type, even after Cajamarca, as to leave no doubt that a given man originated as a merchant. One of the clearest of these cases is Diego Gavilán.

Gavilán's doings first became visible in Lima in 1535. The merchants Francisco and Rodrigo Núñez de Illescas were at that time living in his house, and he had a 2,000-peso investment in merchandise they were to have brought to Lima from Panama. Soon after that he invested 4,000 pesos in a company with the merchant Diego de Cantillana. In the years 1536 to 1538 he was very active in lending money and doing small bits of business for others, doubtless for a commission. He then moved to Huamanga where his day-to-day activity cannot be followed, but we do know that in 1556 he organized a large company to sell merchandise in Lima, himself investing 12,000 pesos and turning over active management to his nephew, the declared merchant Gonzalo de Almonte.

As to other aspects of his career, Gavilán joined the Peru expedition with Hernando de Soto. There is little apparent foundation for later claims by relatives and acquaintances that he was involved in the discovery of Peru, or was one of the Thirteen. Such legends arose because Gavilán outlived most of the other conquerors. He seems to have taken care of some business matters for the Pizarros, and to this he no doubt owed the seat on the council of Lima that he occupied during the year 1535, but he was not an out-and-out Pizarro retainer. He also had connections with other people from his home, Guadalcanal, all of them heavily involved in merchandise, including two alcaldes of Lima, Hernán González and Francisco Núñez de Bonilla. In 1539 Gavilán became a reluctant citizen of the new town of Huamanga, in the highlands, since his encomienda happened to fall within its jurisdiction. Resentful of having to leave the center of Peruvian commerce, Gavilán protested his transfer, appealing all the way up to the royal court. He continued to live in Lima for so long that Francisco Pizarro finally took away some of his Indians. At last he acquiesced, sold four lots he owned, and made the move. In Huamanga he was one of the four or five most important citizens, the others being men of Cajamarca also. His encomienda, even after reduction, was the fourth best in the district; he was regularly on the town council, sometimes alcalde. By 1550 he had married doña Isabel de Chaves. After he had lived out a long life, until 1569, at least, his son and namesake inherited his encomienda.

NOTES. Porras, in Trujillo, *Relación*, p. 94, says that Diego Gavilán was sentenced for involvement in the Gonzalo Pizarro rebellion, but the man in the sentence is not referred to as a *vecino* (encomendero), as would be expected (*CDIAO*, XX, 512). Probably this person was one of two young nephews of Gavilán who took an active part in the Francisco Hernández rebellion of 1554–1555. One of these, also called Diego Gavilán, served as a captain in the rebel forces at that time. Diego Gavilán of

Cajamarca did not fight for the rebels, but he was later fined 5,000 pesos for complicity—which failed to keep him from continuing to harbor his nephews (AGI, Contaduría 1683, records from Lima, August, 1557; AGI, Lima 118, letter of fray Tomás de Santa María, May 20, 1555.

Gavilán's age is calculated merely from the fact that he continued to function on the council of Huamanga until almost 1570. His origin and the names of his parents are given in the will he dictated in 1536, in ANP, PA 791, which tells much about his commercial dealings. The will is published in RANP 4 (1926):25–33. His company with his nephew is documented in BNP, A542, ff.29–32, 202–209, and the relationship between the two in AGI, Contaduría 1683, records from Lima, August, 1557. Other business activity is in AGI, Justicia 1053, no. 5, testimony of Francisco Núñez de Illescas; ANP, PA 272–274, 614; HC 165, 228.

Gavilán's *probanza de servicios*, made in 1540, is in AGI, Patronato 92, no. 10, ramo 1; it is noteworthy that he does not there claim to be an hidalgo. Porras, in Trujillo, *Relación*, p. 94, and Domingo Angulo, in a note in *RANP* 4 (1926):25, give Gavilán's wife as doña Mariana de Cepeda. Yet in a *probanza* instituted by his son and namesake in 1579, it is stated clearly that Gavilán the conqueror married doña Isabel de Chaves, mother of the heir, and the younger Gavilán married doña María de Saravia, daughter of the president of the Royal Audiencia (Barriga, *Mercedarios*, II, 343–345). Possibly the older Gavilán married a second time. The full version of this *probanza*, in AGI, Patronato 123, ramo 12, claims that Gavilán was one of the Thirteen of Gallo Island.

Other references to Gavilán are in AGI, Lima 118, *probanza* of Sebastián de Torres; Lima 204, *probanza* of Jerónimo de Aliaga; Lima 566, vol. IV, May 6, 1541, June 22, 1541; Patronato 93, no. 6, ramo 3; ANP, PA 117, 138, 259, 478, 565, 674, 767; BNP, A203, ff.48, 85, 116, 137, 145; A603, f.13; HC 93, 164, 223, 356, 647, 1227, 1547, 1561, 1562; *RANP* 1 (1920):437; Cieza, *Chupas*, p. 238; Cieza, *Quito* (Jiménez, ed.), p. 109; Cobo, *Obras*, II, 305; *Libros de cabildos de Lima*, I, 15; Loredo, *Los repartos*, pp. 211, 215; Medina, *Descubrimiento*, II, 390, 394.

More information about Gavilán's rebellious nephews is in Diego Fernández, *Historia*, I, 329–331, 349, 384; II, 12.

Crisóstomo de Hontiveros

Age at Cajamarca: About 21
Role: Footman
Share: ¾ share of gold
  and silver

Place of origin: San Miguel de Serrezuela, near Avila in Old Castile
Parents: Crisóstomo de Hontiveros and Catalina Gómez
Extent of literacy: Fully literate

The immediate reason for Hontiveros's quick rise to a certain kind of prominence was his position as a retainer of Hernando Pizarro, but he owed that position in turn to the ability to manage accounts and affairs. Few indeed of the Pizarros' Trujillan friends had such skills. Hontiveros may or may not have been from a merchant family; at any rate he seems to have come out of the broad middle range of society between the obvious plebeians on the one hand and the established hidalgos on the other. He apparently agreed to work for Hernando Pizarro at about the time the expedition left Panama; formal arrangements were not made until May, 1533, when Hernando Pizarro was about to go to Spain with the first shipment of treasure for the crown. Until 1539, when Hernando Pizarro left Peru for the last time, Hontiveros was his chief majordomo in Peru. While he had direct management of the encomiendas, livestock, and properties Hernando possessed in the Lima area, his main function was to coordinate Hernando's far-flung interests. He arranged for the freighting of Hernando's ship, the *Santiago*, and hired its master. He received the large amounts of merchandise that Hernando imported into Peru, and hired people to take it to Cuzco or Arequipa to be sold. He kept accounts of all the debts owed Hernando in Peru, and collected them in Lima, Peru's commercial center and port.

While Hernando Pizarro was at the royal court in 1534, he saw to it that his man Hontiveros was named to a permanent seat on the council of Jauja. Knowing that plans for founding a capital at Jauja were indefinite, Hernando prudently had the appointment made good for Jauja or its region, so that Hontiveros by 1536 was sitting on the council of Lima. Initially, he was a creature of the Pizarros rather than a figure in his own right. But by the late 1530's, as a man of Cajamarca, an encomendero and council member of Lima, now long acquainted with the exercise of power, Hontiveros had outgrown a purely dependent position. In 1539 he rendered account of his activity and Hernando Pizarro discharged him. Apparently the parting was amicable. At this same time the city of Huamanga was founded, and since Hontiveros's encomienda fell in its jurisdiction, he became a citizen there. His encomienda was one of the best in the district, and he was repeatedly alcalde and council member. During the Gonzalo Pizarro rebellion he was in effective charge in Huamanga much of the time; he was reputed to be an avid Pizarrist partisan, but extricated himself in time, retaining his position after Pizarro's defeat. He never became a renowned captain or leader, but maintained his local prominence in Huamanga, where he was still alive and a council member in 1560.

NOTES. The name Hontiveros is the same as Fontiveros, a village in the Avila region. Hontiveros's estimated birthdate of c.1511 rests on his statement in 1536 that he was about twenty-five (AGI, Patronato 93, no. 6, ramo 3), twenty-five being of course the most indefinite of ages. In ANP, Salinas 1538–1540, f.528, he declares himself to be a native of San Miguel de Serrezuela and gives the names of his parents. Hontiveros's contracts with Hernando Pizarro are in HC 220 and 412–414.

Other references are in AGI, Contaduría 1825, records from Cajamarca, May, 1533; Patronato 92, no. 3; ANP, Castañeda, reg. 4, f.45; PA 246, 276, 291, 465, 596, 598, 627; Salinas 1538–1540, f.431; BNP, A203, ff.1, 48, and passim; HC 35, 36, 224, 294, 1269, 1425, 1531, 1547, 1551, 1561, 1562, 1564–1566; Cobo, *Obras*, II, 304; Cieza, *Quito* (Serrano y Sanz, ed.), pp. 55, 279; *Libros de cabildos de Lima*, I, 180; III, 15; Loredo, *Los repartos*, pp. 106, 211, 215; Porras, *Cedulario*, I, 85; 2:30.

Lucas Martínez

Age at Cajamarca: About 21 or 22
Role: Footman
Share: ¾ share of gold and silver

Place of origin: Trujillo
Parents: Francisco Martínez and Francisca de Valencia
Extent of literacy: Fully literate
Trade: Probably merchant

Lucas Martínez owed his special prominence in Peru to the rare combination of two qualities—origin in Trujillo and business ability. Generally speaking, the Trujillans were sorely lacking in managerial talent, and, as a result, the Pizarros' stewards and agents were often Basques, Andalusians, or Castilians who were suspect in their masters' eyes. So it was natural that Lucas, even though not cut out for a warrior or commander, should rise as quickly as his youth permitted.

The only firm evidence that Lucas Martínez might originally have been a merchant is a slip of the pen made by a notary in Lima, who once wrote down, "Lucas Martínez, merchant," at the head of a document, then, on being informed that the gentleman in question was an encomendero, crossed it out and wrote "citizen of Arequipa" instead. Lucas never made any direct claim to be an hidalgo. If not actually a merchant, Lucas was well acquainted with commercial techniques and had a bent for financial and entrepreneurial activity. Together with his inseparable companion and junior business partner, Alonso Ruiz (q.v.), Lucas sold horses and provisions to outfit expeditions, and lent out money, mainly to Trujillo compatriots. His most famous entrepreneurial exploit was to send the first ship with supplies and reinforcements to the struggling Spanish settlement in Chile in 1543. He probably kept up this kind of activity as long as he lived, though it cannot be documented in detail. Various legal testimony left by Lucas Martínez shows him to have had a lively intellect, a retentive memory, and more curiosity about the world than some of his fellows.

There is little reason to doubt that Lucas joined the expedition in his native Trujillo in 1529. After receiving his neophyte's share of the treasure of Cajamarca, he became a citizen and encomendero of Cuzco. Though he did nothing of particular note during the Indian siege, he was sitting on the Cuzco city council by the time the siege was lifted in 1537.

Lucas Martínez's citizenship was transferred to Arequipa when that city was founded in 1539–1540. Probably the Pizarros' intention was to leaven the citizenship, which was quite strongly Almagrist, with a dependable Pizarro partisan. A council member from the first year, Lucas received the large southern encomienda of Tarapacá and Arica, the best, or one of the best, in Arequipa's jurisdiction. Lucas once claimed it was worth more than all of Chile. With the help of many employees, he exploited his encomienda methodically, working the silver mines of Tarapacá and running a supply ship back and forth between encomienda and town.

With such power in his fingers, Lucas began to be anxious for positions of command and honor. Gradually, for dignity's sake, he took an additional surname, becoming Lucas Martínez Vegaso. Yet military leadership and feats of arms were not for him. In 1541 he gained some notoriety by escaping with his ship from the forces of the Almagrists, but achieved no distinction in the ensuing campaign beyond a forehead wound at the battle of Chupas. In the later 1540's he was an early and enthusiastic supporter of the Gonzalo Pizarro rebellion. Though Lucas received no field captaincy, Pizarro finally yielded to his urging to the extent of making him lieutenant governor for the Arequipa region in 1547.

Lucas gloried in his post. He did an excellent job as far as raising money was concerned; he also reported in great detail on his Pizarrist activities and sympathies in a series of letters that royal officials would later use against him. But he was unable to stem the tide of anti-Pizarrist feeling that swept southern Peru when a loyalist army from Panama arrived in the north. In June, 1547, hardly a month after he took office, the citizens of Arequipa seized Lucas as he was trying to conduct some of them to Lima to join Gonzalo Pizarro. The leader of the insurrection was Lucas's *compadre*, Jerónimo de Villegas, to whom Lucas handed over his sword without resistance. The loyalists kept him prisoner for a time, then allowed him to join them. While fighting on the loyalist side at the battle of Huarina in the highlands, he was recaptured by the Pizarrists. So he maintained later, at least, though it is far more likely that at the first opportunity he rejoined the Pizarrists voluntarily. Thenceforth he remained with Gonzalo Pizarro until the final battle of the war at Jaquijahuana in 1548; when it became apparent that a Pizarro rout was taking shape, Lucas Martínez joined the large numbers going over to the loyalist side. The authorities sentenced him at first to exile, loss of his encomienda, and confiscation of half his property. The encomienda went as a reward to Lucas's former friend Villegas. By virtue of a well-financed appeal, the *audiencia* revoked its sentence in March, 1550, but Lucas did not regain his encomienda.

For some years Lucas was left adrift. He still lived in Arequipa and was far from impoverished, but his name was little mentioned, and he never appeared on the municipal council as formerly. He continued to agitate for the return of his encomienda, and probably devoted much attention to business.

In 1555, Jerónimo de Villegas died, leaving neither a widow nor a male heir to inherit Tarapacá; his daughter did not succeed in making good her claim. Thus, in 1557, Lucas was able to get his encomienda back; according to the gossip-mongering royal factor, he achieved his goal by bribing the new viceroy, Cañete. Lucas returned immediately to his old position in the Arequipa community. In 1560 he was alcalde; in 1561 he was Arequipa's representative in the negotiations held in Lima to achieve the perpetuity of encomiendas.

All his life Lucas had spent much of his time in Lima, and this tendency was accentuated in the 1560's. It was in Lima that he married and ten days later died, in April, 1567. Lucas had once had a noble Indian mistress, doña Isabel Yupanqui, but he gave her a dowry and married her off to a small encomendero of Arequipa around 1543. His young bride of 1567, whom he married only so that she could inherit the encomienda, was doña María Dávalos Ribera. She was the daughter of

Nicolás de Ribera, one of the Thirteen, as rich and business-minded a man as Lucas Martínez himself. If Lucas left other heirs, they are not known. He had a son, Francisco Martínez Vegaso, illegitimate and possibly mestizo, who held an encomienda in Chile in 1546, then disappears from the record.

In his final days Lucas was assailed by the wave of moral and legal objections to the conquest, combined with demands for restitution, that swept over Peru in the 1560's. Lucas conceded less to this movement than most. Some of the conquerors made the gesture of leaving handsome legacies to Indian towns or hospitals by way of restitution. Lucas wrote into his will a heated statement that he had considered the conquest to be as justified as any war against infidel Turks or Moors, and that he had never heard otherwise at the time or long afterward, from layman or priest. Reluctantly complying with the importunings of his spiritual advisors, Lucas made the least restitution conceivably justifiable. He added up the exact sums he received at Cajamarca, Jauja, and Cuzco during the conquest (before inflation), discounted all pious donations he had made later (after inflation), and promised restitution of the modest amount remaining.

N O T E S . Lucas's birthplace and parentage are stated by him in *DHA*, I, 84. He gave his age frequently and variously, but two statements will suffice for a general idea. In 1534 he said he was twenty-five (AGI, Patronato 93, no. 6, ramo 4), in 1539 that he was twenty-eight (*DHA*, II, 50–51). The name Lucas Martínez appears with great frequency in the variant of Lucas Martín. Lucas added the "Vegaso" about 1544, but he never used it consistently.

Only certain fragmentary references indicate how Lucas Martínez exploited his encomienda. He speaks of the several *mozos* he kept on the encomienda (*DHA*, II, 175); there are references to his ship supplying the mines of Tarapacá (Pérez de Tudela, *Gasca*, II, 84); and two of his contracts with subordinates are preserved, including one with his chief majordomo, who was empowered to administer his property and encomienda and to hire and fire employees, incuding miners and sailors (BNP, A30, ff.383–385; ANP, Salinas 1546–1548, ff.257–258). The author presumes that Lucas proceeded much in the manner of his rival, Jerónimo de Villegas, whose activities as encomendero of Tarapacá are better documented. (See Lockhart, *Spanish Peru*, pp. 31–33).

There are several mentions of a brother of Lucas Martínez in Peru. One brother is fully authenticated, an Alonso García Vegaso, who was in Arequipa in 1550 (BNP, A171). The chronicler Diego Fernández says that an unnamed brother was in charge of Lucas's ship in 1547 (*Historia*, I, 190). Gutiérrez de Santa Clara, probably following Fernández, says the same, and identifies him as "Pedro Martín Vegaso," but Gutiérrez de Santa Clara is notoriously corrupt when it comes to the names of obscure people (*Quinquenarios*, III, 373–374). Roa y Ursúa asserts that an older brother named Francisco Martínez Vegaso was Lucas's partner in the conquest and in mercantile enterprises. (*Reyno de Chile*, p. 32.) The truth of this is hard to assess, for though Roa y Ursúa is usually a reliable transcriber of documents, he veils his sources, and often makes false identifications. If an older brother was involved in any early stage of the conquest, he certainly would have been a prominent encomendero, but that was not the case. If there was such a brother at all, he was not the merchant Francisco Martínez, from Madrid, who helped finance Pedro de Valdivia's Chile expedition, as asserted by Pocock (*Conquest of Chile*, p. 101). In 1545 a Francisco Martín Camero was acting as master of Lucas Martínez's ship, but does not seem to have been his brother (Pérez de Tudela, *Gasca*, II, 84; conceivably this person was identical with Lucas's son). Another possible relative is Lucas's chief majordomo in 1544, Pedro Alonso de Valencia (BNP, A30, ff.383–385), since Valencia was the name of Lucas's mother; but this man would more likely be a cousin or poor relative than a brother.

The only evidence on Lucas's son is a statement of Pedro de Valdivia that he gave encomiendas in Chile to Diego García de Villalón and to "a son of Lucas Martínez" (*CDIHC*, VII, 315, 330), combined with the presence together, on a list of encomenderos of Santiago in 1546, of Villalón and Francisco Martínez Vegaso (*CDIHC*, VIII, 125). If born in the Indies, he could have been no older than sixteen. For doña Isabel Yupanqui and her husband, Martín Pérez de Villabona, see ANP, RA PC, I, cuaderno 9, and *DHA*, III, 126, 300.

There is a mass of documentation concerning Lucas Martínez, much of it published, though no *probanza de servicios*, as such, is known to exist. His will, in AGI, Lima 124, has not been seen by this writer, but is partially described in Lohmann Villena, "Restitución por conquistadores," *Anuario de Estudios Americanos* 23 (1966):69–70. Many of the records of Lucas's trial for involvement in the Gonzalo Pizarro revolt are published in *CDIHC*, VIII, 398–430, including the letters Lucas wrote to Gonzalo Pizarro and an encomienda grant from Francisco Pizarro in 1540. A slightly different selection of the same materials is in *DHA*, II, 163–193. A set of documents about the partnership between Lucas and Alonso Ruiz is in *DHA*, I, 84–89, 100–102, 107–109.

Other references to Lucas Martínez are in AGI, Contaduría 1824, records from Cuzco, 1536 and 1537; Justicia 1071, no. 2, ramo 3; Lima 118, *probanza* of García Martín; letter of Bernaldino Romani, royal factor, October 15, 1557; letter of Lucas Martínez Vegaso, December 9, 1555; Patronato 93, no. 4, ramo 3; no. 8, ramo 4; 97, no. 1, ramo 1; 109, ramos 4 and 9; 185, ramo 11; ANP, PA 104; Salinas 1542–1543, f.263 (Lucas called merchant); HC 10, 16, 18, 21, 28; *CDIAO*, XX, 526; *CDIHC*, IV, 398; VIII, 62, 89–90, 274; *DHA*, I, 83; II, 81, 84–86, 267, 287–292, 309–313, 318–321; III, 126, 299–301, 308–313; *RANP* 1:565–570; Calvete, *Rebelión de Pizarro*, V, 73–74; Diego Fernández, *Historia*, I, 60, 117, 190; Esteve Barba, *Crónicas del reino de Chile*, p. 19; Esteve Barba, *Descubrimiento y conquista de Chile*, p. 295; Gangotena y Jijón, "La descendencia de Atahualpa," *Boletín de la Academia Nacional de Historia, Quito* 38, no. 91 (1958): 118–119; Gutiérrez de Santa Clara, *Quinquenarios*, II, 335; III, 373–374; Loredo, *Los repartos*, p. 194; Pérez de Tudela, *Gasca*, I, 108–109, 218, 532, 536, 566–567; 2:438, 597; Pedro Pizarro, *Relación*, V, 210; Porras, "Dos documentos esenciales," *Revista Histórica* 17 (1948): 92; Roa y Ursúa, *El reyno de Chile*, pp. 31–32.

For Francisco Martínez, merchant from Madrid, see AGI, Lima 566, vol. 4, August 16, 1541; Patronato 113, ramo 10; ANP, Salinas 1542–1543, ff.204, 205; *CDIHC*, VIII, 53–62; Esteve Barba, *Descubrimiento y conquista de Chile*, p. 242.

Pedro de Mendoza

Age at Cajamarca: About 20
Role: Footman
Share: ¾ share of gold
   and silver

Place of origin: Region of Sahagún
   (Leon)
Extent of literacy: Literate
Trade: Merchant

Pedro de Mendoza is an even clearer example than Diego Gavilán of a man whose activity was so strongly mercantile that one does not hesitate to designate him a merchant. Starting in 1532 and continuing at every opportunity he sold horses, slaves, and stock; he lent money in large amounts; he engaged in such complicated transactions as the trade of thousands of marks of silver for uncollected debts and other assets; he had large dealings with the Basque merchant Domingo de Soraluce; he collected a series of debts for the Florentine merchant Neri Francisqui; he was briefly involved in helping to finance the Chilean expedition of Pedro de Valdivia and Pedro Sancho de Hoz in 1540. He stopped short only at selling merchandise over the counter.

It is not certain that Mendoza was from a family of professional merchants. His relatives, the Escobars, seem to have been mainly tai-

lors. María de Escobar, his sister, had once served the wife of Governor
Pedrarias de Avila of Panama. She came early to Peru, where she far
outshone Mendoza; she was married three times, each time to a notable.
Like her brother she was constantly involved in complex business deals,
which, together with the encomiendas and other assets of her successive husbands, made her one of the wealthiest people in the country.
Though she never acquired the "doña," she did marry one of Peru's
greatest noblemen, don Pedro Portocarrero.

Mendoza's blatant commercial activity appears to have exceeded the
bounds of propriety. His counterpart, Diego Gavilán, took care to di-
lute the flavor of commerce by the use of agents and by developing a
seigneurial façade, so that he eventually became a much honored figure
in Huamanga. Mendoza, on the other hand, was his own agent, and
often even the agent of others. His manner of living was also eccentric;
a report of 1551 complains that he lived most of the time among his
Indians—unusual behavior indeed. He never sat on any municipal
council, and never received mention in accounts of civil wars. Originally a citizen of Lima, he became a founder of Arequipa in 1539–
1540 because his encomienda of Acarí fell on the northern edge of the
new town's jurisdiction; he was still an encomendero of Arequipa as
late as 1556. But when, in 1575, Arequipa began to become curious
about its history and asked some old-timers to name the early settlers,
only one witness could remember that there was such a person as Pedro
de Mendoza.

N O T E S . The name Mendoza was borne by some of the greatest nobles of Spain, and also by other families in every part of the peninsula.
Aside from two viceroys who were Mendozas, many of the Mendozas in
Peru were members of an hidalgo family from the Maestrazgo de Santiago,
in southern Extremadura. But our Pedro de Mendoza showed no tendency
to associate with any of these.

Mendoza's regional origin was established through his connection with
María de Escobar. Though only one source says that Mendoza was María's
brother (*CDIHC*, XXII, 624), the reference is very explicit, and there is
no reason to doubt it, particularly since the resulting regional attribution
is further confirmed by Mendoza's associations (see Pedro Sancho, Notes).
While even María's origin has to be arrived at indirectly, it appears certain
that one is justified in giving her the same origin as her uncle Francisco de
Escobar, who was definitely from Sahagún (Gómara, *Hispania victrix*, I,
254; Garcilaso, *Obras*, III, 231; Gutiérrez de Santa Clara, *Quinquenarios*,

II, 250). An Antonio de Escobar, hosier, who was in Lima in the 1550's, was also from Sahagún, and must have been a relative (ANP, Gutiérrez 1545–1555, f.799). Another probable connection was the tailor Pedro de Escobar, who was in Panama in the 1520's, when María was there too; he was from Villamayor (de Campos), fifty miles down-river from Sahagún (Medina, *Descubrimiento*, II, 452). Garcilaso once said that María was a native of Trujillo, but he was obviously not knowledgeable on the subject, since he gave the name of her husband as Diego de Chaves instead of Francisco. The whole surrounding section, in which Garcilaso is purveying myths about who first introduced European plants and animals to Peru, is one of the most unreliable in all of Garcilaso's writings.

In 1550 Mendoza said he was thirty-eight years old (AGI, Patronato 97, no. 1, ramo 1). The 1575 investigation into Arequipa's history is in *DHA*, II, 341–382, and Mendoza is mentioned on p. 360. Other references are in AGI, Contaduría 1825, Penas de Cámara, 1535; ANP, Juzgado, December 30, 1535; PA 59, 78, 81, 89, 100, 263, 267, 268, 276, 278, 281, 283, 304, 380, 635–637, 647, 679, 680, 755; HC 358, 1013; *CDIHC*, VII, 175. Mendoza appears in two documents among the Peruvian manuscripts of the Lilly Library, once in close conjunction with María de Escobar.

For María de Escobar, see AGI, Justicia 467; ANP, RA PC, I, cuaderno 3; Salinas 1538–1540, f.123; 1542–1543, ff.14, 15 (2nd series); 23, 25, 181, 183, 206, 207, 215; Salinas 1546–1548, f.706; BNP, A33, f.72; HC 485, 486, 525, 526, 535, 539, 555, 558, 578, 579, 607, 612, 647; Gutiérrez de Santa Clara, *Quinquenarios*, II, 173, 175, 178, 254; Lockhart, *Spanish Peru*, pp. 44, 158, Plate 6; Oviedo, *Historia*, III, 262; Porras, *Cartas*, p. 466.

Pedro Navarro

Age at Cajamarca: 30 or over
Role: Footman
Share: 1 full share of gold
 and silver

Place of origin: Pamplona (Navarre)
Parents: Ramón de Iles de Urroz
 and María de Acedo
Extent of literacy: Literate

Though his true name was Pedro de Urroz, in the Indies he took the surname Navarro, indicating his origin in the kingdom of Navarre. Of all the Basque provinces Navarre was the most foreign in the sixteenth century, still new under the crown of Castile. Yet Navarro was thoroughly acclimated to Castile, and there is little evidence of the Basque or Navarre connection in his career in Peru, beyond one or two ephemeral transactions. Generations after Navarro lived, a descendant entering the Order of Santiago "proved" that the family had hidalgo origins in Pamplona, but at that distance in time the proof was tenuous at best. Pedro Navarro was educated and capable, yet he would seem to have been more nearly an entrepreneur, man of affairs, or merchant than an hidalgo. His experience in the New World stretched far back, as far as 1508, according to one vague claim. He had known Francisco Pizarro from about 1526, and may have been on one of the early voyages of discovery. Later legend said he had been one of the Thirteen of Gallo Island.

By 1531 he was in Nicaragua, and it was from there that he came to Peru with Sebastián de Benalcázar. But no sooner did he arrive than he detached himself from Benalcázar's following to become the retainer or servant of his old acquaintance Governor Pizarro. His duties ranged from taking care of his master's gear to managing his financial affairs; whereas Pizarro's other retainer, Juan de Valdevieso, veered toward courtly duties, Navarro was more the steward. His connections and experience put Navarro near the top of the list of footmen on the roll of Cajamarca.

After the conquest Navarro became a citizen of Lima, with an encomienda on the coast south of the city. Though not initially on the council, he was always an important citizen, and he began to advance into posts of honor in Lima: *procurador general* in 1537 and alcalde in 1543. Probably he soon stopped working for Pizarro directly, though he always remained a faithful Pizarrist in the civil wars (in which he was not prominent). He spent most of his energy on his businesses, including one of the first horse-raising enterprises in Peru.

Pedro Navarro married Constanza de León, not a "doña" and not a Ponce de León as later genealogists made her, but the natural daughter of another conqueror, Antón de León. When Navarro died around 1544, he left a minor son, Antonio, who eventually came into his encomienda. Antonio then merged fully into the high society of Lima, marrying the daughter of a judge of the *audiencia*. The family, still retaining the name Urroz, was important in Lima's aristocracy at least until the end of the seventeenth century.

NOTES. Navarro's estimated birthdate of c.1502 or before is based on his declaration that he was over forty in 1544 (AGI, Justicia 467), combined with a statement in a royal cedula issued in 1538 that he had been in the Indies thirty years (AGI, Lima 565, vol. III, December 6, 1538).

Roa y Ursúa (*El reyno de Chile*, p. 3) gives Navarro's birthplace and also a garbled version of his progeny, dividing his son into two and making him both son and grandson. Pedro's son was originally called Juan Antonio Navarro but often dropped the Juan and called himself Antonio Navarro or Antonio Urroz Navarro. He was married twice, first to doña Mencía de Santillán, daughter of Licenciado Hernando de Santillán, judge of the *audiencia*, and second to doña Catalina Manrique de Lara, one of the noblest ladies in Peru. His son by his first marriage (Pedro's grandson) was another Antonio de Urroz Navarro, born in the 1570's. Ignacio de Alarcón y Urroz, the latter's grandson, held high office in Lima and entered the Order of Santiago in 1680 (BNP, A538, July 8, 1556; Cobo, *Obras*, II, 318; Lohmann Villena, *Americanos en las órdenes nobiliarias*, I, 17).

Navarro's *probanza de servicios* is in AGI, Justicia 432, no. 2, ramo 3; information on Navarro as servant of Pizarro is in HC 49 and Trujillo, *Relación*, p. 52. Other references: AGI, Justicia 746, no. 5; Lima 565, vol. III, December 6, 1538; Patronato 92, no. 3; 185, ramo 16; ANP, PA 85, 374, 378, 485, 784; Salinas 1542–1543, f.768; HC 47, 48, 329, 369, 469; several documents of the 1530's among the Peruvian manuscripts of the Lilly Library; Cobo, *Obras*, II, 304; Loredo, *Los repartos*, p. 224; Porras, *Cedulario*, II, 176; Porras, in Trujillo, *Relación*, pp. 95, 96.

For Constanza de León see ANP, Gutiérrez 1545–1555, f.366; AHA, Gaspar Hernández, March 8, 1553; HC 780.

Pedro Pinelo

Role at Cajamarca: Footman   Share: ¾ share of gold and silver

While nothing is known of Pedro Pinelo beyond his name and his modest share of the treasure, the name alone is eloquent, for in the early sixteenth century the Pinelos (originally Pinelli) were among the greatest Genoese merchant families of Seville, along with the Spínolas and the Cataños. (A Cataño was at Cajamarca also.) The Pinelo family had a very strong historical association with the Indies, since the head of the house, Francisco Pinelo, was one of the main backers of the first voyage of Columbus and helped organize the Casa de Contratación. By 1532 there were Pinelos at all stages of assimilation into Sevillian society, some already aristocratic and removed from commerce, some established merchants, and some fresh from Genoa. There is no telling where along this continuum Pedro Pinelo's origins are to be sought, but there can be little doubt that he in some way came out of the Genoese colonies of the Seville-Cádiz area.

NOTES. No reference is known to Pedro Pinelo outside the roll of Cajamarca. For the family background see Pike, *The Genoese in Seville*, pp. 2–4.

Juan de Quincoces

Role at Cajamarca: Horseman
Share: Double share of gold
  and silver

Place of origin: Hermosilla, in the district
  of Burgos in Old Castile
Parents: Pedro de Quincoces and
  Isabel Gómez
Extent of literacy: Could sign,
  doubtless literate

It is not known whether Quincoces had experience in the Indies prior to 1531, when he joined the Peruvian expedition in Panama. Somewhere, however, he had acquired experience in business affairs. After the conquest was over he imported merchandise into Peru in company with his friend Juan de Beranga, also from northern Castile, and a Sevillian merchant named Alvaro Caballero. This and other dealings he had with merchants of Panama lead one to suspect that he may have been from one of those families of "merchants of Burgos" so important in the Indies trade in the earlier part of the sixteenth century. Quincoces was very close to the Pizarros, probably their retainer; at least he often collected debts and managed affairs for full-fledged Pizarro retainers like Crisóstomo de Hontiveros. It was probably as a man expected to represent Pizarro interests that Quincoces received in 1533 a royal appointment to the council of "the city where the governor resides." On the basis of this he sat on the council of Cuzco in 1535, then within the year transferred his citizenship to become a permanent councilman of Lima.

There was more to Quincoces than merely the manager and merchant; he was one of three horsemen who rode ahead of the main group and first entered the valley of Jauja. In 1534 Pizarro chose him for the important mission of retrieving the treasure the citizens of Cuzco had acquired for themselves against the governor's orders. After initial defiance, the men of Cuzco gave in to Pizarro's pressure, their capitulation disguised under a donation of the whole amount to the king, and Quincoces conveyed the 30,000 pesos of gold and 35,000 marks of silver back to Pizarro in Jauja. Quincoces would certainly have become one of the "principal men" of Peru if he had not died in 1536 or 1537, probably a victim of the Indian revolt of those years.

N O T E S . Quincoces's regional origin and parentage are given in Porras, *Cedulario*, II, 336. His company with Beranga and Caballero is mentioned in AGI, Justicia 1074, no. 9, in the accounts of the estates of the deceased.

Other references are in AGI, Contaduría 1825, records from Lima, 1535, 1536; Justicia 1125, proceedings concerning estate of Francisco Martín; 1071, no. 1, ramo 8; Patronato 109, ramo 4; 185, ramo 11; ANP, Juzgado, December 30, 1535; PA 237–239, 245, 248, 291, 762; HC 29, 55; Cieza, *Tercera parte*, in *Mercurio Peruano* 39 (1958):584; *Libros de cabildos de Lima*, I, 174; Porras, *Cedulario*, I, 113; II, 87, 261, 414; Porras, "Jauja," *Revista Histórica* 18 (1949–1950):129, 130, 132, 133; Rivera Serna, *Libro primero de cabildos del Cuzco*, p. 43.

11. MARGINAL HIDALGOS
AND SOLID COMMONERS

THIS CATCH-ALL CATEGORY includes several persons who, if we knew more about them, might be counted with the true hidalgos (Ulloa, Solares), the notaries (Castillo, Palomino), the men of affairs (Herrera, Torres), or the artisans (Cornejo, Morales, and many others). But these men, all in all, did embody very fully and clearly that quality of commonness plus capability which strongly colored the men of Cajamarca as a group. Even such an alleged hidalgo as Juan Ruiz had a strikingly plebeian air. At the same time, most of the conquerors included here were literate, and all had the capacity to rise with time to the highest ranks of Peruvian society, or to find a respectable niche in peninsular Spain.

Francisco de Almendras

Age at Cajamarca: About 23
Role: Footman
Share: 1 full share of gold
and silver

Place of origin: Plasencia
(northern Extremadura)
Extent of literacy: Could sign,
probably could read and write

Almendras was the name of a respected family, neither very noble nor very humble, of Plasencia, to the northwest of Trujillo. Given his age and origin, Francisco must have been with the expedition from its beginnings in the recruiting in Extremadura. His full share of the treasure at Cajamarca shows him already occupying a certain position. By 1537 he was sitting on the council of Cuzco, where he had been a citizen and encomendero from the city's founding. When the town of La Plata was established in the silver region to the south, in 1540, Almendras switched his citizenship there as a perpetual council member.

All his contemporaries agreed that Almendras had an excess of what might be called the Extremaduran temperament; extreme devotion to relatives, close friends, partisans, and compatriots, combined with blunt, arrogant language, an uncontrolled temper, and total indifference to anyone outside the pale. The same complexion can be seen in Alonso de Toro and Hernando Pizarro. Even sympathetic Pedro Pizarro says that Almendras was "ill-dispositioned, cruel, and of bad conscience, with many other public vices."

Almendras was so closely allied to the Pizarros that he may have been one of their "servants" or retainers in the early days. He rushed to the support of the Gonzalo Pizarro rebellion as it took shape in Cuzco in 1544. He was quickly made a captain and managed the crucial act of commandeering the only artillery in Peru, stored at Huamanga. Shortly after Gonzalo Pizarro assumed the governorship of Peru, he sent Almendras to rule the La Plata region in his name. La Plata was soon seething with resistance to the Pizarros, partly because of political sentiments, but partly because no one in La Plata felt safe from the caprice of Almendras, who summarily executed the nobleman don Gómez de Luna for nothing more than words. In June, 1545, anti-Pizarrists took over La Plata and decapitated Almendras, after he refused to deny Pizarro or work for the loyalist cause. When the loyalists won final victory in 1548, officials confiscated Almendras's property, but his mestizo children, who had been legitimated, were absorbed into the Spanish population of La Plata, and his nephew Martín took over the Almendras position there.

NOTES. In 1534 Almendras declared that he was about twenty-five years old, a vague statement at best (AGI, Patronato 93, no. 6, ramo 4). Lists of sentences in the Gonzalo Pizarro revolt say that Almendras was a native of Plasencia (*CDIAO*, XX, 534, and Loredo, "Sentencias," *Mercurio Peruano* 22 [1940]: 265).

Other references are in AGI, Contaduría 1824, Cuzco, August, 1536; Lima 565, vol. III, February 25, 1540; Patronato 93, no. 4, ramo 3; 95, no. 1, ramo 1; 109, ramo 4; 185, ramo 11; HC 1516; *CDIHC*, IV, 399; *CDIHE*, XXVI, 221–232; Cieza, *Chupas*, pp. 156, 157; Cieza, *Quito* (Serrano y Sanz, ed.), pp. 142–143; Diego Fernández, *Historia*, I, 21, 46, 61–62; Garcilaso, *Obras*, III, 238; Gutiérrez de Santa Clara, *Quinquenarios*, II, 186, 195, 338, 380, 383, 384; Loredo, *Los repartos*, p. 170; Pedro Pizarro, *Relación*, V, 234, 275; Porras, *Cedulario*, II, 219; *Relación de las cosas del Perú*, V, 255. More about Almendras's participation in the Gonzalo Pizarro rebellion can be found in the chronicles and in Pérez de Tudela, *Gasca*.

For Almendras's relatives and children see AGI, Lima 565, vol. IV, April 15, 1541; Lima 566, vol. V, April 24, 1545, February 26, 1546; Gutiérrez de Santa Clara, *Quinquenarios*, III, 87, 336, 350; Pérez de Tudela, *Gasca*, I, 216; II, 317.

Francisco de Avalos

Role at Cajamarca: Footman
Share: 1 full share of gold
  and silver

Place of origin: Guareña
  (central Extremadura)
Extent of literacy: Illiterate

Avalos came to the Indies in 1530, presumably among those recruited by the Pizarros in Extremadura. Illiterate and a close associate of Pedro Calderón the horseshoer, he no doubt came of humble origins; but he was a man of some consequence on the expedition, one of the relatively few footmen to get a full share. Like many of the footmen at Cajamarca, he soon joined the riders, with a horse bought in partnership with Calderón. He returned to Spain in 1535 after the founding of Cuzco, apparently without ever having asked for an encomienda. The fortune he carried was large, 30,000 ducats in his own possession plus amounts brought for him by others, but it all suffered the fate of royal confiscation, in return for 8 percent annuities. Not long after arriving home in Guareña he was accused of murdering his wife, Francisca de Ribera, in order to make a better match. The record fails to show whether he was innocent or guilty, but this crime was not unprecedented among men of the Indies, who often found themselves suddenly rich and still tied to humble wives; Hernando Cortés was accused of the same thing.

NOTES. Avalos had a namesake who was a more important man in Peru. The other Francisco de Avalos was from Ubeda in Andalusia, fully literate and of fairly good family. He had been *regidor* on the town council of Granada, Nicaragua, in 1529, and came to Peru with Almagro, arriving at Cajamarca just after the events. He was an encomendero in the jurisdiction of Lima, and held the office of alcalde there in 1537. He died in 1539.

In AGI, Justicia 724, no. 6, the Avalos of Cajamarca is called a citizen of Guareña. Other references are in AGI, Indiferente General 1801, records of ship *Santa Catalina*, 1535; Justicia 1082, no. 1, ramo 4, testimony of Bartolomé Sánchez; ANP, PA 28, 73, 109, 118, 130.

For the second Francisco de Avalos, see AGI, Justicia 1052, no. 7, ramo 2; Lima 204, *probanza* of Hernán González; 565, vol. III, April 18, 1539; 566, vol. 6, October 9, 1549; *CDIHN*, II, 176–178; Torres Saldamando, *Libro primero de cabildos*, I, 113, 115, 116, 349; II, 318; Porras, *Cedulario*, II, 335.

Francisco de Baena

Age at Cajamarca: About 27   Place of origin: Madrid
Role: Horseman   Father: Francisco Márquez
Share: Double share of gold   Extent of literacy: Could sign,
   and silver   probably literate

Baena came to Peru as a known quantity, with both experience in the Indies and connections in Spain. He had been in Nicaragua for five or six years, and by the time he left for Peru he was a *regidor* on the council of Nicaragua's chief town, León. In December, 1532, a royal letter was issued in Madrid (probably obtained through Baena's father) recommending him to the governor of Peru, as a relative of servants of the crown.

Either Baena's riding ability or his horse was quite highly regarded, since he was sent out on such hazardous missions as Soto's ride to interview Atahuallpa, and Hernando Pizarro's expedition to the temple of Pachacámac. Baena may have been the partner of Pedro de Barrera, also from Madrid, who had been in Nicaragua with him; the two appear next to each other on a list of Soto's men, and again on the general list of the men of Cajamarca.

Francisco de Baena was in every respect a man who could have gone far in Peru, but instead he returned with the first group, leaving in July, 1533. By 1534 he was at the royal court in Toledo, giving testimony in favor of a comrade. He was not heard of again in the affairs of the Indies. No doubt he settled in Madrid.

NOTES. In 1530 Baena said he was twenty-five (*CDIHN*, II, 537). The Madrid-born chronicler Oviedo, who may have known Baena slightly, though he thought his first name was Hernando, asserts that he was the "son of Francisco Márquez, citizen of Madrid." (*Historia*, V, 92). See other references in AGI, Patronato 93, no. 4, ramo 4; *CDIHN*, II, 296, 504, 537–540; Porras, *Cedulario*, I, 110–111. In view of his father's name, it seems very likely that Baena is the same person as the Francisco Márquez who was with Hernando Pizarro in Cajamarca in 1533, returned to become a citizen of Madrid, and testified there in favor of Hernando Pizarro sometime in the 1540's. The opposing party in the suit considered Márquez to be of low extraction. See *CDIHC*, V, 408, and VII, 153.

Alonso de la Carrera

Role at Cajamarca: Footman
Share: 1 full share of gold
   and silver

Place of origin: Fuentes de Ropel
   (district of Zamora, in Leon)
Extent of literacy: Very crude signature,
   doubtless illiterate

Carrera was a rather humble and obscure man, though he may have had relatives who were more pretentious. He was never a captain or a member of a city council. Still he held his own, with a full share at Cajamarca and a rich encomienda in Cuzco, where he was a citizen from the day of foundation in 1534 to his death. In 1535 he was nominated for the Cuzco council, but he was not elected. In 1542 Governor Vaca de Castro improved his encomienda still further, presumably for loyalty and aid in the campaign of Chupas. The highest honor Carrera attained was that of appointment as majordomo of the hospital in Cuzco for 1547. Shortly thereafter he died, possibly naturally, but more likely in the bloody battle of Huarina.

NOTES. Carrera's full name, when he used it, was Alonso Alvarez de la Carrera. The evidence for his place of origin is that he sent money in

1536 to his father living in Fuentes de Ropel (AGI, Justicia 1126, no. 2, ramo 1, memorandum of Gregoria de Sotelo). Carrera's encomienda was rated ninth of eighty-three in Cuzco c.1548–1549. There seems to have been some dispute as to whether it belonged in the jurisdiction of Cuzco or Charcas. It included Caquiabo or Caquiabire and Ricaxa (Loredo, *Alardes y derramas*, pp. 116, 128; *Los repartos*, pp. 178, 186–187).

Busto (in *Francisco Pizarro*, p. 222) indicates that Alonso Alvarez, captain of thirty men who intercepted and mistreated Almagro's envoys on the coast south of Lima in 1537, was Alonso Alvarez de la Carrera. This may only be Busto's shrewd guess. The standard original accounts say merely "an Alonso Alvarez" (*CDIAO*, XX, 269; Cieza, *Salinas*, pp. 138–143). A far stronger and more prominent Pizarro partisan was Alonso Alvarez de Hinojosa, from Trujillo and a citizen of Cuzco.

A Sancho de la Carrera appeared at Alonso's side in Cuzco in 1535. He is probably the same as the Sancho de la Carrera from Toro, near Zamora, who appeared in Quito in 1536. This Carrera seems to have been a man of a different stamp; he had a beautiful signature, was *regidor* in Quito in 1537 and alcalde in 1544, then captain for Viceroy Blasco Núñez Vela at the battle of Inaquito in 1546, where he was killed. The relationship is reminiscent of that between Francisco and Hernando Pizarro, where the marginal member of the family goes out to try his luck, then with success quickly draws in the senior branch.

Other references to Alonso de la Carrera are in AGI, Contaduría 1824, records from Cuzco, May–July, 1535, and March–April, 1537; Patronato 109, ramo 4; 185, ramos 10 and 11; ANP, PA 777, 778; AHC, Libros de cabildos, I, f.47; *CDIHE*, XXVI, 221–232; *RANP* 5 (1927):7; Pérez de Tudela, *Gasca*, II, 587.

For Sancho de la Carrera, see AGI, Contaduría 1824, records from Cuzco, May–July, 1535; Cieza, *Quito* (Serrano y Sanz, ed.), p. 89; Gutiérrez de Santa Clara, *Quinquenarios*, II, 355; *Libros de cabildos de Quito*, I, sect. 1, pp. 194, 201, pl. opp. p. 232; I, sect. 2, p. 144.

Gonzalo del Castillo

Role at Cajamarca: Horseman
Share: Double share of gold
   and silver

Place of origin: Lebrija (near Seville)
Parents: Hernando del Castillo and
   Isabel Sánchez Barba
Extent of literacy: Literate

Gonzalo was the son of Hernando del Castillo, notary and attorney of Panama, and in the late 1520's he acted as his father's factor in the budding Indian slave trade between Nicaragua and Panama. In all likelihood he also understood something of his father's profession. It was probably through his father, long acquainted with Pizarro and Almagro, that Gonzalo became involved in the Peruvian venture. In July of 1529 he was in Nicaragua with a ship sent there by Almagro, picking up slaves for use as auxiliaries and secretly trying to persuade the Spaniards he met to abandon Nicaragua in favor of Peru. He must have been with the 1531 expedition from an early stage, taking one of the horses he and his father owned in Nicaragua. In the conquest, Castillo was one of the first line of horsemen, along with his partner, Francisco de Fuentes. After the division of the treasure of Cajamarca, he returned, under Sebastián de Benalcázar, to help maintain security in San Miguel, and he appears to have started off on Benalcázar's campaign toward Quito in 1534. He died in Peru under unknown circumstances before 1536.

NOTES. Busto speculates ("Los fugitivos de Nicaragua," *Mercurio Peruano* 43 [1962]:265–267), that the Gonzalo del Castillo at Cajamarca was a man from Avila (Bermúdez Plata, *Pasajeros*, I, 128) who left Spain in 1514. But as Busto says, basing himself on *CDIHN*, II, 34–35, and as is seen elsewhere, Gonzalo's father was Hernando del Castillo, who appears in a document of 1531 as Hernando del Castillo de Lebrija (Enrique Otte and Miguel Maticorena Estrada, "La isla de la Magdalena," *Mercurio Peruano* 41 [1960]:269). Moreover, Gonzalo's mother was a citizen and resident of Lebrija, as was his brother Pedro (AGI, Justicia 720, no. 6).

It is nowhere specifically stated that Castillo and Francisco de Fuentes were partners. But they appear next to each other on the roll of Cajamarca as do other such sets; they are again listed together on the roster of those who went with Soto to Atahuallpa's camp (Oviedo, *Historia*, V, 92), and they are associated in the days just after Cajamarca (ANP, PA 53). Both went back to San Miguel with Benalcázar, after Cajamarca. To this may be added that both were from the Seville area, had lived in Panama, and were connected with official circles there.

Further references to Castillo are in ANP, PA 33, 40, 78, 111, 154, 159, 162, 771, 773; Loredo, *Los repartos*, pp. 99–100.

Miguel Cornejo

Age at Cajamarca: Probably in his 20's

Role: Footman

Share: ¾ share of gold and silver

Place of origin: Salamanca, in the kingdom of Leon

Extent of literacy: Crude signature

By most indications, Cornejo was a commoner, possibly from an artisan family. He was not pretentious or arrogant, for the time; he never presented a memorial of his numerous services, and when his children finally did so in 1562, they laid no claim to hidalgo connections either for themselves or for their father.

Cornejo had at least brief experience in Nicaragua, and he arrived in Peru with Soto. After the conquest he was at first a citizen of Cuzco, then, with the foundation of Arequipa in 1540, he had to move there, with an encomienda that was far from the best. The transfer was in the nature of a demotion, but in this milieu, much less lordly and brilliant than Cuzco, Cornejo was able to function at a higher level than before. From 1541 on he was repeatedly alcalde in Arequipa. He held the post of local deputy treasurer for eight years, a job most encomenderos shied away from because of the trouble and lack of pay. Cornejo was a conscientious, sedentary man. Before long he married Leonor Méndez, of equally unpretentious lineage, and began to sire a large family.

In the military line Cornejo finally won some local honors. He had performed well on horseback in the siege of Cuzco and the civil war battles, but he was not the type to be a captain. Finally the weight of his experience and seniority made itself felt, and when there was a flare-up in Peru in 1554, the loyalists of Arequipa named Cornejo *maestre de campo*, organizer and field commander. After this he joined the royal forces raised by the *audiencia*, as a cavalryman like all encomenderos. Carried away perhaps by his new prominence, he did more than his age permitted. On a dangerous scouting mission he was suddenly confronted by the enemy, and, to escape, he had to ride so far and hard that he suffocated inside his armor. He left four legitimate and three natural children; the eldest inherited the encomienda, though the family complained of poverty.

N O T E S . Cornejo's close acquaintance Pedro Pizarro said that he was a native of Salamanca (*Relación*, V, 211). No exact indication of his age has been seen, but it may be presumed that he was under thirty in 1532, if he was still riding out on hard scouting missions twenty-two years later. Cornejo's posthumous *probanza de servicios* is in AGI, Patronato 105, ramo 9 and was also partly published in *DHA*, II, 302–313.

Other references are in AGI, Contaduría 1824, records from Cuzco, 1536; Indiferente General 1801, record of the ship *San Miguel*, 1535; Justicia 1052, no. 3, ramo 2; Lima 118, *probanza* of Martín de Salas; Patronato 109, ramo 4; BNP, A512, ff.222–223; *CDIHN*, II, 68; *DHA*, I, 157, 205, 220, 248, 286; II, 140, 194, 215; Diego Fernández, *Historia*, I, 97, 354, 355, 376–378; II, 37; Gutiérrez de Santa Clara, *Quinquenarios*, III, 96, 98, 99, 108, 113, 366; Loredo, *Los repartos*, pp. 195, 201; Pérez de Tudela, in Pedro Pizarro, *Relación*, V, 164; Pedro Pizarro, *Relación*, V, 208; Porras, *Cedulario*, II, 206.

Miguel Estete de Santo Domingo

Age at Cajamarca: About 25
Role: Footman
Share: ¾ share of gold and silver

Place of origin: Santo Domingo de la Calzada (mountains of Old Castile)
Extent of literacy: Fully literate

Estete added "de Santo Domingo" to his name to distinguish himself from his rather more illustrious namesake (chapter 9), whose whole background he presumably shared. His subordinate position might indicate that he was something of a poor relative of the other Estete, but he must have had a very similar education, to judge by his equally superb signature. This Estete, too, had his moment of prominence. According to Cieza, he was the first man to lay hands on Atahuallpa, and the substance of the report is confirmed by other evidence. The feat is not reflected in his share; perhaps he was the man who accidentally wounded Francisco Pizarro while Pizarro was reaching for Atahuallpa.

Estete was first a citizen and encomendero of Jauja, then of Lima, and finally his citizenship was transferred to highland Huamanga at its foundation in 1539. In that provincial town he was a great man, with one of the best encomiendas and repeated terms on the city council. He was never prominent in the civil wars; the only mention of him in the chronicles is Gutiérrez de Santa Clara's false report that he was executed in 1546. Around 1557 the rebellious Inca, Sairi Tupac, came out of his stronghold of Vilcabamba to make peace with the Spaniards. On the Inca's passage through Huamanga, Estete, in a gesture of friendship, presented him with the imperial fringe he had taken away from Atahuallpa in 1532. Estete married doña Beatriz de Guevara and left heirs behind. He was still alive in Huamanga in 1561.

NOTES. No sooner had Miguel Estete the horseman departed from Peru than Miguel Estete the footman began to drop the "Santo Domingo" from his name. It is natural that confusion between the two should arise (see Domingo Angulo's introduction to Estete's chronicle, for one example). The essentials of the distinction between them have been worked out by Porras Barrenechea, though he lacked the concrete data to make categorical statements. Porras did make the very natural mistake of accepting Gutiérrez de Santa Clara's report of the second Miguel Estete's death in 1546, thus he assumed yet a third Miguel Estete was living in Huamanga in the 1550's. No other account of the executions in Cuzco in 1546 mentions Estete, and even more conclusively, there are three separate references to the Estete dwelling in Huamanga after 1546 as a first conqueror (Jiménez de la Espada, *Relaciones geográficas*, I, 196; Loredo, *Los repartos*, pp. 211, 216; Garcilaso, *Obras*, II, 145).

There is no doubt that the man involved in seizing Atahuallpa physically was Miguel Estete de Santo Domingo, not Miguel Estete the horseman. This is probable if only because it was a body of foot under Pizarro which rushed out to take the Inca, and Cieza makes it definite by identifying the man as "Miguel Estete, native of Santo Domingo de la Calzada, foot-soldier" (*Tercera parte*, in *Mercurio Peruano* 38 [1957]:256). The story of Estete's returning the imperial fringe rests on Garcilaso de la Vega, who is certainly often enough a relayer of legends, but in this case he is telling about something that happened when he was nearing eighteen and that he heard discussed shortly after the event (Garcilaso, *Obras*, II, 145). There might seem to be a conflict between Estete's possession of the fringe and Cieza's report that when Atahuallpa was about to be buried with the imperial fringe on his brow, the priest Francisco de Morales appropriated it, and that he later took it to Spain with him (*Tercera parte*, in *Mercurio Peruano* 39 [1958]:579). But an imperial fringe, rather than a physical thing like the crown of a king, would seem to have been an abstraction on the order of a flag, being merely the right to wear a fringe of certain disposition and color, and the Inca could have a new one every day.

The established fact that Miguel Estete of Huamanga was a man of Cajamarca, and specifically a footman, should serve to cement the identities of the two Estetes. However, lest any suspicion remain that a single Estete was shuttling back and forth across the ocean, the documentary proof can be further strengthened. Miguel Estete, without additional surname, who by his own testimony there given was at Cajamarca, was in Panama in September, 1534 (AGI, Patronato 150, no. 6, ramo 2); in Madrid in September, 1535 (*CDIHN*, III, 413–414); in Valladolid in March, 1537 (AGI, Justicia 1124, no. 6, ramo 3), and still there in 1538 (AGI, Justicia 1124, no. 5, ramo 3). Miguel Estete de Santo Domingo, in each case using the surname, was in Jauja as a citizen in December, 1534 (*Libros de cabildos de Lima*, I, 8–10), then in Lima as a citizen in December, 1535 (document in the Lilly Library), in January, 1536 (ANP, PA 780), in June, 1537 (AGI, Lima 204, *probanza* of Francisco de Ampuero), and in May, 1538 (ANP, Castañeda, reg. 9, f.33).

Miguel Estete the footman gave his age as thirty in 1537 (AGI, Lima 204, *probanza* of Francisco de Ampuero). Other references to him are in ANP, PA 279, 290; Salinas 1542–1543, ff.33–38 (2nd series); BNP, A203, ff.1, 63; HC 156, 1547, 1561–1562; Cobo, *Obras*, II, 304; Diego Fernández, *Historia*, I, 349; Gutiérrez de Santa Clara, *Quinquenarios*, III, 84; Porras, *Cronistas*, pp. 106–108.

Francisco de Fuentes

Age at Cajamarca: Over 25   Place of origin: Probably Seville
Role: Horseman   Extent of literacy: Good signature,
Share: Double share of gold and silver   doubtless literate

Fuentes had lived for some time in the Panama region; it was apparently there that he married a natural daughter of Licenciado Gaspar de Espinosa, former *alcalde mayor*, who had much to do with the early stages of the discovery of Peru, both as an actor and as an associate of Hernando de Luque. Fuentes, of necessity an indirect representative of these interests, was a man to be treated carefully by the Pizarros, yet held at arm's length.

Though he had been in Panama and connected with the organizational core of the expedition, Fuentes also had had much experience in Nicaragua and appears to have come to Peru directly from there, with Benalcázar. After receiving his horseman's double share of the treasure at Cajamarca, he went back under Benalcázar to help guard San Miguel, and he therefore got only 1¾ shares of the division made in Jauja, and 1½ shares of the division in Cuzco.

Pizarro gave Fuentes an encomienda in Trujillo, which was a poor region compared to Lima and Cuzco, though that was perhaps not so clear in 1535 as later. The grant was respectable in size, but it was located in a coastal area where Indian mortality was high. By 1549 it was rated only seventeenth best of twenty-nine in the Trujillo area. Nevertheless, Fuentes was always a power in Trujillo; the economy there in any case rested as much on commerce as on encomiendas. In 1538 Pizarro called on the citizens of Trujillo to join his forces against Almagro; the Trujillo contingent was given the assignment of guarding the king's treasure, and Francisco de Fuentes alternated with another leader as captain of the guard. Through the 1540's and 1550's Fuentes was often a council member or alcalde in Trujillo. Like most of the men of the north, he took very little part in the great civil struggles which were the concern of Lima, Cuzco, and Charcas. He died around 1560, leaving a family. In his final days he was affected by the crisis of conscience over the conquest that was beginning to express itself at that time and left large legacies to the Indians of his encomienda by way of restitution.

NOTES. The lower limit on Fuentes's age is estimated from the fact that his daughter was not only married but was having love affairs by 1541, so she must have been fourteen at least, and, following Spanish patterns, Fuentes would hardly have married before the age of twenty—probably some years later.

It seems very likely that Fuentes was from the Seville region. He married his daughter to a Sevillian (AGI, Patronato 105, ramo 10), his sometime partner Gonzalo del Castillo (q.v.) was a Sevillian, and all his life he is seen much in contact with people of Seville. Probably he was connected with another Francisco de Fuentes, from Seville, who was dispenser of Francisco Pizarro in 1536, then became an encomendero and council member in Chachapoyas, adjacent to the Trujillo region; indeed the Fuentes of Cajamarca was called Francisco de Fuentes el Viejo, or the Elder, to distinguish him from the other one. Fuentes may have been the son of García de Fuentes and Beatriz de Escobar, vecinos of Seville, who left Spain in 1527 (Bermúdez Plata, Pasajeros, I, 214).

Fuentes's wife was named Bárbola de Espinosa. Though Guillermo Lohmann Villena considers her the legitimate daughter of Licenciado Espinosa and his wife doña Isabel, he himself quotes evidence proving that such was not the case (Les Espinosa, pp. 97–98). In a will of 1527 Espinosa made a small legacy to Bárbola, called his "servant," toward her dowry, "because she is said to be my daughter." The latter phrase is a formula used to fend off possible larger inheritance claims by those of one's illegitimate children whose mothers were of very low status. Not only was Bárbola not called "doña" like her father's wife, but even Fuentes's legitimate daughter by Bárbola was called plain Francisca de Fuentes, unusual for the daughter of any encomendero, and especially of such an illustrious one. Thus it appears probable that Bárbola's mother had been very low on the social scale, possibly a Morisca or a mulatto woman. Lohmann believes that Fuentes married Bárbola around 1537 or 1538. The age of their daughter Francisca precludes such a late beginning of their relationship, though it might well have been formalized at that time.

Cieza says (in *Tercera parte*, in *Mercurio Peruano* 36 [1955]:470) that Fuentes was among those arriving in Peru with Benalcázar. Porras, in Trujillo, *Relación*, p. 92, says that he saw (in some unnamed source) testimony by Fuentes to the effect that he came with Soto. Fuentes's *probanza* has his participation in the Peruvian conquest begin at Puertoviejo, where Benalcázar joined the expedition, so the probabilities seem to favor Cieza's version.

A posthumous *probanza de servicios* of Francisco de Fuentes is in AGI, Patronato 103, no. 1, ramo 9. Busto's article "El capitán Melchor Verdugo" (in *Revista Histórica* 24 [1959]:329, 371) gives some further detail on Fuentes, his daughter, and his relationship to Verdugo, partly based on sources there given which this writer has not seen.

Other references are in AGI, Contaduría 1681, records from Trujillo, 1551; Contratación 198, ramo 13; Lima 111, letter of *cabildo* of Trujillo, December 6, 1552; Lima 565, vol. III, April 1, 1539; ANP, PA 9, 10, 53, 65, 112, 152, 153, 155, 157, 158, 746; Barriga, *Mercedarios*, II, 181; Borregán, *Crónica*, p. 49; Loredo, *Los repartos*, pp. 251, 256, 258; Lohmann Villena, "Restitución," *Anuario de Estudios Americanos* 23 (1966):49–50; Oviedo, *Historia*, V, 92; Pérez de Tudela, *Gasca*, II, 572; Porras, *Cartas*, pp. 427, 428, 437, 488; Porras, in Trujillo, *Relación*, p. 92; Vargas Ugarte, "Fecha de la fundación de Trujillo," *Revista Histórica* 10 (1936):234–235.

For the second Francisco de Fuentes, see ANP, Juzgado, September 1, 1536; HC 280, 1095; *CDIHC*, VI, 405.

Francisco Gorducho

Role at Cajamarca: Footman   Place of origin: San Martín de Trevejo
Share: ¾ share of gold   (northwestern Extremadura)
  and silver   Parents: Lorenzo Gorducho and
                                                            Juana Martín Galvana
                                                        Extent of literacy: Could sign his name

At home his name had been Francisco Martín Gorducho, but upon seeing how many Francisco Martíns there were in the Indies (at least three others and a Francisco Martínez on the 1531 expedition alone), he dropped the middle name and used only Gorducho, despite its inelegance ("Fatso," approximately). He had been in Nicaragua for at least two or three years and must have come from there directly to Peru with Benalcázar or Soto. After the main surge of the conquest he became a citizen of Lima, apparently with a coastal encomienda. In

late 1535 he took a trip to Cuzco, as many of Lima's citizens were doing, partly to investigate stories of greater wealth to the south, and
partly to sell horses and provisions for the outfitting of Almagro's
great Chile expedition. Gorducho took two slaves to sell, and doubtless
other things, but when he arrived Almagro had already left, and he
was caught in the siege the Indians threw around the city. He seems to
have survived it, since he was still paying the king's fifth in March–
April, 1537, when Almagro returned and ended the Indian threat.
After that, Gorducho disappears. He may have returned to Spain at
that late date, as a few did, or he may have been one of the many
casualties of the first of the civil wars, the "War of Salinas" in 1537–
1538, which began and was largely fought near Cuzco.

N O T E S . Proceedings initiated by his mother to recover money Gorducho sent home (in AGI, Justicia 1124, no. 6, ramo 3) give his origin,
his full name, and the names of his parents. Other references are in AGI,
Contaduría 1824, records from Cuzco, March–April, 1537; 1825, Penas
de Cámara, 1532, 1535; Lima 118, *probanza* of Alvaro Muñoz; ANP, PA
6, 28, 66, 68, 73, 74, 313, 681, 718, 723; *Libros de cabildos de Lima*, I,
128.

Rodrigo de Herrera

Age at Cajamarca: About 25 to 28   Place of origin: Carrión de los Condes,
Role: Musketeer (on foot)   in the kingdom of Leon
Share: ¾ share of gold and silver   Extent of literacy: Signature crude

The expedition had already landed on the north coast of Peru when
Rodrigo de Herrera bought from a comrade the musket he was to use
at Cajamarca. The price was nine pesos, a piddling sum, but perhaps
after all not a great bargain. The musket or harquebus was not a very
effective weapon against Indians who were without number; beyond
this, it was not integrated into the Spaniards' social values as was the
horse, and it lacked the horse's capital value. Possession of a horse
doubled a man's share whenever profits were distributed—possession
of a musket had no visible effect. Neither of the two known musketeers
at Cajamarca got even so much as one full share.

From a very early time Herrera enjoyed the confidence of the Pizarros. In 1533 he received a royal appointment to the council of Túm-

bez, originally intended to be the main settlement. But no Spanish city was ever established there, so in 1535 he was named to the council of the next projected capital, Jauja; officials at the royal court did not realize that he had already settled in Cuzco. Finally, in 1538, he was appointed to the council of Cuzco, where he had already been sitting on a year-to-year basis. Herrera was not personally prominent in any way; he did not achieve such a string of honors through particularly high lineage, education, feats of arms, or standing as a leader. He almost certainly was one of the retainers that the Pizarros tried to place on the town councils to assure obedience. Another Herrera from Carrión de los Condes, Alonso, worked for the Pizarros as a majordomo in Cuzco in the 1540's and was sentenced in 1548 for complicity in the rebellion of Gonzalo Pizarro.

Rodrigo de Herrera returned to Spain around 1539, having lived in Cuzco through the great siege and the first round of the civil wars. Most of those who left the country at this late date had some special reason for doing so. Perhaps Herrera had fallen out with the Pizarros; back in Spain he was one of those persistently suing Hernando Pizarro for money confiscated in Cuzco. He went to Spain with royal license, retaining his Indians, but doubtless he already knew he would not return to Peru. By April, 1540, he had already negotiated the transfer of his council seat to another man, and then soon retired to live in the little village of Lomas in the jurisdiction of Carrión.

NOTES. Herrera gave his age as about thirty in 1534 (AGI, Patronato 93, no. 6, ramo 4); over thirty in 1538 (*DHA*, II, 47–48); and about thirty again in 1540 (AGI, Justicia 1124, no. 5, ramo 2). The latter has been disregarded as inconsistent with the others. In the last-mentioned source and in Justicia 1052, no. 4, ramo 1, he declares himself a citizen of Lomas, subordinate village of Carrión de los Condes; in a petition in AGI, Lima 118, he is called a citizen of Carrión.

Other references are in AGI, Contaduría 1824, records from Cuzco, March, 1536; Indiferente General 1801, records of ship *San Miguel*, 1535; Lima 118, probanza of Alvaro Muñoz; 565, vol. III, April 30, 1540, May 31, 1538; Patronato 93, no. 8, ramo 4; 109, ramo 4; 185, ramo 11; ANP, PA 107, 777; HC 15, 20; *CDIHE*, XXVI, 221–232; Porras, *Cedulario*, I, 111; II, 94, 411.

For Alonso de Herrera, see *CDIAO*, XX, 532; Loredo, "Sentencias," *Mercurio Peruano* 22 (1940):268; Pérez de Tudela, *Gasca*, I, 310–311. Confusingly enough, there was also a Rodrigo Alonso de Herrera acting as a Pizarro majordomo in Cuzco in the 1540's, but he was from Olmedo, not Carrión. See *CDIAO*, XX, 530, and Pérez de Tudela, *Gasca*, passim.

Andrés Jiménez

Age at Cajamarca: About 28 or 29   Place of origin: Cazalla de la Sierra
Role: Footman   (north of Seville)
Share: 1 full share of gold and silver   Extent of literacy: Could sign his name

Though he was from Cazalla "of the mountain," in the hilly wine-growing region north of Seville, Andrés Jiménez seems to have lived in Seville itself for some time, since he was a parishioner there, and in his will he endowed a chaplaincy in Seville rather than one in Cazalla. With a wife, Catalina Martínez, and no less than five children at home in Spain, he must have been quite new to the Indies in 1530. His background appears to have been humble. He put a perfunctory mention of the word "hidalgo" into his petition for a coat of arms, but no such claim was made in the accompanying inquiry into his ancestry carried out in Cazalla, where the people testifying were all good ordinary townsfolk. It would seem then that Jiménez's full share at Cajamarca can be attributed to maturity and sheer ability rather than to experience or connections.

After the main events of the conquest, Jiménez got permission to visit Spain, arriving in 1535. Here, at the royal court, he did more to advance his career than he had ever done in Peru. He negotiated for and received not only a coat of arms, but a permanent seat on the council of Lima. He was also named captain of a party of a hundred men leaving Spain for Peru in early 1537, and thereafter was always styled Captain Jiménez, though he was never captain of an expedition or a company in battle. Back in Peru by 1538, he sat on the council of Lima for a short time, then became a citizen of Arequipa when it was founded in 1540. In 1541 he was alcalde there. He had close connections with a Sevillian merchant in Arequipa, Baltasar de Armenta, who was not only his partner in exploiting mines on his encomienda, but also the executor of his will and guardian of his children. Jiménez was a notable casualty of the civil war battle of Chupas in 1542, where he was on the loyalist side and among the cavalry, but not functioning as captain. His eighteen-year-old son Andrés, who had come to Peru with his father in 1538, inherited Jiménez's encomienda and held it until he too died in 1547.

NOTES. In 1534 Jiménez said he was thirty-one (AGI, Lima 204, *probanza* of Hernán González), in 1541 that he was thirty-six or thirty-seven (AGI, Patronato 93, no. 11, ramo 2). His *probanza de servicios*, made in 1535, is in AGI, Patronato 93, no. 5, ramo 2. His agreements with the merchant Armenta are in ANP, Salinas 1543–1543, ff.61–63, 119–122; the posthumous will Armenta dictated for him is in *DHA*, I, 171–176; there he is called a native of Cazalla. Armenta's biography may be seen in Lockhart, *Spanish Peru*, pp. 92–94.

Other references are in AGI, Indiferente General 1801, records of ship *Santa Catalina*, 1535; Justicia 467; ANP, PA 115, 133, 144; BNP, A591, ff.366, 371–373; HC 347; *DHA*, I, 122, 131, 135, 141–142; II, 89–90; Loredo, *Los repartos*, pp. 198, 204; Porras, *Cedulario*, II, 173, 195, 196, 207, 287–288; Torres Saldamando, *Libro primero de cabildos*, I, 195; Zárate, *Historia*, II, 505.

Pedro de León

Age at Cajamarca: About 29
Role: Horseman
Share: Double share of gold
  and silver

Place of origin: Ciudad Real
  (New Castile)
Extent of literacy: Good signature,
  probably literate

In 1529 a Pedro de León was in the following of Treasurer Diego de la Tovilla of Nicaragua; it is probably right to identify this man with the horseman of Cajamarca, since Nicaragua was the training ground of so many of the conquerors, and in Peru, León is seen often in association with other veterans. He followed the conquest to its conclusion, then left Peru in late 1534, at the time of the general exodus, arriving in Seville in 1535 with wealth even greater than that of many of his comrades. In 1535 another Pedro de León and his brother Francisco de León left Spain for Peru and were subsequently conquerors of Chile with Valdivia. They were from Santa Cruz de Calatrava in the Ciudad Real area, and they may have been relatives of the man of Cajamarca, hoping to match his good fortune.

NOTES. There were yet other Pedro de Leóns in Peru in the early period, one of whom was close enough to give rise to possible confusion. A notary by the name of Pedro de León came to Peru in 1534 with Pedro de Alvarado; he soon went to Cuzco, where he lived through the siege of

1536–1537, and then functioned as notary public in Cuzco for a time, at least until 1539 (AGI, Patronato 93, no. 9, ramo 7).

The Pedro de León of Cajamarca declared in 1535 that he was thirty-two years old and a native of Ciudad Real (AGI, Justicia 719, no. 9). Other references are in AGI, Indiferente General 1801, records from ship *San Miguel*, 1535; Justicia 1126, no. 2, ramo 1, memorandum of Gregorio de Sotelo; ANP, PA 97, 110, 145, 149; *CDIHN*, II, 18–19, 244, 252.

For the Pedro and Francisco de León who went to Chile, see Bermúdez Plata, *Pasajeros*, II, 88, and Thayer Ojeda, *Valdivia y sus compañeros*, p. 47.

Francisco Malaver

Role at Cajamarca: Horseman
Share: 1¾ shares of gold;
  2 shares of silver

Extent of literacy: Could sign
  his name

Because of a misdemeanor, a court in León, Nicaragua, had at some time condemned Malaver to a fine of six pesos (which he never paid). In 1531 he came with Benalcázar directly from Nicaragua to join the expedition. All that is known of his career in Peru is that here, too, his name appears in the accounts of the *penas de cámara*, small fines given out for fighting, gambling, or drinking. Malaver left the country in 1534. Of eleven men of Cajamarca arriving in Seville in 1535 on the ship *San Miguel*, he registered the largest fortune: 30,000 pesos of gold and 1,750 marks of silver, besides some odd gold pieces and emeralds. In Peru in later years, the name Malaver was associated with a respected family from Zafra in southern Extremadura, but there is no sure indication that Francisco Malaver was their relative.

NOTES. The name occurs with about equal frequency in two forms, Malaver and Maraver, either with or without "de." Among the Malavers of Zafra in Peru was a Francisco Malaver in the battle of Huarina in 1547 (Garcilaso, *Obras*, III, 356), and a Pedro Malaver who came to Peru in 1551 (AGI, Lima 567, vol. III, September 28, 1551).

References to Francisco Malaver of Cajamarca are in AGI, Contaduría 1825, Penas de Cámara, 1535; Indiferente General 1801, records of ship *San Miguel*, 1535; Justicia 1124, no. 5, ramo 1, testimony of Pedro de Aguirre; *CDIHN*, II, 296; IV, 559; Porras, in Trujillo, *Relación*, p. 82; Trujillo, *Relación*, p. 48.

Gaspar de Marquina

Age at Cajamarca: Early 20's   Place of origin: Elgoibar, near San Sebastián
Role: Footman   in the Basque country
Share: ¾ share of gold;   Parents: Martín de Gárate and
   no silver   Mari Ramírez de Altamira
                                      Extent of literacy: Fully literate

Much of what we know about Gaspar de Marquina comes from a
letter he wrote to his father in July, 1533, the only one that has
reached us of many personal letters the men of Cajamarca must have
sent to Spain with the first returnees. (The letter, with comment, will
be found in Appendix I.) Gaspar, young and impressionable, was
perhaps a bit more amazed at the land of the Incas than many of his
fellows, but he was typical of many in his burning thoughts of his
homeland and his dreams of how he could use the new wealth to further himself and his family if he could only get back to Spain.

Known as Gaspar de Gárate at home, he adopted the name of Marquina in the Indies as one that was recognized as Basque and yet
familiar to the other Spaniards. He was the illegitimate son of Martín
de Gárate, but his father had recognized him, brought him up, and
given him an education that qualified him to become perhaps a merchant or a notary. Instead, he left Spain while still a boy. By the late
1520's he was serving as a page of Governor Pedrarias de Avila in
Nicaragua. At Pedrarias's death, in March, 1531, Gaspar was left
without prospects, and he came to Peru in the company of some fellow
Basques and other former servants of Pedrarias, probably under Hernando de Soto.

In Peru he was soon back in his former occupation, this time as one
of Governor Pizarro's pages. As such, his name appears near the end
of the roll of Cajamarca, with no share at all of the silver. Yet the gold
was far more important; his 3,330 pesos represented a fortune in absolute terms and a larger portion relatively than the half shares that some
received. At some time while in Peru Gaspar became the partner of
Basque Nicolás de Azpeitia. After Cajamarca he bought a horse in
partnership with Pedro Navarro, also a retainer of Francisco Pizarro
and from Navarre, part of the Basque country. It must have been this
horse Gaspar was riding in Hernando de Soto's vanguard when he was
killed by Indians on the way south to Cuzco, on the slope of Vilcaconga
in November, 1533.

NOTES. AGI, Justicia 1124, no. 5, ramo 1, contains Gaspar's letter and much testimony concerning him. There his comrade, Pedro de Anadel, says Gaspar was about twenty-four or twenty-five when he died in 1533. Other references are in AGI, Justicia 1074, no. 9; ANP, PA 93; HC 48; Busto, "Los caídos en Vilcaconga," pp. 118–119; Loredo, *Los repartos*, p. 105; Porras, *Cedulario*, II, 118, 413; Porras, in Trujillo, *Relación*, p. 121; Trujillo, *Relación*, p. 62.

Diego Mejía

Role at Cajamarca: Horseman
Share: Double share of gold and silver

Place of origin: Probably southern Extremadura
Extent of literacy: Could sign his name

In 1529 Diego Mejía, then living in the area of León, Nicaragua, was one of several Spaniards who allowed themselves to be enticed into the Peruvian venture by the pilot Bartolomé Ruiz. Ruiz took them in his ship to Panama, and thus Diego Mejía was with the 1531 expedition from the beginning. The only measure we have of Mejía's background is that he was connected with two other Mejías in Peru in the early period (both named Francisco), one of whom was alcalde in Cuzco, while the other was a blacksmith. After the division of the treasure of Cajamarca in June, 1533, Diego Mejía disappears; the circumstances make it likely that he was among the immediate returnees to Spain.

NOTES. In his prologue to Diego Gonçález Holguín's *Vocabulario*, p. xxi, Porras says, without indicating source, that the name of the man at Cajamarca was Diego Ruiz Mejía; in this he is probably right, as usual, though in Peru the name was always just Mejía. Porras goes on to associate Mejía generally with several well-known lineages of the Cáceres-Trujillo region, apparently on the basis of name alone, and this is more dubious. There were many, many different Mejía families in Spain. The present writer thinks that Diego Mejía was probably from southern Extremadura, based on the following associations. On June 3, 1533, Diego Mejía lent 530 pesos to a Francisco Mejía, who had just arrived with Almagro, and who shortly became *regidor* and then alcalde in Cuzco (ANP, PA 112). Then in 1536 another Francisco Mejía arrived, who, without even having left Lima, sent general powers of attorney to the Francisco Mejía in Cuzco (ANP, PA 299). This latter Francisco Mejía had been a *vecino* of Natá on the Isthmus (HC 172); he was a blacksmith, and he had been born in

Segura de León on the southern edge of Extremadura (BNP, A505, August 20, 1541).

The indication that Mejía may have left Peru in 1533 is that on August 9, 1533 Francisco Mejía (the future *vecino* of Cuzco) declared that he owed 500 pesos (the amount Diego had previously lent Francisco) to Rodrigo de Chaves, Chaves having paid that amount for Francisco to Diego Mejía (ANP, PA 52). If Diego were staying with the expedition, there would have been no reason for Francisco to pay off his debt so quickly.

Other references to Diego Mejía are in AGI, Contaduría 1825, records from Coaque, August, 1531; HC 27, 30; *CDIHN*, II, 46; Busto, "Los fugitivos," *Mercurio Peruano* 43 (1962):270–271.

Further references to the other Mejías are in ANP, Castañeda, register 13, ff.1–2; PA 347; HC 111, 112, 119, 326; *CDIAO*, XLII, 379.

Diego de Molina

Age at Cajamarca: About 25
Role: Horseman
Share: 1⅞ shares of gold;
   1¾ shares of silver

Place of origin: Baeza
   (eastern Andalusia)
Extent of literacy: Could sign
   his name

Diego de Molina must have been a relative of Alonso de Molina, one of the Thirteen with Pizarro on the first coastal reconnaissance of central Peru, since both men were from the vicinity of Úbeda, in eastern Andalusia near Jaén. Alonso de Molina stayed behind in Peru in 1528, expecting to serve as liaison with the Indians when the conquering expedition would return, but he died in mysterious circumstances before 1531. Instead of his relative, Diego found on the island of Puná—or so one old tale-teller informs us—a group of Indian boys who ran to meet the Spaniards shouting "Jesus Christ" and "Molina." Diego de Molina came to the Indies in 1526. He seems to have been literate, but the Molinas did not presume to high lineage, and the chronicler, Oviedo, who met him and was usually liberal with the word "hidalgo," called him by the more modest term, *hombre de bien*.

Having prior connections with the Peruvian venture, Molina presumably was with the expedition from Panama. He had a good horse, and he was with Hernando de Soto at the first interview with Atahuallpa, but something kept him from getting a horseman's usual double share in the division of treasure. Perhaps he fell ill or was wounded; he left Peru in 1533 with the first returnees, most of whom were sick, wounded, or old veterans, and he certainly was not old. By December,

1533, he was in Santo Domingo in the Caribbean, where even his moderate share was enough to impress onlookers greatly, particularly two great covered golden jars, not to speak of cups and pots made of gold and silver, and woolen Indian clothing of fine workmanship. Molina then went on to Seville, where he may have intended to settle, since he was still there, a citizen, in April, 1535.

N O T E S .   Diego de Molina, citizen of Baeza, received a license to go to the Indies in March, 1526 (Bermúdez Plata, *Pasajeros*, I, 199). Oviedo says he was a native of Baeza (*Historia*, V, 90–92). In Seville in 1535, Molina said he was twenty-eight years old (AGI, Justicia 719, no. 9). Other references are in ANP, PA 36, 79, 94, 109.

For Alonso de Molina, see Cieza, *Tercera parte*, in *Mercurio Peruano* 34 (1953):314; Romero, *Los héroes de la isla del Gallo*, p. 48; Trujillo, *Relación*, p. 51.

Alonso de Morales

Age at Cajamarca: About 30
Role: Horseman
Share: Double share of gold
    and silver

Place of origin: Moral de Calatrava
    (New Castile)
Extent of literacy: Could sign
    his name

To make himself more identifiable, expedition member Alonso. López took an added surname from his home town of Moral; his fellows mistook it for the more common name of Morales, and thus he appears on the roll of Cajamarca as Alonso de Morales. Alonso López left Spain in 1530 with the Pizarros, and by the time the expedition reached Peru, if not earlier, he was acting as a retainer of Juan and Gonzalo Pizarro. Of his social background there is a hint in the company he made with Alonso Jiménez the swordsmith in 1531, to share equally all they earned from their work and other ventures. The agreement is not specific about the type of work, so there is no sure evidence that Alonso López was a smith, but companies of this type were very common among artisans.

During the conquest, Alonso López considered staying in the San Miguel area as an encomendero, but he was persuaded to give that up for the prospect of a better encomienda farther on in Cuzco. Hardly was Cuzco taken, however, than he decided to go home to Spain instead. First he accompanied his Ciudad Real compatriot Almagro north to Jauja and beyond, then he left Peru in late 1534, carrying 1,500 pesos for Gonzalo Pizarro as well as his own money. Back in Spain he had second thoughts; in 1536 he declared his intention of going once again to Peru, claiming that he had come home only temporarily to recover from illness and see about his wife and children. On these grounds he obtained a royal letter to the officials in Peru, recommending that he be considered favorably for an encomienda. It is in fact very possible that Alonso López had left the Indies because of illness, but hardly likely that at that time he meant to return quickly. At any rate, he knew that even with a recommendation he was not likely to be well received in Peru, so he never went back after all and in 1550 was still living in his native Moral de Calatrava.

N O T E S .   In most of the references to him while he was in Peru, our man appears either as plain Alonso López or as Alonso de Morales. In Spain he is referred to as Alonso López del Moral, and once, in provincial fashion, as Alonso López de Benito López (Benito López doubtless being his father). The last version occurs in AGI, Justicia 1082, no. 1, ramo 4, which contains testimony about the money Alonso López brought home for the Pizarros and several other matters of interest. He is seen living in Moral de Calatrava in 1550, forty-eight years old by his declaration. In Seville in 1535, he said he was a citizen of Moral and thirty-three years old (AGI, Patronato 93, no. 5, ramo 2). His company with Alonso Jiménez is in HC 32.

Other references are in ANP, PA 81, 85, 86, 159, 162; HC 19, 32; Porras, *Cedulario*, II, 152–153; Herrera, *Décadas*, XI, 43.

Rodrigo Núñez

Age at Cajamarca: About 35	Place of origin: Probably
Role: Horseman	Extremadura
Share: Double share of gold	Extent of literacy: Could sign
and silver	his name

Occasionally Rodrigo Núñez used the added surname Prado, Núñez de Prado being the name of a lineage of local hidalgos with branches in several parts of Extremadura. But, since Spanish families had so many strata, association with a given family does not by itself greatly clarify an individual's social standing. Rodrigo Núñez could sign his name satisfactorily, and he may have been literate, though the chronicler Cieza said that he was a man of "not much knowledge and less judgment."

Rodrigo Núñez came to the Indies in 1514, with Governor Pedrarias de Avila of Panama. After participating in marginal or unsuccessful conquests in Veragua (western Panama) and Honduras, he came to Nicaragua, and by the late 1520's he held an encomienda, though a small one, in Nicaragua's chief settlement of León. When he arrived in Peru with Benalcázar, therefore, Rodrigo Núñez was one of the most substantial and senior members of the expedition. As such, he demanded a post of responsibility, and the hard-pressed Pizarros made him *maestre de campo*, or fieldmaster, a position of great honor and usually of power as well. The *maestre de campo* customarily was second in command, in charge of daily operations and responsible for tactics in battle. Núñez took his post so much to heart that it became the chief glory of his life; it found mention in the royal letter granting him a coat of arms, and he even began to take his name from it, signing himself, "Rodrigo Núñez, maestre de campo." But the Pizarros had so many captains that they had to apportion power very carefully. Hernando Pizarro as *teniente* was already acting as second in command, not to speak of the inherent power exercised by Soto and Benalcázar. Even judicial authority was given to another man with the title of *alcalde mayor*. The Pizarros' conception of Rodrigo Núñez's function can be seen in Pedro Pizarro's reference to him as a man who distributed provisions and assigned the guards. Their true evaluation of the post came fully to light at the distribution of the treasure of Cajamarca, when Rodrigo Núñez received no more and no less than an ordinary horseman's share.

To this downgrading, Rodrigo Núñez responded by gravitating toward the Pizarros' rival, Diego de Almagro. He accompanied Almagro to Quito, and after that he joined Almagro's great Chile expedition of 1535–1537, one of only three or four men of Cajamarca to do so. Here too he served as *maestre de campo*, but once again only in the narrower sense and not as a great captain. On returning to Peru with the rest, Rodrigo Núñez by circumstance and conviction was Almagro's ally in the civil conflicts that followed. He fought on the losing side at the battle of Salinas in 1538. Later that year the Pizarrist council of Lima refused to seat him despite a royal appointment, alleging sophistic reasons. But since he was a man of considerable prominence, the

Pizarros did not feel it prudent to ignore him completely. Instead they gave him the modest award (which also amounted to exile) of the encomienda of Piscobamba in the new district of Huánuco; he was one of the alcaldes at the town's provisional foundation in 1540.

These relatively small pickings were not enough to satisfy Rodrigo Núñez; when Francisco Pizarro was assassinated in 1541, Núñez was present in Lima, a sympathetic onlooker if not an actual accomplice. He then joined the forces of rebel don Diego de Almagro the younger, and was prominent in his councils. Since he by this time was called *maestre de campo* wherever he went, it is hard to tell whether or not he held any post. He stayed with the Almagrists through the battle of Chupas in 1542 and was almost the only leading figure among them to escape death on the battlefield or execution afterward. He did lose his encomienda and other property, living in relative poverty until the arrival of Viceroy Blasco Núñez Vela in 1544. As the Gonzalo Pizarro revolt began to develop against the harsh measures of the viceroy and most Peruvian Spaniards moved toward Pizarro, it was natural for Rodrigo Núñez to move toward the viceroy, from personal interest and from ancient enmity for the Pizarros. The viceroy won over Rodrigo Núñez completely by giving him back his encomienda. Not long after the Pizarrists occupied Lima in late 1544, they hunted down their old antagonist in the Dominican monastery and executed him as an incorrigible enemy.

Though Rodrigo Núñez did not marry in Peru, he left a heritage. Other Núñez de Prados continued to be important in the following decades. A younger relative was Sebastián Núñez de Prado, council member of Huánuco in the 1550's; Juan Núñez de Prado, conqueror of Tucumán, may also have been related.

NOTES. Busto's "Una relación y un estudio," *Revista Histórica* 27 (1964), contains a section on Núñez's life (pp. 294–297). There Busto gives Núñez's origin as Trujillo, apparently from the mere fact that there were Núñez de Prados in Trujillo, closely connected with the Pizarros. But there were other Núñez de Prados in the area of Llerena-Fuente del Arco-Guadalcanal, and in Badajoz, Talavera, and Salamanca. The treatment accorded Rodrigo Núñez by the Pizarros almost precludes his having been their compatriot and family friend. To follow other hints, three Núñez de Prados coming to the Indies in the 1530's were from Llerena and Fuente del Arco (Bermúdez Plata, *Pasajeros*, II, 120, 251, 332). It is noteworthy that Cieza, from Llerena, has a great deal to say about Rodrigo Núñez.

Núñez received a large loan from Veedor García de Salcedo, who was from Zafra, a little to the west of Llerena (ANP, PA 664). The Núñez de Prados of Llerena had connections in Badajoz, since one of them went to the Indies with Pedro de Alvarado. This leads one by association to Juan Núñez de Prado, from Badajoz, who became governor of Tucumán. Indeed, a Juan Núñez de Prado was in Huánuco with Rodrigo Núñez in 1541, probably the very same man (see HC 490 and Pérez de Tudela, *Gasca*, II, 463). Viewing all of these things together, this writer thinks it more probable that Rodrigo Núñez was connected with the Llerena-Badajoz branches than with any others.

Sebastián Núñez de Prado appeared in Peru in 1536 as "Sebastián Núñez, son of Rodrigo Núñez." If the father was our Rodrigo Núñez, then he must have been born before the c.1497 estimated on the strength of his statement that he was thirty-seven in 1534 (AGI, Patronato 93, no. 4, ramo 1). But Sebastián could also have been Rodrigo's younger brother, or a more distant relative. References to Sebastián are in AGI, Lima 118, papers from Huánuco, 1557, and in ANP, PA 283–284.

Other references to Rodrigo Núñez are in AGI, Lima 566, vol. IV, November 24, 1541; Patronato 93, no. 10, ramo 1; ANP, PA 82, 83, 86, 95, 152, 154, 168; HC 416, 427, 428, 663; *CDIHN*, II, 159, 225; Cieza, *Chupas*, pp. 58, 219 (quoted above); Cieza, *Quito* (Jiménez, ed.), p. 29; Cieza, *Quito* (Serrano y Sanz, ed.), pp. 66, 99; Cieza, *Salinas*, pp. 181, 314; Cieza, *Tercera parte*, in *Mercurio Peruano* 36 (1955):470; Gutiérrez de Santa Clara, *Quinquenarios*, II 289, 339, 340; *Libros de cabildos de Lima*, I, 272; III, 15; Loredo, *Los repartos*, p. 232; Montoto, *Nobiliario*, p. 272; Pedro Pizarro, *Relación*, V, 174; Pérez de Tudela, *Gasca*, II, 92; Porras, *Cedulario*, II, 95, 96, 109, 116; *Relación de las cosas del Perú*, V, 269.

Diego Ojuelos

Age at Cajamarca: About 29
Role: Horseman
Share: Double share of gold
   and silver

Place of origin: Paterna del Campo,
   near Seville
Extent of literacy: Could sign
   his name

A veteran of the Isthmus, Ojuelos had been in Panama as early as 1521 and was a conqueror of Nicaragua with Francisco Hernández de Córdoba in 1523. He had known some of the other men of Cajamarca, like Hernando Beltrán, for as much as ten years. Though he moved in the same circles as the seamen of Huelva and Seville, this might have been from regional affinity alone, since he could sign his name as few sailors could, and his home, Paterna del Campo, was some thirty miles inland, near the foothills of the Castilian plateau. One would expect a first conqueror of Nicaragua to have attained some position there, at least an encomienda; but if Ojuelos did this, there is no record of it. He must have left Nicaragua by 1530, since he joined the 1531 expedition at its starting point in Panama.

Of his action in Peru we know only that he started south from Cajamarca with the main body in 1533 and must have taken part in the main events of the conquest. He left the country in early 1535, arriving back in Spain in time to complete negotiations for a royal grant of a coat of arms (with two eyes, for "ojuelos") by December of that year. In November, 1536, he was living in the San Andrés district of Seville; by 1554 he had moved to Paterna del Campo to live, while retaining citizenship in Seville.

NOTES. The name occurs about as frequently with as without "de." The only specific evidence for Ojuelos's origin in Paterna is his residence there in 1554, but whereas residence in an urban center can be of somewhat ambiguous meaning, residence in an obscure village is not. At that time he was a citizen of Seville and declared he was over fifty (AGI, Patronato 98, no. 4, ramo 3). In 1536, also then a citizen of Seville, he said he was thirty-three (CDIHN, III, 477–481). His testimony there is particularly valuable for reconstructing his life.

Other references are in AGI, Contaduría 1825, Penas de Cámara, 1535; HC 24, 34, 62; Porras, Cedulario, II, 284; Porras, in Trujillo, Relación, p. 83.

Antonio de Oviedo

Role at Cajamarca: Footman
Share: ¾ share of gold
  and silver

Place of origin: León
Extent of literacy: Could sign
  his name

The only indication of Oviedo's background is his ability to sign his name; the name Oviedo, and the other surname of Herrera that he used at times, were not plebeian, but not specifically noble either. From the varying testimony of his comrades, he must have been in Nicaragua for at least a year or two, coming from there directly to Peru with Benalcázar or Soto. Of his action in Peru he has left hardly a trace, except some evidence of a natural tendency to associate with other men from the kingdom of Leon. He left the country around July or August of 1534, without having been a citizen in any town, so far as is known, and arrived in Seville on the ship *Santa Catalina* late in 1535. Oviedo's fortune was seized by royal officials like the rest, in exchange for annuities; some of the money he carried was meant to buy ornaments for the church of Jauja, and this was eventually returned. By 1537 Antonio de Oviedo was living in the town of León, still in contact with several of his Cajamarca comrades from that region who had also returned to Spain.

N O T E S . The main source for Antonio de Oviedo is testimony about some money he brought home for Francisco Gorducho, in AGI, Justicia 1124, no. 6, ramo 3; there he is called a citizen of León. Other references are in AGI, Indiferente General 1801, records of ship *Santa Catalina*, 1535; ANP, PA 16, 136; Busto, "Los presuntos peruleros," *Mercurio Peruano*, 50 (1965):325; Porras, *Cedulario*, II, 142.

Melchor Palomino

Age at Cajamarca: About 23	Place of origin: The Jaén area
Role: Footman	in eastern Andalusia
Share: ¾ share of silver	Extent of literacy: Excellent signature,
and gold	doubtless literate

The Palominos of Jaén or Andújar had been important in the Isthmian region for a long time. One of them was a founder of Panama in 1519, and two or three of them followed the general movement from there to Nicaragua in the 1520's. They were a very miscellaneous family, with both plebeian traits and higher pretensions. The original Palomino in Panama was the son of an *escudero*, a squire, member of the very minor gentry or attendant of a high nobleman. Another of the Jaén Palominos was a notary. But the Palomino who became most famous in Peru, Captain Juan Alonso, was illiterate or nearly so. There was also a Palomino at Cajamarca who was a cooper, though we cannot assert with absolute certainty that he belonged to the clan from Jaén.

Of all these possible niches, the most comfortable for Melchor Palomino would be that of notary, since he had a beautiful signature and was most closely associated with a Diego Palomino, brother of the notary already mentioned. Diego and Melchor joined the expedition together in Panama; they were doubtless brothers or cousins. Diego, the senior, had been in Nicaragua, while Melchor must have been a relatively new arrival in the Indies. They were constantly together, with Diego in the lead, as the expedition worked its way down the Ecuadorian coast to Túmbez. Yet for some reason Diego stayed behind in Piura in 1532. Thus it was only Melchor who received a share at Cajamarca, and after that an encomienda in central Peru, while Diego was left stranded in the marginal north.

Melchor received only a three-fourths share, like most of the young and inexperienced, and it was some time before he achieved any prominence. He was at first a citizen of Jauja, but his encomienda must have been on the southern edge of Jauja's jurisdiction, since he soon afterward appears as a citizen of Cuzco. He changed citizenship once again when the new district of Huamanga was carved out of Cuzco and Lima in 1539. Placed in this smaller pool, Palomino came into his own quickly; his encomienda, the Soras, was Huamanga's best; he was often city councilman or alcalde. Melchor was never a major leader in Peru's civil wars; he did have the reputation of being a fast runner, but that was not the stuff great captains were made of. In the 1548 campaign against Gonzalo Pizarro he achieved a captaincy of infantry, probably through the influence of his relative Juan Alonso. He did not, like Juan Alonso, usually style himself captain. Melchor married in Huamanga and had children, and his son Hernando inherited his encomienda when he died sometime in the later 1550's.

N O T E S . The evidence locating Melchor Palomino's origins in the Jaén region is somewhat complicated. First, because of their constant presence together, there can be no doubt that Diego and Melchor Palomino were the closest kind of relatives. (See AGI, Contaduría 1825, records from Cajamarca, May, 1533; Indiferente General 1801, records of ship *Santa Catalina*, 1535; Lima 565, vol. III, August 1, 1539; HC 28, 644; Cieza, *Tercera parte*, in *Mercurio Peruano* 36 [1955]:465.) Diego was said to be a *deudo* of Captain Juan Alonso Palomino, who was from Andújar, near Jaén. (Pérez de Tudela, *Gasca*, II, 212; Lohmann Villena, *Americanos en las ordenes nobiliarias*, II, 142.) The word "deudo" means relative, but could refer to a distant relative or relative by marriage, so that proof would remain tenuous, except that it is confirmed by yet another piece of evidence: that when Diego Palomino went in 1549 to head an expedition into the area behind Piura, he founded a town which he called Jaén (Pérez de Tudela, *Gasca*, II, 496). We also on occasion find Melchor Palomino and Captain Juan Alonso mentioned in one breath (*CDIHC*, VII, 89).

Melchor's estimated birthdate of c.1509 rests on his statement that he was forty-three in 1552 (AGI, Patronato 105, ramo 16), which is given preference as more exact than statements that he was forty in 1552 (*DHA*, III, 237–240) and thirty in 1541 (AGI, Patronato 93, no. 11, ramo 2).

There were Palominos from Andújar in Francisco de Montejo's party going to Yucatan in 1527: Hernando, the chief constable, and a Francisco, possibly the brother of Diego. This Francisco's parents were Pedro de Parra and Catalina Palomino. (See Bermúdez Plata, *Pasajeros*, I, 215, 218). The Palomino from Andújar who was in Panama in 1519 had the same name as Captain Juan Alonso, but must be a different individual (Góngora, *Grupos*, p. 71).

For Captain Juan Alonso Palomino, see AGI, Patronato 99, no. 1, ramo 3; 97, no. 1, ramo 2; Pérez de Tudela, *Gasca*, I, 406; and the first paragraph above. Many further references will be found in the chronicles of the civil wars and in Pérez de Tudela, *Gasca*. For Diego's brother Francisco, see Loredo, *Los repartos*, p. 267; Pérez de Tudela, *Gasca*, I, 296; II, 295; and above, third paragraph.

Additional references to Melchor Palomino are in ANP, PA 20, 42, 75, 246, 259, 262; BNP, A203, f.72, March 28, 1549; HC 1315, 1375, 1561, 1562, 1571; Cieza, *Salinas*, pp. 53, 54; Diego Fernández, *Historia*, I, 340, 349; Gutiérrez de Santa Clara, *Quinquenarios*, IV, 108; *Libros de cabildos de Lima*, I, 8–10; Loredo, *Los repartos*, pp. 211, 214; Porras, *Cartas*, p. 406.

Additional references to Diego Palomino are in AGI, Justicia 467; ANP, PA 40; Loredo, *Los repartos*, p. 271; Pérez de Tudela, *Gasca*, II, 295, 496; Pedro Pizarro, *Relación*, V, 175.

Gonzalo Pérez

Age at Cajamarca: About 24
Role: Horseman
Share: Double share of gold
   and silver

Place of origin: Jerez de Badajoz
   (southwestern Extremadura)
Extent of literacy: Could sign
   his name

Having been in the Indies since around 1527, Gonzalo Pérez was one of the veterans who came in two contingents from Nicaragua and gave the expedition much of its thrust and staying power. Pérez probably arrived with Hernando de Soto rather than with Benalcázar, for not only is he associated with Miguel Estete, Luis Maza, and Pedro Cataño, all Soto's men, but he was from Soto's home town of Jerez de Badajoz. Nothing is known of what Pérez did in Peru, except that he got a horseman's standard double share of the treasure at Cajamarca. By May, 1535, he was back in Spain, probably having seen the conquest as far as the taking of Cuzco. He was still in Seville in June, 1536, calling himself a citizen, so he may have settled there permanently. This would have been a very normal thing for him to do, since southern Extremadura was very strongly oriented toward Seville.

NOTES. In Seville, in 1535, Pérez said he was a citizen of Jerez de Badajoz (AGI, Indiferente General 1204, no. 44); in 1536 he described himself as twenty-eight years old and a citizen of Seville (AGI, Justicia 719, no. 9).

A Gonzalo Pérez, factor of Hernando Pizarro in Seville in the 1540's, was probably not the same man. (See Calvete, *Rebelión de Pizarro*, V, 7.)

Juan Pérez de Tudela

Age at Cajamarca: About 28   Share: 1 full share of gold and silver
Role: Footman   Extent of literacy: Could sign his name

Juan Pérez de Tudela had been in the region of Honduras and Nicaragua since about 1525, gaining experience in the company of older relatives. Won over to the Peruvian venture in Nicaragua in 1529 or 1530, he accompanied the 1531 expedition from the time it left Panama. He was a fairly prominent man, not far from the top of the list of the footmen on the roll of Cajamarca, with a full share of the treasure. Often his fellows asked him to be a witness, and he was able to judge the quality of silver, or at least so one of his companions thought. So he himself must have thought. After seeing the conquest to its conclusion, he left the country with the large contingent of returnees of late 1534 and arrived in Spain in 1535 with a large fortune. Unlike most of his companions, he had far more silver than gold. Doubtless he was one of those who had been buying up silver in the belief that it was grossly undervalued and underassayed in Peru.

NOTES. Juan Pérez de Tudela may well have been from the region of Navarre. Not only is the large town of Tudela in Navarre, but the combination of names "Pérez de Tudela" has long been attached to a known lineage of that region. Nevertheless, there were other Tudelas in Spain, particularly Tudela de Duero in Old Castile, and the name could have spread anywhere.

In Nicaragua, in 1529, when he was reported to be on the ship of Bartolomé Ruiz, about to go to Panama, Juan Pérez de Tudela was called *el mozo*, "the younger," to distinguish him from some relative. Busto presumes that there was a Juan Pérez de Tudela *el viejo*, "the elder," and that it was the older man who was to be found in León, Nicaragua, in March and April, 1530, in association with some underlings of Hernando de Soto who also later came to Cajamarca. But this man is not specifically called *el viejo*, and he may have been the same man of Cajamarca, who did not go with Bartolomé Ruiz after all; there were others who disembarked. Time still remained to get to Panama before January, 1531, when Pizarro set sail. Juan Pérez may have been called *el mozo* to distinguish him from a Sancho de Tudela who lived in León, Nicaragua, at the time, particularly since Juan Pérez at times was called just Juan de Tudela.

In 1534 Juan Pérez de Tudela said he was thirty years old (AGI, Patronato 93, no. 4, ramo 1). Other references are in AGI, Indiferente General 1801, records of ship *San Miguel*, 1535; Patronato 93, no. 4, ramo 1; ANP, PA 4, 6, 18, 80, 102, 141; HC 30; *CDIHN*, I, 412; II, 35–37; IV, 31, 218, 535–536, 553–554; Busto, "Los fugitivos," *Mercurio Peruano* 43 (1962):271–273; Loredo, *Los repartos*, pp. 99, 103.

Alonso Ruiz

Age at Cajamarca: About 19 or 20	Place of origin: Born in Castronuevo, near Zamora in the kingdom of Leon
Role: Footman	Parents: Rodrigo Ruiz and María Gutiérrez
Share: ¾ share of gold and silver	Extent of literacy: Illiterate

The origin of Alonso Ruiz remains enigmatic. By his own statement he was a native of Castronuevo. Yet he eventually returned to live out his life in Trujillo, the home of his partner, Lucas Martínez. This was a most unusual thing to do. The vast majority of the returnees from the Indies to Spain, whether men of Cajamarca or not, went back to their birthplaces to live; a few settled in a metropolis at some distance. But to go to a provincial center not one's own was almost unheard of, and that Alonso Ruiz did so arouses the suspicion that wherever he was born, he might well have grown up in Trujillo. The chronicler Garcilaso (writing much later) considered him a Trujillo native. Furthermore, Ruiz appears to have been a new recruit in 1530, and Castronuevo was far to the north of Trujillo, well outside the radius of the recruiting effort, although it is true that he could have joined the expedition in Seville or even later in Panama. In 1541 Ruiz still called his parents citizens of Castronuevo, so that in the end one is driven to assume that he was from Castronuevo and that, despite the rarity of the case, Ruiz's own regional ties were overcome by the strength of the new association with Trujillan Lucas Martínez (q.v.).

In Peru, also, Alonso Ruiz lived in the shadow of Lucas Martínez. The two formed a lasting partnership from a very early time. In 1540 they declared that "ten years ago, more or less, we came to these provinces with Marqués don Francisco Pizarro, and in all that time we have been partners, sharing all the hardships that we have passed through in this country and its discovery, eating and drinking together in the same house without any argument or contention, and likewise holding our property together without division or partition." They are listed together on the roll of Cajamarca, and were together citizens first of Cuzco, then of Arequipa when it was founded (though they did receive individual encomiendas). They were inseparable, but not quite equal. Though both were very young, Lucas Martínez was highly literate and an exceptionally energetic and capable man of affairs. Alonso Ruiz was illiterate and doubtless of a more humble background. He learned before long to sign his name, probably having been taught by Martínez, but the difference remained. Lucas Martínez was frequently mentioned, Alonso Ruiz little heard of. It was Martínez rather than Ruiz who was on the council of Arequipa in the first year of its existence, and Martínez had the larger encomienda.

In 1540 Alonso Ruiz and Lucas Martínez divided their wealth and Ruiz set off for Spain. It was very late to be returning; most of the returnees had left in 1533 and 1534, with some stragglers going in 1538–1539. Probably Alonso Ruiz at the time meant to come back to Peru. The immediate occasion of the trip was to effect a marriage between Ruiz and Lucas Martínez's sister Isabel, living in Trujillo. (If she should have died, Ruiz was to marry his sister María instead.) Also, the new city of Arequipa needed to send a representative to court, and Alonso Ruiz could be made to serve this purpose. After the city council and one citizen after another gave him broad powers to negotiate on their behalf, he departed from Arequipa in October, 1540. His encomienda was left in the hands of a majordomo and his natural daughter by a Spanish or Morisca women in the care of Lucas Martínez.

He was at court by October, 1541, and very efficiently obtained the standard "favors" he had seen sent for—the legitimation of mestizo children; the confirmation of encomienda titles; licenses to return to Spain for two years; coats of arms for the city of Arequipa, for many of its citizens, and for himself. He then went to Trujillo, married Lucas Martínez's sister, and began to settle down. Ostensibly he still meant to go back to Peru with his wife. As late as September, 1543, he had his license to stay extended for another year, but the pretense was increasingly hollow. Soon he was a citizen of Trujillo, and by the mid-1550's he had attained a seat on Trujillo's city council; he was the only illiterate plebeian to succeed in doing so. Perhaps the extraordinary wealth and influence of Lucas Martínez were decisive; perhaps Alonso Ruiz as a man from outside the immediate area could mask his origins to a certain extent.

Alonso Ruiz was to all appearances a warm human being with deep feelings. Something of this shows in his partnership with Lucas Martínez, not based on the usual pillars of similar background or common regional origin, and again in Arequipa's choice of him as an envoy to the court, though he was not of the social type likely to move there with ease. Ruiz's life gave rise to legends which, authentic or not, may have some truth at the root. Garcilaso tells an anecdote of how he halted in the midst of the sack of Cuzco to teach Christianity to an Indian who was desirous of it. Back in Spain, again according to Garcilaso, he fell prey to the crisis of conscience about the conquest, that restitution fever that was incubating in Spain long before it reached Peru in the 1560's. Perhaps Alonso Ruiz was one of the men who consulted with the Dominican fray Francisco de Vitoria in Salamanca and heard his strange mixture of prudence and doctrinaire scholasticism. Fearing his great riches were ill-gotten, he is supposed to have offered to make restitution to the crown of the whole fortune, leaving it up to the Emperor how much if any he would allow Ruiz as just reward. But instead of reducing him to poverty, Charles granted Ruiz a handsome annuity of over a thousand ducats situated in a village near Trujillo, a lasting asset that as an entail was still held by Alonso Ruiz's grandson in the seventeenth century.

NOTES. Alonso Ruiz calls himself a native of Castronuevo and gives his parents' names in *DHA*, I, 84. In 1545 he said he was about thirty (AGI, Justicia 1174, no. 1, ramo 3) and in 1545 that he was over forty (AGI, Patronato 98, no. 4, ramo 6) ; in both cases he was a citizen of Trujillo and in the latter a *regidor*. Much information on Ruiz's partnership with Lucas Martínez is in *DHA*, I, 84–89, 100–103, 107–109. Garcilaso's anecdotes about Ruiz are in his *Obras*, III, 91–92.

Other references are in AGI, Contaduría 1824, records from Cuzco, March, 1536, and April, 1537; Justicia 1071, no. 2, ramo 3; Lima 566, vol. IV, September 22, 1541, October 28, 1541, November 29, 1541, March 4, 1542; Patronato 93, no. 4, ramo 3; 109, ramo 4; ANP, Salinas 1542–1543, f.264; *CDIHC*, VII, 153–154, *DHA* I, 91, 93, 97–99, 105, 146–151, 154, 160–161, 163–166, 183; Porras, "Dos documentos esenciales," *Revista Histórica* 17 (1948):91–93. See also under Lucas Martínez, chapter 10.

Juan Ruiz

Age at Cajamarca: About 25 or 26
Role: Horseman
Share: 2 shares of gold;
  1⅞ shares of silver

Place of origin: Alburquerque,
  in western Extremadura
Father: Martín Ruiz (de Arce)
Extent of literacy: Could sign his
  name, probably somewhat literate

In the Indies he sometimes called himself Juan Ruiz de Alburquerque, and after he returned rich to Spain he began to assume the name Juan Ruiz de Arce, but on ordinary occasions he was plain Juan Ruiz, a storybook conqueror who seems to fit the nineteenth-century stereotype almost perfectly. He was from a family of commoners or very petty hidalgos who had long fought for the king of Spain; his grandfather died in a battle against the Portuguese, his father fought under Ferdinand and Isabel against the Moors in Granada. A rough man, not well educated (though apparently able to read), he was expert in the training of horses, given to moralizing, and convinced of the superiority of Hispanic values—a fanatic, another generation might have said. His grandfather had come out of northern Old Castile, but Juan Ruiz himself was from the proverbial Extremadura. Had all the Spaniards been like Juan Ruiz, there would be little apparent need to add to Prescott.

Ruiz came to the Indies after his father died, when he was hardly eighteen, around 1525. He tried his luck in the poor areas of Jamaica and Honduras without success; then a disastrous expedition inland from Honduras led him, with other survivors, to Nicaragua around 1529 or 1530. That area was already well settled, so that when news came of the conquest of Peru, Ruiz had nothing to hold him back, and he joined the first group to leave with Benalcázar. In Peru he gravitated toward Hernando de Soto, who was from the same part of Extremadura as himself, and he rode with the expedition's best horsemen in Soto's vanguard. Apparently Ruiz was not tempted to stay in the country, leaving quickly in 1534 after a general license was issued.

By September, 1535, he was in Madrid at the royal court. He now possessed an income of 600 ducats in annuities, granted in return for the fortune in gold and silver the king's officials seized in Seville. Like other ingenuous returning conquerors, Juan Ruiz spent too much money at court, obtained the grant of a coat of arms, and then went home to Alburquerque. There he lived out his life in considerable magnificence and founded an entail which made substantial citizens of his descendants for several generations. For the edification of each succeeding heir he left a short account of his life (showing every sign of having been dictated), which constitutes one of the six or seven chronicles of the conquest of Peru by eyewitnesses. In it we see a man very naive and quite pontifical, with little breadth of perspective, but with a very good measure of that self-centered strength of character so typical of the conquerors, and perhaps more observant of the natural surroundings than most. Juan Ruiz may have lived on in Alburquerque until about 1560.

NOTES.   Juan Ruiz's elaborate coat of arms did not incorporate, nor did the royal grant even mention, the Ruiz de Arce family arms (Porras, *Cedulario*, II, 112). Yet Juan Ruiz later told his descendants what those arms had been, and he apparently made use of them as well as his personal device. It would be of the greatest interest to know the full facts of this case. The present writer has the strong impression that all those who had any family coat of arms made sure that it was incorporated into their personal arms. Here would appear to be a most interesting case proving the contrary. But the suspicion remains that Juan Ruiz was from a very poor or illegitimate branch and did not feel entitled to use the Ruiz de Arce arms until he had already become a great man in his own community. The extremely elaborate genealogy of the Ruiz family really begins only with Juan Ruiz himself; his father's name is known only accidentally, and his mother's name is not known at all; the woman he married, María Gutiérrez, could not have been of very high lineage, to judge by her name. Royal prosecutor Villalobos once called Juan Ruiz a "persona de baja suerte," the standard deprecatory phrase for people of artisan, peasant, or maritime background (*CDIHC*, VII, 153).

In 1534 Juan Ruiz said he was twenty-seven (AGI, Patronato 150, no. 6, ramo 2); in 1535 he said that he was twenty-nine and a citizen of Alburquerque (AGI, Justicia 719, no. 9). A principal source for Juan Ruiz is his "chronicle," published by Conde de Canilleros (Miguel Muñoz de San Pedro, ed.), in *Tres testigos de la conquista del Perú*, pp. 72–119, under the title "Advertencias de Juan Ruiz de Arce a sus sucesores." Particularly revealing sections on Juan Ruiz personally are on pp. 75–76, 83–85, 90, 95, 107, 115. The same work is published by Antonio del Solar y Taboada and José de Rújula y de Ochotorena as *Servicios en Indias de Juan Ruiz de Arce*, with an elaborate genealogical prologue and excerpts from later legal proceedings. Porras discusses Ruiz's life and writing in *Cronistas*, pp. 109–112.

Other references are in AGI, Indiferente General 1801, records of ship *San Miguel*, 1535; Justicia 1125, proceedings concerning estate of Francisco Martín; *CDIHN*, III, 415.

Juan de Salinas de la Hoz

Age at Cajamarca: Probably over 30
Role: Horseman
Share: 1⅜ shares of gold and silver

Place of origin: Salinas de Añana, near Vitoria in the Basque country
Extent of literacy: Could sign his name

An old veteran of the Indies, Juan de Salinas de la Hoz had been in the Nicaragua area from the early days of its occupation, around 1522, and may have come from Spain considerably before that. As evidence of his background, we have only his adequate signature and the backward reflection of the status of his descendants. A nephew of his, called don Francisco de la Hoz, was a *veinticuatro* ("councilman") of Seville in 1613, and petitioned the crown to be named to a governorship in the Indies.

In Nicaragua, Juan de Salinas had moved around a great deal, following the course of various campaigns, apparently without ever getting an encomienda. He came directly from Nicaragua with Sebastián de Benalcázar, soon taking his place among the horsemen sent on advance missions. His greatest exploit, which gave the motif for his coat of arms, was to go alone on an Indian raft to the isle of Puná as Pizarro's emissary. However, any impression of unusual daring and skill is somewhat belied by Juan de Salinas's share of the treasure of Cajamarca, far below the standard for a horseman.

Immediately after Cajamarca, Salinas was allowed to return to Spain, presumably as an older, perhaps married, man. By 1534 he was at the royal court in Toledo; in October, 1535, he received a coat of arms, and then he must have gone to the north country to live, perhaps to Burgos, like his relative Pedro de Salinas de la Hoz.

NOTES. The name also occurs as Juan de la Hoz Salinas and simply Juan de la Hoz, the form used in the grant of the coat of arms. The estimate of his birthdate as probably before 1502 rests in part on his ten years or more of experience in the Indies, and in part on the fact that mainly older men returned in 1533. It also seems highly probable to this writer that he was identical with the "Juan de Salinas, hijo de Juan Sánchez de Salinas y de Marina su mujer, vecinos de Salinas, que es en la montaña cabe Vitoria," who came to the Indies in 1513, in which case he would no doubt have been born well before 1500 (Bermúdez Plata, *Pasajeros*, I, 105).

Salinas declares himself a native of Salinas de Añana in AGI, Patronato 93, no. 4, ramo 4. The royal letter granting him arms gives a résumé of his career in the Indies (Montoto, *Nobiliario*, pp. 183–187). See also Pedro de Salinas de la Hoz.

Pedro de Salinas de la Hoz

Age at Cajamarca: About 30
Role: Footman
Share: ¾ share of gold;
⁷⁄₁₀ share of silver

Place of origin: Salinas de Añana, near Vitoria in the Basque country
Extent of literacy: Could sign quite well, probably literate

With little doubt this man was a brother, cousin, or other close relative of Juan de Salinas de la Hoz (q.v.), whose background he must have shared. He followed Juan to the Indies by about 1525, and, after a time in Honduras, joined him in Nicaragua. From there Pedro came to Peru, presumably with Benalcázar, as Juan did. Except for bad luck he would have been, like his kinsman, on horseback; the horse he had when he left Nicaragua died in the difficult passage, as many must have.

Pedro stayed in Peru when his older relative returned in 1533, but hardly with any firm intention of settling. One can divine his wavering frame of mind in the two royal directives Juan negotiated for him at the Spanish court in July, 1534, one commanding the governor of Peru to allow Pedro to come home at any time, and the other recommending that the governor favor Pedro in view of his services. But before these documents could reach him, Pedro was on his way home, taking advantage of Pizarro's offer, in that same month of July, of license to return to all who wished it. If he had had any hesitation, his mind was made up by a wound that disabled his right arm. He arrived in Seville in 1535 with a goodly fortune, went to court and obtained a coat of arms, then settled in the city of Burgos, not too far from his home village of Salinas de Añana.

NOTES. Pedro's name also occurs as Pedro de la Hoz Salinas. The attribution of his origin rests on his long association with Juan de la Hoz Salinas and the identity of their surnames, plus the fact that when don Francisco de la Hoz made his petition in 1613 he included copies of the grants of arms of both men as exhibits, indicating close blood relationship beyond reasonable doubt (Montoto, *Nobiliario*, pp. 183–187). It was natural enough for Pedro to settle in Burgos, a metropolitan center for the whole northern mountain region, Basque and non-Basque. Salinas de Añana is toward the edge of the Basque country, and we cannot be sure whether Juan and Pedro were true Basques or not. They did have certain Basque connections. Pedro took home money for the Basque governor of the Río de San Juan, Pascual de Andagoya (AGI, Indiferente General 1801, records of ship *Santa Catalina*, 1535).

In 1537 Pedro de Salinas de la Hoz was a citizen of Burgos and gave his age as thirty-five (AGI, Justicia 1124, no. 6, ramo 3). His cedula of arms tells most of what we know about his career. See also Porras, *Cedulario*, II, 3, 13, 116.

Another Pedro de Salinas appeared at Cajamarca in 1533, with a very crude signature; he seems to be the "Pedro de Salinas color negro" who was present at the founding of Quito. See ANP, PA 61, 128, 135; *Libros de cabildos de la ciudad de Quito*, I, sect. 1, pp. 50–57.

Alonso Sánchez de Talavera

Role at Cajamarca: Footman
Share: ½ share of gold and silver

Place of origin: Cebolla, near Talavera de la Reina (New Castile)

Alonso Sánchez and his partner, Pedro de Valencia, were among the minority getting the rock-bottom share of one half, definitely a slap at either the quality of their participation or their social standing. Sánchez was born in a village not far from Talavera de la Reina. Later his family moved to Triana, the maritime suburb of Seville, but the name

"Talavera" that he took in the Indies shows his roots. The family was plebeian; in an inquiry held into Alonso Sánchez's lineage, most of the witnesses were artisans, and he himself did not claim to be an hidalgo.

In his petition for a coat of arms he mentions no services performed in Panama or Nicaragua, so he must not have been in the Indies long, another factor congruent with his small share. After Cajamarca, Sánchez went south with the main body of conquerors, and in March, 1534, he became a founding citizen and encomendero of Cuzco. He stayed among the forty men guarding Cuzco when the rest returned to Jauja, thus missing the exodus of July of that year. Nevertheless, he then or soon after decided to go to Spain. In November, 1534, in Cuzco, he prepared a memorial of his services; just when he left the country is not known, but by 1537 he was in Seville, and in March, 1538, the crown granted a coat of arms to Alonso Sánchez, conqueror of the province of Peru. He lived in Triana at least into the 1540's.

NOTES. The principal source for Alonso Sánchez's life is AGI, Patronato 93, no. 6, ramo 4, which contains both a *probanza de servicios* and a *probanza de limpieza*. Other references are in AGI, Patronato 109, ramo 4; 185, ramo 1; *CDIHC*, VII, 156; Montoto, *Nobiliario*, p. 365.

Hernán Sánchez

Age at Cajamarca: About 28
Role: Horseman
Share: 2 shares of gold;
   1⅗ shares of silver

Place of origin: Villafranca de los Barros
   (south central Extremadura)
Parents: Francisco Sánchez and
   Isabel Rodríguez
Extent of literacy: Could sign his name

As he came to the Indies around 1530, and his Extremaduran home was within reach of Trujillo, Hernán Sánchez may have been one of the recruits of 1529; in any case, he was with the 1531 expedition from Panama. From his signature, the names of his parents and some incipient entrepreneurial activity he carried on, there emerges the picture of a man from a very unpretentious background, but capable, literate, and not an obvious plebeian. Though almost at the end of the list of horsemen of Cajamarca, he soon made himself respected. After the conquest he became a citizen of Lima with a coastal encomienda;

at the end of the first year of the city's existence, he was nominated, though not selected, to sit on the Lima city council. In 1537 he received a royal appointment to a permanent seat on the Lima council, but it was too late. Around October or November of 1536 he died, apparently killed on his encomienda in the great Indian revolt of that year.

N O T E S . Sánchez's encomienda was Luringancho, south of Lima. The evidence concerning his death is as follows: On October 6, 1536, a friend in Lima assumed he was alive (ANP, PA 791). On November 12, Pizarro gave Luringancho to someone else "because of the end and demise of Hernán Sánchez, former citizen of this city, who they say has died" (HC 539). If Sánchez had died in Lima itself, Pizarro would not have expressed himself in this fashion. There is no reason to doubt the fact of his death, since he is heard of no more and his encomienda was not returned.

Porras and Busto have identified the Hernán Sánchez of Cajamarca with one Hernán Sánchez Morillo, and Busto has written an article in which the biographies of the two are persuasively intertwined, but actually they were two different men (Porras, in Trujillo, *Relación*, p. 103; Busto, "El herrero, el barbero y el gran volteador," *Mercurio Peruano* 43 [1962]:72–78). The identification arose originally because of a remark in the chronicle of Diego de Trujillo that one of just three Spaniards whose life the Indians meant to spare was Hernán Sánchez Morillo, "gran volteador" (Trujillo, *Relación*, p. 55). Trujillo was an eyewitness and is generally very reliable, beyond a certain tendency to shape anecdotes. His one real weakness, since he was writing forty years after the events, was a bad memory for the exact form of names, particularly first names. His editor Porras corrects several mistakes for him. Therefore it is not at all unusual that plain Hernán Sánchez and Hernán Sánchez Morillo should have merged in Trujillo's mind into one.

This reference in Trujillo's chronicle is the only one known in which "Morillo" is added to the name of the Hernán Sánchez of Cajamarca. Otherwise, the man who appears at Cajamarca and then was a citizen of Lima always signed, and was always called, just Hernán Sánchez. On the other hand, there was a man who went to Quito with Benalcázar and became a citizen there, who invariably was called and signed himself Hernán Sánchez Morillo. It should be kept in mind that not a single man of Cajamarca, aside from the leader Benalcázar, settled in Quito. Another weak point in the identification is that since Hernán Sánchez Morillo lived on for many years in the Quito region, one must assume that the report of Hernán Sánchez's death in 1536 was false. Even more conclusive is the physical trail. The Hernán Sánchez of Cajamarca was in Lima on November 23, 1535 (ANP, PA 681); also, by implication, on December 24, 1535, when he was nominated for *regidor* in Lima for the coming year (Torres Saldamando, *Libro primero de cabildos*, I, 55); and again definitely present on March 14, 1536 (ANP, PA 265). Hernán Sánchez Morillo was in far distant Quito most of the year 1535, and specifically on December 27, 1535, and January 1, 1536; he was nominated for *regidor* in Quito for 1536 (*Libros de cabildos de Quito*, I, sect 1, pp. 155, 156–157, 163).

With the two separate identities established, we can return to the question of which of the two was the "gran volteador." This would presumably be the man of Cajamarca, since the episode occurred after the expedition was south of San Miguel, with only the group present who would be there the day Atahuallpa was taken. Yet there can be no certainty. Moreover, we cannot even be positive what "volteador" means. Porras and Busto assume it means a tamer of horses, but in Trujillo there is no explanatory context for the word at all, and the chronicler Oviedo uses the same word to mean "acrobat" pure and simple (*Historia*, III, 261, and elsewhere). Porras assumed the Indians would admire a skill new to them, but it is just as likely that they would be impressed with someone proficient in a skill they themselves admired, acrobatics. From another source, unidentified, Porras relates that "Hernán Sánchez Morillo" played ninepins in Cuzco with Almagro's right-hand man, Rodrigo Orgoños, and lost 11,000 pesos. Once again the man of Cajamarca is the more likely possibility, since he could very well have been in Cuzco in late 1533 and early 1534, while most of the men destined for Quito got no farther into central Peru than San Miguel (Piura) in the north.

Hernán Sánchez of Cajamarca gives his birthplace and the names of his parents in ANP, PA 681. In 1534 he declared he was thirty years old (AGI, Patronato 93, no. 4, ramo 1). Further references are in AGI, Indiferente General 1801, records of ship *San Miguel*, 1535 (though the person referred to may not be our Hernán Sánchez); ANP, PA 80, 121, 136, 231, 232, 688; HC 11, 20; Porras, *Cedulario*, II, 308, 310, 314.

Further references to Hernán Sánchez Morillo are in *Libros de cabildos de Quito*, I, sect. 1, pp. 52, 61, 71–73, 77, 81, 83, 87; *Oficios o cartas del cabildo de Quito, 1552–1558*, p. 569.

Another person altogether was Hernán Sánchez de Badajoz, who arrived with Almagro. In AGI, Patronato 93, no. 4, ramo 1, he and the Hernán Sánchez of Cajamarca testify as separate individuals; the two also appear side by side in ANP, PA 121. Sánchez de Badajoz left the country before many years passed. Also in Peru at the same time was Hernán Sánchez de Pineda, who was a steward or mine operator for the Pizarros; see ANP, PA 693, and HC 92.

Francisco de Solares

Role: Footman
Share: ¾ share of gold;
   ½ share of silver

Place of origin: Probably Cáceres
   or Trujillo (Extremadura)
Extent of literacy: Fully literate

The best testimony as to Solares's background is the original of an agreement between Juan Pizarro de Orellana and Gonzalo Pizarro, written in correct form and in a hand as good as a notary's, by Francisco de Solares himself. Though his share at Cajamarca showed little indication of matching prowess at arms, he acquired a horse, and eventually proved himself very capable in war as well. He came to be a respected member of the dominant Cáceres-Trujillo faction in the conquering expedition, his associations with it being so close and exclusive as to leave very little doubt that he was from that region in Spain, and indeed probably from Cáceres. All in all, he would seem to have been of a respectable family, though the name Solar or Solares was not well known in Cáceres or Trujillo.

After riding south on a horse owned in common with Gonzalo Pizarro, Solares became a citizen and encomendero of Cuzco at its founding. He survived the Indians' siege of Cuzco in 1536–1537—an outstanding horseman in the city's defense, if we are to believe his friend the chronicler Pedro Pizarro. In April, 1537, Almagro ended the Indian threat and started the "War of Salinas" among the Spaniards by entering Cuzco forcibly; Solares was among the men who were jailed as friends and relatives of the Pizarros. Here the trail of Francisco de Solares is lost; though there is no hint of his fate, it is most likely that he was a victim in some fashion of the civil conflict ending in the bloody battle of Salinas, near Cuzco, in 1538.

NOTES. The agreement in Solares's hand is in AGI, Justicia 1082, no. 1, ramo 4. For evidence of his association with men from Cáceres-Trujillo, see that document and AGI, Justicia 1053, no. 5 (buying a horse from Juan Pizarro); Lima 204, *probanza* of Gonzalo de los Nidos (with Nidos and most witnesses from Cáceres); ANP, PA 15, 26, 46, 54, 772.

Other references are in AGI, Contaduría 1824, records from Cuzco, March–April, 1537; Patronato 109, ramo 4; ANP, PA 49; *CDIHC*, IV, 447; Pedro Pizarro, *Relación*, V, 208, 211, 214; Porras, "Dos documentos esenciales," *Revista Histórica* 17 (1948):93.

Hernando de Sosa

Age at Cajamarca: About 22
Role: Footman

Share: ¾ share of gold and silver
Extent of literacy: Could sign his name

Except for his signature, the only clue we have to Hernando de Sosa's background is the suspicion that he was closely connected with the Peru expedition's Sevillian priest, Juan de Sosa, who was an educated man and entrepreneur, but of a quite humble family. There is nothing to indicate that Sosa had any previous experience in the Indies, and at his age he is not likely to have had very much. In Peru he was not outstanding in any way, though he seemed destined eventually to be an important encomendero. He was a citizen of Jauja, and then of Lima, showing a certain interest and ability in encomienda management and other affairs. Around June, 1539, he was killed by Indians while visiting his encomienda, in one of the last outbreaks of Indian rebelliousness.

N O T E S . It is natural to suspect that two members of the expedition with the same name were related, as were the Toros, and it would also be natural for young Hernando de Sosa to be in the company of a more mature relative. However, the two Torreses were unrelated, and there was a Cristóbal de Sosa unrelated to Hernando. To be considered seriously, any connection between Hernando and Juan de Sosa must rest on more than the name alone, and it does, yet the evidence is so tenuous that this writer does not consider a relationship between the two definitely established. The priest Juan de Sosa was definitely connected with a Bernaldino de Sosa, who came to Peru in 1537 and later became an encomendero of Humanga. This Bernaldino occurs in tantalizingly close conjunction with Hernando in a series of notarial documents written in Lima on June 1, 1537. In ANP, PA 353, Hernando makes an agreement with an employee; on the next page (PA 354), Bernaldino acknowledges a debt for passage to Peru from Panama; on the next (PA 355), Hernando is again witness to a document. It looks very much as if Hernando had come to greet his relative on arrival, yet, since he did not actually take over the debt or perform any other definite act of association, the relationship cannot be viewed as proved.

The Hernando de Sosa who was prominent as the elder Almagro's secretary is a different man altogether from the man of Cajamarca; no connection between the two has been established or is likely.

The Sosa of Cajamarca gave his age as twenty-six in 1536 (AGI, Patronato 93, no. 6, ramo 3). Other references are in AGI, Contaduría 1825,

records from Cajamarca, June, 1533; records from Lima, 1535; ANP, PA
30, 353, 355, 777; HC 60, 62, 290; *Libros de cabildos de Lima*, I, 8–10,
347; Torres Saldamando, *Libro primero de cabildos*, I, 444.

For Bernaldino de Sosa, see AGI, Justicia 1125; ANP, PA 354; HC
1242, 1425, 1437, 1438, 1574; Cieza, *Quito* (Jiménez, ed.), p. 134 (showing his connection with Juan de Sosa); Loredo, *Los repartos*, pp. 213, 217.
For Juan de Sosa see Appendix II.

Iñigo Tabuyo

Age at Cajamarca: About 25   Place of origin: Astorga, in the
Role: Footman   kingdom of Leon
Share: 1 full share of gold   Parents: Macías Tabuyo and Mari Cornejos
  and silver   Extent of literacy: Good signature

In all probability, many or most of the men of Cajamarca followed
relatives to the Indies, but whereas a Sánchez or a González is hidden
among the mass, the rare name Tabuyo stands out in the records and
makes it possible to trace antecedents. Iñigo Tabuyo had close relatives
in Zamora, three of whom came to the Indies in 1511. Another went to
Venezuela in 1534, when Iñigo was already on his way home. The
Tabuyos were no great noblemen, but the family has been known in the
Astorga region for centuries.

Iñigo himself left Spain in 1527. Where he spent his time until
1531 is not precisely known, but in Peru he associated very much with
the veterans of Nicaragua, specifically with Benalcázar's men. Therefore he doubtless came to Peru directly from Nicaragua, probably with
Benalcázar. On the roll of Cajamarca his name is near the top of the
list of footmen, among the veterans, with a full share. With part of
that share he bought a white horse, which he rode in Soto's vanguard,
until it was killed by Indians not far from Cuzco. In June or July of
1534, the conquest over, he was one of the large contingent of men of
Cajamarca leaving for Spain with a fortune in precious metals. Arriving in Seville by 1535, he went to the royal court, and later that year he
obtained a coat of arms. He then went to settle in his home town of
Astorga, where he was still living around 1540.

N O T E S .   In 1538 Tabuyo said he was thirty (AGI, Justicia 1124, no.
6, ramo 3), and in 1539 that he was thirty-three (AGI, Justicia 1126, no.
2, ramo 1). In both places he declares himself an Astorga citizen, and, in

the latter, a memorandum by Gregorio de Sotelo calls him a native of Astorga. The names of his parents appear in Bermúdez Plata, *Pasajeros*, I, 236.

Other references are in ANP, PA 46, 107, 113, 126; HC 65; Porras, *Cedulario*, II, 119; Porras, in Trujillo, *Relación*, pp 118–119; Trujillo, *Relación*, p. 61. For Tabuyo's relatives, see Bermúdez Plata, *Pasajeros*, I, 20, 352.

Alonso de Toro

Age at Cajamarca: About 20
Role: Footman
Share: ¾ share of gold and silver

Place of origin: Trujillo (Extremadura)
Parents: Alonso de Toro and Inés Durán
Extent of literacy: Could sign his name, but somewhat crudely

The name Toro was not prominent in Trujillo, and the impression of humbleness or obscurity is increased by the fact that the Toro brothers first appear as direct subordinates or servants of the Pizarros. (Their mother's name, Durán, had a somewhat nobler ring.) Even many years after the conquest, Alonso's old friend Pedro Pizarro, when discussing his origins, made only the noncommittal statement that he "was considered an hidalgo." Three of the Toros joined the Peruvian venture in Spain, but one was killed by Indians early in 1532 as the expedition first entered central Peru at Túmbez. Originally the main figure among them was the oldest brother Hernando, who as Hernando Pizarro's squire was a mounted man. Alonso, though destined to outlive and overshadow his brother, was at first little noticed. By more than one account he too was Hernando Pizarro's servant.

Toro was a citizen of Cuzco from an early time. He and Tomás Vázquez, a former mariner from Palos, received a combined encomienda and continued to hold much of their property in common for as long as Toro lived. By the time of the siege of Cuzco in 1536–1537, Toro was beginning to be mentioned as one of the vigorous young horsemen who were the city's main defense. His services as a strong Pizarro partisan in the "War of Salinas" caused Hernando Pizarro to make him chief constable of Cuzco in 1538, and in this capacity he presided over the execution of the Pizarros' archenemy, Diego de Almagro the elder. There seemed still to be some question about whether Toro was really adequate for the post, since Almagro before dying taunted him with the name "Torico," a jab at his youth and general insignificance.

From this time on, Toro was high in the councils of the Pizarro family, and increasingly an important figure himself. Hernando Pizarro, on leaving Peru in 1539, owed Toro no less than 40,000 pesos. As his personality matured, Toro gave ever more indication of that arrogance and brusqueness so characteristic of the Extremadurans, from Hernando Pizarro down. When Gonzalo Pizarro first organized his rebel forces in Cuzco in 1544, he made Toro, as *maestre de campo*, his second in command, but Toro lasted only a short time in the position because of complaints about his overbearing behavior. Though Pizarro was reluctant to remove him, since he was an old and faithful ally and had now become rich and influential, the demotion became necessary. Toro, as a loyal Pizarrist and Trujillan, acquiesced, accepting a simple captaincy and deflecting his resentment toward the man who replaced him.

To recompense Toro for the loss of face, Pizarro soon afterward gave him the post of lieutenant governor of Cuzco. He managed to hold Cuzco for the Pizarros, and he waged energetic, though militarily not very successful, campaigns against counterinsurgents in the far southern Charcas region. As before, there were complaints about his cruelty and precipitateness. In the spring of 1545, Pizarro sent the nobleman don Pedro Portocarrero to Cuzco as a check on Toro. Deeply offended, Toro wrote to Pizarro accusing him of thinking "that I would not be able to keep this city in peace and quiet just because I am not called don," and maintaining that no don had served the Pizarros better than he. An even worse crisis arose when Pizarro felt it necessary to send Francisco de Carvajal, the very man who replaced Toro as *maestre de campo*, to deal with the opponents Toro had failed to put down. Apparently Toro was on the verge of resisting Carvajal's entrance into Cuzco, but finally the old tie to the Pizarros asserted itself, and Toro gave Carvajal grudging cooperation.

Though he survived the ill effects of his roughness and impetuosity in public affairs, Toro's downfall came through the extension of these same traits into his private life. At some time in the 1540's Toro and his partner Tomás Vázquez married daughters of a Spanish couple who had recently come to Cuzco, probably with just such matches in mind. But though he made this move for the honor of his lineage, Toro was still enamored of the Indian noblewoman who had long been his mistress; even after the marriage he kept her in the house. Toro's wife, doña Francisca de Zúñiga, tried to adjust to the situation, but

Toro abused her to the point that late in 1546 his father-in-law, also part of the household, became desperate and murdered him. Such at least is the version given by the chronicler Gutiérrez de Santa Clara; the fact of the murder and the identity of the murderer are certain. The incident seems unrelated to war and politics, except that resentment of Toro's hard rule in the Cuzco community apparently made it easier than it might otherwise have been for his murderer to find refuge and eventual reintegration into community life. Since Toro left no legitimate heirs, his encomienda went to his widow, who quickly remarried. After the final defeat of the rebels in 1548, Toro's remaining property was confiscated, and, as far as is known, this important family's fortunes did not revive in Peru.

N O T E S .   The accuracy of Gutiérrez de Santa Clara's report (*Quinque-narios*, III, 177–178) cannot be affirmed categorically, even though the chronicler has a special reliability in respect to events occurring in upper Peru in 1546–1547; he apparently either was there at the time or had reports from someone who was. Yet in this instance he gives wrong names for all the principals except Toro himself, and his statement that Toro's mother-in-law had already died of grief is also inaccurate. (She died in 1557.) The present writer is of the opinion that the chronicler was actually there and has reported the substance of the incident correctly, while forgetting the names and some details, since he wrote many years later. See also Lockhart, *Spanish Peru*, p. 211.

Doña Francisca's title was new in the family. An older sister, who was the first wife of Juan Fernández, the plebeian sea captain and great encomendero of Lima, was named plain Isabel de Zúñiga. Her mother was Isabel Díaz de Zúñiga, her father Diego González de Vargas. After Toro's death, doña Francisca's hand was given to a Quirós, of whom nothing more is known than that he betrayed the Pizarrists and was hanged for it in January, 1547. In 1548 doña Francisca married Pedro López de Cazalla, secretary of the governor, who became a prominent council member of Cuzco in the 1550's.

In 1540 Alonso de Toro said he was twenty-eight years old (AGI, Lima, 204, *probanza* of Paullu Inca). He is repeatedly called a native of Trujillo, for example, in Cieza, *Quito* (Jiménez, ed.), p. 106, and Pedro Pizarro, *Relación*, V, 211. His parentage is given in AGI, Justicia 1174, no. 1, ramo 3. Letters from Toro, including a long and revealing one to Gonzalo Pizarro, are in Pérez de Tudela, *Gasca*, I, 335–345. Toro is called a servant of Hernando Pizarro in Enríquez de Guzmán, *Vida y costumbres*, p. 181, and Pérez de Tudela, *Gasca*, I, 454.

Other references are in AGI, Contaduría 1824, records from Cuzco, 1535; Justicia 1082, no. 1, ramo 4; ANP, PA 634; AHC, Libros de cabildos de Cuzco, I, f.37; HC 290; *CDIAO*, XX, 533; Cieza, *Quito* (Serrano y Sanz, ed.), p. 279; Cieza, *Tercera parte*, in *Mercurio Peruano* 37 (1956): 83; Diego Fernández, *Historia*, I, 21, 27, 46, 63; Garcilaso, *Obras*, III, 280; Gutiérrez de Santa Clara, *Quinquenarios*, II, 182, 220–221, 338, 343; III, 104, 177–178; Loredo, *Alardes y derramas*, pp. 117, 128; Pérez de Tudela, *Gasca*, I, 161, 196, 201, 454, 520; Pedro Pizarro, *Relación*, V, 208, 214, 216; *Relación de las cosas del Perú*, V, 277, 278.

For doña Francisca de Zúñiga and her relatives, see ANP, Salinas 1542–1543, ff.4–5, 15–18; AHC, Libro de difuntos for 1557–1560, f.3; Garcilaso, *Obras*, III, 324; IV, 11, 72–73; Gutiérrez de Santa Clara, *Quinquenarios*, III, 1; Pérez de Tudela, *Gasca*, I, 124, 190, 456.

Hernando de Toro

Role at Cajamarca: Horseman
Share: 2 shares of gold;
  1¾ shares of silver

Place of origin: Trujillo, Extremadura
Parents: Alonso de Toro
  and Inés Durán

Hernando shared the background of his brother Alonso, quite obscure, but more nearly plebeian than noble. Though Alonso became more famous eventually because he lived longer, Hernando was the elder and originally the more prominent. He accompanied the Pizarros from Spain in 1530 as Hernando Pizarro's squire or personal attendant; as such his master made sure that he got a horse, whereas young Alonso stayed on foot. He apparently served as aide or bodyguard, as opposed to Crisóstomo de Hontiveros, the man of affairs, who was Hernando Pizarro's steward. As the campaign went on, Hernando de Toro began to emerge as his own man. He rode in Soto's vanguard during the push south toward Cuzco in 1533, and he was one of the firebrands urging that since they were exposed to the greatest danger, they might as well have the greatest gain and honor by hurrying on to take Cuzco themselves. It was in the course of this effort that Hernando was killed in the most serious battle of the conquest, at Vilcaconga near Cuzco in November, 1533. His fortune of over twelve thousand pesos went into the hands of officials, and his heirs in Spain were still litigating over it in 1545.

NOTES. Hernando was older than Alonso, but Alonso was so young (about twenty) that this fact is little help in estimating Hernando's age. Two full sisters of Hernando and Alonso were alive in Trujillo in 1545; Leonor de Toro, widow of Pedro Caballero, and Mari Hernández, wife of Martín de Padilla (AGI, Justicia 1174, no. 1, ramo 3). There Hernando is called a native of Trujillo. Pedro Pizarro calls him Hernando Pizarro's squire in *Relación*, p. 170.

Other references are in HC 220; Loredo, *Los repartos*, p. 99; Porras, in Trujillo, *Relación*, pp. 119, 120; Porras, "Dos documentos esenciales," *Revista Histórica* 17 (1948):23–25; Trujillo, *Relación*, pp. 61, 62. See also the treatment in Busto, "Los caídos en Vilcaconga," pp. 124–125.

Pedro de Torres

Age at Cajamarca: Apparently
   middle 20's
Role: Footman
Share: ¾ share of gold and silver

Place of origin: Valley of Carriedo,
   in the mountains of Old Castile
Extent of liteacy: Fully literate

Torres came to the Indies around 1525 or 1526, arriving first in Panama, but soon going to Nicaragua; he had been in Nicaragua since at least 1527. There he went to work for the two captains and partners, Hernán Ponce de León and Hernando de Soto. By 1530 he was acting as their tribute collector and steward on the encomienda of Tosta in the jurisdiction of León, Nicaragua's principal settlement. Though this kind of position often fell to those on the very lowest level of Spanish society, Torres had a certain amount of education; he may have been more a steward and estate manager and less the lowly tribute collector and stockwatcher. Nevertheless, he neither claimed nor was considered to be an hidalgo, but an honored person, an honest man, and the like.

There can be little doubt that Torres came to Peru with Hernando de Soto, since even after Cajamarca he continued to function as Soto's servant or retainer. He stayed in the country only until the first surge of conquest was completed, then left in later 1534 as many others did, particularly Soto's men. On the Isthmus of Panama, Torres asked Miguel Estete, a fellow veteran of Nicaragua and friend of Soto and a north Castilian, to register all of Torres's gold and silver in his name, thinking no doubt that it was safer in the hands of a man who had acted as a treasury official in Peru. Estete did the favor for Torres, because Soto had asked him to look out for Torres's affairs, and thus it was that the Pedro de Torres arriving in Seville in 1535 on the ship *Santa Catalina* was ostensibly destitute. But like the others he went off to the royal court at Madrid and negotiated for a coat of arms, which was granted him in March, 1536. He then went back to the northern mountains of Castile, and, since his native valley offered no municipality of importance, he settled in nearby Burgos.

N O T E S . Busto thinks Torres may have gone on the Florida expedition with Soto. There was a Pedro de Torres with that expedition, perhaps even more than one. Garcilaso mentions a man of this name from Badajoz, and one from Burgos; it is not clear whether they are the same or not. Garcilaso wrote much later and is not trustworthy on origins. The official register of the expedition lists only one Pedro de Torres, citizen of Medina del Campo, son of Alonso Martín and Elvira de Torres. Therefore it does not seem very probable that the Torres of Cajamarca returned to the Indies. However, Torres as a direct dependent of Soto was the type most likely to join him if anyone did so.

Torres's *probanza de servicios* is in AGI, Patronato 55, no. 2, ramo 1, and is published in *CDIHN*, III, 412–416. There he is called "natural del valle de Carriedo que es en la montaña." In 1537, a citizen of Burgos, he said he was thirty-six years old (AGI, Justicia 1124, no. 6, ramo 3). Yet in Nicaragua in 1530 a court appointed a guardian for Torres on the grounds that he seemed to be between twenty and twenty-five (*CDIHN*, IV, 538). Torres is called "criado de Hernando de Soto" in AGI, Contaduría 1825, records from Cajamarca, May, 1533.

Other references are in AGI, Indiferente General 1801, records of ship *Santa Catalina*, 1535; Justicia 1124, no. 5, ramo 3; *CDIHN*, IV, 31, 72, 124, 218, 259, 531–556, 749; Busto, "Los presuntos peruleros," *Mercurio Peruano* 50 (1965):317–321, 325; Porras, *Cedulario*, II, 149; Solar and Rújula, *El Adelantado Hernando de Soto*, p. 296.

Diego de Trujillo

Age at Cajamarca: About 27 or 28   Place of origin: Trujillo (Extremadura)
Role: Footman   Parents: Hernando de Trujillo
Share: ¾ share of gold;   and Francisca de Ocampo
  ⅞ share of silver   Extent of literacy: Could sign his name

As might be expected from his name, Diego de Trujillo was among the contingent recruited by the Pizarros in Trujillo in 1529. By all indications he was of humble background. The Trujillos did not constitute a lineage like the Pizarros or Orellanas; there were only scattered, miscellaneous individuals of that name. Diego always associated with plebeians like his friend Alonso Díaz the horseshoer; though he could make his signature, it is doubtful that he could do much more.

In Peru he was a close and trusted follower of the Pizarros, in the manner of a henchman, though there is no record that he was their actual retainer. One comrade said of Trujillo that "wherever he might be, he would do whatever Hernando Pizarro ordered him." After the conquest he left Peru with many others in 1534. He formed part of the guard that escorted the disgruntled Pedro de Alvarado back to Guatemala; then he went directly to Spain and Trujillo.

Up to this point Diego de Trujillo's career had nothing extraordinary about it, given that world in which miracles obeyed rules. But Trujillo's life now entered a second, more unusual phase. Though he lived for ten years in his home town, he grew dissatisfied, and finally, around 1546, he went back to Peru. This might be put down to an addiction to the exotic, or the squandering of his fortune, and either explanation may be partly applicable. But certainly there was also an element of social determinism here. The city of Trujillo could give a royal welcome to those of its returning sons who were reasonably well-born, seating them on the municipal council and marrying them to the noblest ladies. For a commoner like Diego de Trujillo this was impossible, even with a fortune in gold and silver, so he naturally yearned for Peru, where as a man of Cajamarca he could hope to achieve such a position.

Those few who came back, however, soon discovered that it was not so easy to convert their undoubted prestige into encomiendas in a country that had changed since they had left it and where great wars were fought precisely because there were not enough encomiendas for the qualified claimants. Trujillo was lucky that he arrived when Peru was under the sway of rebel governor Gonzalo Pizarro, who was willing to make some move to gratify a compatriot and old friend of the Pizarros. Even so, Trujillo received only the very insignificant, actually somewhat humiliating, post of lower constable of Cuzco. By 1549 he had an encomienda in the Cuzco district, though very small pickings compared to the holdings of his old companions who had never left the country. But with this toehold, Trujillo's position improved as time went by; his original seniority loomed larger, his absence smaller. Little by little he achieved his goals. He made a good marriage, by 1559 he was on Cuzco's council, and his encomienda was improved until it was at least respectable, though not enough to make him one of the great of the land. He was in any case not the type for a magnate or a captain.

Perhaps because of his peculiar life history, perhaps because of temperament, Trujillo was forever harping on Cajamarca and the conquest. He became an inveterate teller of anecdotes, and as such he came to the attention of the viceroy don Francisco de Toledo in 1571, when Peruvians were beginning to feel the first symptoms of an antiquarian interest. The viceroy caused Trujillo's memories to be set down in writing, and thus it was that he came to figure among the chroniclers of the conquest. Dictated rather than written, his account shows an untutored mind, manly and direct, magnificently unconcerned with larger issues, able to see and depict what he experienced in vivid anecdotal fashion. He died in 1576, a legendary figure, though still something of the plebeian. Garcilaso de la Vega, who knew him in the 1550's, thought he was one of the Thirteen of Gallo Island and was unaware he had ever left Peru; yet he cites him near the end of his list of men who did momentous things.

N O T E S .   In Seville in 1535 Diego de Trujillo said he was a citizen of Trujillo and thirty years old (AGI, Patronato 93, no. 5, ramo 2). In 1545 he said he was forty (AGI, Justicia 1174, no. 1, ramo 3, which also gives his father's name), and in 1559 that he was fifty-seven (AGI, Lima 205, *probanza* of Juan Sierra de Leguízamo).

For his edition of Trujillo's *Relación*, Porras did extensive biographical research, the results of which are reproduced there, pp. 17–24, and in his *Cronistas*, pp. 116–118; the present writer has in part relied on this material even though Porras does not give his sources. Trujillo's chronicle also appears in Muñoz de San Pedro's *Tres testigos de la conquista*. A manuscript copy, with Trujillo's original signature, is reported to be in an institute in Tulsa, Oklahoma. See Chevy Lloyd Strout's "Literary-Historical Treasures," *Hispanic American Historical Review* 43 (1963):267–270. A letter from Trujillo to Gonzalo Pizarro is extracted in Pérez de Tudela, *Gasca*, II, 565; the original is in the Huntington Library.

Other references are in AGI, Lima 110, Relación de la ciudad del Cuzco; ANP, PA 80; BNP, A542, f.21; AHC, Libro de cabildos, I, f.49; II (59–60), ff.1–3; HC 42, 44; *CDIHC*, VII, 155; *RAHC* 8 (1957):71; Diego

Fernández, *História*, I, 333; II, 3–4; Garcilaso, *Obras*, II, 259; III, 29, 206; IV, 97; Loredo, *Los repartos*, p. 360; Porras, "Dos documentos esenciales," *Revista Histórica* 17 (1948):31.

Pedro de Ulloa

Role at Cajamarca: Footman   Place of origin: Probably Cáceres
Share: ½ share of silver;   (Extremadura)
    no gold   Extent of literacy: Could sign his name

In the Peru of the conquest period the name Ulloa was synonymous with a prominent family of Cáceres (in Extremadura, near Trujillo), the most illustrious representatives being Lorenzo, an early settler in the Trujillo region (of Peru), and Antonio, a captain in the civil wars. There is nothing definite to link Pedro de Ulloa to this clan, and his miserable share of the treasure, the smallest of all the 168 shares if it is not a clerical error, is hardly evocative of gentle birth and good connections. Even so, he is found in association with men from Cáceres and Trujillo often enough to leave the strong impression that he was indeed an Ulloa of Cáceres.

Pedro de Ulloa was a founding citizen of Cuzco in 1534. He briefly returned north to Jauja, as if he intended to join the massive movement toward Spain then in progress, but instead he went back to Cuzco by April, 1535. Though he vanishes from the records after that, everything indicates that he was one of the few men of Cajamarca who accompanied the disastrous expedition of Diego de Almagro to Chile. Ulloa may have resented his small share at Cajamarca, or the influential Lorenzo de Aldana, who was a relative of the Cáceres Ulloas and a leader in the Chile venture, may have persuaded him to go. Whether he died in Chile, was killed in the civil wars like many Almagro followers, or finally reached Spain is unknown.

NOTES. Pedro de Ulloa took part in the series of transactions in Cuzco in the spring of 1535 that formed part of the preparations for the Chiie expedition (ANP, PA 197). While this is not absolute proof that Ulloa was personally committed, the vast majority of those appearing in these documents, written by Almagro's secretary, did in fact go to Chile. From the debt Ulloa contracted at that time it can be deduced that he had just bought goods worth 500 pesos from Juan Martín, Almagro's blacksmith and equipment man. In 1538 Almagro had in his possession a written obligation from Ulloa for 800 pesos; it is listed in the long inventory of debts owed Almagro at his death, and once again, almost all those mentioned went to Chile with him (*CDIHC*, V, 232).

There are other references to Pedro de Ulloa in AGI, Patronato 109, ramo 4; ANP, PA 26, 123, 125, 130, 134, 139, 144, 145, 148, 149; Porras, "Dos documentos esenciales," *Revista Histórica* 17 (1948):92.

For Lorenzo de Ulloa, see Lohmann Villena, "Documentos interesantes a la historia del Perú," *Revista Histórica* 25 (1960–1961):450–476; Lohmann Villena, *Americanos en las órdenes nobiliarias*, II, 14; Porras, *Cedulario*, II, 359; Rubén Vargas Ugarte, "La fecha de la fundación de Trujillo," *Revista Histórica* 10 (1936):234. Antonio de Ulloa appears frequently in the indexed *Crónicas del Perú* and *Gasca*, both edited by Pérez de Tudela. For Ulloa's namesake, fray Pedro de Ulloa, Dominican, in Peru by 1536, see Calvete, *Rebelión de Pizarro*, IV, 381; Porras, in Trujillo, *Relación*, p. 68.

Pedro de Valencia

Age at Cajamarca: About 21
Role: Footman

Share: ½ share of gold and silver
Extent of literacy: Signature rather crude

Valencia was one of the expedition's more insignificant members. As to his importance in the eyes of his fellows, he and his partner, Alonso Sánchez de Talavera, got only one full share between them. As to social origin, the artisan background of Alonso Sánchez gives a hint. Though inseparable, the two had known each other only since the beginning of the 1531 expedition; neither must have had very long experience in the Indies.

After Cajamarca, Valencia acquired a horse and went south to Cuzco with the main body of the expedition. There he and Alonso Sánchez together enrolled as citizens and received adjoining lots, as if they intended to stay. But in November of 1534 Sánchez prepared a memorial of his services and not long afterward left for Spain. Pedro de Valencia's testimony in that memorial is the last we hear of him, in Cuzco or elsewhere, but it is at least highly probable that he meant to accompany his partner home.

NOTES. In 1534, as a witness in Alonso Sánchez's *probanza*, Valencia said he was twenty-three years old, and also mentioned specifically that he was Sánchez's partner (AGI, Patronato 93, no. 6, ramo 4).

Other references are in AGI, Patronato 109, ramo 4; ANP, PA 75; HC

41; *CDIAO*, X, 248–249; Porras, "Dos documentos esenciales," *Revista Histórica* 17 (1948):92.

Lope Vélez

Age at Cajamarca: Probably late 20's or over
Role: Horseman
Share: Double share of gold and silver

Place of origin: Palos (Andalusian coast)
Extent of literacy: Could sign his name

Though Palos usually means the sea, it seems that Vélez was from one of the families who provided sea captains and merchants rather than the lowliest mariners. He could sign his name, he had the second, nobler-sounding surname of Guevara, and his long-time partner in the Indies, Pedro Cataño, was from a commercial-hidalgo family of Seville. Vélez himself did not claim to be an hidalgo (a very rare breed in Palos).

Vélez had been in the Indies since 1524. At that time he, Pedro Cataño, and some others who would someday be at Cajamarca joined the expedition formed in Santo Domingo by Gil González de Avila to conquer the Honduras area. The men found there only a poor territory and endless disputes over jurisdiction by rival governors, so most went elsewhere, many of them, like Vélez and Cataño, to Nicaragua. The two also spent some time in Panama, but it was from Nicaragua that they came to Peru, among the closest and most trusted followers of Hernando de Soto. Both were among the dozen picked horsemen who went with Soto to the first interview with Atahuallpa. After the conquest they went quickly to Spain, like most of Soto's men; in Jauja in June, 1534, Vélez was preparing to leave, and he presumably arrived in Spain in 1535 with Cataño. In May, 1536, he was still in Seville in the company of Cataño, preparing a memorial of his services which led to his receiving a coat of arms in 1537. Then he disappears, but he probably went to live out his life in his birthplace, since both his memorial and the royal grant of arms refer to him as a citizen of Palos.

NOTES. By the name alone one is tempted to suspect there was some connection between Lope Vélez and Bachiller Juan Vélez de Guevara, a lawyer from Jerez de la Frontera who arrived in Peru shortly afterward and became alcalde of Cuzco and captain in the civil wars.

Lope Vélez's *probanza de servicios* is in AGI, Patronato 93, no. 6, ramo 1. There he is called a native of Palos. His age is estimated merely on the basis of his active participation in expeditions since eight years before Cajamarca.

Other references are in ANP, PA 1, 126, 141; Busto, "Una relación y un estudio," *Revista Histórica* 27 (1964):281, 286; Cieza, *Tercera parte*, in *Mercurio Peruano* 39 (1958):578; Montoto, *Nobiliario*, p. 392; Oviedo, *Historia*, V, 92; Porras, *Cedulario*, II, 316.

Sancho de Villegas

Role at Cajamarca: Footman
Share: ¾ share of gold
    and silver

Place of origin: Puebla del Prior
    (south central Extremadura)
Parents: García de Villegas and Elena de Paz
Extent of literacy: Good signature

Puebla del Prior falls within the radius of the recruiting effort in Extremadura in 1529, and it is probable that Villegas came to the Indies in 1530 with the Pizarros. There is no hint of any previous experience in the Indies, and he received the three-fourths share that went to many of the neophytes. Villegas became a citizen and encomendero of Cuzco at its foundation and gradually became a man to be reckoned with, though he seems to have held no posts of honor. He was close to the Pizarros. For one thing, in 1536 he won 2,500 marks of silver gambling with Hernando Pizarro. This did not prevent Hernando from sending him out from Cuzco with three others on the delicate and dangerous mission of making contact with Almagro's forces on their return from Chile in 1537. Villegas seems to have been one of those imprisoned when Almagro seized Cuzco, and for this reason he was still in Cuzco when Hernando Pizarro approached the city at the head of an army in 1538. Villegas began to organize a mass flight by Pizarro followers and tried to enlist the Inca chieftain Paullu in his plans. But the Almagrists discovered the plot and executed Villegas in Cuzco, shortly before the battle of Salinas in April, 1538.

N O T E S .   Villegas's origin and parentage are given in AGI, Justicia 1055, no. 1, ramo 1, which also mentions his gambling with Hernando Pizarro.

Other references are in AGI, Contaduría 1824, records from Cuzco, 1536; Lima 566, September 16, 1545; Patronato 93, no. 6, ramo 4; 109, ramo 4; ANP, PA 195; Cieza, *Salinas*, pp. 23, 310, 313; Oviedo, *Historia*, V, 175, 193; Porras, "Dos documentos esenciales," *Revista Histórica* 17 (1948):92; *Varias relaciones del Perú y Chile*, XIII, 105.

12. ARTISANS

With one or two exceptions, all the men appearing here were actually active in their trades in the years 1531–1532, and many of them were operating in a semiofficial capacity for the expedition. "Artisans" is perhaps too specific a term for them, since they include some musicians and a barber-surgeon, but all had manual skills and belonged in the current social category of "mechanics." One of the captains, Greek artilleryman Candía, had a similar skill, though its special characteristics put him in an unusually advantageous position. Significantly, his colleague Martín de Florencia, included here, also later became a captain.

The group's general flavor is strongly plebeian. Many of these men would find their peers among the seamen (chapter 13) and other lower plebeians (chapter 14). Indeed, one of the seamen, Anadel, was definitely an artisan. (Though listed under the artisans in Part I, Anadel was put under seamen in Part II to associate him with his partner Aguirre.) The cooper Palomino, though put in this section, may well have been a man of the sea. The artisans also stretch somewhat toward the higher end of the scale. We should not ignore the literacy and respectability of such men as Delgado the mason, López the barber, and even Páramo the tailor, who are comparable to the upper commoners in chapter 11. Beyond doubt, more than a few men in that section and elsewhere would prove to have been trained artisans if their backgrounds were known fully.

Pedro de Alconchel

Age at Cajamarca: About 35   Place of origin: La Garganta, near
Role: Footman and trumpeter   Béjar (northern Extremadura)
Share: 1 full share of silver and gold   Extent of literacy: Illiterate

Trumpets and trumpeters were as invariable a part of the Spanish conquest as horses and muskets, and they shared the same mission—to electrify and overwhelm the Indians with an impression of unheard-of power. The Peru expedition had three trumpeters when it left Panama, and two of them got as far as Cajamarca. Despite their value, musicians were not very highly esteemed. Many were from the humblest of families, and Alconchel was a good example. Twice he made his will, but he never cared to reveal who his parents were; he was ignorant of all larger affairs and illiterate, though in Spain he had learned to print a big "P°" (standard for Pedro), expecting someone else to write in the "Alconchel." He had no record of previous experience in the Indies, so it is likely he arrived with the Pizarros in 1530.

His moment of fame came in 1533 when the conquering Spaniards were advancing close to Cuzco. Hernando de Soto, in the vanguard, had become isolated from the main force and was near defeat at Vilcaconga, when at midnight the trumpet of Alconchel sounded from miles away, warning both Indians and beleaguered Spaniards that help was coming. This episode won Alconchel a place in more than one chronicle of the conquest, but it was less cinematic and more typically Spanish than might appear. Soto's men had gotten into trouble by rushing too far ahead, trying to reach the riches of Cuzco before the rest. The rescuers were hurrying, not so much to save their comrades as to keep them from getting to Cuzco first. And Alconchel was not trying to signal that help was coming, but to inform some stragglers where camp had been made for the night.

Alconchel settled down in Lima for the rest of his life, too set in his ways as an obvious and incorrigible plebeian to play a role among the great of the capital. His encomienda of Chilca and Mala was far from the most lucrative, rated thirty-fifth of about forty-five in Lima's jurisdiction, and he never held any post on the municipal council or received any other kind of honors. Though not poor, he owned only one house, his own, and his lands could not match those of a magnate like Diego de Agüero. His closest associates were people of the stamp of his *compadre*, Rogel de Loria, an illiterate old veteran of the Indies who came to Peru too late to get an encomienda and eked out a living with carpentry and furniture-making. Alconchel also sheltered in his house the trumpeter Diego de Segovia, relative of Juan de Segovia, his fellow trumpeter at Cajamarca.

He did make quite a good marriage in 1543 to doña María de Aliaga from Segovia, a relative of Jerónimo de Aliaga, and through this avenue his progeny advanced into more aristocratic circles. Both of his daughters were surnamed Aliaga rather than Alconchel, and one of them, after a life of some notoriety, married into one of Lima's greatest families. Alconchel lived on until 1562 in relative obscurity, not involved in the civil wars after 1540, devoting some of his time to petty business ventures like a fishery and an inn, his only recognition the "street of Alconchel" that passed in front of his house.

N O T E S.   Alconchel was vague about his age. In 1536, unless some mistake is involved, he thought he was about fifty-five (AGI, Patronato 93, no. 6, ramo 3); in 1549, about fifty (*RANP* 1 [1920]:524); and in 1552, again about fifty-five (AGI, Lima 118, *probanza* of Licenciado Mercado de Peñalosa). Since the last two are consistent with each other and with common sense, the first was disregarded. A will Alconchel dictated in 1544 is in BNP, A30, ff.367–372, with a codicil, ff.391–392. Another, of 1562, is published in *RANP* 9 (1936):117–121; there Alconchel declares himself a native of La Garganta de Campos in the jurisdiction of Béjar. Busto's article "Pedro de Alconchel, trompeta de caballería," *Mercurio Peruano* 41 (1960):505–515, contains much narrative detail.

Pedro de Alconchel may be at the bottom of the apocryphal "don Francisco de Alconcher" mentioned in the late, extraordinarily corrupt Pero López, *Rutas*, pp. 46–47. According to López, this don Francisco de Alconcher, citizen of Lima, gave the Mercedarian friars a site on which to build their establishment; a few days later, while bullbaiting on horseback in the square, he was cornered by the bull and took refuge in the church, horse and all, entering unharmed by a postern gate through which the horse later could not be extricated without unsaddling. The story is full of inconsistencies and impossibilities, and the donation as described cannot have taken place, but some such incident may have occurred.

Other references are in AGI, Patronato 92, no. 3; ANP, PA 32, 103, 143; Juzgado, October 9, 1535; BNP, A33, ff.61–64; HC 14, 18, 26, 35, 599, 747; *RANP* 1:509, 524–535; Domingo Angulo, "El conquistador Pedro de Alconchel," *RANP* 9 (1936):111–115; Busto, "Una relación y un estudio sobre la conquista," *Revista Histórica* 27 (1964):318; Cobo, *Obras*, II, 304; Diego Fernández, *Historia*, I, 38–39; Gangotena y Jijón, "La descendencia de Atahualpa," *Boletín de la Academia Nacional de Historia, Quito* 38, no. 91 (1958):112–114; *Libros de cabildos de Lima*, I, 8–10; IV, 170; Loredo, *Los repartos*, p. 228; Pedro Pizarro, *Relación*, V, 189; Raúl Porras Barrenechea, in Trujillo, *Relación*, p. 121; Diego de Trujillo, *Relación*, p. 62.

Pedro Calderón

Age at Cajamarca: About 27
Role: Footman
Share: ¾ share of silver; no gold

Place of origin: Trujillo (Extremadura)
Extent of literacy: Illiterate
Trade: *Herrador* (horseshoer and veterinarian)

Calderón no doubt came from Spain in 1530; he had no known record in the Indies, and he was the partner of Francisco de Avalos, who left Extremadura with the Pizarros at that time. Why his share of treasure was so small we do not know. He took part in the conquest all the way to Cuzco. Though he did not in the end decide to settle there, a lot in Cuzco in October, 1534, was still known as Calderón's. Perhaps it was merely the place where he had carried on his trade. He left Peru in 1534, arriving in Seville by 1535 and quickly proceeding to his birthplace of Trujillo. Though a seat on Trujillo's municipal council proved beyond the reach of an illiterate artisan, he basked in his prosperity, and, to emphasize its source, by 1545 he was calling himself resoundingly Pedro Calderón del Perú.

NOTES. The identification of Calderón's trade rests on the fact that Antonio de Herrera, another of the men of Cajamarca, who died before July 1534, had had dealings with "Calderón herrador" (ANP, PA 117). No other Calderón has appeared either among those at Cajamarca or among Almagro's contingent, who came shortly afterward. A bit of confirmation can be found in the association at one point of Pedro Calderón with the other herrador, Juan de Salinas (ANP, PA 118). Furthermore, Calderón was present as witness at the weighing of the treasure of Cuzco, where a man knowledgeable with metals would have been in place (Loredo, *Los repartos*, p. 117).

Busto (in "Los presuntos peruleros," *Mercurio Peruano* 50 [1965]:314–317) associates Calderón with an hidalgo family of Trujillo, but Calderón's trade, his illiteracy, and his failure to become a *regidor* on his return all speak most strongly against any such association. It is true that there was in Trujillo a member of that family called Pedro Calderón, of the same generation as Calderón herrador, but this certainly would be the man who was the son of Pedro Calderón Loaysa and doña Aldonza de Orellana, and who left Spain for Santa Marta in 1536 (Bermúdez Plata, *Pasajeros*, II, 142).

Busto further speculates that the Pedro Calderón of Cajamarca may have been the man of that name who was a captain with Hernando de Soto on the Florida expedition. This would be conceivable, if somewhat incongruous, except that Soto's Captain Calderón is described as a citizen of Badajoz by Garcilaso de la Vega and other sources, and he returned to Badajoz to live by 1558, whereas Pedro Calderón of Cajamarca was a citizen of Trujillo in 1545.

The Calderón of Cajamarca said in 1535 that he was thirty (AGI, Patronato 93, no. 5, ramo 2), and in 1545, when he was a citizen of Trujillo, that he was forty (AGI, Justicia 1174, no. 1, ramo 3). Other references are in ANP, PA 28, 147; *RAHC* 8 (1957):117.

Juan Chico

Role at Cajamarca: Footman
Share: ¾ share of gold and silver
Place of origin: Seville

Parents: Antón Chico and
   Inés Hernández
Extent of literacy: Illiterate
Trade: Tailor

Juan's father was a baker of Seville, and he himself was trained in the trade of tailoring. What business there was for a tailor in the early stages of the conquest of Peru is hard to see, yet on the expedition itself he was still identified with his trade, indeed almost defined by it. While the Spaniards were still on the north coast he had dealings with the tailor Juan Jiménez; on the roll of Cajamarca he is listed next to the tailor Robles, both with small shares. For a time Juan Chico and Sevillian mulatto Miguel Ruiz were business partners, investing their first gains in merchandise to be brought back to the expedition from Panama. The two were probably also partners in the broader sense of being close friends and constant companions, until Ruiz was killed by Indians on the way to Cuzco.

Chico became a citizen and encomendero of Jauja, then moved to the successor city of Lima at its foundation in 1535. With his associate Ruiz gone, Chico now gravitated to Pedro Navarro, but more as a dependent than as a partner; Navarro was a capable, literate man closely connected with the Pizarros. Chico lived unassumingly in Navarro's house with the Indian mistress he had brought from Cuzco. In 1536, during the Indian rebellion, Chico was killed on an expedition sent to relieve Cuzco from a protracted siege. Though he died without a will, his friend Navarro saved his estate from official hands, giving one fourth to his three mestizo children and sending the rest back to Spain to his relatives. One senses that, had he lived, Chico would have had great difficulty in finding a role in the ever more pretentious society his companions were building up around him.

NOTES. The most comprehensive source for Chico's life is the litigation over recovery of his estate contained in AGI, Justicia 746, no. 5. This document reveals that Chico was born and grew up in Seville, tells the names of his relatives, establishes their social milieu, and gives much information on Chico in the Indies as well. Other references are in AGI, Contaduría 1825, records from Lima, January, 1536; Justicia 1126, no. 2, ramo 1; HC 13, 21, 22, 75, 76; Cieza, *Chupas*, p. 256; *Libros de cabildos de Lima*, I, 8–10; Porras, *Cedulario*, II, 356.

Juan Delgado

Age at Cajamarca: About 25
Role: Footman
Share: ¾ share of gold and silver

Place of origin: Salamanca
Extent of literacy: Could sign his name
Trade: Stonemason

Stonemasons, with silversmiths, were the aristocrats of artisanship, so Juan Delgado might be reckoned in the middle range of the men of Cajamarca as to rank within Spanish society. Delgado was probably either a new arrival in the Indies or one of those recruited in Spain for the Peruvian conquest—most likely the latter, since he appears to have been a direct dependent of the Pizarros from an early time. By 1535 he was a citizen of Cuzco, with an encomienda that brought him a respectable income but was mediocre compared to others (it was forty-eighth on a list of eighty-three in Cuzco around 1548). Even as an encomendero he continued to act as steward for Gonzalo Pizarro, and he never became one of the great lords of Cuzco. Having worked for Gonzalo Pizarro, it was natural for him to be drawn deeply into Pizarro's rebellion. For this he received a sentence in 1548 and lost his encomienda. He was in Lima in 1554, and died in Cuzco in December, 1556.

NOTES. It appears that there may have been another Juan Delgado from Salamanca in Peru, no doubt a relation of the man of Cajamarca (Bermúdez Plata, *Pasajeros*, I, 306), with some consequent possibilities of false identifications. However, the main lines are clear, since the man who was *vecino* and encomendero in Cuzco in 1539 was, by his own declaration, at Cajamarca (AGI, Lima 118, *probanza* of Garci Martínez), and there is another contemporary statement that Juan Delgado, *vecino* of Cuzco, was Gonzalo Pizarro's majordomo in 1537–1538 (AGI, Justicia 1054, no. 3, ramo 2). A letter of 1546 refers to Juan Delgado, *vecino* of Cuzco, as a former servant of Gonzalo Pizarro (Pérez de Tudela, *Gasca*, 1:292), and the man in Lima in 1554 declared he took part in Atahuallpa's capture (*Boletín de la Academia Nacional de Historia, Quito* 38, no. 91 [1958]: 110–112). He there says that he was godparent of one of Atahuallpa's sons, don Juan, who lived in Cuzco.

The Caravantes-Salinas y Córdoba version of the roll of Cajamarca lists Juan Delgado as "Juan Delgado Monzón," or "Menzón." It is not clear whether this is a mistake, a corrupt version of a trade or position, or a second surname that never appears again.

Delgado's trade and origin appear in AGI, Contaduría 1825, records from Coaque, April, 1531, where he is referred to as a stonemason from Salamanca. His origin is also given in *CDIAO*, XX, 524, and *RIPIG* 10 (1957):88. Delgado gave his age as over twenty-five in 1539 (AGI, Patronato 93, no. 9, ramo 7), thirty in 1540 (AGI, Lima 204, *probanza* of Pedro del Barco), and forty-eight in 1554 (*Boletín de la Academia Nacional de Historia, Quito* 38, no. 91 [1958]:111).

Other references are in AGI, Contaduría 1824, records from Cuzco, March, 1536; Patronato 185, ramo 10; ANP, PA 135; Loredo, *Los repartos*, pp. 122, 131.

Escalante

Age at Cajamarca: About 40
Role: Footman
Share: ¾ share of gold;
    1 full share of silver

Place of origin: Escalante
    (mountains of Old Castile)
Extent of literacy: Illiterate
Trade: Carpenter

Juan de Escalante was the carpenter of the company, with a modest salary paid by the royal officials. No doubt he had had long experience in the Indies, apparently in Nicaragua, but he was with the expedition only from the time it left Panama. After the conquest proper was over, Escalante became a founding citizen of Lima, with a good encomienda on the southern coast in the region of Ica. He was too set in his ways to attempt to hide his identity as Escalante the carpenter, so he became in effect a test case of whether a man could be both artisan and encomendero in rich Peru, as had been possible in impoverished Panama and Nicaragua. For a time he was tolerated in both capacities. In 1536 the city council appointed Juan de Escalante, "carpenter and citizen," to inspect carpentry work done in Lima and to assign prices. But before long Governor Pizarro forced him to relinquish his encomienda in favor of the well-connected Nicolás de Ribera. He had to sell his livestock for less than their real price, and his house and lot in Lima went to someone else. Such at least was Escalante's story, which is probably not far from the truth. The Pizarros would no doubt have replied that Escalante wanted to go home, and there would be some truth in that too. He reached Seville by 1538, and by 1540 was living in Cartagena, still protesting to royal officials of the injustices done.

NOTES. A man from the mountains of Castile going to a place as out of the way as Cartagena is an anomaly that this writer is hard put to explain. Perhaps Escalante was a ship's carpenter and sought a maritime environment. Escalante said in 1538 that he was over forty-five years old and was a citizen of Escalante, "que es en las montañas" (AGI, Justicia 734, no. 6); in 1536 he said he was forty-five (AGI, Patronato 93, no. 6, ramo 3). AGI, Contaduría 1679, shows that Escalante was paid 133 pesos as his salary as the expedition's carpenter from April, 1531, to April, 1532.

Other references to Escalante are in AGI, Indiferente General 1801, records from ship *San Miguel*, 1535; Lima 565, vol. III, April 15, 1540, June 10, 1540; ANP, PA 783; HC 2, 23, 46, 48; Busto, "Los innominados en el reparto de Cajamarca," *Anales del III Congreso Nacional de la Historia del Perú*, p. 92; *Libros de cabildos de Lima*, I, 56, 98; Porras, *Cedulario*, II, 30; Torres Saldamando, *Libro primero de cabildos*, I, 90.

Another Juan de Escalante appeared in Jauja in 1534 as notary public and clerk of the council; he was replaced when Lima was founded at the beginning of 1535, and is not heard of again, in Lima or elsewhere.

For Juan de Escalante, the notary, see AGI, Contaduría 1825, records from Jauja, November, 1534; Lima 204, *probanza* of Hernán González; Justicia 1126, no. 2, ramo 1; Patronato 93, no. 4, ramo 1.

Martín de Florencia

Role at Cajamarca: Footman
Share: ¾ share of gold
  and silver

Place of origin: Barbastro (kingdom
  of Aragon)
Parents: Martín de Florencia and
  María Leonarda de Santángel
Extent of literacy: Could sign his name

Martín de Florencia was cast in the role of a foreigner among the Spaniards of Peru. Aragon itself was foreign enough to the Castilians; added to Martín's Aragonese birth were his Italian name and ancestry. He was often called Machín, the Basque form of Martín, which the Spaniards used as a derogatory nickname for foreigners. Most of Florencia's associates were either Aragonese or such true foreigners as the Greeks Jorge Griego and Pedro de Candía. And though his father had been a merchant, Florencia, like Candía, followed the typical foreigner's calling of artilleryman. His home town of Barbastro was known for its crossbow production, in which one of Florencia's in-laws was involved. Florencia had probably been a crossbow expert from an early age and moved from there into the related field of artillery. At Cajamarca he was doubtless one of artillery captain Candía's men. During the siege of Cuzco by the Indians in 1536–1537, he acted as chief of a contingent of crossbowmen and musketeers, and at the battle of Chupas in 1542 he directed the loyalist artillery. That these posts were captaincies is not certain, but by the early 1540's there begins to be a mention of Captain Martín de Florencia.

The taint of foreignness (and possibly of Jewish descent as well) may have held Florencia back a bit, but did not halt his advance toward a position of importance in Cuzco. His encomienda there, while not of the very highest order of size and wealth, was better than most (it was once rated twenty-third of eighty in the Cuzco district), and he exploited his holdings methodically; before his death he was one of Cuzco's richest men. He was granted a coat of arms in 1543. In time he certainly would have taken his place on the council of Cuzco, if a conflict with the rebel forces of Gonzalo Pizarro had not put an end to his career. In 1544, as the movement of rebellion gathered strength in Cuzco, Florencia was drawn into it, voluntarily or not, and as a man useful in war he was high in the Pizarrist councils. But before Pizarro's army got far from Cuzco, he and others fled to Lima to support the viceroy. On the triumphant entry of the Pizarrists into Lima in October, 1544, they sought out Martín de Florencia and quickly hanged him, the first of several of the men of Cajamarca to die in Peru's most virulent civil war.

NOTES. In his article "Tres conversos en la captura de Atahualpa," *Revista de Indias* 27 (1967):427–442, Busto maintains that Florencia was one of three *conversos*, or men of Jewish descent, at Cajamarca. Florencia is indeed the strongest case of the three. On the basis of published sources to which he there refers, Busto establishes that a *converso* family by the name of Santángel existed in Aragon at the time, and that it had a branch in Barbastro. There is no known documentary link between this family and Florencia's mother, but the concurrence of names, the name's rarity, and the small size of Barbastro all add up to a certain probability that Florencia was of *converso* origin at least on the maternal side. Busto also points to the Jewish ring of the Old Testament motto on Florencia's coat of arms.

Florencia's foreign connection is more strongly established than his Jewishness. He appears next to Jorge Griego on the list of founding citizens of Cuzco (Porras, "Dos documentos esenciales," *Revista Histórica* 17 [1948]:92), near him on the roll of Cajamarca, and as witness for him at Coaque (HC 16). Florencia's house in Cuzco stood beside that of Pedro de Candía, who collected Florencia's share of the silver of Cuzco in 1534 (Loredo, *Alardes y derramas*, p. 110). Eventually Florencia bought or inherited Candía's house (BNP, A33, f.279). See also Busto, "Pedro de Candía," *Revista Histórica* 25 (1960–1961):392, 403. The foreign tie endured in the second generation. In Lima, in 1567, Florencia's apparently mestizo son, also named Martín, married a woman of half-Italian parentage, her father being from Siena, near Florence. (*RIPIG*, 1947, no. 2, p. 44). Given this, we can hardly doubt in retrospect that the original Martín de Florencia, merchant, father of the man of Cajamarca, was himself Florentine. Even the name Santángel, *converso* or not, was Florentine. In the 1580's there lived in Cuzco a painter and sculptor from Florence named Pedro Santángel (*RAHC* 4 [1953]:141, 148).

Information about Florencia's regional origin, relatives, and much else is to be found in the litigation carried on by his sister to recover his estate (AGI, Justicia 1074, no. 6), and in a posthumous testament of 1544, incorporating his own instructions and a rough inventory of his estate (BNP, A33, f.279). In the latter place Florencia gives his mother's name as María Leonarda de Santángel; in the other set of documents she is referred to as María Santángel or María Santángel Leonardo.

In the will Florencia recognized three mestizo children, Luis and Pedro de Florencia and Isabelica, by "his" Indian women, Isabel and Tocto. For their sustenance he left them each a thousand pesos to be invested in live-stock. At the time of Florencia's death Isabelica was living on his enco-mienda; the boys were presumably in Cuzco. It is quite possible that who-ever raised the children renamed one of them Martín in his father's mem-ory. The youngest Martín de Florencia might also have been a posthumous son by Marina Bernáldez, an eighteen-year-old Spanish girl from Huelva with whom Martín had been having an affair in Lima just before his death. He left her 150 pesos "to satisfy his conscience."

The will gives considerable information on the nature of Florencia's estate. He owned two, possibly three, houses in Cuzco. Some of his en-comienda Indians were working the gold mines of Carabaya under the direction of Antonio de Torres, a barber. Torres was a thousand pesos in debt to his employer. Florencia owned six Negro slaves, some in the Cara-baya mines and some in his house in Cuzco. One was his trusted henchman, whom he freed in his will, and one was on long-term loan to a fellow artilleryman, Captain Pedro de Vergara. On his encomienda in the Cuzco district, or "at his cacique" as he expressed it, he had (besides his daugh-ter) some cloth or clothing with gold woven into it, a horse, mare, and colt, and "many" pigs and llamas. Florencia also owned a house and a mine in the upper Peruvian silver-mining region of Charcas.

In various parts of Peru Florencia had a good amount of liquid wealth hidden away, a surprising amount of it in the care of Indians. Two thou-sand pesos were in his house in Cuzco, in a place known to his Indian Callaquiz; another thousand was buried near a llama pen in an Indian town. In Lima, tailor Domingo de Destre, a fellow Aragonese, had an emerald of Florencia's, and an Indian Huaman was keeping a golden chain and other items of gold that Florencia thought sufficient to pay all his local debts.

Other references to Florencia are in AGI, Contaduría 1824, records from Cuzco, March, 1536; 1825, records from Cuzco, August 14, 1541; Lima 566, vol. V, September 28, 1543; Patronato 90, no. 1, ramo 11; 109, ramo 4; 185, ramo 11; ANP, PA 23; CDIHE, XXVI, 221–232; RANP 1 (1920):582; Atienza, Diccionario nobiliario español, 376–377; Calvete, Rebelión de Pizarro, IV, 256; Diego Fernández, Historia, I, 25, 45; II, 127; Gutiérrez de Santa Clara, Quinquenarios, II, 281–283; 384–385; Lo-redo, Alardes y derramas, pp. 109–111, 119, 129; Pedro Pizarro, Relación, V, 233–234; Relación de las cosas del Perú, V, 259, 268, 276. Busto's "Tres conversos" gives yet more references from the chronicles.

Juan García pregonero

Age at Cajamarca: Probably
  over 30
Role: Footman
Share: ⅛ share of gold;
  ⅚ share of silver

Place of origin: Las Barcas de Albalá, near
  Jaraicejo (northeastern Extremadura)
Parents: García [de Xeda?] and
  Catalina Clemente
Extent of literacy: Illiterate
Trade: Crier and piper

A Spanish social convention demanded that criers (also serving variously as executioners, auctioneers, and constables) should be black or mulatto. The crier of the expedition that conquered Peru was no exception. He too had auxiliary skills, since he was the company's piper (as such often called Juan García *gaitero*), and he was responsible for weighing much of the gold and silver of Cajamarca.

Juan García was functioning among the expedition's Spaniards as at least nominally an equal, though in a lowly function. The records in which he appears directly contain no reference to his ethnic characteristics; however, twice other Spaniards referred to him in litigation as a *negro* (Negro, or black). Despite this term, he was probably a dark mulatto of partially mixed parentage, rather than fully African in origin. Juan García was born in Spain, in the hinterland of Trujillo, as the product of a legitimate marriage; he had a cousin there who was a priest, and one can hardly imagine a black man in that position at that time and place. The mixture might have been on either side of the family. Juan García's brothers and sisters bore the maternal and paternal surnames equally, and in the Jaraicejo area he acknowledged relatives on both sides, some living and some buried in local churches. Juan García himself had been married and widowed in the locality, and had two legitimate daughters; his mother-in-law was still living in the area. Thus it appears that Juan García was integrated in the usual fashion into the local society of the rural hamlets near Jaraicejo, unless we can presume the existence of a whole functioning free black community. At any rate, Juan García's Spanish social position was not a high one. After his return to Spain he was to be referred to once as a "low and vile person," standard legal terminology for a lower plebeian. His highest hope for his two daughters' future, despite the wealth they might inherit from him, was that they be married to "honorable people."

Coming as he did from the Trujillo area, Juan García was presumably among those newly recruited there in 1530. In Peru he was with the expedition all the way to Cuzco, where he continued to act as crier and to help with the division of the treasure. After having been one of the founding citizens of Cuzco and actually residing there for some months, he decided early in 1535 to return to Spain. From August to December of that year he was in Lima making various preparations, including a will, and by February, 1536, he was in Nombre de Dios on the Isthmus, ready to embark for Spain. A budding inclination to unfold socially can be seen in his assumption of a double surname as Juan García Clemente, an appellation he was to continue to use at least part of the time after his return to his homeland.

While many of the men needed little urging to be allowed to go home rich, one wonders to what extent Juan García's departure was voluntary. There was at least one other humble old conqueror (Juan de Escalante) who was pushed out of his position. Juan García's share at Cajamarca was adjusted downward in view of his social condition (of course tailors and other lowly people got the same treatment). In Cuzco he was one of the very few citizens not formally assigned a lot. People had complained about the impropriety of a man of his type using the royal seal to mark precious metals. In short, there probably was no comfortable place in ever wealthier, ever more conservative Peru for a black encomendero of Cuzco. Conditions in Peru permitted the reestablishment of the main lines of the peninsular order of society, which had fallen into some disarray in the impoverished backwoods of Panama and Nicaragua in the 1520's. Juan García was prudent to leave with his fortune while he had it.

It was Juan García's intention, whether actually carried out or not we do not know, to take with him to Spain his natural daughter Magdalena and her mother, Isabel, his Peruvian Indian servant woman. He reached home, and well into the 1540's he was a citizen of the village of Casas del Puerto, near Jaraicejo. Still an associate or partisan of the Pizarros, he testified on their behalf when the occasion demanded. This connection makes it likely that he was the same person as an illiterate Juan García Pizarro who was living at an unidentified place called Las Piñuelas somewhere in the Trujillo area in 1545.

N O T E S . The evidence on the life of Juan García *pregonero* is a very tangled skein, and the thought processes applied to it need to be brought out into the open so that future research can confirm them, build on them, or demolish them, as the case may be, though the writer believes that the identification will stand. At Coaque, in 1531, there was a Juan García gaitero, or piper, much in the company of the expedition's trumpeters (HC 18, 25, 26, 28). At Cajamarca, and at the division of the treasure, there appears Juan García pregonero, or crier. The prima facie reasons for considering these two as one are (1) that the two professions were often practiced together, as two ways of attracting the attention of numbers of people, and (2) that the two names never appear together, but always in a way that fits into a single line. This writer thinks that the name varied with Juan García's function of the moment and with the notary writing the document.

Juan García pregonero is distinguished in the records from Juan García escopetero and Juan García de Santa Olalla, first at Cajamarca in 1532–1533 (roll of Cajamarca; AGI, Contaduría 1825; ANP, PA 103), and then in Cuzco in early 1534 (Loredo, *Los repartos*, pp. 98, 103, 132). In Cuzco, Juan García pregonero continued to function as a crier and was closely connected with the division of the treasure (Loredo, *Los repartos*, pp. 98, 132). In March, 1534, Juan Garcia gaitero became a citizen of Cuzco; he then stayed among the forty citizens guarding the city in the second half of 1534 (AGI, Patronato 185, ramo 11, or *CDIAO*, X, 249; Porras, "Dos documentos esenciales," *Revista Histórica* 17 [1948]:92–93; RAHC 8 [1957]:73). On September 4, 1534, he was mentioned in the Cuzco cabildo records as the person to receive money from fines for improper disposition of horse dung. This confirms once again his identity with Juan García pregonero (Rivera Serna, *Libro primero de cabildos de la ciudad del Cuzco*, p. 31). He then appears no more in Cuzco.

In 1535 Juan García pregonero appeared in Lima, paying the royal fifth (AGI, Contaduría 1825). At the same time, in August–September, 1535, a Juan García, *vecino* of Cuzco, going to Spain, a native of Las Barcas de Albalá, testified in Lima during an investigation of the royal treasury officials, saying that he had weighed the gold and silver of Cajamarca. The fact that this Juan García is a *vecino* of Cuzco, going to Spain at the same time that Juan García gaitero, *vecino* of Cuzco, disappears, is another proof that Juan García gaitero and Juan García pregonero are one. In this same investigation another witness complained that he had seen a "Negro" who was crier in Cuzco carrying around the royal seal to mark gold and silver. The investigator picked up the charge, and Francisco Pizarro admitted its validity. Since Juan García acted as a crier at Cuzco and was involved in weighing gold and silver, he must be the man. In February, 1536, Juan García Clemente, a native of Las Barcas de Albalá, was in Nombre de Dios, and testified that he had personally proclaimed the ordinances on gold and silver in Cuzco. Another witness there said the ordinances were proclaimed by Juan García pregonero.

The matter of the preceding paragraph comes from an inquiry into the functioning of the royal exchequer in Peru, made in 1535 by Bishop Tomás de Berlanga of Panama. The original is in AGI, Patronato 185, ramo 11. It has been twice published, though with some mistakes: in *CDIAO*, X, 237–332, and in Torres Saldamando, *Libro primero de cabildos*, III, 65–83.

On December 14, 1535, still in Lima, Juan García, native of Las Barcas de Albalá, near Jaraicejo, issued a will. The document is in the Peruvian section of the Latin American manuscripts of Indiana University's Lilly Library. The will contains many valuable personal details, of which for the present purpose the most important is that Clemente was one of the surnames common in Juan García's family. (An ink blot has obscured part of the name of García ———, Juan García's father. Instead of "de Xeda," the reading suggested above, it could conceivably be "texedor" ("weaver"), but I have not been able to attain certainty.) Juan García's age is estimated on the basis not only of the existence of a wife and children as seen in the will, but of his probable identity with Juan García Pizarro (see Juan García escopetero).

Juan García pregonero was capable of making a rubric (Berlanga inquiry), though he did not always do so; it is possible that he once tried to learn at least to write his name. At Cajamarca in June, 1533, Pedro de Alconchel sold a Nicaraguan slave woman on credit to a Juan García; the name is unmodified, but we must suspect that it is our García because of the two men's close association. The debtor signed with an abbreviated "Juan García" of consummate crudity, surrounded by rubrics consisting of a cross inside a circle, with dots in the quarters thus formed (PA 103).

As if there were not enough complications in identifying Juan García pregonero, during the conquest a certain Juan Clemente was in Peru, and specifically in Cuzco. Since the man of Cajamarca called himself Juan García Clemente, it would be natural to suspect that the two men are one. Yet they are not. In Jauja in 1534 Juan Clemente testified that he had taken part in the early stages of the conquest of Peru but was not at Cajamarca. He was forty years old at this time, and could not write his name (AGI, Lima 204, *probanza* of Hernán González). Clemente stayed in Peru after Juan García left; he was in the siege of Cuzco of 1536–1537, then disappears (AGI, Justicia 1071, no. 2, ramo 3; Contaduría 1824, records from Cuzco, 1536–1537; Pedro Pizarro, *Relación*, V, 205). This Juan Clemente may well be the sailor of the same name who was in Panama in 1514

(Medina, *Descubrimiento*, II, 425). There is no telling whether Juan García pregonero and Juan Clemente were in any way connected. The name Clemente, which sounds Portuguese, was rare among the Spaniards.

Since the social type of the crier seems to have been little described, and particularly the association with piping is unfamiliar, I will give another example—illiterate Pedro de la Peña, who functioned as town crier in Lima during the 1540's. It is not certain that he was black, though he may well be identical with "Pedro de color negro," a crier in Lima in March, 1535 (*Libros de cabildos de Lima*, I, 19). In 1546 he appears as piper for a company of musketeers in the forces of rebel Gonzalo Pizarro (Loredo, *Alardes y derramas*, p. 104). In 1549 he dictated a will (BNP, A35, f.112), in which it can be seen that his chief income was from auction fees. Most of his associations were with foreigners and lower plebeians. Among his possessions was a green case holding some flutes.

Francisco González

Age at Cajamarca: About 27	Place of origin: Zalamea de la Serena
Role: Footman	(eastern Extremadura)
Share: ½ share of gold	Extent of literacy: Illiterate
and silver	Trade: Tailor

Since he came from a town some fifty miles south of Trujillo, Francisco González may well have been recruited by the Pizarros in 1529. At Cajamarca he had as low a place and as small a share as the three or four other practicing tailors. He started to settle in Cuzco in 1534, but changed his mind, and was in Seville by September, 1535, doubtless on his way home to Zalamea.

N O T E S . In Seville, in 1535, Francisco González testified to his participation at Cajamarca, gave his age as thirty, and declared himself a citizen of Zalamea de la Serena (AGI, Patronato 93, no. 5, ramo 2). He is called a tailor in a document written at Cajamarca on July 23, 1533 (ANP, PA 2), and in AGI, Contaduría 1825, Penas de Cámara, January, 1532. Other references to him are in AGI, Patronato 185, ramo 11, and ANP, PA 22.

Alonso Jiménez

Age at Cajamarca: Probably 25
  or more
Role: Footman
Share: 1 full share of gold
  and silver

Place of origin: Miajadas
  (central Extremadura)
Parents: Juan Jiménez and
  Catalina Alonso
Extent of literacy: Illiterate
Trade: Swordsmith

Alonso Jiménez had married in his home town of Miajadas before he left Spain in 1527, along with the party of Francisco de Montejo, destined for Yucatan. Apparently he deserted Yucatan after a short time and went to Santa Marta, on the Caribbean coast of South America, since in Peru he was sometimes called Jiménez de Santa Marta. With this background, he must have already been at least in his midtwenties by 1532, even though he answered a query about his age in 1535 only with the standard formula that he was "over twenty-five."

Jiménez was with the main group of conquerors from the time they left Panama. His essential skill as a swordsmith explains his full share at Cajamarca, exceptional for a practicing artisan; he is the only known blacksmith of the expedition, as opposed to the two *herradores* (horseshoers). He settled in Cuzco at the Spanish founding in 1534. The next year he went to Lima to arrange to send money home to Spain, and, while there, he testified in the memorial of services of his friend, the *herrador* Juan de Salinas. Then he returned to Cuzco, where he died well before 1539.

N O T E S . Jiménez's origin and the names of his parents are given in Seville's Archivo de Protocolos, oficio XV, libro II, October 4, and Bermúdez Plata, *Pasajeros*, I, 227. The name of his wife, Marina Magaña, appears in AGI, Lima 565, vol. III, January 31, 1539. Records from Coaque, May, 1531, in AGI, Contaduría 1825, show Jiménez's trade.

Other references are in AGI, Contaduría 1824, records from Cuzco, May–July, 1535; Lima 204, *probanza* of Juan de Salinas; Patronato 109, ramo 4; 185, ramos 10 and 11; HC 32, 153; Porras, "Dos documentos esenciales," *Revista Histórica* 17 (1948):92.

Juan Jiménez

Age at Cajamarca: Probably near 30,
  or over
Role: Footman
Share: ¾ share of gold;
  1 full share of silver

Place of origin: Probably Consuegra
  (New Castile)
Extent of literacy: Illiterate
Trade: Tailor

Juan Jiménez the tailor was with the 1531 expedition from the time it left Panama. During the long stay at Coaque on the north coast he is seen associating with other artisans—his colleague Juan Chico and the swordsmith Alonso Jiménez. At Cajamarca he came closer than any of the other tailors to getting a full share of the treasure. He seems to have gone on to Cuzco, and may have lived there for some years, but after Cajamarca he never again called himself tailor. In the post-Cajamarca period it is very hard to distinguish him from the second Juan Jiménez who arrived with Almagro in 1533, and the half-dozen others who were in the country by 1540. He appears to be the same man as a Juan Jiménez de Consuegra, who had been in the Indies since about 1522.

NOTES. As far as is known, only one other Juan Jiménez arrived with Almagro, thus there were just two of them going south to Cuzco. Two Juan Jiménezes appear as founding citizens of Cuzco in 1534, called respectively Juan Jiménez de Consuegra and Juan Jiménez de Jamaica (Porras, "Dos documentos esenciales," *Revista Histórica* 17 [1948]:92). One of them must have been Juan Jiménez the tailor. Unfortunately, neither of these names ever appears in this form after 1534.

The Juan Jiménez who arrived with Almagro can be traced fairly well. He was born around 1498, was illiterate, may have been a carpenter, and came from Santa Cruz de la Sierra, near Trujillo; he usually styled himself Juan Jiménez de Trujillo. He was a citizen and encomendero of Cuzco, lived through the siege of 1536–1537, and was still there in April, 1540. Some time after that he went to Spain, and he was living in Santa Cruz de la Sierra in 1545.

Now since this Juan Jiménez (de Trujillo) was almost certainly one of the two at the founding of Cuzco, he must have been Juan Jiménez de Jamaica. He could very well have been on the Caribbean island of Jamaica, but he was definitely not from the Spanish town of Consuegra. So it appears that Juan Jiménez the tailor was Juan Jiménez de Consuegra, and hence in all probability actually from the town of Consuegra, south of Toledo. In the New World for ten years, he must have been about thirty, at least.

One of the two Juan Jiménezes was *alguacil menor* ("lower constable") of Cuzco at its founding (AGI, Patronato 109, ramo 4). Either one would have graced the post, so there is no basis for deciding which one it was, but regional affinity with the Pizarros and subsequent connection with them make Juan Jiménez de Trujillo the more likely candidate.

In April, 1540, a Juan Jiménez was in Cuzco, definitely not Juan Jiménez de Trujillo, because both testified to the same memorial of services (AGI, Lima 204, *probanza* of Pedro del Barco). This Jiménez was then about thirty, was illiterate, and had been in the Indies at least fifteen years. The man could very well be Juan Jiménez the tailor, except that he is not called a citizen (encomendero), which any participant at Cajamarca would have been, under ordinary circumstances. However, if Juan Jiménez the tailor really was from Consuegra, only some thirty miles from Almagro's birthplace, he, like others from the Ciudad Real–Toledo area, might have sided with Almagro in the "War of Salinas" in 1537–1538 and have lost his encomienda as a result.

The Juan Jiménez of the original Peruvian expedition is called a tailor in HC 13 and 32. Testimony by Juan Jiménez de Consuegra, illiterate, in Cuzco in 1534, appears in AGI, Patronato 93, no. 4, ramo 3. Other references are in AGI, Contaduría 1825, records from Jauja, November, 1534; ANP, PA 10, 11, 45, 49, 50, 54, 56, 57, 62, 105. It is quite possible that the man in some of the documents just above is Juan Jiménez de Trujillo, particularly in ANP, PA 62.

For Juan Jiménez de Trujillo, see AGI, Contaduría, 1824, records from Cuzco, March–August, 1536, March–April, 1537; Justicia 833, letter of Hernando Pizarro, June 8, 1549; 1053, no. 2; Lima 204, *probanza* of Pedro del Barco; ANP, PA 718, 761; Porras, *Testamento de Pizarro*, p. 17. In AGI, Lima 118, *probanza* of García Martín, Juan Jiménez de Trujillo states that he arrived in Peru with Almagro, after the taking of Atahuallpa.

Francisco López

Role at Cajamarca: Horseman
Share: 1½ share of gold;
   2⅕₀ shares of silver

Place of origin: Cádiz
   (Andalusian coast)
Extent of literacy: Could sign his name
Trade: Barber

López had been in Nicaragua since perhaps 1525. In 1529 he had an encomienda there in partnership with an Alonso Lozano who may be the Lozano of Cajamarca. Both of them joined the 1531 expedition in Panama. Barbers were almost always practical surgeons as well; most had some education and a capacity for affairs. They were accorded a certain amount of respect, so that it is quite natural to find Francisco López among the horsemen at Cajamarca. His smaller-than-usual share is probably more a reflection on his horse than on his calling. While the expedition was at Cajamarca, López took an active part in the immensely lucrative horse-trading going on there, doubtless recouping his share and more.

He went on with the rest to Jauja, then stayed there while the main body proceeded to Cuzco. Bachiller Juan de Balboa, with an academic title, replaced López as surgeon. López left Peru in late 1534 and arrived in Seville by May, 1535, carrying his own fortune and large amounts entrusted to him by others.

NOTES. The 1531–1532 expedition had a second surgeon-barber, Alvaro Muñoz, who stayed behind in San Miguel instead of going to Cajamarca; he was stricken blind by a disease that affected many Spaniards upon arrival there.

In Seville in 1535 López said he was a citizen of Cádiz (AGI, Indiferente General 1204, no. 44). Other references are in AGI, Contaduría 1825, records from Coaque, May, 1531; ANP, PA 51, 82, 83, 98, 101, 649, 681; HC 8, 23, 27, 50, 51; *CDIHN*, II, 225; Busto, "El herrero, el barbero y el gran volteador," *Mercurio Peruano* 43 (1962):70–71; Porras, in Trujillo, *Relación*, p. 102. For the other surgeons, see AGI, Lima 118, *probanza* of Alvaro Muñoz; Loredo, *Los repartos*, p. 103; Porras, "Dos documentos esenciales," *Revista Histórica* 17 (1948):90.

Francisco Martínez

Role at Cajamarca: Footman
Share: ½ share of gold;
   ¾ share of silver

Trade: Tailor
Extent of literacy: Could sign
   his name

Francisco Martínez is the only one of the tailors at Cajamarca who has left any evidence of activity directly connected with his trade. He is known to have sold a cape to one of his companions, and another man owed him a small debt, about the price of an article of clothing. He stayed in Jauja in 1533–1534 rather than going south to Cuzco. After the main body returned from Cuzco, he went to San Miguel with Almagro and then, it seems, accompanied him to Quito in late 1534. Probably he returned to Spain after that, though the proof is not definite.

NOTES. The precise evidence needs to be brought to light when the man being trailed has a name as common as Francisco Martínez. However, there appears to have been no other of this name either at Cajamarca or among Almagro's men. Often Spaniards interchanged Martín and Martínez, but the notaries in this case were careful to write Martínez, because they already had three Francisco Martíns to deal with.

The first hint that Francisco Martínez was a tailor comes from his position on the roll of Cajamarca next to the tailor Francisco González. At Cajamarca in May, 1533, we hear that Francisco Martínez has sold a cape and a dagger to Hernando de Montalbo (ANP, PA 66). In the account of the estates of the deceased we find that Pedro de Contreras, who died at Cajamarca before the division of the treasure, owed a small debt to Francisco Martínez (AGI, Justicia 1074, no. 9). On March 1, 1534, Francisco Martínez was in Jauja, in the company of a Francisco de Robles who was probably the "Robles, tailor," of Cajamarca (HC 61). On June 6, 1534, "Francisco Martínez, tailor," is in the village of Canga near San Miguel (ANP, PA 161).

The question of whether or not Francisco Martínez definitely returned to Spain turns on his identity with a Francisco Martínez, hosier, born about 1508, who had been in Lima around 1536, and in 1538 was a citizen of Seville in the district of Santa María. Another witness at the side of this Martínez was Juan de Escalante, of Cajamarca (AGI, Justicia 734, no. 6). The present writer feels that there is a high probability that this man is the Martínez at Cajamarca, but can make no stronger statement.

In López de Caravantes's version of the Cajamarca list it is said that Francisco Martínez appears on the gold list as Francisco Cazalla. No other version repeats this, and the name does not appear in any other kind of contemporary record.

Those experienced in Spanish calligraphy of the sixteenth century realize that nothing regarding anyone named Martínez is ever clear beyond a doubt. Even strict contemporaries often confused the name with Núñez and other names, not to speak of the sins of transcription of a score of later generations. Therefore this writer feels it his duty at least to mention a man by the name of Francisco Muñiz from La Bañeza (Leon), born about 1498, who took part in the conquest of Cuzco, then left Peru in late 1534. In Spain he went to the royal court and was granted a coat of arms. The six men to receive this honor before him were all at Cajamarca, as were the six immediately after him. In 1538 he was living in La Bañeza.

Other homonyms of Francisco Martínez appear in ANP, PA 90; CDIAO, XX, 500; Porras, Cedulario, I, 138. There are references to Francisco Muñiz in AGI, Contaduría 1825, records from Jauja, 1534; Justicia 1124, no. 6, ramo 3; ANP, PA 131, 133, 144; Porras, Cedulario, II, 119.

Palomino tonelero

Role at Cajamarca: Footman   Trade: Cooper
Share: 1 full share of gold and silver

The main business of *toneleros* (coopers) in the Indies in the sixteenth century was to make water casks for ships, so that most of them
were men of the sea. This particular man was quite highly valued either
for his craft or for other qualities, since he received a full share of the
treasure of Cajamarca, well above average for the infantry, whether
well-born or plebeian.

One can only be glad that the secretaries of the expedition wrote
down Palomino's trade, which speaks volumes about his background.
But the price of this inclusion is the loss of his first name, and without
that it is not possible to identify him with certainty among the conquerors of Peru. Two seventeenth-century sources mention a Pedro Palomino who might have been the man, but the most likely person is an
Alonso Palomino, related to Melchor (above) and doubtless from the
Jaén region. Alonso was on Lima's city council in the year of its founding and alcalde in Lima in 1541 and 1544. He was one of Peru's important men until he left the country because of illness just before
Gonzalo Pizarro occupied Lima, and he died very soon afterward in
Spain, around 1545.

N O T E S .   Salinas y Córdoba's early seventeenth-century version of the
roll of Cajamarca includes "Pedro Palomino." However, we know that his
source said merely "Palomino tonelero," and we must assume he was simply
guessing, as he did elsewhere. Herrera mentions a "Pedro Palomino" supposed to have been in Piura in 1534 (*Década* V, lib. IV, cap. XI).

Alonso was definitely connected with the other Palominos (AGI, Lima
565, vol. III, August 1, 1539; PA 728; HC 662, 663, 664). There is no
indication of how long he had been in the Indies. He was apparently literate. By 1542 he had married Beatriz de Rojas, who was a sister of fellow
conqueror Pedro Díaz (de Rojas), a silversmith and assayer who missed
the events of Cajamarca but got there in time to officiate at the distribution.
Palomino was a solid man, active in the community rather than a civil war
leader. Back in Spain he wrote or dictated a report on recent events in Peru
which betrays a shrewd grasp of political and economic essentials and an
admirable directness of expression.

Several pieces of evidence tend to point to Alonso as Palomino *tonelero*.

First, no other candidate appears in the actual contemporary records. Then there is Alonso's appointment to the council of Lima for 1535, which means that he must have been in the country for some time, and establishes a presumption that he was either a man of Cajamarca or a conqueror of Cuzco. Also, the relative positions of Alonso, immediately eminent, and Melchor, obscure at first, correspond well with the relative shares of the two Palominos at Cajamarca. Finally, there was a noticeable tendency to refer to Alonso Palomino without his first name, just like Palomino tonelero. (See Torres Saldamando, *Libro primero de cabildos*, I, passim, particularly the votes for alcalde.)

Yet there are certain reasons to draw back from a positive identification. Whereas Diego and Melchor Palomino appear several times in the documents of the 1531–1532 expedition, Alonso does not. There is no trace of him in Peru before 1535, except by extrapolation. Perhaps most ominously, Alonso, despite his prominence and his easy availability, was, to this writer's knowledge, never asked to testify to any of the memorials of services of the men of Cajamarca, so that we do not have his own statement that he was there, as we have for most of those who lived on for any length of time in Lima. Busto's rejection of Alonso because he was alcalde is not decisive ("Los innominados en el reparto de Cajamarca," p. 93). Other very humble men, including Martín Pizarro, served as alcaldes of Lima.

References to Alonso Palomino are in ANP, Salinas 1542–1543, ff.231, 579; Salinas 1546–1548, ff.486, 556; BNP, A31, f.153; *RANP* 1 (1920): 429–430, 599, 602; 10: 217; 11: 228; Busto, "Una relación y un estudio," *Revista Histórica* 27 (1964):299; Cobo, *Obras*, II, 304; Gutiérrez de Santa Clara, *Quinquenarios*, II, 178; Loredo, *Los repartos*, pp. 226, 228; Porras, *Cartas*, pp. 169, 524; Torres Saldamando, *Libro primero de cabildos*, I, 11–13 and passim; Alonso Palomino, *Relación sumaria de lo sucedido en el Perú después de la llegada del virrey*, Appendix III to Diego Fernández, *Historia*, II.

Pedro del Páramo

Role at Cajamarca: Horseman
Share: 1⅜ shares of gold;
 1½ shares of silver

Place of origin: Probably Carrión de los
 Condes (Leon)
Extent of literacy: Could sign his name
Trade: Tailor

Tailor Páramo comes last on the list of the cavalry of Cajamarca, with one of the smallest shares for a horseman. The relative rarity of his name makes it highly probable that he is the Pedro del Páramo,

born in Carrión de los Condes in the kingdom of Leon, who left Spain
in 1528. In 1531 he was working in his trade in the city of Panama.

Páramo may have been one of the last of the men of Cajamarca to
arrive in Peru. Two ships from Panama registered in San Miguel or
Piura in August, 1532, shortly after the city was founded and a month
and a half or more before the main body headed south to face Atahuallpa's forces. One of the larger importers of merchandise on these
vessels was Pedro del Páramo, who paid duties on some 700 pesos'
worth, a large sum before Inca treasure brought inflation. The "merchandise" may have included Páramo's horse, equipment, and provisions. But such an amount implies commercial purposes; Páramo the
tailor very likely brought cloth to be made up or clothing to be sold.
We cannot be sure that he physically accompanied the ships, but since
he was still in Panama in early March, 1532, there is hardly any other
possibility.

In July of 1533 Páramo appears for the last time in Peruvian documents, selling an Indian slave. Perhaps he left Peru with the first contingent; he is not heard of again.

NOTES. Pedro del Páramo, native of Carrión de los Condes, son of
Juan del Páramo and María del Campo, received permission to go to the
Indies on February 28, 1528 (Bermúdez Plata, *Pasajeros*, I, 249). To indicate something of the name's rarity, there is no other Páramo in the
whole first volume, running from 1509 to 1534; one Páramo occurs in the
second volume, and two are in the third, none of them a Pedro.

Busto's valuable treatment of Páramo is in his "Tres conversos," *Revista
de Indias* 17 (1967):435–438. His source for Páramo's activity in Panama
is AGI, Justicia 363, which this writer has not seen. Busto assumes that
Páramo was of Jewish descent, apparently for no better reason than that
another man called him a Jew in an argument.

The only known documentary references to Páramo in Peru, aside from
the roll of Cajamarca, are in AGI, Contaduría 1825, records from San
Miguel, August, 1532, and ANP, PA 96, PA 117.

Robles sastre

Role: Footman   Trade: Tailor
Share: ½ share of gold and silver

Only this man's trade of tailoring and his correspondingly small reward are known to us with certainty. He was probably the Francisco de

Robles seen in the company of Francisco Martínez, one of the other tailors, at Jauja on March 1, 1534. If so, he did not take a direct part in the conquest of Cuzco.

NOTES. The Francisco de Robles who was at Jauja in March, 1534 (HC 61), is not to be confused with a Francisco de Robles from Segovia who left Spain in September, 1534, and was in Peru for many years thereafter (Bermúdez Plata, *Pasajeros*, I, 335; AGI, Lima 566, vol. IV, August 16, 1541).

Among the men recruited for the Peru venture in Nicaragua in 1529 was a Pedro de Robles, shoemaker; but the Spaniards were not prone to confuse shoemakers and tailors, and this is no doubt a different man altogether (*CDIHN*, II, 35–37, 41, 46, 56, 62). Present at the same time and place as Pedro de Robles was "a tailor called Rojas," but there is even less reason to assume that he is the person sought (*CDIHN*, II, 35). He is mentioned only because there has been some uncertainty about the name of the man at Cajamarca; while three versions of the general list have "Robles," the fourth and best known gives "Rodas." This writer believes that "Robles" is correct because of the three-to-one preponderance and because a Robles appears in another contemporary record, whereas no Rodas does. Busto continues to believe the man's name was Rodas, and asserts by a further deduction that he was killed at Vilcaconga on the way to Cuzco in 1533 ("Los innominados en el reparto de Cajamarca," pp. 93–94; "Los caídos en Vilcaconga," I: 117).

Juan de Salinas herrador

Age at Cajamarca: Probably over 30
Role: Horseman
Share: Double share of gold and silver

Place of origin: Born in Córdoba, grew up in Jerez de la Frontera (Andalusia)
Extent of literacy: Could sign his name
Trade: *Herrador* (horseshoer and veterinarian)

Juan de Salinas was born in Córdoba into a family of artisans or other humble people, though he had an uncle who was a friar. When Juan was seven or eight this uncle took him to Jerez de la Frontera, where he taught him some rudiments of writing, and put him to the trade of *herrador* or horseshoer. By about 1515 Salinas was in the Indies, and in the early 1520's he took part in the conquest of Mexico, the only one of the men of Cajamarca known to have done so. In all probability he was involved only marginally or in the later phases;

otherwise he would never have left Mexico. In 1524–1525 he accompanied Cortés on his expedition to Honduras, and from that impoverished and strife-torn region he went to Nicaragua in 1527. From Nicaragua he came to Peru with Benalcázar.

In the conquest of Peru, Salinas was a man to be reckoned with, though there were limits beyond which a practicing artisan could not rise. He was one of the most experienced even among the veterans of Nicaragua, and his trade was of special importance. The *herrador*, as both horseshoer and veterinarian, was responsible for the welfare of horses, which were an expedition's principal weapon against Indians and the individual conquerors' principal fortune. Juan de Salinas cannot have been the original *herrador* of the Peru expedition, since he was not in Panama when it was organized. (He was listed as *herrador* on the roll of Cajamarca only to distinguish him from another Juan de Salinas.) As an expert on horses, Salinas was a good horseman and owned a good horse, a fast-running silver-grey mare that kept him at the front when the Spaniards were engaged in pursuit. At Cajamarca he got a horseman's full double share, though his name comes near the end of the list.

Salinas resisted the first urges to return to Spain. He became a citizen and encomendero of Jauja, then moved to Lima at its founding in 1535, but no sooner was he there than he started planning to leave. He sold his mare, prepared a memorial of his services, and was on his way home by late 1535 or early 1536. On the way across the Atlantic he disembarked with all his gold and silver in the Azores in order to enter Spain through Portugal and avoid having his fortune seized by the officials in Seville. Apparently he got away with it. By November, 1536, he was in Córdoba arranging for an inquiry into the orthodoxy of his lineage, and in 1537 the royal court granted him a coat of arms. Nothing more is known of him, but he doubtless settled in Córdoba or Jerez de la Frontera, if he lived.

NOTES. The presumption that Salinas was born before 1502 rests mainly on his assertion in 1535 that he had been in the Indies for twenty years, or since about 1515. He lived in Córdoba until he was seven or eight, and he must have been in Jerez de la Frontera for several years, since he once called himself a native of Jerez (*CDIAO*, X, 276). Salinas's *probanza de servicios*, made in Lima in 1535, and his *probanza de limpieza*, made in Córdoba in 1536, are in AGI, Lima 204.

There were several other people named Juan de Salinas in Peru in the conquest period, some of them prominent enough and close enough in time to give rise to confusion. There was Juan de Salinas de la Hoz (q.v.), also at Cajamarca. Another Juan de Salinas arrived in 1533 with Almagro, became a citizen of Cuzco at its founding, then left for Spain in the late 1530's, having been in the siege of Cuzco; he was sometimes called Juan de Salinas Farfán. He was an educated man, cousin of a Licenciado Pedro Farfán, and could write beautifully and fluently. His home was Jerez, but we do not know which one, because one source names Jerez de Badajoz, another Jerez de la Frontera; the writer suspects the first is correct. After living in Madrid for many years, this Juan de Salinas returned to Peru in 1555, now calling himself Juan Pantiel de Salinas. He seems to have held government posts in Peru, and he was alive in Lima in 1562.

Yet another man of the same name, calling himself at times Juan de Salinas Loyola, came to Peru in 1535. He was in the siege of Lima and various civil conflicts until, in the late 1540's, he had a hand in settling the inland area of southern Ecuador and northern Peru, containing the towns of Loja, Zamora, and Jaén. For a time he served as governor of this area, with Piura as his headquarters. He was still living in Peru in 1565.

Further references to Juan de Salinas herrador are in AGI, Contaduría 1825, records from Lima, 1535; ANP, PA 75, 118, 721, 722, 725, 734; Busto, "El herrero, el barbero y el gran volteador," *Mercurio Peruano* 43 (1962):67–70; *Libros de cabildos de Lima*, I, 8–10; Porras, *Cartas*, p. 219; Porras, *Cedulario*, II, 354; Porras, in Trujillo, *Relación*, p. 102.

For Juan de Salinas Farfán see AGI, Justicia 1074, no. 6; Lima 566, vol. IV, July 27, 1540; Patronato 90, no. 1, ramo 11; 105, ramo 9; 109, ramo 4; 185, ramo 10; ANP, PA 58; HC 421; Bermúdez Plata, *Pasajeros*, III, 183; Enríquez de Guzmán, *Vida y costumbres*, p. 325; Porras, "Dos documentos esenciales," *Revista Histórica* 17 (1948):91–93.

For Juan de Salinas Loyola, see AGI, Patronato 113, ramo 7.

Juan de Segovia

Role at Cajamarca: Trumpeter
Share: ¾ share of gold
and silver

Place of origin: Cogolludo, near Guadalajara
in northeastern New Castile
Parents: Juan de Segovia and
Juana de Buruébano

Juan de Segovia was the junior of the two trumpeters at Cajamarca; his colleague Pedro de Alconchel received a full share of the treasure to his three-fourths. The two trumpeters and the black piper and crier, Juan García, were often together, from Coaque on the north coast to

Cajamarca, and beyond to Cuzco. Since Juan García and Alconchel were the most obvious sort of plebeians, the same may be presumed of Segovia. In 1533 Alconchel achieved a certain fame at Vilcaconga by alerting Hernando de Soto and his surrounded vanguard with trumpet blasts sounding across the miles, that help was on the way. No one recorded the name of the trumpeter of Soto who replied to Alconchel, but it must have been Segovia. He enrolled among the citizens of Cuzco at its Spanish foundation in March, 1534, then went back north to Jauja with the main body of the conquerors. Perhaps he meant to return to Spain as other men were then doing, perhaps not; the issue was settled when he died in Jauja in late 1534.

Since he had not made a will, the fortune he left behind went into the hands of the custodians of the estates of the deceased—notoriously reluctant to disgorge what they were so quick to take—and when Juan's uncle, Diego de Segovia, also a trumpeter, decided to come to Peru to collect the inheritance, he had little apparent luck. In 1544 he was living in the house of Juan's old trumpeter companion Pedro de Alconchel, now an encomendero of Lima. Diego's fate was no better than Juan's; in 1554 his widow sold his trumpets to be used by some Mexican Indian trumpeters who played in Lima on festive occasions.

NOTES. Segovia's regional origin is given in a cedula mentioning him, in AGI, Lima 566, vol. IV, November 22, 1544. The names of his parents appear there and in Porras, *Cedulario*, II, 97.

Other references to Juan de Segovia are in AGI, Contaduría 1825, records from Coaque, August, 1531; Justicia 1074, no. 9; Lima 566, vol. IV, November 22, 1540; HC 19, 26, 28, 58; Porras, "Dos documentos esenciales," *Revista Histórica* 17 (1948):91–93.

For Diego de Segovia, see AGI, Contaduría 1680, records from Lima, 1554; BNP, A30, ff.367–372; Porras, *Cedulario*, II, 97, 100.

13. MEN FROM THE SEA

W E CANNOT ASSERT that more than two or three of the conquerors in this section had actually been sailors, either in the Indies or on the other side of the Atlantic. But they were from maritime regions, in most cases had the diagnostic characteristics of seamen, and above all lived in close association with each other. Of the eleven men included here, no less than eight had a partner or constant companion within the group. The pairs are Aguirre and Anadel, Beltrán and Pérez, Bueno and Moguer, and González and Romero. If the habit of close and long-lasting relationships like this did not originate in the maritime world, it was at least unusually prevalent there.

Only two of our men, Peto and Alonso Pérez, were in origin much above the status of the lowest plebeian, though several eventually rose beyond that position. Among men in other chapters, one of the expedition's hidalgos, Sebastián de Torres, was somehow connected with the sea; so may have been the two Greeks, Candía and Griego, and some of the artisans, not to speak of the more obscure figures.

Pedro de Aguirre

Age at Cajamarca: About 33   Place of origin: Biscay
Role: Horseman   Extent of literacy: Could sign
Share: Double share of silver and gold   his name

Among the expedition's Basque contingent were Pedro de Aguirre and his partner Pedro de Anadel. The two had shared an encomienda in León, Nicaragua, from 1529, if not earlier. They came to Peru together, probably directly from Nicaragua, with Hernando de Soto. All their business dealings were in common, and they were still together when they left for Spain with the first group of returnees in July, 1533.

Aguirre and Anadel had broad contacts within their Basque circle of sailors, merchants, and artisans. Of the Basques on the expedition, the partners were on close terms with Pizarro's page Gaspar de Marquina and the accountant Nicolás de Azpeitia. They also had connections with Domingo de Soraluce, a merchant important in the discovery of Peru, and with Pascual de Andagoya, would-be rival of Pizarro as hypothetical governor of a district to the north. After reaching Seville in early 1534, the two companions went separate ways, Anadel to the Basque country and Aguirre to Málaga, where he became a citizen, but they still talked together whenever Aguirre visited the north. The best hint we have as to the nature of Aguirre's activities is that in the five years between 1534 and 1539 he visited Biscay four times. This circumstance suggests he had some connection with the sea, as do for that matter his residence in Málaga and the fact that his friend Anadel was a seaman by origin.

NOTES. In 1539 Aguirre said that he was about forty years old and that Biscay was his native country (AGI, Justicia 1124, no. 5, ramo 1). Other references are in AGI, Contratación 576, f.45; ANP, PA 10, 77; *CDIHN*, II, 226.

Pedro de Anadel

Age at Cajamarca: About 46   Place of origin: San Sebastián (Biscay)
Role: Horseman   Extent of literacy: Could not sign his name
Share: Double share of gold   Trade: Probably seaman and carpenter
   and silver   or wood-dresser

Most of the known particulars of Anadel's life—his Basque connections, his residence in Nicaragua, his early return to Spain—are treated under his partner Pedro de Aguirre, just above. Anadel may have had even longer experience in the Indies than Aguirre; his name appears among the conquerors of Nicaragua in 1524, and there is good reason to believe that he had been in Panama for several years before that. His illiteracy points to a humble origin. Apparently one of the many seamen and artisans the Basque country sent to America, he can almost certainly be identified with an encomendero of Panama who in 1522 declared himself a mariner and wood-worker. Like many Basque names, his had several versions, including Pedro de Oyanader and Pedro Martínez de Oyanader. Not long after arrival in Seville, Anadel went home to San Sebastián, where he was living in 1539.

NOTES. Chaos reigned concerning Basque names. The Basques themselves were affected by chronic indecision, and the Castilian notaries made a hash of all versions. Given this state of things, Pedro de Anadel probably is identical with a Pedro de Onardes (final "s" is almost indistinguishable from "l"), who was an encomendero in Panama in 1522. This person, who had come to the Indies around 1517, was Basque, and gave his trades as man of the sea and *hachero*, presumably wood-cutter, lumberman, or the like (Góngora, *Grupos*, p. 74). The same man is listed in Medina, *Descubrimiento*, II, 455, as Pedro de Lonardes. Another indication of the contemporary use of *hachero* can be seen in the description of an Ortuño de Baracaldo, also in Panama in 1522, as a Basque seaman who had served "as carpenter and *hachero* and in making canoes and in other useful trades." (Medina, *Descubrimiento*, II, 448). The fact that this very Baracaldo, with the same origin and trades as "Onardes," appears as a trusted associate of Pedro de Anadel in Nicaragua, in 1524, is strong circumstantial proof that "Onardes" and Anadel are the same man (Góngora, *Grupos*, p. 51).

Anadel's age and origin are given in AGI, Justicia 1124, no. 5, ramo 1. There Pedro Martínez de Oyanader, citizen of San Sebastián, declares in 1539 that he is about fifty-three.

Other references are in AGI, Contaduría 576, f.45; ANP, PA 10, 67, 77; *CDIHN*, I, 500; II, 226; IV, 125, 238–239, 277.

Hernando Beltrán

Age at Cajamarca: About 30 or 35
Role: Horseman
Share: Double share of gold and silver

Place of origin: The Seville-Huelva region, probably Triana
Extent of literacy: Illiterate

There can be little doubt that Hernando Beltrán was by origin a sailor. His first reported activity in the Indies was helping to build ships; in Peru he was in constant association with the seamen of Seville and Huelva. Back in Spain, he chose Seville's maritime district of Triana for his residence, and most of the witnesses to the memorial of services he prepared in Seville in 1536 were sailors. He was, however, ambitious to be more than a sailor, as he showed by riding a horse in the conquest of Peru. On the basis of his exploits he obtained an elaborate coat of arms, referring to his action in the Quito campaign of taking a mountain defended by Indians. In the memorial, one of his best friends in Triana told vaguely of hearing that Beltrán's grandparents had come from the mountains of Castile and were hidalgos, but all the other witnesses described him only as a good and honored person or an Old Christian.

Beltrán had been on the Pacific Coast since about 1520, taking part in all phases of the discovery and conquest of Nicaragua. He came to Peru directly from Nicaragua with Sebastián de Benalcázar and was one of those who went back with Benalcázar to guard the coastal town of San Miguel after Cajamarca. He also followed Benalcázar's trail north to Quito, rather than going south like most to Cuzco. After the foundation of Quito, Beltrán returned to Spain in 1535, without ever having been a citizen of any of the new towns. He settled in Triana immediately, and he was still living there ten years later, in 1546.

NOTES. In 1543 Beltrán was a citizen of Triana, declaring himself to be about forty (AGI, Patronato 90, no. 1, ramo 11); Porras says that in 1546 he was still living Triana, fifty years old (in Trujillo, *Relación*, p. 82). In the document granting him a coat of arms, he is called a citizen of Seville (Porras, *Cedulario*, II, 315, or Montoto, *Nobiliario*, p. 47). Most of the references listed below, from ANP, PA, show Beltrán consorting with people from Seville or Huelva. Beltrán's *probanza de servicios* is in *CDIHN*, III, 462–487, and in AGI, Patronato 93, no. 6, ramo 1. There Beltrán claims to be one of thirteen men who rode out with Soto to interview Atahuallpa for the first time. His name does not appear on Diego de Molina's list of the men (Oviedo, *Historia*, V, 92), but in the *probanza* his partner, Alonso Pérez de Vivero, who is on that list, corroborates Beltrán's claim.

There are references to Beltrán in ANP, PA 55, 63, 65, 66, 69, 71, 82, 84, 85, 97, 106, 159; HC 65; Góngora, *Grupos*, p. 50.

Martín Bueno

Age at Cajamarca: About 35
Role: Footman
Share: 1 share of gold; ¾ share of silver

Place of origin: Moguer
(coast of Andalusia)
Extent of literacy: Illiterate

The chronicler Cieza de León was so impressed with the inequities of the division of the treasure of Cajamarca that he refrained from giving the amounts, in order not to cause his readers trouble of mind. The failure to give a full share or better to Martín Bueno might seem one of the most striking of the injustices. Bueno was one of three men sent from Cajamarca to Cuzco, while the city was still under Inca control, to survey the riches there and expedite their transportation. Bueno and his companions made but poor ambassadors, says Cieza, since they did not respect the sanctities of the Incas, and laughed aloud at the fuss the Incas made over three such ordinary fellows as themselves. But they succeeded in their principal mission and escorted untold amounts of gold back to Cajamarca.

While Moguer, Bueno's home, was synonymous with the sea, and illiteracy was a badge of the seaman, there is no specific evidence that Bueno had been a sailor. Some modest commercial activity that he engaged in around the time of Cajamarca does not serve to distinguish him from the many others doing the same thing. Bueno arrived in Peru with Benalcázar, so he must have had some experience in Nicaragua. Having seen the conquest through, he returned to Spain in 1535 and settled in Moguer, where he was living in 1543.

NOTES. In 1543 Bueno declared that he was forty-seven years old and a citizen of Moguer (Patronato 90, no. 1, ramo 11). Busto asserts that the man of Cajamarca was a Pero Martín Bueno, shipmaster, who was sailing between the Isthmus and Spain in 1526 ("Pero Martín Bueno," *Mercurio Peruano*, no. 478 [March–April, 1969], pp. 746–753). Busto's only reasons for thinking so are the name and the fact that the master of 1526 was involved with a sailor named Jorge Griego (like one of the men of Cajamarca). There is no reason to accept this identification. There must have been scores of sailors on the Atlantic named Jorge Griego. Moreover, the Martín Bueno and the Jorge Griego of Cajamarca are never seen in any kind of association. It would have been most unusual for a shipmaster on the Atlantic not only to venture onto the Pacific Coast but to accept a lower position. Also, the Pero Martín Bueno of 1526 seems to have been able to sign his name, which Martín Bueno of Cajamarca could not. Above all, Busto never faces the question of the difference in name of the two men. The shipmaster is always called Pero Martín Bueno or Pero Martín. The name of the man of Cajamarca appears many times in documents drafted at Cajamarca and in Spain, as well as in chronicles, but never does it assume any other form than simple Martín Bueno.

There are references to Martín Bueno in AGI, Indiferente General 1801, records of ship *Santa Catalina*, 1535; ANP, PA 14, 48, 56, 57, 80, 116; Cieza, *Tercera parte*, in *Mercurio Peruano* 38 (1957):263, 266; Muñoz de San Pedro, *Tres testigos*, 3rd ed., p. 121; Pedro Pizarro, *Relación*, V, 183; Porras, *Relaciones primitivas*, p. 82; Porras, in Trujillo, *Relación*, p. 83.

Pedro Catalán

Role at Cajamarca: Footman   Place of origin: Probably Catalonia
Share: ½ share of silver;
  ¾ share of gold

From his name alone there is a strong likelihood that Pedro Catalán was a seaman, like the Luis Catalán who was a sailor on one of the ships supplying the expedition of 1531–1532. That Pedro's name also indicates his birthplace (very probable, in any case) is made nearly certain by a reference to him as "the Catalan." A citizen of Lima at its founding, he died there before August of 1536, leaving behind a fortune. His widow, Antonía de Sosa, later came to Lima to try to recover his estate, but, failing in that, married another encomendero of Lima.

NOTES. In Lima on August 14, 1536, Royal Factor Illán Suárez de Carvajal asked for the grant of a lot "que era del catalán" (Torres Saldamando, *Libro primero de cabildos*, I, 95). "Pedro Catalán, vecino desta ciudad de Los Reyes" figures in a 1535 document among the Peruvian manuscripts of the Lilly Library. Pedro Catalán is listed on accounts of the estates of the deceased, written in Lima in 1541 (AGI, Justicia 1074, no. 9). In Lima, on February 10, 1543, Antonía de Sosa, wife of Francisco de Talavera, empowered him to recover the estate of her first husband, Pedro Catalán (ANP, Salinas 1542–1543, ff.713–714).

Luis Catalán is mentioned in HC 3, 7, and 11.

Nuño González

Age at Cajamarca: Probably about 30   Share: 1 share of silver; no gold
Role at Cajamarca: Footman   Extent of literacy: Illiterate

González was a veteran of the Indies. He and his partner, Alonso Romero, had known each other since the early 1520's, when they met in Santo Domingo. Fortune carried them eventually to Nicaragua, and from there they came with Benalcázar to Peru. Together they followed the conquest as far as Cuzco and then in 1534 returned to Jauja, where, we are told, both were involved in a fight that left a fellow Spaniard dead. Romero then returned to Spain. At that point we lose González's trail; if he lived, he no doubt did the same as his partner. González's long association with Romero, their illiteracy, and their association with the earlier, more maritime and Andalusian phase of the conquest, arouse the suspicion that González was from the Huelva area as Romero was, and that both were seamen.

NOTES.   A rough estimate of Nuño Gonzalez's age is made on the basis of his long experience alone. In AGI, Patronato 93, no. 4, ramo 3 (Romero's *probanza de servicios*), González directly states that he is Romero's partner.

In 1550 a man named Iñigo González testified in Seville in a memorial of services of Benalcázar (AGI, Justicia 1160, no. 1, ramo 1, published in Quito, *Colección de documentos relativos al . . . Benalcázar*, pp. 418–421). His record is so much like Nuño González's that it is hard to believe that the two men are not one. Iñigo González was a citizen of Seville, forty-seven years old in 1550, and illiterate. He came to Peru with Benalcázar, and in answer to a question about whether Benalcázar accompanied Pizarro in the whole conquest, until Atahuallpa was taken and the land was under control, he said he had been present at it all. Iñigo González then remained in Peru proper while Benalcázar conquered Quito, but he returned to Spain shortly after that and lived in Seville the whole time to 1550. Since González could not sign his name, the officiating notary could very easily have written down "Iñigo" for the very similar name "Nuño." Moreover, downright lying about participation at Cajamarca was extremely rare. Nevertheless, since conclusions based on the assumption that contemporaries made a mistake are extremely dubious, it seems best to leave the reader to judge the probabilities of the case.

Other references to Nuño González are in AGI, Lima 565, vol. III, September 5, 1539; ANP, PA 19, 118, 126, 146; HC 56.

Pedro de Moguer

Role at Cajamarca: Footman
Share: 1 full share of gold
   and silver

Place of origin: Moguer
   (Andalusian coast)
Extent of literacy: Illiterate

His full name, which he used more as he became more established
in Peru, was Pedro Martín de Moguer. While we cannot be sure of
his background, there are the congruent signs that his home town of
Moguer lived from the sea, and he was illiterate as were most seamen.

Pedro de Moguer achieved mention in several of the chronicles of
the conquest as one of three men, along with his companion from Moguer, Martín Bueno, and the Basque notary Juan de Zárate, who were
sent to Cuzco, before it was occupied by Spaniards, to collect treasure
and take possession in the name of the king. Moguer seems to have
been the senior man of the party. Some accounts, including that of the
contemporary Pedro Pizarro, leave out the notary as a mere adjunct.
Of the other two, Moguer received the larger share at the distribution
of treasure. Apparently he had a reputation as a good scout or runner,
since he was again chosen (with Diego de Agüero) to reconnoiter upper Peru as far as Lake Titicaca after the Spanish foundation of Cuzco
in 1534. He then settled in the town he was one of the first Spaniards
to see, but he had hardly lived there two years when he was killed by
Sana Indians of his encomienda, as a massive Indian rebellion began to
take shape in 1536.

NOTES. Porras says (in Trujillo, *Relación*, p. 83), without giving a
source, that Pedro de Moguer was from Moguer; this is in any case highly
likely from the very name of Pedro Martín de Moguer, he having doubtless
adopted the name of his home town to distinguish himself from the many
other Pedro Martíns in the Indies. A final confirmation of his origin is his
constant association with people from the Huelva-Seville area, and particularly the fact that his fellow explorer of Cuzco, Martín Bueno, was from
Moguer.

References to Pedro de Moguer are in AGI, Contaduría 1824, records
from May to July, 1535; 1825, records from Cuzco, 1535; Patronato 185,
ramo 10; ANP, PA 3, 6, 7, 14, 29, 53, 55, 56, 57, 81, 89, 96; HC 86;
CDIAO, IX, 576; Cieza, *Tercera parte*, in *Mercurio Peruano* 38 (1957):
263, 266; Pedro Pizarro, *Relación*, V, 183, 198; Porras, "Dos documentos
esenciales," *Revista Histórica* 17 (1948): 92; Porras, *Relaciones primitivas*,
p. 92.

Alonso Pérez

Age at Cajamarca: About 40   Place of origin: The Seville area,
Role: Horseman   possibly Triana
Share: Double share of gold and silver   Extent of literacy: Literate

Though listed on the roll of Cajamarca as plain Alonso Pérez, he had long called himself Alonso Pérez de Vivero or Viveros, which in this case was not a dubious surname added after the man had become rich and well known. Actually, Alonso Pérez was already quite well known among the veterans of Nicaragua, for he was one of the oldest and most experienced of them all. He had been in the Caribbean, in Darién and Santo Domingo, as early as 1518 or 1519. He took part in the discovery of Nicaragua under Gil González de Avila in 1522, and returned there the next year with Francisco Hernández de Córdoba, both times in the company of his inseparable friend, Hernando Beltrán. He seems to have shared a maritime origin with Beltrán, though he was more literate. Ever since he had been in the Indies he had known and at times followed Sebastián de Benalcázar; with Benalcázar he and Beltrán came to Peru.

In Peru Alonso Pérez was a man of consequence, called upon as a witness to documents much more frequently than most of his fellows. He also had one of the best horses, since he was picked to go on the most dangerous and prestigious exploit of the whole campaign, Soto's ride with a dozen men into the Inca camp to interview Atahuallpa. He did not, as might have been expected, return to Spain immediately in 1533 with the old veterans, but saw the conquest through before leaving with the largest contingent of returnees in late 1534, and he arrived in Seville on the *San Miguel* in 1535. He carried only gold, since he had already sold his silver to a merchant, payable in Seville, thus avoiding the risk of loss and the near certainty of seizure. In general, Alonso Pérez seems to have been a capable man of affairs.

Once back in Spain, he settled in Triana, the maritime district of Seville, and lived there the rest of his life. In 1537 the king granted him the coat of arms to which many returning conquerors aspired. Alonso Pérez was frequently sought out to testify in matters concerning Peru; having spent so much of his life in the Indies, he was not able to dismiss them from his mind but carried on correspondence across the sea and questioned fresh arrivals in Seville. He is last seen in 1550, testifying on behalf of his old companion Sebastián de Benalcázar.

NOTES. Alonso Pérez's constant association with men from the Seville-Huelva area leaves no doubt that he was originally from there; moreover, settling in Triana was a very specific act. He is described as a citizen of Triana in AGI, Patronato 90, no. 1, ramo 11; *CDIHN*, III, 469–474; and Quito, *Colección de documentos relativos al . . . Benalcázar*, pp. 389–393. There he declared his age in 1536 as forty-five; in 1543 as fifty-one; in 1550 as sixty. His testimony there, and particularly in the Benalcázar collection, is basic for tracing his life.

Other references are in AGI, Indiferente General 1801, records of ship *San Miguel*, 1535; Lima 204, *probanza* of Hernán Gonzales; Patronato 93, no. 6, ramo 1; ANP, PA 45, 55, 56, 69–71, 77, 85, 97, 106, 127, 130; Oviedo, *Historia*, V, 92; Porras, *Cedulario*, II, 316; Porras, in Trujillo, *Relación*, p. 82.

Alonso Peto

Role at Cajamarca: Horseman
Share: 1¾ shares of gold
   and silver

Place of origin: Palos
  (Andalusian coast)
Extent of literacy: Could sign his name

Alonso Peto, or Prieto, belonged to one of several Palos families prominent in navigation and commerce. The whole maritime region of Huelva, Palos, and Moguer was strongly plebeian in flavor, with few of the hidalgo pretensions of inland Castile, yet the Petos were substantial people. They were literate, unusual enough in Palos; a namesake of Alonso Peto's was a shipmaster on the route between the Isthmus and Seville and another relative became a member of the town council of Niebla, a few miles from Palos.

Peto had experience in Nicaragua, probably in conjunction with a kinsman, Alvaro Alonso Peto, who had been there since 1529 at least. Both men seem to have left active navigation to pursue wealth and honors on land. Alonso came to Peru from Nicaragua with Sebastián de Benalcázar. As far as is known he was in no way outstanding among the conquerors, and his share of the treasure at Cajamarca was less than standard for a horseman. Most of his contacts were with his modest compatriots of the Andalusian maritime area. After staying in Peru through the main events of the conquest, he left in 1534, when general license was given, and arrived in Seville in 1535, with a large fortune. Alvaro Alonso Peto followed him to Peru by 1534, saw the conquest of Quito, and then in his turn went back to Spain.

NOTES. The evidence for Peto's place of origin and his relationships is purely circumstantial, but so strong as to be certain. The alternation between the names Peto and Prieto is exceedingly rare, yet it is observed in both of the Alonso Petos and in Alvaro Alonso Peto. The principals and witnesses in three documents mentioning Alonso Peto in Peru are heavily from Palos, Moguer, and Triana (ANP, PA 55, 142; HC 56). When Alonso returned he carried money for only one other person, Rodrigo Alvarez, a merchant of Palos. (AGI, Indiferente General 1801, records of ship *San Miguel*; Contratación 2715, no. 1, ramo 2. In the latter, Rodrigo Alvarez appears as a partner of a Juan Quintero, Quintero being a specific Palos name.) Alvaro Alonso, when he returned, was a citizen of Palos, lived in Trigueros, and was *regidor* in Niebla (AGI, Justicia 734, no. 3; Patronato 90, no. 1, ramo 11).

Busto also thinks Alonso Peto was Andalusian, but identifies him with Alvaro Alonso ("Una relación y un estudio," *Revista Histórica* 27 [1964]: 315). This is natural enough, yet Alonso was in Jauja on July 27, 1534, when Alvaro Alonso was well on his way to Quito (ANP, PA 142, 172). And Alvaro Alonso then came back to Lima when it was founded, while Alonso was already on his way across the sea (PA 692). In AGI, Patronato 90, no. 1, ramo 11, all the men who were at Cajamarca are asked to testify about it, and Alvaro Alonso is not so asked.

Further references to Alonso Peto are in AGI, Justicia 723, list of gold and silver seized in 1535; Herrera, *Décadas*, XI, 43; Cieza, *Tercera parte*, in *Mercurio Peruano* 36 (1955):470; the "Diego" Prieto in the latter is doubtless a mistake or mistranscription for Alonso. Further references to Alvaro Alonso Peto are in AGI, Patronato 150, no. 6, ramo 1; ANP, PA 171, 694, 703; *CDIHN*, II, 225.

Other information about the Petos of Palos is in AGI, Contratación 2715, no. 1, ramo 1, records of galleon *San Salvador*, 1533 (mention of Alonso Prieto, merchant, *vecino* of Palos); no. 1, ramo 2, records of galleon *San Antón*, 1533 (with passenger Alonso Peto from Palos); and records of ship *San Marcos* (whose master, Alonso Prieto, is connected with Nuño Rodríguez, *vecino* of Palos); *CDIHN*, III, 142.

Alonso Romero

Age at Cajamarca: Probably over 30
Role: Standard-bearer (and footman)
Share: 1 full share of gold and silver

Place of origin: Lepe (Andalusian coast near Portugal)
Extent of literacy: Illiterate

Romero's illiteracy and his origin in the seaside town of Lepe point to a maritime background, confirmed to a certain extent by his choice of Seville's portside district of San Lorenzo for a residence after his return to Spain. He came to the Indies around 1520 or 1522, and was successively in Santo Domingo, Honduras, Nicaragua, Panama, and then in Nicaragua again, most of the time with his partner Nuño González (q.v.). From Nicaragua the two came to Peru in the contingent of Benalcázar. On arrival or thereafter, Romero achieved the distinction of appointment as ensign or standard-bearer; he claimed to have been "chief" or "royal" ensign, but we know that Diego de Agüero, a horseman and man of importance, served as ensign too. In the pre-Cajamarca phase the Pizarros saw themselves forced to lavish often meaningless titles and posts of command on their men, particularly the reinforcements, to keep them satisfied. Since Romero was a footman at Cajamarca, he must have been the man beside Governor Pizarro who hoisted his standard as the signal for the onslaught to begin. Romero is near the top of the list of footmen on the general roll, with the full share that went only to a minority.

After Cajamarca, Romero became a horseman and followed the conquest on to Cuzco, still collecting minor honors. He was the first man to enter the great fortress of Cuzco, Sacsahuamán, and Pizarro made him its alcaide or warden. He enrolled as a citizen at the founding of Cuzco but almost immediately thereafter left for Jauja and then Spain, arriving in 1535. In Seville he resumed life with his wife, whom he had married before going to the Indies. She was the daughter of a merchant, and their children advanced in station, some becoming nuns and friars; one served as treasurer of the Duke of Béjar. After some years in Seville, Alonso Romero died, but his children and even his grandchildren continued to seek favors from the crown on the basis of the merit he had acquired in the Indies.

NOTES. Romero's estimated age rests on the fact that he was already married in about 1520–1521. A *probanza de servicios*, made partly in Cuzco in 1534 and partly posthumously in Spain in 1577, is the main source for Romero's life (AGI, Patronato 93, no. 4, ramo 3). There a priest, Alonso de Jerez, citizen of Lepe, says that he and Romero are from the same town. See also Busto, "Una relación y un estudio," *Revista Histórica* 27 (1964):310–313; Busto there uses certain sources not directly consulted by this writer.

Other references are in AGI, Contaduría 1825, records from Jauja, November, 1534; Lima 565, vol. III, September 5, 1539; ANP, PA 51, 52, 70, 111; Porras, "Dos documentos esenciales," *Revista Histórica* 17 (1948): 91–93.

Bartolomé Sánchez marinero

Role: Footman   Trade: Sailor
Share: ¾ share of gold and silver

The most revealing bit of information we have about Bartolomé Sánchez—that he was a man of the sea—comes from the roll of Cajamarca itself. Definite confirmation that *marinero* was not merely some kind of epithet can be seen in a list of fines imposed on various miscreants in January, 1532, where "Bartolomé Sánchez, marinero" appears in the midst of a dozen other sailors. From this it would appear that Sánchez had not been a member of the expedition proper until that time, when the Spaniards had reached the island of Puná and were about to enter central Peru at Túmbez. Sánchez's calling constitutes a fairly good definition of his background, since sailors were mainly plebeian and illiterate, looked down upon by the inland Castilians. Almost all of them came from coastal lands, whether of Iberia or of the Mediterranean; with an Hispanic name, Bartolomé Sánchez was most likely from Seville-Huelva, Portugal, or the north coast. He may have headed south from Cajamarca with the expedition in 1533; then he disappears.

N O T E S . There are only two authenticated references to Bartolomé Sánchez marinero: on the roll of Cajamarca and in AGI, Contaduría 1825, Penas de Cámara, January, 1532.

Surely a different man was Bartolomé Sánchez de Terrazas, usually called Bartolomé de Terrazas, who first appears in the records of the conquerors in 1533 and would seem to have arrived in Peru with Almagro. He was from Talavera de la Reina, far inland in New Castile, and the son of an apothecary. A founding citizen of Cuzco and at some point a councilman, he was associated with Almagro's side in the civil conflicts, then managed to recuperate his position to some extent, retaining an encomienda in Cuzco. Garcilaso knew him in the 1550's and thought him a noble, liberal man with all the virtues of a cavalier. He also thought him a "first conqueror."

In September, 1533, a Bartolomé Sánchez, definitely not Terrazas, because both appear in the same document, was in Huaylas, between Cajamarca and Jauja (ANP, PA 62). We cannot be sure that this was the man of Cajamarca, however, because yet a third Bartolomé Sánchez took part in the conquest of Peru, a man from Miajadas in Extremadura, who returned to Spain in 1535 (AGI, Justicia 1082, no. 1, ramo 4). Another namesake in the early period was the Galician Bartolomé Sánchez, who was town crier in Lima in 1535–1536 (ANP, Juzgado, December 15, 1536; *Libro de cabildos de Lima*, 1:47). The regional origin is plausible, but the post was too lowly for a man who had shared in the gold of Cajamarca.

For Bartolomé de Terrazas, see AGI, Contaduría 1824, records from Cuzco, March, 1536; Patronato 185, ramo 11; ANP, PA 50, 62; Bermúdez Plata, *Pasajeros*, I, 174; Garcilaso, *Obras*, II, 366; Diego Fernández, *Historia*, I, 333; Porras, *Cartas*, 301–302; Porras, *Cedulario*, II, 312; Porras, "Dos documentos esenciales," *Revista Histórica*, 17 (1948):92.

14. LOWER PLEBEIANS

THE HUMBLE CONQUERORS INCLUDED HERE were all illiterate. With certain notable exceptions, they tended to receive small shares of the treasure of Cajamarca, and few honors and rewards in after times. Several equally lowly persons, with the same hallmarks, can be found among the artisans (chapter 12) and seamen (chapter 13). Humbleness or marginality usually expresses itself in a conjuncture of traits rather than in a single specific one. For that reason no clear line can be drawn between these men and the upper commoners to be found in chapter 11. If the full background were known, Juan Muñoz, who appears here, might go in that category, while such men as the partners Sánchez de Talavera and Valencia might well join the lower grouping.

Juan García de Santa Olalla

Age at Cajamarca: About 26
Role: Footman
Share: ¾ share of gold and silver

Place of origin: Santa Olalla del Cala (Andalusia, north of Seville)
Degree of literacy: Illiterate

Though under the jurisdiction of Seville in the sixteenth century, the town of Santa Olalla lies inland on the edges of the Castilian plateau, where Andalusia and Extremadura come together. For this reason it is hardly likely that Juan García de Santa Olalla was a seaman as were so many of the Andalusians from Seville and Huelva. Perhaps he was the Juan García, carpenter, who was present in Cuzco in 1534. That he was some variety of plebeian is beyond doubt; even when unusual circumstances earned him a royal recommendation, no mention was made of his lineage or connections.

Juan García de Santa Olalla followed the course of the conquest all the way to Cuzco, where he showed some inclination to take root, since he enrolled as a founding citizen and received an encomienda. But soon changing his mind, he joined the last small group of returnees to Spain in 1536. His ship had come within sight of Spanish territory when, just outside the harbor of Sanlúcar de Barrameda, French corsairs seized it and robbed him of his whole fortune, some 16,000 ducats in gold and silver. The loss was too much for him to absorb; unlike the king, who also seized the conquerors' money, the pirates gave no compensating annuities.

Thus it happened that Juan García de Santa Olalla was one of the only three or four of the men of Cajamarca who came back to Peru after having abandoned it, as they thought, for the rest of their lives. Sometime in the later 1530's Juan García arrived in Lima, equipped with royal letters recommending that in view of his great loss he be treated well and reinstated in his encomienda or an equivalent one. But when a man once relinquished his claims and left the country, he broke beyond mending the magic thread of seniority. Then too, encomiendas did not fall vacant every day. So Juan García had to content himself with the grant of a lot and lands in Lima, where he stayed, very much on the margin of things, until a violent episode in the civil wars allowed him to accumulate new merits and become an encomendero in the Cuzco district in 1542. He thereby recouped much of his loss, yet his encomienda was a poor thing compared to the lordly estates of some of his old comrades who had never gone back to Spain.

Perhaps it was the discontent arising from this that caused Juan García to commit himself to the great Gonzalo Pizarro rebellion of 1544–1548 more deeply than most of his fellows and to stay with the movement even as its defeat grew imminent. Juan García died sometime before the final battle in 1548, but royal authorities later confiscated his estate as that of an unrepentant rebel, putting the final touches on a life ruined by French pirates off Sanlúcar in 1536.

NOTES. Juan García's trail can be followed with some confidence as far as his return to Peru and receipt of an encomienda in Cuzco. His participation in the Gonzalo Pizarro rebellion is somewhat obscured by the improbable circumstance that there was in Peru at the same time another Juan García de Santa Olalla, from the Santa Olalla near Toledo, who was also involved in the rebellion and sentenced for it. Nevertheless, since the one who died before sentencing was a citizen and encomendero of Cuzco and the other was not, the main lines are clear enough (Loredo, "Sentencias," *Mercurio Peruano* 22 [1940]:265–266; *CDIAO*, XX, 534).

In Seville, in 1536, Juan García said he was thirty years old, and a native of "Santolalla, tierra de esta ciudad de Sevilla" (AGI, Justicia 1126, no. 2, ramo 1); back in Lima, in 1541, he said he had been present at Cajamarca and gave his age as "over twenty-five" (AGI, Patronato 93, no. 11, ramo 2). Royal cedulas in Porras, *Cedulario*, II, 222–234, 238–239, tell the story of how Juan García lost his fortune and planned to go back to Peru.

Other references are in AGI, Patronato 109, ramo 4; 185, ramo 11; ANP, Salinas 1542–1543, f.130; AHC, Libros de cabildos, I, f.55; *CDIHE*, XXVI, 221–232; Cobo, *Obras*, II, 304; Loredo, *Alardes y derramas*, pp. 123, 127; Loredo, *Los repartos*, p. 103; Pérez de Tudela, *Gasca*, II, 67.

Gómez Gonzáles

Age at Cajamarca: About 33
Role: Footman
Share: ¾ share of gold and silver
Extent of literacy: Illiterate

In March, 1530, Gómez González was living in an Indian village in the jurisdiction of León, Nicaragua, to all appearances working as a tribute collector for some encomendero of León. This was a position usually delegated to the lowly, the incapable, or the recently arrived. González seems to have been lowly enough, but by no means recently arrived, since he had been in Darién to see Balboa go off to discover the Pacific in 1513.

Among González's friends and gambling companions were two other men of Cajamarca: Pedro de Torres, an employee of Hernando de Soto, and Juan Pérez de Tudela. González must have arrived in Peru with one of the groups coming straight from Nicaragua, either

Benalcázar's or Soto's—probably the latter, since he was close to Soto's circle. But though these facts give a partial understanding of González's background, there is not the slightest trace of his action in Peru itself.

N O T E S . In León, Nicaragua, in 1529, Gómez González said he was about thirty and stated that he had arrived in Darién sixteen years previous to that time (Medina, *Descubrimiento*, II, 342). Other references are in *CDIHN*, IV, 534–535, 545–547, 550. In one document transcribed there, González is referred to as an *escribano* (notary), a reading roundly contradicted by three separate indications that he could not write or sign. The word should have been *estante*. See also Busto, "Los presuntos peruleros," *Mercurio Peruano* 50 (1965):317–318.

Jorge Griego

Age at Cajamarca: About 28   Place of origin: Probably Greece
Role: Footman   Extent of literacy: Illiterate
Share: 1 full share of gold and silver

"Jorge Griego" means "George Greek." Neither element of the name sat well on a sixteenth-century Spaniard, not even the "Jorge," which sounded Portuguese. It was the most popular combination of names among the many Greeks in the Spanish Indies, except possibly "Juan Griego." Therefore a Greek connection for the owner of this name can be taken as established beyond reasonable doubt. There does remain the somewhat remote possibility that Jorge Griego was of the second generation, with a Greek father and a Spanish mother, though such people usually adopted Spanish names. Most likely Jorge was a born Greek, attracted to the enterprise in Panama, where he had been for a year or two, by his compatriot Pedro de Candía.

Most Greeks in the Indies were seamen or artillerymen. Griego may well have been both. He seems to have gravitated to Candía and the Italian-Aragonese Martín de Florencia, both of them involved in artillery. After his return to Spain he lived in maritime Triana.

Griego had gained the respect of the Spaniards. He was among the minority of footmen receiving a full share of the treasure of Cajamarca. By the time he reached Cuzco he was on horseback, and his Spanish companion, Sancho de Villegas, entrusted him with collecting his share of the treasure. Back in Jauja he became a full-fledged citizen and encomendero. He was still there to cast his vote when the move to

Lima was decided in December, 1534. Sometime after that he went to Spain. It is possible, but not probable, that he was the Jorge Griego who was in Cuzco during the siege of 1536–1537. In 1544 he was a citizen of Triana, the maritime district across the river from Seville. Having come up in the world, he had taught himself to sign his name, though hardly, one would imagine, to read and write.

NOTES. Torres Saldamando, without giving evidence, asserts that Jorge Griego was from Crete, but he cannot be taken very seriously, for he identifies the man of Cajamarca with practically every Jorge Griego in Peru up to 1570 (*Libro primero de cabildos*, I, 392). Since there were so many men of this name, it means little that the one sentenced in 1548 for complicity in the Gonzalo Pizarro rebellion was a Cretan native (Loredo, "Sentencias," *Mercurio Peruano* 22 [1940]:269; CDIAO, XX, 501). There is no reason either to accept Busto's identification of the man of Cajamarca with a sailor in Nombre de Dios in 1526 ("Pero Martín Bueno," *Mercurio Peruano*, no. 478 [March–April, 1969], pp. 746–753).

In Seville, in 1544, Jorge Griego declared himself a citizen of Triana, forty years old (AGI, Justicia 1125, proceedings concerning the estate of Francisco Martín de Alburquerque). Other references are in AGI, Justicia 724, no. 6; ANP, PA 143; HC 1, 16; Loredo, *Los repartos*, p. 105; Porras, "Dos documentos esenciales," *Revista Histórica* 17 (1948):92.

The presence of a Jorge Griego in Cuzco is documented by AGI, Contaduría 1679, records from Cuzco, 1536, and Contaduría, 1824, records from Cuzco, March–April, 1537. The action of a Jorge Griego during the Gonzalo Pizarro rebellion is described in Calvete, *Rebelión de Pizarro*, IV, 247.

García Martín

Age at Cajamarca: Probably over 25   Share: 1 full share of gold and silver
Role: Footman   Extent of literacy: Illiterate

García Martín was a thorough plebeian who even some years after the conquest claimed only to be an honored person of good life and reputation, qualities far more estimable than high lineage but invariably alleged only in its absence. He had been in the Indies since 1525 or before, in Santo Domingo, Santa Marta, Cartagena, and then Panama. As a veteran and a man skillful with a crossbow, he received a full share of the treasure of Cajamarca.

Martín was at first a citizen of Cuzco and then of Huamanga, since his encomienda was inside the boundaries of the new district carved out in 1539. He was alcalde the first year, and after that perpetual council member. By now certain pretensions were emerging; he acquired a coat of arms, began to call himself García Martín de Castañeda, and learned how to sign his name with surprising success, far better than other old illiterates like Martín Pizarro and Pedro de Alconchel. His encomienda had originally been a good one, but it was near the area where the rebellious Inca still held out, with consequent desertion of Indians and damage, so that by 1548 it was rated seventeenth among the twenty-two encomiendas of the Huamanga district. Still, he maintained his position. He made a good marriage to doña Leonor de Valenzuela, and his son, Juan Pérez de Valenzuela, characteristically named after his mother's lineage, inherited what was left of the encomienda when García Martín died around 1555.

NOTES. García Martín was often called García Martínez, and it was this form that he learned to write. The estimate of his birthdate as probably before 1507 rests on the presumption that he was eighteen or over when he left Santo Domingo for the mainland. His *probanza de servicios*, made in Cuzco in 1539, is in AGI, Lima 118. A posthumous *probanza* is in AGI, Patronato 124, ramo 10.

Busto, in *Francisco Pizarro*, p. 97, says that Pizarro made García Martín leader of a body of twenty crossbowmen while the expedition was on its way from San Miguel to Cajamarca. Such a body was formed, as can be seen in Jerez, *Verdadera relación*, II, 325; and García Martín claims in his *probanza* that he served as a crossbowman, but this writer knows of no other evidence, nor does Busto present any. Jerez speaks of a "captain" of the crossbowmen, and plebeian Martín, listed far down on the roll of Cajamarca, with a good but not unusual share, does not seem a likely candidate for the post.

Other references are in AGI, Contaduría 1824, records from Cuzco, March–April, 1537; Lima 566, vol. IV, July 19, 1540; Patronato 109, ramo 4; 185, ramo 10; HC 34, 41, 60, 61, 1209, 1273, 1315, 1547, 1570; Diego Fernández, *Historia*, I, 349; Loredo, *Los repartos*, pp. 213, 215; Pedro Pizarro, *Relación*, V, 205; Porras, *Cartas*, p. 406.

Juan Muñoz

Age at Cajamarca: About 24
Role: Footman
Share: ¾ share of gold
  and silver

Place of origin: Quesada
  (eastern Andalusia)
Extent of literacy: Crude signature,
  probably illiterate

His blocky signature and the plebeian names of his brother and sister, Pedro Pérez and Mari Muñoz, are sufficient grounds for assuming that Juan Muñoz was of humble origin. In the conquest, he went all the way to Cuzco, and expressed his intention of becoming a citizen there, only to leave the area at the first opportunity. In July, 1534, when Governor Pizarro gave general license to those first conquerors who wished to return and distributed encomiendas to those who were staying, Juan Muñoz chose an encomienda and citizenship in Jauja. In December, 1534, he gave his opinion on moving the city to Lima. Yet almost immediately thereafter he was on his way home. He may have been the "Captain Juan Muñoz" that the newly arrived nobleman and chronicler don Alonso Enríquez de Guzmán found in San Miguel, on the north coast, on July 31, 1535; by September he was in Seville, destined for his home town of Quesada.

NOTES. The Juan Muñoz of Cajamarca was not, as Porras thought (*Relaciones primitivas*, p. 98), a Juan Muñoz Cornejo, who was born c.1500, took some part in the discovery of Peru in the years 1524–1527, and had become an *alcalde ordinario* in Seville by 1554; by his own declaration (AGI, Patronato 98, no. 4, ramo 3) it can be seen that he was not present at the capture of Atahuallpa.

In 1534 Juan Muñoz, the man of Cajamarca, said once that he was thirty (AGI, Lima 204, *probanza* of Hernán González) and once that he was twenty-six (AGI, Patronato 93, no. 4, ramo 1); in 1535 he declared that he was twenty-seven and a citizen of Quesada (AGI, Patronato 93, no. 5, ramo 2).

Other references are in AGI, Contaduría 1825, records from Jauja, December, 1534; ANP, PA 30, 47, 91, 144; HC 58; Enríquez de Guzmán, *Vida y costumbres*, p. 143; *Libros de cabildos de Lima*, I, 8–10; Porras, "Dos documentos esenciales," *Revista Histórica* 17 (1948):92.

Martín Pizarro

Age at Cajamarca: About 23 or 24
Role: Footman
Share: ½ share of gold; ¾ share of silver

Place of origin: Trujillo
Extent of literacy: Illiterate

Contemporaries distinguished between the "good" Pizarros of Extremadura, and the others. Martín, for better or worse, belonged to the others. His small share at Cajamarca in itself suffices to prove that he was no near relative of the Pizarro brothers. Whether there was some very distant connection remains in doubt. By one piece of late and dubious testimony, Martín was Francisco's *deudo*, or relative of some kind (the term extended to the most tenuous ties). By the equally late and dubious Gutiérrez de Santa Clara, Martín was not related in any way to the other Pizarros. The best clue to Martín's background is his brother Juan Pizarro, who later came to Lima and ran a shoemaker's shop for many years. Martín was, then, of a humble family of artisans, not only illiterate, but unable to learn to sign his name as most others of his kind did. Though he had much occasion to sign documents, all his life he contented himself with a pair of rubrics, leaving the name between them to a more practiced hand.

Yet, while not starting on a high level, Martín had certain advantages. He was from Trujillo, he had that special loyalty to the Pizarros, and dependence on them, of the men who were recruited there in 1529. Even if not a relative of the governor's family, his name was one to conjure with. And personally Martín was strong, steady, evenhanded and likable, without the vindictiveness so pronounced in Francisco and Hernando Pizarro; perhaps he was also a bit simple-minded. He became a citizen of Lima and held the encomienda of Huamantanga, with a good income but far from the best in the district. In the first year of the city's existence Martín was made chief constable, an important post though at that time still a subsidiary one, without a seat on the town council. Then from 1540 to 1558 he was four times named alcalde, his seniority and his fairness as a judge outweighing his illiteracy.

Martín lived much more in the center of Lima's society than the equally plebeian Pedro de Alconchel, but there were limits to his rise. He was not a captain in the civil wars, and though he lived in a lordly style, he lacked the business acumen to manage and increase his wealth like some of his companions. He was a close friend of powerful men such as Jerónimo de Aliaga and Diego de Agüero, but his marriage was not as resplendent as theirs. Around 1545 he married Catalina Cermeño, who was not a "doña" and could not be transformed into one, though she was connected with an important family of early conquerors.

When Martín died, in 1557, he was already becoming legendary, and realization of the distinction between him and the other Pizarros was receding. He left numerous heirs—mestizo as well as Spanish, illegitimate and legitimated as well as legitimate. Their lives were not always happy, since they were not too wealthy, and a daughter who suffered from hallucinations was called "the bedeviled," but they found a place in Peru's aristocracy. One son inherited Martín's encomienda; another was among the first Peruvian-born Spaniards to enter the Jesuit order; and a daughter married the son of chronicler Pedro Pizarro, establishing a link with the "good" Pizarros after all.

N O T E S . Busto, in his good and informative article on Martín Pizarro ("El conquistador Martín Pizarro," *Mercurio Peruano* 44 [1963], part 1, pp. 111–125), understands that Martín was a plebeian of some kind, and extends this to the point of saying that Martín's wife was of low origin. However, most of the evidence about the Cermeño women concerns their bad conduct, a trait as often found in ladies as in peasant women. Actually, the marriage was nothing to be ashamed of. In Peruvian marriages, the lady's lineage had to be balanced off against the influence, wealth, and reputation of her relatives in Peru. Some important men married women of plebeian background in order to associate themselves with powerful allies. Martín's marriage was of this type. His wife Catalina was sister of Cristóbal Cermeño, a renowned conquerer of Cuzco, though he died in the 1530's, and of Pedro Cermeño, who was Gonzalo Pizarro's captain of musketeers. Gonzalo Pizarro probably arranged the match to cement relationships among his followers. The Cermeños were not noble, but they were not of the lowest origin either; their father was official gunpowder manufacturer for the Casa de Contratación in Seville. One of Catalina's sisters married Tomás Farel, a Spanish-born Englishman who became an encomendero in Arequipa. Yet another was the wife of Captain Juan Fernández, who was of very humble origin, but became alcalde of Lima; after his death she married the aristocratic Jerónimo de Silva.

An example of Martín's open ingenuousness or simple-mindedness may be found in his testimony in favor of his friend Jerónimo de Aliaga. Aliaga in an interrogatory alleged that the followers of rebel Gonzalo Pizarro had plotted to assassinate him (Aliaga) as their enemy. Martín replied that it was true: before Gonzalo Pizarro's army reached Lima, Martín and Jerónimo strolled out to Pizarro's camp for a friendly chat; Martín got wind that some of the men were angry with Jerónimo, warned him, and the two left hurriedly (*RANP* 1 [1920]:564).

Martín Pizarro gave his age as forty in both 1548 (AGI, Patronato 92, no. 3) and 1549 (*RANP*, 1:556). His posthumous *probanza de servicios* is in AGI, Patronato 132, no. 2, ramo 1. A will of 1542 is in ANP, Salinas 1542–1543, f.775. A substantial biographical note by Porras is in *Testamento de Pizarro*, pp. 77–78.

Other references are in AGI, Justicia 1082, no. 1, ramo 4; Lima 566, vol. IV, August 23, 1541; Patronato 93, no. 11, ramo 1; 97, no. 1, ramo 3; ANP, PA 125, 128, 253, 404, 571, 576; Salinas 1542–1543, ff.656, 701; Salinas 1546–1548, ff.578–579; J. Fernández 1557–1598, f.145; HC 31, 620; *RANP* 1 (1920):460–461, 499, 556–564; 6 (1928):164; 13 (1940):233; Cobo, *Obras*, II, 303; Gutiérrez de Santa Clara, *Quinquenarios*, IV, 171; *Libros de cabildos de Lima*, VI, 1, p. 218; Lockhart, *Spanish Peru*, pp. 19–20; Loredo, *Los repartos*, pp. 115, 221, 227; Torres Saldamando, *Libro primero de cabildos*, II, 318–320.

For the Cermeños, see Busto's article and ANP, Alzate, f.554; Salinas 1542–1543, f.515; AHA, Gaspar Hernández, July 10, 1553; HC 818–821, *RANP* 6 (1928):164; Bermúdez Plata, *Pasajeros*, I, 246; Jiménez de la Espada, *Relaciones geográficas*, I, 162–163.

Pedro Román

Role at Cajamarca: Footman   Extent of literacy: Illiterate
Share: ½ share of gold and silver

His illiteracy and his half share of the treasure of Cajamarca would seem to point to a man humble in more than one respect. However, some accident may account for his small share; Pedro Román subsequently proved to have merit. He became a citizen and encomendero of Cuzco from its founding and distinguished himself as a horseman in resisting the Indians' siege of Cuzco in 1536–1537. At the same time, in Spain, a royal appointment to a seat on Cuzco's council was being issued in his favor. It probably never reached him. Román was one of the minority of Cuzco's citizens so exasperated by the rule of Hernando Pizarro that they joined the forces of Almagro when he came back from Chile in 1537 and seized the city. Thus Román was caught up on the losing side of the first major civil conflict and lost his life fighting for Almagro at the battle of Salinas in April, 1538. He left behind a mestizo daughter, Francisca, and 1,800 marks of silver that in better days he had given to a Pizarro retainer to be taken to Spain.

N O T E S . The chronicler Pedro Pizarro, writing forty years later, gives Román's first name as Juan, but there was only one Román who was encomendero of Cuzco.

Román's place of origin is unknown, but there are two separate, conflicting hints which might lead to the truth if combined with more information. First, a Pero Román, native of Salamanca, son of Pero Román and Marta García, registered to come to the Indies in 1527, which would be about the right time (Bermúdez Plata, *Pasajeros*, I, 217); and the Pedro Román of Cajamarca chose a man from Salamanca (Miguel Cornejo) as one of the executors of his will. However, another of the executors was not from Salamanca (Gonzalo de Zayas; see Justicia 1056, no. 4). Second, pointing in a different direction, Pedro Román showed a certain tendency to associate with men from the Huelva-Palos-Moguer region, and the money he sent home to Spain was destined for Nuño Rodríguez, citizen of Palos, and Hernán Sánchez, citizen of Seville. The present writer's instincts tell him Román was probably from Palos, but this is unscientific.

The most comprehensive document on Román is his power to the executors of his will, contained in AGI, Justicia 1052, no. 3, ramo 2. Other references are in AGI, Contaduría 1824, records from Cuzco, 1536 and 1537; 1825, Penas de Cámara, 1535; Patronato 109, ramo 4; ANP, PA 51; *CDIAO*, XX, 363; *CDIHC*, VI, 397; Pedro Pizarro, *Relación*, V, 208, 211; Porras, "Dos documentos esenciales," *Revista Histórica* 17 (1948): 91–93.

Miguel Ruiz

Role: Horseman
Share: Double share of gold
    and silver

Place of origin: Seville
Parents: Juan Rodríguez de Bañares
    and Argenta Rodríguez
Extent of literacy: Illiterate

"Miguel Ruiz de color loro" was part of the 1531 expedition from the time it left Panama. "Loro" was a term originally used by the Spaniards to describe a tawny or yellowish cast of skin as opposed to the darker mulatto. In practice, however, it was a meliorative synonym for mulatto; a man's friends would call him "loro," his enemies mulatto. Miguel Ruiz would seem to have been the son of a Spaniard and a slave woman, since not only was the name of Miguel's mother—Argenta—very common for a slave, but her last name was the same as that of Miguel's father, indicating that she had doubtless adopted her master's name, as was the common practice in such cases. Argenta may have been black, mulatto, or Morisca, since slave women of all three types were common in Seville; probably she had been freed, and may even have married Juan Rodríguez.

It was not uncommon for a light mulatto, particularly if he had been recognized by his father and given a certain upbringing, to advance to a position of respect in the Indies. Such cases are hard to trace, because the flexibility consisted in a willingness to ignore the ancestry of a cer-

tain individual rather than in a theoretical respect and tolerance for all
mulattoes, and the successful individual was never called a mulatto
again. Such cases were becoming very rare in rich Peru after Cajamarca, but even there the Pizarros' captain of artillery at the battle of
Salinas in 1538 was a "loro" (though it is true they afterward uncere-
moniously hanged him).

Miguel Ruiz was functioning within the Peruvian expedition as a
full-fledged member and man of some weight, far above the level of
the black crier Juan García, with whom, by the way, he does not seem
to have associated. He did not move in the circles of the captains and
hidalgos; rather he was involved in a company with one of the more
obvious plebeians, his Sevillian compatriot Juan Chico, and on the roll
of Cajamarca his name comes toward the end of the list of horsemen.
But to be a horseman at all put a man in the upper third of the conquerors, and Miguel Ruiz received a horseman's full double share, as
some did not. The horse he rode was not his own, however, and he had
to divide his share with its owner, the notary Juan Alonso. After Cajamarca Ruiz followed the course of conquest south, now riding usually
in the vanguard with Hernando de Soto. In November, 1533, when
Soto's men were nearing Cuzco, the Indians attacked them at Vilcaconga near the top of a steep slope, causing the heaviest Spanish casualties yet suffered. One of the men killed was Miguel Ruiz.

At the new distribution of treasure in Cuzco in 1534, Ruiz received
a large share posthumously; his associate Juan Alonso collected the
horse's share, and the rest went to the official custodians of the estates
of the deceased. Ruiz left behind a son, Miguel, probably by one of the
Nicaraguan Indian servant women who accompanied the conquest.
Juan Alonso, who settled in Lima, took in mother and son, and was
appointed Miguel's guardian. At one time he meant to take both Ruiz's
son and his estate back to Spain with him, but he appears not to have
done so. Ruiz's mother in Seville continued to carry on litigation to recover his estate until 1550.

NOTES. The words "Miguel Ruiz de color loro" appear in Contaduría 1825, records from Coaque, 1531. The names and residence of Ruiz's
parents are in AGI, Lima 566, vol. IV, July 31, 1540, and APS, 1550,
oficio XV, libro II, f.332. His relationship with Juan Chico is seen in HC
13, 21, and 22 and his relationship with Juan Alonso in ANP, PA 72 and
Porras, *Cedulario*, II, 351. It is probable that our Miguel Ruiz is the same

as a man of that name who took part in an expedition from Acla on the Isthmus in June, 1529 (Góngora, *Grupos*, p. 28).

Other references are in AGI, Justicia 1079, no. 9, accounts of estates of the deceased; ANP, PA 109; HC 4; Busto, "Los caídos en Vilcaconga," pp. 122–123; Busto, *Francisco Pizarro*, p. 179; Loredo, *Los repartos*, p. 105; Porras, in Trujillo, *Relación*, p. 120; Trujillo, *Relación*, p. 62 .

Cristóbal de Sosa

Age at Cajamarca: Probably early 20's   Share: ¾ share of gold and silver
Role: Footman   Extent of literacy: Illiterate

Cristóbal de Sosa had been in Nicaragua since 1529 or earlier, acting as a page, though it is not quite clear for whom. He was acquainted with the circle of Hernán Ponce de León and Hernando de Soto; probably he accompanied Soto to Peru. After Cajamarca he became joint owner of a horse with another of Soto's men and rode south in the main body of conquerors all the way to Cuzco. He enrolled as a citizen of Cuzco at its foundation and stayed there among the few men guarding the town in late 1534. Most of the guards of Cuzco remained in the region for the rest of their lives.

Sosa, however, was one of the very few men of Cajamarca who gave up an encomienda in Peru to go with Almagro's expedition of discovery and conquest to Chile. The motive of the four or five men who did this may have been the expectation (and not a totally unreasonable one) of yet greater wealth, but more important in most cases was regional affinity with Almagro, or active disaffection with the Pizarros. This is readily imaginable in one of Hernando de Soto's men, most of whom left the country very quickly. Soto himself had negotiated with Almagro for the position of field commander of the expedition, and Sosa might have taken his interest in the venture from his former chief. He may also have been from New Castile like his associate, Vasco de Guevara. At any rate he was to be seen in April and June, 1535, in the company of Almagro's men, making ready for the journey.

He survived the two-year trek, one of the most disappointing the Spaniards ever undertook, and returned to Cuzco with the rest in 1537. Inevitably he was drawn into the War of Salinas on the side of the Almagrists, and though he lived through Almagro's defeat, he was left in Cuzco in 1539 without an encomienda. The repeated disappointment and injustice must have rankled with him as with the other men of Chile, so there is little doubt that he was the Cristóbal de Sosa who was prominent in the rebellion of the younger Almagro and died at the battle of Chupas in 1542, shouting defiantly "I killed Francisco Pizarro." Some chroniclers say he was among Pizarro's actual assassins, but this does not seem likely.

N O T E S . Sosa's age is estimated first partly on the basis that pages were invariably young, and second because in 1539 he gave his age with the formula of "over twenty-five," which, though sometimes used by men up to fifty, was most common for relatively young men. If "over twenty-five" is to be taken in a fairly strict sense of about twenty-six, Sosa would have been born around 1513. Luis de Roa y Ursúa (El reyno de Chile, p. 15) asserts that the Sosa in Chile was from Benavente (Zamora), identifying him with a man of that name who left Spain in 1534 (Bermúdez Plata, Pasajeros, I, 281). This is impossible if he was the man of Cajamarca.

Since it was so very rare for a man of Cajamarca to go to Chile, it seems well to be explicit about the evidence. The Cristóbal de Sosa, page in León, Nicaragua, 1529–1530 (CDIHN, II, 250; IV, 532), is identified with the man of Cajamarca in the first instance because several of his associates also came to Peru (Soto, Pedro de Torres, Ponce, and others). Then on arrival, the Cristóbal de Sosa of Cajamarca, illiterate, enters into a deal about a horse with Luis Maza, who came to Peru from Nicaragua with Soto (ANP, PA 93). This Cristóbal de Sosa became a citizen of Cuzco (Porras, "Dos documentos esenciales," Revista Histórica 17 [1948]:92). In Cuzco, in 1535, Cristóbal de Sosa, illiterate, engages in a horse trade; the witnesses are all men going to Chile and among them is Vasco de Guevara (ANP, PA 201). In Cuzco, in February, 1539, Cristóbal de Sosa testifies in the probanza of Vasco de Guevara (CDIHC, VI, 275): Sosa went to Chile with Almagro, and he has known Guevara ten years, or since 1529 (when Guevara was indeed in León, Nicaragua [CDIHN, II, 288] as was the Cristóbal de Sosa of Cajamarca). The name Cristóbal de Sosa also appears on a list of Almagro's debtors, most of whom went to Chile (CDIHC, V, 234).

As to his possible part in the assassination of Pizarro, the rather distant Gómara, and Gutiérrez de Santa Clara, following Gómara, say that a Cristóbal de Sosa was one of the assassins (Gómara, Hispania victrix, I, 244; Gutiérrez de Santa Clara, Quinquenarios, III, 230). Cieza, closer to the source, mentions no Sosa among the assassins, but says a Sosa "el Galán," or the Gallant (that is, wearing flashy clothes) was part of the conspiracy (Chupas, pp. 108–109). The official interrogatory of the prosecution in 1542, lumping together assassins and principal conspirators, lists toward the end a Sosa, "caballerizo del Marqués," or Pizarro's groom (*CDIHC*, VI, 284). That might very well have been Cristóbal's function around the time of Cajamarca, but hardly in more recent years. The shout at the battle of Chupas was not a confession, since Martín Carrillo, definitely not one of the assassins, joined Sosa in it; rather it was meant to call down certain death upon men who did not want to survive Almagro's defeat (Gómara, *Hispania victrix*, I, 248; Zárate, *Historia*, II, 505).

Further references are in AGI, Patronato 109, ramo 4; ANP, PA 223; *CDIAO*, X, 248–249; Cieza, *Salinas*, p. 11.

Hernando del Tiemblo

Age at Cajamarca: Probably 20 or less
Role: Footman

Share: ½ share of gold; ⅜ share of silver
Extent of literacy: Illiterate

Hernando del Tiemblo must have been a humble man, of little importance in the expedition that conquered Peru. He followed the conquest south to Cuzco and may have thought of settling there, since he was assigned a lot; but he did not enroll as a citizen, and by 1535 he was on his way back to Spain.

The more unusual part of his career began after he had reached home. Possibly having lost his fortune in Spain, he joined the tiny minority of the men of Cajamarca who returned to Peru, once having left it definitively. He entered the country around 1547 or 1548, and settled once again in Cuzco. The most exceptional thing of all about his life is that the prestige of a first conqueror did not win him an encomienda, not even a small one, not even later in the 1560's, when the men of Cajamarca had become legendary patriarchs. The only conclusion one can draw is that Hernando del Tiemblo labored under some severe personal or social handicap. He was still alive in Cuzco in 1570, having lived there most of the time since his return.

NOTES. The estimate of Tiemblo's age rests partly on the mere fact of his having lived to 1570, partly on his statement that he was about fifty in 1570. Taken literally, this would have made him twelve years old at Cajamarca, but since precision in these statements decreased with age, and fifty is a good round number, it can be given only the most approximate value.

Tiemblo's testimony in Cuzco in 1570 is in Barriga, *Mercedarios*, I, 153–154. See also *RAHC* 8 (1957):73, and Diego Fernández, *Historia*, I, 332.

15. THE OBSCURE

THE LIVES OF ALMOST ALL the men of Cajamarca are obscure, in the sense of not being known in abundant detail. We do have in most cases a coherent outline, or at least a few salient traits—enough to allow us to place the individuals in various groupings. With the men in the following section, even this skeleton cannot be assembled; we are left with fragments which, though suggestive and capable of integration into the group's total statistical picture, lack internal coherence. Only two or three career outlines will appear here, of men like Francisco Martín and Cristóbal Gallego who have not left any certain indication whether we should put them among the upper or the lower plebeians.

A question that naturally arises is whether these twenty-nine men who are so little known might not tend to be of the very humblest origin and thus perceptibly alter the group characteristics worked out on the basis of the members who are better documented. There are several reasons, however, for thinking that this is not so. First, we can definitely assign some of these men to the middle or upper ranks; on the strength of their signatures alone, Antón García and Hernando de Montalbo could have been no less than upper plebeians. Second, we can directly discern that many of the factors rendering these men obscure have little or nothing to do with the status of the individual. One of these factors is an early death, which accounts for at least seven cases. Another is the chance circumstance of being listed on the roll of Cajamarca without a Christian name, often making certain identification impossible; this applies to four cases. Another reason is that individuals with simple patronymics are hard to trace in the records. A high proportion of the men here are named Sánchez, Pérez, and the like. These are not of course noble surnames, at least unless modified, but those better-known individuals among the conquerors who bore the names of Sánchez and Pérez were not of the humblest, by any means.

One might also suspect that most of the unknowns went quickly back to Spain, which would significantly change the proportion of settlers to returnees. This is within the realm of possibility. On the other hand, most of those here whose fates are documented died in Peru in the first years of the conquest, and presumably such was the destiny of several others as well. The two possibilities—early return and early death—probably account between them for almost all the men. We can be reasonably sure that none were in Peru after about 1538 or 1540.

Alonso de Alburquerque

Role at Cajamarca: Footman   Share: ½ share of silver and gold

All that can be offered on the subject of Alburquerque is a bare deduction or two. First, according to a general rule formulated by Peter Boyd-Bowman, there is a probability that a sixteenth-century Spaniard who bore only a place name for a surname was from that place, particularly if the place name was Andalusian or Extremaduran, as is the case here. Second, the obscurity of Alburquerque's fate and the smallness of his share point toward a man of few connections and little importance in the eyes of his fellows. He may have returned to Spain, but it seems more probable that he died very early and no relatives ever came forward to claim his estate.

NOTES. The author has found no definite reference to Alburquerque outside the roll of Cajamarca itself. A possible reference exists in Diego de

Trujillo's *Relación*, p. 62. There Trujillo lists among the dead at Vilcaconga in 1533 a Juan Alonso who cannot be identified from any other
source. The various Juan Alonsos who are known to have been in Peru
around this time either disappeared before Vilcaconga, or survived beyond
it. Diego de Trujillo's work has excellent general reliability, since he was
an eyewitness, but his memory was not perfect, and, writing many years
after the events, he made numerous mistakes about the names of individuals. The suspicion arises that "Juan Alonso" is one such mistake, and that
the person meant is Alonso de Alburquerque. This would readily account
for his early disappearance. For the present, however, such a hypothesis
remains in the realm of unprovable.

Bonilla

Role at Cajamarca: Footman   Share: 1 full share of gold and silver

Although the identification cannot be regarded as established beyond
all doubt, this man appears to have been Francisco de Bonilla or Francisco Díaz de Bonilla, from Bonilla de la Sierra near Avila (Old Castile). He died in Peru sometime before 1539, leaving enough money
to cause litigation and inquiry from his relatives in Spain. He would
seem to have been a Lima citizen, probably one of those who had their
encomiendas in the San Gallán area to the south.

NOTES. Francisco Díaz de Bonilla would appear to be the same person as a Francisco Díaz who was with the expedition at Coaque on the
north coast on June 9, 1531 (HC 24). The main evidence for the identification of Bonilla is simply that a royal cedula was issued in Madrid, August
22, 1539, inquiring into the fate of the estate of Francisco Díaz de Bonilla
who died in Peru, on behalf of his brother in Bonilla de la Sierra (AGI,
Lima 565, vol. III, August 22, 1539). In this writer's experience, almost all
such inquiries in the 1530's concerned the large amounts of silver and gold
left by the first conquerors who shared the treasures of Cajamarca and
Cuzco. In Lima in October, 1539, Juan de Barbarán, who had been custodian of the property of the deceased, was arranging to make settlements
with the Spanish heirs of three men, one of whom was a Francisco de
Bonilla. The other two men concerned were definitely early conquerors,
and one of them had been at Cajamarca. The others both died in 1538 or
1539 (HC 443, 447).
    Busto speculates that Bonilla might have been a Juan de Bonilla who
was in Natá on the Isthmus, then himself rejects the proposal because this
Bonilla stayed too long in the Panama region. In Busto's opinion the man

of Cajamarca was probably a Juan de Padilla, but since all versions of the Cajamarca list clearly say "Bonilla," this is unacceptable. See "Los innominados en el reparto de Cajamarca," *Anales del III Congreso de la Historia del Perú*, pp. 90–91.

Generally speaking, in Peru the name Bonilla was synonymous with a family from the area of Guadalcanal, north of Seville on the border between Andalusia and Extremadura. One member of this clan, Francisco Núñez de Bonilla, was a very important man in the early days of Lima, the city's majordomo and *procurador* in 1537, then alcalde in 1539. But in no records is he seen to have been in Peru before 1536, and when he does appear it is as a wealthy entrepreneur in association with Dr. Hernando de Sepúlveda, who arrived in 1536. Though he lived until 1542 and his prominence would have made him a desirable witness, no one ever asked him to testify for the many memorials of services presented by the men who participated in Atahuallpa's capture. Thus one must assume that he was not the Bonilla of Cajamarca. There are references to this Francisco Núñez de Bonilla in ANP, Juzgado, February 24, 1536; PA 271, 279, 619; Salinas 1538–1540, ff.7–9, 216, 242; HC 99, 133, 223, 240, 350, 497; Busto, "Una relación y un estudio," *Revista Histórica* 27 (1964):301; Cobo, *Obras*, II, 305; *Libros de cabildos de Lima*, I, 183; Porras, *Cedulario*, II, 230–231; Torres Saldamando, *Libro primero de cabildos*, I, 164, 171, 172, 179, 218, 219, 249, 259–260, 299, 318, 320, 326–328.

Juan Borrallo

Role at Cajamarca: Footman   Extent of literacy: Illiterate
Share: 1 full share of gold and silver

Of Borrallo we can only say that there was a person of this name (a name which smacks of Portugal) at Cajamarca, that his illiteracy points to a humble origin, and that his full share of the treasure indicates an able-bodied man with a certain amount of skill, or influence of some kind. From the horse-trading he engaged in at Cajamarca, one may deduce that he intended to continue on the conquest of the mainland. In these dealings he appears in conjunction with four men of maritime background from the Seville-Huelva region, making it tempting to speculate that Borrallo might have been a seaman himself, but both his trade and his fate remain uncertain.

NOTES. Borrallo figures in documents in ANP, PA 69, 83, 95. A Juan Borrallo who was in Mexico from the middle 1520's into the 1540's can hardly have been our man. This Borrallo was from Braga, Portugal (Francisco A. de Icaza, *Conquistadores y pobladores de Nueva España*, II, 204).

Contreras difunto

Role: Footman   Place of origin: Talavera de la Reina
Share: ⅝ share of gold;   (New Castile)
  ¾ share of silver

His full name was Pedro López de Contreras, and he came to the Indies with Pizarro in 1530, leaving behind his wife, Mari Vázquez. He was the only Spaniard to die before the division of the treasure, of an illness not further specified. That he did not receive a full share can perhaps be put down to this circumstance rather than to any moral or social attributes of his person. The remarkable thing is that he was assigned a share at all. His sister in Talavera, María de Arévelo, attempted to recover his estate, but since Contreras died without a will, the money went first to the official custodians of the property of the deceased, from whose hands little emerged.

N O T E S . Most of what we know about Contreras and his origins comes from proceedings in AGI, Justicia 1071, no. 1, ramo 7. Other references are in AGI, Contaduría 1825, records from Coaque, August, 1531; Justicia 1074, no. 9; Porras, *Cedulario*, I, 153. See also Busto, "Los innominados en el reparto de Cajamarca," *Anales del III Congreso Nacional de la Historia del Perú*, p. 91.

Diego Escudero

Role: Footman   Share: 1 full share of gold; no silver

Escudero was in León, Nicaragua, in July, 1529, having taken refuge in a church after cutting off another man's ear in a fight. Opportunely for him, Bartolomé Ruiz, the pilot of the Peruvian venture, appeared in Nicaragua's port to recruit men for the conquest; he was prepared to take anyone he could get, whether openly or clandestinely, legally or illegally. When the news reached Escudero, he fled to the ship; from there he must have gone to Panama, and then from Panama on to

Peru with the main body of the 1531 expedition. In 1533, not long after Cajamarca, he died, possibly of natural causes, since he had time to appoint Rodrigo de Chaves from Ciudad Rodrigo as executor of his will.

NOTES. AGI, Contaduría 1825, Penas de Cámara, 1533; Justicia 1126, no. 2, testimony of Rodrigo de Chaves; *CDIHN*, II, 38–39, 61–62; Busto, "Los fugitivos," *Mercurio Peruano* 43 (1962): 267.

Cristóbal Gallego

Age at Cajamarca: About 28 to 30   Share: 1¾ shares of silver; no gold
Role: Horseman   Extent of literacy: Could sign his name

Gallego was allowed to return to Spain in 1533 because of a bad arm wound, possibly received in some skirmish before the events of Cajamarca, since certainly the dividers of the treasure, harsh though they were, would not have penalized a man for being wounded in the fighting of that day. Then, too, there is the widespread report that the only wound any Spaniard received in the fighting at Cajamarca was a scratch on Francisco Pizarro's hand. Conceivably, Gallego is the unfortunate conqueror who lost an arm in a fight with two fellows in the days shortly after Atahuallpa's capture. Back in Spain, Gallego settled in Seville. In 1535 he could not use his right hand for writing, but by 1554, still in Seville, he had either recovered or had taught himself to sign with his left hand.

Most people with the name Gallego were either actual Galicians or, even more frequently, Andalusians, in either case often connected with the sea; there was no ship without a Gallego on it. Names alone rarely yield certainty, but, given his long residence in Seville and his friendship with Francisco de Jerez, a native of Seville, there is a certain probability that Cristóbal Gallego was originally from Seville or the surrounding area.

NOTES. In 1535 Gallego declared himself a citizen of Seville, thirty-two or thirty-three years old (AGI, Justicia 719, no. 9). In 1554 he was a citizen of Seville in the district of La Magdalena, and said he was fifty (AGI, Justicia 98, no. 4, ramo 3). The incident of the lost arm is described in Mena, *Conquista*, p. 91.

Francisco Gallego

Role at Cajamarca: Footman   Share: ¾ share of gold and silver

Francisco's life is as obscure as that of the other Gallego, Cristóbal. There is no particular reason to assume a relationship between the two of them, since the name (the implications of which are discussed just above) was reasonably common. Francisco Gallego was a founding citizen of Cuzco in March, 1534, and was one of the small body of men staying there in July and August to guard the city. In October, 1534, like the other citizens, he received a lot for his house. After that he disappears from Cuzco. There is reason to believe that he went to Chile with Almagro in 1535, and he must be the Francisco Gallego who figures in chronicler Zárate's list of those who distinguished themselves at the battle of Chupas in 1542. According to Zárate, Governor Vaca de Castro gave encomiendas to most or all of these men. However, Gallego does not seem to appear among Peru's encomenderos after that date, making it likely that he died soon afterward.

NOTES. The first reason for suspecting that Gallego went to Chile is his disappearance at the time Almagro's expedition was being formed. The possibility is converted into a probability by the fact that Gallego owed Almagro money. His name appears on a list of Almagro's debtors, the great majority of whom accompanied him to Chile (*CDIHC*, V, 233). He probably gave up his Cuzco encomienda in 1535, then on return was on the losing side of the battle of Salinas in 1538 and maintained a marginal existence until 1542. The Gallego on the loyalist side in the battle of Chupas would very likely be the man of Cajamarca, in any case, but Zárate adds to the probability by specifically including him among the former supporters of Almagro (*Historia*, II, 506).

Other references to Gallego are in *CDIAO*, X, 248–249; *RAHC* 8 (1957): 74; Porras, "Dos documentos esenciales," *Revista Histórica* 17 (1948):93.

Antón García

Role at Cajamarca: Footman   Extent of literacy: Very good
Share: ⁵⁄₁₁ share of gold;   signature, probably literate
  1 full share of silver

Antón García was part of the 1531 expedition from the time it left

Panama. He followed the main course of the conquest as far as Jauja, where he stayed in late 1533 and early 1534 while most of the men went on to take Cuzco. He is last seen in Jauja in June, 1534.

NOTES. In July of 1529 the pilot Bartolomé Ruiz came to the port of Nicaragua to recruit men clandestinely for the Peru expedition. Officials ordered an inquiry, and one of the witnesses reported that he had seen Antón García, shoemaker, on the ship. This would seem, under ordinary circumstances, to be the Antón García of Cajamarca, particularly since most of the other men on Ruiz's ship did indeed join the expedition. But in this case the officials asked the witnesses to name all the men they could remember; consequently there was uncertainty with those the witnesses knew less well, and the accounts varied. Only one witness named Antón García, shoemaker; the other four omitted him but did name a Cristóbal García, shoemaker. So this hint of García's origin is dubious at best, though it still seems likely that there was an Antón García there, even if not a shoemaker. (See *CDIHN*, II, 35–37, 41, 46, 51, 56.)

The most widely diffused version of the roll of Cajamarca contains an Antón Esteban García, but this is an error stemming from confusion with Esteban García. Cieza and Herrera give Antón García and Esteban García as two separate individuals, and this is the way they occur in all the records.

Other references are in AGI, Justicia 724, no. 6; ANP, PA 15, 114, 147; HC 11, 41, 42, 66.

Esteban García

Role at Cajamarca: Footman   Share: 1 full share of gold; ½ share of silver

This man was with the expedition from Panama; he was still at Cajamarca in June, 1533, and presumably also in the following month at the division of the treasure. Nothing more is known of his origin or his fate.

NOTES. There are references to Esteban García in AGI, Contaduría 1825, records from Cajamarca, June, 1533, and in HC 2. The name Esteban, not at all common among Spaniards of the time, is found in more frequent use by the Portuguese and some of the other semi-foreign groups of the Iberian peninsula. But of course it did appear on occasion among Castilians, so no conclusions can be drawn.

Juan García escopetero

Role at Cajamarca: Musketeer (afoot)   Share: ¾ share of gold and silver

Since two Juan Garcías have been identified, and there were only three at Cajamarca, it would seem that a Juan García Pizarro, who was living in a little village near Trujillo in 1545, must have been Juan García *escopetero*, or musketeer. Yet there is much reason to think that this person was none other than Juan García *pregonero* (q.v.) or Juan García Clemente. He was illiterate, he was the right age and he returned to Spain at about the right time, 1535. It would have been natural enough for Juan García Clemente to adopt the Pizarro surname on occasion, it being a common practice for dependents to use the surname of a patron. It is true that "Juan García Pizarro" was a resident of a hamlet called Las Piñuelas, while Juan García Clemente is known to have been a citizen of Casas del Puerto, near Jaraicejo, at much the same time. Yet neither place appears on maps, and it can be deduced from Juan García Clemente's will that the area where he lived was not very nucleated. All in all we must conclude that we are dealing with but one man, and that Juan García escopetero remains a blank, except that he was present in Cuzco in 1534.

N O T E S .   There were still other Juan Garcías in Peru in the early days. One was Juan García de Calzadilla (yet another illiterate), who was in Jauja in 1533 and again in 1534, then appeared in Cuzco in July, 1535, apparently headed for Chile. He also called himself Juan García de Palos, and he must have actually come from Palos, since he is found in constant association with men from there. (ANP, PA 142; HC 45, 60, 83). He might be the Juan García, former Almagrist, who did well on the loyalist side of the battle of Chupas in 1542 (Zárate, *Historia*, II, 506). He is hardly likely to have been the musketeer of Cajamarca.

As to Juan García escopetero, the only evidence about him is his presence on the general Cajamarca list and in treasury records written in Cuzco in 1534 (Loredo, *Los repartos*, p. 193). Juan García Pizarro testifies in AGI, Justicia 1174, no. 1, ramo 3.

Antonio de Herrera

Role at Cajamarca: Footman   Parents: Alvaro Rodríguez
Share: ¾ share of gold and silver   and Leonor Gallego

Herrera was with the 1531 expedition from Panama. He died in Peru (probably at Jauja) before July 2, 1534, leaving as executors of his will two other men of Cajamarca. One of them, Antonio de Vergara, took 3,000 pesos of Herrera's to Spain in 1535, to be given to his father.

NOTES. The place of origin of the man taking money to Spain is often a clue to the origin of the man who sent it, and it was also standard to choose compatriots as executors of wills. In this case, however, the two executors were from different places, and Vergara, who took the money, was from Oropesa, but settled in Seville. ANP, PA 117 gives the executors' names (the other was Diego Gavilán) and those of Herrera's parents, as well as a list of Herrera's creditors. Other references are in AGI, Indiferente General 1801, records of ship *Santa Catalina*, 1535; Patronato 185, ramo 11, testimony of Pedro Díaz (or *CDIAO*, X, 284); ANP, PA 124; HC 20.

Diego López

Role at Cajamarca: Footman   Share: ¾ share of gold and silver

Diego López accompanied the main body of the expedition from Panama as far as Jauja, where in stayed in 1533–1534, during the time of the conquest of Cuzco. He seems to have intended to settle in Jauja, since he is seen in July, 1534, sending money home with one comrade and lending a large sum to another. This makes it seem possible that he is the Diego López de la Mota who was named a permanent member of the council of Jauja by a royal order signed in August, 1535, before news had reached the court that Jauja, having been incorporated into Lima, had ceased to exist. Diego López does not appear among the citizens of Jauja who were consulted about moving the city in December, 1534, nor is he heard of again in any other way.

NOTES. If Diego López was indeed the Diego López de la Mota who received the royal appointment (Porras, *Cedulario*, II, 103), it would be likely also that he was in some way related to a Francisco López de la Mota, from Plasencia, who went to the Indies in 1538 with Pedro de Alvarado (Bermúdez Plata, *Pasajeros*, II, 326).

The only direct hint we have as to López's origin is that Francisco Muñiz, who was to take money to his father, was from La Bañeza in the kingdom of Leon. Of course López's father might have lived anywhere between there and Seville.

It is noticeable that most of the people appearing in documents with López are on the plebeian side. There are references to López in AGI, Contaduría 1825, records from Coaque, August 1531; ANP, PA 29, 59, 89, 130–133; HC 55, 63; Porras, *Cedulario*, II, 103.

García López

Role at Cajamarca: Footman   Extent of literacy: Could sign
Share: ¾ share of gold and silver   his name

Of García López it can only be said that he was an original member of the 1531 expedition and that he was still in Peru in June, 1534. At that time he gave general powers to Juan de Herrera, who was leaving the country, so that by implication López meant to stay. He is seen once in conjunction with Alonso López del Moral and an Antón López, conjuring up the possibility of a whole López family from Moral de Calatrava, the home of Alonso López. But the name is too common to deduce anything with certainty.

NOTES. The only certain references to García López, outside the roll of Cajamarca, are in ANP, PA 121 and HC 19. Sometime in the 1540's a group of men testified in Spain in behalf of Hernando Pizarro in the suit brought against him for killing Almagro. All of the witnesses had known Pizarro in Peru; some had been at Cajamarca, and others had not. We do not have their original testimony, but only the prosecutor's statement objecting to the witnesses. Among a group of persons "of low extraction" appears a García López de Avilés. This may or may not be the López of Cajamarca, and Avilés may be either a surname or the man's place of origin. See *CDIHC*, VII, 155.

Lozano

Role at Cajamarca: Footman   Share: ½ share of gold and silver

Placed toward the end of the roll of Cajamarca, with one of the smallest shares, this man must have been one of the humblest members of the expedition. It is not even possible to identify him with certainty among the three Lozanos involved in the conquest. He may have been illiterate Alonzo Lozano, who had been an associate of Francisco López the barber, in Nicaragua, and who was with López in Coaque in May and June of 1531. This Lozano is not heard of again. Or he may have been a Domingo Lozano who was with the expedition by 1533 and took part in the conquest of Cuzco, getting as small a share as the Lozano of Cajamarca would have. He too then disappears.

NOTES. A Rodrigo Lozano, from Salvatierra in Extremadura, was with the 1531–1532 expedition and soon became a prominent citizen of Trujillo (Peru). It has been very naturally assumed that he was the Lozano of Cajamarca, but such is not the case. By his own repeated assertion Rodrigo Lozano stayed behind in San Miguel and was already on his way to Nicaragua to get his wife when Atahuallpa was taken. Further, there is no special reason to assume that he was associated with either of the other Lozanos. In no records does he appear in conjunction with them; Lozano was a reasonably common name, and there were other Lozanos in Peru, from Andalusia. Rodrigo and Alonso Lozano were in Nicaragua at the same time but had different partners in their encomiendas, and while Rodrigo was highly literate, Alonso could not sign his name.

Rafael Loredo, in *Los repartos*, p. 101, reports the apparent presence of a Domingo Lozano in Cuzco in 1534, and considers this to be a mistake for Rodrigo (thought by Loredo to have been at Cajamarca). But Rodrigo Lozano did not go to Cuzco, and the name Domingo Lozano also occurs in Contaduría 1825, in the expedition's Penas de Cámara for 1533. There is little doubt that a person by this name arrived in Peru with Almagro or earlier. Busto, unaware of Alonso's existence, decides in favor of Domingo as the man of Cajamarca. See "Los innominados en el reparto de Cajamarca," *Anales del III Congreso Nacional de la Historia del Perú*, pp. 92–93.

For Alonzo Lozano, see HC 15, 27; *CDIHN*, II, 225.

For Rodrigo Lozano, see AGI, Lima 118, *probanza* de Sebastián de Torres, and papers concerning Lozano's inn concession in the valley of Guañape; Patronato 93, no. 8, ramo 1; 97, no. 1, ramo 4; *CDIHN*, II, 225; Bermúdez Plata, *Pasajeros*, I, 92; Pérez de Tudela, introduction to Pedro Pizarro, *Relación*, V, 245–247; Porras, *Cartas*, p. 107; Porras, *Cedulario*, II, 380; Porras, *Crónicas perdidas*, pp. 15–19.

Martín de Marquina

Role at Cajamarca: Footman   Place of origin: Biscay
Share: ¾ share of gold and silver

Though nothing more is known of this man than his name, that alone suffices to establish his origin quite firmly, since Marquina was a rare name, and all of the four or five bearers of it in Peru and Nicaragua in this period were from the Basque country. Presumably Martín was not a relative of the young Basque Gaspar de Marquina (above), in view of the fact that Gaspar failed to mention him in the newsy letter he wrote home to his father.

NOTES. Not only is Marquina a Basque place name, but Martín as a first name has a Basque flavor. In 1548 a Martín de Marquina, from Marquina in the Basque country, was sentenced in Cuzco for guilt in the Gonzalo Pizarro rebellion; but without more details there is no reason to assume that this was the man of Cajamara (*CDIAO*, XX, 506; Pérez de Tudela, *Gasca*, II, 563). A Pedro de Marquina in Lima in 1535 was a Basque (HC 75). Closest of all, in a way, was a Martín (or Machín) de Marquina, an illiterate shoemaker, who was in León, Nicaragua, from the early 1520's to 1535, and who worked for the Basque merchant Domingo de Soraluce, one of the Thirteen of Gallo Island. (*CDIHN*, I, 321; II, 262, 269, 271, 362, 367–368; IV, 518). The man of Cajamarca may well have been this Marquina's relative and namesake.

Francisco Martín

Age at Cajamarca: About 25 or 26
Role: Footman
Share: ¾ share of gold and silver

Place of origin: Alburquerque (western Extremadura)
Parents: Francisco Soitino and Leonor Martín
Extent of literacy: Illiterate

Francisco Martín joined the expedition in Panama, having been in the Indies since about 1527. Of his social origins we know no more than can be deduced from his illiteracy and the names of his parents. But because there was a dispute about his identity, we know something of his appearance and manner. His family and his comrades of Cajamarca agreed that he was in size medium to large, as lean and spare as a Spaniard should be, dark, with a large nose, and vivacious of speech. He had known one of the other men, Juan Ruiz, from boyhood, and the two met again by chance in the Indies. He survived a serious illness during the expedition's first stopover at Coaque in 1531, only to get killed in the notable battle of Vilcaconga near Cuzco in November, 1533.

NOTES. Martín's estimated birthdate of c.1506–1507 is based on Juan Ruiz's statement that he was twenty-six or twenty-seven when he died. He sometimes called himself Francisco Martín de Alburquerque, and his relatives at home called him Francisco Martín Soitino. The principal source for his life is the official record of the proceedings initiated by his family to recover his estate, in AGI, Justicia 1125. Portions of the testimony there are quoted in Busto, "Los caídos en Vilcaconga," pp. 120–122.

As Porras Barrenechea already knew, the Francisco Martín at Cajamarca was not Francisco Pizarro's half brother Francisco Martín de Alcántara; the share alone would prove that with absolute certainty. Pizarro's brother was with the expedition, but he stayed behind when the main body went on toward Cajamarca. (See Porras, in Trujillo, *Relación*, p. 121, and Cieza, *Tercera parte*, in *Mercurio Peruano* 37 [1956]:86.)

Also with the expedition from Panama was Francisco Martín Albarrán, distinguishable from the others by his ability to sign. He, too, stayed behind in San Miguel and became a citizen and encomendero there (AGI, Contaduría 1825, records from Cuzco, March, 1534; Lima 566, vol. IV, July 27, 1540; HC 3, 7).

Other references to the Francisco Martín of Cajamarca are in AGI, Lima 565, vol. III, July 20, 1538; ANP, PA 65, 85; HC 29; Herrera, *Historia general*, X, 35; Trujillo, *Relación*, p. 62.

Hernando de Montalbo

Role at Cajamarca: Footman   Extent of literacy: Could sign well
Share: ¾ share of gold;
  1 full share of silver

Hernando de Montalbo's signature would seem to imply a good background in Spain. There is no definite evidence to connect him with the family of that name which was prominent in Leon and Old Castile, though one member of it, a relative of Governor Vaca de Castro, did later come to Peru. All we know is that while at Cajamarca Montalbo bought a cape, a dagger, a horse, and a black slave, then headed south with the main body of the expedition toward Jauja in 1533. Nothing more is heard of him.

NOTES. See ANP, PA 14, 27, 64, 66, 67; Atienza, *Nobiliario*, p. 547; Zárate, *Historia*, II, 505.

Hernán Muñoz

Role at Cajamarca: Footman   Extent of literacy: Illiterate
Share: ¾ share of gold and silver

One of the few things we can assert about this man is that he was indeed Hernán Muñoz, as he is listed on the traditional roll of Cajamarca, and not Hernán Martínez as he appears in some versions. In 1533, with the Spaniards still encamped at Cajamarca, he bought one of the horses which were then being sold for great fortunes, so he must have been among those who followed the conquest south and not one of the immediate returnees. After the distribution of treasure, he disappears.

N O T E S . It is possible, though it would need further confirmation, that this Hernán Muñoz was the same as the Fernando Muñoz, son of Juan Muñoz, *vecino* of Plasencia, who went to Yucatan with Francisco de Montejo in 1527 (Bermúdez Plata, *Pasajeros*, I, 223). At least one other man of Cajamarca, Alonso Jiménez, was with that group. References to Hernán Muñoz are in ANP, PA 105, and HC 65.

Juan de Niza

Role at Cajamarca: Footman   Share: ¾ share of gold; 1⅛ shares of silver

All that is known about this man is his presence at Cajamarca and his share. His name alone would appear to say much, to speak of origins in the town of Nice in Savoy and of concomitant maritime associations. But his name is not clearly established. Though it appears as Juan de Niza on two versions of the roll of Cajamarca, on the other two it is totally different. The only strictly contemporary written sample of the name seems to say "Juan de Nizar." In August, 1533, before the expedition left Cajamarca, he lent money to Simón Suárez, a Portuguese. This would be consonant with, yet does not decisively confirm, a foreign origin for Niza (or Nizar).

N O T E S . The Cajamarca roll, as given by Francisco López de Caravantes and by Salinas y Córdoba (both taken from the same source), shows Juan de Niza, but Cieza, in the corrupt version we know, has Juan Deuscar, and Herrera, though mainly based on Cieza, has Juan de Urfán. The reading Juan de Nizar is in ANP, PA 48. Two of the renderings agree on the ending in "r," so it would appear probable that "Juan de Niza," tempting as that version is, is not right. It still remains possible that Spanish notaries could have turned Niza into Nizar.

Juan Pérez

Role at Cajamarca: Footman   Share: ¾ share of gold and silver

There were four men named Juan Pérez at Cajamarca; three of them had, or received, additional surnames to distinguish them; but one of them, the man in question here, was left as plain Juan Pérez. He could hardly be called *the* Juan Pérez, however, since he got the smallest share of all four, and never stood out in any other way. Though he seems to figure in several documents from Cajamarca, Jauja, and Cuzco as the conquest swept through them, there is no way of being sure that the person involved is not another of the four, with his provisional surname omitted. After the foundation of Cuzco there were so many Spaniards of this name in the country that the search becomes fruitless.

Busto identifies this Juan Pérez with a tailor who had a shop in Panama in March, 1531, and was associated with Pedro del Páramo. The identification is conceivable, but remains unestablished.

N O T E S . "Juan Pérez" was at Cajamarca in May, June, and August, 1533 (ANP, PA 49, 73, 75, 94); was joint owner of a horse with Diego de Trujillo in Jauja, in October, 1533 (HC 42); and was assigned a lot in Cuzco in October, 1534 (AGI, Patronato 109, ramo 4). Since there are indications that the other three Juan Pérezes were leaving the country in 1534, the man getting a lot in Cuzco was probably indeed plain Juan Pérez. Busto's mention of Juan Pérez, tailor, is in "Tres conversos," *Revista de Indias* 27 (1967):436.

Juan Pérez de Oma

Role at Cajamarca: Footman   Extent of literacy: Could sign
Share: ⅞ share of gold;   his name
  ¾ share of silver

As obscure as his namesakes, this Juan Pérez joined the expedition in Panama. He followed the conquest south to Cuzco, then returned to Jauja along with the bulk of the conquerors in mid-1534. Of the few facts known about him, the only suggestive items are his adequate signature and his association with Pedro Navarro, man of affairs and retainer of Francisco Pizarro. In July, 1534, Juan Pérez de Oma delegated general powers to a comrade; this act often signaled a departure, and since July, 1534, was the time when the fever to return ran highest, it is likely that Juan Pérez was on his way out of Peru.

N O T E S . The name also occurs as Juan Pérez de Osma, though Juan Pérez himself seems to have preferred Oma. Since this name in any case is quite rare, it is of some interest to observe that a Francisco Pérez de Osma, son of Juan Pérez de Osma and Juana de la Pena (?), *vecinos* of Cáceres, registered to come to the Indies in June, 1534 (Bermúdez Plata, *Pasajeros*, I, 315).

References to Juan Pérez de Oma are in AGI, Contaduría 1825, records from Jauja, 1534; ANP, PA 36, 123, 126; HC 31, 47, 48.

Juan Pérez de Zamora

Role at Cajamarca: Footman   Extent of literacy: Could sign
Share: 1 full share of gold and silver   his name

From his predilection for associating with old veterans, one gathers that Juan Pérez de Zamora had had his share of experiences in Panama or Nicaragua; he also got the full share that was the veteran's portion at Cajamarca. He was still in Peru, in Jauja, in July, 1534, when many of his comrades were arranging their affairs for return to Spain. As he left general powers at that time with a comrade, we may presume that Juan Pérez de Zamora also intended to leave.

N O T E S . While Pérez de Oma (or Osma) and Pérez de Tudela sound like true names of Spanish lineages, Pérez de Zamora has the ring of improvisation. It is most likely that this Juan Pérez was a native of Zamora and added the name of his hometown to his own, as did Pedro Martín de Moguer, Francisco Martín de Alburquerque, and Juan Ruiz de Alburquerque. Nevertheless, though a strong possibility, this is not a certainty, and Juan Pérez de Zamora showed no particular tendency to congregate with people from the Zamora region.

References to Juan Pérez de Zamora are in ANP, PA 18, 39, 46, 71, 95, 104, 109, 114, 129.

Juan Ronquillo

Role at Cajamarca: Footman
Share: 1 full share of gold and silver

Extent of literacy: Could sign
his name

On the roll of Cajamara, Ronquillo's name stands near the top of the list of infantry, in the midst of ten or a dozen men who soon made their mark in one way or another. Of all these, Ronquillo is the most obscure. He bought a horse after Cajamarca, as almost everyone did, and he took part in the conquest of Cuzco. There he became a citizen and encomendero. For the year 1535 he attained a seat on the powerful Cuzco town council. He was still in Cuzco in July, 1535, but thereafter disappears. He may have gone to Spain, died of an illness, or conceivably have accompanied Almagro's Chile expedition. However, the first hints of the coming Indian rebellion showed themselves at this time; some citizens of Cuzco were killed in the countryside by Indians of their encomiendas, and this was very likely Ronquillo's fate.

N O T E S . The name Ronquillo seems to have been felt adjectively, and therefore usually had no "de" with it. Thus it is probably not relevant, even as a speculation, that there is a village called El Ronquillo in the jurisdiction of Seville.

References to Juan Ronquillo are in AGI, Contaduría 1824, records from Cuzco, May–July, 1535; Lima 204, *probanza* of Gonzalo de los Nidos; Patronato 109, ramo 4; 185, ramo 10; ANP, PA 60, 99, 136, 144; Rivera Serna, *Libro primero de cabildos de la ciudad del Cuzco*, pp. 39, 43–44.

Juan de Salvatierra

Role at Cajamarca: Footman
Share: ¾ share of gold and silver

Neither this man's share, small but respectable, nor his name is by itself enough to shed much light on him. Since his name is a place name, there is a certain probability that it indicates his origin, but Spain boasted several Salvatierras (the largest, now called Salvatierra de los Barros, is in central-western Extremadura). Presumably he was the same Juan de Salvatierra who returned to Spain on the ship *San Miguel* in 1535, along with a dozen other men of Cajamarca, but even this is thrown somewhat into doubt by the fact that Salvatierra regis-

tered only 500 pesos of gold, whereas the others registered many
thousands.

N O T E S . See AGI, Indiferente General 1801, records of ship *San
Miguel*. No definite reference to the Salvatierra of Cajamarca is known beyond his appearance on the general list.

Juan Sánchez

Role: Footman   Share: ⅜ share of gold; ½ share of silver

From the obscurity surrounding this man there emerges a single
item: it appears that in 1535 he sent some 5,000 pesos to Spain with
the barber Francisco López. If so, he had improved his fortune somewhat after having been allotted one of the smallest shares any Spaniard
received of the treasure of Cajamara. Sending money home would
seem to imply that Juan Sánchez himself was staying in Peru.

N O T E S . The above passage is couched in somewhat speculative terms
because it rests on an unsuppported statement by Porras (in Trujillo, *Rela-
cion*, p. 102). Porras is highly reliable, yet, since his source is veiled, one
must suspect that he might have the wrong Sánchez; it is definitely established that Francisco López took home 5,000 pesos for Hernán Sánchez
(ANP, PA 681).
A Juan Sánchez, reputed to be a tailor, was killed when Almagro's men
entered Cuzco in April, 1537, but the name is too common to draw any
conclusions (AGI, Patronato 185, ramo 16).

Lázaro Sánchez

Role: Footman   Extent of literacy: Illiterate
Share: ½ share of gold and silver,
   plus a token 100 pesos

Taking his less than princely share of the treasure of Cajamarca,
Lázaro Sánchez followed the conquest south in 1533 to Cuzco and enrolled there as a founding citizen. He was among the forty men left to
guard the city in late 1534. The official distribution of lots of October,
1534, mentions his name, but in the following June the lot destined
for him seems to have been given to someone else, implying his previous departure or death.

NOTES. The passage in the distribution of lots, as it has reached us in a somewhat corrupt version, is as follows: "Señalóse a Lázaro Sánchez un solar donde está por linderos la calle real, . . . y por encima Su Señoria, . . . lo dieron a Pedro Díaz fundidor a 7 de Junio de 1535 anos." (Rivera Serna, *Libro primero de cabildos de la ciudad del Cuzco*, p. 35; other versions in *RAHC* 8 [1957]:72, and AGI, Patronato 109, ramo 4). See also PA 65, *CDIAO*, X, 248–249, and Porras, "Dos documentos esenciales," *Revista Histórica* 17 (1948):92.

Miguel Sánchez

Role: Footman   Share: ¾ share of gold and silver

Miguel Sánchez was a member of the expedition from the time it first left Panama, was still with it at Cajamarca, and received a semi-respectable three-quarters share. This is not, like a full share, enough to deduce some skill or influence, nor, like a half share, little enough to deduce humbleness or worthlessness. Otherwise, the record of Miguel Sánchez is blank.

NOTES. The only known mention of Miguel Sánchez outside the roll of Cajamarca is in HC 25. A Miguel Sánchez who saw the Pacific with Balboa in 1513 is definitely not our man, since he was killed by Indians not long afterward (Oviedo, *Historia*, III, 213; Medina, *Descumbrimiento*, I, 322).

Sandoval

Role: Footman   Share: ¾ share of gold and silver

Sandoval has left very little trace of himself. Apparently he can be identified with the Rodrigo de Sandoval who was in Coaque in April, 1531; therefore he must have been part of the expedition when it left Panama. This, together with his share, typically that of the young and inexperienced, makes it likely that he was relatively new to the Indies. To testify to his origins we have only his name, which despite its rather noble sound could have been borne by a plebeian. The chronicler Diego de Trujillo says that a young man named Juan de Sandoval, who was killed a few months before Cajamarca, was from Extrema-dura. There might be some connection, but, on the other hand, there was a nobleman named don Juan de Sandoval in Peru a little later who was from Old Castile. Also, Sandoval was the name of the maternal side of the family of Diego de Agüero, from Deleitosa in northeastern Extremadura.

N O T E S . Rodrigo de Sandoval appears in AGI, Contaduría 1825, records from Coaque, April, 1531. See also Trujillo, *Relación*, p. 53, and AGI, Lima 204, *probanza* of don Juan de Sandoval. The writer cannot accept Busto's suggestion that the man of Cajamarca was probably an Alonso de Sandoval who spent much of his career in Chachapoyas, too peripheral a situation for a first conqueror ("Los innominados en el reparto de Cajamarca," pp. 94–95). Busto is unaware of Rodrigo.

Francisco de la Torre

Role: Footman   Share: ⅝ share of gold; ¾ share of silver

The reason for the almost total obscurity of this man is his early death. We know only that he bought a horse after Cajamarca and participated in the conquest of Jauja but died before the expedition reached Cuzco in late 1533. Posthumously he received a share of the treasure of Cuzco, again a modest one, as at Cajamarca.

N O T E S . The only references to Francisco de la Torre are in PA 109 —merely confirming his name and his presence at Cajamarca—and in Loredo, *Los repartos*, p. 99, an extract from the distribution of treasure at Cuzco.

16. AUXILIARIES

THE INDIAN AND BLACK AUXILIARIES who were with the Spaniards at Cajamarca have left hardly a trace in the records. A black slave of Jerónimo de Aliaga was killed there, the only casualty the Spaniards mention. Another black started off to inspect Cuzco with Moguer, Bueno, and Zárate, then came back to Cajamarca conveying over a hundred loads of gold and silver found in Jauja. (One presumes that the person referred to was a slave, not black crier Juan García, who was counted among the Spaniards.) Black slaves were few until Inca treasure gave the Spaniards the means to import them. Much more numerous were the Indian slaves and servants brought from Nicaragua, particularly women. While the expedition was at Coaque, in the north, several such Indian women changed hands. How many got as far as Cajamarca we cannot know. Some did, like the woman named Ana who accompanied Captain Juan de Salcedo. When Salcedo departed for Spain in July, 1533, he left Ana and their mestizo son in the hands of his compatriot Antonio de Vergara. During the whole progress southward from Coaque the Spaniards accumulated further Indian bearers, servants, and mistresses, sometimes commandeered and sometimes given to them by Indian chieftains.

Only two Indians emerge from the general anonymity. The roll of Cajamarca specifies that Governor Pizarro's huge share was to reward the contributions made by his person, his horse, and the *lenguas* ("interpreters"). Though the interpreters did not share in the treasure directly, their presence at Cajamarca had at least as great an effect on their lives, and the same kind of effect, as on the lives of the Spaniards. They achieved great notoriety; their names, or at least their Christian names, are well known to us from the chronicles and histories, and it is not hard to get some impression of the shape of their lives, though large gaps remain. Both were among the tiny handful of Indians who became important actors inside the Spanish world. The more famous of the two is Felipillo, also on occasion called Felipe and don Felipe. Yet, in the end, his life is more hidden than that of the other, who when still a boy was called Martinillo, and then don Martín; at times he used the surname Pizarro.

It has not been known just where and when the two interpreters came among the Spaniards. Many have assumed, and not without reason, that pilot Bartolomé Ruiz took them when he first encountered central Peruvian Indians, toward the end of Pizarro's "second voyage," in late 1526 or very early 1527. At that time, leaving Pizarro far behind, Ruiz sailed along the coast until he was three and a half degrees south of the equator, the exact vicinity of Túmbez. There he sighted and captured an Indian vessel which the Spaniards thought worthy of the name "ship." Over half of the twenty Indians aboard swam to shore, and Ruiz let the others go too, except for three that he kept to be interpreters. The Indians were thought to be from a city or land called Calangane. This at any rate is what we read in an account dating from around late 1527, probably written by Francisco de Jerez, which adds that as of that time the three Indians were with Pizarro, and had taken very well to Spanish.

Yet no names are given for the Indians, and they are apparently not the interpreters of Cajamarca. In 1527–1528 Pizarro, in person, with Ruiz and the Thirteen (or some of them) reconnoitered the Peruvian coastal populations, perhaps as far south as Chincha. According to Cieza, the only early chronicler to tell of this trip in any detail, Pizarro landed, on the way back, at a place somewhat south of Cabo Blanco and Túmbez, and asked for boys to learn the language. The Indians gave him two, "one whom they named Felipillo, and another that they called don Martín." Farther north the Spaniards collected two more boys. One of these died a little later in Spain. Another, don Juan, was from Puertoviejo and probably not a speaker of Quechua.

The place where Pizarro got don Martín and Felipillo seems to have been the valley the Spaniards knew as Poechos, well south of Túmbez and just north of the main river valley of Piura. Gómara refers to Felipillo as "Felipillo de Poechos." The problems of don Martín's origin is more complex. In his testament don Martín does not give his birthplace, saying merely that he was a nephew of "Maicavílica, cacique of Chincha." Years later a Spaniard testified that in his opinion don Martín was a native of the valley of Chincha, though he was not sure. Despite this, other evidence tends to place don Martín's origin in the Piura region. Hernando Pizarro once declared him to be a native of the valley of San Miguel (Piura); he could not recall whether he was from the land of the cacique Lachira (Piura proper), or of Maicavilca, the two being right together. In the geographical part of Cieza's chronicle we can read that the valley of Poechos was sometimes called Maicavilca, "because in the lower part of the valley was a chief or lord called by that name."

There can thus be little doubt that don Martín as well as Felipillo had lived in Poechos, but some sort of association with Chincha remains. We can find a hint of its nature in the words of Atahuallpa to Hernando Pizarro at their first meeting; the Inca said he had a "captain" (thus the Spanish translation) on the river of Zuricara, named Maicavílica, who had told him of the Spaniards' vulnerability. No doubt, then, Maicavilca was not the native lord of Poechos, but its governor for the Incas, and as such he could easily have been from Chincha. The name Maicavilca, or Maicavílica, sounds much like names that appear on the map in the Chincha area, such as Huancavélica and Chilca. A cacique of nearby Ica was named Chayavílica. As Maicavilca's nephew, don Martín was close to the Inca imperial nobility; though he perhaps grew up in Poechos, he retained a loyalty to Chincha and may even have been born there.

From a very early time Felipillo and don Martín were rivals and enemies. The rivalry may well have had a regional and social dimension: Chincha against Piura, Quechua against Tallán, Inca noble against local chieftain or commoner. One cannot help noticing that though the Spaniards called both boys by diminutives until around the time of Cajamarca, afterward one was called "don Martín," like the caciques, or chiefs, and the other mainly retained the familiar "Feli-

pillo," like the Spaniards' Indian servants. Atahuallpa is said to have
felt mortally affronted that such a low creature as Felipillo should
aspire to one of his women.

Both boys accompanied Pizarro back to Spain in 1529, already baptized as Christians, and both were members of the expedition from its
formal inception in Toledo. By the time they got back to Túmbez they
had traversed most of the Hispanic world and had lived among Spaniards for some years of their adolescence. The linguistic results were
excellent. Garcilaso, much later, had a bad concept of the interpreters'
abilities, but this seems to rest very largely on his opinion as a Cuzco
native that no one born more than a few miles away from the Inca
capital could speak good Quechua. At the time no one complained,
and eyewitness chronicler Miguel Estete says that from Túmbez on, the
conquerors communicated readily with the Indians because "those two
Indian boys that Pizarro took to Spain understood our language very
well." Don Martín, who lived longer, aroused considerable comment
with the excellence of his spoken Spanish, though of course it may
have been better in later years that it was at the time of Cajamarca.

The supreme moments for the interpreters are also in a way their
most obscure. Probably both of them went out to the Inca encampment
for the Spaniards' first interview with Atahuallpa, since two bodies of
horse rode out at different times, one under Soto and a second under
Hernando Pizarro. Most accounts fail to say who interpreted on this
occasion; two chroniclers assert that don Martín was there, and one
mentions Felipillo's presence. But when it comes to the climactic scene
between fray Vicente de Valverde and Atahuallpa, minutes before the
capture, there is no basis for deciding whether the intermediary was
don Martín or Felipillo. All reports of the events mention only one
interpreter. Several say that he was a boy, and Cristóbal de Mena says
that the boy, whatever his name, boldly ran to retrieve the breviary
Atahuallpa had thrown among his people. Few give the boy's name.
Two writers say it was don Martín, and one of these, Miguel Estete,
was present; but Cieza, prince of chroniclers, says it was Felipillo. In
his will don Martín claimed he had been assigned a share of ten thousand pesos for his part at Cajamarca and other conquests. Such an
amount would correspond to an important personal contribution; on
the other hand, we have no idea how much may have been assigned to
Felipillo. Don Martín's share had no legal standing in any case, as it
was included in Francisco Pizarro's, and Pizarro never paid him any of

it. (This was not unusual; Pizarro also withheld the share assigned his page and relative, Pedro Pizarro, in the taking of Cuzco.)

After Cajamarca the paths of Felipillo and don Martín began to separate. Felipillo, a constant intriguer, got involved in one incident after another, and thereby earned prominent mention in the chronicles. Don Martín remained a loyal follower of the Pizarros, achieving more success with less fame. To their rivalry was now added a new dimension, that of Spanish civil strife. Felipillo became an Almagrist, don Martín a Pizarrist.

Felipillo's name is closely associated with the death of Atahuallpa. While the first Spanish reports and chronicles take very seriously the hostile forces that Atahuallpa was said to be raising and fail to mention Felipillo in this connection, the best chronicles of the 1540's and the 1550's are unanimous in saying that Felipillo maliciously invented the whole story in order to be rid of Atahuallpa, and then proved it by falsifying the testimony of Indian witnesses. Some maintain that Felipillo's reason was his love for one of Atahuallpa's wives or concubines; it is also said that he was influenced or bribed by the Spaniards newly arrived with Almagro, who feared that the whole wealth of Peru would go into Atahuallpa's ransom, and they would get nothing. In the Spanish reports there is much ill will, ignorance, and legend; we can have no idea whether there is truth at the core or not. At any rate, Felipillo's reputation was established. Cieza, Zárate, and Góngora all call him traitorous, lying, inconstant, and the like.

After Atahuallpa's death Felipillo went in Almagro's retinue, and his further behavior is better authenticated. When Almagro came to Quito in 1534 to ward off the threat of Pedro de Alvarado's intrusion into Peru, Felipillo deserted Almagro, went to Alvarado's camp, and told him how few men Almagro had. The two Spanish leaders finally came to a peaceful agreement, and Almagro came close to burning Felipillo at the stake for his attempted treason.

Somehow Felipillo got back in Almagro's favor. He was with him in Cuzco in 1535, a little before Almagro's Chilean expedition set off, and after a Pizarro-Almagro dispute ending in a fragile reconciliation. We hear that Felipillo was hobnobbing with the new Inca, Manco, to win him over to Almagro, while don Martín, who was also there, threatened the Inca for unfriendliness to Pizarro. But both were acting as much out of mutual rivalry as out of loyalty to their party.

The predictable downfall of Felipillo came while he was with Almagro on the way to Chile. The Villaumac, or Inca high priest, who was with the expedition, is supposed to have planned a revolt simultaneous with Manco Inca's siege of Cuzco. The chronicles allege that Felipillo was part of the conspiracy. At any rate, before reaching Chile proper, both fled from Almagro's camp. The Villaumac escaped, but the Spaniards finally found Felipillo, captured him, and executed him. By this time he was much more than a boy interpreter. Spanish captain Martín Monje later claimed that one of his great services to the crown was to win a mountain stronghold "where a captain called Felipillo had fortified himself with many warriors." Felipillo was caught between two cultures, or indeed three. Removed from his native Poechos before maturity, he probably also lacked any deep sense of identification with Spaniards or Incas. He had reached great prominence, always by playing one party off against another; but without a complete grasp of Spanish society and mores, this method was like dancing on quicksand.

Don Martín's procedure was far better geared to the situation. He attached himself unconditionally to Francisco and Hernando Pizarro, and followed the Pizarro family unswervingly as long as he lived. Had it not been for the accident of the Gonzalo Pizarro rebellion, he and his descendants might have entered fully into the upper levels of Spanish Peruvian society. Don Martín's life patterns are in many ways like those of any other man of Cajamarca, and so presumably could Felipillo's have been, if he had chosen a different path and a different master.

After seeing the conquest through, don Martín became a citizen and encomendero of Lima; before long he had his house there, with a Spanish wife, Spanish guests and employees, and all the appurtenances of a seigneurial life in the Spanish style, from horses to black slaves. Like the other conquerors, he accumulated honors: not it is true a seat on the council, but at least a coat of arms from the Spanish king and the title of "interpreter general." He was influential with Governor Pizarro and sought after by the Spaniards for that reason.

Even so, don Martín was no Spaniard. He lacked regional and family roots in Spain and a grasp of the subtle workings of Spanish politics. For all the positions and honors accorded him, many Spaniards naturally enough continued to view him as they would any other Indian. There was no other of his kind. His place was therefore precarious, and he failed to work his way gradually toward independence as most of the Pizarro retainers did. This mattered little, and indeed it was the best possible course for don Martín, until finally in 1548 Pizarro dominance in Peru came to an end with Gonzalo Pizarro's defeat and execution. Don Martín had followed rebel Gonzalo too long; the new authorities took his property and his encomienda and sent him into exile. He died in Seville shortly afterward. His treatment was more unceremonious than most, and possibly, unlike most of the condemned rebels, he actually received the two hundred lashes to which he was sentenced. But even here don Martín was not without parallel. All of the unrepentant followers of Gonzalo Pizarro were punished, and some important figures were executed. There were other men of Cajamarca besides don Martín who were unconditional followers of Pizarro, such as Francisco de Almendras, who died rather than abjure him, and Lucas Martínez, who stayed by his side until all hope of victory was lost and forfeited his encomienda for his obstinancy.

Don Martín's wife and his daughter, doña Francisca Pizarro, followed him to Spain, not completely destitute. In 1567 doña Francisca was at the royal court in Madrid, petitioning the crown for favors like many other descendants of the men of Cajamarca.

N O T E S .   A somewhat more detailed account of don Martín's career by this writer can be found in Lockhart, *Spanish Peru*, 213–215. Pedro Pizarro would have it (*Relación*, V, 174) that one of the two boys with the Spaniards in the Túmbez area was "don Francisquillo." This can hardly be correct in the face of so much testimony to the contrary, but don Francisquillo may well have been the third boy, who died in Spain.

For the origins of the interpreters and the pre-Cajamarca phase of their lives, see AGI, Patronato 114, ramo 9, testimony of Juan Cortés and Hernando Pizarro; ANP, Salinas 1542–1543, f.729; Cieza, *Crónica del Perú*, II, 411–412; Cieza, *Tercera parte*, in *Mercurio Peruano* 34 (1953):314–315; Estete, *Relación*, p. 23; Gómara, *Hispania victrix*, I, 238; Jerez, *Verdadera relación*, II, 324, 331; Pedro Pizarro, *Relación*, V, 168–169; Porras, *Relaciones primitivas*, pp. 21, 65–67; Zárate, *Historia*, II, 475; and the will of don Martín below. Garcilaso (*Obras*, III, 48) claims that Felipillo was a native of the island of Puná; Garcilaso wrote so late and is so manifestly corrupt on matters of the conquest that the assertion has little value despite his special knowledge about Indians. It is *conceivable* that Felipillo was born on Puná and was at Poechos as prisoner, hostage, or servant.

For the role of the interpreters in the events of Cajamarca, see Jerez, *Verdadera relación*, II, 331–332, or Zárate, *Historia*, II, 476, as typical of the many accounts that give no name; but more especially Cieza, *Tercera parte*, in *Mercurio Peruano* 38 (1957):225; Estete, *Relación*, pp. 26, 30;

Gómara, *Hispania victrix*, I, 228; Mena, "Conquista del Perú," p. 86; Pedro Pizarro, *Relación*, V, 177–178. The Cuzco rivalries of the two appear in *CDIHC*, VII, 460, and Herrera, *Historia general*, XI, 140.

For the further career of Felipillo in particular, see *CDIHC*, VII, 338; Cieza, *Tercera parte*, in *Mercurio Peruano* 39 (1958):576–578; Gómara, *Hispania victrix*, I, 231, 238; Herrera, *Historia general*, XI, 55, 319; Pedro Pizarro, *Relación*, V, 185; Zárate, *Historia*, II, 479, 482, 484.

The most comprehensive sources for don Martín's life are his will of 1545, in *Revista Histórica* 16 (1943):128–135, and the *probanza* instituted in Madrid in 1566–1567 by his daughter doña Francisca, in AGI, Patronato 114, ramo 9. A royal grant of a coat of arms, with a summary of don Martín's career up to 1537, is in Porras, *Cedulario*, II, 340 (a second, similar grant is in AGI, Lima 566, vol. IV, August 20, 1540). Further references are in AGI, Contaduría 1679, records of August, 1534, and December, 1535; Contaduría 1680, records from Cuzco, 1535, and a passage from c.1550 about Lope Martín, citizen of Cuzco, who owed don Martín money; Contaduría 1825, records from Jauja, October, 1534; Justicia 467, testimony of don Martín; ANP, Castañeda, reg. 8, f.45; Salinas 1538–1540, f.365; RA PP, I, trial of Pedro de Salinas; Salinas 1546–1548, f.208; Alzate, f.41; BNP, A29, f.37; A36, f.8; *CDIAO*, XX, 518; *CDIHE*, XLIX, 231; Calvete, *Rebelión de Pizarro*, V, 30; Cobo, *Obras*, II, 305; Loredo, *Los repartos*, pp. 226, 228; Pérez de Tudela, *Gasca*, I, 153–154.

In 1557 a don Martín, native of the valley of Lachira or la Chira (Piura), was interperter for the Royal Audiencia in Lima. Not as accomplished as his namesake and possible relative, he was unable to sign his name. (See AGI, Lima 204, *probanza* of Francisco de Ampuero.)

There was also a don Pedro, native of Túmbez, alive in Lima in 1555, who said he had been an interpreter for Marqués Pizarro (AGI, Lima 204, *probanza* of don Gonzalo, cacique of the valley of Lima). A don Francisco also interpreted for Pizarro and received an encomienda in Chachapoyas. He died sometime before the late 1540's; his wife (whether Indian or Spanish is not known) inherited the encomienda and married a Melchor Ruiz (Loredo, *Los repartos*, pp. 261–262).

Busto's article "Martinillo de Poechos," in his *Dos personajes de la conquista del Perú*, contains several assertions that it is necessary to contest. He feels that Felipillo was from Túmbez, not Poechos (pp. 14–15). The evidence on Felipillo's origin is slim enough, to be sure; there seems no reason, however, to disbelieve Cieza's statement that he joined Pizarro with don Martín at Poechos. Some other matters are clearer.

1. Busto believes don Martín definitely to have been from Poechos, and resolves the difficulty of Chincha by moving the valley hundreds of miles north to the vicinity of Piura. This is untenable. He himself quotes testi-

mony (p. 15), seen also by this writer, that the area where don Martín was born was "the valley of Chincha, which is under the head of His Majesty": that is, was administered directly by royal officials instead of given in encomienda, as was indeed the case with the famous valley south of Lima.

2. Busto declares that don Martín lied all his life about joining Pizarro in 1528; he arrives at this conclusion through an interpretation he gives to statements made by Hernando Pizarro in 1567 (AGI, Patronato 114, ramo 9). According to this, don Martín joined the Spaniards only around July, 1532, at Poechos (pp. 2–3, 8). This writer did not give Hernando Pizarro's remarks quite that construction when he read them; at any rate, Hernando specifically said he did not remember well. We have Cieza's statement on the other side, as well as statements of eyewitnesses Miguel Estete and Pedro Pizarro, that the two boy interpreters had been to Spain. Common sense also tells us that it takes more than four months to make an interpreter. Such presistent lying by don Martín lacks verisimilitude.

3. Busto thinks that don Martín's petition for a coat of arms was denied, on what evidence is unclear (p. 8). It is true that the first royal order of 1537 is phrased somewhat tentatively; but there is another, of which Busto was unaware, in the clearest words granting arms to don Martín Pizarro, *vecino* of Lima, issued at Madrid on August 20, 1540 (AGI, Lima 566, vol. IV).

4. Busto has uncovered direct testimony (AGI, Justicia 399) that don Martín took a trip to Spain in 1543–1544 on behalf of the Pizarros, apparently to carry a secret message. Yet a more conspicuous messenger is hard to imagine, and, as Busto points out, don Martín's presence in Lima in August, 1543, is documented in Lima parochial records (*RANP* 12 [1939]:106), whereas the testimony would have him leaving Spain on the way back only two months later. The contradiction remains unresolved.

John Hemming's recent *Conquest of the Incas* goes into the lives of the interpreters thoroughly, on the basis of primary and secondary materials very similar to those used here, though the overlap is not complete; he gives much detail on the career of Felipillo. A careful comparison of his treatments with mine will uncover much congruity, some direct dependence, and some conflict on interesting points which must remain undiscussed for the present.

Appendix I
A Letter from Cajamarca

Correspondence written from Cajamarca before the Spaniards left the site is extremely rare, and, to this writer's knowledge, no private letters have appeared at all until now, though many must have accompanied the first group of men who left for Spain in July, 1533. In the course of scanning papers in the Archive of the Indies, Justicia 1124, no. 5, ramo 1, the writer came upon a copy of such a letter, which is here published in English and Spanish, probably for the first time. (As old document detective Rafael Loredo once said, only the naive or foolhardy would make an outright claim that any given Spanish document had not been published before, somewhere or sometime.)

The letter is from Gaspar de Marquina, or Gárate, one of Pizarro's pages, to his father in the valley of Mendaro in the Basque country. In Gaspar's biography above, some details of his life may be found, but the reader of the letter needs only to know that he was Basque and an illegitimate son (though recognized), and that he was killed shortly afterward in an Indian skirmish.

Gaspar wrote hastily, repeating himself and making occasional mistakes (some of which are slightly rectified in the English version). The result is freshness, an impression of reality, and an excellent psychological portrait that emerges as Gaspar, writing what comes naturally to his mind, reveals what is important and unimportant to him. Whether Gaspar can be considered typical is problematic, since he was Basque and without long experience in the Indies. At least we have here the private views of a young man who was literate, but who was not compromised by any position of leadership.

An interesting aspect of the letter is the light it throws on the meaning of religion to the "ordinary" Spaniard in the Indies in the conquest period. Nowhere does Gaspar mention that the Indians might be converted to Christianity, or should be. Valverde's sermon to Atahuallpa, for many commentators the most dramatic and significant episode in the whole chain of

events at Cajamarca, is totally ignored. Gaspar merely says that when Atahuallpa got to where the Spaniards were, they rushed out and seized him.
It is apparent that the whole question of the religious and moral justification of the conquest does not concern Gaspar in the least; he takes that as
a given.

Yet his language is sprinkled with God and Jesus Christ and "the service of our Lord." Partly this is the usage of the time; partly it reflects how
religion has indeed touched Gaspar deeply in two ways. The old veterans
among the Spaniards understood what an advantage steel and horses gave
them on flat ground, but this was not so obvious to the young or inexperienced, like Gaspar, and even the veterans were often taken aback by the
Indians' overwhelming numbers and the stunning effect of Spanish
weapons and devices. Thus they readily grasped at miracles to explain their
victories, an explanation that still tempts agnostics four hundred years
later, and they prayed for divine favor before every battle.

Even more basic than the God of Battles was the social religion of the
time. The whole ambition of most Spaniards in the Indies, "conquerors"
or not, was to amount to something. This was in the first instance an individual goal, but inherent in it was the idea of raising the prestige of one's
whole lineage. Some of the most essential vehicles for giving generational
depth to a family's renown were religious: chaplaincies for future generations and masses for the dead. Hence Gaspar's strongly expressed desire
to "do good" for the souls of his parents. It may appear incongruous, if
charming, that Gaspar leaps from money to high drama, from cousins to
the souls of the dead, but all are strung on the same thread. Gaspar's letter
tells how he has won wealth and honor, and how he desires and intends
to share these things with his lineage.

Observers often fail to recognize the intensity of Spanish self-preoccupa-
tion in the conquest period, or, if they recognize it, fail to understand it.
For the ordinary Spaniard of the time, Spain and his home town were
everything, and his family more than everything. It was very hard for any
outside element to touch the Spaniards in their vitals. Gaspar admires the
resources of Peru as something to be used. He is amazed at the Incas as a
spectacle, and more than a little afraid of them; but they do not touch him.
As far as he is concerned he is in the "new country" of New Castile, whose
governor is Francisco Pizarro. There is no malice in Gaspar's attitude toward the Indians, merely heedlessness. In his own Spanish context, Gaspar
emerges as an observant and well-trained boy with a good heart.

Gaspar also illustrates the truly ambivalent attitude of the Spaniards
toward home and returning home. It is evident that Gaspar is deeply
rooted, and when he thinks about home he falls into a deep longing, made
more poignant by his imminent and not totally unexpected death. Yet, as
he says, he has hardly had time to think of such things; first the battle

with poverty absorbed him, then the momentum of the conquest carried him forward. Only in the Indies can he gain the wealth that brings honor at home. Had Gaspar lived until 1534 and the general license to leave Peru, there is no telling whether he would have stayed or gone; either way, he would have been torn.

The phrase Gaspar uses to describe the riches of Peru, "more gold and silver than iron in Biscay," is not original with him, nor did it occur to him because he was a Basque. Rather it was constantly on the lips of the Spaniards when they talked of mineral wealth. The following translation is slightly free in places. It seemed more important to communicate with the English-speaking reader of the twentieth century than to give a false impression of quaintness through excessive accuracy. For example, Gaspar calls his father "Vuestra merced," or "Your grace"; even at that time this had the force of a formal pronoun, and is rendered simply as "you." In any case, the Spanish version is appended.

To my longed-for father, Martín de Gárate, in Mendaro
Dear Sir,

It must be about three years ago that I got a letter from you, in which you asked me to send some money. God knows how sorry I was not to have anything to send you then, because if I had anything then there wouldn't have been any need for you to write; I've always tried to do the right thing, but there wasn't any possibility till now. You also told me to remember my homeland, God knows if I remember my homeland or not, but as I said, till now there hasn't been time to think of it, because I give you my word that I never had a penny the whole time since I came to these parts until six months ago, when God was pleased to give me more than I deserved, and now I have over 3,000 ducats; please God that it will be for his holy service.

Sir, I'm sending you 213 pesos of good gold in a bar with an honorable man from San Sebastián; in Seville he'll have it turned into coin and then bring it to you. I'd send you more except he's taking money for other people too and couldn't take more. His name is Pedro de Anadel, I know him, and he's the kind of person who will get the money to you, so that's why I asked him to do me a favor and take you the money.

Sir, I would like to be the messenger myself, but it couldn't be, because we're in new country and haven't been here long, and they aren't giving license to leave except to married men who have been in these parts for a long time. I expect to be there with you in two years with the aid of our Lord; I swear to God that I have a greater desire to be there than you have to see me, so that I can give you a good old age.

Sir, I'll tell you something of my life since I came to these parts; you must know how I went to Nicaragua with Governor Pedrarias as his page, and I was with him till God was pleased to take him from this world. He died very poor and so all of his servants were left poor too, as the carrier of this letter can very well tell you when he sees you, and then a few days after he died we got news of how Governor Francisco Pizarro was coming to be governor of this kingdom of New Castile and so, hearing this news and having few prospects in Nicaragua, we came to this district, where there's more gold and silver than iron in Biscay, and more sheep than in Soria, and great supplies of all kinds of provisions, and fine clothing and the best people that have been seen in the whole Indies, and many great lords among them, one of them rules over 500 leagues. We have him prisoner in our power, and with him prisoner, a man can go by himself 500 leagues without getting killed, instead they give you whatever you need and carry you on their shoulders in a litter.

We took this lord by a miracle of God, because our forces wouldn't be enough to take him nor to do what we did, but God gave us the victory miraculously over him and his forces. You must know that we came here with Governor Francisco Pizarro to the land of this lord where he had 60,000 warriors, and there were 160 Spaniards with the governor, and we thought our lives were finished because there was such a horde of them, and even the women were making fun of us and saying they were sorry for us because we were going to get killed; but afterward their bad thoughts turned out the opposite. The lord came with all his armed men within two shots of a crossbow from where we were camped and pitched his camp there, and then from there he came to see the Governor and what kind of people we were, with about 5,000 men all dressed in his livery, and him in a litter covered with gold, with a hundred nobles carrying him and sweeping the ground in front of his litter, and all of them singing in unison, and when he arrived where we were, the Governor rushed out with all his men and we attacked them and seized the lord and killed many of his people, most of the ones that came with him, and then we went out where all the rest of the warriors were, all armed with lances 15 feet long, and we routed them all. In the rout we killed 8,000 men in about two hours and a half, and we took much gold and clothing and many people, it would be too long to tell if it all were told; the bearer of the present letter can inform you, and I won't say more because as I say, it would be too long to tell.

Give my greetings to Catalina and my brothers and sisters and my uncle Martín de Altamira and his daughters, especially the older one, because I am much in her debt, and also to my cousins Martín de Altamira and Marina de Gárate and my uncle San Juan de Gárate and my uncle Pedro Sánchez de Arizmendi and all the rest of my relatives, because I've already forgotten many of their names. I really want you to greet them all from me and tell them that I greatly desire to see them, and pleasing God I'll be there soon. Sir, the only thing I want to ask you is to do good for the souls of my mother and all my relatives, and if God lets me get there, I'll do it very thoroughly myself. There is nothing more to write at present except that I'm praying to our Lord Jesus Christ to let me see you before I die. From Cajamarca, in the kingdom of New Castile, July 20, 1533.

Your son who would rather see than write you,
Gaspar de Gárate

On the outside is a memorandum to Anadel, bearer of the letter:

Sir, I implore you to write me with the first people who come, and if by chance God our Lord has been pleased to take my father from this world, give the 213 pesos to my uncle Martín de Altamira and to San Juan de Gárate, jointly to both, and if one of them is dead, to either of them, so that with 100 pesos they can do good for the souls of my parents Martín de Gárate and María Ramírez de Altamira, and divide the other 113 pesos among my brothers and sisters, and in case both my uncles are dead, to my brother Jorge de Gárate with a guardian, who as I say should do good for my parents with the hundred and divide all the rest between himself and his and my brothers and sisters, all equally.

Gaspar de Marquina

In the following Spanish version the orthography has been modernized and to some extent the punctuation as well. The copy in AGI, Justicia 1124, no. 5, ramo 1, on which the following is based, is not Gaspar's holograph, but an authorized contemporary copy by a notary.

A mi muy deseado señor padre Martín de Gárate
Muy deseado señor padre,

Una carta de vuestra merced recibí habrá bien tres años poco más o menos, en la cual me enviaba a mandar que le enviase algunos dineros. Dios sabe la pena que yo recibí por no tenerlos entonces para enviárselos, que si yo entonces los tuviera no hubiera necesidad que vuestra merced me escribiere, que yo he tenido el cuidado que era razón, empero no ha habido lugar hasta ahora, y también encargándome que tuviese memoria de mi tierra; Dios sabe si tengo memoria o no de mi tierra, sino que como digo no ha habido tiempo de acordarme de ella hasta ahora, porque yo le doy mi fe que hasta ahora yo no he tenido un real después que en estas partes pasé sino de seis meses a esta parte, que Dios me ha querido dar más que yo merecía, que hoy día de la fecha tengo tres mil ducados largos. Plega a Dios que será para su santo servicio.

Señor, allá envío a vuestra merced 213 castellanos de buen oro en una barra con una persona honrada de San Sebastián; en Sevilla la hará moneda y se lo llevará, y más le enviara a vuestra merced, sino que lleva muchos dineros de otras personas y no pudo llevar más, el cual se llama Pedro de

Anadel, porque le conozco, y es persona que los dará a vuestra merced, por eso le rogué que me hiciese merced de se los llevar.

Señor, yo quisiera ser el mensajero, empero no pudo ser, porque estábamos en tierra nueva y ha poco que estamos en ella, y no dan licencia sino a hombres casados que ha mucho tiempo que están en estas partes. De hoy en dos años pienso ser allá con vuestra merced con el ayuda de Nuestro Señor, que juro a Dios que más deseo tengo de estar allá que vuestra merced de verme, por darle buena vejez.

Señor, quiero dar a vuestra merced la cuenta de mi vida que ha sido después que pasé e estas partes. Vuestra merced sabrá como yo fui a Nicaragua con el gobernador Pedrarias por su paje, y estuve con él hasta que Dios fue servido de llevarle de este mundo, el cual murió muy pobre, y así quedamos pobres todos sus criados, como el que la presente lleva se lo podrá bien contar si con él se ve, y despues de él muerto de a pocos días, tuvimos nueva como el gobernador Francisco Pizarro venía por gobernador de estos reinos de la Nueva Castilla, y así sabida nueva con el poco remedio que teníamos en Nicaragua pasamos a su gobernación, donde hay más oro y plata que hierro en Vizcaya, y más ovejas que en Soria, y muy bastecida de otras muchas comidas, mucha ropa muy buena, y la mejor gente que se ha visto en todas las Indias, y muchos señores grandes. Entre ellos hay unos que sujetan quinientas leguas en largo, el cual tenemos preso en nuestro poder, que teniendo a él preso, puede ir un hombre solo quinientas, sin que le maten, sino que antes le den todo lo que ha menester para su persona, y le lleven a cuestas en una hamaca, al cual dicho señor le prendimos por milagro de Dios, que nuestras fuerzas no bastaran prenderle ni hacer lo que hicimos, sino que Dios milagrosamente nos quiso dar victoria contra él y de su fuerza.

Vuestra merced sabrá que con el gobernador Francisco Pizarro venimos a su tierra de este señor donde tenía sesenta mil hombres de guerra 160 españoles con el gobernador, donde pensamos que nuestras vidas eran fenecidas porque tanta era la pujanza de la gente que hasta las mujeres hacían burla de nosotros y nos habían lástima como nos habían de matar, aunque despues nos salió al través su mal pensamiento, que vino aquel señor con toda su gente armada dos tiros de ballesta de donde nosotros teníamos asentado nuestro real, y allí asentó su real, y de allí vino a ver al señor gobernador qué gente eramos con obra de cinco mil hombres, todos de su librea, y él en unas andas guarnecidas de oro, y con cien señores que lo traían a cuestas, limpiándole las pajas del suelo por donde sus andas pasaban, todos cantando a una voz, y de que llegó donde nosotros estábamos saltó el gobernador con toda su gente y dimos en ellos y prendimos al señor y matámosle mucha gente, toda la más que con él venía, y salimos donde estaba toda la gente de guerra, todos con sus lanzas de a 25 palmos, y desbaratamos toda, en el cual desbarate matamos ocho mil hombres en obra de dos horas y media, y tomamos mucho oro y mucha ropa y mucha gente, lo cual sería largo de contar si todo lo hubiese de contar. El que la presente lleva se podrá bien informar.

En esta no diré más porque como digo será largo de contar, sino que vuestra merced dé mis encomiendas a la señora Catalina y a mis hermanos y hermanas y a mi tío Martín de Altamira y a sus hijas, en especial a la mayor, que le soy mucho en cargo, y también a mi tío San Juan de Gárate y a mi tío Pedro Sánchez de Arezmendi y a todos los otros mis parientes y parientas, que ya de muchos de ellos no se me acuerda. Tomo a mucho que se la dé allá a todos y diga que tengo mucho deseo de verlos, que placiendo a Dios, presto seré allá. Señor, no quiero encargar a vuestra merced otra cosa sino que haga bien por el ánima de mi madre y de todos mis parientes, y si Dios me deja ir allá yo lo haré cumplidamente. No hay más que le escribir más al presente, sino que quedo rogando a nuestro señor Jesucristo me deje ver a vuestra merced antes que muera. Fecha en Cajamarca en los reinos de la Nueva Castilla, en 20 de julio de 1533 años.

Vuestro hijo que más ver que escribir os desea,
Gaspar de Gárate

And on the outside, to Anadel:

Señor, suplico a vuestra merced me escriba con los próximos que pudiere, y digo que si por ventura Dios nuestro señor ha querido llevar a mi padre de este mundo, le dé los 213 castellanos a mi tío Martín de Altamira y San Juan de Gárate juntamente a entrambos, y si alguno de ellos fuere muerto a cualquier de ellos, para que con los 100 pesos haga bien por las ánimas de mis padres Martín de Gárate y María Ramírez de Altamira, y los otros 113 pesos repartan entre mis hermanos, y si por caso fueren muertos entrambos mis tíos, a mi hermano Jorge de Gárate con un tutor, que como digo haga bien por mis padres con los ciento y lo otro reparta entre él y sus hermanos míos y hermanas a todos por igual.

Gaspar de Marquina

As explained in Part I, chapter 4, the roll of Cajamarca is a list of shares rather than of participants. Therefore some Spaniards might have been present who received no share and consequently are absent from the list, fray Vicente de Valverde being a known example. It is also a possibility— one that has been less considered—that some of those on the list might not have taken part in the events. There is thus room for error and uncertainty, and an assessment of the list's reliability is called for.

We now know definitely that one man on the distribution list, Juan de Sosa, not only did not participate in Atahuallpa's capture, but was not even physically present in the Cajamarca area at the time. Despite this deviation, it is quite certain that appearance on the list can generally be equated with participation, because the distribution of treasure was so closely tied to pres-ence at Cajamarca. Those who were there shared in all the gold and silver that came into the Spanish camp for months after the capture, while all others got only token amounts. The whole distinction between the two groups was actual presence when the Inca was taken, for many of those left at San Miguel had been important expedition members all the way from Panama. If even they do not appear on the list, we may conclude that Sosa was the only exception made, one which was politically possible because he was an ecclesiastic.

An extremely close correspondence between participants and recipients of treasure can be seen also through comparison of the Cajamarca list with other reports. Most contemporary commentators, eyewitnesses or not, limit themselves to rounded estimates that there were something on the order of 150 to 170 men. Such accounts establish a general framework but lack the necessary precision. Fortunately there exists an exact statement by the man in the best position to know: Francisco de Jerez, Pizarro's secretary, who had chief responsibility for drawing up the distribution lists. In his chroni-cle-report, written before he left Peru in 1533, he says that a general muster was held south of San Miguel in September, 1532. There were found to be 67 horsemen and 110 footmen; 5 horsemen and 4 footmen then returned to San Miguel, leaving Pizarro with 62 horse and 106 foot to carry on the campaign.[1] If we count the names on the roll of Cajamarca, we find that, omitting Juan de Sosa, there are 62 horse and 105 foot. The missing footman would seem to be fray Vicente de Valverde. The men of Cajamarca are thus accounted for completely; all those listed, except Sosa, were present, and all those present are known, except that there could possibly have been one more footman if fray Vicente was not counted at the muster. This is highly unlikely, since Jerez says that they counted "Christians."

There is a strong presumption, then, against the truth of any claims raised for the participation of men not on the general list. In this light we can discuss some cases in which error has arisen or might arise.

1. On the List but Not Present: Juan de Sosa

Secular priest Juan de Sosa is a unique case. His name appears near the top of the Cajamarca list, where he is assigned a very respectable 1¾ shares of gold and silver. Though one might have suspected that he was not in fact a horseman, there has been no reason to assume that he was not present at the events. Nevertheless, in testimony given in Seville in 1535, participant Pedro de Barrera says in so many words that Pizarro ordered Juan de Sosa to stay behind in Piura and that Sosa did so, with the understanding that he would receive his share as if he had been there. He came to Cajamarca only afterward.[2] Chronicler Cieza was apparently aware of all this, for he dropped Sosa from his version of the Cajamarca list.[3]

Though not a participant in the strict sense, Sosa is so closely associated with the men and events studied in this book that it will be well to discuss his life briefly. He was probably related to Hernando de Sosa, footman at Cajamarca. The Cajamarca gold he brought back to Spain in 1533 is mentioned in the chronicles in the same breath as Captain Cristóbal de Mena's. Perhaps Sosa deliberately misrepresented his role, perhaps not, but chronicler Oviedo had the impression from listening to Sosa's friends that he had literally taken part in the capture. Sosa's subsequent career shows patterns often seen in the lives of the other men; he is another of those who, like Soto, Benalcázar, and Pedro Sancho, tried to use the fame and wealth of Peru to carve out new jurisdictions for themselves in other parts of the Indies. He offers an example of a type, the priest-entrepreneur, which was

[1] Francisco de Jerez, *Verdadera relación*, II, 325. The number of footmen going on with Pizarro is there given incorrectly as 102. That there is a mistake can be seen from the fact that the figures as given do not tally with each other. They appear correctly in the other version of Jerez's report in Gonzalo Oviedo, *Historia*, V, 39.

[2] AGI, Justicia 719, no. 9.

[3] See Part I, ch. 5.

common in the conquest period and, in the person of Hernando de Luque, was important for the conquest of Peru, yet chances not to appear among the men of Cajamarca themselves.

Juan de Sosa was born in Seville, the son of Ana Martín and Luis de Sosa, who is said to have been a baker. His birthdate is unknown, but he was already an ordained priest when he came to the Indies in 1528, so he could hardly have been born after 1505. His exact whereabouts and activities between 1528 and 1532 are also a mystery, but it is apparently this time of his life that Oviedo is referring to when he says he knew Sosa in Panama, "involved in the things of the world." By the time we find him in San Miguel in late 1532 he had become the vicar of the Peruvian expedition; since no other such appears in any record, it is probable that he was with the conquerors from Panama.

Our first direct glimpse of Sosa shows him still absorbed in secular affairs. In effect he refused to stay in San Miguel unless he was given a share of Inca treasure. No sooner was Atahuallpa captured than Sosa hurried from San Miguel to Cajamarca. In order to expedite his departure for Spain, he sold his share in advance to secretary Pedro Sancho, who also took over Sosa's outstanding debts and credits. One can see that Sosa had been engaging in entrepreneurial activity in the course of the expedition. In the matter of speed Sosa was successful, since he arrived in Seville in December, 1533, on the galleon *San Salvador*, the first ship to bring Peruvian treasure to Spain. As a speculation, his maneuver went awry, for Pedro Sancho made a large profit. When Sancho himself arrived in Spain in 1536, Sosa sued him in vain for the excess.

Even so, Sosa had great wealth, and he went as many other conquerors did to display it at the royal court. His purpose at court was not merely frivolous, however. Like his business rival, Sancho, and like Benalcázar and Soto on a larger scale, Sosa wanted royal sanction to undertake some enterprise in the Indies, in which he could gain honor and wealth independently and not be under the thumb of the Pizarros. But though custom sanctioned the involvement of clerics in the organization, financing, and supplying of expeditions, a priest could hardly be made Adelantado or captain general.

Thus Sosa's interest in the conquest of Veragua, on the Caribbean coast west of Panama, resulted in a four-hundred–man expedition in 1536 of which Sosa may have been the eminence grise, but a young pseudo-courtier named Felipe Gutiérrez bore the title of governor. Life in the Indies was hard indeed for ambitious secular priests; they could not have encomiendas, coats of arms, or council seats, and all the bishoprics went to friars. One of the Veragua venture's three large ships belonged to Sosa personally, and he loaded in it many supplies and provisions to be sold at the right time to expedition members. The expedition itself was a frightful disaster, as might have been predicted. Tropical, mountainous Veragua had been the graveyard of Spanish intruders before and often would be again. The command was divided; Sosa did what he pleased. Once he attempted to go as captain of a contingent of men exploring the interior, causing a bitter argument with Felipe Gutiérrez. But in Oviedo's account, on which we must rely for the whole Veragua episode, Sosa's behavior appears to stem mainly from the fact that he was far superior to Gutiérrez in experience and judgment. As the men died off from disease, Indian fighting, and hunger, Sosa adjusted to the situation, abandoned his capitalism, and accepted his loss, freely giving his investment in food and stock to those in greatest need.

Before a year was out the few survivors evacuated the area; from Panama both Gutiérrez and Sosa went impoverished to Peru. In June of 1537 Bernaldino de Sosa, who was apparently the nephew Juan de Sosa had with him in Veragua, arrived in Lima. Juan probably came at much the same time, though he does not appear in the records until 1539. Juan de Sosa now faced the same lot as others who returned to Peru. The desirable positions, lay or ecclesiastic, were filled; qualified claimants by the score were already standing in line; society was hardening. With no capital and little hope of a benefice, Sosa was left in a very marginal position. He floated from city to city; for a while, in 1540, he was curate in highland Huamanga, where his relative Bernaldino by now held an encomienda.

Such a situation bred discontent and made the Gonzalo Pizarro revolt, when it came, even more attractive to Sosa than it might otherwise have been. (The same was true of Sosa's lay counterpart Juan García de Santa Olalla, who lost his fortune to French pirates and then came back to Peru.) As Pizarro began to organize his forces in Cuzco in 1544, Bishop Loaysa in Lima started toward the highland to attempt to pacify the incipient rebellion. In his retinue went Juan de Sosa. Loaysa was stopped in Huamanga by Pizarro's advance men; Sosa, instead of aiding Loaysa, sent a message by Bernaldino de Sosa's Indians to Pizarro, urging him to be steadfast in his purpose and not to listen to the bishop, who came to deceive him.

During the time that Gonzalo Pizarro was in power, Sosa's affairs flourished. Gonzalo, as a man of Cajamarca, was a respecter of seniority, and he was also very grateful for allies among the clergy. Sosa now received generous subsidies from the royal treasury; in 1547 he was the vicar-general of the diocese of Cuzco. Naturally he became ever more passionately identified with the rebellion. After the cruel battle of Huarina he granted Gonzalo Pizarro absolution, and his gestures of strong support continued even as most Peruvian Spaniards were going over to the other side.

If Sosa ever repented, he did so too late. In June, 1548, after Pizarro's defeat, Bishop Loaysa made him stand in the cathedral of Cuzco with a rope around his neck and a candle in his hand, to hear a sentence of suspension from the priesthood for two years, confiscation of all property, and exile from Peru. It appears that Sosa did in fact depart for Spain shortly afterward, unlike the many "exiles" who never stirred from the country. His further fate is not known. Cajamarca was central to Sosa's twenty-year career in the Indies. His first phase as a small entrepreneur was aimed at it; his Veragua venture was the result of it; and his second stay in Peru was marked by his inability to reduce the expectations it had raised.[4]

2. Contemporary False Claims

Given the fame of Cajamarca, it is amazing to discover how few Spaniards lied about being there. In the strictly contemporary period, up to about 1550, when there were many participants still alive, no fully authenticated case of misrepresentation has come to this writer's attention. Sometimes the very form of an interrogatory would mislead witnesses into an apparent untruth. Particularly there is the blanket question which enumerates all the events of the conquest, perhaps from the founding of San Miguel to the taking of Cuzco, and then asks if the witness saw a given person there. The witness will usually say yes, he saw it all, without really meaning to claim specific presence at Atahuallpa's capture.[5]

The nearest approach to a direct false claim in the earlier time is in the royal grant of a coat of arms to Pedro Díaz, the expedition's assayer and founder, dated August 1, 1539. After summarizing Díaz's past services, it goes on to say "and you took part in the capture of the cacique Atahuallpa." Yet Pedro Díaz himself refutes this in his testimony of 1535, where his statement reads "the Governor went toward Cajamarca and Jerónimo de Aliaga with him, and after Atahuallpa was captured this witness went to Cajamarca and found Aliaga there with the others who were in the capture of Atahuallpa." Usually the services recited in a coat of arms reproduced the statement made by the applicant, but conceivably there was some mistake involved in this case. Pedro Díaz had a crucial role in the distribution of treasure at Cajamarca, as the man who evaluated the gold and silver. He

[4] Sosa's parents and birthplace are given in Cristóbal Bermúdez Plata, *Pasajeros*, I:264. AGI, Justicia 719, no. 9, contains litigation between Sosa and Pedro Sancho. Oviedo's account of the Veragua expedition, with many valuable details on Sosa personally, is in his *Historia*, III, 187–194. Other references are in AGI, Contratación 2715, no. 1; Contaduría 1679; ANP, PA 88; Salinas 1538–1540, f.29; Salinas 1546–1548, ff.371–372; HC 403, 1241; Juan Cristóbal Calvete, *Rebelión de Pizarro*, V, 28, 55; Pedro de Cieza, *Quito* (Jiménez, ed.), pp. 119, 134–135; Diego Fernández, *Historia*, I, 230; Pedro Gutiérrez de Santa Clara, *Quinquenarios*, IV, 26; Jerez, *Verdadera relación*, II:344; Juan Pérez de Tudela, *Gasca*, II, 264. For further examples of the type of the priest-entrepreneur in the conquest of Peru, see James Lockhart, *Spanish Peru*, p. 55.

[5] Francisco de Talavera and Pedro Martín de Sicilia answer this way, for example, in *RANP* 1 (1920):463, 465. The testimony of Iñigo González in Benalcázar's *probanza* may be of this kind, if the person is not indeed Nuño González (see under Nuño González, notes).

probably even received some of the treasure in payment for his work. Perhaps he alluded to this in his statement, and the subtleties were lost on the officials at the Spanish royal court.[6]

3. Later False Claims

As the years passed, Cajamarca spawned myths and legends, good examples of which can be seen in Garcilaso's account. By 1565 or 1570 the survivors of the events were few indeed. The second and third generations of Peruvian Spaniards tended to think that all the veterans of the conquest had been at Cajamarca, or were among the Thirteen. Claims of this kind are too frequent and too insubstantial to take cognizance of them all. Garcilaso says once that by the phrase "first conqueror" he means only men of Cajamarca. But in fact he uses the word loosely, including conquerors of Cuzco and indeed apparently anyone in the country by 1535. A 1570 interrogatory by the Mercedarian order claims that a Luis de Atienza and Lozano, citizens of Trujillo, were of "those of Cajamarca." Actually Atienza's name was Blas, and both he and Rodrigo Lozano declared specifically that they were not at Cajamarca.[7] Chronicler Herrera was probably basing himself on similar legends when he added Pedro Alonso Carrasco, a conqueror of Cuzco, to his version of the Cajamarca list. This writer has found no direct statement proving Herrera in error, but in all the many years Pedro Alonso lived in Peru, no one asked him to testify about Cajamarca, as he did about the siege of Cuzco. Herrera's addition of Pedro de Vergara need hardly be mentioned, since Vergara does not appear in Peruvian records before 1536.

The changed atmosphere of the times and the increasing absence of those who could contradict induced the old veterans to begin telling lies themselves. Juan de la Torre, who was an authentic member of the Thirteen and had little apparent need to fabricate, claimed in 1565 that he had seen the capture of Atahuallpa.[8] His instinct was right, however; the conquest brought far greater rewards than the discovery. The most prominent old liar was Mancio Sierra de Leguízamo, who fibbed not only about Cajamarca, but about the great golden image of the sun he supposedly got at the taking of Cuzco, and many other marvels. Finally he was caught in his own net. When it came time to make his will the priests urged him to make restitution for his share at Cajamarca as some others of the more long-lived conquerors had done. Rather than admit the truth, Mancio Sierra in this solemn document continued to affirm his presence at Cajamarca and claimed

---

[6] CDIAO, X, 239–240; RANP 1 (1920):434–435; Santiago Montoto, Nobiliario, p. 97.

[7] AGI, Lima 118, probanza of Blas de Atienza. For Lozano see under Lozano, above, p. 437. See also p. 105.

[8] DHA, II, 321; Raúl Porras, in Diego de Trujillo, Relación, pp. 79–81.

that in the formal distribution he had received a share of 2,000 pesos—a patent falsehood—for which he then ordered his heirs to arrange restitution.[9]

4. Final Doubts

This writer was for some time under the impression that the Francisco Martín of Cajamarca was Francisco Pizarro's half brother Francisco Martín de Alcántara, but such is not the case, as is seen under Francisco Martín above.

Another cloudy matter was the presence or absence of Pedro Pizarro, the chronicler, who in the conquest was one of Governor Pizarro's pages. Though several scholars have correctly said that he was not present, they did so on the basis of Pedro's absence from the general list, and this is not completely conclusive evidence in his case, because sometimes pages were omitted from distribution lists, or only included under their masters. Thus, in the distribution of Cuzco in 1534, Pizarro's share was said to be "for his person, two horses, the interpreters and Pedro Pizarro his page." Yet we know that Gaspar de Marquina, also apparently Pizarro's page, received an independent share at Cajamarca. The issue is resolved in favor of Pedro's staying behind in San Miguel by his own testimony: that "this witness saw Pedro Navarro in Cajamarca, and he must have been in the capture of Atahuallpa with the others."[10]

[9] *RAHC* 4:95; Porras, in Trujillo, *Relación*, pp. 111–113.
[10] AGI, Justicia 432, no. 2, ramo 3; Rafael Loredo, *Los repartos*, p. 101.

BIBLIOGRAPHY

Most of what needs to go into a bibliographical essay has already been said. The Preface describes the antecedents of the present work. Sources, both printed and archival, for the individual biographies, have been thoroughly evaluated in the notes. A general discussion of sources for early Peruvian social history may be seen in Lockhart, *Spanish Peru*, pp. 269–272.

Perhaps a specific statement of the relation of the research for this project to that carried out by Raúl Porras Barrenechea and José Antonio del Busto Duthurburu would be in place here. Almost but not quite all of the original materials—chronicles and AGI documents—on which their publications are based have been consulted. When an important point in their work rested on something not seen by the author, as occasionally happened, it was accepted, after careful analysis, in view of the two scholars' general reliability, even though in Porras's case this meant taking his word pure and simple. In addition to what Porras and Busto saw, the author used other material in the AGI, above all Contaduría 1825 (which deserves publication in its entirety), and several items in the section "Justicia." This book's documentation gained much from the general survey of sources carried out for *Spanish Peru*, considerably broader than any Porras or Busto ever undertook; particularly their portrayals lack the social-economic dimension that comes out of the Peruvian notarial records.

Aside from the idea of the complete sample, the research techniques employed here are mainly those of *Spanish Peru*, except that even more use has been made of the historian's classic detective work. The tracing of individuals, drawing every implication from each scrap of data, and subjecting all to the closest kind of comparison, here reaches an intensity more often associated with biblical exegesis or the study of prehistoric man. It pays dividends in sharpening the eye for social distinctions and patterns, in retrieving coherent careers from disconnected fragments, and occasionally in relatively spectacular discoveries, such as the fact that Juan García pregonero was black.

John Hemming's *Conquest of the Incas* appeared when preparation of

the present book was almost complete. Hemming's work combines popular-
ization with a rather high degree of bibliographical thoroughness. Its contribution lies primarily in its concentration of a great deal of scattered work
on Indians, especially on the high nobles. There is very little information
about the first conquerors or the conquering expedition that is not given in
greater depth here. Therefore in the notes no attempt has been made to
give specific references to Hemming. Specialists may find it useful to consult Hemming's Index for individuals of interest to them. As a narrative,
the work is the fullest and most reliable yet to appear, but we must still
await an account of the conquest that is balanced, multidimensional, and
analytical.

The following bibliography does not make distinctions between primary
and secondary sources. Almost all items were used for the primary information in them. Only Porras, Góngora, and Pérez de Tudela had any influence
of an interpretational nature on the author.

Archival Sources

Notes to the individual biographies give the best idea as to the true extent of the archival sources. Whereas in *Spanish Peru* the Peruvian notarial
archives were more important than the Archive of the Indies, the two elements are more equally balanced here. The AGI's "Patronato," in the sections on sixteenth-century Peru between legajos 90 and 185, contained
testimonials crucial to the research. Others were in the section "Lima."
"Justicia" contained much litigation of relatives trying to recover fortunes
left by the men of Cajamarca. The importance of Contaduría 1825 and Indiferente General 1801 has been emphasized above.

Notarial records in the Archivo Nacional del Perú, Archivo Histórico de
Arequipa, Archivo Histórico Nacional del Cuzco, and Biblioteca Nacional
del Perú told much about the daily lives of the conquerors. All-important
was the early Protocolo Ambulante in the Archivo Nacional. The Library
of Congress holds some equally crucial notarial documents in its Harkness
Collection. The published calendar of the latter is useful, but not thoroughly reliable paleographically. A small number of related documents are in
the Lilly Library of Indiana University.

Published Sources

Altolaguirre y Duvale, Angel de. *Vasco Núñez de Balboa*. Madrid, 1914.
Alvarez Rubiano, Pablo. *Pedrarias Dávila*. Madrid, 1944.
Anghiera, Pietro Martire d'. *De orbe novo*. 2 vols. Madrid, 1892.
Angulo, Domingo. "El Capitán Gerónimo de Aliaga." *RANP* 2 (1921).
————. "El conquistador Pedro de Alconchel." *RANP* 9 (1936).
Atienza, Julio de. *Nobiliario español. Diccionario heráldico de appellidos
    españoles y de títulos nobiliarios*. Madrid, 1954.

Barriga, Víctor M., ed. *Documentos para la historia de Arequipa* [*DHA*]. 3 vols. Arequipa, 1939–1955.

———, ed. *Los mercedarios en el Perú en el siglo XVI. Documentos inéditos del Archivo de Indias.* 5 vols. Vol. I, Rome, 1933; vols. II–V, Arequipa, 1939–1954.

Bermúdez Plata, Cristóbal, ed. *Catálogo de pasajeros a Indias.* 3 vols. Seville, 1940–1946.

Blanco Castillo, Francisco. *Hernando de Soto, el centauro de las Indias.* Madrid, n.d.

Borregán, Alonso. *Crónica de la conquista del Perú.* Edited by Rafael Loredo. Seville, 1948.

Bourne, Edward Gaylord, ed. *Narratives of the Career of Hernando de Soto.* Translated by Buckingham Smith. 2 vols. London: D. Nutt, 1905.

Boyd-Bowman, Peter. *Indice geobiográfico de cuarenta mil pobladores españoles de América en el siglo XVI.* Vol. I, 1493–1519, Bogotá, 1964; vol. II, 1520–1539, Mexico City, 1968.

Busto Duthurburu, José Antonio del. "Alonso Briceño, el de la Isla del Gallo." *Mercurio Peruano* 42 (1961):479–485.

———. "Los caídos en Vilcaconga." *Historia y Cultura* (Órgano del Museo Nacional de Historia, Lima) 1 (1965):115–125.

———. "El capitán Melchor Verdugo, encomendero de Cajamarca." *Revista Histórica* 24 (1959):318–387.

———. "El conquistador Martín Pizarro, primer alguacil de Lima." *Mercurio Peruano* 44, part 1 (1963):111–125.

———. "La expedición de Hernando Pizarro a Pachacámac." *Humanidades* (Revista de la Facultad de Letras, Pontificia Universidad Católica del Perú) 1 (1967).

———. *Francisco Pizarro, el marqués gobernador.* Madrid, 1966.

———. "Los fugitivos de Nicaragua en la conquista del Perú." *Mercurio Peruano* 43 (1962):264–273.

———. "El herrero, el barbero y el gran volteador en la conquista del Perú." *Mercurio Peruano* 43 (1962):66–78.

———. "Los innominados en el reparto de Cajamarca." *Anales del III Congreso Nacional de la Historia del Perú,* pp. 90–101. Lima, 1965.

———. "Maldonado el Rico, señor de los Andahuaylas." *Revista Histórica* 26 (1962–1963):113–145.

———. "La marcha de Francisco Pizarro de Cajamarca al Cusco." *Revista Histórica* 26 (1962–1963):146–174.

———. "Martinillo de Poechos." In *Dos personajes de la conquista del Perú.* Lima, 1969.

———. "Pedro de Alconchel, trompeta de caballería." *Mercurio Peruano* 41 (1960): 505–515.

———. "Pedro de Candía, artillero mayor del Perú." *Revista Histórica* 25 (1960–1961):379–405.

———. "Pero Martín Bueno, el marino que recogió el primer oro del Cuzco." *Mercurio Peruano*, no. 478 (March–April, 1969), pp. 746–753.

———. "Los presuntos peruleros en la conquista de la Florida." *Mercurio Peruano* 50 (1965):313–326.

———. "Ruy Hernández Briceño, el guardián de Atahualpa." *Cuadernos del Seminario de Historia del Instituto Riva- Agüero* (Lima), no. 7 (December, 1964), pp. 5–7.

———. "Tres conversos en la captura de Atahualpa." *Revista de Indias* 27 (1967):427–442.

———. "Una relación y un estudio sobre la conquista." *Revista Histórica* 27 (1964):280–319.

Cabero, Marco A. "El corregimiento de Saña y el problema histórico de la fundación de Trujillo." *Revista Histórica* 1 (1906).

Calvete de Estrella, Juan Cristóbal. *Rebelión de Pizarro en el Perú y vida de don Pedro Gasca.* In *Crónicas del Perú.* Edited by Juan Pérez de Tudela. Vols. IV and V. Madrid, 1963–1965.

Casas, Bartolomé de las, O.P. *Historia de las Indias.* Edited by Agustín Millares Carlo, with a preliminary study by Lewis Hanke. 3 vols. Mexico City, 1951.

Castellanos, Juan de. *Elegías de varones ilustres de Indias.* Madrid, 1857.

Chevalier, François. *Land and Society in Colonial Mexico: The Great Hacienda.* Berkeley and Los Angeles: University of California Press, 1963.

Cieza de León, Pedro de. *La crónica del Perú.* In *Historiadores primitivos de Indias.* Edited by Enrique de Vedia. Vol. II. Madrid, 1946–1947.

———. *Guerra de Chupas.* Madrid, n.d.

———. *Guerra de Quito.* In *Historiadores de Indias.* Edited by Manuel Serrano y Sanz. Vol. II. Madrid, 1909.

———. *Guerra de Salinas.* Madrid, n.d.

———. *Tercera parte de la crónica del Perú.* Chapters 1–54. Edited by Rafael Loredo. *Mercurio Peruano* 27 (1946):409–440; 32 (1951):148–159; 34 (1953):305–317; 36 (1955):456–473; 37 (1956):77–95; 38 (1957):247–268; 39 (1958):565–585.

———. *Tercero libro de las guerras civiles del Perú, el cual se llama la Guerra de Quito.* Edited by Marcos Jiménez de la Espada. Madrid, 1877.

Cobo, Bernabé, S.J. *Obras.* Edited by Francisco Mateos, S.J. 2 vols. Madrid, 1964.

Colección de documentos inéditos para la historia de España [*CDIHE*]. Madrid, 1842–1895.

Colección de documentos inéditos relativos al descubrimiento, conquista y colonización de las posesiones españolas en América y Oceanía [*CDIAO*]. Madrid, 1864–1884.

Colección Somoza. Documentos para la historia de Nicaragua [*CDIHN*]. Madrid, 1954–1956.

Cuesta, Luisa. "Una documentación interesante sobre la familia del conquistador del Perú." *Revista de Indias* 8 (1947):865–892.

Cúneo-Vidal, R. *Vida del conquistador del Perú, don Francisco Pizarro, y de sus hermanos.* Barcelona, 1925.

Domínguez Bordona, Jesús. *Manuscritos de América. Catálogo de la Biblioteca de Palacio, IX.* Madrid, 1935.

Egaña, Antonio de. *Historia de la iglesia en la América Española desde el descubrimiento hasta comienzos del siglo XIX: Hemisferio sur.* Madrid, 1966.

Enríquez de Guzmán, don Alonso. *Libro de la vida y costumbres de don Alonso Enríquez de Guzmán.* Edited by Hayward Keniston. Madrid, 1960.

Estete, Miguel de. *El descubrimiento y la conquista del Perú.* Edited by Carlos M. Larrea. Quito, 1918.

———. *Relación de la conquista del Perú.* In *Colección de libros y documentos referentes a la historia del Perú.* Vol. VIII (Second series). Edited by Horacio H. Urteaga and Carlos A. Romero, q.v.

Esteve Barba, Francisco. *Descubrimiento y conquista de Chile.* Barcelona, 1946.

———, ed. *Crónicas del reino de Chile.* Madrid, 1960.

Fernández, Diego. *Historia del Perú.* In *Crónicas del Perú.* Edited by Juan Pérez de Tudela. Vols. I and II. Madrid, 1963–1965.

Foster, George M. *Culture and Conquest: America's Spanish Heritage.* Chicago: Quadrangle Books, 1960.

Gangotena y Jijón, C. "La descendencia de Atahualpa." *Boletín de la Academia Nacional de Historia, Quito,* 38, no. 91 (1958):107–124.

Garcilaso de la Vega. *Obras Completas.* Edited by Carmelo Sáenz de Santa María, S.J. 4 vols. Madrid, 1960.

Gibson, Charles. *Spain in America.* New York: Harper and Row, 1966.

Gómara, Francisco López de. *Hispania victrix: Historia general de las Indias.* In *Historiadores primitivos de Indias.* Edited by Enrique de Vedia. Vol. I. Madrid, 1946–1947.

Gonçalez Holguín, Diego, S.J. *Vocabulario de la lengva general de todo el Peru llamada lengua qquichua o del Inca.* Edited, with prologue, by Raúl Porras Barrenechea. Lima, 1952.

Góngora, Mario. *Los grupos de conquistadores en Tierra Firme (1509–1530).* Santiago de Chile, 1962.

Góngora Marmolejo, Alonso. *Historia de todas las cosas que han acaecido en el reino de Chile y de todos los que lo han gobernado.* In *Crónicas del reino de Chile.* Edited by Francisco Esteve Barba. Madrid, 1960.

Gutiérrez de Santa Clara, Pedro. *Quinquenarios o historia de las guerras civiles del Perú.* In *Crónicas del Perú.* Edited by Juan Pérez de Tudela. Vols. II–IV. Madrid, 1963–1965.

The Harkness Collection in the Library of Congress. See U.S., Library of Congress.

Hemming, John. *The Conquest of the Incas.* New York: Harcourt Brace Jovanovich, 1970.

Herrera, Antonio de. *Historia general de los hechos de los castellanos en las islas y tierra firme del mar océano (Décadas).* Publicado por acuerdo de la Real Academia de la Historia. Notes by Miguel Gómez del Campillo. Madrid, 1934–1957.

Icaza, Francisco A. de. *Conquistadores y pobladores de Nueva España.* 2 vols. Madrid, 1923.

Jerez, Francisco de. *Verdadera relación de la conquista del Perú y provincia del Cuzco, llamada la Nueva Castilla.* In *Historiadores primitivos de Indias.* Edited by Enrique de Vedia. Vol. II. Madrid, 1946–1947.

Jijón y Caamaño, Jacinto. *Sebastián de Benalcázar.* 2 vols. Quito, 1936.

Jiménez de la Espada, Marcos, ed. *Relaciones geográficas de Indias.* Vol. I, *Perú.* Edited by José Urbano Martínez Carreras. Madrid, 1965.

Keniston, Hayward F. *Francisco de los Cobos, Secretary of the Emperor Charles V.* Pittsburgh: University of Pittsburgh Press, 1959.

Kirkpatrick, F. A. *The Spanish Conquistadores.* Cleveland and New York: World Publishing Co., 1962.

Lee, Bertram T. "Algunos documentos sobre los primeros conquistadores del Perú." *Revista Histórica* 8 (1925).

Lima. *Libros de cabildos de Lima.* Vols. I–VI. Lima, 1935–.

Lockhart, James. "The Social History of Colonial Latin America: Evolution and Potential." *Latin American Research Review* 7, no. 1 (Spring, 1972):6–45.

——. *Spanish Peru, 1532–1560.* Madison: University of Wisconsin Press, 1968.

Lohmann Villena, Guillermo. *Los americanos en las órdenes nobiliarias.* 2 vols. Madrid, 1947.

——. "Documentos interesantes a la historia del Perú en el Archivo Histórico de Protocolos de Madrid." *Revista Histórica* 25 (1960–1961): 450–476.

——. *Les Espinosa: Une famille d'hommes d'affaires en Espagne et aux Indes à l'époque de la colonisation.* Paris, 1968.

——. "La restitución por conquistadores y encomenderos: Un aspecto de la incidencia lascasiana en el Perú." *Anuario de Estudios Americanos* 23 (1966):21–89.

López, Pero. *Rutas de Cartagena de Indias a Buenos Aires y sublevaciones de Pizarro, Castilla, y Hernández Girón, 1540–1570.* Edited by Juan Friede. Madrid, 1970.

Loredo, Rafael. *Alardes y derramas*. Lima, 1942.

——, ed. "Documentos sobre el conquistador Aliaga." *Revista Histórica* 12 (1939):183–203.

——. *Los repartos*. Lima, 1958.

——. "Sentencias contra los que participaron en el alzamiento de Gonzalo Pizarro." *Mercurio Peruano* 22 (1940):257–287.

Mariño de Lobera, don Pedro. *Crónica del reino de Chile*. In *Crónicas del reino de Chile*. Edited by Francisco Esteve Barba. Madrid, 1960.

Martínez, Santiago. *Fundadores de Arequipa*. Arequipa, 1936.

Matienzo, Juan de. *Gobierno del Perú*. Edited by Guillermo Lohmann Villena. Paris and Lima, 1967.

Maynard, Theodore. *De Soto and the Conquistadores*. New York: AMS Press, 1969.

Medina, José Toribio. *Colección de documentos inéditos para la historia de Chile* [*CDIHC*]. Santiago de Chile, 1888–1902.

——. *El Descubrimiento del Océano Pacífico*. 2 vols. Santiago de Chile, 1914.

Mellafe, Rolando. "Descubrimiento del Perú." In *Diego de Almagro*, by R. Mellafe and Sergio Villalobos. Santiago de Chile, 1954.

Mena, Cristóbal de. "La conquista del Perú." In *Las relaciones primitivas de la conquista del Perú*, by Raúl Porras Barrenechea, pp. 79–101. Paris, 1937.

Mendiburu, Manuel de. *Diccionario histórico-biográfico del Perú*. 2d edition. 11 vols. Lima, 1931–1935.

Montesinos, Fernando. *Anales del Perú*. Edited by Víctor M. Maúrtua. 2 vols. Madrid, 1906.

Montoto, Santiago. *Nobiliario hispano-americano del siglo XVI*. Madrid, n.d.

Moreyra Paz Soldán, Manuel. "Dos oidores del primer tercio del siglo XVII." *Mercurio Peruano* 27 (1946).

Muñoz de San Pedro, Miguel. "Doña Isabel de Vargas, esposa del padre del conquistador del Perú." *Revista de Indias* 11 (1951):9–28.

——. "Francisco Pizarro debió apellidarse Díaz o Hinojosa." *Revista de Estudios Extremeños* 6 (1950):403–542.

——. "Información sobre el linaje de Hernando Pizarro." *Revista de Estudios Extremeños* 22 (1966):209–227.

——. "La total extinguida descendencia de Francisco Pizarro." *Revista de Estudios Extremeños* 20 (1964):467–472.

——, ed. *Tres testigos de la conquista del Perú*. 3d ed. Madrid, 1964.

O'Gorman, Edmundo. *Catálogo de pobladores de Nueva España*. Mexico City, 1941.

Otte, Enrique. "Mercaderes vascos en Tierra Firme a raíz del descubrimiento del Perú." *Mercurio Peruano* 45, nos. 443–444 (Libro Jubiliar de Víctor Andrés Belaúnde) (March–April, 1964):81–89.

————, and Miguel Maticorena Estrada. "La isla de La Magdalena en el segundo viaje de Pizarro y Almagro para el descubrimiento del Perú." *Mercurio Peruano* 41 (1960):259–270.

Oviedo, Gonzalo Fernández de. *Historia general y natural de las Indias.* Edited by Juan Pérez de Tudela. 5 vols. Madrid, 1959.

Palomino, Alonso. "Relación sumaria de lo sucedido en el Perú después de la llegada del virrey." Appendix 3 of Diego Fernández, *Historia del Perú.* Vol. II, 124–127.

Parry, J. H. *The Spanish Seaborne Empire.* New York: Alfred A. Knopf, 1966.

Pasajeros a Indias. See Bermúdez Plata, Cristóbal.

Pérez de Tudela, Juan, ed. *Crónicas del Perú.* 5 vols. Madrid, 1963–1965.

————, ed. *Documentos relativos a don Pedro de la Gasca y a Gonzalo Pizarro.* 2 vols. Madrid, 1964.

Pike, Ruth. *Enterprise and Adventure: The Genoese in Seville and the Opening of the New World.* Ithaca: Cornell University Press, 1966.

Pizarro, Pedro. *Relación del descubrimiento y conquista de los reinos del Perú.* In *Crónicas del Perú.* Edited by Juan Pérez de Tudela. Vol. 5. Madrid, 1963–1965.

Pocock, H. R. S. *Conquest of Chile.* New York: Stein and Day, 1967.

Porras Barrenechea, Raúl, ed. *Cartas del Perú (1524–1543).* Lima, 1959.

————, ed. *Cedulario del Perú.* 2 vols. Lima, 1944–1948.

————. "Las conferencias del Dr. Raúl Porras Barrenechea sobre el conquistador del Perú." *Documenta*, I (1948):159–174.

————. *Crónicas perdidas, presuntas y olvidadas sobre la conquista del Perú.* Lima, 1951.

————. *Los cronistas del Perú (1528–1650).* Lima, 1962.

————. "Diego de Silva, cronista de la conquista del Perú." *Mar del Sur* 5, no. 15 (1950–1951):14–33.

————. "Dos documentos esenciales sobre Francisco Pizarro y la conquista del Perú." *Revista Histórica* 17 (1948):9–95.

————. "Jauja, capital mítica, 1534." *Revista Histórica* 18 (1949–1950): 117–148.

————. "El nombre del Perú." *Mar del Sur* 6, no. 18 (1951):2–39.

————. *Las relaciones primitivas de la conquista del Perú.* Paris, 1937.

————, ed. *El Testamento de Pizarro. Prólogo y notas por.* Paris, 1936.

————. "Medina y su contribución a la historia peruana." *Mercurio Peruano* 33 (1952):491–523.

Prescott, William H. *History of the Conquest of Peru.* New York: The Modern Library, n.d.

Quito. *Libros de cabildos de la ciudad de Quito.* Vols. I–III. Quito, 1934.

————. *Oficios o cartas del cabildo de Quito, 1552–1558*. Quito, 1934.

————. *Testamento del señor don Sebastián de Benalcázar*. Quito, 1935.

————. *Colección de documentos inéditos relativos al Adelantado Capitán don Sebastián de Benalcázar, 1535–1565*. Publicaciones del Archivo Municipal, X. Quito, 1936.

Relación de las cosas del Perú. In *Crónicas del Perú*. Edited by Juan Pérez de Tudela. Vol. 5. Madrid, 1963–1965.

Revista del Archivo Histórico del Cuzco [*RAHC*]. Cuzco, 1950 ff.

Revista del Archivo Nacional del Perú [*RANP*]. Lima, 1920 ff.

Revista del Instituto Peruano de Investigaciones Genealógicas [*RIPIG*]. Lima, 1964 ff.

Rivera Serna, Raúl, ed. *Libro primero de cabildos de la ciudad del Cuzco*. Lima, 1965.

Roa y Ursúa, Luis de. *El reyno de Chile (1538–1810)*. Valladolid, 1945.

Romero, Carlos A. *Los héroes de la Isla del Gallo*. Lima, 1944.

Ruiz de Arce, Juan. *Advertencias de Juan Ruiz de Arce a sus sucesores*. In *Tres testigos de la conquista del Perú*. Edited by Miguel Muñoz de San Pedro. Madrid, 1964.

————. *Servicios en Indias de Juan Ruiz de Arce*. Edited by Antonio del Solar y Taboada and José de Rújula y de Ochotorena. Madrid, 1933.

Rye, William B., ed. *The Discovery and Conquest of Terra Florida by Don Ferdinando de Soto, . . . written by a Gentleman of Elvas*. Translated by Richard Hakluyt. London: Hakluyt Society, 1851.

Salinas y Córdoba, Buenaventura de, O.F.M. *Memorial de las historias del nuevo mundo Pirú*. Edited by Luis E. Valcárcel and Warren L. Cook. Lima, 1957.

Sancho, Pedro. *Relación de la conquista del Perú*. Translated and edited by Joaquín García Icazbalceta. Madrid, 1962.

Schaefer, Ernst. "El proceso de Hernando Pizarro por la muerte del Adelantado Almagro." *Investigación y Progreso* 5 (1931):43–46.

Solar y Taboada, Antonio del, and José de Rújula y de Ochotorena. *El Adelantado Hernando de Soto. Breves noticias y nuevos documentos para su biografía*. Badajoz, 1929.

Strout, Chevy Lloyd. "Literary-Historical Treasures in the Thomas Gilcrease Institute of American History and Art." *Hispanic American Historical Review* 43 (1963):267–270.

Temple, Ella Dunbar. "Don Carlos Inca." *Revista Histórica* 17 (1948): 134–179.

Thayer Ojeda, Tomás. *Formación de la sociedad chilena y censo de la población de Chile en los años de 1540 a 1565*. 3 vols. Santiago de Chile, 1939–1941.

————. *Valdivia y sus compañeros*. Santiago de Chile, 1950.

Torres, Alberto María, O.P. *El padre Valverde. Ensayo biográfico y crítico.* Quito, 1932.

Torres Saldamando, Enrique. *Libro primero de cabildos de Lima.* 3 vols. Paris, 1888.

Trujillo, Diego de. *Relación del descubrimiento del reino del Perú.* Edited by Raúl Porras Barrenechea. Seville, 1948.

U. S., Library of Congress. *The Harkness Collection in the Library of Congress. Documents from Early Peru.* 2 vols. Washington, 1936.

Urteaga, Horacio H., and Carlos A. Romero, eds. *Colección de libros y documentos referentes a la historia del Perú.* 2d series. Lima, 1920–1935.

————. "Don Diego de Agüero y Sandoval, conquistador y poblador del Perú." *RANP* 6 (1928).

————. "Algunas provisiones de Pizarro sobre encomiendas." *RANP* 15 (1942): 7–24.

Vargas Ugarte, Rubén, S.J. "La fecha de la fundación de Trujillo." *Revista Histórica* 10 (1936):229–244.

————. *Historia de la iglesia en el Perú.* Vol. I. Lima, 1953.

————. "El monasterio de la Concepción de la Ciudad de Los Reyes." *Revista de Indias* 6 (1945):419.

Varias relaciones del Perú y Chile. Colección de libros españoles raros o curiosos. Vol. XIII. Madrid, 1879.

Zárate, Agustín de. *Historia del descubrimiento y conquista de la provincia del Perú.* In *Historiadores primitivos de Indias.* Edited by Enrique de Vedia. Vol. II. Madrid, 1946–1947.

————. *The Discovery and Conquest of Peru.* Translated by J. H. Cohen. Baltimore: Penguin Books, 1968.

Zúñiga, don Francesillo de. *Crónica de don Francesillo de Zúñiga.* In *Curiosidades bibliográficas.* Edited by Adolfo de Castro. Madrid, 1855.

INDEX

Acarí: 280 n., 306

Acla: 268, 423 n.

Africans. *See* Blacks

Agüero, Diego de: on roll of Cajamarca, 98; biography of, 209–212; mentioned, 60, 85, 208, 259, 289 n., 371, 404, 408, 418, 446

Aguilar, María de: 173

Aguirre, Pedro de: on roll of Cajamarca, 98; biography of, 398; mentioned, 45 n., 57 n., 73 n., 263, 397, 399

Alarcón y Urroz, Ignacio de: 309 n.

Albítez, Diego: 124

Alburquerque, Alonso de: on roll of Cajamarca, 100; biography of, 427–428

Alconchel, Pedro de: on roll of Cajamarca, 99; biography of, 370–372; mentioned, 34, 37 n., 51, 95, 260, 396, 416, 418

Alconcher, don Francisco de. *See* Alconchel, Pedro de

Aldana, Hernando de: on roll of Cajamarca, 99; biography of, 212–214; mentioned, 272

Aldana, Lorenzo de: 213–214, 365

Aliaga, doña María de: 371

Aliaga, Jerónimo de: possible Jewish descent of, 36; on roll of Cajamarca, 97; testimony of Francisco Pizarro for, 149; biography of, 258–263; mentioned, 34, 37 n., 57, 60, 69, 73 n., 91, 117, 240, 244, 249, 254, 284 n., 289, 371, 418, 419, 447, 468

Almagro, Diego de (the elder): narrative details concerning, 5, 6, 12, 15–16; as Isthmian type, 24–25; role in organizing expeditions, 67–72, 82–85;

supporters of, fellow New Castilians and men associated with, 78, 88, 104–105, 134, 210–211, 235, 269, 283–284, 333, 335, 365 n., 386, 388, 451; and Sebastián de Benalcázar, 122–123, 125, 126; and Francisco Pizarro, 142–144, 147, 150, 151, 154 n., 269; and Hernando Pizarro, 159; and Juan Pizarro, 170; and Hernando de Soto, 197; and fray Vicente de Valverde, 204; mentioned, 79 n., 131, 170, 325, 357, 368

Almagro, don Diego de (the younger): 16, 132, 205, 336

Almendras, Francisco de: on roll of Cajamarca, 100; biography of, 312–314; mentioned, 87

Almendras, Martín de: 313, 314 n.

Almonte, Gonzalo de: 297

Alonso, Juan (notary): 75, 269, 422, 428

Alonso, María: 173 n., 186 n.

Alonso, Martín: on roll of Cajamarca, 98; biography of, 288–289; mentioned, 45 n., 58, 174, 295

Alvarado, Alonso de: 159

Alvarado, Diego de: 204

Alvarado, Pedro de: and expedition to Quito, 15, 125, 126, 197, 363, 451; as typical Badajoz native, 150; mentioned, 210, 277, 337 n.

Alvarez, Rodrigo (merchant of Palos): 407 n.

Alvarez de la Carrera, Alonso. *See* Carrera, Alonso de la

Ampuero, Francisco de: 154 n.

Anadel, Pedro de: on roll of Cajamar-

Gonzalo Pizarro rebellion, 16, 181–185, 228, 252, 375; as stability factor, 19–20, 44; social qualifications of holders of, 51, 375, 376, 381; inheritance of, 60, 154 n., 165, 211, 302; as basis of position of men of Cajamarca, and where held, 60–63; comparative view of, 113–114, 376; importance of Francisco Pizarro's in Panama, 142, 144; examples of exploitation of, 167 n., 188 n., 204–205, 211, 221–223, 229, 251–252, 254 n., 288, 301, 303 n., 377, 379 n., 452; mentioned, under individual men, and *passim*
Enríquez de Guzmán, don Alonso: 140, 162, 417
entradas: examples of, 16, 111, 114, 131–132, 180–181, 187 n., 222, 278–279; discussion of, 65–77, 89
Escalante, Juan de (carpenter): on roll of Cajamarca, 100; biography of, 375–376; mentioned, 37 n., 51, 56, 76, 389 n.
Escalante, Juan de (notary): 376 n.
Escobar, Antonio de (hosier): 307 n.
Escobar, María de: 306–307
Escobar, Pedro de (tailor, of Panama): 307 n.
Escudero, Diego: on roll of Cajamarca, 102; biography of, 430–431; mentioned, 91 n.
Espinosa, Bárbola de: 323 n.
Espinosa, Licenciado Gaspar de: 67, 71–72, 142, 143, 192, 204, 247, 250–251, 322, 323 n.
Espinosa, Juan de: 134
Estete, Martín: 265, 277
Estete, Miguel (author of chronicle, horseman): on roll of Cajamarca, 97; biography of, 265–267; and Miguel Estete (de Santo Domingo), 320 n.–321 n.; mentioned, 26 n., 34, 37 n., 94, 147, 291, 320, 341, 361, 450, 455 n.
Estete (de Santo Domingo), Miguel (footman): on roll of Cajamarca, 99; biography of, 320–322; mentioned, 11, 26 n., 37 n., 94, 265
Extremadurans: numbers and origins of, in Peru expedition, 27–31; characteristics of, 32, 40, 77, 136, 147, 148–149, 150, 152, 165, 299, 300, 313,

358; favored treatment of, 85–86, 109, 152. *See also* individual men from Extremadura

Farel, Tomás: 419 n.
Federmann, Nicolás: 126
Felipillo (interpreter): 448–455
Félix, Gabriel: on roll of Cajamarca, 98; biography of, 267; mentioned, 37 n.
Félix de Morales, Alonso: 267 n.
Fernández, Juan (sea captain): 73, 125, 359 n.
Fernández el Palentino, Diego: 265
Florencia, Martín de: on roll of Cajamarca, 100; biography of, 377–379; mentioned, 22, 36, 37 n., 73 n., 89, 95, 369
Florencia, Martín de (son of the man of Cajamarca): 378 n., 379 n.
Flores, Bartolomé de: 282 n.
Florida: 198, 199, 281 n.
foreigners: 28, 282 n., 305, 384 n., 419 n., 429 n.–430 n., 440–441. *See also* Candía, Pedro de; Florencia, Martín de; Griego, Jorge
Foster, George M.: ideas of, 116–117
Francisco, don (interpreter): 454 n.
Francisqui, Neri (Florentine merchant): 305
Fuentes, Francisca de: 252, 323 n., 324 n.
Fuentes, Francisco de: on roll of Cajamarca, 98; biography of, 322–324; mentioned, 73 n., 95, 252, 318

Gallego, Cristóbal: on roll of Cajamarca, 98; biography of, 431; mentioned, 45 n., 426
Gallego, Francisco: on roll of Cajamarca, 100; biography of, 432
Gallo Island: 5, 67–68, 130, 149, 152, 217, 268, 308, 438
Gárate, Gaspar de. *See* Marquina, Gaspar de
Garay, Adelantado Francisco de: 211
Garay, doña Luisa de: 211
García, Antón: on roll of Cajamarca, 101; biography of, 432–433; mentioned, 427
García, Esteban: on roll of Cajamarca, 102; biography of, 433

marca, 100; biography of, 325–326; mentioned, 76, 95, 312
hidalgo: discussion of, as term, 31–33, 111, 208. *See also* chaps. 2, 7, 8
Hispaniola. *See* Santo Domingo
Holguín, Perálvarez: 213 n.
Honduras: 24, 124, 125, 225, 294, 335, 342, 346, 349, 367, 394, 408
Hontiveros, Crisóstomo de: on roll of Cajamarca, 99; biography of, 298–300; mentioned, 77, 87, 310, 360
horses: importance of, 47, 70, 79, 231; commercial dealings and, 74–75, 283, 308, 388; facility of certain leaders with, 147, 163, 177, 195; mentioned, *passim. See also* Calderón, Pedro, and Salinas herrador, Juan de (horseshoers)
Hoz, don Francisco de la: 348, 350 n.
Hoz, Pedro Sancho de. *See* Sancho (de Hoz), Pedro
Huaco Ocllo, doña Catalina: 229
Huamanga: 16, 53, 61–62, 63, 313, 467 n.; citizens of, *see* Estete de Santo Domingo, Miguel; Gavilán, Diego; Hontiveros, Crisóstomo de; Martín, García; Palomino, Melchor
Huamantanga: 418
Huancavélica: 449
Huánuco: 16, 245, 336
Huarina, battle of: 302, 316, 467
Huayna Capac: 154 n., 199 n.

Ica: 376
Inca, don Carlos: 199 n.
illegitimacy: 138–139, 308, 322, 323 n., 330. *See also* mestizos
Indians: Some narrative aspects of battles and skirmishes with, 8, 11, 12, 13, 15, 149, 171, 196, 205–206, 231, 245, 370, 404, 457–463; number of Spaniards lost in fighting with, 59–61, 114; as structural factor more than as cultural influence on Spaniards, 117; as mistresses of conquerors, 153 n.–154 n., 174, 199 n., 222, 229, 248, 272, 302, 304 n., 358–359, 374, 378 n., 381, 422, 447; Spanish attitudes toward, 159–160, 161, 169, 178, 191, 204, 252, 306, 332, 458; as auxiliaries and interpreters, 199 n., 379 n., 447–455; as slaves, 317–318, 392,

447; mentioned, *passim. See also* Atahuallpa; Hemming, John; mestizos; military tactics; restitution; slaves
Inquill Coya, doña Francisca: 174 n.
investment patterns: of repatriates, 55, 57, 58–59; of men staying in Peru, 63; in expeditions, 66–75, 89, 133, 143–144, 193–194, 278–279, 466; of individuals, 161–162, 167 n., 247, 270, 277, 287–311 *passim*, 342, 392, 405, 466. *See also* companies; encomiendas; horses; slaves

Jamaica: 346, 386 n.
Jaquijahuana, battle of: 16, 183, 260
Jauja: Spanish in, 12, 13, 14, 78, 154 n., 196, 203, 231, 244, 339, 396, 447; men staying in, in late 1533, 13, 263, 294, 388; men of Cajamarca, as citizens of, 61–62; council members of, 216, 219, 221, 231, 237, 241, 290, 326, 435; other Spanish citizens of, 233, 340, 374, 394, 417; notaries in, 259, 283, 276 n., 285 n.; mentioned, *passim*
Jerez, Francisco de (official secretary and chronicler): 18, 91, 134, 265, 276, 464–465; on roll of Cajamarca, 97; biography of, 268–270; mentioned, 34, 37 n., 45 n., 95, 448
Jews (converted): reputed or suspected, 36–37, 201, 206, 285 n., 378 n., 392 n.
Jiménez, Alonso: on roll of Cajamarca, 100; biography of, 385; mentioned, 37 n., 73 n., 333, 386, 440
Jiménez, Andrés: on roll of Cajamarca, 100; biography of, 327–328
Jiménez, Francisca: 244, 245 n., 246 n.
Jiménez, Juan (tailor): on roll of Cajamarca, 100; biography of, 386–387; mentioned, 37 n., 88, 373
Jiménez (de Trujillo), Juan: arrives with Almagro, 386 n.–387 n.
juros: 55, 56, 160, 247, 289 n., 345, 347

La Conquista. *See* La Zarza
Lachira: 449
La Plata: 16, 62, 180, 313
La Zarza: 157, 166 n., 169, 288, 289 n.
León, Antón de: 308
León, Constanza de: 308, 309 n.

Martín Soitino, Francisco. *See* Martín, Francisco

Martínez, Francisco (merchant): 304, 305

Martínez, Francisco (tailor): on roll of Cajamarca, 101; biography of, 388–389; mentioned, 37 n., 95, 393

Martínez (Vegaso), Francisco: 303, 304

Martínez (Vegaso), Lucas: on roll of Cajamarca, 100; biography of, 300–305; and partner, Alonso Ruiz, 343–345; mentioned, 63, 73 n., 87, 95, 295

Martinillo. *See* Martín, don

Maza, Bernaldino de: 225

Maza, Luis: on roll of Cajamarca, 97; biography of, 225–226; mentioned, 58, 73 n., 216, 217, 341, 424 n.

Mazuelas, Rodrigo de: 145, 146, 235 n., 286 n.

Medina, Alonso de: on roll of Cajamarca, 97; biography of, 226–227; mentioned, 73 n., 191, 219

Medrano, doña Beatriz de. *See* Vázquez, Beatriz

Mejía, Diego: on roll of Cajamarca, 98; biography of, 331–332

Mejía, Francisco (alcalde in Cuzco): 331

Mejía, Francisco (blacksmith): 331

Mejía, doña Jordana: 254

Mella, Antonía de: 241, 243 n.

Mellafe, Rolando: comment on writings of, 68, 71–72, 144

Mena, Cristóbal de: as Almagro compatriot and ally, 80, 83–84, 85, 88; on roll of Cajamarca, 97; biography of, 133–135; mentioned, 18, 23, 45 n., 69, 125, 189, 450

Méndez, Leonor: 319

Mendoza, Pedro de: on roll of Cajamarca, 101; biography of, 305–307; mentioned, 26 n., 63, 280 n., 294

Mercado, doña Isabel: 166 n.

Mesa, Alonso de: on roll of Cajamarca, 99; biography of, 227–230; mentioned, 37 n., 88, 208, 247, 271, 272

Mesa, don Alonso de: 230 n.

Mesa, Bernardo de: 229 n.

mestizos: among conquerors, 108–109; among children of conquerors, 127, 128, 132, 153 n.–155 n., 174 n., 186 n., 199 n., 222, 229–230 n.,

245 n., 247, 248, 249–250, 252, 261, 272, 281 n., 282 n., 313, 344–345, 374, 378 n., 379 n., 381, 418, 420, 447; mentioned, *passim*

Mexico: 24, 107, 211, 393, 396

military orders: Order of Santiago, 36, 53, 123, 159, 198, 206, 252, 253–254, 255 n.; others, 246, 250

military tactics: 10, 68, 147, 178, 189, 192, 194, 231, 325, 370. *See also* Candía, Pedro de, and Florencia, Martín de (artillerymen); horses; Indians

Mogrovejo, Toribio de: 230

Moguer, Pedro de: on roll of Cajamarca, 99; biography of, 403–404; mentioned, 73 n., 196, 285, 397, 442, 447

Molina, Alonso de: 332–333

Molina, Diego de: on roll of Cajamarca, 98; biography of, 332–333; mentioned, 26 n., 45 n., 266, 294 n.

Monje, Martín: 452

Montalbo, Hernando de: on roll of Cajamarca, 101; biography of, 439; mentioned, 389 n., 427

Montejo, Francisco de: 341 n., 385, 440 n.

Morales, Alonso de: on roll of Cajamarca, 98; biography of, 333–334; mentioned, 73 n., 312, 436

Morales, Francisco de (priest): 321 n.

Morales, Gaspar de: 142

Morgovejo (de Quiñones), Juan: on roll of Cajamarca, 98; biography of, 230–232; mentioned, 33, 34, 85, 157

Moriscos: 35, 146, 249, 323, 344, 421

mozos: 303 n. *See* majordomos

mulattoes. *See* Blacks

municipal offices. *See* town councils

Muñiz, Francisco: 389 n., 435 n.

Muñoz, Alvaro (barber-surgeon): 388 n.

Muñoz, Hernán: on roll of Cajamarca, 99; biography of, 440; mentioned, 94

Muñoz, doña Inés: 154 n., 157 n.

Muñoz, Juan: on roll of Cajamarca, 102; biography of, 416–417; mentioned, 94, 411

Muñoz Cornejo, Juan: 417 n.

Muñoz de San Pedro, Miguel (Conde de Canilleros): comment on writings of, 136, 155 n., 167 n., 237 n.–238 n.

Narváez, Andrés de: 272 n.

Pizarro, doña Isabel (daughter of Juan): 174 n., 186 n.

Pizarro, Juan (brother of Francisco): owner of three horses in conquest, 75; in relation to brothers, 80, 122, 139, 153, 158, 175, 177; accession to leadership, 85; on roll of Cajamarca, 97; biography of, 168–175; close associates of, 220, 295, 333; mentioned, *passim*

Pizarro, Juan (shoemaker, brother of Martín Pizarro): 148, 156 n., 418

Pizarro, don Juan (son of Francisco): 154 n.

Pizarro, don Juan (son of Hernando): 166 n.

Pizarro, Juan (uncle of Francisco): 141

Pizarro, don Juan Fernando (grandson of Hernando): 166 n.

Pizarro, Martín: on roll of Cajamarca, 101; biography of, 417–420; mentioned, 391 n., 416

Pizarro, don Martín de. *See* Martín, don

Pizarro, Pedro: 220 n., 319 n., 419, 451, 470; comment on writings of, 79 n., 156 n., 188 n., 193, 248, 404, 453 n.

Pizarro de Orellana, Juan: on roll of Cajamarca, 97; biography of, 236–238; mentioned, 166 n.

Pizarro family: 136–137, 220. *See also* individual Pizarros

Poechos: 449, 452

Ponce de León, Hernán: associate of Hernando de Soto, 73, 192–193, 194, 197, 199 n., 200 n.; and other conquerors of Peru, 256, 361, 423

Popayán: 126, 127

Porco: 161

Porras, Antonio de: 238

Porras, Juan de: on roll of Cajamarca, 99; biography of, 238–239; mentioned, 26 n., 241, 257 n., 273

Porras, Bachiller Juan de: 238

Porras Barrenechea, Raúl: comment on writings of, xiv, 71–72, 135 n., 136, 155 n., 167 n., 191, 471, 472

Portocarrero, don Pedro: 358

Potosí: 161, 222

Prescott, William H.: comment on writings of, 3, 169, 346

Prieto. *See* Peto

Puertoviejo: 8, 449

Puná (island): arrival of Soto at, 8, 68, 194; fighting on, in 1531, 8, 149; deaths of Valdevieso and Valverde at, in 1541, 205–206, 248; The Thirteen on, 332; mentioned, 9, 169, 225, 235 n., 348

Puñoenrrostro, Count of: 155 n., 164

Quechua: 213, 450

Quesada, Licenciado Gonzalo Jiménez de: 126

Quincoces, Juan de: on roll of Cajamarca, 98; biography of, 310–311; mentioned, 73 n., 74, 291

Quiñones, Antonio de: 230

Quiñones, Francisco de: 230

Quiñones, Juan de: 231 n., 232 n.

Quiñones, Juan Morgovejo de. *See* Morgovejo (de Quiñones), Juan

Quintero, Juan: 407 n.

Quito: and Benalcázar, 15, 85, 125, 126–127; and men of Cajamarca, 62, 352 n.; and Gonzalo Pizarro, 180–181, 182; and Soto, 195, 197; mentioned, 210, 247, 317 n., 352 n., 353 n., 388, 400, 451

Quízquiz: 196

Ramírez, Ana: 260

Reconquest, Spanish: 66, 74

religion: role of, in the conquerors' minds, 117–118, 152, 457–458. *See also* chaplaincies; church; restitution

restitution: general atmosphere of, to Indians, 105, 118; instances of, 105 n., 229, 323, 345, 469–470; resistance to, 303

retainers, *See* majordomos

Ribera, don Antonio de: 154 n.

Ribera, Nicolás de: 105 n., 216, 303, 376

Ríos, Pedro de los (governor of Panama): 5, 67, 69, 129–130, 271

Riquelme, Alonso (royal treasurer): 13, 75, 263, 273, 277, 294

Roa y Ursúa, Luis de: comment on writings of, 304 n.

Robles, Francisco de. *See* Robles sastre

Robles, Martín de: 260

Robles, Pedro de (shoemaker): 393 n.

Robles sastre: on role of Cajamarca, 101;

biography of, 392–393; mentioned, 37 n., 39, 95, 373, 389 n.
"Rodas sastre": 393 n. *See also* Robles sastre
Rodríguez, Diego: 149
Rodríguez, Francisca (sister of Juan Pizarro): 174
Rodríguez de Hontiveros, Francisco: 110 n.
Rodríguez de Monroy, Hernán: 281 n.
Rojas, Beatriz de: 390 n.
Rojas, Juan de: on roll of Cajamarca, 98; biography of, 239–240; mentioned, 73 n., 233
Román, Pedro: on roll of Cajamarca, 100; biography of, 420–421
Romero, Alonso: on roll of Cajamarca, 99; biography of, 407–408; mentioned, 57, 73 n., 397, 403
Romero, Juan: 110 n., 281 n.
Ronquillo, Juan: on roll of Cajamarca, 99; biography of, 443
Ruiz, Alonso: on roll of Cajamarca, 100; biography of, 343–346; mentioned, 73 n., 95, 301, 304 n.
Ruiz, Bartolomé (pilot): 5, 6, 227, 331, 342 n., 430, 433 n., 448
Ruiz, Juan: as example of repatriate, 54–55, 56, 57; on roll of Cajamarca, 98; biography of, 346–348; mentioned, 22, 95, 312, 438, 442 n.
Ruiz, Miguel: on roll of Cajamarca, 98; biography of, 421–423; mentioned, 36, 73 n., 75, 373
Ruiz de Alburquerque, Juan. *See* Ruiz, Juan
Ruiz de Arce, Juan. *See* Ruiz, Juan

Sacsahuamán: 171, 408
Sairi Tupac: 320
Salcedo, García de (royal *veedor*): 337 n.
Salcedo, Juan de: on roll of Cajamarca, 97; biography of, 189–190; mentioned, 23, 45 n., 80, 83–84, 85, 447
Salinas, battle of: 15–16, 131, 158–159, 163, 211, 235, 283, 335, 420, 423
Salinas y Córdoba, fray Buenaventura: comment on writings of, 92–94
Salinas, Juan de. *See* Salinas de la Hoz;

Salinas Farfán; Salinas herrador; Salinas Loyola
Salinas de la Hoz, Juan: on roll of Cajamarca, 98; biography of, 348–349; mentioned, 45 n., 57, 395 n.
Salinas de la Hoz, Pedro: on roll of Cajamarca, 101; biography of, 349–350; mentioned, 26 n., 57
Salinas Farfán, Juan de: 395 n.
Salinas herrador, Juan de: on roll of Cajamarca, 98; biography of, 393–395; mentioned, 37 n., 56, 373 n., 385
Salinas Loyola, Juan de: 395 n.
Salvatierra, Juan de: on roll of Cajamarca, 102; biography of, 443–444
Sámano, Juan de: 259, 262 n.
Sánchez, Alonso. *See* Sánchez de Talavera, Alonso
Sánchez, Bartolomé. *See* Sánchez marinero, Bartolomé
Sánchez, Hernán: on roll of Cajamarca, 98; biography of, 351–353
Sánchez, Juan: on roll of Cajamarca, 101; biography of, 444
Sánchez, Lázaro: on roll of Cajamarca, 101; biography of, 444–445
Sánchez, Miguel: on roll of Cajamarca, 101; biography of, 445
Sánchez de Badajoz, Hernán: 353 n.
Sánchez de Pineda, Hernán: 353 n.
Sánchez de Talavera, Alonso: on roll of Cajamarca, 101; biography of, 350–351; mentioned, 73 n., 366, 411
Sánchez de Terrazas, Bartolomé: 409 n., 410 n.
Sánchez marinero, Bartolomé: on roll of Cajamarca, 101; biography of, 409–410; mentioned, 37 n.
Sánchez Morillo, Hernán: 352 n., 353 n.
Sancho (de Hoz), Pedro: in Chile, 16, 109; in Peru, 76, 91, 92, 134; on roll of Cajamarca, 97, 99; biography of, 276–283; mentioned, 37 n., 58 n., 265, 273, 305, 466
Sandoval: on roll of Cajamarca, 99; biography of, 445–446
Sandoval, don Juan de: 445
Sandoval, Juan de: 445
Sandoval, Rodrigo de. *See* Sandoval
San Juan, Juan de (mariner): 9 n.
San Miguel (Piura): men who stayed behind in (in general), 9, 78, 103–

104, 464–465; ships at, in August, 1532, 9 n., 76, 392; Benalcázar in, 15, 84–85, 126, 318, 322, 400; men who stayed behind in (instances of), 339–340, 388 n.; mentioned, 40, 247, 333, 388
San Millán, Luis de: 283, 284 n.
San Millán, Pedro de: on roll of Cajamarca, 100; biography of, 283–285; mentioned, 37 n., 89
Santa: 6
Santa Clara, Pedro Gutiérrez de. *See* Gutiérrez de Santa Clara, Pedro
Santa Marta: 385, 415
Santiago, Order of. *See* military orders
Santillán, Licenciado Hernando de: 309 n.
Santillán, doña Mencía de: 309 n.
Santo Domingo: men of Cajamarca in, 124, 125, 141, 293, 367, 405, 408, 415; men returning from Cajamarca in, 164, 332–333; Spanish woman born in, in Peru, 244, 245 n. *See also* Caribbean Sea
Saravia, doña María: 298 n.
Segovia, Diego de (trumpeter): 371, 396
Segovia, Juan de: on roll of Cajamarca, 99; biography of, 395–396; mentioned, 37 n., 95, 371
Segura, María: 229 n.
seigneurial ideal: 57, 63, 64, 118 *passim*
seniority: 23–24, 116, 142, 145–146 *passim*
Sierra de Leguízamo, Mancio: 469
signatures: as index of literacy, 34–35, 176; mentioned, *passim*
slaves: mentioned, 67, 133, 219, 229 n., 231, 280, 325. *See also* Blacks; Indians
Solares, Francisco de: on roll of Cajamarca, 101; biography of, 354; mentioned, 312
soldada: 20
"soldiers": meaning and application of term, 17–22
Soraluce, Domingo: 263, 305, 398, 438
Sosa, Antonía de: 402
Sosa, Bernaldino de: 355 n., 356, 467
Sosa, Cristóbal de: on roll of Cajamarca, 102; biography of, 423–425

Sosa, Hernando de: on roll of Cajamarca, 101; biography of, 355–356; mentioned, 26 n., 465
Sosa, Hernando de (secretary to Almagro): 355 n.
Sosa, Juan de: on roll of Cajamarca, 97; biography of, 465–468; mentioned, 90, 201, 203, 277, 282 n., 355 n., 465
Sotelo, Antonio de: 241, 243 n.
Sotelo, Cristóbal de: 242, 243 n.
Sotelo, Gaspar de: 242, 243 n.
Sotelo, Gregorio de: on roll of Cajamarca, 99; biography of, 241–243; mentioned, 26 n., 37 n., 54, 218 n., 261, 262 n., 284 n., 357 n.
Soto, Bartolomé de: 168, 173 n.
Soto, Blas de: 173 n.–174 n., 186 n.
Soto, Hernando de: narrative details concerning, 4, 8, 10, 13–14; in 1531–1532 Peru expedition, 68, 77, 80, 82–85, 95; company of, with Hernán Ponce, 73; and Benalcázar, 82–85, 124–125; on roll of Cajamarca, 97; and Francisco Pizarro, 142, 151; at Badajoz, 150; and Juan Pizarro, 169–170; biography of, 190–201; supporters and associates of, 216, 225, 226, 233, 237, 244, 265, 294, 297, 319, 330, 341, 361, 367, 398, 414, 423; mentioned, *passim*
Soto, Isabel de: 173 n., 186 n.
Soto, doña Leonor de: 199 n., 201 n.
Soto, doña María de: 199 n.
stewards. *See* majordomos
Suárez, Simón (Portuguese): 440
Sucre. *See* La Plata

Tabuyo, Iñigo: on roll of Cajamarca, 99; biography of, 356–357; mentioned, 26
Talavera, Francisco de: 402 n., 468 n.
Tangarará: 9 n. *See also* San Miguel
Téllez de Guzmán, Antonio: 236 n.
Terrazas, Bartolomé de. *See* Sánchez de Terrazas, Bartolomé
Thayer Ojeda, Tomás: comment on writings of, xiii, 108, 110, 110 n., 111–112, 281 n.
Thirteen of Fame (or of Gallo Island): actions of, 5–6, 68; some of, in Peru later, 105 n., 303, 469; among men of Cajamarca, 130–131, 215–216; anecdotes relating to, 150, 152, 332, 448;

men falsely thought to be among, 297, 308, 364, 469; mentioned, 217, 268

Tiemblo, Hernando del: on roll of Cajamarca, 101; biography of, 425; mentioned, 50

Titicaca, Lake: 210, 404

Tocto Chimbu (doña Leonor): 199 n.

Toledo, don Francisco de (viceroy): 364

Toro, Alonso de: on roll of Cajamarca, 100; biography of, 357–360; mentioned, 26 n., 87, 313, 360

Toro, Hernando de: on roll of Cajamarca, 98; biography of, 360–361; mentioned, 76, 357

Torre, Francisco de la: on roll of Cajamarca, 100; biography of, 446; mentioned, 272 n.

Torre, Juan de la: 469

Torres, Antonio de (barber and miner): 379 n.

Torres, Cristóbal de: 245

Torres, Hernando de: 245 n.

Torres, doña Juana de: 245

Torres, Pedro de: on roll of Cajamarca, 100; biography of, 361–362; mentioned, 77, 291, 413, 424 n.

Torres, Sebastián de: on roll of Cajamarca, 98; biography of, 243–246; mentioned, 26 n., 73 n., 193, 208, 312, 397

Tosta: 361

Tovilla, Diego de la: 292, 328

town councils: membership on, as reward, 52–53, 114; membership on, in Spain, by men of Cajamarca, 57–58, 220, 345; membership on, in Peru, by men of Cajamarca, 62–63; Pizarro domination of, 86–87, 145–146, 159, 185, 235, 247, 326, 335. See also biographies of individual men

treasure: distribution of, 12–13, 14, 76, 78–82, 104 n., 105 n.; effects of, in determining conquerors' actions, 44, 47, 85, 113, 114; conveyance of, to Spain, 54–55, 216, 220, 241–242, 243 n., 266, 361, 394, 412; attempts of relatives in Spain to recover, 59, 360, 396, 422; individuals speculating in, 277, 342, 405; mentioned, passim

Trujillo, Diego de: on roll of Cajamarca, 100; biography of, 362–365; mentioned, 50, 58, 159, 352 n.

Trujillo (Peru): 14, 62, 265, 267 n., 290, 365; men of Cajamarca as citizens of, 250–255, 322–324

Trujillo (Spain): recruiting for Peru expedition in, 6, 27; as source of favored group of men of Cajamarca, 28–29, 75, 84, 86, 152; Peruvian veterans on council of, 58, 215, 220, 237, 295, 345; Francisco Pizarro as a son of, 136–140, 148–150, 152–153; position of Hernando Pizarro in, 157–158, 164–165; mentioned, passim. See especially biographies of men of Cajamarca born in Trujillo

Tucumán: 114, 336, 337 n.

Túmbez: seen by Spaniards 1527–1528, 6, 130, 448; as intended capital, 9, 194, 217, 325; in conquest of 1532, 9, 70, 152, 194, 195; mentioned, 205, 454

Ulloa, Antonio de: 365

Ulloa, Lorenzo de: 365–366

Ulloa, María de: 186

Ulloa, Pedro de: on roll of Cajamarca, 101; biography of, 365–366; mentioned, 89, 312

Ulloa, fray Pedro de: 366 n.

Vaca de Castro, Licenciado Cristóbal: associates and compatriots of, 87, 211, 230, 247, 248 n., 439; activities of, as governor, 16, 127, 181, 316, 432; mentioned, 132, 205

Valdevieso, Juan de: high social status of, 33, 34, 157, 224; related to men of affairs, 37 n.; close friends of, 73 n., 224, 225 n., 228; as Pizarro retainer, 76, 77, 86–87; on roll of Cajamarca, 99; biography of, 246–248

Valdivia, Pedro de: Extremaduran regional ties and activities of, 109; compared to Pizarro, 150; and Pedro Sancho de Hoz, 278–280; mentioned, 16, 151, 304 n., 305

Valencia, Pedro de: on roll of Cajamarca, 101; biography of, 366–367; mentioned, 73 n., 350, 411

Valencia, Pedro Alonso de (majordomo): 304 n.

St. Francis College Library
180 Remsen Street
Brooklyn, NY 11201

CPSIA information can be obtained
at www.ICGtesting.com
Printed in the USA
LVOW11s1135190118
563195LV00001B/53/P

9 780292 735637